Contents

CONTINUUM & THE PUBLISHERS ASSOCIATION

DIRECTORY OF PUBLISHING
2010

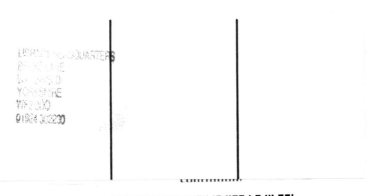

Continuum
The Tower Building
11 York Road
London SE1 7NX

80 Maiden Lane
Suite 704
New York, NY 10038

Thirty-fifth Edition 2009

British Library Cataloguing-in-Publication Data
A catalogue entry for this book is available from the British Library.

ISBN: 9781441110886

Research and editing by First Edition Translations, Cambridge
Text input, processing and typesetting by John Ainslie Consultancy
Printed and bound in the UK by MPG Books Ltd, Bodmin, Cornwall

1 Introduction

FOREWORD

The 35th edition of the *Directory of Publishing*, published by Continuum in association with The Publishers Association, provides an indispensable guide to book publishing in the United Kingdom and Republic of Ireland and contains details of nearly 900 publishers. In addition to the detailed entries on publishers, the *Directory* offers in depth coverage of the wider UK book trade, and lists over 500 organizations associated with the industry, including packagers, distributors, library suppliers, authors' agents and translation services. An appendix analyses publishers by field of speciality. Indexes include ISBN prefix numbers; names of key personnel and publishers' imprints; and a listing of UK publishers by postcode.

The directory is updated annually. Previous entrants are sent last year's entry and new entrants a questionnaire. We are grateful to all those who have provided information for this edition. We have done all we can to ensure accuracy and completeness, but cannot accept responsibility for errors or omissions that escaped us. New entrants either approached the publisher or were discovered by monitoring various sources – the trade press, publishers' catalogues, exhibitions, book fairs, and the files of the Publishers Association itself.

As in the previous edition we have not excluded all organizations which have failed to reply to our mailings. Instead we have re-run their 2009 entries (in abbreviated form) and marked them with an asterisk. However, such organizations will be deleted from the next edition if they fail to update their entries for the second year running.

We welcome all comments and suggestions from readers for improvements. We are also happy to receive details of possible new entries, but please note these must meet our criteria for inclusion. Publishers must either be a PA or CLÉ member or be of a certain size, publishing at least 5 new titles a year or employing at least 4 people.

All organizations are entered free of charge.

Continuum

ABBREVIATIONS

UK Book Trade Association Membership
Publishers Association
APD – Publishers Association: Academic & Professional Division
BA – Booksellers Association
EPC – Educational Publishers Council

IGSMTP – International Group of Scientific, Medical & Technical Publishers
IPG – Independent Publishers Guild

* Asterisked entries indicate 2008 data.
<u>Underlined entries</u> indicate members of the Publishers Association.

HOW TO OBTAIN BRITISH BOOKS

This introduction is particularly intended for booksellers ordering from a British publisher for the first time.

HOW TO ORDER

1   If you have not previously ordered from a publisher, you should write for details on:
   trade discounts;
   credit facilities;
   catalogue mailing.
Please enclose in your letter information including:
   name and address of your bank;
   names and addresses of one or two publishers, preferably British, with whom you already do business. In certain circumstances you may be directed to a local stockist, agent or representative.

2   When the publisher agrees to supply you, your order should include:
   your full name and address;
   order date and order number;
   dispatch instructions: where you want the books to be sent and where you want the invoice sent;
   carriage instructions:
      surface post
      special carrier (e.g. shipper)
      air freight
   invoicing instructions:
      if you want a separate invoice by airmail
      minimum number of copies you require
   full details of the book:
      number of copies you need
      title
      author/editor
      cased/limp/paperback
      international standard book number (ISBN)

3   Orders Clearing, Mardev Ltd, Quadrant House, The Quadrant, Sutton, Surrey SM2 5AS (tel: +44 (0)20 8652 3899, fax: +44 (0)20 8652 4597, email: enquiries@mardev.com, web site: http://www.mardevlists.com) have an Orders Clearing system: by sending all your orders for different publishers to the one address, you can save yourself money. Similarly, Orders Clearing operates a service for the payment of publishers' accounts, the Overseas Booksellers' Clearing House (OBCH). Booksellers may send one cheque for various accounts and OBCH will then distribute the payments to the different publishers.

4   An Orders Clearing Service is also offered by the Booksellers Order Distribution Ltd (BOD). Their address is 49 Victoria Road, Aldershot, Hampshire GU11 1SJ (tel: +44 (0)1252 20697, fax: +44 (0)1252 20697).

5   Nielsen BookNet provides a range of e-commerce services that allow electronic trading between booksellers, distributors, publishers, libraries and other suppliers, regardless of their size and location. Services include BookNet for booksellers and publishers/distributors, TeleOrdering and EDI messaging. Contact Nielsen BookData, 3rd Floor, Midas House, 62 Goldsworth Road, Woking, GU21 6LQ (tel: +44 (0)870 777 8710, fax: +44 (0)870 777 8711, email: sales@nielsenbookdata.co.uk, website: http://www.bookdata.co.uk).

FOR REFERENCE

1   **Nielsen BookData:**
Provides monthly and quarterly content-rich book information for English-language titles published internationally. Available on CD-ROM and online by subscription from Nielsen BookData, 3rd Floor, Midas House, 62 Goldsworth Road, Woking, GU21 6LQ (tel: +44 (0)870 777 8710, fax: +44 (0)870 777 8711, email: sales@nielsenbookdata.co.uk, website: http://www.bookdata.co.uk).

2   **The Bookseller:**
The British book trade journal, published weekly by Bookseller Publications, containing correspondence, articles, trade news, together with a list of books published each week (web site: http://www.theBookseller.com). See also section 6.12 for details of other periodicals and reference books of the trade.

3   **British National Bibliography:**
A subject list of new British books arranged by Dewey classification. Published weekly with interim cumulations and an annual cumulation by the British Library, National Bibliographic Service, Boston Spa, Wetherby, West Yorkshire LS23 7BQ (tel: +44 (0)1937 546585, fax: +44 (0)1937 546586, email: nbs-info@bl.uk, web site: http://www.bl.uk).

4   Individual publishers will normally provide catalogues of their own publications on request.

HOW TO PAY

You can pay by:
   cheque, bank draft or letter of credit
   bill of exchange drawn by the publisher on your giro or postal account
   international money order/postal order

IMPORTANT

Please make sure that:
   the publisher receives the *full amount* of the invoice value, free of all bank charges and transfer fees;
   you pay *promptly*;
   if you have any problems, raise them *promptly*;
   if you have any difficulty in paying, consult your local bank manager, or the British Embassy, Consulate or High Commission.

WHEN YOU HAVE DIFFICULTY IN OBTAINING BRITISH BOOKS

1   If you have a problem of a *general* nature, please write to the Publishers Association, 29b Montague Street, London WC1B 5BH (email: mail@publishers.org.uk, tel: +44 (0)20 7691 9191, fax: +44 (0)20 7691 9199). The Association cannot intervene in problems which may arise between individual booksellers and publishers.

2   British Council

Your nearest office may be able to help you with enquiries about UK publishing. Details of its network of offices are available from: British Council Information Centre, tel: +44 (0)161 957 7755, fax: +44 (0) 161 957 7762, email: general.enquiries@britishcouncil.org, minicom: +44 (0)161 957 7188, web site: http://www.britishcouncil.org.

PUBLISHERS' ABBREVIATED ANSWERS

Most publishers use one of the answers below when books are not available, and give an explanation of their answer codes at the bottom of the invoice.

NK	Not known, not ours, or so far in the future or so long out of print that it is unknown to the trade department
OO/TF	On order, to follow shortly
B8 *or* **BDG8**	Binding, will be available in August
B/ND	Binding (no date)
RP/June *or* **RP/6**	Reprint available in June
RP/2M	Reprint available in 2 months
NYP	Not yet published
NEP	New edition in preparation
RPUC	Reprint under consideration
OP	Out of print
OO/USA	On order, to be supplied by USA
TOP	Temporarily out of print
OS	Out of stock
RP/ND	Reprinting, no date

TECHNICAL TERMS

Firm

Books are normally supplied 'firm'. This means you will accept the books, pay for them, and will not be able to return them.

See-safe or On approval

Some publishers are prepared to supply books on the basis that they are paid for at normal credit terms, but if the books remain unsold they may be returned with the publisher's authorization for crediting against future orders. You will be expected to return the books at your own expense. You should always obtain in writing details from publishers of any such agreements they are prepared to offer to their customers.

Standing Orders

Some publishers operate a scheme which allows a bookseller automatically to receive books in given subjects as they are published. These are normally supplied 'on approval'. You should write to individual publishers for details of their schemes.

Continuation Orders

Continuation Orders can be placed for books published in series and multi-volume works. This means that each new volume that appears will be sent to you automatically.

Pro-forma Invoice

Some publishers may prefer to supply initial orders by means of a pro-forma invoice which has to be paid before the books are sent.

THE PUBLISHERS ASSOCIATION

29b Montague Street, London WC1B 5BW
Telephone: +44 (0)20 7691 9191 **Fax:** +44 (0)20 7691 9199
Email: mail@publishers.org.uk
Web site: http://www.publishers.org.uk

Chief Executive: Simon Juden
Director of Educational, Academic & Professional Publishing:
  Graham Taylor
Director of International Services: Emma House

Making the case for UK publishers
– **The Publishers Association** is the leading organisation working on the behalf of book, journal and electronic publishers based in the UK. We bring publishers together to discuss the critical issues facing the industry and to define the practical policies, which will drive our lobbying and campaigns in the UK and Internationally. The aim of The Publishers Association is to ensure a secure future for the UK publishing industry.
– **Acting for the Industry:** The PA's mission is to strengthen the trading environment for UK publishers by ensuring that the needs and concerns of the industry are heard at all levels of Government in the UK, in Europe and internationally. We are actively involved in issues such as: copyright legislation, the adaptation of legislation to digital technology, copyright licensing arrangements for education, business, and public bodies, legislation on VAT, e-commerce and other issues affecting publishers, funding for learning and information resources in schools, colleges and universities, the promotion of books and reading, export promotion of books and journals, anti-piracy campaigns (terrestrial and internet), efficiency in supply and marketing, the protection of freedom to publish.
– **Front Line Information:** PA posts front line information to our website and communicates with members through our regular e-mail bulletins. The Members Only section of the PA website contains detailed information prepared exclusively for members including: the latest market statistics, copyright law updates, comments on current government policy, PA briefs and reports on market concerns, anti-piracy action updates, digital rights information, updates on EU legislation.

Home and Export Markets
Market development is at the heart of the PA's activities, which include:
– **International trade fairs**, operating with UK Trade & Investment a subsidy scheme for companies wishing to exhibit. Additionally, our TurnKey Exhibition Services offer publishers a complete exhibition service for major fairs.

– **Market intelligence**, including free online access to the Global Publishing Information website (http://www.publishers.org.uk/gpi.nsf), and exclusive access to the Aid Digest.
– **Trade delegations and seminars** organised with UK Trade & Investment support, to gain knowledge of and exposure in growth markets such as China, Africa, Asia and Eastern Europe.
– **Home trade initiatives**, such as World Book Day, which result in a significant increase in sales, particularly of children's books, during the period of promotion.

Join the PA now – add your voice, have your say
As a PA member you can add your voice and have your say on the vital issues affecting our industry today. Membership is open to any company registered in the UK engaged in book, journal or electronic publishing as a bona fide and continuing operation. Subscription rates are based on turnover, with special introductory rates for new members and discounted rates for journal publishers.

The International Division
The International Division actively supports the international sales activities of PA members. We act against piracy, and on copyright and trade barrier issues, organise trade missions and UK representation at international trade fairs.

Trade Publishers Council
The Trade Publishers Council determines PA policy on consumer market matters, and acts on specific issues with the objectives of expanding the market and increasing efficiency. Other trade groups include our Children's Book Group and Religious Books Group.

Academic and Professional Publishing
The Academic and Professional Division provides a forum for higher education, monograph, journal and reference publishers. We represent publishers' concerns to key stakeholders, conduct market research and run a number of events.

The Educational Publishers Council (EPC)
The Educational Publishers Council provides a voice for school and college publishers. We campaign for better funding for learning resources and represent the industry in the development of the electronic market, as well as running seminars and compiling market statistics.

Digital Publishing Forum
Provides support for on-line and off-line electronic publishers, and organises a programme of seminars and meetings.

2   Publishers

2001

AA PUBLISHING
[trading as Automobile Association Media Ltd]
Fanum House, Basingstoke, Hants
RG21 4EA
Telephone: 01256 491578
Fax: 01256 322575
Web Site: www.theAA.com

Distribution (UK):
Littlehampton Book Services Ltd,
Faraday Close, Durrington, Worthing,
West Sussex BN13 3RB

Directors: R. C. A. Miles (Chief Executive)
D. Watchus (Publisher)
T. A. Lee (Sales & Marketing)
R. Firth (Production)
L. Hopkins (Finance)
S. Gold (Human Resources)

Atlases & Maps; Gardening; Guide Books;
Natural History; Photography; Transport;
Travel & Topography; General Illustrated

ISBNs, Imprints & Series:
978 0 7495 Travel Series: Citypacks; Travel
Series: Essentials; Travel Series: Key
Guides; Travel Series: Spiral Guides
978 0 7495, 978 0 86145 Automobile
Association

Distributor for:
AAA Road Maps of USA, Canada, Mexico;
Thomas Cook; Scottish Tourist Board

2002

*ABSOLUTE PRESS
Scarborough House, 29 James Street West,
Bath BA1 2BT
Telephone: 01225 316013
Fax: 01225 445836
Email: sales@absolutepress.co.uk
Web Site: www.absolutepress.co.uk

**Accounts, Warehouse, Trade Enquiries
& Orders:**
Central Books Ltd, 99 Wallis Road, London
E9 5LN
Telephone: (020) 8986 4854
Fax: (020) 8533 5821

Publisher & Editorial: Jon Croft
Art Director: Matt Inwood
Commissioning Editor: Meg Avent

Cookery, Wines & Spirits; Gardening; Guide
Books; Illustrated & Fine Editions; Sports &
Games; Travel & Topography

ISBNs, Imprints & Series: 978 0 948230

Overseas Representation:
Australia: Peribo Pty Ltd, Mount Kuring-Gai,
NSW
South Africa: Stephan Phillips (Pty) Ltd,
Umdloti Beach
USA (Outlines only): BHB International Inc,
Seneca, SC, USA

2003

ACAIR LTD
Unit 7, 7 James Street, Stornoway,
Isle of Lewis HS1 2QN
Telephone: 01851 703020
Fax: 01851 703294
Email: info@acairbooks.com
Web Site: www.acairbooks.com

Distribution:
BookSource, 50 Cambuslang Road,
Glasgow G32 8NB
Telephone: 0845 370 0067
Fax: 0845 370 0068

Editor: Norma Macleod
Designer: Margaret Anne Macleod
Administrator: Margaret Martin
Stock: Donalda Riddell

Children's Books; Educational & Textbooks;
Fiction; History & Antiquarian; Poetry

New Titles: 14 (2008) , 16 (2009)
No of Employees: 4
Annual Turnover: £90,000

ISBNs, Imprints & Series: 978 0 86152

Book Trade Association Membership:
BA

2004

ACCENT PRESS LTD
The Old School, Upper High Street,
Bedlinog CF46 6SA
Telephone: 01443 710930
Fax: 01443 710940
Email: info@accentpress.co.uk
Web Site: www.accentpress.co.uk

Distribution:
Macmillan Distribution (MDL), Brunel Road,
Houndmills, Basingstoke, Hants RG21 6XS
Telephone: 01256 802692
Email: trade@macmillan.co.uk

Directors: Hazel Cushion (Managing)
Robert Cushion (Finance)
Administration: Karen Smart
Marketing: Cory Hughes
Production: Alison Stokes

Biography & Autobiography; Children's
Books; Cookery, Wines & Spirits; Crafts &

Hobbies; Crime; Educational & Textbooks;
Fiction; Guide Books; Humour; Industry,
Business & Management; Medical (incl. Self
Help & Alternative Medicine); Poetry

Associated Companies:
Curriculum Concepts UK; Green Fuse;
Wedding Bible Co; Xcite Books

Overseas Representation:
Australia, New Zealand, Papua New Guinea
& Fiji: DA Information Services Pty Ltd,
Mitcham, Vic, Australia
South Africa: Shirley Cooksley, Quartet
Sales & Marketing, Northcliffe
USA: National Book Network Inc, Blue Ridge
Summit, PA

Book Trade Association Membership:
BA; IPG

2005

ACUMEN PUBLISHING LTD
Stocksfield Hall, Stocksfield,
Northumberland NE43 7TN
Telephone: 01661 844865
Fax: 01661 844865
Email:
steven.gerrard@acumenpublishing.co.uk
Web Site: www.acumenpublishing.co.uk

**Warehouse, Trade Enquiries, Orders &
Distribution:**
Marston Book Services, 160 Milton Park,
Abingdon, Oxon OX14 4YN
Telephone: 01235 465521
Fax: 01235 465555
Email: trade.orders@marston.co.uk
Web Site: www.marston.co.uk

Publisher: Steven Gerrard
Prepress Manager: Kate Williams

Academic & Scholarly; Biography &
Autobiography; Educational & Textbooks;
History & Antiquarian; Philosophy; Politics &
World Affairs; Reference Books, Directories
& Dictionaries; Religion & Theology;
Sociology & Anthropology

New Titles: 30 (2008) , 30 (2009)

ISBNs, Imprints & Series:
978 1 84465, 978 1 902683

Overseas Representation:
Australia & New Zealand: Palgrave
Macmillan, South Yarra, Vic, Australia
Austria, Germany & Switzerland: Bernd
Feldmann, Oranienburg, Germany
Belgium, Luxembourg & Netherlands:
Kemper Conseil Publishing, De Star,
Netherlands
Botswana, Lesotho, Namibia, South Africa,

Swaziland & Zimbabwe: The African
Moon Press, Kelvin, South Africa
Brunei, Cambodia, Indonesia, Laos,
Philippines, Singapore, Thailand &
Vietnam: APD Singapore Pte Ltd,
Singapore
China, Hong Kong, Korea & Taiwan: Asia
Publishers Services Ltd, Hong Kong
France, Italy, Portugal & Spain: Flavio
Marcello Publishers' Agents &
Consultants, Padua, Italy
Greece, Cyprus & Malta: Charles Gibbes
Associates, Louslitges, France
India: Maya Publishers Pvt Ltd, New Delhi
Scandinavia: Colin Flint Ltd, Harlow, UK

Book Trade Association Membership:
IPG

2006

ADAM MATTHEW DIGITAL LTD
Pelham House, London Road,
Marlborough, Wiltshire SN8 2AA
Telephone: 01672 511921
Fax: 01672 511663
Email: david@amdigital.co.uk
Web Site: www.amdigital.co.uk

Publishers: William Pidduck (Chairman)
David Tyler (Managing Director)
Khal Rudin (Sales & Marketing Director)

Academic & Scholarly; Electronic
(Educational); Electronic (Professional &
Academic); Gender Studies; History &
Antiquarian; Literature & Criticism; Military
& War

New Titles: 8 (2008) , 8 (2009)
No of Employees: 20
Annual Turnover: £2.66M

Parent Company:
Hanfrageo Holdings Ltd

Associated Companies:
Adam Matthew Publications Ltd

Overseas Representation:
Italy: Licosa SPA, Florence
Japan: Maruzen Co Ltd, Tokyo
Korea: GDI, Seoul, Republic of Korea
Taiwan: Transmission Books & Microforms
Co Ltd, Taipei

2007

ADAM MATTHEW PUBLICATIONS
LTD
Pelham House, London Road,
Marlborough, Wiltshire SN8 2AA
Telephone: 01672 511921
Fax: 01672 511663
Email: david@ampltd.co.uk
Web Site: www.ampltd.co.uk

Publishers: William Pidduck (*Chairman*)
David Tyler (*Managing Director*)
Khal Rudin (*Sales & Marketing Director*)

Academic & Scholarly; Economics; Gender Studies; History & Antiquarian; Literature & Criticism; Reference Books, Directories & Dictionaries

New Titles: 10 (2008) , 7 (2009)
No of Employees: 20
Annual Turnover: £1.6M

ISBNs, Imprints & Series: 978 1 85711

Parent Company:
Hanfrageo Holdings Ltd

Associated Companies:
Adam Matthew Digital Ltd

Overseas Representation:
Japan: Maruzen Co Ltd, Tokyo
Taiwan: Transmission Books & Microforms
Co Ltd, Taipei

2008

ADAMSON PUBLISHING LTD
8 The Moorings, Norwich NR3 3AX
Telephone: 01603 623336
Fax: 01603 624767
Email: stephen@adamsonbooks.com
Web Site: www.adamsonbooks.com

Chairman: Stephen Adamson

Educational & Textbooks; Reference Books, Directories & Dictionaries

New Titles: 3 (2008) , 4 (2009)
No of Employees: 1

ISBNs, Imprints & Series: 978 0 948543

2009

ADLARD COLES NAUTICAL
36 Soho Square, London W1D 3QY
Telephone: (020) 7758 0200
Fax: (020) 7758 0333
Email: acn@acblack.com
Web Site: www.adlardcoles.com

Directors: Janet Murphy (*Editorial*)
David Wightman (*Sales*)
Jill Coleman (*Managing*)

Nautical

New Titles: 35 (2008) , 36 (2009)
No of Employees: 5

ISBNs, Imprints & Series:
978 0 7136, 978 0 85177

Parent Company:
A. & C. Black (Publishers) Ltd

Associated Companies:
Thomas Reed Publications; Reeds Almanac

Overseas Representation:
See: A. & C. Black (Publishers) Ltd, London,
UK

2010

AEON BOOKS
118 Finchley Road, London W5 4YX
Telephone: (020) 7431 1075
Fax: (020) 7435 9076
Email: shop@karnacbooks.com
Web Site: www.karnacbooks.com

Warehouse, Distribution:
NBN International, Estover Road, Plymouth
PL6 7PY
Telephone: 01752 202301
Fax: 01752 202333

Email: orders@nbninternational.com
Web Site: nbninternational.com

Managing Director: Oliver Rathbone

Magic & the Occult

New Titles: 10 (2008) , 10 (2009)
No of Employees: 8
Annual Turnover: £20,000

ISBNs, Imprints & Series: 978 1 904658

Overseas Representation:
USA: Stylus Publishing Inc, Sterling, VA

Book Trade Association Membership:
BA

2011

AGE CONCERN BOOKS
1268 London Road, Norbury, London
SW16 4ER
Telephone: (020) 8765 7200
Fax: (020) 8765 7211
Email: books@ace.org.uk
Web Site: www.ageconcern.org.uk

Trade Distributor:
Orca Book Services, Stanley House,
3 Fleets Lane, Poole, Dorset BH15 3AJ
Telephone: 01202 665432
Fax: 01202 666219
Email: orders@orcabookservices.co.uk

Commissioning Editor: (vacant)
Production Controller: Keith Hawkins
Marketing Officer: Donna Colbourne
Publications & Marketing Manager:
Kate Pearce

Academic & Scholarly; Accountancy & Taxation; Computer Science; Educational & Textbooks; Gardening; Guide Books; Health & Beauty; Medical (incl. Self Help & Alternative Medicine); Reference Books, Directories & Dictionaries; Sociology & Anthropology

New Titles: 10 (2008) , 8 (2009)
No of Employees: 3

ISBNs, Imprints & Series:
Plan it! (series); Your Rights (series); Can do computing; We've Made It Easy
978 0 86242

Parent Company:
Age Concern

Book Trade Association Membership:
IPG

2012

AIR-BRITAIN (HISTORIANS) LTD
41 Penshurst Road, Leigh, Tonbridge, Kent
TN11 8HL
Telephone: 01732 835637
Fax: 01732 835637
Email: mike@absales.demon.co.uk
Web Site: www.air-britain.com

Directors: Michael Graham Rice (*Sales*)
Howard Nash
Dr C. Chatfield
Treasurer: Don Schofield
Chairman: Geoff Negus

Aviation; Military & War

New Titles: 12 (2008) , 12 (2009)
No of Employees: 4
Annual Turnover: £200,000

ISBNs, Imprints & Series: 978 0 85130

Overseas Representation:
Australia & New Zealand: Aviation
Worldwide, Oamaru, New Zealand

2013

AL-FURQAN ISLAMIC HERITAGE FOUNDATION
22A Old Court Place, London W8 4PL
Telephone: (020) 3130 1530
Fax: (020) 7937 2540
Email: info@al-furqan.com
Web Site: www.al-furqan.com

Office Manager: Susan John-Richards

Academic & Scholarly; History & Antiquarian; Mathematics & Statistics; Religion & Theology

ISBNs, Imprints & Series:
978 1 873992 Al-Furqan Publications

Book Trade Association Membership:
Publishers Association; BA

2014

ALBAN BOOKS LTD
14 Belford Road, Edinburgh EH4 3BL
Telephone: 0131 226 2217
Fax: 0131 225 5999
Email: sales@albanbooks.com
Web Site: www.albanbooks.com

Warehouse, Invoicing, Customer Services:
c/o Marston Book Services
Telephone: 01235 465500
Fax: 01235 465555

Managing Director: Jane Grounsell
Sales Manager: Nigel Parkinson
Marketing Executive: Elaine Reid
Accounts & Special Orders: Margaret Reid
Sales Representative: Kate Dennis

Academic & Scholarly; Children's Books; Educational & Textbooks; Philosophy; Reference Books, Directories & Dictionaries; Religion & Theology; Spirituality

No of Employees: 6

Distributor for:
USA: Abingdon Press; Augsburg Fortress
Publishers; Ave Maria Press; Baylor
University Press; Wm B. Eerdmans
Publishing Co; Hendrickson Publishers;
Orbis Books; Templeton Foundation
Press; Westminster John Knox Press

2015

ALBYN PRESS
2 Caversham Street, Chelsea, London
SW3 4AH
Telephone: (020) 7351 4995
Fax: (020) 7351 4995
Email:
leonard.holdsworth@btopenworld.com

Director: James Hughes (*Editorial*)
Production: Leonard Holdsworth
Sales: Margaret Fletcher

Fiction; Fine Art & Art History; Geography & Geology; Guide Books; History & Antiquarian; Illustrated & Fine Editions; Literature & Criticism; Poetry; Reference Books, Directories & Dictionaries; Transport; Scottish Books

New Titles: 12 (2008) , 15 (2009)
No of Employees: 4

ISBNs, Imprints & Series: 978 0 284

Parent Company:
Christchurch Publishers Ltd

Associated Companies:
Charles Skilton Publishing Group; Tallis
Press

Book Trade Association Membership:
IPG

2016

IAN ALLAN PUBLISHING LTD
Riverdene Business Park, Molesey Road,
Hersham, Surrey KT12 4RG
Telephone: 01932 266600
Fax: 01932 266601
Email: info@ianallanpublishing.co.uk
Web Site: www.ianallanpublishing.com

Distribution:
Littlehampton Book Services,
Faraday Close, Durrington, Worthing,
West Sussex BN13 3RB
Telephone: 01903 828800 (trade orders)
Fax: 01903 828802
Email: orders@lbsltd.co.uk

Mail Order:
Midland Counties Publications,
4 Watling Drive, Hinckley, Leics LE10 3EY
Telephone: 01455 254450
Fax: 01455 233737
Email: orders@midlandcounties.com
Web Site:
www.midlandcountiessuperstore.com

Representation (England & Wales):
Amalgamated Book Services,
The Old Mill House, Mill Lane, Uckfield,
East Sussex TN22 5AA
Telephone: 01825 746050
Fax: 01825 764925

Representation (Scotland):
Alan Scollan, Earnockmuir Cottage,
Meikle Earnock Road, Hamilton ML3 8RL
Telephone: 01698 459371

Chairman: David Allan
Directors: Iain Aitken (*Managing*)
Jonathan King (*Sales & Marketing*)
Managers: Nick Grant (*Publisher*)
Nigel Passmore (*Sales*)
Sue Frost (*Marketing*)
Alan Butcher (*Production*)

Atlases & Maps; Aviation; Biography & Autobiography; History & Antiquarian; Military & War; Nautical; Reference Books, Directories & Dictionaries; Sports & Games; Transport

ISBNs, Imprints & Series:
978 0 7110 Ian Allan
978 0 85318 Lewis; Lewis Masonic (only
available from Midland Counties
Publications)
978 0 86093 OPC
978 1 85780 Aerofax; Midland Publishing
978 1 903223 Classic Publications

Parent Company:
Ian Allan Group Ltd

Distributor for:
KRB (formerly Kestrel Railway Books);
Millstream; Noodle Books; Pendragon;
Polygon Press; Red Kite; Runpast; John
Sullivan

Overseas Representation:
Australia, New Zealand, New Guinea & Papua: DLS Australia (Pty) Ltd, Braeside,
Vic, Australia
Austria, Belgium, France, Germany, Netherlands & Switzerland: European
Marketing Services, London, UK
Canada: Vanwell Publishing Ltd, St
Catharines, Ont
Central & Eastern Europe: Tony Moggach,
InterMedia Americana (IMA) Ltd,
London, UK
Middle & Far East: Julian Ashton, Ashton
International Marketing Services,
Sevenoaks, Kent, UK
Republic of Ireland & Northern Ireland:
Sales Office, Ian Allan Publishing Ltd,
Hersham, UK

Scandinavia: Gill Angell & Stewart Siddall, Angell Eurosales, Berwick-on-Tweed, UK
Spain, Portugal, Gibraltar, Italy, Malta, Greece, Slovenia, Croatia, Bosnia & Montenegro: Bookport Associates, Corsico (MI), Italy
USA (Aviation titles only): Specialty Press, North Branch, MN, USA
USA (Masonic titles only): Atlas Books (a division of BookMasters Inc), Ashland, OH, USA
USA (Military titles only): Casemate Publishers & Book Distributors LLC, Havertown, PA, USA

Book Trade Association Membership:
BA; IPG

2017

PHILIP ALLAN PUBLISHERS LTD
Market Place, Deddington, Oxon OX15 0SE
Telephone: 01869 338652
Fax: 01869 338803
Email: sales@philipallan.co.uk
Web Site: www.philipallan.co.uk

Editorial Director: Paul Cherry
Marketing Manager: Ceri Jenkins

Educational & Textbooks

New Titles: 200 (2008) , 216 (2009)
No of Employees: 28

ISBNs, Imprints & Series:
978 0 86003, 978 1 84489 Philip Allan Updates

Parent Company:
Hodder Education

Book Trade Association Membership:
EPC

2018

*R. L. ALLAN & SON PUBLISHERS
[Ltd]
53 Bothwell Street, Glasgow G2 6TS
Telephone: 0141 204 1285
Fax: 0141 204 1285
Email: rlallan@btinternet.com
Web Site: www.bibles-direct.com

Managing Director: Nicholas Gray
Company Secretary: Wendy Gray
Administration: Margaret Milligan
Distribution: Eric Campbell

Religion & Theology

ISBNs, Imprints & Series: 978 0 948643

Parent Company:
Chapter House Ltd

2019

J. A. ALLEN
[an imprint of Robert Hale Ltd]
45–47 Clerkenwell Green, London EC1R 0HT
Telephone: (020) 7251 2661
Fax: (020) 7490 4958
Email: allen@halebooks.com
Web Site: www.halebooks.com

Warehouse & Shipping:
Combined Book Services Ltd, Units I/K, Paddock Wood Distribution Centre, Paddock Wood, Tonbridge, Kent TN12 6UU
Telephone: 01892 837171
Fax: 01892 837272
Email: orders@combook.co.uk

Commissioning Editor: Lesley Gowers *(Publisher)*

Dogs; Equine & Equestrian

ISBNs, Imprints & Series: 978 0 85131

Parent Company:
Robert Hale Ltd

Overseas Representation:
See: Robert Hale Ltd, London, UK

2020

*ALLIED MOUSE LTD
Mayfield, High Street, Dingwall IV15 9SS
Telephone: 01349 865400
Fax: 01349 866066

Directors: Sitakumari
Nick Sidle

Children's Books

ISBNs, Imprints & Series: 978 0 9513492

Book Trade Association Membership:
Publishers Association

2021

ALLISON & BUSBY
13 Charlotte Mews, London W1T 4EJ
Telephone: (020) 7580 1080
Fax: (020) 7580 1180
Email: susie@allisonandbusby.com
Web Site: www.allisonandbusby.com

Warehouse/Distribution:
Turnaround Publisher Services Ltd, Unit 3, Olympia Trading Estate, Coburg Road, London N22 6TZ
Telephone: (020) 8829 3000
Fax: (020) 8881 5088
Email: orders@turnaround-uk.com

Publishing Director: Susie Dunlop *(UK Sales)*
Managers: Chiara Priorelli *(Publicity)*
Lara Dafert *(Editorial)*
Lesley Brown *(Sales & Marketing)*
Finance: John Gardner
Editors: Louise Watson
Christina Griffiths *(Art)*

Biography & Autobiography; Crime; Fiction; History & Antiquarian; Humour; Literature & Criticism

ISBNs, Imprints & Series:
978 0 7490, 978 0 85031

Parent Company:
Spain: Editorial Prensa Iberica SA

Overseas Representation:
Africa, Middle East & Gulf: InterMedia Americana (IMA) Ltd, London, UK
Australia & New Zealand: Keith Ainsworth (Pty) Ltd, Penrith, NSW, Australia
Canada: Georgetown Publications Inc, Toronto, Ont
France, Belgium & Netherlands: Michael Geoghegan, London, UK
Germany: Gabriele Kern Publishers Services, Frankfurt-am-Main
India: Maya Publishers Pvt Ltd, New Delhi
Italy: Ted Dougherty, London, UK
Scandinavia: Angell Eurosales, Berwick-on-Tweed, UK
South & Central America & Caribbean: InterMedia Americana (IMA) Ltd, London, UK
South & South East Europe, Eastern Europe & Egypt: IMA, Greece
South Africa: Trinity Books CC, Randburg
Spain, Portugal & Malta: Peter Prout Iberian Book Services, Madrid, Spain
USA: International Publishers Marketing Inc, Sterling, VA

Book Trade Association Membership:
IPG

2022

ALMA BOOKS LTD
London House,
243–253 Lower Mortlake Road, Richmond, Surrey TW9 2LL
Telephone: (020) 8948 9550
Fax: (020) 8948 5599
Email: info@almabooks.com
Web Site: www.almabooks.com

Directors: Alessandro Gallenzi *(Managing)*
Elisabetta Minervini *(Sales & Marketing)*

Biography & Autobiography; Crime; Fiction; Humour; Poetry

New Titles: 15 (2008) , 15 (2009)

ISBNs, Imprints & Series: 978 1 84688

Associated Companies:
UK: Herla Publishing

Overseas Representation:
Australia: Tower Books Pty Ltd, Frenchs Forest, NSW
South Africa: Penguin Books South Africa (Pty) Ltd, Johannesburg
USA & Canada: Trafalgar Square Publishing / IPG, Chicago, IL, USA

2023

ALPHA SCIENCE INTERNATIONAL LTD
7200 The Quorum,
Oxford Business Park North,
Garsington Road, Oxford OX4 2JZ
Telephone: 01865 481433
Fax: 01865 481482
Email: info@alphasci.com
Web Site: www.alphasci.com

Trade Orders:
Marston Book Services,
Trade Order Department, PO Box 269, Abingdon, Oxon OX14 4YN
Telephone: 01235 465500
Fax: 01235 465655
Email: direct.trade@marston.co.uk

Director: Sascha Mehra

Academic & Scholarly; Biology & Zoology; Chemistry; Computer Science; Educational & Textbooks; Electronic (Educational); Electronic (Professional & Academic); Engineering; Environment & Development Studies; Mathematics & Statistics; Medical (incl. Self Help & Alternative Medicine); Physics; Reference Books, Directories & Dictionaries; Scientific & Technical

New Titles: 100 (2008) , 100 (2009)

ISBNs, Imprints & Series: 978 1 84265

Distributor for:
India: Narosa Publishing House Pvt Ltd

Book Trade Association Membership:
Publishers Association; IPG

2024

*AMBERWOOD PUBLISHING LTD
Unit 4, Stirling House, Sunderland Quay, Culpeper Close, Medway City Estate, Rochester, Kent ME2 4HN
Telephone: 01634 290115
Fax: 01634 290761
Email: books@amberwoodpublishing.com
Web Site:
www.amberwoodpublishing.com

Warehouse:
Mulberry Court, Stour Road, Bournemouth, Dorset
Telephone: 01202 488333
Fax: 01202 476872

Managing Director: June Crisp
Co Secretary: Henry Crisp
Chairman: Victor Perfitt
Administration & Accounts, Dispatch:
Chris Derby
Yvonne James

Health & Beauty; Medical (incl. Self Help & Alternative Medicine)

ISBNs, Imprints & Series:
978 0 9517723, 978 1 899308

2025

AMERICAN PSYCHIATRIC PUBLISHING INC
5 Victoria House, 138 Watling Street East, Towcester NN12 6BT
Telephone: 01327 357770
Fax: 01327 359572
Email: appi@oppuk.co.uk
Web Site: www.appi.org

Warehouse & Distribution:
NBN International, Estover Road, Plymouth PL6 7PY
Telephone: 01752 202301
Fax: 01752 202331
Email: orders@nbninternational.com
Web Site: www.nbninternational.com

Manager: Gary Hall

Academic & Scholarly; Educational & Textbooks; Medical (incl. Self Help & Alternative Medicine); Psychology & Psychiatry; Reference Books, Directories & Dictionaries

ISBNs, Imprints & Series: 978 1 5856

Parent Company:
USA: American Psychiatric Publishing Inc

2026

AMNESTY INTERNATIONAL INTERNATIONAL SECRETARIAT
1 Easton Street, London WC1X 0DW
Telephone: (020) 7413 5500
Fax: (020) 7956 1157
Email: amnestyis@amnesty.org &
orderpubs@amnesty.org
Web Site: www.amnesty.org &
shop.amnesty.org

Secretary General: Irene Khan
Director, Publications Program: Sarah Wilbourne

Academic & Scholarly; Law; Politics & World Affairs; Human Rights

New Titles: 8 (2009)
No of Employees: 529

ISBNs, Imprints & Series: 978 0 86210

Overseas Representation:
see website: www.amnesty.org, UK

2027

A.M.S. EDUCATIONAL LTD
38 Parkside Road, Leeds LS6 4NB
Telephone: 0113 275 5500
Fax: 0113 275 7799
Email: admin@amseducational.co.uk
Web Site: www.amseducational.com

Directors: Stan Sharp *(Managing)*
Margaret Sharp *(Finance)*
Manager: Victoria Keys *(Publishing)*

Children's Books; Educational & Textbooks; Military & War; Poetry

New Titles: 18 (2008) , 20 (2009)
No of Employees: 5

ISBNs, Imprints & Series:
978 0 946947 New Education Press (N.E.P.)
978 1 86029 A.M.S. Educational;
Educational Fun Factory; Propagator
Press
978 1 899929 Leopard Learning
978 1 900899 Falconwood Series
978 1 902751 Senter Series

Distributor for:
Claire Publications; Desktop Publications;
Prim-Ed Publishing
New Zealand: Sunshinebooks UK

Book Trade Association Membership:
IPG

2028

ANDERSEN PRESS LTD
20 Vauxhall Bridge Road, London
SW1V 2SA
Telephone: (020) 7840 8701
Fax: (020) 7233 6263
Email:
andersenpublicity@randomhouse.co.uk
Web Site: www.andersenpress.co.uk

Warehouse, Orders & Payments:
TBS Ltd, Colchester Road, Frating Green,
Colchester, Essex CO7 7DW
Telephone: 01206 255678
Fax: 01206 255930

Address for Returns Requests:
Sales Department,
Random House Children's Books,
61-63 Uxbridge Road, London W5 5SA
Telephone: (020) 8231 6800
Fax: (020) 8231 6767
Web Site: www.andersenpress.co.uk

Directors: Klaus Flugge *(Managing &*
Publisher)
P. W. Durrance
Rona Selby *(Editorial)*
Company Secretary: Mark Hendle
Rights & Permissions: Sarah Pakenham
Marketing & Publicity: Eloise King

Children's Books

ISBNs, Imprints & Series:
978 0 86264, 978 0 905478, 978 1 84270,
978 1 84939 Andersen Artists (greetings
cards); Andersen Press; Andersen Young
Readers' Library; Children's Picture Books

Associated Companies:
Random House

Overseas Representation:
Other overseas markets See: Random
House Group Ltd, London, UK
USA: Lerner Publishing Group

2029

PETER ANDREW PUBLISHING CO
LTD
4 Charlecot Road, Droitwich, Worcs
WR9 7RP
Telephone: 01905 778543
Email: sales@peterandrew.com
Web Site: www.peterandrew.com

Directors: Philip Checkley
Joan Checkley *(Sales)*

Academic & Scholarly; Accountancy &
Taxation; Economics; Engineering; Health &
Beauty; Industry, Business & Management;
Law; Sports & Games; Theatre, Drama &
Dance

ISBNs, Imprints & Series: 978 0 946796

Book Trade Association Membership:
Book Data

2030

CHRIS ANDREWS PUBLICATIONS
LTD
15 Curtis Yard, North Hinksey Lane, Oxford
OX2 0LX
Telephone: 01865 723404
Fax: 01865 725294
Email: chris.andrews1@btclick.com
Web Site: www.cap-ox.co.uk

Partners: Chris Andrews
Virginia Andrews
Personal Assistant: Annabel Matthews

Travel & Topography

New Titles: 30 (2008) , 25 (2009)
No of Employees: 3

ISBNs, Imprints & Series:
978 0 9509643, 978 0 9540331, 978 1
905385, 978 1 906725

Book Trade Association Membership:
IPG

2031

ANGLO-SAXON BOOKS
25 Brocks Road, Swaffham, Norfolk
PE37 7XG
Telephone: 0845 430 4200
Email: enq@asbooks.co.uk
Web Site: www.asbooks.co.uk

Contact: Tony Linsell

Academic & Scholarly; Educational &
Textbooks; History & Antiquarian;
Languages & Linguistics; Military & War;
Poetry; Reference Books, Directories &
Dictionaries

New Titles: 4 (2008) , 5 (2009)

ISBNs, Imprints & Series:
978 1 898281 Anglo-Saxon Books
978 1 903313 Athelney

Overseas Representation:
USA & Canada: The David Brown Book Co,
Oakville, CT, USA

2032

ANN ARBOR PUBLISHERS LTD
PO Box 1, Belford, Northumberland
NE70 7JX
Telephone: 01668 214460
Fax: 01668 214484
Email: enquiries@annarbor.co.uk
Web Site: www.annarbor.co.uk

Managing Director: Peter D. Laverack

Children's Books; Educational & Textbooks;
Psychology & Psychiatry; High Interest Low
Reading Level Novels; Tests for Learning
Difficulty; Work Books for Dyslexic Pupils

New Titles: 2 (2008) , 4 (2009)
No of Employees: 4

ISBNs, Imprints & Series:
978 0 87879, 978 0 931421, 978 1 900506

Distributor for:
Academic Therapy Publications; Ann Arbor
Publishers; High Noon Books; PAR; Pro-
Ed; SlossEn; Wester Psychological
Services

Book Trade Association Membership:
BEEA

2033

ANSHAN LTD
6 Newlands Road, Tunbridge Wells, Kent
TN4 9AT
Telephone: 01892 557767

Fax: 01892 530358
Email: info@anshan.co.uk
Web Site: www.anshan.co.uk

Warehouse:
CBS, Unit Y,
Paddock Wood Distribution Centre,
Paddock Wood, Tonbridge, Kent TN12 6UU
Telephone: 01892 837171
Fax: 01892 837272
Email: orders@combook.co.uk
Web Site: www.combook.co.uk

Representation (UK):
Quantum Publishing Solutions Ltd,
2 Cheviot Road, Paisley PA2 8AN

Directors: Shân White *(Managing)*
Andrew White *(Sales)*

Academic & Scholarly; Chemistry;
Computer Science; Educational &
Textbooks; Engineering; Environment &
Development Studies; Mathematics &
Statistics; Medical (incl. Self Help &
Alternative Medicine); Physics; Psychology
& Psychiatry; Scientific & Technical

New Titles: 24 (2008) , 53 (2009)

ISBNs, Imprints & Series:
978 1 848290, 978 1 904798, 978 1
905740

Overseas Representation:
Central Europe: Andrew Durnell Marketing
Ltd, Tunbridge Wells, UK
China: Access Asia Media Services,
Shanghai, P. R. of China
Japan (Science Titles): Nankodo Co Ltd,
Tokyo, Japan; United Publishers Services
Ltd, Tokyo, Japan
Republic of Ireland & Northern Ireland:
Quantum Publishing Solutions Ltd,
Paisley, UK
Scandinavia: Colin Flint Ltd, Harlow, UK
Taiwan: Unifacmanu Trading Co Ltd, Taipei
USA: Princeton Selling Group Inc, Wayne,
PA

2034

ANTIQUE COLLECTORS' CLUB LTD
Sandy Lane, Old Martlesham, Woodbridge,
Suffolk IP12 4SD
Telephone: 01394 389950
Fax: 01394 389999
Email: sales@antique-acc.com
Web Site: www.antique-acc.com

Directors: Diana Steel *(Managing)*
Sarah Smye *(Marketing)*
Vanessa Shorten *(Financial)*
James Smith *(Sales)*
Mario Jellinek *(Business Development)*

Antiques & Collecting; Architecture &
Design; Children's Books; Cookery, Wines &
Spirits; Fashion & Costume; Fine Art & Art
History; Gardening; Humour; Natural
History; Reference Books, Directories &
Dictionaries

New Titles: 33 (2008) , 35 (2009)
No of Employees: 30
Annual Turnover: £3.5M

ISBNs, Imprints & Series:
978 0 902028, 978 0 907462, 978 1
85149, 978 1 870673

Associated Companies:
ACC Books; Garden Art Press; Natural
Wonders Press
UK: National Galleries of Scotland

Distributor for:
Acanthus Press; ACR Edition; Adelson
Galleries; Adler Planetarium and
Astronomy; Alinari 24 Ore; Umberto
Allemandi; Architectura & Natura;
Arnoldsche Verlagsanstalt; Arsenale

Editrice; Artmedia Press; The Azur
Corporation Ltd; Baldini Castoldi; Chris
Beetles; Beta Plus; George Braziller;
Brioni Books; Centro Di; The Chippendal
Society; Christie's Books; Deben Gallery;
Editions Vausor; Fine Arts Museum of
San Francisco; Fine Arts Society; Fiske &
Freeman; Fry Art Gallery; Gambero
Rosso; GML Publishing; Grafiche
Vianello; Alan & Simone Hartman; Heel
Verlag; Hudson Hills Press LLC; Intelligent
Layman; Jaca Book SPA; Kew Publishing;
Lannoo/Terra Publishers; Laynforah;
Mandragora; Merrick & Day; David
Messum; Motta; Museum SRL; New
Cavendish Books; Newark Museum; P. I.
Global; Palace Editions; Pandora; Panini;
Parkstone; Philadelphia Museum of Art;
Pointed Leaf Press; Randall
International; Ritika; River Books;
Riverside Book Company; Royal Ontario
Museum; Royal Pavilion Libraries &
Museums; Scala Publishers; J. & C. Smith;
Sotheby's NY; Stichting Kunstboek;
Storm King; Texstyle Solutions; Thieme
Art; M. T. Train; Verba Volant; Waanders
Publishers; The Walters Art Museum
Australia: Images
France: Alain de Gourcuff Editeur

Overseas Representation:
All other territories: Antique Collectors'
Club, Woodbridge, Suffolk, UK
Australia: Peribo Pty Ltd, Mount Kuring-Gai,
NSW
Belgium & Luxembourg: Altera Diffusion,
Belgium
Central Europe (excluding Russia): Csaba &
Jackie Lengyel de Bagota, Budapest,
Hungary
Far East (including Hong Kong, Taiwan,
Philippines & China): Asia Publishers
Services Ltd, Hong Kong
France: Interart SARL, Paris, UK
Germany, Austria & Switzerland: Michael
Klein, Vilsbiburg, Germany
India: Timeless, The Art Book Studio, New
Delhi
Iran: Jahan Adib Publishing, Tehran
Italy, Spain, Portugal & Greece: Penny
Padovani, London, UK
Japan & South Korea: Ralph & Sheila
Summers, Woodford Green, Essex, UK
Malaysia: APD Kuala Lumpur Pte Ltd,
Selangor
Near & Middle East & Turkey: Avicenna
Partnership, Dumfries, UK
Netherlands: Nilsson & Lamm BV, Weesp
New Zealand: Book Reps NZ Ltd, Auckland
Republic of Ireland & Northern Ireland:
Robert Towers, Monkstown, Co Dublin,
Republic of Ireland
Scandinavia & Iceland: Elisabeth Harder-
Kreimann, Hamburg, Germany
South & Central America, Caribbean &
Mexico: InterMedia Americana (IMA) Ltd,
London, UK
South Africa: Peter Hyde Associates (Pty)
Ltd, Cape Town
South East Asia (including Singapore,
Thailand, Vietnam, Cambodia, Indonesia
& Brunei): APD Singapore Pte Ltd,
Singapore
USA: Antique Collectors Club, New York,
NY
West, Central & East Africa (excluding
Sudan): InterMedia Africa Ltd (IMA),
London, UK

Book Trade Association Membership:
IPG

2035

ANVIL PRESS POETRY LTD
Neptune House, 70 Royal Hill, London
SE10 8RF
Telephone: (020) 8469 3033
Fax: (020) 8469 3363
Email: anvil@anvilpresspoetry.com
Web Site: www.anvilpresspoetry.com

Distributors:
Littlehampton Book Services,
Columbia Building, Faraday Close,
Durrington, Worthing, West Sussex
BN13 3RB
Telephone: 01903 828800
Fax: 01903 828801 & 828802
Email: orders@lbsltd.co.uk
Web Site: www.lbsltd.co.uk

Editorial, Administration & Production:
Peter Jay (Managing Director)
Manager: Kit Yee Wong (Administrative)

Poetry

ISBNs, Imprints & Series:
978 0 85646, 978 0 900977 Anvil
Editions; Poetica

Overseas Representation:
Australia: Eleanor Brasch Enterprises,
Artarmon, NSW
Eastern Europe, Greece & Israel: Tony
Moggach, InterMedia Americana (IMA)
Ltd, London, UK
France, Benelux, Germany, Austria &
Switzerland: Ted Dougherty, London, UK
Republic of Ireland: Robert Towers,
Monkstown, Co Dublin
Spain: Peter Prout Iberian Book Services,
Madrid
USA: Consortium Book Sales & Distribution
Inc, St Paul, MN

Book Trade Association Membership:
IPG

2036

APEX PUBLISHING LTD
PO Box 7086, Clacton-on-Sea, Essex
CO15 5WN
Telephone: 01255 428500
Email: mail@apexpublishing.co.uk
Web Site: www.apexpublishing.co.uk

Marketing Manager: Jackie Bright
Managing Editor: Chris Cowlin

Academic & Scholarly; Biography &
Autobiography; Children's Books; Crafts &
Hobbies; Crime; Fiction; Fine Art & Art
History; Guide Books; Health & Beauty;
Humour; Medical (incl. Self Help &
Alternative Medicine); Military & War;
Philosophy; Poetry; Politics & World Affairs;
Reference Books, Directories &
Dictionaries; Religion & Theology; Science
Fiction; Sports & Games

ISBNs, Imprints & Series:
978 1 904444, 978 1 906358

Book Trade Association Membership:
IPG

2037

APPLETREE PRESS LTD
The Old Potato Station,
14 Howard Street South, Belfast BT7 1AP
Telephone: (028) 9024 3074
Fax: (028) 9024 6756
Email: reception@appletree.ie
Web Site: www.appletree.ie

Distribution:
BookSource, 50 Cambuslang Road,
Cambuslang, Glasgow G32 8NB
Telephone: 0141 642 9182
Fax: 0141 641 9181

Director: John Murphy (Managing)
Editor: Jean Brown
Managers: Paul McAvoy (Production)
Mark Elliott (Sales)

Cookery, Wines & Spirits; Guide Books;
History & Antiquarian; Humour; Music;
Reference Books, Directories &

Dictionaries; Sports & Games; Travel &
Topography; Irish Interest Non-Fiction

New Titles: 22 (2008) , 20 (2009)
No of Employees: 10

ISBNs, Imprints & Series:
978 0 86281, 978 0 904651

Overseas Representation:
Australia & New Zealand: Peribo Pty Ltd,
Mount Kuring-Gai, NSW, Australia
France, Belgium, Scandinavia, Germany,
Austria, Switzerland & Spain: Appletree
Press, Belfast, UK
Greece, Cyprus, Israel, Russia, Eastern
Europe & the Baltic States: IMA, Greece
Italy: Penguin Italia srl, Milan
Netherlands: Novelty Books, Weesp
Republic of Ireland: Compass Independent
Book Sales Ltd, Naas, Co Kildare
USA & Canada: Independent Publishers
Group (IPG), Chicago, IL, USA

Book Trade Association Membership:
CLÉ (Irish PA)

2038

ARC PUBLICATIONS LTD
Nanholme Mill, Shaw Wood Road,
Todmorden, Lancs OL14 6DA
Telephone: 01706 812338
Fax: 01706 818948
Email: arc.publications@btconnect.com
Web Site: www.arcpublications.co.uk

Directors: Tony Ward (Publishing)
Angela Jarman (Development)

Music; Poetry

New Titles: 16 (2008) , 22 (2009)
No of Employees: 3
Annual Turnover: £64,000

ISBNs, Imprints & Series:
978 0 902771, 978 0 946407, 978 1
900072, 978 1 904614, 978 1 906570

Overseas Representation:
Australia & New Zealand: Eleanor Brasch
Enterprises, Artarmon, NSW, Australia

Book Trade Association Membership:
IPG

2039

ARCADIA BOOKS LTD
15–16 Nassau Street, London W1W 7AB
Telephone: (020) 7436 9898
Email: info@arcadiabooks.co.uk
Web Site: www.arcadiabooks.co.uk

Distribution:
Turnaround, Unit 3, Olympia Trading Estate,
Coburg Road, London N22 6TZ
Telephone: (020) 8829 3000
Fax: (020) 8881 5088
Email: orders@turnaround-uk.com
Web Site: www.turnaround-uk.com

Publisher: Gary Pulsifer
Associate Publisher: Daniela de Groote
Editor: Angeline Rothermundt

Biography & Autobiography; Crime;
Fiction; Gay & Lesbian Studies; Gender
Studies; Photography; Politics & World
Affairs; Travel & Topography; Translations

New Titles: 40 (2008) , 45 (2009)
No of Employees: 3

ISBNs, Imprints & Series:
BlackAmber; Bliss Books; EuroCrime; The
Maia Press
978 1 900850
978 1 905147

Overseas Representation:
Australia: Tower Books Pty Ltd, Brookvale,
NSW
Israel (selected titles only): Steimatzky Ltd,
Bnei Brak, Israel
New Zealand: Addenda Ltd, Grey Lynn
North America: Independent Publishers
Group (IPG), Chicago, IL, USA
South Africa: Quartet Sales & Marketing,
Johannesburg

Book Trade Association Membership:
IPG; Hite Research Foundation; English PEN
– Writers in Prison & Books to Prisoners
Committee; BTBS (The Book Trade Charity)

2040

ARCHETYPE PUBLICATIONS LTD
6 Fitzroy Square, London W1T 5HJ
Telephone: (020) 7380 0800
Fax: (020) 7380 0500
Email: info@archetype.co.uk
Web Site: www.archetype.co.uk

Managing Director: James Black

Academic & Scholarly; Archaeology; Fine
Art & Art History; Scientific & Technical

New Titles: 11 (2008) , 12 (2009)
No of Employees: 3

ISBNs, Imprints & Series:
978 1 873132, 978 1 904982

Overseas Representation:
USA (All titles): Antique Collectors Club Ltd,
Easthampton, MA, USA; JG Publishing
Services, Los Angeles, CA, USA

2041

**ARCHITECTURAL ASSOCIATION
PUBLICATIONS**
36 Bedford Square, London WC1B 3ES
Telephone: (020) 7887 4021
Fax: (020) 7414 0782
Email: publications@aaschool.ac.uk
Web Site: www.aaschool.ac.uk

Sales & Marketing Manager: Marilyn
Sparrow
Publications Co-ordinator: Kirsten
Morphet
Editors: Pamela Johnston
Thomas Weaver

Architecture & Design

New Titles: 8 (2008) , 8 (2009)
Annual Turnover: £150,000

ISBNs, Imprints & Series:
978 1 870890, 978 1 902902

Parent Company:
Architectural Association Inc

Overseas Representation:
Australia: Robyn Ralton, Collingwood, Vic
France: Muriel Fischer, Paris
Germany & Austria: Kurt Salchli, Berlin,
Germany
Netherlands & Belgium: Berend Bosch,
Noordwijk, Netherlands
Southern Europe: Bookport Associates,
Milan, Italy

Book Trade Association Membership:
Publishers Association

2042

*ARCTURUS PUBLISHING LTD
26/27 Bickels Yard,
151–153 Bermondsey Street, London
SE1 2EJ
Telephone: (020) 7407 9400
Fax: (020) 7407 9444

Email:
ian.mclellan@arcturuspublishing.com
Web Site: www.arcturuspublishing.com

Directors: Ian McLellan (Managing)
Roberta Bailey (Managing, Children's
Books)
Mr Chok (Finance)
Tom Oakes (Marketing)
Tessa Rose (Editorial)
Peter Ridley (Design)
Managers: David Meads (Production)
Charlie Cooper (Rights)

Children's Books; Cookery, Wines & Spirits;
Crafts & Hobbies; Crime; Educational &
Textbooks; Fine Art & Art History;
Gardening; History & Antiquarian;
Humour; Magic & the Occult; Medical (incl.
Self Help & Alternative Medicine); Military
& War; Music; Natural History; Philosophy;
Poetry; Reference Books, Directories &
Dictionaries; Religion & Theology; Sports &
Games

ISBNs, Imprints & Series:
978 1 84193 Arcturus; Capella

Overseas Representation:
Worldwide: Gunnar Lie & Associates Ltd,
London, UK

2043

ARENA BOOKS (PUBLISHERS)
6 Southgate Green, Bury St Edmunds,
Suffolk IP33 2BL
Telephone: 01284 754123
Fax: 01284 754123
Email: arenabooks@tiscali.co.uk
Web Site: www.arenabooks.co.uk

Directors: James Farrell (Managing)
Robert Corfe
Editor: Russell Corfe
Sales Manager: June Hardy

Academic & Scholarly; Economics; Fiction;
History & Antiquarian; Industry, Business &
Management; Literature & Criticism;
Philosophy; Politics & World Affairs;
Religion & Theology; Sociology &
Anthropology; Travel & Topography

New Titles: 10 (2008) , 15 (2009)

ISBNs, Imprints & Series:
978 0 9538460, 978 0 9543161, 978 0
9556055, 978 1 906791

Overseas Representation:
Egypt: Abdul Radder Al-Bakkar, Cairo
Poland: Graal Sp, Warsaw
USA: Ingram Publisher Services, La Vergne,
TN

Book Trade Association Membership:
IPG

2044

*ARGYLL PUBLISHING
Glendaruel, Argyll PA22 3AE
Telephone: 01369 820229
Fax: 01369 820372
Email: argyll.publishing@virgin.net
Web Site: www.argyllpublishing.com

Publisher: Derek Rodger

Biography & Autobiography; Fiction; Guide
Books; Health & Beauty; Medical (incl. Self
Help & Alternative Medicine); Natural
History

ISBNs, Imprints & Series:
Douglas Press; Thirsty Books
978 0 906938 West Dunbartonshire
Libraries & Museums
978 1 874640, 978 1 902831, 978 1
906134

2045

ARRIS PUBLISHING LTD
12 Main Street, Adlestrop,
Moreton in Marsh, Glos GL56 0YN
Telephone: 01608 659328
Fax: 01608 659345
Email: gcs@arrisbooks.com
Web Site: www.arrisbooks.com

Distribution (for Arris titles):
Orca Book Distribution, Unit A3,
Fleets Corner, Poole, Dorset BH17 0HL
Telephone: 01202 665432
Fax: 01202 666219

**Distribution (for Chastleton titles –
Travel):**
Portfolio Books, Suite 3/
4 Great West House, Brentford, Middx
TW8 9DF
Telephone: (020) 8326 5620
Fax: (020) 8326 5621
Email: info@portfoliobooks.com

Directors: Geoffrey Smith *(Joint Managing)*
Victoria Huxley *(Editorial)*

*Guide Books; History & Antiquarian;
Natural History; Politics & World Affairs;
Travel & Topography*

New Titles: 15 (2008) , 15 (2009)
No of Employees: 2

ISBNs, Imprints & Series:
978 1 84437
978 1 905214 Chastleton Travel

Overseas Representation:
*Germany, Eastern Europe, Switzerland,
Austria, Italy & Greece:* Portfolio Books,
Brentford, UK
Spain & Portugal: Iberian Book Services,
Madrid, Spain

2046

ASHGATE PUBLISHING LTD
Wey Court East, Union Road, Farnham,
Surrey GU9 7PT
Telephone: 01252 331551
Fax: 01252 736736
Email: info@ashgatepublishing.com
Web Site: www.ashgate.com

Warehouse & Mailing Shop, Orders:
Ashgate Publishing Direct Sales,
Bookpoint Ltd, 39 Milton Park, Abingdon,
Oxon OX14 4TD
Telephone: 01235 400400
Fax: 01235 400454

Chairman: Nigel Farrow
Managing Director: Rachel Lynch
Publishers: John Smedley *(History
(Variorum))*
Jonathan Norman *(Business (Gower))*
Directors: Lucy Myers *(Managing – Lund
Humphries)*
Adrian Shanks *(Social Sciences)*
Darren Wise *(Finance/Accounting)*
Anne Nolan *(Ashgate Marketing)*
Richard Dowling *(Sales)*
Jo Burges *(Editorial & Production)*

*Academic & Scholarly; Architecture &
Design; Aviation; Bibliography & Library
Science; Economics; Educational &
Textbooks; Electronic (Professional &
Academic); Environment & Development
Studies; Fine Art & Art History; Gender
Studies; Geography & Geology; History &
Antiquarian; Illustrated & Fine Editions;
Industry, Business & Management; Law;
Literature & Criticism; Military & War;
Music; Philosophy; Politics & World Affairs;
Reference Books, Directories &
Dictionaries; Religion & Theology; Sociology
& Anthropology; Theatre, Drama & Dance;
Transport*

ISBNs, Imprints & Series:
978 0 291, 978 1 85628, 978 1 85972
Avebury
978 0 566, 978 1 85904 Gower Publishing
978 0 576 Gregg International
978 0 7045 Wildwood House
978 0 7512 Gregg Revivals
978 0 7546, 978 1 84014 Ashgate
Publishing
978 0 85331 Lund Humphries
978 0 85967, 978 1 85928 Scolar Press
978 0 86078 Variorum
978 1 85521 Dartmouth
978 1 85742 Arena

Parent Company:
Ashgate Publishing Group

Associated Companies:
Gower Publishing Co Ltd; Lund Humphries;
Scolar Fine Art Ltd
USA: Ashgate Publishing Co

Overseas Representation:
*Australia, South East Asia, Malaysia,
Philippines, China, Hong Kong, Taiwan,
Myanmar (Burma), & South Korea:*
Ashgate Publishing Asia-Pacific,
Newport, NSW, Australia
India: Maya Publishers Pvt Ltd, New Delhi
Japan: United Publishers Services Ltd, Tokyo
USA: Ashgate Publishing Co, Burlington, VT

Book Trade Association Membership:
IPG

2047

ASHGROVE PUBLISHING
27 John Street, London WC1N 2BX
Telephone: (020) 7242 4820

Warehouse & Distribution:
Vine House Distribution Ltd, Waldenbury,
North Common, Chailey, East Sussex
BN8 4DR
Telephone: 01825 723398
Fax: 01825 724188
Email: gmo73@dial.pipex.com
Web Site: www.ashgrovepublishing.co.uk

Managing Director: Brad Thompson

*Audio Books; Biography & Autobiography;
Cookery, Wines & Spirits; Fiction; Health &
Beauty; Medical (incl. Self Help &
Alternative Medicine); Psychology &
Psychiatry; Religion & Theology*

New Titles: 2 (2008) , 8 (2009)
Annual Turnover: £20,000

ISBNs, Imprints & Series:
978 0 906798, 978 1 85398

Parent Company:
Hollydata Publishers Ltd

Associated Companies:
Childrens Corner Ltd

2048

**ASHMOLEAN MUSEUM
PUBLICATIONS**
Ashmolean Museum, Beaumont Street,
Oxford OX1 2PH
Telephone: 01865 278010
Fax: 01865 278106
Email: publications@ashmus.ox.ac.uk
Web Site: www.ashmolean.org

Warehouse, Trade Enquiries & Orders:
Gazelle Book Services Ltd,
White Cross Mills, Hightown, Lancaster
LA1 4XS
Telephone: 01524 68765
Fax: 01524 63232

Publishing Managers: D. McCarthy *(Sales
& Marketing)*

E. Jolliffe *(Deputy, Editorial, Production,
Web Editor)*
Photographic Services: H. Statham
K. Wodehouse

*Academic & Scholarly; Archaeology; Fine
Art & Art History; History & Antiquarian;
Numismatics*

New Titles: 5 (2008) , 8 (2009)

ISBNs, Imprints & Series:
978 0 900090, 978 0 907849, 978 1 85444

Parent Company:
Ashmolean Museum, University of Oxford

Overseas Representation:
Australia: Inbooks, c/o James Bennett Pty
Ltd, Belrose, NSW
Europe: Gazelle Book Services Ltd,
Lancaster, UK
USA: Antique Collectors Club Ltd,
Easthampton, MA

Book Trade Association Membership:
BA; IPG; Museums & Galleries Publishing
Group

2049

**ASSOCIATION FOR LEARNING
TECHNOLOGY**
Gipsy Lane, Headington, Oxford OX3 0BP
Telephone: 01865 484125
Fax: 01865 484165
Email: admin@alt.ac.uk
Web Site: www.alt.ac.uk

Chief Executive: Seb Schmoller

Academic & Scholarly

New Titles: 4 (2008) , 4 (2009)
No of Employees: 8

ISBNs, Imprints & Series:
978 0 9545870 Beyond Control (Research
Proceeding)

2050

**ASSOCIATION FOR SCOTTISH
LITERARY STUDIES**
c/o Dept of Scottish Literature,
University of Glasgow,
7 University Gardens, Glasgow G12 8QH
Telephone: 0141 330 5309
Fax: 0141 330 5309
Email: office@asls.org.uk
Web Site: www.asls.org.uk

Trade Enquiries:
BookSource, 50 Cambuslang Road,
Glasgow G32 8NB
Telephone: 0845 370 0063
Fax: 0845 370 0064
Email: orders@booksource.net
Web Site: www.booksource.net

General Manager: Duncan Jones

*Academic & Scholarly; Educational &
Textbooks; Languages & Linguistics;
Literature & Criticism; Poetry; Theatre,
Drama & Dance*

New Titles: 8 (2008) , 6 (2009)
No of Employees: 2
Annual Turnover: £115,860

ISBNs, Imprints & Series:
ASLS Annual Volumes (series); New Writing
Scotland (series); Scotnotes (series)
978 0 948877, 978 1 906841

Overseas Representation:
USA & Canada: Independent Publishers
Group (IPG), Chicago, IL, USA

Book Trade Association Membership:
Publishing Scotland

2051

ATLANTIC BOOKS
Ormond House, 26–27 Boswell Street,
London WC1N 3JZ
Telephone: (020) 7269 1610
Fax: (020) 7430 0916
Email: enquiries@groveatlantic.co.uk
Web Site: www.groveatlantic.co.uk

Distribution:
TBS Ltd, Colchester Road, Frating Green,
Colchester, Essex CO7 7DW
Telephone: 01206 255678
Fax: 01206 255930
Email: sales@tbs-ltd.co.uk
Web Site: www.thebookservice.co.uk

Company Secretary: Guy Newton
Directors: Toby Mundy *(Chief Executive
Officer & Publisher)*
Daniel Scott *(Managing)*
Nicolas Cheetham *(Publishing, Corvus)*
Sarah Castleton *(Editorial)*
Production: Alan Craig
Rights: Valerie Duff
Publicity: Karen Duffy
Editor-in-Chief: Ravi Mirchandani
Financial Controller: Irina Stoyanova

*Biography & Autobiography; Crime;
Economics; Fiction; History & Antiquarian;
Humour; Industry, Business &
Management; Law; Literature & Criticism;
Mathematics & Statistics; Military & War;
Music; Natural History; Philosophy; Poetry;
Politics & World Affairs; Psychology &
Psychiatry; Reference Books, Directories &
Dictionaries; Religion & Theology; Science
Fiction; Sports & Games; Transport*

New Titles: 65 (2008) , 65 (2009)
No of Employees: 22
Annual Turnover: £5.5M

ISBNs, Imprints & Series: 978 1 84354

Associated Companies:
USA: Grove/Atlantic Inc

Overseas Representation:
Australia: Penguin, Scoresby, Vic
Caribbean: David Willians, InterMedia
Americana (IMA) Ltd, London, UK
Europe: Faber & Faber, London, UK
Far East: Julian Ashton, Ashton
International Marketing Services,
Sevenoaks, Kent, UK
New Zealand: Penguin Books (New
Zealand) Ltd, Auckland
Republic of Ireland: Repforce Ireland,
Irishtown, Dublin
South Africa: Penguin Group SA, Rosebank

Book Trade Association Membership:
IPG

2052

***ATLANTIC EUROPE PUBLISHING
CO LTD**
Greys Court Farm, Greys Court,
Henley on Thames, Oxon RG9 4PG
Telephone: 01491 628188
Fax: 01491 628189
Email: e-mail addresses on website
Web Site: www.AtlanticEurope.com &
www.CurriculumVisions.com

Director: Dr B. J. Knapp

*Chemistry; Children's Books; Educational &
Textbooks; Electronic (Educational);
Environment & Development Studies;
Geography & Geology; History &
Antiquarian; Mathematics & Statistics;
Physics; Reference Books, Directories &
Dictionaries; Religion & Theology; Scientific
& Technical*

ISBNs, Imprints & Series:
978 1 862140, 978 1 869860

2053

ATTIC PRESS
[an imprint of Cork University Press]
c/o Cork University Press,
Youngline Industrial Estate, Pailaduff Road,
Togher, Cork, Republic of Ireland
Telephone: +353 (021) 432 1725
Fax: +353 (021) 431 5329
Web Site: www.corkuniversitypress.com

Representation (Republic of Ireland & Northern Ireland):
Mullet Fitzpatrick, 58 New Vale Cottages,
Shankhill, Dublin, Republic of Ireland

Orders & Distribution:
Gill & Macmillan, Hume Avenue,
Park West, Dublin 12, Republic of Ireland

Publications Director: Mike Collins

*Biography & Autobiography; Cookery,
Wines & Spirits; Gender Studies; Music;
Politics & World Affairs*

New Titles: 2 (2008) , 3 (2009)

ISBNs, Imprints & Series:
978 0 946211, 978 0 9535353, 978 1
85594

Parent Company:
Republic of Ireland: Cork University Press

Overseas Representation:
Netherlands & Germany: Brigitte Axster,
Frankfurt, Germany
UK: Quantum Publishing Solutions Ltd,
Paisley
UK (excluding Northern Ireland): Marston
Book Services Ltd, Abingdon, UK
USA: Dufour Editions Inc, Chester Springs,
PA

Book Trade Association Membership:
CLÉ (Irish PA)

2054

**AUDIO-FORUM - THE LANGUAGE
SOURCE**
World Microfilms, PO Box 35488,
St John's Wood, London NW8 6WD
Telephone: (020) 7586 4499
Email: microworld@ndirect.co.uk
Web Site: www.microworld.uk.com

Director: S. C. Albert

*Academic & Scholarly; Languages &
Linguistics*

ISBNs, Imprints & Series:
978 1 86013 with Sussex Pubs

Associated Companies:
Sussex Publications Ltd; World Microfilms
Publications Ltd

Distributor for:
USA: Audio-Forum USA; Jeffrey Norton
Publishing

2055

AURELIAN INFORMATION LTD
4(A) Alexandra Mansions, West End Lane,
London NW6 1LU
Telephone: (020) 7794 8609
Fax: (020) 7794 8609
Email: aurelian@dircon.co.uk
Web Site: www.dircon.co.uk/aurelian/

Distribution:
Wyvern DM Ltd, Harrier House,
Sedgeway Business Park, Witchford, Ely,
Cambs CB6 2HY
Telephone: Database enquiries: 01353
667733
Fax: 01353 669030 (Database enquiries)
Web Site: www.dircon.co.uk/aurelian/

Directors: Paul Petzold
Julia Kaufmann OBE *(Company
Secretary)*

*Industry, Business & Management;
Reference Books, Directories &
Dictionaries; Charities & Voluntary
Organizations; Internet for Business;
Internet for Charity Sector*

ISBNs, Imprints & Series:
978 1 899247 Aurelian; National Charities
Database

2056

AUREUS PUBLISHING LTD
Castle Court, Castle-upon-Alun,
St Bride's Major, Vale of Glamorgan
CF32 0TN
Telephone: 01656 880033
Fax: 01656 880033
Email: info@aureus.co.uk
Web Site: www.aureus.co.uk

Director: Meuryn Hughes

*Biography & Autobiography; Fine Art & Art
History; Music; Sports & Games*

New Titles: 10 (2008) , 10 (2009)
Annual Turnover: £28,000

ISBNs, Imprints & Series: 978 1 899750

2057

***AURORA METRO PUBLICATIONS
LTD**
67 Grove Avenue, Twickenham, London
TW1 4HX
Telephone: (020) 3261 0000
Fax: (020) 3261 0000
Email: info@aurorametro.com
Web Site: www.aurorametro.com

Distribution:
Central Books, 99 Wallis Road, Hackney,
London E9 5LN
Telephone: (020) 8986 4854
Fax: (020) 8533 5821
Email: info@centralbooks.com &
orders@centralbooks.com
Web Site: www.centralbooks.com

Publisher: Cheryl Robson
Sales & Marketing: Steve Robson
Aidan Jenkins

*Academic & Scholarly; Children's Books;
Cinema, Video, TV & Radio; Cookery, Wines
& Spirits; Educational & Textbooks; Fiction;
Gay & Lesbian Studies; Gender Studies;
Humour; Reference Books, Directories &
Dictionaries; Theatre, Drama & Dance;
Travel & Topography*

ISBNs, Imprints & Series:
978 0 9515877, 978 0 9536757, 978 0
9542330, 978 0 9546912, 978 0
9551566, 978 1 906582 Aurora Metro
Press

Overseas Representation:
Canada: Playwrights Press Canada, Toronto,
Ont
South Africa: Quartet Sales & Marketing,
Johannesburg
USA: TCG/Consortium, St Paul, MN

Book Trade Association Membership:
IPG

2058

AURUM PRESS
7 Greenland Street, London NW1 0ND
Telephone: (020) 7284 7160
Fax: (020) 7485 4902
Email:
firstname.secondname@aurumpress.co.
uk

Web Site: www.aurumpress.co.uk

Distribution & Warehouse:
Littlehampton Book Services,
Columbia Building, Faraday Close,
Durrington, Worthing, West Sussex
BN13 3RB
Telephone: 01903 828800
Fax: 01903 828801

Directors: W. J. McCreadie *(Managing)*
Graham Eames *(Sales)*
Graham Coster *(Editorial)*

*Architecture & Design; Biography &
Autobiography; Cinema, Video, TV &
Radio; Cookery, Wines & Spirits; Crafts &
Hobbies; Fashion & Costume; Gardening;
Health & Beauty; Humour; Military & War;
Music; Natural History; Photography;
Sports & Games; Transport; Travel &
Topography*

New Titles: 60 (2008) , 58 (2009)

ISBNs, Imprints & Series:
978 1 84513, 978 1 85410, 978 1 902538,
978 1 903221, 978 1 906417

Parent Company:
Quarto Group Plc

Overseas Representation:
*Africa (excluding South Africa) & Eastern
Europe:* InterMedia Americana (IMA) Ltd,
London, UK
Australia: Bookwise International, Adelaide,
SA
Canada: Manda Group, Toronto, Ont
Europe: Bill Bailey Publishers
Representatives, Newton Abbot, UK
Far East: Ashton International Marketing
Services, Sevenoaks, Kent, UK
Latin America & Caribbean: Humphrys
Roberts Associates, London, UK
New Zealand: Hachette Livre New Zealand,
Auckland
Scandinavia: McNeish Publishing
International, East Sussex, UK
South Africa: Trinity Books CC, Randburg
USA: IPG Trafalgar Square, Chicago, IL

Book Trade Association Membership:
IPG

2059

**AUSTIN & MACAULEY PUBLISHERS
LTD**
CGC-33-01, 25 Canada Square,
Canary Wharf, London E14 5LB
Telephone: (020) 7038 8212
Fax: (020) 7038 8100
Email: mail@austinmacauley.com
Web Site: www.austinmacauley.com

Editors: Annette Longman *(Chief)*
David Calvert *(Executive)*
Marketing Executive: Ross Malik

*Academic & Scholarly; Animal Care &
Breeding; Antiques & Collecting; Audio
Books; Biography & Autobiography;
Biology & Zoology; Children's Books;
Cinema, Video, TV & Radio; Computer
Science; Cookery, Wines & Spirits; Crime;
Educational & Textbooks; English as a
Foreign Language; Environment &
Development Studies; Fashion & Costume;
Fiction; Gardening; Gay & Lesbian Studies;
Health & Beauty; Humour; Literature &
Criticism; Magic & the Occult; Medical (incl.
Self Help & Alternative Medicine); Military
& War; Natural History; Nautical;
Philosophy; Politics & World Affairs;
Psychology & Psychiatry; Religion &
Theology; Science Fiction; Sociology &
Anthropology; Sports & Games; Theatre,
Drama & Dance; Travel & Topography;
Vocational Training & Careers*

2060

**AUSTRALIAN CONSOLIDATED
PRESS UK**
10 Scirocco Close,
Moulton Park Office Village, Northampton
NN3 6AP
Telephone: 01604 642200
Fax: 01604 642300
Email: books@acpuk.com
Web Site: www.acpuk.com

Directors: Linda Ayres *(Sales)*
Laura Bamford
Managers: Anna Pisani *(Office)*
Nick Lympany *(Key Account)*

*Children's Books; Cookery, Wines & Spirits;
Crafts & Hobbies*

New Titles: 37 (2008) , 40 (2009)
No of Employees: 5

ISBNs, Imprints & Series:
978 0 94989, 978 1 86396, 978 1 90377
Australian Women's Weekly Home Library

Parent Company:
Australia: ACP Publishing Pty Ltd

Overseas Representation:
Germany, Austria & Switzerland: Gabriele
Kern Publishers Services, Frankfurt-am-
Main, Germany
*Hungary, Poland, Slovakia, Czech Republic,
Romania, Albania, Yugoslavia, Croatia
Slovenia, Bosnia & Herzegovina,
Macedonia & Bulgaria:* Csaba Lengyel,
Pendragon Trading Bt, Budapest,
Hungary
*Lebanon, Egypt, Jordan, Dubai, Saudi
Arabia & United Arab Emirates:* Michael
Morris Associates, Saffron Walden, UK

2061

AUTHENTIC MEDIA
9 Holdom Avenue, Bletchley,
Milton Keynes, Bucks
Telephone: 01908 364205
Fax: 01908 648592
Email: donna.harris@authenticmedia.co.uk
Web Site: www.authenticmedia.co.uk

Head Office:
IBS-STL UK, PO Box 300,
Kingstown Broadway, Carlisle, Cumbria
CA3 0HA
Telephone: 01228 512512
Fax: 01228 514949
Web Site: www.stldistribution.co.uk

Publishers: Mark Finnie
Malcolm Down *(Fiction & Children)*
Manager: Pete Barnsley *(Marketing)*
Editorial: Robin Parry *(Paternoster
(Academic))*
Sarah Gallegher *(Authentic (General) –
Administration)*
Liz Williams *(Authentic (General) –
Supervisor)*
Production Controller: Peter Little

*Academic & Scholarly; Biography &
Autobiography; Children's Books; Religion
& Theology*

New Titles: 77 (2008)

ISBNs, Imprints & Series:
978 0 8500 Authentic Bibles
978 1 84227, 978 1 85364 Paternoster
978 1 85078, 978 1 86024 Authentic
Lifestyle
978 1 93406 Authentic US Lifestyle

Parent Company:
IBS-STL UK

Overseas Representation:
India: OM Book Services, Delhi
USA: STL Inc, Waynesboro, GA

2062

AUTHORHOUSE UK LTD
500 Avebury Boulevard, Milton Keynes,
Bucks MK9 2BE
Telephone: 01908 309250
Fax: 01908 309259
Email: tdavies@authorhouse.co.uk
Web Site: www.authorhouse.co.uk

Directors: Tim Davies (Managing)
Daniel Cooke (Business Development)

Biography & Autobiography; Children's
Books; Cookery, Wines & Spirits; Crime;
Fiction; Humour; Poetry; Religion &
Theology; Science Fiction

New Titles: 800 (2008) , 1000 (2009)
No of Employees: 16

ISBNs, Imprints & Series:
978 1 4208, 978 1 4259, 978 1 4343

Parent Company:
USA: Author Solutions Inc

Associated Companies:
USA: Authorhouse (USA); iUniverse;
Trafford; Wordclay; Xlibris

2063

AVA PUBLISHING (UK) LTD
56A Chapel Road, Worthing, West Sussex
BN11 1BE
Telephone: 01903 204455
Fax: 01903 237346
Email: enquiries@avabooks.com
Web Site: www.avabooks.com

Publisher: Brian Morris
Managers: Terry Hancock (Finance)
Sarah Turner (Marketing)
Editor in Chief: Caroline Walmsley

Architecture & Design; Cinema, Video, TV &
Radio; Educational & Textbooks; Electronic
(Educational); Fashion & Costume; Industry,
Business & Management; Photography;
Reference Books, Directories & Dictionaries

New Titles: 20 (2008)

ISBNs, Imprints & Series:
978 2 88479, 978 2 940373, 978 2 940411

Overseas Representation:
Rest of Europe: Thames & Hudson Ltd,
London, UK
USA & Canada: Ingram Publisher Services,
La Vergne, TN, USA

2064

AWARD PUBLICATIONS LTD
The Old Riding School, Welbeck Estate,
Worksop, Notts S80 3LR
Telephone: 01909 478170
Fax: 01909 484632
Email: info@awardpublications.co.uk
Web Site: www.awardpublications.co.uk

Directors: Anna Wilkinson (Managing)
David King (International Sales)
David Meggs (UK Sales)

Children's Books

New Titles: 50 (2008) , 50 (2009)

ISBNs, Imprints & Series:
978 0 86163, 978 1 84135, 978 1 89976

2065

B & D PUBLISHING
PO Box 4658, Stratford upon Avon,
Warwickshire CV37 1EP
Telephone: 01789 417824
Fax: 01789 417826
Email: postmaster@banddpublishing.co.uk
Web Site: www.banddpublishing.co.uk

Academic & Scholarly; Educational &
Textbooks

Book Trade Association Membership:
Publishers Association

2066

B SMALL PUBLISHING LTD
The Book Shed, 36 Leyborne Park, Kew,
Richmond, Surrey TW9 3HA
Telephone: (020) 8948 2884
Fax: (020) 8948 6458
Email: books@bsmall.co.uk
Web Site: www.bsmall.co.uk

**Sales Representation, UK Trade
Enquiries & Orders:**
Bounce! Sales & Marketing Ltd,
14 Greville Street, London EC1N 8SB
Telephone: (020) 7138 3650
Fax: (020) 7138 3658
Email: sales@bouncemarketing.co.uk
Web Site: www.bouncemarketing.co.uk

Publisher & Managing Director:
Catherine Bruzzone

Children's Books; Languages & Linguistics

ISBNs, Imprints & Series:
978 1 874735, 978 1 902915, 978 1
905710

Overseas Representation:
Australia (languages only): Intext Book Co
Pty Ltd, Hawthorn, Vic, Australia
South Africa: Phambili Agencies CC,
Johannesburg

Book Trade Association Membership:
IPG

2067

*B SQUARED
4c Vulcan Close, Sandhurst, Berks
GU47 9DD
Telephone: 0845 466 0141
Fax: 0845 466 0191
Email: info@bsquared.co.uk
Web Site: www.bsquared.co.uk

Executives: Brenda Byrom
Brian Pickles
Dale Pickles

Academic & Scholarly; Educational &
Textbooks

2068

**BERNARD BABANI (PUBLISHING)
LTD**
The Grampians, Shepherds Bush Road,
London W6 7NF
Telephone: (020) 7603 2581/7296
Fax: (020) 7603 8203
Email: enquiries@babanibooks.com
Web Site: www.babanibooks.com

Director: Michael H. Babani (Sales,
Production, Managing)

Computer Science; Crafts & Hobbies;
Educational & Textbooks; Electronic
(Educational); Electronic (Entertainment);
Electronic (Professional & Academic);
Engineering; Mathematics & Statistics;
Scientific & Technical; Radio & Electronics

ISBNs, Imprints & Series:
978 0 85934, 978 0 900162 Babani Press

Associated Companies:
Bernards (Publishers) Ltd

Book Trade Association Membership:
IPG

2069

BACK-IN-PRINT BOOKS LTD
PO Box 47057, London SW18 1YW
Telephone: (020) 8637 0975
Email: rolf@backinprint.co.uk
Web Site: www.backinprint.co.uk

Orders:
Gardners Books,1 Whittle Drive,
Eastbourne BN23 6QH

Orders:
Bertrams, Norwich

Directors: Rolf Stricker
Gillian Cutress

Biography & Autobiography; Crime;
Educational & Textbooks; Fiction; Guide
Books; Literature & Criticism; Military & War

ISBNs, Imprints & Series: 978 1 903552

Associated Companies:
Italy: Editoriale Shopping Italia srl

2070

BADGER PUBLISHING LTD
15 Wedgwood Gate,
Pin Green Industrial Estate, Stevenage
SG1 4SU
Telephone: 01438 356907
Fax: 01438 747015
Email: enquiries@badger-publishing.co.uk
Web Site: www.badger-publishing.co.uk

Managers: David Jamieson (General &
Publisher)
Jean Constantine (Sales & Marketing)
Accountant: Melanie Forder

Educational & Textbooks

New Titles: 45 (2008) , 56 (2009)
No of Employees: 15

ISBNs, Imprints & Series:
978 1 84424, 978 1 84691, 978 1 85880

Parent Company:
UK: Haven Books Ltd

Book Trade Association Membership:
Publishers Association; EPC

2071

DUNCAN BAIRD PUBLISHERS
29 Jewry Street, Winchester, Hants
SO23 8RY
Telephone: 01962 841411
Fax: 01962 841413
Email: enquiries@dbp.co.uk
Web Site: www.dbp.co.uk

Directors: Duncan Baird (Managing)
Alex Mitchell (Sales)
Bob Saxton (Editorial)
Roger Walton (Art)
Adela Cory (Production)
Ryan Tring (Finance)

Architecture & Design; Cookery, Wines &
Spirits; Fine Art & Art History; Health &
Beauty; Magic & the Occult; Medical (incl.
Self Help & Alternative Medicine); Natural
History; Philosophy; Reference Books,
Directories & Dictionaries; Religion &
Theology

New Titles: 75 (2008) , 60 (2009)

ISBNs, Imprints & Series:
978 1 84483, 978 1 90585

Associated Companies:
Watkins Publishing

Overseas Representation:
Australia: Simon & Schuster (Australia) Pty
Ltd, Pymble, NSW
Canada: Raincoast Book Distribution Ltd,
Vancouver, BC
New Zealand: HarperCollins (NZ) Ltd,
Glenfield, Auckland

2072

THE BANNER OF TRUTH TRUST
3 Murrayfield Road, Edinburgh EH12 6EL
Telephone: 0131 337 7310
Fax: 0131 346 7484
Email: info@banneroftruth.co.uk
Web Site: www.banneroftruth.co.uk

Warehouse:
17 Bankhead Drive,
Sighthill Industrial Estate, Edinburgh
EH11 4DW
Telephone: 0131 442 2945
Fax: 0131 442 2945

General Manager: John Rawlinson
Editor: Jonathan Watson

Religion & Theology

New Titles: 27 (2008) , 30 (2009)
No of Employees: 11
Annual Turnover: £900,000

ISBNs, Imprints & Series:
978 0 85151, 978 1 84871

Associated Companies:
USA: The Banner of Truth

Overseas Representation:
New Zealand: Sovereign Grace Books,
Auckland
Nigeria: Amazing Grace Ltd, Kano
Philippines: Evangelical Outreach Inc,
Quezon City
South Africa: Barnabas Book Room, Durban
North; Farel Distributors (Pty) Ltd, North
Riding
USA: The Banner of Truth, Carlisle, PA

2073

THE BANTON PRESS
Dippin Cottage, Kildonan, Isle of Arran
KA27 8SB
Telephone: 01770 820231
Fax: 01770 820231
Email: bantonpress@ndo.co.uk
Web Site: www.bantonpress.co.uk

Managing Director: Mark Brown

Fiction; Magic & the Occult; Religion &
Theology

New Titles: 4 (2008) , 4 (2009)

ISBNs, Imprints & Series: 978 1 85652

2074

BARDDAS
Pen-Rhiw, 71 Pentrepoeth Road, Morriston,
Swansea SA6 6AE
Telephone: 01792 792829
Fax: 01792 792829
Email: alan.llwyd@googlemail.com

Assistant Officer:
Bod Aeron, Heol Pen-Sarn, Y Bala,
Gwynedd LL23 7SR
Telephone: 01678 521051
Fax: 01678 521051
Email: elwyn@barddas.fsnet.co.uk
Web Site: www.barddas.com

Administrative Officer: Alan Llwyd
Assistant Officer: Elwyn Edwards

Poetry

New Titles: 10 (2008) , 10 (2009)

No of Employees: 2
Annual Turnover: £60,000

ISBNs, Imprints & Series: 978 1 900437

2075

BAREFOOT BOOKS
124 Walcot Street, Bath BA1 5BG
Telephone: 01225 322400
Fax: 01225 322499
Email: info@barefootbooks.com
Web Site: www.barefootbooks.com

Trade Sales (Orders):
Littlehampton Book Services Ltd,
Faraday Close, Durrington, Worthing,
West Sussex BN13 3RB
Telephone: 01903 828800
Fax: 01903 828801

Publisher: Tessa Strickland (Editorial)
Director: Nancy Traversy (Managing)
Managers: Melisa Schulman (US Trade
Sales)
Jeanne Nicholson (Marketing)
Sarah Spencer (Rights)

Audio Books; Children's Books; Educational
& Textbooks; Gift Books

New Titles: 52 (2008), 38 (2009)
No of Employees: 24

ISBNs, Imprints & Series:
978 1 84148, 978 1 84686, 978 1 898000,
978 1 901223, 978 1 902283, 978 1
905236

Overseas Representation:
Australia: Willow Connection Pty Ltd,
Brookvale, NSW
East Africa: A–Z Africa Book Services,
Rotterdam, Netherlands
Europe (Trade), Indian Sub-Continent &
Middle East: Gabriele Kern Publishers
Services, Frankfurt-am-Main, Germany;
Penny Padovani, Montanare di Cortona,
Italy; Jenny Padovani, Barcelona, Spain
Latin America & Caribbean: David Williams,
InterMedia Americana (IMA) Ltd,
London, UK
New Zealand: Addenda Ltd, Grey Lynn
Republic of Ireland & Northern Ireland:
Conor Hackett, Dublin, Republic of
Ireland
South Africa: Phambili Agencies CC,
Germiston; Salmonberry Press
South East Asia, Far East, North Asia, Hong
Kong, Singapore, Brunei & Malaysia
(Libraries), Singapore, Brunei & Malaysia
(Trade & Special Sales): Chris Ashdown,
Publishers Marketing Services Pte Ltd,
Singapore
South East, Far East & North Asia:
Publishers International Marketing,
London, UK
USA: Barefoot Books Inc, Cambridge, MA

2076

BARNY BOOKS
Hough on the Hill, Grantham NG32 2BB
Telephone: 01400 250246
Fax: 01400 251737
Email: barnybooks@hotmail.co.uk
Web Site: www.barnybooks.biz

Editor: Molly Burkett
Business Manager: Jayne Thompson

Biography & Autobiography; Children's
Books; Fiction; History & Antiquarian;
Humour; Industry, Business &
Management; Medical (incl. Self Help &
Alternative Medicine); Military & War;
Transport

New Titles: 6 (2008), 10 (2009)
No of Employees: 2
Annual Turnover: £10,000

ISBNs, Imprints & Series:
Events, People to be Remembered (Joseph
Banks – Sir John Hawrins)
978 0 948204
978 1 903172 Once upon a Wartime
(Series)
978 1 906542

2077

*BARTSKY LTD
39A Welbeck Street, London W1G 8DH
Email: email@bartsky.com

Contact: Richard Astor

Law; Medical (incl. Self Help & Alternative
Medicine)

ISBNs, Imprints & Series:
978 1 873994 Bartsky Law; Bartsky
Medicine; JurisPrudent

2078

BATSFORD
[an imprint of Anova Books Group]
10 Southcombe Street, London W14 0RA
Telephone: (020) 7605 1400
Fax: (020) 7605 1401
Email: reception@anovabooks.com
Web Site: www.anovabooks.com

Distribution, Warehouse & Enquiries:
HarperCollins Distribution, Campsie View,
Westerhill Road, Bishopbriggs, Glasgow
G64 2QT
Telephone: 0141 306 3100
Fax: 0141 306 3767

Publisher: Tina Persaud
Marketing Manager: Komal Patel
Head of International Rights: Sinead
Hurley

Archaeology; Architecture & Design; Crafts
& Hobbies; Fashion & Costume;
Gardening; History & Antiquarian

New Titles: 190 (2008), 161 (2009)
No of Employees: 65

ISBNs, Imprints & Series: 978 0 7134

Parent Company:
Anova Books Co Ltd

Overseas Representation:
Australia: Capricorn Link (Australia) Pty Ltd,
Windsor, NSW
Canada: Sterling Publishing Co Inc, New
York, NY, USA
Eastern Europe: Tony Moggach, InterMedia
Americana (IMA) Ltd, London, UK
Far East: Ashton International Marketing
Services, Sevenoaks, Kent, UK
France, Netherlands & Luxembourg: Ted
Dougherty, London, UK
Germany, Switzerland & Austria: Gabriele
Kern Publishers Services, Frankfurt-am-
Main, Germany
Mexico & Central America: Christopher
Humphrys, Humphrys Roberts
Associates, London, UK
New Zealand: HarperCollins (NZ) Ltd,
Glenfield, Auckland
Scandinavia & Italy: McNeish Publishing
International, East Sussex, UK
Singapore: Pansing Distribution Sdn Bhd
South Africa: Trinity Books CC, Randburg
South America: Terry Roberts, Cotia SP,
Brazil
Spain, Portugal, Malta & Greece: Penny
Padovani, London, UK

Book Trade Association Membership:
IPG

2079

*BBC ACTIVE
80 Strand, London WC2R 0RL

Telephone: (020) 7010 2731
Fax: (020) 7010 6965
Email: jonathan.scott@pearson.com
Web Site: www.bbcactive.com

Customer Services:
Edinburgh Gate, Harlow, Essex CM20 2JE
Telephone: 01279 623623
Web Site: www.bbcactive.com

Head: Susan Ross
Head of Digital & Brand Development:
Julia King
Head of Sales & Marketing: Valerie de la
Rochette (Product Development)
Publisher: Maureen Gallagher

Chemistry; Children's Books; Computer
Science; Educational & Textbooks;
Electronic (Educational); English as a
Foreign Language; Geography & Geology;
History & Antiquarian; Languages &
Linguistics; Mathematics & Statistics;
Physics; Religion & Theology; Audio & Video
Cassettes; CD-ROMs; DVDs

ISBNs, Imprints & Series:
978 0 563, 978 1 4066

Parent Company:
Pearson Education

Book Trade Association Membership:
EPC

2080

BBC AUDIOBOOKS LTD
St James House, The Square,
Lower Bristol Road, Bath BA2 3BH
Telephone: 01225 878000
Fax: 01225 310771
Email: jan.paterson.01@bbc.com
Web Site: www.bbcaudiobooks.com

Directors: Mike Bowen (Managing)
Jan Paterson (Publishing & Marketing)
Sam Newman (Sales)
Tracy Leeming (Operations)
Bradley Whittock (Finance)

Audio Books

New Titles: 184 (2008), 139 (2009)
No of Employees: 72

ISBNs, Imprints & Series:
978 0 563, 978 1 8460 Radio Collection
(Audio Cassettes, CDs & MP3 CDs)
978 0 754 Word for Word (Audio Cassettes
& CDs)
978 1 85549 Cover to Cover Cassettes
(Audio Cassettes & CDs)

Parent Company:
BBC Worldwide

Overseas Representation:
USA: BBC Audiobooks America

2081

*BCR PUBLISHING LTD
3 Cobden Court, Wimpole Close, Bromley,
Kent BR2 9JF
Telephone: (020) 8466 6987
Fax: (020) 8466 0654
Email: info@bcrpub.co.uk
Web Site: www.bcrpub.co.uk

Managing Director: Michael Bickers
Editor: Roopi Makkar
Marketing Manager: Anya Tatyanchenko

Industry, Business & Management

ISBNs, Imprints & Series:
978 0 9522351, 978 0 9539877

2082

BEAM EDUCATION
Maze Workshops, 72A Southgate Road,
London N1 3JT
Telephone: (020) 7684 3323
Fax: (020) 7684 3334
Email: info@beam.co.uk
Web Site: www.beam.co.uk

Directors: Sheila Ebbutt (Managing)
Mike Askew
Managing Editor: Marion Dill
Business Manager: Seraphina Granelli

Educational & Textbooks; Mathematics &
Statistics

No of Employees: 14

ISBNs, Imprints & Series:
978 1 874099, 978 1 903142, 978 1
906224

Parent Company:
Nelson Thornes Ltd

2083

RUTH BEAN PUBLISHERS
Victoria Farmhouse, Carlton, Bedford
MK43 7LP
Telephone: 01234 720356
Fax: 01234 720590
Email: ruthbean@onetel.com

Partners: Ruth Bean
Nigel Bean

Academic & Scholarly; Antiques &
Collecting; Crafts & Hobbies; Fashion &
Costume; Theatre, Drama & Dance

New Titles: 1 (2008), 2 (2009)

ISBNs, Imprints & Series: 978 0 903585

Book Trade Association Membership:
IPG

2084

BEAUTIFUL BOOKS LTD
36–38 Glasshouse Street, London W1B 5DL
Telephone: (020) 7734 4448
Fax: (020) 3070 0764
Email: simon@beautiful-books.co.uk
Web Site: www.beautiful-books.co.uk

Sales & Distribution:
Turnaround Publisher Services, Unit 3,
Olympia Trading Estate, Coburg Road,
London N22 6TZ
Telephone: (020) 8829 3000
Fax: (020) 8881 5088
Email: claire@turnaround-uk.com
Web Site: www.turnaround-uk.com

Publisher: Simon Petherick
Production Manager: Tamsin Griffiths
Editor: Anthony Nott
Publicity: Katherine Josselyn

Audio Books; Fiction; Humour; Literature &
Criticism; Music; Psychology & Psychiatry;
Travel & Topography

New Titles: 20 (2008), 25 (2009)
No of Employees: 4
Annual Turnover: £500,000

ISBNs, Imprints & Series:
978 0 95494, 978 1 905636 Beautiful
Books; Bloody Books; Burning House

Overseas Representation:
Australia & New Zealand: Peribo Pty Ltd,
Mount Kuring-Gai, NSW, Australia
Europe (including Ireland): Turnaround
Publisher Services Ltd, London, UK
Worldwide (foreign rights): The Marsh
Agency, London, UK

2085

BEDFORD FREEMAN WORTH (BFW)
at Palgrave Macmillan, Houndmills,
Basingstoke, Hants RG21 6XS
Telephone: 01256 302983

Trade Orders & Warehouse:
Macmillan Direct, Customer Services,
Brunel Road, Houndmills, Basingstoke,
Hants RG21 6XS
Telephone: 01256 302699
Fax: 01256 364733
Email: mdl@macmillan.co.uk
Web Site: www.macmillan-mdl.co.uk

Publishing Director (College): Margaret
Hewinson

*Academic & Scholarly; Biology & Zoology;
Chemistry; Geography & Geology;
Mathematics & Statistics; Physics;
Psychology & Psychiatry; Astronomy/
Cosmology*

ISBNs, Imprints & Series: 978 0 7167

Parent Company:
USA: W. H. Freeman & Co

Distributor for:
Palgrave Macmillan; University Science
Books; Worth Publishers
USA: Sinauer Associates

Overseas Representation:
Australia & New Zealand: Macmillan
Education Australia, South Yarra, Vic,
Australia
USA: W. H. Freeman & Co, New York

Book Trade Association Membership:
IGSMTP; CAPP

2086

THE BELMONT PRESS
29 Tenby Avenue, Harrow HA3 8RU
Telephone: (020) 8907 4700
Fax: (020) 8907 7354
Web Site: www.waterways.co.uk &
www.belmont1948.co.uk

Directors: John Lawes *(Managing)*
Mark Lawes *(Technical)*

*Atlases & Maps; Children's Books; History &
Antiquarian; Nautical; Transport; Travel &
Topography; Inland Waterways*

New Titles: 6 (2008) , 6 (2009)

ISBNs, Imprints & Series:
978 0 905366 Belmont series of books;
Navigator series of maps; Working
Waterways series

Parent Company:
Belmont (1948) Ltd

Associated Companies:
Belmont Books; Chris Deucher; John
Reeve; Waterway Books; Waterways
Book Service

Distributor for:
Enigma Publishing; Remus Publishing; W.H.
Walker & Bros; Robert Wilson Designs;
Working Waterways Series

2087

BENE FACTUM PUBLISHING LTD
PO Box 58122, London SW8 5WZ
Telephone: (020) 7720 6767
Email: inquiries@bene-factum.co.uk
Web Site: www.bene-factum.co.uk

Representation:
Compass DSA, 13 Progress Business Park,
Whittle Parkway, Slough SL1 6DQ
Telephone: 01628 559500

Fax: 01628 663876
Email: sales@compass-dsa.co.uk

Distribution:
Marston Book Services, PO Box 269,
Abingdon, Oxon OX14 4YN
Telephone: 01235 465500
Fax: 01235 465555
Email: direct.orders@marston.co.uk

Managing Director: Anthony Weldon

*Aviation; Biography & Autobiography;
Children's Books; Gardening; History &
Antiquarian; Humour; Illustrated & Fine
Editions; Industry, Business &
Management; Law; Medical (incl. Self Help
& Alternative Medicine); Military & War;
Reference Books, Directories &
Dictionaries; Vocational Training & Careers*

New Titles: 10 (2009)

ISBNs, Imprints & Series:
978 0 9522754, 978 1 903071

Book Trade Association Membership:
IPG

2088

BERG PUBLISHERS
1st Floor, Angel Court,
81 St Clements Street, Oxford OX4 1AW
Telephone: 01865 245104
Fax: 01865 791165
Email: kearle@bergpublishers.com
Web Site: www.bergpublishers.com

Distribution & Returns:
Macmillan Distribution Ltd (MDL),
Brunel Road, Houndmills, Basingstoke,
Hants RG21 6XS
Telephone: 01256 302692
Fax: 01256 812521/812558 (Home),
01256 842084 (Export)
Email: trade@macmillan.co.uk

Trade Enquiries & Orders:
A. & C. Black, 36 Soho Square, London
W1D 3QY
Telephone: (020) 7758 0345

Directors: Kathryn Earle *(Managing &
Editorial)*
Tristan Palmer *(Editorial)*
Managers: Jennifer Howell *(Marketing &
Sales)*
Ken Bruce *(Production)*

*Academic & Scholarly; Architecture &
Design; Cinema, Video, TV & Radio;
Educational & Textbooks; Fashion &
Costume; Sociology & Anthropology*

New Titles: 42 (2008) , 50 (2009)
No of Employees: 15
Annual Turnover: £1.3M

ISBNs, Imprints & Series:
978 0 485 19, 978 0 85496, 978 1 84520,
978 1 84788, 978 1 85973

Parent Company:
A. & C. Black

Associated Companies:
Fairchild Books

Overseas Representation:
Australia & New Zealand: InBooks, Frenchs
Forest, NSW, Australia
China & Hong Kong: Access Asia Media
Services, Shanghai, P. R. of China
Europe: Andrew Durnell Marketing Ltd,
Tunbridge Wells, UK
India: Maya Publishers Pvt Ltd, New Delhi
Japan: United Publishers Services Ltd, Tokyo
Korea: Information & Culture Korea (ICK),
Seoul, Republic of Korea

Middle East & Africa: International
Publishing Services (IPS) Middle East Ltd,
Dubai, UAE
Pakistan: World Press, Lahore
Philippines: AdBox Distributors, Quezon
City
South Africa: Juta Publishing, Cape Town
Taiwan: Unifacmanu Trading Co Ltd, Taipei
USA: Palgrave Macmillan, New York, NY

2089

*BERGHAHN BOOKS
3 Newtec Place, Magdalen Road, Oxford
OX4 1RE
Telephone: 01865 250011
Fax: 01865 250056
Email: publisher@berghahnbooks.com
Web Site: www.berghahnbooks.com

Warehouse & Orders:
Marston Book Services, PO Box 269,
Abingdon, Oxon OX14 4YN
Telephone: 01235 465500
Fax: 01235 465555
Email: enquiries@marston.co.uk

Representation (UK):
Compass Academic Ltd,
The Barley Mow Centre,
10 Barley Mow Passage, Chiswick, London
W4 4PH
Telephone: (020) 8994 6477
Fax: (020) 8400 6132

Managing Director: Marion Berghahn
(Publisher)
Managers: Mark Stanton *(Production)*
David Crabtree *(Publicity)*
Lore Cortis *(Rights)*
Rupert Jones-Parry *(Sales)*

*Academic & Scholarly; Biography &
Autobiography; Cinema, Video, TV &
Radio; Economics; Electronic (Professional &
Academic); Environment & Development
Studies; Gender Studies; History &
Antiquarian; Languages & Linguistics;
Literature & Criticism; Military & War;
Politics & World Affairs; Religion &
Theology; Sociology & Anthropology;
Theatre, Drama & Dance; Travel &
Topography*

ISBNs, Imprints & Series:
978 1 57181, 978 1 84545

Associated Companies:
USA: Berghahn Books Inc

Distributor for:
Durkheim Press; Yad Vashem [English
language titles only]
India: Social Science Press

Overseas Representation:
Australia & New Zealand: Woodslane Pty
Ltd, Warriewood, NSW, Australia
Benelux: Jos de Jong, Belgium
Canada: Renouf Books, Ottawa, Ont
China & Hong Kong: Access Asia Media
Services, Malaysia
Eastern Europe: Dr László Horváth
Publishers Representative, Budapest,
Hungary
Europe: Berghahn Books, Oxford, UK
Germany (stockholding): Missing Link
International Booksellers, Bremen,
Germany
Greece & Cyprus: Charles Gibbes
Associates, London, UK
India: Julian Russ, Oxford, UK
Italy & France: Flavio Marcello Publishers'
Agents & Consultants, Padua, Italy
Japan (stockholding): United Publishers
Services Ltd, Tokyo, Japan
Latin/Central America: Cranbury
International LLC, Montpelier, VT, USA
Middle East & Turkey: Avicenna Partnership,
Oxford, UK
North America & Rest of the World:
Berghahn Books, New York, NY, USA

Scandinavia: David Towle International,
Stockholm, Sweden
South Africa: Nigel Doyle
Spain & Portugal: Iberian Book Services,
Madrid, Spain

2090

BIBLE READING FELLOWSHIP
15 The Chambers, Vineyard, Abingdon,
Oxon OX14 3FE
Telephone: 01865 319700
Fax: 01865 319701
Email: enquiries@brf.org.uk
Web Site: www.brf.org.uk

Distribution:
STL Distribution, Kingstown, Broadway,
Carlisle CA3 0HA
Telephone: 01228 512512
Fax: 01228 514949
Email: info@stl.org
Web Site: www.stldistribution.co.uk

Chief Executive Officer: R. Fisher
General Manager: Karen Laister
Commissioning Editors: Sue Doggett
Naomi Starkey

*Children's Books; Educational & Textbooks;
Religion & Theology*

New Titles: 30 (2008) , 31 (2009)
No of Employees: 24

ISBNs, Imprints & Series:
Barnabas; Day by Day with God;
Guidelines; New Daylight; People's Bible
Commentary Series; Quiet Spaces; The
Upper Room
978 0 7459, 978 1 84101

Overseas Representation:
Australia: Willow Connection Pty Ltd,
Brookvale, NSW
New Zealand: Scripture Union Wholesale,
Wellington
USA: The Bible Reading Fellowship, Winter
Park, FL

2091

JOSEPH BIDDULPH PUBLISHER
32 Stryd Ebeneser, Pontypridd CF37 5PB
Telephone: 01443 662559

Sole Proprietor: Joseph Biddulph

*Academic & Scholarly; Architecture &
Design; Languages & Linguistics; Law;
Poetry; Reference Books, Directories &
Dictionaries; Heraldry*

New Titles: 4 (2008)

ISBNs, Imprints & Series:
978 0 948565 Languages Information
Centre
978 1 897999 Joseph Biddulph Publisher

2092

BIRLINN LTD
West Newington House,
10 Newington Road, Edinburgh EH9 1QS
Telephone: 0131 668 4371
Fax: 0131 668 4466
Email: info@birlinn.co.uk
Web Site: www.birlinn.co.uk

Distribution:
BookSource, 50 Cambuslang Road,
Glasgow G32 8NB
Telephone: 0845 370 0067
Fax: 0845 370 0068
Email: info@booksource.net
Web Site: www.booksource.net

Managing Director: Hugh Andrew
Finance: Rona Stewart
Production: Liz Short
Publisher: Neville Moir

Editorial: Andrew Simmons
Sales: Helen Stanton
Rights: Maria White
Publicity: Jan Rutherford
Key Accounts Manager: Bob Smith *(Sales)*

Fiction; Guide Books; History & Antiquarian; Humour; Illustrated & Fine Editions; Military & War; Adventure; Local Interest

New Titles: 145 (2009)
No of Employees: 20
Annual Turnover: £3M

ISBNs, Imprints & Series:
978 0 7486, 978 0 9544075, 978 1 84697, 978 1 904598 Polygon
978 0 85976 John Donald
978 1 84158, 978 1 874744 Birlinn
978 1 84183, 978 1 87364 Mercat
978 1 84341 Birlinn General (Military & Adventure titles)
978 1 904607 John Donald (Print on demand titles)

Associated Companies:
John Donald Publishers Ltd; Polygon

Distributor for:
Clar; Maclean Press

Overseas Representation:
Australia: UNIREPS University and Reference Publishers' Services, Sydney, NSW
Austria, Belgium, France, Germany, Greece, Italy, Luxembourg, Netherlands & Switzerland: Ted Dougherty, London, UK
Canada: Vanwell Publishing Ltd, St Catharines, Ont
Denmark, Finland, Iceland, Norway, Portugal, Spain, Sweden & Eastern Europe: Bill Bailey Publishers Representatives, Newton Abbot, UK
USA (academic): Interlink Publishing Group Inc, Northampton, MA, USA
USA (for military & adventure titles only): Casemate Publishers & Book Distributors LLC, Havertown, PA, USA

Book Trade Association Membership:
IPG

2093

BITTER LEMON PRESS
37 Arundel Gardens, London W11 2LW
Telephone: (020) 7727 7927
Fax: (020) 7460 2164
Email: books@bitterlemonpress.com
Web Site: www.bitterlemonpress.com

Crime; Fiction

New Titles: 7 (2008) , 7 (2009)

ISBNs, Imprints & Series: 978 1 94738

Book Trade Association Membership:
IPG

2094

BLACK ACE BOOKS
PO Box 7547, Perth PH2 1AU
Telephone: 01821 642822
Fax: 01821 642101
Web Site: www.blackacebooks.com

Publisher & Rights: Hunter Steele
Publicity & Sales: Boo Wood

Academic & Scholarly; Biography & Autobiography; Fiction; History & Antiquarian; Philosophy

ISBNs, Imprints & Series: 978 1 872 988

Overseas Representation:
Italy: Piergiorgio Nicolazzini Literary Agency, Milan

Japan: The English Agency (Japan) Ltd, Tokyo

2095

BLACK DOG PUBLISHING LTD
10A Acton Street, London WC1X 9NG
Telephone: (020) 7713 5097
Fax: (020) 7713 8682
Email: sales@blackdogonline.com
Web Site: www.blackdogonline.com

Warehouse & Distribution:
Marston Book Services, PO Box 269, Abingdon, Oxon OX14 4YN
Telephone: 01235 465500
Fax: 01235 465555
Email: direct.orders@marston.co.uk

Editorial: Nikos Kotsopoulos
Sales: Annabell Power
Office Manager: Amy Visram
Press: Rosie French
Production: Irene Amore

Architecture & Design; Cinema, Video, TV & Radio; Crafts & Hobbies; Fashion & Costume; Fine Art & Art History; History & Antiquarian; Illustrated & Fine Editions; Music; Philosophy; Photography; Travel & Topography

New Titles: 40 (2008) , 30 (2009)
No of Employees: 16

ISBNs, Imprints & Series:
Artworld; Labels Unlimited
978 1 901033 Architecture & Urbanism (Serial books); -De, -Dis, -Ex; Revisions; Serial Books Design
978 1 904772, 978 1 906155

Overseas Representation:
Australia & New Zealand: Peribo Pty Ltd, Mount Kuring-Gai, NSW, Australia
Canada & USA: Perseus Group, Jackson, TN, USA
Europe, Asia & New Zealand: Marston Book Services Ltd, Abingdon, UK
France: Critiques Livres Distribution, Bagnolet
Germany: Bugrim, Berlin

2096

BLACK SPRING PRESS LTD
Curtain House, 134–146 Curtain Road, London EC2A 3AR
Telephone: (020) 7613 3066
Fax: (020) 7613 0028
Email: general@blackspringpress.co.uk
Web Site: www.blackspringpress.co.uk

Distribution:
Turnaround Publisher Services Ltd, Unit 3, Olympia Trading Estate, Coburg Road, London N22 6TZ
Telephone: (020) 8829 3000
Fax: (020) 8881 5088
Email: orders@turnaround-uk.com
Web Site: www.turnaround-psl.com

Publisher: Robert Hastings

Biography & Autobiography; Cinema, Video, TV & Radio; Fiction; Music

ISBNs, Imprints & Series: 978 0 948238

Overseas Representation:
Europe, Middle East & Far East: Turnaround Publisher Services Ltd, London, UK

2097

A. & C. BLACK (PUBLISHERS) LTD
36 Soho Square, London W1D 3QY
Telephone: (020) 7758 0200
Fax: (020) 7758 0222
Email: rbortoli@acblack.com
Web Site: www.acblack.com

Distribution:
Macmillan Distribution (MDL), Brunel Road, Houndmills, Basingstoke, Hants RG21 6XT
Telephone: 01256 302699
Fax: 01256 812521
Email: direct@acblack.com

Directors: Nigel Newton *(Chairman)*
Jill Coleman *(Managing)*
Jonathan Glasspool *(Deputy Managing)*
Janet Murphy *(Adlard Coles Nautical)*
Oscar Heini *(Production)*
David Wightman *(Rights, Sales & Marketing)*
Colin Adams *(Group Finance)*
Chris Facey *(Finance)*
Jayne Parsons *(Children's Books)*
Head of Publicity & Marketing: Rosanna Bortoli

Architecture & Design; Children's Books; Crafts & Hobbies; Educational & Textbooks; English as a Foreign Language; Fashion & Costume; Fine Art & Art History; Health & Beauty; Humour; Music; Natural History; Nautical; Reference Books, Directories & Dictionaries; Sports & Games; Theatre, Drama & Dance; Ornithology

ISBNs, Imprints & Series:
Adlard Coles Nautical; The Arden Shakespeare; Andrew Brodie Publications; Featherstone Education; Know the Game; Methuen Drama; New Mermaids; Thomas Reeds; Whitaker's Almanacks; Who's Who; Wisden Cricketer's Almanack

Parent Company:
Bloomsbury Plc

Distributor for:
Little Tiger Press; V & A Publications; Wisden

Overseas Representation:
Australia & New Zealand: Allen & Unwin Pty Ltd, Crows Nest, NSW, Australia
Canada (excluding V&A titles): Penguin Group Canada, Toronto, Ont, Canada
Central & Eastern Europe: Grazyna Soszynska, Penguin Poland, Poznan-Baranowo, Poland
France (excluding V&A titles): Jean-Luc Morel, Penguin France, Paris, France
Germany: Edith Strommen, Penguin Books Deutschland GmbH, Frankfurt am Main
Germany & Austria: Klaus Melz, Penguin Books Deutschland GmbH, Mannheim, Germany
India (excluding V&A titles): Penguin Books India, New Delhi, India
Italy: Umberto Vigoni, Penguin Italia srl, Milan
Laos, Cambodia, Vietnam & Thailand: Keith Hardy, International Sales Dept, Penguin UK, London, UK
Malaysia (excluding V&A titles): Penguin Books Malaysia, c/o Pearson Malaysia Sdn Bhd, Selangor Darul Ehsan, Malaysia
Middle East, Hong Kong, Thailand & Indonesia: Sarah Davison-Aitkins, International Sales Dept, Penguin UK, London, UK
Netherlands, Belgium & Luxembourg: Feico Deutekom, Penguin Books BV, Amsterdam, Netherlands
Portugal: Adelino Abrantos, Penguin Books SA, Madrid, Spain
Republic of Ireland: Brian Blennerhassett, Butler Sims Ltd, Dublin
Scandinavia & Latin America: Tamsin Pagella, International Sales Dept, Penguin UK, London, UK
Singapore (excluding V&A titles): Penguin Books Singapore, c/o Pearson Education South Asia Pte Ltd, Singapore
South America, Latin America & Caribbean: David Williams, InterMedia Americana (IMA) Ltd, London, UK

South East Europe & Africa: Amy Elkington, International Sales Dept, Penguin UK, London, UK
South Korea, Taiwan, Japan, China & Philippines: Yvonne Francis, International Sales Dept, Penguin UK, London, UK
Southern Africa: Book Promotions (Pty) Ltd/ Horizon Books (Pty) Ltd, Cape Town, South Africa
Spain: Javier Rivera, Penguin Books SA, Madrid
Switzerland & Malta: Kathy John, International Sales Dept, Penguin UK, London, UK
USA (excluding V&A titles): Consortium Book Sales & Distribution, Minneapolis, MN, USA

Book Trade Association Membership:
EPC; Music Publishers Association

2098

BLACKHALL PUBLISHING
Lonsdale House, Avoca Avenue, Blackrock, Co Dublin, Republic of Ireland
Telephone: +353 (01) 278 5090
Fax: +353 (01) 278 4800
Email: blackhall@eircom.net
Web Site: www.blackhallpublishing.com

Managing Director: Gerard O'Connor
Commissioning Editor: Elizabeth Brennan
Financial Controller: Conor O'Mahony
Editor: Eileen O'Brien
Marketing: Sarah Franklin
Production Assistant: Zoe Faulder
Typesetting Manager: Benil Shah

Academic & Scholarly; Accountancy & Taxation; Economics; Industry, Business & Management; Law; Medical (incl. Self Help & Alternative Medicine); Psychology & Psychiatry; Sociology & Anthropology

ISBNs, Imprints & Series:
978 1 842180, 978 1 901657

Overseas Representation:
UK: CMD BookSource, Blackrock, Republic of Ireland

2099

BLACKSTAFF PRESS
4C Heron Wharf, Sydenham Business Park, Belfast BT3 9LE
Telephone: 028 9045 5006
Fax: 028 9046 6237
Email: info@blackstaffpress.com
Web Site: www.blackstaffpress.com

Distribution (UK & Northern Ireland):
Gill & Macmillan, Hume Avenue, Park West, Dublin 12, Republic of Ireland
Telephone: +353 (01) 5009 500
Fax: +353 (01) 5009 599
Email: sales@gillmacmillan.ie
Web Site: www.gillmacmillan.ie

Editors: Patricia Horton *(Managing)*
Helen Wright
Michelle Griffin *(Production)*
Publicist: Sarah Bowers

Academic & Scholarly; Agriculture; Archaeology; Biography & Autobiography; Cinema, Video, TV & Radio; Cookery, Wines & Spirits; Crime; Fiction; Geography & Geology; Guide Books; Health & Beauty; History & Antiquarian; Humour; Illustrated & Fine Editions; Literature & Criticism; Mathematics & Statistics; Medical (incl. Self Help & Alternative Medicine); Military & War; Music; Natural History; Photography; Poetry; Politics & World Affairs; Reference Books, Directories & Dictionaries; Religion & Theology; Sports & Games; Theatre, Drama & Dance; Travel & Topography

ISBNs, Imprints & Series:
978 0 85640 The Blackstaff Press

Parent Company:
W. G. Baird (Holdings) Ltd

Overseas Representation:
All other areas: Blackstaff Press, Belfast, UK
USA: Dufour Editions Inc, Chester Springs, PA

Book Trade Association Membership:
BA; IPG; CLÉ (Irish PA)

2100

BLACKTHORN PRESS
Blackthorn House, Middleton Road, Pickering, North Yorks YO18 8AL
Telephone: 01751 474043
Email: blackthornpress@yahoo.com
Web Site: www.blackthornpress.com

Proprietor: Alan Avery

Fine Art & Art History; History & Antiquarian; Literature & Criticism

New Titles: 12 (2008), 12 (2009)
Annual Turnover: £120,000

ISBNs, Imprints & Series: 978 0 9540535

2101

BLACKWELL PUBLISHING
see: Wiley-Blackwell

2102

JOHN BLAKE PUBLISHING LTD
[incorp. Smith Gryphon Publishers Ltd & Metro Publishing Ltd]
3 Bramber Court, 2 Bramber Road, London W14 9PB
Telephone: (020) 7381 0666
Fax: (020) 7381 6868
Email: rosie@blake.co.uk

Distribution:
Littlehampton Book Services,
Faraday Close, Durrington, Worthing,
West Sussex BN13 3RB
Telephone: 01903 828800
Fax: 01903 828802
Email: orders@lbsltd.co.uk
Web Site: www.lbsltd.co.uk

Directors: John Blake *(Managing)*
Rosie Ries *(Deputy Managing)*
Ray Mudie *(Sales)*
Editor-in-Chief: Michelle Signore
Accounts Executive: Joanna Kennedy
Head of Marketing: Clare Tillyer
Sales & Logistics Manager: Stuart Finglass
Editor: John Wordsworth
Production: Moira Ashcroft

Audio Books; Biography & Autobiography; Cookery, Wines & Spirits; Crime; Humour; Music; Sports & Games

New Titles: 150 (2008), 150 (2009)
No of Employees: 14

ISBNs, Imprints & Series:
978 1 84358, 978 1 84454, 978 1 85782

Associated Companies:
Metro Books; Smith Gryphon Publishers Ltd

Overseas Representation:
Australia & New Zealand: Bookwise
International, Adelaide, SA, Australia
Germany: Michael Mellor, Munich
South Africa: Peter Hyde Associates (Pty)
Ltd, Cape Town
USA: Trafalgar Publishing, Chicago, IL

Book Trade Association Membership:
BA

2103

BLOODAXE BOOKS LTD
Highgreen, Tarset, Northumberland NE48 1RP
Telephone: 01434 240500 (editorial)
01678 521550 (sales)
Fax: 01434 240505 (editorial) 01678 521544 (sales)
Email: editor@bloodaxebooks.com
(editorial), sales@bloodaxebooks.com
Web Site: www.bloodaxebooks.com

Warehouse, Trade Enquiries & Orders:
Littlehampton Book Services,
Faraday Close, Durrington, Worthing,
West Sussex BN13 3RB
Telephone: 01903 828800
Fax: 01903 828802
Email: orders@lbsltd.co.uk

Chairman: Simon Thirsk
Managing Director: Neil Astley *(Editorial)*
Company Secretary: Alison Davis
Managers: Bethan Jones *(Finance)*
Christine Macgregor *(Publicity)*
Permissions & Foreign Rights: Suzanne Fairless-Aitken
Finance & Sales Assistant: Jean Smith
Prizes & Administration: Rebecca Hodkinson
Marketing: Annette Charpentier

Literature & Criticism; Poetry

New Titles: 35 (2008), 35 (2009)
No of Employees: 8

ISBNs, Imprints & Series:
978 0 906427, 978 1 85224 Bloodaxe Books
978 1 85557 Pandon Press

Associated Companies:
Pandon Press Ltd

Overseas Representation:
Australia: John Reed Book Distribution, Tea Gardens, NSW
Caribbean: Hugh Dunphy, Kingston, Jamaica
Europe: Michael Geoghegan, London, UK
India: Surit Mitra, New Delhi
Italy, Spain & Portugal: Penny Padovani, London, UK
North America: Dufour Editions Inc, Chester Springs, PA, USA
Republic of Ireland: Repforce Ireland, Irishtown, Dublin
South & Central America, Africa (excluding South Africa), Eastern Europe, Middle East, Turkey, Israel, Greece & Cyprus: InterMedia Americana (IMA) Ltd, London, UK

2104

BLOOMSBURY PUBLISHING PLC
36 Soho Square, London W1D 3QY
Telephone: (020) 7494 2111
Fax: (020) 7434 0151
Web Site: www.bloomsbury.com

Distributor:
Macmillan Distribution (MDL), Houndmills,
Basingstoke, Hants RG21 6XS
Telephone: 01256 329242
Fax: 01256 364733

Directors: Nigel Newton *(Chief Executive)*
Richard Charkin *(Executive)*
Alexandra Pringle *(Editor-in-Chief)*
Kathleen Furran *(Marketing)*
Colin Adams *(Finance)*
Ruth Logan *(Rights)*
Colin Midson *(Publicity)*
Penny Edwards *(Production)*
David Ward *(Sales)*
Sarah Odedina *(Children's)*

Audio Books; Biography & Autobiography; Children's Books; Cinema, Video, TV &

Radio; Cookery, Wines & Spirits; Fiction; Health & Beauty; History & Antiquarian; Humour; Literature & Criticism; Military & War; Music; Politics & World Affairs; Reference Books, Directories & Dictionaries; Theatre, Drama & Dance

No of Employees: 300

ISBNs, Imprints & Series: 978 0 7475

Parent Company:
USA: Bloomsbury

Associated Companies:
A & C Black
Germany: Berlin Verlag

Overseas Representation:
Africa & Middle East: Penguin International Sales, London, UK
Australia & New Zealand: Allen & Unwin Pty Ltd, Sydney, NSW, Australia
Canada: Penguin Group Canada, Toronto, Ont
Central & Eastern Europe: Grazyna Soszynska, Penguin Poland, Poznan-Baranowo, Poland
France, Morocco, Tunisia & Algeria: Jean-Luc Morel, Penguin Group, Roissy, France
Germany & Austria: Uli Hoernemann, Berlin Verlag, Berlin, Germany
Hong Kong, Macau, China, Philippines, Thailand, Indonesia, Vietnam, Cambodia, Taiwan & Korea: Yvonne Francis, Penguin International Sales, London, UK
India: Penguin Books India, New Delhi
Italy: Penguin Italia srl, Milan
Japan: Lisa Finch, Bloomsbury International Sales, Bloomsbury Publishing, London, UK
Netherlands, Belgium & Luxembourg: Penguin Books BV, Amsterdam, Netherlands
Pakistan: Julian Russ, Tula Publishing Ltd, Oxford, UK
Republic of Ireland & Northern Ireland: Louise Dobbin, Repforce Ireland, Irishtown, Dublin, Republic of Ireland
Scandinavia: Sarah Davison-Aitkens, Penguin International Sales, London, UK
Singapore & Malaysia: Penguin Books Malaysia, c/o Pearson Malaysia Sdn Bhd, Selangor Darul Ehsan, Malaysia; Penguin Books Singapore, c/o Pearson Education South Asia Pte Ltd, Singapore
South Africa: Jonathan Ball Publishers (Pty) Ltd, Johannesburg
South East Europe, Cyprus, Greece, Gibraltar, Turkey, Israel, Caribbean & Latin America: Tamsin Pagella, Penguin International Sales, London, UK
Spain & Portugal: Geraldine Kilpatrick, Penguin Books SA, Madrid, Spain
Sri Lanka: Shan Rajaguru, Colombo
Switzerland & Malta: Kathy John, Penguin International Sales, London, UK

Book Trade Association Membership:
Publishers Association; IPG

2105

BLUE SKY PRESS
57 Longfield Avenue, Fareham, Hants PO14 1BU
Telephone: 07816 411341
Fax: 01329 221969
Email: press@mrbluesky.net
Web Site: www.mrbluesky.net,
www.thealicefactor.com &
www.blueskypress.co.uk

Executive Assistant: Victoria Stone
Managing Editor: Cfyn Markwick-Day

Fiction; Music; Poetry

ISBNs, Imprints & Series: 978 9 544983

Parent Company:
Mr Blue Sky Ltd

2106

BODLEIAN LIBRARY PUBLISHING
Bodleian Library, Broad Street, Oxford OX1 3BG
Telephone: 01865 277627
Fax: 01865 277187
Email: publishing@bodley.ox.ac.uk
Web Site: www.bodleianbookshop.co.uk

Trade Enquiries & Orders:
Turpin Distribution Ltd,
Stratton Business Park, Pegasus Drive,
Biggleswade, Beds SG18 8QS
Telephone: 01767 604968
Fax: 01767 601640
Email: custserve@turpin-distribution.com
Web Site: www.turpin-distribution.com

Representation (UK Book Trade):
Yale University Press

Publisher: Samuel Fanous
Project Manager: Deborah Susman

Academic & Scholarly; Antiques & Collecting; Architecture & Design; Biography & Autobiography; Children's Books; Fine Art & Art History; History & Antiquarian; Humour; Literature & Criticism; Military & War; Reference Books, Directories & Dictionaries

New Titles: 9 (2008), 9 (2009)
No of Employees: 4

ISBNs, Imprints & Series:
Postcards from ...; Treasures of the Bodleian Library
978 1 85124

Parent Company:
University of Oxford

Overseas Representation:
North America & Canada: Chicago University Press, Chicago, IL, USA

Book Trade Association Membership:
IPG; Association of Cultural Enterprises

2107

BOOK CASTLE PUBLISHING LTD
2a Sycamore Business Park, Copt Hewick, North Yorkshire HG4 5DF
Telephone: 01582 344321
Fax: 01582 344318
Email: info@bookcastlepublishing.co.uk
Web Site: www.book-castle.co.uk

Publisher, Manager: Paul Bowes
Production Manager: Sally Siddons *(External Sales & Marketing)*

Biography & Autobiography; History & Antiquarian; Travel & Topography

New Titles: 12 (2008), 7 (2009)
No of Employees: 3

ISBNs, Imprints & Series:
978 0 950 9773, 978 1 871199, 978 1 903747, 978 1 906632

Book Trade Association Membership:
BA

2108

BOOK MARKETING LTD
39 Store Street, London WC1E 7DS
Telephone: 0870 870 2345
Email: steve@bookmarketing.co.uk
Web Site: www.bookmarketing.co.uk

Managing Director: Jo Henry
Research Editor: Steve Bohme

Academic & Scholarly; Electronic (Professional & Academic); Reference Books, Directories & Dictionaries; Trade

Book Trade Association Membership:
Publishers Association; IPG

2109

BORTHWICK PUBLICATIONS
Borthwick Institute, University of York,
Heslington, York YO10 5DD
Telephone: 01904 321160
Web Site: www.york.ac.uk/borthwick

Publications Manager: Sara Slinn

*Academic & Scholarly; Archaeology;
Educational & Textbooks; History &
Antiquarian; Law; Religion & Theology*

New Titles: 4 (2008) , 4 (2009)

ISBNs, Imprints & Series:
978 0 903857 Borthwick List & Indexes;
Borthwick Papers; Borthwick Studies in
History; Borthwick Texts & Calendars;
Borthwick Wallets; Monastic Research
Bulletin
978 1 094497 Borthwick Publications

Parent Company:
University of York

2110

BOSSINEY BOOKS LTD
Hillside, Langore, Launceston, Cornwall
PL15 8LD
Telephone: 01566 774176
Email: bossineybooks@btinternet.com
Web Site: www.bossineybooks.com

Distribution:
Tor Mark Press, PO Box 4, Redruth,
Cornwall TR16 5YX
Telephone: 01209 822101
Fax: 01209 822035
Email: office@tormark.co.uk
Web Site: www.tormark.co.uk

Directors: Jane White
Paul White

*Cookery, Wines & Spirits; Guide Books;
History & Antiquarian; Magic & the Occult;
Local Interest Books*

New Titles: 10 (2008) , 10 (2009)
No of Employees: 2

ISBNs, Imprints & Series:
Tamar Books
978 1 899383, 978 1 906474

Book Trade Association Membership:
IPG

2111

BOWKER (UK) LTD
1st Floor, Medway House, Cantelupe Road,
East Grinstead, West Sussex RH19 3BJ
Telephone: 01342 310450
Fax: 01342 310486
Email: sales@bowker.co.uk
Web Site: www.bowker.co.uk

Directors: Doug McMillan *(Managing)*
Pam Roud *(Sales)*
Marketing Manager: Jo Grange

*Academic & Scholarly; Bibliography &
Library Science; Electronic (Educational);
Electronic (Professional & Academic);
Reference Books, Directories & Dictionaries*

ISBNs, Imprints & Series: 978 0 8352

Associated Companies:
USA: Cambridge Information Group

Overseas Representation:
see: www.bowker.co.uk, UK

Book Trade Association Membership:
BA; Data Publishers Association

2112

MARION BOYARS PUBLISHERS LTD
24 Lacy Road, London SW15 1NL
Telephone: (020) 8788 9522
Fax: (020) 8789 8122
Email: catheryn@marionboyars.com
Web Site: www.marionboyars.co.uk

Distribution:
Central Books, 99 Wallis Road, London
E9 5LN
Telephone: (020) 8986 4854
Fax: (020) 8533 5821
Email: orders@centralbooks.com

Managing Director: Catheryn Kilgarriff
*(Publicity, Rights & Permissions,
Production)*
Managers: Rebecca Gillieron *(Editorial)*
Katharine Bright-Holmes *(Editorial)*
Kit Maude *(Sales Co-ordinator)*

*Biography & Autobiography; Children's
Books; Cinema, Video, TV & Radio; Fiction;
Literature & Criticism; Music; Philosophy;
Theatre, Drama & Dance*

New Titles: 10 (2008) , 10 (2009)
No of Employees: 4
Annual Turnover: £260,000

ISBNs, Imprints & Series:
978 0 7145 Marion Boyars

Associated Companies:
USA: Marion Boyars Publishers Inc

Overseas Representation:
Australia & New Zealand: Tower Books Pty
Ltd, Frenchs Forest, NSW, Australia
France, Germany & Switzerland: Michael
Geoghegan, London, UK
Italy, Spain, Portugal & Greece: Penny
Padovani, London, UK
South Africa: Stephan Phillips (Pty) Ltd,
Cape Town
USA: Consortium Book Sales & Distribution
Inc, MN

Book Trade Association Membership:
IPG

2113

BOYDELL & BREWER LTD
PO Box 9, Woodbridge, Suffolk IP12 3DF
Telephone: 01394 610615
Fax: 01394 610316
Email: trading@boydell.co.uk
Web Site: www.boydell.co.uk

Directors: R. W. Barber *(Group Managing)*
P. Clifford *(Managing)*
M. J. Richards *(Sales)*
C. L. Palmer *(Editorial)*
W. Ellis *(Accounts)*
Managers: J. M. Jordan *(Customer Orders)*
M. L. Webb *(Production)*

*Academic & Scholarly; Archaeology; History
& Antiquarian; Literature & Criticism;
Military & War; Music; Philosophy;
Reference Books, Directories &
Dictionaries; Travel & Topography*

New Titles: 200 (2009)

ISBNs, Imprints & Series:
978 0 85115 Boydell Press
978 0 85991 D. S. Brewer
978 1 57113 Camden House
978 1 84701 James Currey
978 1 85566 Tamesis
978 1 900639 Companion Guides

Associated Companies:
USA: Boydell & Brewer Inc; University of
Rochester Press

Distributor for:
Bedfordshire Historical Record Society;
Henry Bradshaw Society; Burke's
Peerage; Canterbury & York Society;
Church of England Record Society; Early
English Text Society; Ecclesiastical History
Society; Lincoln Records Society;
Plumbago Books; Royal Society of
Literature; Suffolk Records Society;
Surtees Society; Victoria County History;
Yorkshire Archaeological Society
USA: Toccata Press; University of Rochester
Press

Overseas Representation:
Australia: DA Information Services Pty Ltd,
Mitcham, Vic
Belgium, Luxembourg & Netherlands:
Kemper Conseil Publishing,
Leidschendam, Netherlands
Eastern Europe: Marek Lewinson, Warsaw,
Poland
France: Mare Nostrum, Paris
Germany, Austria & Switzerland: Bernd
Feldmann, Oranienburg, Germany
Greece & Cyprus: Charles Gibbes
Associates, Louslitges, France
India & Sri Lanka: Viva Group, New Delhi,
India
Italy: David Pickering, Mare Nostrum
Publishing Consultants, Rome
Middle East & North Africa: Publishers
International Marketing, Storrington, UK
Pakistan: T.M.L. Publishers' Consultants &
Representatives, Lahore
Philippines: Edwin Makabenta, Quezon City
Republic of Ireland: Mullett Fitzpatrick,
Shankill, Co Dublin
Scandinavia: Colin Flint Ltd, Publishers
Scandinavian Consultancy, Cambridge,
UK
South East Asia & Korea: Publishers
International Marketing, London, UK
Spain & Portugal: Iberian Book Services,
Madrid, Spain

2114

BRADT TRAVEL GUIDES LTD
23 High Street, Chalfont St Peter, Bucks
SL9 9QE
Telephone: 01753 893444
Fax: 01753 892333
Email: info@bradtguides.com
Web Site: www.bradtguides.com

British Orders (Distributor):
NBN International, 10 Estover Road,
Plymouth PL6 7PY
Telephone: 01752 202301
Fax: 01752 202331
Email: orders@nbninternational.com

Directors: Donald Greig *(Executive)*
Peter Jay *(Finance)*
Adrian Phillips *(Editorial)*
Managers: Mrs Debbie Hunter *(Finance)*
Debbie Everson *(Export)*
Helen Anjomshoaa *(Rights & Publishing
Services)*
Helen Calderon *(Sales)*
Deborah Gerrard *(Advertising)*
Assistant – Editorial/Production: Anna
Moores
Emma Thomson
Elspeth Beidas
Book Keeper: Julie May

Guide Books; Travel & Topography

New Titles: 42 (2008) , 33 (2009)
No of Employees: 14

ISBNs, Imprints & Series:
978 1 84162 Mini Guide Series
978 1 84162, 978 1 898323 Backpacking
Guide Series; Eccentric Series; Guide to
Series; Rail Guide Series; Wildlife Series

Overseas Representation:
Africa (excluding South Africa, Namibia, &

Zimbabwe): A–Z Africa Book Services,
Rotterdam, Netherlands
Australia: Woodslane Pty Ltd, Warriewood,
NSW
Austria: Freytag & Berndt, Vienna
Belgium: Craenen bvba, Herent (Winksele)
Eastern Europe: CLB Marketing Services,
Budapest, Hungary
France: Cartothèque EGG, Notre Dame
D'Oé
Germany: GeoCenter ILH, Stuttgart
Israel: Steinhard Katzir, Netanya
Netherlands: Nilsson & Lamm BV, Weesp
Portugal: Iberian Book Services, Madrid,
Spain
Scandinavian Europe: Angell Eurosales,
Berwick-on-Tweed, UK
Singapore: Pansing Distribution Pte Ltd
South & Central America: David Williams,
InterMedia Americana (IMA) Ltd,
London, UK
South Africa: Wild Dog Press, Johannesburg
Spain: Altair, Barcelona
Switzerland: Distribution OLF SA, Fribourg
USA: Globe Pequot Press, Guilford, CT

Book Trade Association Membership:
IPG

2115

BRANDON/MOUNT EAGLE
PUBLICATIONS
PO Box 32, Dingle, Co Kerry,
Republic of Ireland
Telephone: +353 (066) 915 1463
Fax: +353 (066) 915 1234
Web Site: www.brandonbooks.com

Warehouse, Trade Orders:
Gill & Macmillan, Hume Avenue,
Park West, Dublin 12, Republic of Ireland
Telephone: +353 (01) 500 9500
Fax: +353 (01) 500 9599
Email: sales@gillmacmillan.ie

Publisher & Managing Director: Steve
MacDonogh

*Biography & Autobiography; Fiction;
Literature & Criticism; Politics & World
Affairs; Travel & Topography*

New Titles: 12 (2008) , 14 (2009)
No of Employees: 2

ISBNs, Imprints & Series:
978 0 86322 Brandon
978 1 902011 Mount Eagle

Associated Companies:
Republic of Ireland: Brandon Book
Publishers Ltd

Overseas Representation:
UK (excluding Northern Ireland):
Turnaround Publisher Services Ltd,
London, UK
USA: Dufour Editions Inc, Chester Springs,
PA

Book Trade Association Membership:
CLÉ (Irish PA)

2116

NICHOLAS BREALEY PUBLISHING
3–5 Spafield Street, London EC1R 4QB
Telephone: (020) 7239 0360
Fax: (020) 7239 0370
Email: rights@nicholasbrealey.com
Web Site: www.nicholasbrealey.com

Orders & Warehouse:
TBS Ltd, Colchester Road, Frating Green,
Colchester, Essex CO7 7DW
Telephone: 01206 256000
Fax: 01206 819587

Managing Director: Nicholas Brealey
(Editorial & Rights)

Managers: Kim Cope *(Sales/Office)*
Sally Lansdell *(Publishing)*

*Biography & Autobiography; Economics;
Industry, Business & Management;
Psychology & Psychiatry; Travel &
Topography; Vocational Training & Careers*

ISBNs, Imprints & Series:
978 0 85290 Industrial Society (acquired
  titles)
978 0 89106 Davies-Black
978 1 85788 Nicholas Brealey
978 1 877864, 978 1 93193 Intercultural
  Press
978 1 90483 Nicholas Brealey International

Associated Companies:
USA: NB Publishing Inc

Overseas Representation:
Asia (excluding Singapore & Malaysia):
  Sales East, Bangkok, Thailand
Australia: Allen & Unwin Pty Ltd, Sydney,
  NSW
*Europe (excluding Scandinavia) &
  Switzerland:* Michael Geoghegan,
  London, UK
India: Research Press, New Delhi
Republic of Ireland: Gill Simpson, Dublin
Scandinavia: Angell Eurosales, Berwick-on-
  Tweed, UK
Singapore & Malaysia: Horizon Books Pte
  Ltd, Singapore
South Africa: Wild Dog Press, Highlands
  North
USA: Nicholas Brealey Publishing North
  America, Boston, MA; National Book
  Network, Lanham, MD

Book Trade Association Membership:
IPG

2117 ▬▬▬

***BREEDON BOOKS PUBLISHING CO
LTD**
3 The Parker Centre, Derby DE21 4SZ
Telephone: 01332 384235
Fax: 01332 292755
Email:
  steve.caron@breedonpublishing.co.uk
Web Site: www.breedonbooks.co.uk

Directors: Stephen Caron *(Chairman &
  Managing)*
  Jane Caron *(Finance)*
Marketing: Claire Lynes
Editorial: Michelle Grainger *(Publishing
  Manager)*

*Biography & Autobiography; Sports &
Games; Transport*

ISBNs, Imprints & Series:
978 0 907969, 978 1 85983, 978 1 873626

2118 ▬▬▬

BREWIN BOOKS LTD
Doric House, 56 Alcester Road, Studley,
Warwickshire B80 7LG
Telephone: 01527 854228
Fax: 01527 852746
Email: admin@brewinbooks.com
Web Site: www.brewinbooks.com

Warehouse:
Supaprint Works, Unit 19,
Enfield Industrial Estate, Redditch, Worcs
B97 6BZ
Telephone: 01527 62212
Fax: 01527 60451
Email: admin@supaprint.com
Web Site: www.supaprint.com

Directors: Alan Brewin *(Managing)*
  Alistair Brewin *(Art, Book design and
  production)*
Company Secretary: Julie Brewin

Biography & Autobiography; History &

Antiquarian; Military & War; Transport

New Titles: 25 (2008) , 30 (2009)

ISBNs, Imprints & Series:
978 0 947731, 978 0 9505570, 978 1
  85858 Brewin Books
978 1 85858 Alton Douglas Books; History-
  into-Print

Distributor for:
City of Birmingham Libraries [Local History];
Hereford County Council [Trail Path
Guides]; Hunt End Books [Local History
(Worcs)]

2119 ▬▬▬

BRIDGE BOOKS
61 Park Avenue, Wrexham LL12 7AW
Telephone: 01978 358661 & 0845 166
2851
Email: enquiries@bridgebooks.co.uk

Partners: W. Alister Williams
Susan A. Williams

*Aviation; History & Antiquarian; Military &
War; Travel & Topography*

New Titles: 15 (2008) , 12 (2009)
No of Employees: 2

ISBNs, Imprints & Series:
978 0 9508285, 978 1 84494, 978 1
  872424

Associated Companies:
Maelor Interactive Publishing

2120 ▬▬▬

BRILLIANT PUBLICATIONS
Unit 10, Sparrow Hall Farm, Edlesborough,
Dunstable LU6 2ES
Telephone: 01525 222292
Fax: 01525 222720
Email: info@brilliantpublications.co.uk
Web Site: www.brilliantpublications.co.uk

Sales & Distribution:
BEBC Distribution, Albion Close, Parkstone,
Poole, Dorset BH12 3LL
Telephone: 01202 712910
Fax: 0845 130 9300
Email: brilliant@bebc.co.uk

Publisher: Priscilla Hannaford
Finance Director: Richard Dorrance
Marketing: Alison Marshall

*Educational & Textbooks; Languages &
Linguistics*

New Titles: 20 (2008) , 30 (2009)
No of Employees: 5

ISBNs, Imprints & Series:
978 1 897675
978 1 903853
978 1 905780

Book Trade Association Membership:
Publishers Association; EPC; IPG

2121 ▬▬▬

**BRITISH ASSOCIATION FOR
ADOPTION & FOSTERING**
[BAAF]
Saffron House, 6–10 Kirby Street, London
EC1N 8TS
Telephone: (020) 7421 2602
Fax: (020) 7421 2601
Email: shaila.shah@baaf.org.uk
Web Site: www.baaf.org.uk

Trade Enquiries:
Turnaround Distribution, Unit 3,
Olympia Trading Estate, Coburg Road,
London N22 6TZ
Telephone: (020) 8829 3000

Fax: (020) 8881 5088
Email: orders@turnaround-uk.com

Chief Executive: David Holmes
Director of Publications: Shaila Shah
  (Editorial, Production, Sales & Rights)

*Academic & Scholarly; Children's Books;
Psychology & Psychiatry; Reference Books,
Directories & Dictionaries; Sociology &
Anthropology*

New Titles: 30 (2008) , 30 (2009)
No of Employees: 100

ISBNs, Imprints & Series:
978 0 903534, 978 1 873868, 978 1
  903699, 978 1 905664

Overseas Representation:
Australia (selected titles): Innovative
  Resources, Bendigo, Vic, Australia

Book Trade Association Membership:
The Publishers Forum for the Voluntary
Sector

2122 ▬▬▬

BRITISH GEOLOGICAL SURVEY
Keyworth, Nottingham NG12 5GG
Telephone: 0115 936 3241 (sales) & 0115
  936 3147 (returns)
Fax: 0115 936 3488
Email: sales@bgs.ac.uk & ikp@bgs.ac.uk
  (returns)
Web Site: www.bgs.ac.uk &
  www.geologyshop.com (online shop)

Distribution & Representation:
Cordee Ltd, 11 Jacknell Road,
Dodswell Bridge Industrial Estate, Hinckley,
Leics LE10 3BS
Telephone: 01455 611185
Fax: 01455 635687
Email: info@cordee.co.uk
Web Site: www.cordee.co.uk

Director: Prof John Ludden
Head of Graphics Communications: Jim
  Rayner
Copyright & IPR: Chris Luton
Head of Sales: Ms Elaine Johnston

*Atlases & Maps; Geography & Geology;
Guide Books; Scientific & Technical*

New Titles: 60 (2008) , 50 (2009)
No of Employees: 800

ISBNs, Imprints & Series:
978 0 7518 British Geological Survey
  (Maps)
978 0 85272 British Geological Survey
  (Books & Reports)

Parent Company:
Natural Environment Research Council

Distributor for:
Durham County Council; Journal of Mines
& Minerals

2123 ▬▬▬

BRITISH LIBRARY
96 Euston Road, London NW1 2DB
Telephone: (020) 7412 7535
Fax: (020) 7412 7768
Email: blpublications@bl.uk
Web Site: www.bl.uk

Orders:
The British Library, Turpin Distribution Ltd,
Stratton Business Park, Pegasus Drive,
Biggleswade, Beds SG18 8QB
Telephone: 01767 604955
Fax: 01767 601640
Email: custserv@turpin-distribution.com
Web Site: www.turpin-distribution.com

Head of Publishing: David Way

Editorial & Rights: Catherine Britton
Sales: Martin Oestreicher

*Academic & Scholarly; Bibliography &
Library Science; Biography &
Autobiography; Fine Art & Art History;
History & Antiquarian; Illustrated & Fine
Editions*

ISBNs, Imprints & Series:
978 0 7123 Bibliography of British
  Newspapers; The British Library; British
  Library Guides; British Library Occasional
  Papers; The British Library Studies in
  Medieval Culture; The British Library
  Studies in the History of the Book;
  Corpus of British Medieval Library
  Catalogues; The Panizzi Lectures

Parent Company:
The British Library

Overseas Representation:
Australia: InBooks, Belrose, NSW
Canada: University of Toronto Press, North
  York, Ont
USA: University of Chicago Press, Chicago,
  IL

Book Trade Association Membership:
Publishers Association; BA; CAPP

2124 ▬▬▬

BRITISH MUSEUM PRESS
38 Russell Square, London WC1B 3QQ
Telephone: (020) 7323 1234
Fax: (020) 7436 7315
Email: rbradley@britishmuseum.co.uk
Web Site: www.britishmuseum.org

Trade Distributor:
Littlehampton Book Services,
Faraday Close, Durrington, Worthing,
West Sussex BN13 3RB
Telephone: 01903 828501
Fax: 01903 828801/2
Email: enquiries@lbsltd.co.uk

Directors: Brian Oldman *(Managing)*
  Helen Watts *(Finance & Administration)*
  Rosemary Bradley *(Publishing)*
Editorial: Teresa Francis
Production: Susan Walby
Rights: Louise Fletcher
Marketing/Publicity: Margaret Robe

*Academic & Scholarly; Antiques &
Collecting; Archaeology; Children's Books;
Fine Art & Art History; Natural History;
Reference Books, Directories &
Dictionaries; Sociology & Anthropology*

ISBNs, Imprints & Series: 978 0 7141

Parent Company:
The British Museum Co Ltd

Overseas Representation:
USA (Trade orders): British Museum Press,
  London, UK
Worldwide (excluding USA): Thames &
  Hudson (Distributors) Ltd, Farnborough,
  Hants, UK

Book Trade Association Membership:
Publishers Association

2125 ▬▬▬

BROOKLANDS BOOKS LTD
PO Box 146, Cobham, Surrey KT11 1LG
Telephone: 01932 865051
Fax: 01932 868803
Email: sales@brooklands-books.com
Web Site: www.brooklands-books.com

Directors: I. Dowdeswell
  J. Powell
Sales Manager: B. Cleveland

Aviation; Military & War; Transport

New Titles: 40 (2008) , 40 (2009)
No of Employees: 7

ISBNs, Imprints & Series: 978 1 85520

Parent Company:
USA: Robert Bentley Publishers; Cartech; SA Design

Distributor for:
USA: Robert Bentley Inc; SA Design

Overseas Representation:
Southern Europe: Bookport Associates, Corsico (MI), Italy

2126 ▬▬▬▬▬▬▬▬▬▬

BROWN DOG BOOKS
6 The Old Dairy, Melcombe Road, Bath BA2 3LR
Telephone: 01225 478444
Fax: 01225 478440
Email: sales@manning-partnership.co.uk
Web Site: www.manning-partnership.co.uk

Directors: Garry Manning *(Managing)*
Roger Hibbert *(Sales & Marketing)*
Heather Morris *(Editorial)*
Managers: Karen Twissell *(Office)*
James Wheeler *(Sales)*

Children's Books; Humour; Sports & Games

New Titles: 5 (2008) , 3 (2009)
No of Employees: 6

ISBNs, Imprints & Series:
978 1 903056 Brown Dog Books
978 1 903222 Nightingale

Parent Company:
Manning Partnership Ltd

Distributor for:
Brimax; Carroll & Brown; Five Mile Press; Globe Pequot Press; Interpet Publishing; Lorenz; Nightingale Press; Peter Pauper; Tony Potter; Powerfresh; Mathew Price; RICS Books; Search Press; Selectabook; Source Books; Southwater

2127 ▬▬▬▬▬▬▬▬▬▬

BROWN, SON & FERGUSON, LTD
4–10 Darnley Street, Glasgow G41 2SD
Telephone: 0141 429 1234/5922
Fax: 0141 420 1694
Email: info@skipper.co.uk
Web Site: www.skipper.co.uk

Chairman & Production Director: T. Nigel Brown
Company Secretary & Editorial Director: L. Ingram-Brown
Sales Manager: R. P. B. Brown

Nautical; Theatre, Drama & Dance

New Titles: 2 (2008) , 3 (2009)
No of Employees: 11
Annual Turnover: £1.2M

ISBNs, Imprints & Series: 978 0 85174

Associated Companies:
James Munro & Co

Book Trade Association Membership:
Publishing Scotland

2128 ▬▬▬▬▬▬▬▬▬▬

BROWN & WHITTAKER PUBLISHING
Stronsaule, Tobermory, Isle of Mull PA75 6PR
Telephone: 01688 302381
Email: olivebrown@msn.com
Web Site: www.brown-whittaker.co.uk

Partners: Olive Brown
Jean Whittaker

Archaeology; Biography & Autobiography; Biology & Zoology; Cookery, Wines & Spirits; Guide Books; History & Antiquarian; Natural History; Poetry

New Titles: 1 (2008) , 3 (2009)
Annual Turnover: £15,000

ISBNs, Imprints & Series:
978 0 9528428, 978 0 9532775, 978 1 9043530

Book Trade Association Membership:
Publishing Scotland

2129 ▬▬▬▬▬▬▬▬▬▬

*BRYNTIRION PRESS
Bryntirion, Bridgend, Mid Glamorgan CF31 4DX
Telephone: 01656 655886
Fax: 01656 665919

Representation:
Evangelical Press, Faverdale North, Darlington DL3 0PH
Telephone: 01325 380232
Fax: 01325 466153
Email: sales@evangelical-press.org

Press Officer: Huw Kinsey

Religion & Theology

ISBNs, Imprints & Series:
978 0 900898, 978 0 9502686, 978 1 85049 Evangelical Library of Wales
978 0 900898, 978 1 85049 Evangelical Movement of Wales; Evangelical Press of Wales

Parent Company:
Evangelical Movement of Wales

Distributor for:
Association of Christian Teachers of Wales; Evangelical Library (London); Yr Undeb Cristnogol

Book Trade Association Membership:
BA; Undeb Cyhoeddwyr a Llyfrwerthwyr Cymru; (The Union of Welsh Publishers and Booksellers)

2130 ▬▬▬▬▬▬▬▬▬▬

BURNS & OATES
see: Continuum International Publishing Group

2131 ▬▬▬▬▬▬▬▬▬▬

BUSINESS EDUCATION PUBLISHERS
evolve Business Centre, Cygnet Way, Rainton Bridge Business Park, Houghton-le-Spring, Tyne & Wear DH4 5QY
Telephone: 0191 305 5165
Fax: 0191 305 5504
Email: info@bepl.com
Web Site: www.bepl.com

Warehouse:
Unit 18, Hartlepool Workshops, Usworth Road Industrial Estate, Usworth Road, Hartlepool, Cleveland TS25 1PD
Telephone: 01429 234153
Fax: 01429 234153

Managing Director: Paul Callaghan
Managers: Andrea Murphy *(Publications)*
Joe McQuilling *(Warehouse)*

Academic & Scholarly; Biography & Autobiography; Computer Science; Educational & Textbooks; History & Antiquarian; Industry, Business & Management; Law; Military & War

New Titles: 4 (2008) , 3 (2009)
No of Employees: 2

ISBNs, Imprints & Series:
978 0 907679, 978 1 901888

Book Trade Association Membership:
BA; Book Data

2132 ▬▬▬▬▬▬▬▬▬▬

BUTTERFINGERS BOOKS
The Rose House, 19 Tor View Avenue, Glastonbury, Somerset BA6 8AE
Telephone: 01458 832035
Email: laurie@butterfingersbooks.co.uk
Web Site: www.butterfingers.co.uk

Director: L. H. R. Collard *(Rights)*

Educational & Textbooks; Sports & Games

ISBNs, Imprints & Series:
978 0 9513240, 978 1 898591

Distributor for:
Circusstuff
Germany: Die Jonglerie
USA: Brian Dubé Inc; Finesse Press; Renegade Juggling

Overseas Representation:
North America: Brian Dube Inc, New York, NY, USA

2133 ▬▬▬▬▬▬▬▬▬▬

*CABI
Nosworthy Way, Wallingford, Oxon OX10 8DE
Telephone: 01491 832111
Fax: 01491 833508 & 829292 (order fulfilment)
Email: publishing@cabi.org
Web Site: www.cabi.org/

Directors: Ms Caroline McNamara *(Executive, Commercial)*
Ms Andrea Powell *(Executive, Publishing)*
Shaun Hobbs *(Database Publishing)*
Elizabeth Dodsworth *(Knowledge for Development)*
Nigel Farrar *(Books Publishing)*

Academic & Scholarly; Agriculture; Animal Care & Breeding; Biology & Zoology; Environment & Development Studies; Medical (incl. Self Help & Alternative Medicine); Scientific & Technical; Veterinary Science

ISBNs, Imprints & Series:
978 0 85198, 978 0 85199, 978 1 84593

Parent Company:
CAB International

Distributor for:
International Food Information Service; Royal Society of Edinburgh

Overseas Representation:
Africa: CABI Africa, Nairobi, Kenya
All other areas: Commercial Department, Wallingford, UK
Asia: CABI South East & East Asia, Serdang, Malaysia
Australia, New Zealand & Papua New Guinea: DA Information Services Pty Ltd, Mitcham, Vic, Australia
Canada: CABI North America, Cambridge, MA, USA
Caribbean: CABI Caribbean & Latin America, Curepe, Trinidad
Denmark, Finland, Iceland, Norway & Sweden: Colin Flint Ltd, Harlow, UK
Germany, Austria & Switzerland: Missing Link International Booksellers, Bremen, Germany
India: Book Marketing Services, Chennai

Middle East (excluding Iran): James & Lorin Watt Ltd, Publishing Consultants, Oxford, UK
South Africa: Academic Marketing Services (Pty) Ltd, Craighall
USA, Central America, Caribbean, Mexico, Puerto Rico & Guam: Oxford University Press, Cary, NC, USA

Book Trade Association Membership:
BA

2134 ▬▬▬▬▬▬▬▬▬▬

CALYPSO PUBLICATIONS
2 Gatcombe Road, London N19 4PT
Telephone: (020) 7281 4948
Fax: (020) 7281 4948
Email: Gerald@calypso.org.uk & enquiries@calypso.org.uk
Web Site: www.calypso.org.uk/ourbooks & www.calypso.org.uk/bookshop

Proprietor: G. H. Jennings

Academic & Scholarly; Animal Care & Breeding; Biology & Zoology; Crafts & Hobbies; Educational & Textbooks; Natural History; Reference Books, Directories & Dictionaries; Scientific & Technical; Travel & Topography

ISBNs, Imprints & Series:
978 0 906301, 978 1 902788

Parent Company:
The Calypso Organization

Overseas Representation:
Australia: Andrew Isles Bookshop, Melbourne, Vic
Cyprus: Soloneion Book Centre, Nicosia
USA: The Aquatic Bookshop, Placerville, CA

2135 ▬▬▬▬▬▬▬▬▬▬

CAMBRIDGE ARCHIVE EDITIONS LTD
7 Ashley House, The Broadway, Farnham Common, Slough SL2 3PQ
Telephone: 01753 646633
Fax: 01753 646746
Email: info@archiveeditions.co.uk
Web Site: www.archiveeditions.co.uk

Head of Customer Relations & Finance: Jeanette Wood
Managers: Ann Greenwood *(Production)*
Jessica Lagan *(Marketing)*

Academic & Scholarly; History & Antiquarian; Politics & World Affairs

New Titles: 3 (2008) , 3 (2009)
No of Employees: 4

ISBNs, Imprints & Series:
978 1 84097, 978 1 85207

Parent Company:
UK: Cambridge University Press

2136 ▬▬▬▬▬▬▬▬▬▬

CAMBRIDGE UNIVERSITY PRESS
The Edinburgh Building, Shaftesbury Road, Cambridge CB2 8RU
Telephone: 01223 312393
Fax: 01223 315052
Email: information@cambridge.org
Web Site: www.cambridge.org

Orders:
Telephone: 01223 325577
Fax: 01223 325151
Email: intcustserve@cambridge.org
Web Site: www.cambridge.org

Chief Executive of the Press: Stephen R. R. Bourne
Press Board: Christopher Boughton *(Managing Director, Asia-Pacific)*

Andrew Brown *(Managing Director, Academic)*
Hanri Pieterse *(Managing Director, Cambridge Learning)*
Andrew Gilfillan *(Managing Director, Europe, Middle East & Africa)*
Steven Miller *(Chief Financial Officer)*
Richard Ziemacki *(President, Americas)*
Directors: Ron Bennett *(Legal Services)*
Peter Davison *(Corporate Affairs)*
Richard Fisher *(Academic & Professional)*
David Harrison *(ELT Sales & Marketing)*
Ron Ragsdale *(ELT Editorial)*
Maralyn Johnson *(Chief Technology Officer)*
Simon Ross *(Journals)*
Rohan Segry *(Academic Sales & Marketing)*
Simon Read *(Education)*
Howard Buckley *(Chief Financial Officer, EH)*
Cheryl Park *(Human Resources)*
Andy Williams *(Academic & Professional)*
Geoff Staff *(Cambridge Learning)*
Sandra Ward *(Operations)*

Academic & Scholarly; Accountancy & Taxation; Agriculture; Archaeology; Architecture & Design; Bibliography & Library Science; Biography & Autobiography; Biology & Zoology; Chemistry; Children's Books; Computer Science; Economics; Educational & Textbooks; Electronic (Educational); Electronic (Professional & Academic); Engineering; English as a Foreign Language; Environment & Development Studies; Fine Art & Art History; Gender Studies; Geography & Geology; History & Antiquarian; Industry, Business & Management; Languages & Linguistics; Law; Literature & Criticism; Mathematics & Statistics; Medical (incl. Self Help & Alternative Medicine); Music; Natural History; Philosophy; Physics; Politics & World Affairs; Psychology & Psychiatry; Reference Books, Directories & Dictionaries; Religion & Theology; Scientific & Technical; Sociology & Anthropology; Theatre, Drama & Dance; Animal Behaviour; Astronomy; Biotechnology; Classics; Ecology; History & Philosophy of Science

New Titles: 2500 (2008) , 2500 (2009)
No of Employees: 1882
Annual Turnover: £180M

ISBNs, Imprints & Series: 978 0 521

Associated Companies:
Greece: Cambridge University Press (Greece) EPE
Hong Kong: Cambridge Knowledge (China) Ltd; United Publishers Services Ltd
India: Cambridge University Press India (Pvt) Ltd
Japan: Cambridge University Press Japan KK; Kabushiki Kaisha Phoenic
Mexico: ELT Trading SA de CV
South Africa: Cambridge University Press South Africa (Pty) Ltd
UK: Cambridge Global Grid for Learning; Cambridge Hitachisoft Educational Solutions PLC; Cambridge Printing Services Ltd; Cambridge University Press (Holdings) Ltd; Greenwich Medical Media Ltd; Oncoweb Ltd

Overseas Representation:
Contact: Chris Boughton, Managing Director, Asia-Pacific, Cambridge University Press, Cambridge, UK; Peter Langworth, Cambridge University Press, Cambridge, UK; Richard Ziemacki, President, The Americas, Cambridge University Press, Cambridge, UK

Book Trade Association Membership:
Publishers Association; BA; EPC; IGSMTP; CAPP; IPG; Association of Learned &

Professional Society Publishers; BML; IBD; PIRA

2137

CAMRA BOOKS
230 Hatfield Road, St Albans, Herts AL1 4LW
Telephone: 01727 798458
Fax: 01727 848795
Email: camra@camra.org.uk
Web Site: www.camra.org.uk

UK Sales & Distribution:
Pan Macmillan, 20 New Wharf Road, London N1 9RR
Telephone: (020) 7014 6000

Head of Marketing: Louise Ashworth
Managing Editor: Simon Hall
Marketing Manager: Kim Carvey

Biography & Autobiography; Cookery, Wines & Spirits; Guide Books; Reference Books, Directories & Dictionaries; Travel & Topography

New Titles: 6 (2008) , 6 (2009)

ISBNs, Imprints & Series: 978 1 85249

Parent Company:
Campaign for Real Ale Ltd

Overseas Representation:
USA: Trafalgar (Pan Macmillan), Chicago, IL

2138

CANONGATE BOOKS
14 High Street, Edinburgh EH1 1TE
Telephone: 0131 557 5111
Fax: 0131 557 5211
Email: info@canongate.co.uk
Web Site: www.meetatthegate.com

Warehouse & Orders:
The Book Service Ltd, Distribution Centre, Colchester Road, Frating Green, Colchester, Essex CO7 7DW
Telephone: 01206 256000
Fax: 01206 255715
Email: helpdesk@tbs-ltd.co.uk
Web Site: www.thebookservice.co.uk

Publisher: Jamie Byng
Directors: Kathleen Anderson *(Finance)*
Caroline Gorham *(Production)*
Polly Collingridge *(Rights)*
Jenny Todd *(Sales & Marketing)*
Anya Serota *(Publishing (Fiction))*
Nick Davies *(Editorial (Non-Fiction))*
Managing Editor: Stephanie Gorton

Audio Books; Biography & Autobiography; Crime; Fiction; Fine Art & Art History; Guide Books; History & Antiquarian; Humour; Illustrated & Fine Editions; Literature & Criticism; Music; Philosophy; Poetry; Politics & World Affairs; Scottish

New Titles: 75 (2008) , 75 (2009)
No of Employees: 28
Annual Turnover: £15M

ISBNs, Imprints & Series:
978 0 86241, 978 1 84195 Canongate; Canongate Classics; Myths

Associated Companies:
Australia: Text Publishing
USA: Canongate US

Overseas Representation:
Australia: Penguin Books Australia Ltd, Camberwell, Vic
Canada: Penguin Group Canada, Toronto, Ont
Eastern Europe: Csaba & Jackie Lengyel de Bagota, Budapest, Hungary

Far East: Julian Ashton, Ashton International Marketing Services, Sevenoaks, Kent, UK
India: Rave Media, Nandan Jha
Latin America & Caribbean: InterMedia Americana (IMA) Ltd, London, UK
Netherlands, Africa & Pakistan: Export Sales Department, Canongate Books, Edinburgh, UK
New Zealand: Penguin Books (New Zealand) Ltd, Auckland
Northern Europe: Bridget Lane, Faber & Faber, London, UK
South Africa: Penguin Books South Africa, Gardenview
Southern Europe: Melissa Elders, Faber & Faber, London, UK
USA: Publishers Group West, Berkeley, CA

Book Trade Association Membership:
IPG; Publishing Scotland

2139

*CANOPUS PUBLISHING LTD
27 Queen Square, Bristol BS1 4ND
Telephone: 0117 972 6660
Email: robin@canopusbooks.com
Web Site: www.canopusbooks.com

Managing Director: Robin Rees
Publisher, Physical Science: Tom Spicer

Academic & Scholarly; Physics; Reference Books, Directories & Dictionaries; Scientific & Technical

ISBNs, Imprints & Series: 978 0 9549846

Overseas Representation:
Europe: Andrew Durnell Marketing Ltd, Tunbridge Wells, UK

2140

CAPALL BANN PUBLISHING
Auton Farm, Milverton, Somerset TA4 1NE
Telephone: 01823 401528
Fax: 01823 401529
Email: enquiries@capallbann.co.uk
Web Site: www.capallbann.co.uk

Publishers: Jon Day *(Sales & Rights)*
Julia Day *(Administration & Editorial)*

Animal Care & Breeding; Archaeology; Cookery, Wines & Spirits; Crafts & Hobbies; Educational & Textbooks; Environment & Development Studies; Gardening; Gender Studies; Guide Books; Health & Beauty; History & Antiquarian; Magic & the Occult; Medical (incl. Self Help & Alternative Medicine); Music; Natural History; Philosophy; Psychology & Psychiatry; Religion & Theology; Theatre, Drama & Dance

ISBNs, Imprints & Series:
978 1 86163, 978 1 898307

Overseas Representation:
Australia (New Age): Brumby Books Holdings Pty Ltd, Kilsyth South, Vic, Australia
South Africa: Bacchus Books, Cresta
USA: Holmes Publishing Group, Edmunds, WA; New Leaf Distributing Co, Lithia Springs, GA

2141

CAPITAL TRANSPORT PUBLISHING
PO Box 250, Harrow, Middlesex HA3 5ZH
Email: info@capitaltransport.com
Web Site: www.capitaltransport.com

Trade Orders:
The Trade Counter, Mendlesham Industrial Estate, Norwich Road, Mendlesham, Norfolk IP14 5NA
Telephone: 01449 766629

Fax: 01449 767122
Email: orders@tradecounter.co.uk

Publisher: James Whiting

Transport

New Titles: 10 (2008) , 10 (2009)
Annual Turnover: £450,000

ISBNs, Imprints & Series:
978 1 85414 Capital History; Capital Transport

Book Trade Association Membership:
IPG

2142

*CAPUCHIN CLASSICS
128 Kensington Church Street, London W8 4BH
Telephone: (020) 7221 7166
Fax: (020) 7792 9288
Email: info@capuchin-classics.co.uk
Web Site: www.capuchin-classics.co.uk

Director: Max Scott
Editor-at-Large: Emma Howard
Editor: Christopher Ind

Fiction

Parent Company:
Stacey Arts Ltd

Book Trade Association Membership:
IPG

2143

CAREERS EUROPE
72–74 Godwin Street, Bradford BD1 3PT
Telephone: 01274 829600
Fax: 01274 829610
Email: info@careerseurope.co.uk
Web Site: www.careerseurope.co.uk

Managers: Michael Carey
Leila Shkodra *(Sales & Business Development)*

Educational & Textbooks

ISBNs, Imprints & Series:
978 1 899483 Gap Year Resource Pack; Languages & Careers Pack; Science & Careers Pack

Associated Companies:
UK: Aspire-i Ltd

2144

CAREL PRESS
4 Hewson Street, Carlisle, Cumbria CA2 5AU
Telephone: 01228 538928
Fax: 01228 591816
Email: info@carelpress.com
Web Site: www.carelpress.com & www.shortershakespeare.com

Publisher: Chas White

Atlases & Maps; Educational & Textbooks; Electronic (Educational); Languages & Linguistics; Literature & Criticism; Mathematics & Statistics; Reference Books, Directories & Dictionaries; Sports & Games; Theatre, Drama & Dance

ISBNs, Imprints & Series:
978 1 872365, 978 1 905600, 978 1 905600

Distributor for:
Arc Theatre Co; ODT Inc (Maps); One Page Book Co

Book Trade Association Membership:
IPG

2145

CARLTON PUBLISHING GROUP
20 Mortimer Street, London W1T 3JW
Telephone: (020) 7612 0400
Fax: (020) 7612 0408
Email: sales@carltonbooks.co.uk &
editorial@carltonbooks.co.uk

Distribution:
HarperCollins Publishers, PO Box Glasgow
G4 0NB
Telephone: 0141 306 3100
Fax: 0141 306 3767
Email: uk.orders@harpercollins.co.uk

Directors: J. Goodman (Chairman/
Publisher)
B. Rasmussen (Managing)
P. Murray Hill (Publishing)
R. Porter (Design)
A. Whitton (Financial)
J. Greenhough (Sales)

Antiques & Collecting; Architecture &
Design; Children's Books; Cinema, Video,
TV & Radio; Computer Science; Cookery,
Wines & Spirits; Crafts & Hobbies; Crime;
Fashion & Costume; Health & Beauty;
History & Antiquarian; Humour; Military &
War; Music; Natural History; Science
Fiction; Sports & Games; Transport

No of Employees: 60
Annual Turnover: £15M

ISBNs, Imprints & Series:
978 0 233 Andre Deutsch
978 1 84222 Carlton Books
978 1 84796 Goodman Books
978 1 85375 Prion
978 1 85868

Overseas Representation:
All Other Markets: Gunnar Lie & Associates
Ltd, London, UK
Australia & New Zealand: c/o Jonathan
Goodman, Carlton Publishing Group,
London, UK
North America & Foreign Language: c/o
Belinda Rasmussen, Carlton Publishing
Group, London, UK

2146

CARNEGIE PUBLISHING LTD
Carnegie House, Chatsworth Road,
Lancaster LA1 4SL
Telephone: 01524 840111
Fax: 01524 840222
Email: anna@carnegiepublishing.com
Web Site: www.carnegiepublishing.com

Directors: Alistair Hodge (Managing)
Anna Goddard (Production)

Academic & Scholarly; Agriculture;
Archaeology; History & Antiquarian;
Industry, Business & Management; Natural
History

New Titles: 17 (2008) , 18 (2009)
No of Employees: 6
Annual Turnover: £430,000

ISBNs, Imprints & Series:
978 1 85936 Carnegie Publishing Ltd
978 1 874181 Palatine Books
978 1 904244 Scotforth Books
978 1 905472 Crucible Books

Book Trade Association Membership:
IPG

2147

JON CARPENTER PUBLISHING
Alder House, Market Street, Charlbury
OX7 3PH
Telephone: 01608 811969
Fax: 01608 811969
Email: jon@joncarpenter.co.uk

Trade Orders:
Central Books, 99 Wallis Road, London
E9 5LN
Telephone: (020) 8986 4854
Fax: (020) 8533 5821
Email: orders@centralbooks.com

Contact: Jon Carpenter

Academic & Scholarly; Cookery, Wines &
Spirits; Economics; Environment &
Development Studies; History &
Antiquarian; Medical (incl. Self Help &
Alternative Medicine); Philosophy; Politics &
World Affairs; Sociology & Anthropology

New Titles: 8 (2008) , 8 (2009)
Annual Turnover: £50,000

ISBNs, Imprints & Series:
978 0 9549727, 978 1 897766, 978 1
906067 Jon Carpenter
978 1 902279 Wychwood Press

Distributor for:
Australia: Envirobook Pty

Overseas Representation:
Australia: Envirobook, Annandale, NSW
South Africa: New Horizon Distributors,
Claremont
USA: Independent Publishers Group (IPG),
Chicago, IL

Book Trade Association Membership:
BA

2148

CARROLL & BROWN LTD
20 Lonsdale Road, London NW6 6RD
Telephone: (020) 7372 0900
Fax: (020) 7372 0460
Email: mail@carrollandbrown.co.uk
Web Site: www.carrollandbrown.co.uk

Directors: Amy Carroll (Managing)
Chrissie Lloyd (Art)
Rights: Simonne Waud (Sales)
UK Sales: Derek Thornhill

Animal Care & Breeding; Cookery, Wines &
Spirits; Crafts & Hobbies; Health & Beauty;
Medical (incl. Self Help & Alternative
Medicine); Mind, Body, Spirit; Parenting &
Pregnancy

New Titles: 5 (2008) , 5 (2009)
No of Employees: 6
Annual Turnover: £1M

ISBNs, Imprints & Series:
978 90 3258, 978 90 4760

Associated Companies:
Carroll & Brown Publishers Ltd

Overseas Representation:
Worldwide: Derek Thornhill, Carroll &
Brown Ltd, London, UK

Book Trade Association Membership:
Book Packagers Association

2149

CATCHER LTD
Honeysuckle Cottage,
4 Weaverhead Close, Thaxted, Essex
CM6 2PP
Telephone: 01371 831087
Email: juliaheron@btinternet.com
Web Site: www.catcher.me

Managing Director: Julia Heron

Biography & Autobiography; Children's
Books; Educational & Textbooks; Electronic
(Educational); Fiction; Poetry; Science
Fiction

New Titles: 1 (2009)

No of Employees: 2
Annual Turnover: £100,000

ISBNs, Imprints & Series:
978 0 9544619 Storycatcher Books /
children's fiction
978 0 9554992 Memorycatcher Books

Overseas Representation:
Canada: Martine Jacquot
China: David Zou / CNN, P. R. of China
USA: Pinnock & Co

2150

THE CATHOLIC TRUTH SOCIETY
40–46 Harleyford Road, London SE11 5AY
Telephone: (020) 7640 0042
Fax: (020) 7640 0046
Email: info@cts-online.org.uk
Web Site: www.cts-online.org.uk

Retail Bookshop & Mail Order:
25 Ashley Place, London SW1P 1LT
Telephone: (020) 7834 1363
Fax: (020) 7821 7398
Email: bookshop@cts-online.org.uk
Web Site: www.cts-online.org.uk

Directors: Rt Rev Paul Hendricks
(Chairman)
Fergal Martin (General Secretary,
Publisher, Rights & Permissions,
Accounts, Editorial)
John Dilger (Hon Treasurer)
Production: Stephen Campbell
Sales: Richard Brown
Systems: Carlo Boi

Biography & Autobiography; Children's
Books; Educational & Textbooks; Guide
Books; History & Antiquarian; Religion &
Theology

New Titles: 65 (2008) , 70 (2009)
No of Employees: 24
Annual Turnover: £1.2M

ISBNs, Imprints & Series:
978 1 86082 The Incorporated Catholic
Truth Society; CTS Publications

Distributor for:
Vatican City: Osservatore Romano

Overseas Representation:
Australia & New Zealand: St Pauls
Publications, Strathfield, NSW, Australia

Book Trade Association Membership:
BA

2151

JOHN CATT EDUCATIONAL LTD
12 Deben Mill Business Centre, Melton,
Woodbridge, Suffolk IP12 1BL
Telephone: 01394 389850
Fax: 01394 386893
Email: enquiries@johncatt.co.uk
Web Site: www.johncatt.com

Directors: Jonathan Evans (Managing)
Christine Evans (Information)
Derek Bingham (Publishing)

Academic & Scholarly; Educational &
Textbooks

No of Employees: 14

ISBNs, Imprints & Series:
978 1 901577, 978 1 904724

Book Trade Association Membership:
Periodical Publishers' Association

2152

CAXTON PUBLISHING GROUP LTD
20 Bloomsbury Street, London WC1B 3JH
Telephone: (020) 7636 7171

Fax: (020) 7636 1922
Email: office@caxtonpublishing.com
Web Site: www.caxtonpublishing.com

Directors: Finbarr McCabe (Managing)
James Birney (Sales & Marketing,
Operations)

Antiques & Collecting; Architecture &
Design; Atlases & Maps; Aviation;
Children's Books; Cookery, Wines & Spirits;
Crafts & Hobbies; Crime; Do-It-Yourself;
Fiction; Fine Art & Art History; Gardening;
Magic & the Occult; Medical (incl. Self Help
& Alternative Medicine); Military & War;
Natural History; Reference Books,
Directories & Dictionaries; Transport

ISBNs, Imprints & Series:
978 1 84067 Caxton Editions; Knight
Paperbacks
978 1 84186 Brockhampton Press
978 1 84447 TimeLife
978 1 904449 Chaucer Press
978 1 904668 Mercury Books

2153

CBD RESEARCH LTD
Chancery House, 15 Wickham Road,
Beckenham, Kent BR3 5JS
Telephone: (020) 8650 7745
Fax: (020) 8650 0768
Email: cbd@cbdresearch.com
Web Site: www.cbdresearch.com

Crime; Reference Books, Directories &
Dictionaries

ISBNs, Imprints & Series:
978 0 900 246 CBD Research; Chancery
House Press
978 0 9554514

Book Trade Association Membership:
IPG; Data Publishers Association

2154

*CENGAGE LEARNING EMEA
50–51 Bedford Row, London WC1R 4LR
Telephone: (020) 7067 2500
Fax: (020) 7067 2600
Web Site: www.CengageLearning.co.uk

Directors: Tom Davy (Managing, Chief
Executive Officer)
Ross Clayton (Finance, Chief Financial
Officer)
Andrew Robinson (Sales)
Diane Thomas (Sales)
Rossella Proscia (Marketing)
John Yates (Publishing)
Production: Kay Larkin

Academic & Scholarly; Educational &
Textbooks; English as a Foreign Language;
Industry, Business & Management;
Vocational Training & Careers

Distributor for:
Arden Shakespeare; Brooks/Cole; Cengage
Learning; Delmar Learning; Gale;
Heinle; South Western; Wadsworth

Book Trade Association Membership:
Publishers Association

2155

**CENTRE FOR ALTERNATIVE
TECHNOLOGY PUBLICATIONS**
Machynlleth, Powys SY20 9AZ
Telephone: 01654 705980
Fax: 01654 702782
Email: allan.shepherd@cat.org.uk
Web Site: www.cat.org.uk/catpubs

Production Manager: Graham Preston
Publisher: Allan Shepherd
Publishing Assistant: Annika Lundqvist

Architecture & Design; Do-It-Yourself; Educational & Textbooks; Environment & Development Studies; Gardening; Travel & Topography

New Titles: 2 (2009)
No of Employees: 3
Annual Turnover: £120,000

ISBNs, Imprints & Series:
978 1 898049, 978 1 902175 New Futures

Overseas Representation:
USA & Canada: New Society Publishers, Gabriola Island, BC, Canada

Book Trade Association Membership:
IPG

2156

CENTRE FOR ECONOMIC POLICY RESEARCH
53–56 Great Sutton Strreet, London, EC1V 0DG
Telephone: (020) 7183 8801
Fax: (020) 7183 8820
Email: cepr@cepr.org
Web Site: www.cepr.org

Chief Executive Officer: Stephen Yeo
Publications Manager: Anil Shamdasani

Academic & Scholarly; Economics; Industry, Business & Management; Politics & World Affairs

New Titles: 3 (2008) , 5 (2009)
No of Employees: 14

ISBNs, Imprints & Series:
978 0 9557009, 978 1 898128, 978 1 907142

Overseas Representation:
USA & Canada: The Brookings Institution, Washington, DC, USA

2157

CENTRE FOR POLICY ON AGEING
25–31 Ironmonger Row, London EC1V 3QP
Telephone: (020) 7553 6500
Fax: (020) 7553 6501
Email: cpa@cpa.org.uk
Web Site: www.cpa.org.uk/

Warehouse, Trade Enquiries & Orders:
Central Books, 99 Wallis Road, London E9 5LN
Telephone: 0845 458 9911
Fax: 0845 458 9912
Email: orders@centralbooks.com
Web Site: www.centralbooks.co.uk

Director: Gillian Crosby
Manager: Angela Clark

Academic & Scholarly; Electronic (Professional & Academic); Sociology & Anthropology

New Titles: 4 (2008) , 5 (2009)
No of Employees: 7

ISBNs, Imprints & Series:
978 0 904139, 978 1 901097

Book Trade Association Membership:
IPG

2158

CHALKSOFT LTD
PO Box 49, Spalding, Lincs PE11 1NZ
Telephone: 01775 769518
Fax: 01775 762618
Email: chalksoft@clara.co.uk
Web Site: www.chalksoft.clara.co.uk

Managing Director: David Baldwin
Office Manager: Mrs Gillian Baldwin (*Sales & Rights*)

Academic & Scholarly; Animal Care & Breeding; Children's Books; Educational & Textbooks; Electronic (Educational); Gardening; Geography & Geology; Mathematics & Statistics; Music; Natural History; Scientific & Technical

New Titles: 24 (2008) , 15 (2009)

ISBNs, Imprints & Series:
978 1 85116 Chalksoft; Nene Valley Publishing; School Garden Co; SGC Books

Associated Companies:
Nene Valley Publishing; School Garden Co

Book Trade Association Membership:
IPG

2159

CHAMBERS HARRAP PUBLISHERS LTD
7 Hopetoun Crescent, Edinburgh EH7 4AY
Telephone: 0131 556 5929
Fax: 0131 556 5313
Email: admin@chambersharrap.co.uk
Web Site: www.chambersharrap.com

Distributor:
Bookpoint, 130 Milton Park, Abingdon, Oxon OX14 4SB
Telephone: 01235 400400
Fax: 01235 400401

Managing Director & Publisher: Patrick White
Managers: Jane Camillin (*Sales & Marketing*)
Ian Scott (*Production*)
Vivian Marr (*Editorial*)

Reference Books, Directories & Dictionaries

New Titles: 74 (2008) , 102 (2009)
No of Employees: 28

ISBNs, Imprints & Series:
978 0 245 Harrap
978 0 550 Chambers

Parent Company:
France: Hachette Livre

Overseas Representation:
Africa: Anita Zih, A–Z Africa Book Services, Rotterdam, Netherlands
All other international enquiries: Hema Shah, Export Sales Dept, Hodder, London, UK
Australia: Hachette Livre Australia, Sydney, NSW
Caribbean: Christopher Humphrys, Humphrys Roberts Associates, London, UK
China: Ian Taylor Associates Ltd, London, UK
Eastern Europe: Jacek Lewinson, Warsaw, Poland
Europe & Middle East (schools enquiries): Gill Dee, International Schools Sales Manager, Hodder, London, UK
France & French-speaking countries: Larousse, Paris, France
Germany, Austria & Switzerland: Giana Elyea, Hodder, London, UK
Greece, Malta & Cyprus: Zitsa Seraphimidi, J & L Watt, Paleo Faliro, Greece
Hong Kong, Taiwan & Japan: Andrew White, The White Partnership, Tunbridge Wells, UK
India: Sunil Sachdev, Allied Publishers Ltd, New Delhi
Italy, Spain & Portugal: Anna Kelsall, Hodder, London, UK
Korea: Information & Culture Korea (ICK), Seoul, Republic of Korea

Middle East: James & Lorin Watt Ltd, Publishing Consultants, Oxford, UK
New Zealand: Hachette Livre New Zealand, Auckland
Pakistan: Salahuddin Iqbal, Paramount Books (Pvt) Ltd, Karachi
Scandinavia & Benelux: Bea Dorning, Hodder, London, UK
Singapore, Malaysia & Brunei (schools only): APD Malaysia, Malaysia
Singapore, Malaysia & Brunei (trade): MPH Distributors, Singapore
South Africa: Pan Macmillan SA Pty Ltd, Hyde Park
South America: Terry Roberts, Humphrys Roberts Associates, Cotia SP, Brazil
USA: Katrina Kruse, Houghton Mifflin, Boston, MA

Book Trade Association Membership:
Publishing Scotland

2160

*CHANNEL VIEW PUBLICATIONS LTD
Frankfurt Lodge, Clevedon Hall, Victoria Road, Clevedon, North Somerset BS21 7HH
Telephone: 01275 876519
Fax: 01275 871673
Email: info@multilingual-matters.com
Web Site: www.multilingual-matters.com

Distribution:
Marston Distributors, PO Box 269, Unit 160, Milton Park, Abingdon OX14 4YN
Telephone: 01235 465500
Fax: 01235 465555
Email: trade.order@marston.co.uk
Web Site: www.marston.co.uk

Directors: Mike Grover (*Chair*)
T. Grover (*Managing*)
Editors: Anna Roderick (*Commissioning, Permissions & Foreign Rights*)
Elinor Robertson (*Marketing*)
Production Manager: Sarah Williams

Academic & Scholarly; Educational & Textbooks; Environment & Development Studies; Languages & Linguistics; Psychology & Psychiatry; Sociology & Anthropology; Travel & Topography

ISBNs, Imprints & Series:
978 0 905028, 978 1 85359 Bilingual Education & Bilingualism; Child Language and Child Development; Communication Disorders Across Languages; Critical Language and Literary Studies; Language & Education Library; Language Planning and Policy; Languages for Intercultural Communication and Education; Linguistic Diversity & Language Rights; Modern Languages in Practice; Multilingual Matters; New Perspectives on Language and Education; Non Writing Viewpoints; Parents' and Teachers' Guides; Professional Interpreting in the Real World; Second Language Acquisition; Topics in Translation; Translating Europe
978 1 84541, 978 1 873150 Aspects of Tourism; Channel View Publication; Tourism & Cultural Change
978 1 84769 New Multilingual Matters

Associated Companies:
Multilingual Matters

Overseas Representation:
Australia: DA Information Services Pty Ltd, Mitcham, Vic
Canada: University of Toronto Press, North York, Ont
China: Access Asia Media Services, Shanghai, P. R. of China
Hong Kong: Aromix Books

India: Viva Books, New Delhi
Iran: Kowkab Publishers, Tehran
Japan: Koro Komori
Korea: Se-Jun Jung, Seoul, Republic of Korea
Malaysia: PMS Marketing Services, Selangor
Pakistan: Book Bird Publishers Representatives, Lahore
Singapore: Publishers Marketing Services Pte Ltd
USA: UTP, Tonawanda, NY

Book Trade Association Membership:
IPG; Association of Learned & Professional Society Publishers; UK Serials Group

2161

CHARTERED INSTITUTE OF PERSONNEL & DEVELOPMENT
151 The Broadway, London SW19 1JQ
Telephone: (020) 8612 6570
Fax: (020) 8543 4371
Email: publishing@cipd.co.uk
Web Site: www.cipd.co.uk/bookstore

Distribution:
McGraw-Hill Education, McGraw-Hill House, Shoppenhangers Road, Maidenhead, Berks SL6 2QL
Telephone: 01628 502700
Fax: 01628 770224
Web Site: www.cipd.co.uk/bookstore

Managers: Ruth Lake (*Publishing/ Commissioning*)
Margaret Marriott (*Business Development*)
Tim Runacre (*Business Development*)
Dawn Wood (*Sales & Marketing*)
Nathan Harris (*Operations*)
Senior Sales & Marketing Executive: Sinead Burke
Marketing Executive: Roger Dickens
Operations Executives: Caroline Windle (*Senior*)
Robert Williams
Editors: Andrea Blue (*Senior – Commissioning*)
Ruth Aderson (*Senior – Commissioning*)
Kirsty Smy (*Assistant – Commissioning*)
Lindsay Anderson (*Online Content*)
Abi Sugden (*Development*)
Administrators: Rob Jones (*Commissioning*)
Georgie Smith (*Publishing*)

Academic & Scholarly; Educational & Textbooks; Industry, Business & Management; Personnel Management

New Titles: 27 (2008) , 16 (2009)
No of Employees: 300

ISBNs, Imprints & Series:
978 0 85292, 978 1 84398

2162

THE CHARTERED INSTITUTE OF PUBLIC FINANCE & ACCOUNTANCY
3 Robert Street, London WC2N 6RL
Telephone: (020) 7543 5600
Fax: (020) 7543 5607
Email: sara.hackwood@cipfa.org
Web Site: www.cipfa.org.uk/shop

Publcations Manager: Sara Hackwood

Accountancy & Taxation; Economics

New Titles: 30 (2008) , 30 (2009)

ISBNs, Imprints & Series:
978 0 85299, 978 1 84508

Book Trade Association Membership:
Association of Learned & Professional Society Publishers

2163

CHATHAM PUBLISHING
3 Barham Avenue, Elstree, Herts WD6 3PW
Telephone: (020) 8953 4969
Fax: (020) 8953 4969
Email: l.leventhal@hotmail.co.uk
Web Site: www.chathampublishing.com

Trade Enquiries & Orders:
Bookpoint Ltd, 39 Milton Park, Abingdon,
Oxon OX14 4TD
Telephone: 01235 400400

Publisher: Lionel Leventhal

*Military & War; Nautical; Transport;
Maritime and Naval History*

ISBNs, Imprints & Series: 978 1 86176

Parent Company:
Lionel Leventhal Ltd

Overseas Representation:
Australia & New Zealand: Peribo Pty Ltd,
Mount Kuring-Gai, NSW, Australia
*Austria, Switzerland, Czech & Slovak
Republics, Hungary, Poland, Croatia,
Slovenia, Spain (including Gibraltar) &
Portugal:* Sandro Salucci, Florence, Italy
Belgium: De Krijger, Erps
Canada: Vanwell Publishing Ltd, St
Catharines, Ont
France & Netherlands: Casemate Books,
Newbury, UK
Germany: Robbert J. Pleysier, Heerde,
Netherlands
India: Knowledge World International, Delhi
Middle East & Far East: Publishers
International Marketing, Burmarsh, UK
New Zealand: South Pacific Books (Imports)
Ltd, Auckland
South Africa: Peter Renew, Titles SA,
Johannesburg
USA: MBI Publishing Co, St Paul, MN

2164

CHEMCORD LTD
16 Inch Keith, St Leonards, East Kilbride,
Glasgow G74 2JZ
Telephone: 01355 235447
Fax: 01355 235447
Email: office@chemcord.co.uk
Web Site: www.chemcord.co.uk

Directors: Jim Melrose
Douglas Buchanan
Sales Manager & Company Secretary:
Pat Buchanan

Educational & Textbooks

2165

CHICKEN HOUSE PUBLISHING LTD
2 Palmer Street, Frome, Somerset
BA11 1DS
Telephone: 01373 454488
Fax: 01373 454499
Email: chickenhouse@doublecluck.com
Web Site: www.doublecluck.com

Warehouse, Trade Enquiries & Orders:
Scholastic Ltd, Westfield Road, Southam,
Warwickshire CV47 0RA
Telephone: 0845 850 1144
Email: tradeorders@scholastic.co.uk
Web Site: www.scholastic.com

Directors: Barry Cunningham *(Managing)*
Rachel Hickman *(Deputy Managing)*
Fiction Editor: Imogen Cooper
Managers: Elinor Bagenal *(Rights)*
Esther Waller *(Publishing)*
Publishing Officer: Claire Skuse

Children's Books

ISBNs, Imprints & Series:
978 1 903434, 978 1 904442, 978 1
905294

Parent Company:
USA: Scholastic

Overseas Representation:
Bermuda: Mary Winchell, Flatts
Central & Eastern Europe & Israel: Vincent
Walsh, Yellow Brick Media, Scarborough,
UK
Hong Kong & China: Jolie Li, Scholastic
Asia, Causeway Bay, Hong Kong
Jamaica & other Caribbean Islands: Sharon
Neita, The Book Merchant Ltd, Kingston,
Jamaica
Japan: Keiko Niwano, Scholastic, Saitama
Korea: Helen Yang, Scholastic Asia, Seoul,
Republic of Korea
Latin America: Janine Kelly, Scholastic,
Buenos Aires, Argentina
Middle East & Northern Africa: Michelle
Alwan & Bassem Badran, Bab Idriss,
Beirut, Lebanon
Philippines: Henry Chua, Scholastic, Makati
City
Puerto Rico: Darlene Vazquez, Caribe
Grolier/Scholastic Inc, Santurce
Singapore, Malaysia & Indonesia: Selina
Lee, Scholastic, Kuala Lumpur, Malaysia
Southern & East Africa: Brian Mey,
Scholastic, Cape Town, South Africa
Taiwan: Sonia Dung, Scholastic, Taipei
Thailand: Maneerat Kurdmanee, Scholastic
Asia, Bangkok
West Africa: Joyce Agyare, Scholastic,
Tema, Ghana

2166

**CHILD'S PLAY (INTERNATIONAL)
LTD**
Ashworth Road, Bridgemead, Swindon,
Wilts SN5 7YD
Telephone: 01793 616286
Fax: 01793 512795
Email: allday@childs-play.com
Web Site: www.childs-play.com

Publisher, Chief Executive: Neil Burden
Sales Director: Paul Gerrish
Managers: Alan Johnson *(Production)*
Beth Cox *(Education)*
Chair: Adriana Twinn

Children's Books

New Titles: 50 (2008) , 50 (2009)
No of Employees: 12

ISBNs, Imprints & Series:
978 0 85953, 978 1 84643, 978 1 904550
Child's Play

Overseas Representation:
Australia: Child's Play Australia, Terrey Hills,
NSW
Canada: Monarch Books of Canada Ltd,
Downsview, Ont
New Zealand: Educational Equipment
Wholesale Ltd, Auckland
South Africa: Phambili Agencies CC,
Germiston
United Arab Emirates: Child's Play Dubai,
Dubai, UAE
USA: Child's Play Inc, Auburn, ME

Book Trade Association Membership:
EPC; IPG

2167

CHRISTIAN EDUCATION
1020 Bristol Road, Selly Oak, Birmingham
B29 6LB
Telephone: 0121 472 4242
Fax: 0121 472 7575
Email: enquiries@christianeducation.org.uk
Web Site: www.christianeducation.org.uk

Director: Peter Fishpool *(Chief Executive
Officer)*
Editors: Azhar Lodhi *(Design & Production)*
Anstice Hughes *(Publications Team
Leader)*
Finance Officer: Gill Neuenhaus
Managers: Diane Horton *(Office, Sales &
Administration)*
Harvinder Rai *(Marketing)*
Sales Administrator: Pete Johnson

*Academic & Scholarly; Children's Books;
Educational & Textbooks; Religion &
Theology*

New Titles: 13 (2008) , 12 (2009)
Annual Turnover: £1M

ISBNs, Imprints & Series:
978 1 904024 International Bible Reading
Association; RE Today Services
978 1 904024, 978 1 905893 Christian
Education Publications

Associated Companies:
Christian Education Publications; RE Today
Services

Book Trade Association Membership:
Publishers Association; EPC; Christian
Booksellers Convention

2168

CHRISTIAN FOCUS PUBLICATIONS
Geanies House, Fearn, Tain, Ross-shire
IV20 1TW
Telephone: 01862 871005
Fax: 01862 871699
Email: info@christianfocus.com
Web Site: www.christianfocus.com

Managing Director: William MacKenzie
Managers: Anthony Gosling *(General &
Sales)*
Willie Mackenzie *(Editorial (Adult))*
Jonathan Dunbar *(Production)*
Catherine Mackenzie *(Editorial (Child))*
Danie van Straaten *(Design)*
Philip Magee *(Marketing)*

*Biography & Autobiography; Children's
Books; Educational & Textbooks; History &
Antiquarian; Religion & Theology; Sports &
Games*

ISBNs, Imprints & Series:
Christian Focus; Christian Focus 4 Kids;
Christian Heritage; Mentor
978 0 906731, 978 1 84550, 978 1 85792,
978 1 871676

Parent Company:
UK: Balintore Holdings

Overseas Representation:
Australia: Word, Nunawaping, Vic
New Zealand: Soul Distributors, Auckland
South Africa: Struik Christian Books, Cape
Town
USA & Canada: STL Inc, Johnson City, TN,
USA

Book Trade Association Membership:
Evangelical Christian Publishers Association
(USA); Christian Booksellers Association
(USA)

2169

*THE CHRYSALIS PRESS
7 Lower Ladyes Hills, Kenilworth, Warks
CV8 2GN
Telephone: 01926 855223
Email: brian@margaretbuckley.com
Web Site: www.margaretbuckley.com

Director: Brian Boyd
Editor: Jane Buckley
Officers: B. R. Buckley *(Finance)*
Stephen Mackey *(Marketing)*

*Academic & Scholarly; Biography &
Autobiography; Fiction; History &
Antiquarian; Literature & Criticism; Travel &
Topography*

ISBNs, Imprints & Series: 978 1 897765

Book Trade Association Membership:
IPG

2170

CHURCH HOUSE PUBLISHING
The Archbishops' Council, Church House,
Great Smith Street, London SW1P 3AZ
Telephone: (020) 7898 1451
Fax: (020) 7898 1449
Email: publishing@c-of-e.org.uk
Web Site: www.chpublishing.co.uk

Sales, Customer Service & Warehouse:
Norwich Books & Music, St Mary's Works,
St Mary's Plain, Norwich NR3 3BH
Telephone: 01603 612914
Fax: 01603 624483
Email:
orders@norwichbooksandmusic.co.uk
Web Site: www.chpublishing.co.uk

Head of Publishing: Thomas Allain-
Chapman
Managers: Cynthia Hamilton *(Sales)*
Tracy Somorjay *(Marketing)*
Kathryn Pritchard *(Product Development)*
Katherine Allenby *(Production)*
Andrew Sweeney *(New Media)*
Commissioning Editor: Tracey Messenger
Copyright Administrator: Linda Foster

*Reference Books, Directories &
Dictionaries; Religion & Theology*

New Titles: 37 (2008) , 40 (2009)
No of Employees: 12
Annual Turnover: £1M

ISBNs, Imprints & Series: 978 0 7151

Parent Company:
UK: The Archbishops' Council

Overseas Representation:
*Africa, Caribbean, Hong Kong, Korea,
Malaysia, Singapore, Taiwan & Thailand:*
Kelvin van Hasselt Publishing Services,
Brininghaim, Norfolk, UK
Australia & New Zealand: Willow
Connection Pty Ltd, Brookvale, NSW,
Australia
Canada: Bayard/Novalis Distribution,
Toronto, Ont
USA: Westminster John Knox Press,
Louisville, KY

Book Trade Association Membership:
IPG; Christian Suppliers' Group

2171

CHURCH OF IRELAND PUBLISHING
Church of Ireland House, Church Avenue,
Rathmines, Dublin 6, Republic of Ireland
Telephone: +353 (01) 492 3979
Fax: +353 (01) 492 4770
Email: susan.hood@rcbdub.org
Web Site: www.cip.ireland.anglican.org

Publications Officer: Susan Hood

*Academic & Scholarly; History &
Antiquarian; Religion & Theology*

New Titles: 3 (2008) , 5 (2009)

ISBNs, Imprints & Series: 978 1 904884

Book Trade Association Membership:
CLÉ (Irish PA); Church Publishers Network
(UK & Ireland)

2172

CICERONE PRESS LTD
2 Police Square, Milnthorpe, Cumbria
LA7 7PY
Telephone: 015395 62069
Fax: 015395 63417
Email: info@cicerone.co.uk
Web Site: www.cicerone.co.uk

Directors: Jonathan Williams *(Managing)*
Lesley Williams *(Sales & Marketing)*

Guide Books; Sports & Games; Travel & Topography

New Titles: 30 (2008), 30 (2009)
No of Employees: 7

ISBNs, Imprints & Series:
978 0 902363, 978 1 85284

Overseas Representation:
Europe: Bill Bailey Publishers
Representatives, Newton Abbot, UK
France: Editeur, Vaison la Romaine
Netherlands: Nilsson & Lamm BV, Weesp
Spain: Map Iberia FeB SL, Avila
USA: Midpoint Trade Books Inc, New York

Book Trade Association Membership:
IPG

2173

CILT, THE NATIONAL CENTRE FOR LANGUAGES
111 Westminster Bridge Road, London
SE1 7HR
Telephone: 0845 612 5885
Fax: 0845 612 5995
Email: books@cilt.org.uk
Web Site: www.cilt.org.uk

Distribution & Orders:
Central Books Ltd, 99 Wallis Road, London
E9 5LN
Telephone: 0845 458 9911
Fax: 0845 458 9912
Email: mo@centralbooks.com
Web Site: www.centralbooks.com

Director, Communications: Teresa Tinsley
Publishing Manager: Isabelle Almeida
Marketing Co-ordinator: Julie
Manandhar

Academic & Scholarly; Educational & Textbooks; Languages & Linguistics; Vocational Training & Careers

New Titles: 6 (2008), 10 (2009)

ISBNs, Imprints & Series:
Advanced Pathfinder; Classic Pathfinder;
Curriculum Guides; Info Tech; New
Pathfinder; Pathfinder; Reflections on
Practice; Resource File; Young Pathfinder

Book Trade Association Membership:
EPC; CAPP

2174

CLAIRE PUBLICATIONS
Unit 8, Tey Brook Centre, Great Tey,
Colchester, Essex CO6 1JE
Telephone: 01206 211020
Fax: 01206 212755
Email: mail@clairepublications.com
Web Site: www.clairepublications.com

Managing Director: Noel Graham
(Production)
Finance: Elaine Hayward
Rights: Dorcas Smith

Educational & Textbooks; Electronic (Educational); Languages & Linguistics; Mathematics & Statistics

New Titles: 4 (2008), 4 (2009)

No of Employees: 4
Annual Turnover: £250,000

ISBNs, Imprints & Series: 978 0 904572

Book Trade Association Membership:
British Educational Supplies Association

2175

T. & T. CLARK
see: Continuum International Publishing
Group

2176

JAMES CLARKE & CO
PO Box 60, Cambridge CB1 2NT
Telephone: 01223 350865
Fax: 01223 366951
Email: publishing@jamesclarke.co.uk &
orders@jamesclarke.co.uk
Web Site: www.james.clarke.co.uk

Managing Director: Adrian Brink
Customer Service: Anna Januszkiewicz
Accounts Department: Penny Bull
Sales & Publicity: Antoaneta Ouzuonova
Megan Waddington
Editorial: Aidan van de Weyer
Ian Bignall

Academic & Scholarly; Bibliography & Library Science; Biography & Autobiography; History & Antiquarian; Literature & Criticism; Philosophy; Reference Books, Directories & Dictionaries; Religion & Theology

New Titles: 14 (2008), 41 (2009)
No of Employees: 9

ISBNs, Imprints & Series: 978 0 227

Associated Companies:
The Lutterworth Press

Overseas Representation:
Asia: Access Asia Media Services, Shanghai,
P. R. of China
Philippines: Edwin Makabenta, Quezon City
USA: Ingram Publisher Services Inc,
Chambersburg, PA

Book Trade Association Membership:
EPC; CAPP; IPG

2177

CLASS PUBLISHING
Barb House, Barb Mews, London W6 7PA
Telephone: (020) 7371 2119
Fax: (020) 7371 2878
Email: post@class.co.uk
Web Site: www.class.co.uk

Trade Enquiries & Orders & Distribution:
Macmillan Distribution (MDL), Brunel Road,
Houndmills, Basingstoke, Hants RG21 6XS
Telephone: 01256 329242
Fax: 01256 331413
Email: mdl@macmillan.co.uk
Web Site: www.macmillan-mdl.co.uk

Managing Director: Richard Warner
Managers: Judith Wise *(Healthcare Marketing)*
Rebecca Hirst *(Healthcare Special Sales)*
Sylvia Hotchin *(Legal Customer Services)*

Health & Beauty; Law; Medical (incl. Self Help & Alternative Medicine)

ISBNs, Imprints & Series:
978 1 85959, 978 1 872362

Associated Companies:
Class Health; Class Legal; Jones & Bartlett
International

Book Trade Association Membership:
IPG

2178

CLASSICAL COMICS LTD
PO Box 7280, Litchborough, Towcester,
Northants NN12 9AR
Telephone: 0845 812 3000
Fax: 0845 812 3005
Email: info@classicalcomics.com
Web Site: www.classicalcomics.com

Chairman: Clive Bryant
Creative Director: Jo Wheeler

Children's Books; Educational & Textbooks; English as a Foreign Language; Fiction; Literature & Criticism; Theatre, Drama & Dance

New Titles: 25 (2008), 30 (2009)
No of Employees: 4
Annual Turnover: £130,000

ISBNs, Imprints & Series: 978 1 906332

Parent Company:
UK: Providence Press

Overseas Representation:
Australia, New Zealand & Fiji: Book &
Volume, Birregurra, Vic, Australia
USA & Canada: Publishers Group West,
Berkeley, CA, USA

Book Trade Association Membership:
IPG

2179

CLEAR ANSWER MEDICAL PUBLISHING LTD
128A Queens Court, Queensway, London
W2 4QS
Telephone: (020) 7229 0893
Email: info@camp-books.com

Managing Director: Dr Frank Seibert-Alves
Company Secretary: Mrs Catarina A.
Seibert-Alves

Academic & Scholarly; Biology & Zoology; Educational & Textbooks; Medical (incl. Self Help & Alternative Medicine)

New Titles: 2 (2008), 2 (2009)

ISBNs, Imprints & Series: 978 1 903573

Book Trade Association Membership:
IPG

2180

*CLÓ IAR-CHONNACHTA
Indreabhán, Conamara, Co Galway,
Republic of Ireland
Telephone: +353 (091) 593307
Fax: +353 (091) 593362
Email: cic@iol.ie
Web Site: www.cic.ie

Representation:
AIS, 31 Fenian Street, Dublin 2,
Republic of Ireland
Telephone: +353 (01) 661 6522
Fax: +353 (01) 661 2378

Managing Director: Micheal Ó Conghaile
Sales & Marketing: Caitriona Ní Bhaoill
General Manager: Deirdre Ní Thuathail
Rights: Toner Quinn

Audio Books; Biography & Autobiography; Children's Books; Educational & Textbooks; Fiction; Gay & Lesbian Studies; History & Antiquarian; Languages & Linguistics; Literature & Criticism; Music; Photography; Poetry; Theatre, Drama & Dance; Travel & Topography

ISBNs, Imprints & Series:
978 1 874700, 978 1 900693, 978 1
902420, 978 1 905560

Overseas Representation:
USA: Dufour Editions Inc, Chester Springs,
PA; Galway Traders, Seattle, WA

Book Trade Association Membership:
CLÉ (Irish PA)

2181

COACHWISE LTD
Chelsea Close, off Amberley Road, Armley,
Leeds LS12 4HP
Telephone: 0113 231 1310
Fax: 0113 203 8826
Email: enquiries@coachwisesolutions.co.uk
Web Site: www.coachwisesolutions.co.uk

Directors: Kath Leonard *(Commercial)*
Melanie Mallinson *(Marketing & Mail
Order)*
Head of Publications & Design: Martin
Betts
Design & Print Manager: Keith Loveday

Academic & Scholarly; Children's Books; Educational & Textbooks; Electronic (Educational); Sports & Games

ISBNs, Imprints & Series:
978 1 905540, 978 1 902523

Parent Company:
UK: The National Coaching Foundation

Distributor for:
UK: The Association for Physical Education;
The National Coaching Foundation
[Sports Coach UK]

Overseas Representation:
USA: Soccer Learning Systems, Pleasanton,
CA

Book Trade Association Membership:
Publishers Association

2182

COASTAL PUBLISHING
The Studio, Puddletown Road, Wareham,
Dorset BH20 6AE
Telephone: 01929 554195
Fax: 01929 554502
Email: orders@coastalpublishing.co.uk
Web Site: www.coastalpublishing.co.uk

Academic & Scholarly; Trade

New Titles: 2 (2008), 1 (2009)

Book Trade Association Membership:
Publishers Association

2183

COIS LIFE
62 Páirc na Rós, Ascaill na Cille,
Dún Laoghaire, Co Dublin,
Republic of Ireland
Telephone: +353 (01) 280 7951
Fax: +353 (01) 280 7951
Email: eolas@coislife.ie
Web Site: www.coislife.ie

Trade - Wholesaler:
Áis, 31 Fenian Street, Dublin 2,
Republic of Ireland
Telephone: +353 (01) 661 6522

Directors: C. Nic Pháidín *(Company
Secretary)*
S. Ó Cearnaigh *(Chairman)*

Academic & Scholarly; Audio Books; Children's Books; Educational & Textbooks; Fiction; Languages & Linguistics; Literature & Criticism; Poetry; Theatre, Drama & Dance

New Titles: 9 (2008), 9 (2009)
Annual Turnover: £100,000

ISBNs, Imprints & Series: 978 1 901176

Book Trade Association Membership:
CLÉ (Irish PA)

2184

COLLINS & BROWN
Anova Books, 10 Southcombe Street,
London W14 0RA
Telephone: (020) 7605 1400
Fax: (020) 7605 1401
Email: rleeds@anovabooks.com
Web Site: www.anovabooks.com

Warehouse & Trade Orders:
HarperCollins, Glasgow
Telephone: 0141 306 3100
Fax: 0141 306 1401

Associate Publisher: Katie Cowan
Head of Marketing & Publicity: Jane Ellis

*Animal Care & Breeding; Cookery, Wines &
Spirits; Crafts & Hobbies; Do-It-Yourself;
Fashion & Costume; Fiction; Health &
Beauty; Magic & the Occult; Medical (incl.
Self Help & Alternative Medicine); Music;
Photography; Reference Books, Directories
& Dictionaries; Sports & Games; Theatre,
Drama & Dance*

ISBNs, Imprints & Series: 978 1 84340

Parent Company:
Anova Books

Overseas Representation:
Australia: HarperCollins Publishers, Pymble,
  NSW
*Belgium, France, Netherlands &
  Luxembourg:* Anova Books, London, UK
Caribbean, Mexico & Central America:
  Christopher Humphrys, Humphrys
  Roberts Associates, London, UK
Eastern Europe: Csaba Lengyel de Bagota,
  CLB Marketing Services, Budapest,
  Hungary
Far East: Julian Ashton, Ashton
  International Marketing Services,
  Sevenoaks, Kent, UK
Germany, Switzerland & Austria: Gabriele
  Kern Publishers Services, Frankfurt-am-
  Main, Germany
India: Mr Seshadri, Overleaf, New Delhi
Italy, Spain, Portugal & Greece: Padovani
  Books Ltd, London, UK
New Zealand: HarperCollins (NZ) Ltd,
  Glenfield, Auckland
Pakistan: Tahir M. Lodhi, Lahore
Russia & Baltic States: Tony Moggach,
  InterMedia Americana (IMA) Ltd,
  London, UK
Scandinavia: Katie McNeish, McNeish
  Publishing International, East Sussex, UK
Singapore & Malaysia: Pansing Distribution
  Sdn Bhd, Singapore
South Africa: Trinity Books CC, Randburg
South America: Terry Roberts, Humphrys
  Roberts Associates, Cotia SP, Brazil
USA & Canada: Sterling Publishing Co Inc,
  New York, NY, USA

Book Trade Association Membership:
IPG

2185

COLLINS GEO
[a division of HarperCollins Publishers]
Westerhill Road, Bishopbriggs, Glasgow
G64 2QT
Telephone: 0141 306 3576
Fax: (020) 8237 4209
Email:
  elizabeth.mclachlan@harpercollins.co.uk
Web Site: www.collinsbartholomew.com

Directors: Sheena Barclay *(Managing)*
  James Graves *(Production)*
  Jamie Moore *(Marketing)*

Financial Controller: David Alford
Manager: Helen Gordon *(General)*

*Atlases & Maps; Educational & Textbooks;
Electronic (Educational); Guide Books;
Travel & Topography*

ISBNs, Imprints & Series:
978 0 00 360 Collins Longman
978 0 00 447 Collins Cartographic
978 0 7028 Bartholomew; Nicholson
978 0 7230 Times Books

Parent Company:
HarperCollins

Overseas Representation:
Australia: HarperCollins Publishers, Pymble,
  NSW
Canada: HarperCollins Publishers, Toronto
  & Scarborough, Ont
Denmark: Scanvik Books ApS, Copenhagen
France: Editions Geographiques Generales,
  Paris
Germany & Austria: Internationales
  Landkartenhaus Geocenter, Stuttgart,
  Germany
India: Maya Publishers Pvt Ltd, New Delhi;
  Rupa, New Delhi
Italy: InterOrbis Media Distribution srl Ed,
  Corsico (Milan)
Japan: Maruzen Co Ltd, Tokyo
Netherlands: Nilsson & Lamm BV, Weesp
New Zealand: HarperCollins (NZ) Ltd,
  Glenfield, Auckland
Singapore & Malaysia: MPH Distributors,
  Singapore
South Africa: Jonathan Ball, HarperCollins
  Publishers, Johannesburg & Jeppestown
Sweden: Lantmateriet Kartbutiken,
  Stockholm & Vällingby
Thailand: Asia Book Co Ltd, Bangkok
USA: Hammond Inc, Maplewood, NJ

Book Trade Association Membership:
Publishers Association; Publishing Scotland

2186

COLOURPOINT BOOKS
Colourpoint House, Jubilee Business Park,
21 Jubilee Road, Newtownards, Co Down
BT23 4YH
Telephone: (028) 9182 6339
Fax: (028) 9182 1900
Email: info@colourpoint.co.uk
Web Site: www.colourpoint.co.uk

Representation:
Bookworld, Unit 10, Hodfar Road,
Sandy Lane Industrial Estate,
Stourport on Severn, Worcs DY13 9QB
Telephone: 01299 823330

Distribution:
MIMO Distribution (as principal address)
Telephone: (028) 9182 0505
Email: sales@mimodistribution.co.uk

Partners: Norman Johnston *(Editorial)*
  Sheila Johnston *(Editorial)*
  Wesley Johnston *(Editorial)*
  Malcolm Johnston *(Finance)*
Company Administrator: Denise Martin
  (Administration & Marketing Manager)

*Biography & Autobiography; Educational &
Textbooks; Fiction; History & Antiquarian;
Transport*

New Titles: 36 (2008) , 18 (2009)

ISBNs, Imprints & Series:

978 1 898392, 978 1 904242, 978 1
  906578

Distributor for:
MIMO Distribution

Book Trade Association Membership:
Irish Educational PA

2187

COLUMBA
55A Spruce Avenue,
Stillorgan Industrial Park, Blackrock,
Co Dublin, Republic of Ireland
Telephone: +353 (01) 294 2556
Fax: +353 (01) 294 2564
Email: info@columba.ie
Web Site: www.columba.ie

Managing Director & Publisher: Séan O
  Boyle
Sales Director: Cecilia West
Sales Manager: Michael Brennan
Public Relations & Marketing Executive:
  Gráinne Ross

*History & Antiquarian; Medical (incl. Self
Help & Alternative Medicine); Psychology &
Psychiatry; Religion & Theology*

New Titles: 40 (2008) , 40 (2009)
No of Employees: 5

ISBNs, Imprints & Series:
978 0 948183, 978 1 85607 The Columba
  Press
978 1 85607 Currach Press

Overseas Representation:
Australia: Rainbow Books, Melbourne, Vic
Canada: Bayard Distribution, Toronto, Ont
New Zealand: Pleroma, Central Hawkes Bay
USA: Dufour Editions Inc, Chester Springs,
  PA

Book Trade Association Membership:
CLÉ (Irish PA); Booksellers Association

2188

COMMONWEALTH SECRETARIAT
Marlborough House, Pall Mall, London
SW1Y 5HX
Telephone: (020) 7747 6342
Fax: (020) 7839 9081
Email: g.bentham@commonwealth.int
Web Site: www.thecommonwealth.org

Orders:
BEBC Distribution, Albion Close, Parkstone,
Poole, Dorset BH12 3LL
Telephone: 01202 724292
Email: commonwealth@bebc.co.uk
Web Site: www.bebcdistribution.co.uk

Publications Manager: Guy Bentham

*Academic & Scholarly; Agriculture;
Economics; Electronic (Educational);
Environment & Development Studies;
Gender Studies; Industry, Business &
Management; Law; Politics & World
Affairs; Reference Books, Directories &
Dictionaries; Scientific & Technical*

New Titles: 30 (2008) , 30 (2009)

ISBNs, Imprints & Series:
978 0 85092, 978 1 84859

Overseas Representation:
Canada: Renouf Publishing Co Ltd, Ottawa,
  Ont
Ghana: F. Reimmer Book Services, Accra
Hong Kong: Transglobal Publishers Services
  Ltd
Iberia: Iberian Book Services, Madrid, Spain
India: Parrot Reads Publishers, New Delhi
Malawi & Zambia: Anglia Book Distributors
  Ltd, Blantyre, Malawi
Malaysia: Globe Enterprise, Selangor; MDC
  Publishers, Kuala Lumpur
Middle East, Mediterranean & North Africa:
  Avicenna Partnership, Oxford, UK
Nigeria: Mosuro The Booksellers Ltd, Ibadan
Pakistan: Book Bird Publishers
  Representatives, Lahore
Singapore: Horizon Books Pte Ltd; Select
  Books Pte Ltd
South Africa: Anglia Book & Freight Pty Ltd,

Knysna; Hargraves Library Service,
  Claremont & Cape Town
USA: Stylus Publishing Inc, Sterling, VA

Book Trade Association Membership:
Publishers Association; IPG

2189

CONRAN OCTOPUS
2–4 Heron Quays, London E14 4JP
Telephone: (020) 7531 8400
Fax: (020) 7531 8627
Web Site: www.octopusbooks.co.uk

Distribution:
Littlehampton Book Services Ltd,
Faraday Close, Durrington, Worthing,
West Sussex BN13 3TG
Telephone: 01903 828500
Fax: 01903 828802

Directors: Lorraine Dickey *(Publisher)*
  Jonathan Christie *(Art)*

*Architecture & Design; Cookery, Wines &
Spirits; Crafts & Hobbies; Gardening*

Parent Company:
Hachette UK

Overseas Representation:
See: Octopus Publishing Group, London, UK

2190

CONSTABLE & ROBINSON LTD
3 The Lanchesters,
162 Fulham Palace Road, London W6 9ER
Telephone: (020) 8741 3663
Fax: (020) 8748 7562
Email: enquiries@constablerobinson.com
Web Site: www.constablerobinson.com

Warehouse & Distribution:
TBS Ltd, Colchester Road, Frating Green,
Colchester, Essex CO7 7DW
Telephone: 01206 256000
Fax: 01206 819587

Directors: Nick Robinson *(Publisher)*
  Pete Duncan *(Managing)*
  Nova Jayne Heath *(Publishing)*
  Adrian Andrews *(Finance)*
  Andrew Hayward *(Commercial)*
  Leo Hollis *(Editorial - History)*
  Eryl Humphrey Jones *(Rights)*
  Sam Evans *(Publicity)*
  Haydn Jones *(Sales)*
  Rob Nichols *(Marketing)*
Senior Commissioning Editor: Krystyna
  Green *(Robinson - Crime - Fiction & Non-
  Fiction)*
Editors: Duncan Proudfoot *(Non-Fiction)*
  Becky Hardie *(General Non-Fiction)*
  Andreas Campomar *(General Non-
  Fiction)*

*Biography & Autobiography; Children's
Books; Crime; Fiction; Health & Beauty;
Humour; Medical (incl. Self Help &
Alternative Medicine); Military & War;
Psychology & Psychiatry; Science Fiction;
Travel & Topography*

New Titles: 150 (2008) , 165 (2009)
No of Employees: 35
Annual Turnover: £6.3M

ISBNs, Imprints & Series:
978 0 094, 978 1 84119, 978 1 84529, 978
  1 84961, 978 1 85487 Constable
978 0 094, 978 1 84119, 978 1 85487
  Magpie Books
978 0 094, 978 1 84119, 978 1 84529, 978
  1 85487 Robinson

Overseas Representation:
*Australia (Constable & Robinson - Library
  Supplies):* DLS Australia (Pty) Ltd,
  Braeside, Vic, Australia

Australia (Constable & Robinson - Retail): Tower Books Pty Ltd, Frenchs Forest, NSW, Australia
Central & Eastern Europe, Russia, CIS, Middle East, North & Central America: Tony Moggach, IMA, London, UK
France: Anselm Robinson, London, UK
India: Maya Publishers Pvt Ltd, New Delhi
Italy & Greece: Ted Dougherty, London, UK
Japan & China: Timberham, Ferndown, UK
Japan, China & South East Asia: Publishers International Marketing, London, UK
Middle East: Ray Potts, Polfages, France
New Zealand: Southern Publishers Group, Auckland
Republic of Ireland: Vivienne Lavery, Blackrock, Co Dublin
Scandinavia & Iceland: McNeish Publishing International, East Sussex, UK
South Africa: Penguin Books South Africa, Parklands
Spain & Portugal: Iberian Book Services, Madrid, Spain
West Indies & West Africa: Kelvin van Hasselt Publishing Services, Briningham, Norfolk, UK
Western Europe: Michael Geoghegan, London, UK

Book Trade Association Membership:
Publishers Association; IPG

2191 ▪

*CONSTRUCTION INDUSTRY RESEARCH & INFORMATION ASSOCIATION (CIRIA)
Classic House, 174–180 Old Street, London EC1V 9BP
Telephone: (020) 7549 3300
Fax: (020) 7253 0523
Email: enquiries@ciria.org
Web Site: www.ciria.org

Publishing Director: John Tomlin
Publishing Executive: Clare Drake

Academic & Scholarly; Archaeology; Architecture & Design; Engineering; Environment & Development Studies; Industry, Business & Management; Scientific & Technical

ISBNs, Imprints & Series:
978 0 86017 CIRIA Publications

Overseas Representation:
Hong Kong: Wardell Armstrong China Ltd
USA (non exclusive distributors): Balogh International Inc, Champaign, IL, USA

Book Trade Association Membership:
IPG; PIRA

2192 ▪

THE CONTINUUM INTERNATIONAL PUBLISHING GROUP LTD
The Tower Building, 11 York Road, London SE1 7NX
Telephone: (020) 7922 0880
Fax: (020) 7922 0881
Email: info@continuumbooks.com
Web Site: www.continuumbooks.com

Distribution:
Orca Book Services, Stanley House, 3 Fleets Lane, Poole, Dorset BH15 3AJ
Telephone: 01202 665432
Fax: 01202 666219
Web Site: www.orcabookservices.co.uk

Chief Executive: Oliver Gadsby
Directors: Bob Marsh *(Finance)*
Robin Baird-Smith *(Publishing)*
Ken Rhodes *(Sales & Marketing)*
Publishers: Anna Fleming
Sarah Campbell
Rights Manager: Elizabeth White *(Special Sales & Rights)*

Academic & Scholarly; Bibliography &
Library Science; Biography & Autobiography; Cinema, Video, TV & Radio; Economics; Educational & Textbooks; Electronic (Educational); Electronic (Professional & Academic); History & Antiquarian; Languages & Linguistics; Literature & Criticism; Music; Philosophy; Politics & World Affairs; Reference Books, Directories & Dictionaries; Religion & Theology; Theatre, Drama & Dance

New Titles: 650 (2008) , 650 (2009)
No of Employees: 75
Annual Turnover: £10M

ISBNs, Imprints & Series:
978 0 225 Geoffrey Chapman
978 0 264 Mowbray
978 0 304 Cassell Academic; Cassell Reference
978 0 485 Athlone
978 0 567 T. & T. Clark International
978 0 5829 Claridge Press
978 0 7136 A. & C. Black (New Testament Commentaries)
978 0 7185 Leicester University Press
978 0 7201 Mansell
978 0 7220 Sheed & Ward
978 0 8264 Continuum
978 0 8601 Burns & Oates
978 0 8618, 978 1 8556 Pinter
978 1 56338 Trinity Press International
978 1 84127, 978 1 85075 Sheffield Academic Press
978 1 84371, 978 1 85506 Thoemmes Continuum
978 1 84714 Continuum Collection
978 1 84725 Hambledon Continuum
978 1 85539 Network Continuum Education
978 1 87062, 978 1 90051 Claridge Press

Associated Companies:
USA: The Continuum International Publishing Group Inc

Overseas Representation:
Australia: Palgrave Macmillan, Melbourne, Vic
Australia (Religion titles only): Rainbow Books, Melbourne, Vic, Australia
Austria, Greece, Cyprus & Eastern Europe: Tyers Book Sales, UK
Hong Kong, China, Taiwan & Philippines: Asia Publishers Services Ltd, Hong Kong
India & Sri Lanka: Palgrave Macmillan, New Delhi, India
Japan: United Publishers Services Ltd, Tokyo
Korea: Information & Culture Korea (ICK), Seoul, Republic of Korea
Mexico, Central & South America: Cranbury International LLC, Montpelier, VT, USA
Middle East, North Africa & Malta: International Publishing Services (IPS) Middle East Ltd, Dubai, UAE
Netherlands, Germany, France, Switzerland, Italy, Israel & Caribbean: The Continuum International Publishing Group Ltd, London, UK
Nigeria: Bounty Press Ltd, Ibadan
Pakistan: T.M.L. Publishers' Consultants & Representatives, Lahore
Scandinavia: Colin Flint Ltd, Publishers Scandinavian Consultancy, Cambridge, UK
Singapore, Malaysia, Indonesia & Thailand: APD Singapore Pte Ltd, Singapore
Southern Africa: Book Promotions (Pty) Ltd/ Horizon Books (Pty) Ltd, Cape Town, South Africa
Spain, Portugal & Gibraltar: Iberian Book Services, Madrid, Spain

Book Trade Association Membership:
IPG

2193 ▪

CONWAY
10 Southcombe Street, London W14 0RA
Telephone: (020) 7605 1400
Fax: (020) 7605 1401
Email: jlee@anovabooks.com
Web Site: www.anovabooks.com

Distribution:
HarperCollins, Campsie View, Westerhill Road, Bishopbriggs, Glasgow G64 2QT
Telephone: 0141 306 3100
Fax: 0141 306 3767

Associate Publisher: John Lee *(Editorial)*
Publicity & Marketing Manager: Komal Patel

Aviation; Engineering; History & Antiquarian; Military & War; Nautical; Politics & World Affairs; Transport

ISBNs, Imprints & Series:
978 0 85177 Conway Maritime Press; Putnam Aeronautical Books
978 1 84486
978 1 85753 Brassey's (UK)

Overseas Representation:
Australia: Capricorn Link (Australia) Pty Ltd, Windsor, NSW
Canada: Vanwell Publishing Ltd, St Catharines, Ont
Caribbean: Humphrys Roberts Associates, London, UK
Eastern Europe: CLB Marketing Services, Budapest, Hungary
Far East: Ashton International Marketing Services, Sevenoaks, Kent, UK
France, Netherlands & Luxembourg: Anova Books, London, UK
Germany, Austria & Switzerland: Gabriele Kern Publishers Services, Frankfurt-am-Main, Germany
New Zealand: HarperCollins (NZ) Ltd, Glenfield, Auckland
Russia & Baltic States: Tony Moggach, InterMedia Americana (IMA) Ltd, London, UK
Scandinavia: McNeish Publishing International, East Sussex, UK
Singapore & Malaysia: Pansing Distribution Sdn Bhd, Singapore
South Africa: Trinity Books CC, Randburg
South America: Terry Roberts, Cotia SP, Brazil
Spain, Portugal, Malta, Greece & Italy: Padovani Books Ltd, London, UK
USA: Casemate Publishers & Book Distributors LLC, Havertown, PA

2194 ▪

COORDINATION GROUP PUBLICATIONS LTD (CGP LTD)
Kirkby-in-Furness, Cumbria LA17 7WZ
Telephone: 01229 715700
Fax: 01229 716958
Email: customerservices@cgpbooks.co.uk
Web Site: www.cgpbooks.co.uk

Directors: Graham Servante *(Managing)*
Jane Barnes *(Publishing)*

Educational & Textbooks

ISBNs, Imprints & Series:
978 1 84146, 978 1 84762

Associated Companies:
USA: CGP Study; Coordination Group Publications Inc [trading as CGP Education]

Book Trade Association Membership:
IPG

2195 ▪

COPPER BEECH PUBLISHING LTD
PO Box 159, East Grinstead, Sussex RH19 4FS
Telephone: 01342 314734
Fax: 01342 312196
Email: sales@copperbeechpublishing.co.uk
Web Site: www.copperbeechpublishing.co.uk

Rights: Jan Barnes
Editorial: Julie Hird
Finance: Elizabeth Moreira

Cookery, Wines & Spirits; Fashion & Costume; Gardening; History & Antiquarian; Sports & Games; Transport

ISBNs, Imprints & Series:
English Eccentricities; The Etiquette Collection
978 0 9516295, 978 1 898617

Book Trade Association Membership:
IPG

2196 ▪

CORK UNIVERSITY PRESS
Youngline Industrial Estate, Pailaduff Road, Togher, Cork, Republic of Ireland
Telephone: +353 (021) 490 2980
Fax: +353 (021) 431 5329
Email: corkuniversitypress@ucc.ie
Web Site: www.corkuniversitypress.com

Orders & Distribution (Republic of Ireland, Northern Ireland & Europe):
Gill & Macmillan Distribution, Hume Avenue, Park West, Dublin 12, Republic of Ireland
Telephone: +353 (01) 500 9500
Fax: +353 (01) 500 9596

Representation (Republic of Ireland & Northern Ireland):
Robert Towers, 2 The Crescent, Monkstown, Co Dublin, Republic of Ireland
Telephone: +353 (01) 280 6532
Fax: +353 (01) 280 6020

Publications Director: Mike Collins
Editors: Sophie Watson *(Commissioning)*
Maria O'Donovan *(Production)*

Academic & Scholarly; Archaeology; Architecture & Design; Atlases & Maps; Environment & Development Studies; Fine Art & Art History; Gay & Lesbian Studies; Gender Studies; History & Antiquarian; Literature & Criticism; Music; Philosophy; Photography

New Titles: 15 (2008) , 15 (2009)
No of Employees: 4

ISBNs, Imprints & Series:
Atrium; Attic Press
978 0 902561, 978 1 85918 Field Day Essays; Irish Narratives; Undercurrents

Overseas Representation:
Germany, Austria & Switzerland (Rights only): Brigitte Axster, Frankfurt, Germany
Japan: United Publishers Services Ltd, Tokyo
North America: Stylus Publishing LLC, Herndon, VA, USA
UK & Europe: Quantum Publishing Solutions Ltd, Paisley, UK
UK (excluding Northern Ireland) (Distribution): Marston Book Services Ltd, Abingdon, UK

Book Trade Association Membership:
CLÉ (Irish PA)

2197 ▪

CORNWALL EDITIONS LTD
8 Langurtho Road, Fowey, Cornwall PL23 1EQ
Telephone: 01726 832483
Fax: 01726 832483
Email: info@cornwalleditions.co.uk
Web Site: www.cornwalleditions.co.uk

Publisher: Ian Grant
Manager: Judy Martin *(Customer Services)*

Archaeology; Children's Books; Fiction; History & Antiquarian; Natural History

Annual Turnover: £11,000

ISBNs, Imprints & Series:
978 1 904880 Cornwall Editions; Ian Grant Publishers

Book Trade Association Membership:
IPG

2198

COUNCIL FOR BRITISH ARCHAEOLOGY
St Mary's House, 66 Bootham, York YO30 7BZ
Telephone: 01904 671417
Fax: 01904 671384
Email: books@britarch.ac.uk
Web Site: www.britarch.ac.uk

Distribution:
Central Books Ltd, 99 Wallis Road, London E9 5LN
Telephone: 0845 458 9910
Fax: 0845 458 9912
Email: mo@centralbooks.com
Web Site: www.centralbooks.com

Directors: Michael Heyworth
Peter Olver *(Finance)*
Senior Officers: Gill Chitty *(Head of Conservation)*
Donald Henson *(Head of Education)*
Officers: Lynne Walker *(Listed Buildings)*
Dan Hull *(Head of Information & Communication)*
Marcus Smith *(Information)*
Sophie Cringle *(Marketing & Events)*
Nicky Milsted *(Young Archaeologists' Club Magazine)*
Mike Pitts *(Magazine Editor)*
Catrina Appleby *(Publications)*

Archaeology

New Titles: 6 (2008) , 6 (2009)
No of Employees: 25

ISBNs, Imprints & Series:
Archaeology of York; British and Irish Archaeological Bibliography; British Archaeology; CBA Research Reports
978 1 902771 Practical Handbooks in Archaeology

Book Trade Association Membership:
BA; Association of Learned & Professional Society Publishers

2199

COUNCIL OF MORTGAGE LENDERS
Bush House, Aldwych, London WC2B 4PJ
Telephone: (020) 7438 8908
Email: pat.gauntlett@cml.org.uk
Web Site: www.cml.org.uk

Director General: Michael Coogan
Chief Economist: Bob Pannell
Head of External Affairs: Sue Anderson
Senior Legal Advisor: Samantha Barnett

Economics; Housing

ISBNs, Imprints & Series:
978 0 954457, 978 1 872423, 978 1 905257

2200

COUNTRYSIDE BOOKS
2 Highfield Avenue, Newbury, Berks RG14 5DS
Telephone: 01635 43816
Fax: 01635 551004
Email: info@countrysidebooks.co.uk
Web Site: www.countrysidebooks.co.uk

Publisher: Nicholas Battle

Partner: Suzanne Battle
Sales Manager: Jackie Arrowsmith
Managing Editor: Paula Leigh

Architecture & Design; Aviation; Guide Books; History & Antiquarian; Humour; Military & War; Reference Books, Directories & Dictionaries; Sociology & Anthropology; Transport; Travel & Topography; Local History

ISBNs, Imprints & Series:
978 0 86368, 978 0 905392, 978 1 84674, 978 1 85306, 978 1 85455

Parent Company:
Countryside Book UK

Distributor for:
Boomerang Family Ltd; Cube Publications Ltd; The Dovecote Press; Historical Publications Ltd; Kent County Council; Meridian Books; Power Publications

Overseas Representation:
USA & Canada: The David Brown Book Co, Oakville, CT, USA

Book Trade Association Membership:
IPG

2201

COUNTYVISE LTD
14 Appin Road, Birkenhead CH41 9HH
Telephone: 0151 647 3333
Fax: 0151 647 8286
Email: info@birkenheadpress.co.uk
Web Site: www.countyvise.co.uk

Directors: John Emmerson *(Managing)*
Jean Emmerson

Academic & Scholarly; Biography & Autobiography; Children's Books; Crime; Fiction; History & Antiquarian; Humour; Natural History; Nautical; Poetry; Religion & Theology; Sports & Games; Transport

New Titles: 24 (2008) , 25 (2009)
No of Employees: 6

ISBNs, Imprints & Series:
978 0 907768, 978 1 901231, 978 1 906823
978 0 9516129 Merseyside Port Folios
978 1 871201 Liver Press
978 1 873245 Picton Press (Liverpool)
978 1 906205 Appin Press

2202

*CQ PRESS
PO Box 317, Oxford OX2 9RU
Telephone: 01865 861669
Email: smiller@cqpress.com
Web Site: www.cqpress.com

Distribution:
Marston Book Services, PO Box 269, Milton Park, Abingdon, Oxon OX14 4YN
Telephone: 01235 465521
Fax: 01235 465555
Email: direct.orders@marston.co.uk

Representation:
Quantum Publishing Solutions, 2 Cheviot Road, Paisley PA2 8AN
Telephone: 0141 884 1398
Fax: 0141 884 5322
Email: quantumjim@btopenworld.com

Contact: Sue Miller

Academic & Scholarly; Educational & Textbooks; Environment & Development Studies; Politics & World Affairs; Reference Books, Directories & Dictionaries

ISBNs, Imprints & Series:
978 0 87187, 978 0 87289, 978 1 56643, 978 1 56802, 978 1 933116

Overseas Representation:
Europe: Andrew Durnell Marketing Ltd, Tunbridge Wells, UK

2203

CRÉCY PUBLISHING LTD
Unit 1A, Ringway Trading Estate, Shadowmoss Road, Manchester M22 5LH
Telephone: 0161 499 0024
Fax: 0161 499 0298
Email: books@crecy.co.uk
Web Site: www.crecy.co.uk

Managing Director: Jeremy M. Pratt
Managers: Gill Richardson *(Customer Services)*
Julia Nash *(Financial)*
Chris Tordoff *(Marketing)*

Aviation; History & Antiquarian; Military & War; Nautical; Transport

ISBNs, Imprints & Series:
978 0 85979 Airdata Publications
978 0 907579 Goodall Publications
978 0 947554 Crécy
978 0 954560 Flight Recorder Publications
978 1 874783 Airplan Flight Equipment Ltd
978 1 902109 Hikoki Publications

Distributor for:
Air Research Publications; Airplan Flight Equipment Ltd; Airtime Publishing; Aviation Publications Inc; Camber Publications Ltd; Independent Books; Pacific Century; Specialty Press

Overseas Representation:
Australia: J. B. Wholesalers, Bibra Lake, WA
Canada: Vanwell Publishing Ltd, St Catharines, Ont
Europe: Bookport Associates, Corsico (MI), Italy
New Zealand: South Pacific Books (Imports) Ltd, Auckland
USA: Specialty Press, North Branch, MN

2204

*CRESCENT MOON PUBLISHING
PO Box 393, Maidstone, Kent ME14 5XU
Telephone: 01622 729593
Email: cresmopub@yahoo.co.uk
Web Site: www.crescentmoon.org.uk

Director: Jeremy Robinson
Editors: C. Hughes
C. Hellawell
Design: Jean Kazan

Academic & Scholarly; Biography & Autobiography; Cinema, Video, TV & Radio; Fine Art & Art History; Gardening; Gender Studies; Literature & Criticism; Magic & the Occult; Music; Philosophy; Photography; Poetry; Religion & Theology; Sociology & Anthropology; Theatre, Drama & Dance; Travel & Topography

ISBNs, Imprints & Series:
Art in Close-Up Series; British Poets Series; European Writers Series; Thomas Hardy Studies Series; Painters Series; John Cowper Powys Studies Series; Sculptors Series
978 1 86171, 978 1 871846 Crescent Moon
978 1 898283 Joe's Press

Overseas Representation:
USA: State Mutual Book & Periodical Service Ltd, New York

Book Trade Association Membership:
Small Press Group

2205

CRESSRELLES PUBLISHING CO LTD
10 Station Road Industrial Estate, Colwall, Malvern WR13 6RN

Telephone: 01684 540154
Fax: 01684 540154
Email: simon@cressrelles.co.uk
Web Site: www.cressrelles.co.uk

Directors: Simon Smith *(Sales)*
Leslie Smith

Theatre, Drama & Dance

No of Employees: 2

ISBNs, Imprints & Series:
978 0 7155 Kenyon-Deane
978 0 85343 J. Garnet Miller
978 0 85956 Cressrelles
978 0 90002 Actinic Press

Associated Companies:
New Playwrights' Network

Distributor for:
USA: Anchorage Press Inc

Overseas Representation:
Australia: Origin Theatrical, Sydney, NSW
New Zealand: Play Bureau of New Zealand Ltd, New Plymouth
Republic of Ireland: Drama League of Ireland, Dublin
South Africa: Dalro (Pty) Ltd, Braamfontein
USA: Bakers Plays, Quincy, MA

2206

CRIMSON PUBLISHING
2nd Floor, Westminster House, Kew Road, Richmond, Surrey TW9 2ND
Telephone: (020) 8334 1600
Fax: (020) 8334 1601
Email: info@crimsonpublishing.co.uk
Web Site: www.crimsonpublishing.co.uk

Bookshop Orders:
Portfolio Books
Telephone: (020) 8334 1730
Fax: (020) 8334 1609
Email: info@portfoliobooks.com

Directors: David Lester *(Managing)*
Allison Harper *(Financial)*
Managers: Jo Jacomb *(Production – Trotman)*
Helen Shelmardine *(International Sales & Rights)*
Head of Marketing: Lucy Smith
Commissioning Editor: Lucy McLoughlin

Biography & Autobiography; Educational & Textbooks; Guide Books; Industry, Business & Management; Reference Books, Directories & Dictionaries; Travel & Topography; Vocational Training & Careers

ISBNs, Imprints & Series:
978 1 84455 Trotman
978 1 85458 Crimson / Vacation Work
978 1 90604 Trotman Education

Distributor for:
Italy: Green Volunteers

Overseas Representation:
Australia: Woodslane Pty Ltd, Warriewood, NSW
Benelux: Nilsson & Lamm BV, Weesp, Netherlands
South Africa: Trinity Books CC, Randburg
USA: Globe Pequot Press, Guilford, CT

2207

*PAUL H. CROMPTON LTD
94 Felsham Road, London SW15 1DQ
Telephone: (020) 8780 1063 & 8788 9130
Fax: (020) 8780 1063
Email: cromptonph@aol.com

Distribution:
Airlift Book Co, 8 The Arena, Mollison Avenue, Enfield EN3 7NJ

Telephone: (020) 8804 0400
Fax: (020) 8804 0044

Editorial, Production: Paul Crompton
(*Information Co-ordination*)
Sales: Rosalie Brookhouse
Peter Howcroft
Artistic, Design Director: Richard
Batchelor
Administration, Office: Tirzah Christian

*Health & Beauty; Medical (incl. Self Help &
Alternative Medicine); Religion & Theology;
Sports & Games; Martial Arts; Survival*

ISBNs, Imprints & Series:
978 0 901764, 978 1 874250

Distributor for:
USA: Ryukyu Imports; Smiling Tiger
Publications; Unique Publications; YMAA

Overseas Representation:
Australia: Banyan Tree Book Distributors,
Darra, Qld
USA & Canada: Ryukyu Imports, USA;
Unique Publications, USA

2208

CROSSBOW EDUCATION LTD
41 Sawpit Lane, Brocton, Staffs ST17 0TE
Telephone: 01785 660902
Fax: 01785 661431
Email: sales@crossboweducation.co.uk
Web Site: www.crossboweducation.co.uk

Chief Executive Officer: Robert Hext
(*Sales & Research UK & USA*)
General Director: Anne Hext (*UK & USA*)
Manager: Pelle Johansson (*UK Sales &
Production*)
Finance & Wages: Ruth Johansson (*UK*)

*Academic & Scholarly; Educational &
Textbooks*

Annual Turnover: £375,000

ISBNs, Imprints & Series: 978 1 900891

Overseas Representation:
USA: Crossbow Education Corp, Cornelius,
NC

Book Trade Association Membership:
EPC

2209

THE CROWOOD PRESS LTD
The Stable Block, Crowood Lane,
Ramsbury, Marlborough, Wiltshire SN8 2HR
Telephone: 01672 520320
Fax: 01672 520280
Email: enquiries@crowood.com
Web Site: www.crowood.com

Distribution:
Grantham Book Services, Trent Road,
Grantham, Lincs NG31 7XQ
Telephone: 01476 541000
Fax: 01476 541060
Email: orders@gbs.tbs-ltd.co.uk
Web Site: www.crowood.com

Chairman: John Dennis (*Publisher*)
Director: Ken Hathaway (*Managing*)
Sales & Marketing: Julie Sankey

*Agriculture; Animal Care & Breeding;
Antiques & Collecting; Aviation; Crafts &
Hobbies; Do-It-Yourself; Gardening;
Military & War; Natural History; Nautical;
Sports & Games; Theatre, Drama & Dance;
Transport*

New Titles: 65 (2008) , 70 (2009)

ISBNs, Imprints & Series:
978 0 946284, 978 1 84797, 978 1 85223,
978 1 86126

Overseas Representation:
Australia: Peribo Pty Ltd, Mount Kuring-Gai,
NSW
Canada: Vanwell Publishing Ltd, St
Catharines, Ont
Scandinavia: Angell Eurosales, Berwick-on-
Tweed, UK
Singapore, Malaysia & Brunei: Publishers
Marketing Services Pte Ltd, Singapore
South Africa: Peter Hyde Associates (Pty)
Ltd, Cape Town
Southern Europe: Bookport Associates,
Corsico (MI), Italy
USA: Trafalgar Square Publishing, North
Pomfret, VT
Western Europe: Anselm Robinson,
London, UK

2210

G. L. CROWTHER
224 South Meadow Lane, Preston PR1 8JP
Telephone: 01772 257126

Sole Proprietor/Executive: G. L.
Crowther

*Atlases & Maps; Geography & Geology;
Transport*

New Titles: 20 (2008) , 14 (2009)
Annual Turnover: £1000

ISBNs, Imprints & Series:
978 1 85615 National Series of Waterway
Tramway and Railway Atlases

2211

CRW PUBLISHING LTD
6 Turville Barns, Eastleach, Cirencester, Glos
GL7 3QB
Telephone: 01367 850448
Fax: 0870 751 7073
Email: clive.reynard@btinternet.com
Web Site: www.collectors-library.com

Trade Orders:
Macmillan Distribution (MDL), Brunel Road,
Basingstoke, Hants RG21 6XS
Telephone: 01256 302692 & 0845 070
5656 (automated line – orders & availability)
Fax: 01256 812558
Email: orders@macmillan.co.uk

Directors: Ken Webb (*Production*)
Marus Clapham (*Editorial*)
Clive Reynard (*Sales*)
Cameron Brown (*Chairman*)

Children's Books; Fiction; Humour

New Titles: 18 (2008) , 18 (2009)
No of Employees: 3
Annual Turnover: £1M

ISBNs, Imprints & Series:
978 1 904633, 978 1 904919, 978 1
905716 Collector's Library; Collector's
Library Editions/Cases/Omnibus Editions

Overseas Representation:
Australia: Gary Allen Pty Ltd, Wetherill Park
BC, NSW
Far East: Pan Macmillan Asia, Hong Kong
Germany, Eastern Europe, Russia: Pan
Macmillan, London, UK
New Zealand: David Bateman Ltd, Auckland
Spain, Portugal & Italy: Penguin Books SA,
Madrid, Spain

2212

CSA WORD
[the trading name for CSA Telltapes Ltd]
6a Archway Mews, London SW15 2PE
Telephone: (020) 8871 0220
Fax: (020) 8877 0712
Email: info@csaword.co.uk
Web Site: www.csaword.co.uk

Distribution:
Orca Book Services, Unit A3, Fleets Corner,
Poole, Dorset BH17 0HL
Telephone: 01202 665432
Fax: 01202 666219
Email: orders@orca-book-services.co.uk

Managing Director: Clive Stanhope
Managers: Victoria Williams (*Sales*)
Rebecca Fenton (*Digital Rights &
Marketing*)
Vanessa Brown (*Production*)

Audio Books

New Titles: 24 (2008) , 17 (2009)

ISBNs, Imprints & Series:
978 1 873859, 978 1 901768, 978 1
904605, 978 1 906147, 978 1 934997

Overseas Representation:
USA & Canada: Publishers Group West,
Jackson, TN, USA

Book Trade Association Membership:
Audiobook Publishers Association (APA)

2213

CUALANN PRESS
6 Corpach Drive, Dunfermline, Fife
KY12 7XG
Telephone: 01383 733724
Fax: 01383 733724
Email: info@cualann.com &
cualann@btinternet.com
Web Site: www.cualann.com

Director: Brid Hetherington

*Biography & Autobiography; History &
Antiquarian; Military & War; Sports &
Games; Travel & Topography*

ISBNs, Imprints & Series:
978 0 9535036, 978 0 9544416, 978 0
9554273

Book Trade Association Membership:
Publishing Scotland

2214

CURRACH PRESS
55A Spruce Avenue,
Stillorgan Industrial Park, Blackrock,
Co Dublin, Republic of Ireland
Telephone: +353 (01) 294 2556
Fax: +353 (01) 294 2564
Email: jo@currach.ie
Web Site: www.currach.ie

Trade Enquiries & Orders:
CMD Book Source
Telephone: +353 (01) 294 2560
Fax: +353 (01) 294 2564
Email: cmd@columba.ie

Publisher: Jo O'Donoghue
Publicity Officer: Gráinne Ross
Sales Manager: Michael Brennan

*Biography & Autobiography; Cinema,
Video, TV & Radio; Cookery, Wines &
Spirits; Guide Books; History &
Antiquarian; Humour; Music;
Photography; Psychology & Psychiatry;
Sports & Games; Transport; Travel &
Topography*

New Titles: 20 (2008) , 20 (2009)
No of Employees: 5

ISBNs, Imprints & Series: 978 1 85607

Parent Company:
Republic of Ireland: The Columba
Bookservice Ltd

Overseas Representation:
Australia: Rainbow Books, Fairfield, Vic

Europe: Andrew Durnell Marketing Ltd,
Tunbridge Wells, UK
New Zealand: Pleroma Christian Supplies,
Otane, Central Hawkes Bay
USA & Canada: Dufour Editions Inc, Chester
Springs, PA, USA

Book Trade Association Membership:
CLÉ (Irish PA)

2215

CYHOEDDIADAU'R GAIR
Ael y Bryn, Chwilog, Pwllheli, Gwynedd
LL53 6SH
Telephone: 01766 819120
Fax: 01766 819120
Email: aled@ysgolsul.com
Web Site: www.ysgolsul.com

Director: Aled Davies

Children's Books; Religion & Theology

New Titles: 40 (2008) , 35 (2009)

ISBNs, Imprints & Series: 978 1 85994

Parent Company:
Welsh Sunday School Council

Overseas Representation:
Worldwide: Welsh Books Council,
Aberystwyth, UK

Book Trade Association Membership:
IPG

2216

DANCE BOOKS LTD
The Old Bakery, 4 Lenten Street, Alton,
Hants GU34 1HG
Telephone: 01420 86138
Fax: 01420 86142
Email: dwl@dancebooks.co.uk
Web Site: www.dancebooks.co.uk

Warehouse, Trade Enquiries & Orders:
Vine House Distribution, Waldenbury,
North Common, Chailey, East Sussex
BN8 4DR
Telephone: 01825 723398
Fax: 01825 724188
Email: sales@vinehouseuk.co.uk
Web Site: www.vinehouseuk.co.uk

Chairman: John O'Brien
Directors: David Leonard (*Managing,
Editorial & Production*)
Richard Holland (*Sales*)

*Academic & Scholarly; Music; Theatre,
Drama & Dance*

ISBNs, Imprints & Series:
978 0 903102, 978 1 85273

Distributor for:
USA: Dance Horizons; Princeton Book Co

Overseas Representation:
Australia: Footprint Books Pty Ltd,
Warriewood, NSW
USA: Princeton Book Company,
Hightstown, NJ

Book Trade Association Membership:
BA

2217

DARTON, LONGMAN & TODD LTD
1 Spencer Court,
140–142 Wandsworth High Street, London
SW18 4JJ
Telephone: (020) 8875 0155
Fax: (020) 8875 0133
Email: tradesales@darton-longman-
todd.co.uk
Web Site: www.dltbooks.com

Distribution:
Norwich Books and Music,
St Mary's Works, St Mary's Plain, Norwich
NR3 3BH
Telephone: 01603 612914

Directors: David Jones *(Accounts)*
Brendan Walsh *(Editorial)*
Helen Porter *(Managing Editor)*
Ken Ruskin *(Production)*
Aude Pasquier *(Sales & Marketing)*

*Academic & Scholarly; Biography &
Autobiography; Educational & Textbooks;
Philosophy; Psychology & Psychiatry;
Religion & Theology*

New Titles: 33 (2008) , 32 (2009)
No of Employees: 8

ISBNs, Imprints & Series: 978 0 232

Overseas Representation:
*Africa, Caribbean Commonwealth, Far East
& South Africa:* Kelvin van Hasselt
Publishing Services, Briningham, Norfolk,
UK
Australia: Rainbow Books, Fairfield, Vic
Canada: Novalis Inc, Toronto, Ont
Malta: Preca Library, Societas Doctrinae
Christianae, M.U.S.E.U.M., Bajda
New Zealand: Pleroma Christian Supplies,
Otane, Central Hawkes Bay

Book Trade Association Membership:
Publishers Association

2218 ▬▬▬

THE DAVENANT PRESS
PO Box 323, Burford OX18 4XN
Telephone: 01865 292148
Fax: 01993 824129
Email: judith@history.u-net.com
Web Site: www.davenantpress.co.uk

Proprietor: Judith Ann Loades

*Academic & Scholarly; Animal Care &
Breeding; Archaeology; Biography &
Autobiography; Educational & Textbooks;
History & Antiquarian; Religion & Theology*

New Titles: 20 (2008) , 34 (2009)

ISBNs, Imprints & Series:
978 1 85944 Davenant Press General
Academic Titles; Notes on English
Literature; Notes on History; Notes on
Politics

Book Trade Association Membership:
BA

2219 ▬▬▬

DAVID & CHARLES LTD
Brunel House, Newton Abbot, Devon
TQ12 4PU
Telephone: 01626 323200
Fax: 01626 323317
Web Site: www.davidandcharles.co.uk

Directors: Stephen Bateman *(Managing/
Publisher)*
Richard Dodman *(Sales & New Business)*
Roger Lane *(Production)*
Ali Myer *(Editorial)*
James Woollam *(Marketing)*

*Crafts & Hobbies; Do-It-Yourself; Fine Art &
Art History; Humour; Military & War;
Natural History; Photography; Equestrian*

New Titles: 70 (2008) , 60 (2009)
No of Employees: 80

ISBNs, Imprints & Series:
978 0 7153 David & Charles
978 0 907115 Pevensey Press

Parent Company:
USA: F & W Media Inc

Distributor for:
Dover Books; F & W Media (North Light
Books, Writer's Digest Books, Betterway
Books); Reader's Digest Books
USA: Adams Media; Krause Publications

Overseas Representation:
Asia, Middle East & Caribbean: Michelle
Morrow Curreri, Beverly, MA, USA
Australia: Capricorn Link (Australia) Pty Ltd,
Windsor, NSW
Belgium, France & Netherlands: Ted
Dougherty, London, UK
*Denmark, Finland, Norway, Sweden &
Netherlands (Foreign Rights Agent):*
Candida Buckley, Leeds, Kent, UK
Denmark, Sweden, Norway & Finland:
Angell Eurosales, Berwick-on-Tweed, UK
Germany, Austria & Switzerland: Gabriele
Kern Publishers Services, Frankfurt-am-
Main, Germany
India, Bangladesh, Nepal & Sri Lanka: Maya
Publishers Pvt Ltd, New Delhi, India
Italy, Spain, Portugal, Greece & Gibraltar:
Penny Padovani, London, UK
*Mauritius, Kenya, Gambia, Botswana &
Zimbabwe:* Pat Bence, Export Sales
Manager, David & Charles Ltd, Newton
Abbot, UK
New Zealand: David Bateman Ltd, Auckland
*Poland, Croatia, Hungary, Czech Republic,
Romania, Slovak Republic, Yugoslavia,
Bulgaria, Slovenia & Bosnia:* Casba &
Jackie Lengyel de Bagota, Bill Bailey
Publishers Representatives, Newton
Abbot, UK
South Africa: Trinity Books CC, Randburg
USA & Canada: F & W Media Ltd,
Cincinnati, USA

2220 ▬▬▬

DAY ONE PUBLICATIONS
Ryelands Road, Leominster HR6 8NZ
Telephone: 01568 613740
Fax: 01568 611473
Email: info@dayone.co.uk
Web Site: www.dayone.co.uk

Director: John Roberts
Managers: Mark Roberts
Jim Holmes *(Marketing & Sales)*

*Audio Books; Biography & Autobiography;
Children's Books; Guide Books; Religion &
Theology; Travel & Topography*

New Titles: 32 (2008) , 26 (2009)
No of Employees: 6

ISBNs, Imprints & Series:
978 0 902548, 978 1 846250, 978 1
903087

Parent Company:
Day One Christian Ministries

Overseas Representation:
Canada: Sola Scriptura Ministries, Guelph,
Ont
USA: Day One Christian Ministries (Inc),
Greenville, SC

Book Trade Association Membership:
BA; Christian Booksellers Convention (UK);
CBA (USA)

2221 ▬▬▬

DEDALUS LTD
Langford Lodge, St Judith's Lane, Sawtry,
Cambs PE28 5XE
Telephone: 01487 832382
Email: info@dedalusbooks.com
Web Site: www.dedalusbooks.com

Distribution, Warehouse & Invoicing:
Central Books Ltd, 99 Wallis Road, London
E9 5LN

Telephone: 0845 458 9911
Fax: 0845 458 9912
Email: orders@centralbooks.com

UK Sales:
Turnaround Publisher Services Ltd, Unit 3,
Olympia Trading Estate, Coburg Road,
London N22 6TZ
Telephone: (020) 8829 3000
Fax: (020) 8881 5088

Directors: Robert Irwin *(Editorial)*
Juri Gabriel *(Chairman & Rights)*
Eric Lane *(Managing)*
Mike Mitchell *(Translations)*

*Cookery, Wines & Spirits; Fiction;
Gardening; Literature & Criticism; Travel &
Topography*

New Titles: 14 (2008) , 12 (2009)
Annual Turnover: £175,000

ISBNs, Imprints & Series:
Dedalus Euro Shorts
978 0 946626, 978 1 873982 Dedalus
European Classics; Empire of the Senses;
Europe 1992–2010; Modern English
Fiction
978 1 903517 Dedalus Concept Books

Overseas Representation:
Australia & New Zealand: Peribo Pty Ltd,
Mount Kuring-Gai, NSW, Australia
Canada: Disticor Book Division, Toronto,
Ont
*France, Belgium, Germany, Switzerland,
Austria & Netherlands:* Michael
Geoghegan, London, UK
Spain, Portugal, Greece & Italy: Penny
Padovani, London, UK
USA: SCB Distributors, Gardena, CA

Book Trade Association Membership:
IPG

2222 ▬▬▬

DELANCEY PRESS LTD
23 Berkeley Square, London W1J 6HE
Telephone: (020) 7665 6605
Email: delanceypress@aol.com
Web Site: www.delanceypress.co.uk &
www.peoplesbookprize.com

Managing Director: Tatiana Wilson
(Marketing)
Finance: Jackie Naish
Rights Manager: Rupert Jones-Parry
Editor: Alexandra Shelly
PA to Managing Director: Rashmi Shastri

*Children's Books; Fiction; Humour;
Psychology & Psychiatry*

New Titles: 1 (2008) , 3 (2009)

ISBNs, Imprints & Series:
978 0 9539119, 978 1 907205

Book Trade Association Membership:
Publishers Association; BA; IPG

2223 ▬▬▬

DELTA ALPHA PUBLISHING LTD
19H John Spencer Square, London N1 2LZ
Telephone: (020) 7359 1822
Fax: (020) 7359 1822
Email: dap@deltaalpha.com
Web Site: www.deltaalpha.com

Director: Damien Abbott
Marketing Managers: Deborah Lloyd
John Knox

*Law; Reference Books, Directories &
Dictionaries*

ISBNs, Imprints & Series: 978 0 9668946

Associated Companies:
USA: Delta Alpha Publishing

Overseas Representation:
Australia: Delta Alpha, Scarborough, Qld
USA: Port City Fulfilment, Kimball, MI

Book Trade Association Membership:
IPG; Publisher Marketing Association, USA;
Australian PA

2224 ▬▬▬

DELTA ELT PUBLISHING LTD
Hoe Lane, Peaslake, Surrey GU5 9SW
Telephone: 01306 731770
Web Site: www.deltapublishing.co.uk

*Educational & Textbooks; Languages &
Linguistics*

New Titles: 10 (2008) , 10 (2009)
No of Employees: 2
Annual Turnover: £200,000

ISBNs, Imprints & Series:
978 0 953309, 978 0 954198, 978 1
900783, 978 1 905085

2225 ▬▬▬

*RICHARD DENNIS PUBLICATIONS
The Old Chapel, Shepton Beauchamp,
Ilminster, Somerset TA19 0LE
Telephone: 01460 240044
Fax: 01460 242009
Email:
books@richarddennispublications.com
Web Site:
www.richarddennispublications.com

Production: Richard Dennis
Administration: Sharon Pearce
Accounts: Tracie Welch
Photographer: Magnus Dennis
Marketing: Buchan Dennis

*Academic & Scholarly; Antiques &
Collecting; Architecture & Design;
Biography & Autobiography; Fine Art & Art
History; History & Antiquarian; Illustrated &
Fine Editions*

ISBNs, Imprints & Series:
978 0 903685, 978 0 9553741

Overseas Representation:
USA: Antique Collectors Club Ltd,
Easthampton, MA

2226 ▬▬▬

*DENOR PRESS LTD
PO Box 12913, London N12 8ZR
Telephone: (020) 8343 7368
Fax: (020) 8446 4504
Email: denor@dial.pipex.com
Web Site: www.denorpress.com

Directors: Lucille Leader *(Production &
Editorial)*
Dr Geoffrey Leader
Consultant/Accountant: Philip Woolfson
Marketing/Administration: Felicia Beder

*Biography & Autobiography; Fiction;
Medical (incl. Self Help & Alternative
Medicine)*

ISBNs, Imprints & Series: 978 0 9526056

Overseas Representation:
USA: Lightning Source Inc (US), Lavergne,
TN

2227 ▬▬▬

J M DENT
[Imprint of The Orion Publishing Group Ltd]
Orion House, 5 Upper St Martins Lane,
London WC2H 9EA
Telephone: (020) 7240 3444

Fax: (020) 7240 4822

Trade Counter & Warehouse:
Littlehampton Book Services Ltd,
Faraday Close, Durrington, Worthing,
West Sussex BN13 3RB
Telephone: 01903 828500
Fax: 01903 828625

*Academic & Scholarly; Biography &
Autobiography; Children's Books;
Economics; Fiction; Gardening; History &
Antiquarian; Law; Literature & Criticism;
Music; Reference Books, Directories &
Dictionaries; Scientific & Technical;
Everyman classics*

ISBNs, Imprints & Series:
978 0 460 J M Dent; Everyman Paperbacks

Parent Company:
The Orion Publishing Group Ltd

Overseas Representation:
see: The Orion Publishing Group Ltd,
London, UK

2228 ▬▬▬▬

DIONYSIA PRESS LTD
7 Duddingston House Courtyard,
127 Milton Road West, Edinburgh
EH15 1JG

Directors: Eve Smith
Denise Smith *(Marketing, Editorial,
Secretary)*
Editor: Thom Nairn

Literature & Criticism

New Titles: 7 (2008), 6 (2009)
No of Employees: 6

ISBNs, Imprints & Series: 978 1 903171

Distributor for:
Greece: Dionysia Press

Overseas Representation:
Greece: Dionysia Zervanou, Athens

Book Trade Association Membership:
Publishing Scotland

2229 ▬▬▬▬

DISCOVERY WALKING GUIDES LTD
10 Tennyson Close, Dallington,
Northampton NN5 7HJ
Web Site: www.walking.demon.co.uk

Company Secretary: David Brawn
Director: Ros Brawn

*Atlases & Maps; Guide Books; Travel &
Topography*

New Titles: 10 (2008), 12 (2009)

ISBNs, Imprints & Series:
978 1 904946 Drive! Touring Maps; Tour &
Trail Maps; Walk! Guide Books

Overseas Representation:
Spain: Map Iberia FeB SL, Avila

2230 ▬▬▬▬

DONHEAD PUBLISHING LTD
Lower Coombe, Donhead St Mary,
Shaftesbury, Dorset SP7 9LY
Telephone: 01747 828422
Fax: 01747 828522
Email: enquiries@donhead.com
Web Site: www.donhead.com

Directors: Jill Pearce *(Managing, Publisher)*
Chris Hall *(Finance)*

Architecture & Design; Scientific &

*Technical; Building Conservation; Heritage
& Museum Studies*

No of Employees: 4

ISBNs, Imprints & Series: 978 1 873394

Overseas Representation:
USA: Port City Fulfilment, Kimball, MI

Book Trade Association Membership:
IPG

2231 ▬▬▬▬

THE DOVECOTE PRESS
Stanbridge, Wimborne Minster, Dorset
BH21 4JD
Telephone: 01258 840549
Fax: 01258 840958
Email: online@dovecotepress.com
Web Site: www.dovecotepress.com

Managing Director: David Burnett
Secretary: Elizabeth Dean

*Archaeology; Biography & Autobiography;
Geography & Geology; Guide Books;
History & Antiquarian; Military & War;
Natural History; Transport; Travel &
Topography*

New Titles: 10 (2008), 12 (2009)
No of Employees: 2
Annual Turnover: £100,000

ISBNs, Imprints & Series:
978 0 946159, 978 1 874336, 978 1
904349

2232 ▬▬▬▬

ASHLEY DRAKE PUBLISHING LTD
PO Box 733, Cardiff CF11 7ZY
Telephone: (029) 2021 8187
Email: post@ashleydrake.com
Web Site: www.ashleydrake.com

Distribution:
NBN International, Estover Road, Plymouth
PL6 7PY

Directors: Ashley Drake *(Managing)*
Siwan Drake *(Company Secretary)*

*Academic & Scholarly; Biography &
Autobiography; Children's Books; Cookery,
Wines & Spirits; Educational & Textbooks;
History & Antiquarian; Industry, Business &
Management; Languages & Linguistics;
Literature & Criticism; Military & War;
Politics & World Affairs; Psychology &
Psychiatry; Sports & Games; Theatre,
Drama & Dance*

New Titles: 10 (2009)

ISBNs, Imprints & Series:
978 1 86057 Welsh Academic Press
978 1 874312 Hisarlik Press
978 1 899869 Gwasg Addysgol Cymru
978 1 899877 Y Ddraig Fach
978 1 902719 St David's Press (formerly
Ashley Drake Publishing)
978 1 903532 Morgan Publishing
978 1 904609 Scandinavian Academic
Press

2233 ▬▬▬▬

DRAMATIC LINES
PO Box 201, Twickenham TW2 5RQ
Telephone: (020) 8296 9502
Fax: (020) 8296 9503
Email: mail@dramaticlinespublishers.co.uk
Web Site: www.dramaticlines.co.uk

Managing Editor: John Nicholas
Sales, Marketing & Production: Heather
Stephens
Development: Irene Palko

*Children's Books; Educational & Textbooks;
History & Antiquarian; Theatre, Drama &
Dance*

New Titles: 1 (2008), 2 (2009)

ISBNs, Imprints & Series:
978 0 952222, 978 0 953777

Book Trade Association Membership:
Publishers Association

2234 ▬▬▬▬

DREF WEN CYF/LTD
28 Church Road, Whitchurch, Cardiff
CF14 2EA
Telephone: (029) 2061 7860
Fax: (029) 2061 0507
Email: gwil@drefwen.com
Web Site: www.drefwen.com

Directors: Roger Boore
Anne Boore
Gwilym Boore
Alun Boore
Rhys Boore

*Audio Books; Children's Books; Educational
& Textbooks; Fiction; Welsh Language
Learners*

New Titles: 28 (2008), 56 (2009)
No of Employees: 4

ISBNs, Imprints & Series:
978 0 85596, 978 0 946962

Book Trade Association Membership:
Cwlwm Cyhoeddwyr Cymru (Union of
Welsh Publishers)

2235 ▬▬▬▬

GERALD DUCKWORTH & CO LTD
90–93 Cowcross Street, London EC1M 6BF
Telephone: (020) 7490 7300
Fax: (020) 7490 0080
Email: info@duckworth-publishers.co.uk
Web Site: www.ducknet.co.uk

Distribution:
Grantham Book Services, Trent Road,
Grantham, Lincs NG31 7XQ

Directors: Peter Mayer *(Owner &
Managing)*
Ray Davies *(Production)*
Deborah Blake *(Editorial)*
Editor: Mary Morris *(Editorial)*
Manager: Suzannah Rich *(Publicity)*

*Academic & Scholarly; Archaeology;
Architecture & Design; Biography &
Autobiography; Crime; Fiction; Fine Art &
Art History; History & Antiquarian;
Humour; Literature & Criticism; Military &
War; Philosophy; Politics & World Affairs;
Reference Books, Directories &
Dictionaries; Religion & Theology; Science
Fiction; Travel & Topography*

New Titles: 78 (2008), 85 (2009)
No of Employees: 9

ISBNs, Imprints & Series:
Ardis
978 0 7156
978 1 85399 Bristol Classical Press

Overseas Representation:
Australia & New Zealand (Duckworth):
Tower Books Pty Ltd, Frenchs Forest,
NSW, Australia
Canada: Publishers International Marketing,
Dulles, VA, USA
Europe & Scandinavia: Bill Bailey Publishers
Representatives, Newton Abbot, UK
Middle East & Indian Subcontinent:
Publishers International Marketing,
Storrington, UK

South Africa: Book Promotions Pty Ltd, Diep
River
South East Asia & North East Asia:
Publishers International Marketing,
London, UK
USA: Books International Inc, Dulles, VA

2236 ▬▬▬▬

DUNEDIN ACADEMIC PRESS
Hudson House, 8 Albany Street, Edinburgh
EH1 3QB
Telephone: 0131 473 2397
Fax: 01250 870920
Email: mail@dunedinacademicpress.co.uk
Web Site:
www.dunedinacademicpress.co.uk

Representation (UK):
Compass Academic Ltd,
The Barley Mow Centre,
10 Barley Mow Passage, Chiswick, London
W4 4PH
Telephone: (020) 8994 6477
Fax: (020) 8400 6132
Email: AS@compass-academic.co.uk

**Distribution (excluding North America
& Australasia):**
Dunedin Academic Press, c/
o Turpin Distribution, Pegasus Drive,
Stratton Business Park, Biggleswade, Beds
SG18 8TQ
Telephone: 01767 604951
Fax: 01767 601640
Email: books@turpin-distribution.com

Consultant Editor: Dr Douglas Grant
Directors: Anthony Kinahan
Norman Steven

*Academic & Scholarly; Geography &
Geology; Philosophy; Politics & World
Affairs; Sociology & Anthropology*

New Titles: 18 (2008), 18 (2009)

ISBNs, Imprints & Series:
978 1 903765, 978 1 906716

Overseas Representation:
Arab World & Iran: Dar Kreidieh, Beirut,
Lebanon
Australasia: Inbooks, c/o James Bennett Pty
Ltd, Belrose, NSW, Australia
Benelux: Netwerk Academic Book Agency,
Rotterdam, Netherlands
Hong Kong & Macau: Transglobal
Publishers Services Ltd, Hong Kong
India: Overseas Press India Pvt Ltd, New
Delhi
Korea South, Taiwan & Philippines: Edwin
Makabenta, Quezon City, Philippines
Malaysia, Singapore & Thailand: Inthanon
Publishing, Bangkok, Thailand
North America: International Specialized
Book Services Inc, Portland, OR, USA
*Republic of Ireland (including Northern
Ireland):* Brookside Publishing Services,
Dublin, Republic of Ireland
Scandinavia: Jan Norbye, Ølstykke,
Denmark
Spain & Portugal: Chris Humphrys, Gaucin,
Spain

Book Trade Association Membership:
Publishing Scotland

2237 ▬▬▬▬

EAGLE PUBLISHING LTD
3–4 The Drove, West Wilts Trading Estate,
Westbury, Wilts BA13 4JE
Telephone: 01225 899141
Fax: 01225 768811
Email: eaglepublishing@btconnect.com

Distributors:
IVP Books, Norton Street, Nottingham
NG7 3HR
Telephone: 0115 978 1054

Fax: 0115 942 2694
Web Site: www.ivpbooks.com

Managing Director: David Wavre

Religion & Theology; Colour gift book; Self-Help

ISBNs, Imprints & Series:
978 0 86347 Eagle

Overseas Representation:
Australia & South Africa: IVP Books,
Nottingham, UK
New Zealand: Scripture Union Wholesale,
Wellington
Republic of Ireland: Columba Book Service,
Blackrock, Co Dublin

2238

EARTHSCAN
Dunstan House, 14A St Cross Street,
London EC1N 8XA
Telephone: (020) 7841 1930
Fax: (020) 7242 1474
Email: earthinfo@earthscan.co.uk
Web Site: www.earthscan.co.uk

Distribution:
Macmillan Distribution (MDL), Brunel Road,
Houndmills, Basingstoke, Hants RG21 6XS
Telephone: 01256 329242
Fax: 01256 842084
Email: orders@macmillan.co.uk

Executive Chairman: Edward Milford
Managing Director: Jonathan Sinclair
Wilson
Production: Gina Mance
Head of Sales & Marketing: Veruschka
Selbach

*Academic & Scholarly; Agriculture;
Architecture & Design; Atlases & Maps;
Biology & Zoology; Economics; Educational
& Textbooks; Electronic (Professional &
Academic); Engineering; Environment &
Development Studies; Geography &
Geology; Industry, Business &
Management; Law; Politics & World
Affairs; Reference Books, Directories &
Dictionaries; Scientific & Technical;
Sociology & Anthropology; Transport*

New Titles: 100 (2008) , 100 (2009)
No of Employees: 25

ISBNs, Imprints & Series:
978 0 907383, 978 1 873936, 978 1
902916 James & James
978 1 84407, 978 1 85383 Earthscan

Overseas Representation:
Africa (excluding North & South Africa):
Tony Moggach, InterMedia Africa Ltd
(IMA), London, UK
*Australia, New Zealand & Papua New
Guinea:* DA Information Services Pty Ltd,
Mitcham, Vic, Australia
Canada: UBC Press, Georgetown, Ont
China & Hong Kong: Nicola Everitt, Access
Asia Media Services, Shanghai, P. R. of
China
India: Vinod Vasishtha, Viva Books, New
Delhi
Japan: United Publishers Services Ltd, Tokyo
Korea: Se-Yung Jun, Information & Culture
Korea (ICK), Seoul, Republic of Korea
Latin America & Caribbean: Ethan Atkin,
Cranbury International LLC, Montpelier,
VT, USA
Malaysia & Brunei: UBSD, Selangor,
Malaysia
Middle East & North Africa: Zoe Kaviani,
International Publishing Services (IPS)
Middle East Ltd, Dubai, UAE
Pakistan, Afghanistan & Tajikistan: Book
Bird Publishers Representatives, Lahore,
Pakistan
Philippines: Megatexts Phil Inc, Cebu City

South Africa: Book Promotions (Pty) Ltd,
Plumstead
Taiwan: Unifacmanu Trading Co Ltd, Taipei
USA: Stylus Publishing LLC, Herndon, VA

Book Trade Association Membership:
IPG

2239

ECO-LOGIC BOOKS
Mulberry House, 19 Maple Grove, Bath
BA2 3AF
Telephone: 01225 484472
Fax: 0871 522 7054
Email: books@eco-logicbooks.com
Web Site: www.eco-logicbooks.com

Senior Executive: Peter Andrews

*Agriculture; Architecture & Design; Crafts &
Hobbies; Environment & Development
Studies; Gardening*

New Titles: 3 (2008) , 4 (2009)

ISBNs, Imprints & Series: 978 1 899233

Distributor for:
Common Ground; Verey & von Kanitz Rural
Classics
Australia: Holmgren Design Services
USA: Alan C. Hood & Co Inc; Mole
Publishing Co; Oasis Design; Post
Carbon Publishing; Trucking Turtle
Publishing

2240

EDINBURGH UNIVERSITY PRESS
22 George Square, Edinburgh EH8 9LF
Telephone: 0131 650 4218
Fax: 0131 662 0053
Email: university.press@ed.ac.uk
Web Site: www.eup.ed.ac.uk

Trade Enquiries:
Marston Book Services, PO Box 269,
Abingdon, Oxon OX14 4SP
Telephone: 01235 465500
Fax: 01235 465555
Web Site: www.marston.co.uk

Chairman (Non-Executive): Ivon Asquith
Executive Board: Timothy Wright *(Chief
Executive)*
Jackie Jones *(Head of Publishing)*
Ian Davidson *(Head of Production)*
Jan Thomson *(Head of Finance)*
Catriona Murray *(Head of Sales &
Marketing)*
Managers: Claire Abel *(Rights & Co-
Publications)*
Wendy Gardner *(Marketing)*
Anna Skinner *(Marketing)*
**Sales Administrator & Digital Print Co-
ordinator:** Rebecca Mackenzie

*Academic & Scholarly; Archaeology;
Educational & Textbooks; Gender Studies;
History & Antiquarian; Languages &
Linguistics; Law; Literature & Criticism;
Philosophy; Politics & World Affairs;
Reference Books, Directories &
Dictionaries; Religion & Theology; Sociology
& Anthropology; American Studies; Botany
& Environment; Celtic Studies; Cultural
Studies, Media Studies; Islamic Studies;
Scottish Studies*

New Titles: 110 (2008) , 115 (2009)
No of Employees: 20
Annual Turnover: £1.3M

ISBNs, Imprints & Series:
978 0 7486, 978 0 85224 Edinburgh
University Press
978 1 85331 Keele University Press
978 1 902930 Polygon @ Edinburgh

Parent Company:
University of Edinburgh

Overseas Representation:
*Albania, Bosnia, Bulgaria, Croatia, Czech &
Slovak Republics, Herzegovina, Hungary,
Macedonia, Romania, Serbia, Slovenia,
Yugoslav Republics & Israel:* Contact
Sales Department, Edinburgh, UK
Australia & New Zealand: UNIREPS
University and Reference Publishers'
Services, Sydney, NSW, Australia
Benelux: Kemper Conseil Publishing,
Voorburg, Netherlands
China: Ian Taylor Associates Ltd, London, UK
Germany, Austria & Switzerland: SHS
Publishers' Consultants and
Representatives, Oranienberg, Germany
Greece: Charles Gibbes Associates,
Louslitges, France
Hong Kong, Taiwan, Malaysia & Singapore:
Taylor & Francis Asia Pacific, Singapore
India: Maya Publishers Pvt Ltd, New Delhi
Japan: United Publishers Services Ltd, Tokyo
Korea: Se-Yung Jun, Seoul, Republic of
Korea
Middle East: James & Lorin Watt Ltd,
Publishing Consultants, Oxford, UK
Pakistan: Mohammad Dahir, Karachi
Scandinavia: Colin Flint Ltd, Harlow, UK
South Africa: Academic Marketing Services
(Pty) Ltd, Craighall
Southern Europe (including Spain): Charles
Gibbes Associates, London, UK
USA & Canada (most titles, enquiries):
Columbia University Press, New York,
USA
USA & Canada (most titles, orders):
Columbia University Press, New York,
USA

Book Trade Association Membership:
Publishers Association; CAPP; IPG;
Publishing Scotland

2241

**EDUCATIONAL PLANNING BOOKS
LTD**
PO Box 63, Hathersage, Hope Valley,
Derbyshire S32 1DJ
Telephone: 01433 651010
Fax: 01433 650000
Email: sales@epb-ltd.co.uk

Warehouse:
Bamford Works, Bamford, Hope Valley,
Derbyshire S33 0EB
Telephone: 01433 651010
Fax: 01433 650000
Email: sales@epb-ltd.co.uk
Web Site: www.edplanbooks.com

Managing Director: G. N. S. Garner

Educational & Textbooks

Book Trade Association Membership:
Publishers Association

2242

EGMONT UK LTD
239 Kensington High Street, London
W8 6SA
Telephone: (020) 7761 3500
Fax: (020) 7761 3510
Email: info@euk.egmont.com
Web Site: www.egmont.co.uk

Egmont Press & Sales Departments:
3rd Floor, Beaumont House,
Kensington Village, Avonmore Road,
London W14 8TS
Telephone: (020) 7605 6600
Fax: (020) 7605 6601

**Senior Vice-President & UK Managing
Director:** Rob McMenemy
Chief Financial Officer: Jimmy Weir
Directors: Gillian Laskier *(Group Sales)*
Cally Poplak *(Press)*
David Riley *(Publishing)*
Debbie Cook *(Magazines)*

Children's Books

New Titles: 459 (2008)
No of Employees: 230
Annual Turnover: £44.8M

ISBNs, Imprints & Series:
978 0 416 Methuen
978 0 6035 Dean
978 0 7497 Mammoth
978 1 4052 Egmont

Parent Company:
Denmark: Egmont Fonden

Book Trade Association Membership:
Publishers Association; BA

2243

ELAND PUBLISHING LTD
3rd Floor, 61 Exmouth Market, London
EC1R 4QL
Telephone: (020) 7833 0762
Fax: (020) 7833 4434
Email: info@travelbooks.co.uk
Web Site: www.travelbooks.co.uk

Trade Distribution:
Grantham Book Services, Trent Road,
Grantham, Lincs NG31 7XG
Telephone: 01476 541080
Fax: 01476 541061
Email: orders@gbs.tbs-ltd.co.uk

Trade Representation (UK):
Publishers Group UK, 8 The Arena,
Mollison Avenue, Enfield, Middx EN3 7NL
Telephone: (020) 8804 0400
Fax: (020) 8804 0044
Email: info@pguk.co.uk
Web Site: www.pguk.co.uk

Production Director: Rose Baring
Co-Publisher: Barnaby Rogerson

Travel & Topography

New Titles: 12 (2008) , 15 (2009)
No of Employees: 12
Annual Turnover: £250,000

ISBNs, Imprints & Series:
978 0 907871, 978 0 955010

Associated Companies:
UK: Baring & Rogerson; Sickle Moon Books

Overseas Representation:
Australia & New Zealand: UNIREPS
University and Reference Publishers'
Services, Sydney, NSW, Australia
*Eastern Europe, Russia & Sub-Saharan
Africa:* Tony Moggach, London, UK
*France, Benelux, Germany, Austria &
Switzerland:* Ted Dougherty, London, UK
Italy, Spain, Portugal, Greece & Gibraltar:
Penny Padovani, London, UK
Mexico, Central & Southern America: David
Williams, InterMedia Americana (IMA)
Ltd, London, UK
Middle East, North Africa, Turkey & Iran:
Peter Ward Book Exports, London, UK
Thailand, Burma, Laos & Vietnam: Orchid
Press, Bangkok, Thailand
USA & Canada: Dufour Editions Inc, Chester
Springs, PA, USA

Book Trade Association Membership:
IPG

2244

EDWARD ELGAR PUBLISHING LTD
The Lypiatts, 15 Lansdown Road,
Cheltenham, Glos GL50 2JA
Telephone: 01242 226934
Fax: 01242 262111
Email: info@e-elgar.co.uk
Web Site: www.e-elgar.co.uk

Distribution:
Marston Book Services Ltd, PO Box 269,
Abingdon, Oxon OX14 4YN
Telephone: 01235 465500
Fax: 01235 465555
Email: client@marston.co.uk
Web Site: www.marston.co.uk

Personnel Director & Secretary: Sandy
Elgar
Managing Director: Edward Elgar
Senior Commissioning Editor: Francine
O'Sullivan
Rights & Permissions: Jennie Hawden
Head of Editorial & Production Services:
Julie Leppard
Marketing, Publicity & Sales: Hilary
Quinn
Publisher: Tim Williams

*Academic & Scholarly; Agriculture;
Economics; Educational & Textbooks;
Environment & Development Studies;
Industry, Business & Management; Law;
Reference Books, Directories &
Dictionaries; Transport*

New Titles: 276 (2008) , 280 (2009)
No of Employees: 50

ISBNs, Imprints & Series:
978 1 84064, 978 1 84376, 978 1 84542,
978 1 84720, 978 1 84844, 978 1 85278
978 1 85898

Associated Companies:
USA: Edward Elgar Publishing Inc

Overseas Representation:
Japan: United Publishers Services Ltd, Tokyo
North & South America: Edward Elgar
Publishing Inc, Northampton, MA, USA
*Singapore, Malaysia, Thailand, Indonesia,
Philippines, Brunei, Vietnam, Myanmar,
Laos & Cambodia:* Taylor & Francis Asia
Pacific, Singapore

2245

ELLIOTT & THOMPSON
27 John Street, London WC1N 2BX
Telephone: (020) 7831 5013
Fax: (020) 7831 5011
Email: mark@eandtbooks.com
Web Site: www.eandtbooks.com

Chairman: Lorne Forsyth
Publisher: Mark Searle
Assistant: Ellen Marshall

*Cookery, Wines & Spirits; Fiction; History &
Antiquarian; Military & War; Music; Sports
& Games*

New Titles: 3 (2008) , 10 (2009)
Annual Turnover: £500,000

ISBNs, Imprints & Series:
978 1 904027 Gold Editions; Spitfire;
Young Spitfire

Distributor for:
Al Madad Foundation

Book Trade Association Membership:
IPG

2246

*ELM PUBLICATIONS
Seaton House, Kings Ripton, Huntingdon
PE28 2NJ
Telephone: 01487 773238
Fax: 01487 773359
Email: elm@elm-training.co.uk
Web Site: www.elm-training.co.uk

Managing Director: Sheila Ritchie *(Home
& Export Sales)*
Managers: Duncan Ritchie *(IT Director/
Secretary)*
Jacqueline Wieczovek *(Sales)*

*Educational & Textbooks; Electronic
(Educational); Industry, Business &
Management; Transport; Travel &
Topography; Training*

ISBNs, Imprints & Series:
978 0 946139, 978 0 9505828, 978 1
85450

Parent Company:
Elm Consulting Ltd

Book Trade Association Membership:
BA

2247

ELSEVIER LTD
The Boulevard, Langford Lane, Kidlington,
Oxford OX5 1GB
Telephone: 01865 843000
Fax: 01865 853010
Email: initial.surname@elsevier.com
Web Site: www.elsevier.com

Also at:
Elsevier, Trends,
Current Opinion and Academic Press
imprints, 84 Theobald's Road, London
WC1X 8RR
Telephone: (020) 7611 4000
Fax: (020) 7611 4501

Also at:
Mosby & W. B. Saunders imprints,
32 Jamestown Road, London NW1 7BY
Telephone: (020) 7424 4200
Fax: (020) 7424 4431

Also at:
Churchill Livingstone imprint,
20–22 East Street, Edinburgh EH7 4BQ
Telephone: 0131 524 1700
Fax: 0131 524 1800

Managing Director: Jim Donohue *(Book
Publishing (S & T))*
Directors: Helen Gainford *(Global Rights)*
Mark Carnegie-Brown *(Editorial)*
Nick Pym *(Production)*

*Academic & Scholarly; Chemistry;
Educational & Textbooks; Medical (incl. Self
Help & Alternative Medicine); Scientific &
Technical*

ISBNs, Imprints & Series:
Harcourt Ltd; Harcourt Health Sciences;
Harcourt Publishers Ltd; Scutari Press
978 0 08 Elsevier Advanced Technology;
Elsevier Applied Science; Elsevier Trends
Journals; Pergamon
978 0 12 Academic Press
978 0 443 Churchill-Livingstone
978 0 7020 W. B. Saunders
978 0 7243 Mosby

Parent Company:
Netherlands: Elsevier BV

Associated Companies:
USA: Elsevier Inc

Overseas Representation:
Australia: Elsevier Australia, Marrickville,
NSW
Brazil: Editora Campus Ltda, Rio de Janeiro
India: Elsevier India, New Delhi
Japan: Elsevier Japan, Tokyo
Korea: Elsevier, Seoul, Republic of Korea
Pakistan: Rae & Sons Publishers
Representatives, Lahore

Book Trade Association Membership:
Publishers Association; IGSMTP; STM

2248

*EMERALD GROUP PUBLISHING LTD
Howard House, Wagon Lane, Bingley,
West Yorkshire BD16 1WA
Telephone: 01274 777700

Web Site: www.emeraldinsight.com

Chairman: Martin Fojt
Chief Executive Officer: John Peters
Head of Editorial: Niki Haunch
Head of Strategic Marketing: Moyna
Keenan

*Academic & Scholarly; Accountancy &
Taxation; Archaeology; Computer Science;
Economics; Educational & Textbooks;
Electronic (Educational); Electronic
(Professional & Academic); Engineering;
Environment & Development Studies;
Industry, Business & Management;
Languages & Linguistics; Philosophy;
Psychology & Psychiatry; Sociology &
Anthropology; Vocational Training &
Careers*

2249

**ENCYCLOPAEDIA BRITANNICA (UK)
LTD**
2nd Floor, Unity Wharf, 13 Mill Street,
London SE1 2BH
Telephone: (020) 7500 7800
Fax: (020) 7500 7578
Email: enquiries@britannica.co.uk
Web Site: www.britannica.co.uk

Distributors:
Encyclopaedia Britannica (UK) Ltd, Unit Y,
Paddock Wood Distribution Centre,
Paddock Wood, Tonbridge, Kent TN12 6UU
Telephone: 01892 839814
Fax: 01892 837272
Email: britannica@combook.co.uk

Director: Ian Grant *(Managing)*
Vice-President: Jane Helps *(Operations)*
Managers: Patrick McGuire *(Print & CD/
DVD Sales)*
Diane Franklyn *(Consumer Marketing)*
Nick Harris *(Online Sales)*
Chrysandra Halstead *(Marketing
Executive)*

*Atlases & Maps; Children's Books;
Electronic (Educational); Reference Books,
Directories & Dictionaries*

ISBNs, Imprints & Series:
978 0 85229, 978 1 59339, 978 1 84326,
978 2 85229

Parent Company:
USA: Encyclopaedia Britannica Inc

Distributor for:
France: Encyclopaedia Universalis

Overseas Representation:
*Germany, Austria, Switzerland &
Netherlands:* Ted Dougherty, London, UK
Italy: Mare Nostrum Publishing Consultants,
Rome
Scandinavia: Colin Flint Ltd, Harlow, UK
*South-East Europe, North Africa & Middle
East (excluding GCC):* Avicenna
Partnership, Oxford, UK
Spain & Portgual: Iberian Book Services,
Madrid, Spain
*Sub-Saharan Africa (excluding South
Africa), Eastern Europe (excluding
Russia):* InterMedia Americana (IMA) Ltd,
London, UK

Book Trade Association Membership:
IPG

2250

ENERGY INSTITUTE
61 New Cavendish Street, London
W1G 7AR
Telephone: (020) 7467 7100

Publishing Manager: Erica Sciolti

Academic & Scholarly; Chemistry; Electronic

*(Professional & Academic); Engineering;
Environment & Development Studies;
Industry, Business & Management;
Reference Books, Directories &
Dictionaries; Scientific & Technical*

ISBNs, Imprints & Series: 978 0 85293

Book Trade Association Membership:
Association of Learned & Professional
Society Publishers

2251

ENGLISH HERITAGE
Kemble Drive, Swindon SN2 2GZ
Telephone: 01793 414619
Fax: 01793 414769
Email: robin.taylor@english-
heritage.org.uk
Web Site: www.english-heritage.org.uk

Distribution:
Central Books, 99 Wallis Road, London
E9 5LN
Telephone: 0845 458 9910
Fax: (020) 8533 5821
Email: eh@centralbooks.com

Managing Editor: Robin Taylor
Head of Publishing: John Hudson
Sales & Publicity Manager: Clare Blick

*Academic & Scholarly; Archaeology;
Architecture & Design; Children's Books;
Educational & Textbooks; Guide Books;
History & Antiquarian; Military & War;
Scientific & Technical; Travel & Topography;
Conservation (UK)*

New Titles: 10 (2008) , 20 (2009)
No of Employees: 12

ISBNs, Imprints & Series:
978 1 84802, 978 1 85074, 978 1 873592,
978 1 905624

Overseas Representation:
Australia: James Bennett Pty Ltd, Belrose,
NSW
USA: The David Brown Book Co, Oakville,
CT

Book Trade Association Membership:
Association of Learned & Professional
Society Publishers

2252

ENITHARMON PRESS
26B Caversham Road, London NW5 2DU
Telephone: (020) 7482 5967
Fax: (020) 7284 1787
Email: books@enitharmon.co.uk
Web Site: www.enitharmon.co.uk

Warehouse:
Central Books, 99 Wallis Road, London
E9 5LN
Telephone: (020) 8986 4854
Fax: (020) 8533 5821

Director: Stephen Stuart-Smith
Managers: Jacqueline Gabbitas
(Marketing)
Isabel Britten *(Editorial)*

*Fiction; Illustrated & Fine Editions;
Literature & Criticism; Poetry*

ISBNs, Imprints & Series:
978 1 870612, 978 1 900564, 978 1
904634

Associated Companies:
Enitharmon Editions Ltd

Overseas Representation:
USA & Canada: Dufour Editions Inc, Chester
Springs, PA, USA

Book Trade Association Membership:
IPG

2253

EQUINOX PUBLISHING LTD
Unit 6, The Village, 101 Amies Street,
London SW11 2JW
Telephone: (020) 7350 2836
Fax: (020) 7350 2836
Email: jjoyce@equinoxpub.com
Web Site: www.equinoxpub.com

Distribution:
Marston Book Services Ltd, PO Box 269,
Abingdon, Oxon OX14 4YN
Telephone: 01235 465521
Fax: 01235 465555
Email: trade.orders@marston.co.uk

Publisher: Janet Joyce
Editorial & Rights: Valerie Hall

*Academic & Scholarly; Archaeology;
Biography & Autobiography; Cookery,
Wines & Spirits; Educational & Textbooks;
Electronic (Professional & Academic);
Gender Studies; History & Antiquarian;
Languages & Linguistics; Music;
Philosophy; Reference Books, Directories &
Dictionaries; Religion & Theology; Sociology
& Anthropology*

New Titles: 50 (2008) , 50 (2009)
No of Employees: 2
Annual Turnover: £650,000

ISBNs, Imprints & Series:
978 1 84553, 978 1 904768

Distributor for:
J R Collis Publications; Contact Pastoral
Trust

Overseas Representation:
Australia & New Zealand: Eleanor Brasch
Enterprises, Artarmon, NSW, Australia
China, Hong Kong & Taiwan: Ian Taylor &
Associates, Beijing, P. R. of China
Europe: Andrew Durnell Marketing Ltd,
Tunbridge Wells, UK
India: Maya Publishers Pvt Ltd, New Delhi
Japan: United Publishers Services Ltd, Tokyo
North America: The David Brown Book Co,
Oakville, CT, USA
Singapore, Malaysia & Brunei: Publishers
Marketing Services Pte Ltd, Singapore
*South Africa, Botswana, Lesotho, Namibia,
Swaziland & Zimbabwe:* Chris Reinders,
The African Moon Press, Kelvin, South
Africa

Book Trade Association Membership:
IPG; Association of Learned & Professional
Society Publishers (UK Serials Interest
Group)

2254

THE ERSKINE PRESS
The White House, Sandfield Lane, Eccles,
Norwich, Norfolk NR16 2PB
Telephone: 01953 887277
Fax: 01953 888361
Email: erskpres@aol.com
Web Site: www.erskine-press.com

Director: Crispin de Boos
Commissioning Editor: Lesley de Boos

*Academic & Scholarly; Biography &
Autobiography; History & Antiquarian;
Illustrated & Fine Editions; Medical (incl. Self
Help & Alternative Medicine); Military &
War; Natural History; Travel & Topography*

New Titles: 6 (2008) , 5 (2009)
Annual Turnover: £60,000

ISBNs, Imprints & Series:
978 0 948285, 978 1 85297 Archival
Facsimiles; Erskine Press

Parent Company:
jack afrika Publishing Ltd

2255

ETHICS INTERNATIONAL PRESS LTD
[publishes for Centre for Business & Public
Sector Ethics]
St Andrews Castle,
St Andrews Street South, Bury St Edmunds,
Suffolk IP33 3PH
Telephone: 01954 710086
Fax: 01954 710103
Email: info@ethicspress.com
Web Site: www.ethicspress.com

Director: Dr Rosamund Thomas
Managers: Robert Willis *(Marketing)*
Christopher Thomas *(General)*

*Academic & Scholarly; Educational &
Textbooks; Electronic (Educational);
Electronic (Professional & Academic);
Environment & Development Studies;
Industry, Business & Management; Politics
& World Affairs; Vocational Training &
Careers*

New Titles: 2 (2009)

ISBNs, Imprints & Series:
978 1 871891 Teaching Ethics (Book series)

Associated Companies:
Ethics International MultiMedia Ltd

Book Trade Association Membership:
Publishers Association

2256

***EUROMONITOR INTERNATIONAL
PLC**
60–61 Britton Street, London EC1M 5UX
Telephone: (020) 7251 8024
Fax: (020) 7608 3149
Email: info@euromonitor.com
Web Site: www.euromonitor.com

Directors: Trevor Fenwick *(Managing)*
Robert Senior *(Chairman)*
David Gudgin

*Economics; Industry, Business &
Management; Reference Books, Directories
& Dictionaries*

ISBNs, Imprints & Series:
978 0 86338, 978 1 84264

Associated Companies:
Dubai: Euromonitor International
Lithuania: Euromonitor International
P. R. of China: Euromonitor International
(Shanghai) Co Ltd
Singapore: Euromonitor International (Asia)
Pte Ltd
USA: Euromonitor International Inc

Book Trade Association Membership:
Data Publishers Association; European
Association of Directory Publishers

2257

***EVANGELICAL PRESS & SERVICES
LTD**
Grange Close, Faverdale,
North Industrial Estate, Darlington DL3 0PH
Telephone: 01325 380232
Fax: 01325 466153
Email: sales@evangelicalpress.org
Web Site: www.evangelicalpress.org

Managers: A. L. Gosling *(General)*
P. Cooper *(Production)*
A. Williamson *(Senior Editor)*

*Academic & Scholarly; Archaeology;
Biography & Autobiography; History &
Antiquarian; Reference Books, Directories &
Dictionaries; Religion & Theology*

ISBNs, Imprints & Series:
978 0 85234 Evangelical Press
978 0 946462 Grace Publications
978 0 95279 Carey Publications
978 1 85049 Bryntirion Press

Associated Companies:
France: Europresse SARL

Distributor for:
Bryntirion Press; Carey Publications; Free
Presbyterian Publishing; Gospel Standard
Publications; Knox Press; Sovereign
Publications
Canada: Joshua Press
USA: Baker Book House; Calvary Press;
Hendricksen Publishers; P & R
Publishing; Pilgrim Publications;
Reformation Heritage Books;
Reformation Trust; Solid Ground
Publications

Book Trade Association Membership:
Christian Booksellers Association;
Evangelical Christian Publishers Association

2258

EVANS PUBLISHING GROUP
2A Portman Mansions, Chiltern Street,
London W1U 6NR
Telephone: (020) 7487 0920
Fax: (020) 7487 0921
Email: sales@evansbrothers.co.uk
Web Site: www.evansbooks.co.uk

Trade Office:
Zero to Ten, Suite 1.3, Coomb House,
7 St John's Road, Isleworth, Middx
TW7 6NH
Telephone: (020) 8758 9777
Fax: (020) 8758 9888
Web Site: www.evansbooks.co.uk

Directors: Stephen Pawley *(Managing)*
Brian Jones *(International)*
Andrew Macmillan *(UK Sales)*
Ms Alex Evans *(Marketing)*
UK Publisher: Ms Su Swallow
Accountant: Danny Daly
Managers: Ms Jenny Mulvanny
(Production)
Ms Britta Martins-Simon *(Foreign Rights)*
Jason McGovern *(Export Sales)*

*Children's Books; Educational & Textbooks;
Electronic (Educational)*

ISBNs, Imprints & Series:
978 0 237 Evans
978 1 84089 Zero to Ten
978 1 84234 Cherrytree

Associated Companies:
Kenya: Evans Brothers (Kenya) Ltd
Nigeria: Evans Brothers (Nigeria Publishers)
Ltd
Sierra Leone: Evans Brothers (Sierra Leone)
Ltd

Book Trade Association Membership:
Publishers Association; EPC

2259

EVERYMAN'S LIBRARY
Northburgh House, 10 Northburgh Street,
London EC1V 0AT
Telephone: (020) 7566 6350
Fax: (020) 7490 3708
Email: books@everyman.uk.com

Trade Orders & Enquiries:
GBS, Isaac Newton Way,
Alma Park Industrial Estate, Grantham
NG31 9SD
Telephone: 01476 541000
Fax: 01476 541061

Managing Director: David Campbell

Managers: Clémence Jacquinet *(Editorial
(Travel Guides))*
Jane Holloway *(Editorial (Classics))*

*Academic & Scholarly; Children's Books;
Fiction; Guide Books; Illustrated & Fine
Editions; Literature & Criticism; Philosophy;
Travel & Topography*

ISBNs, Imprints & Series:
Everyman Children's Classics; Everyman
Classics; Everyman Guides; Everyman
Pocket Classics; Everyman Pocket Poets;
Everyman Wodehouse

Parent Company:
USA: Alfred A. Knopf [(a division of Random
House US)]

Overseas Representation:
Worldwide (excluding North America):
Random House International (Everyman's
Library), UK

2260

EX LIBRIS PRESS
16A New St John's Road, St Helier, Jersey
JE2 3LD
Telephone: 01534 780488
Fax: 01534 780488
Email: roger.jones@ex-librisbooks.co.uk
Web Site: www.ex-librisbooks.co.uk

Stockists:
Gardners Books, 1 Whittle Drive,
Willingdon Drove, Eastbourne, East Sussex
BN23 6QH
Telephone: 01323 521777
Fax: 01323 521666

Proprietor: Roger Jones

*Archaeology; Biography & Autobiography;
Cookery, Wines & Spirits; Gardening;
Geography & Geology; Guide Books;
History & Antiquarian; Natural History;
Nautical; Poetry; Transport; Travel &
Topography*

New Titles: 3 (2008) , 1 (2009)
Annual Turnover: £30,000

ISBNs, Imprints & Series:
ELSP (Ex Libris Self Publishing)
978 0 948578, 978 0 9506563, 978 1
903341 Seaflower Books
978 1 906641

2261

**EXECUTIVE GRAPEVINE
INTERNATIONAL LTD**
Rosanne House, Parkway,
Welwyn Garden City AL8 6HG
Telephone: 01707 351451
Fax: 01707 390143
Email: enquiries@executive-
grapevine.co.uk
Web Site: www.askgrapevine.com

Chief Executive Officer: Helen Barrett
Managing Director: Anna Weston
Head of Sales & Marketing: Sabrina
Ponte
Head of Business Operations: Sally
Griffin

*Industry, Business & Management;
Reference Books, Directories &
Dictionaries; Human Resources; Talent
Management*

New Titles: 2 (2008) , 2 (2009)
No of Employees: 20

ISBNs, Imprints & Series:
978 1 903530, 978 1 903550

Book Trade Association Membership:
Data Publishers Association

2262

EXLEY PUBLICATIONS LTD
16 Chalk Hill, Watford, Herts WD19 4BG
Telephone: 01923 474480
Fax: 01923 818733
Email: sales@exleypublications.co.uk
Web Site: www.helenexleygiftbooks.com

Warehouse:
Trade Counter, The Airfield, Norwich Road,
Mendlesham, Suffolk IP14 5NA
Telephone: 01449 766629
Fax: 01449 767122

Directors: Helen M. Exley *(Managing & Editorial)*
Richard A. Exley *(Finance & Production)*
Lincoln Exley *(Associate/Export Sales)*
Managers: Charlotte Markey *(Head of UK Sales)*
Keith Allen-Jones *(Foreign Rights)*

Humour; Gift Books

ISBNs, Imprints & Series:
978 1 84634, 978 1 85015, 978 1 86187,
978 1 90513

Associated Companies:
France: Exley SA
USA: Exley Giftbooks

Overseas Representation:
Australia: Card & Paper House; New
Holland Publishers Pty Ltd, French's
Forest, NSW
Canada: Pierre Belvedere, Montreal
Hong Kong: Pacific Century Distribution Ltd
India: Maya Publishers Pvt Ltd, New Delhi
Israel: Astra Agency, Jerusalem
Korea: Union Enterprise Co Ltd, Seoul,
Republic of Korea
Lebanon: Librarie Samir Editeur, Beirut
Malta: Audio Visual Centre Ltd, Sliema
New Zealand: David Bateman Ltd, Auckland
Pakistan: Mackwin & Co, Karachi
Philippines: Balatbat & Sons International,
Filinvest
Republic of Ireland: Island Publications Ltd,
Dublin
Singapore: Cards n Such Pte Ltd
Southern Africa: Struik Book Distributors,
Johannesburg, South Africa
Spain: Editorial Edaf SA, Madrid
Vietnam: Fahasa Companie, Ho Chi Minh
City

Book Trade Association Membership:
IPG

2263

EXPRESS NEWSPAPERS
The Northern and Shell Building,
10 Lower Thames Street, London EC3R 6AE
Telephone: 0871 520 7887
Fax: 0871 434 7966
Email: leila.palmer@express.co.uk
Web Site: www.express.co.uk

Head of Enterprise: Leila Palmer

*Atlases & Maps; Biography &
Autobiography; Crime; Do-It-Yourself;
Gardening; Guide Books; Health & Beauty;
Humour; Illustrated & Fine Editions; Poetry;
Reference Books, Directories &
Dictionaries; Sports & Games; Transport;
Travel & Topography*

ISBNs, Imprints & Series: 978 0 85079

Parent Company:
Northern and Shell Media

Overseas Representation:
Canada: Canadian Manda Group, Toronto,
Ont
India: Wilco International

2264

FABER & FABER LTD
Bloomsbury House,
74–77 Great Russell Street, London
WC1B 3DA
Telephone: (020) 7927 3800
Fax: (020) 7927 3801
Email: mailbox@faber.co.uk
Web Site: www.faber.co.uk

Accounts:
16 Burnt Mill, Elizabeth Way, Harlow, Essex
CM20 2HX
Fax: 01279 417366
Web Site: www.faber.co.uk

Distribution & Orders:
TBS Ltd, Colchester Road, Frating Green,
Colchester, Essex CO7 7DW
Telephone: 01206 256004
Fax: 01206 255912

Chief Executive: Stephen Page
Directors: Walter Donohue *(Publisher &
Film)*
Valerie Eliot
Julian Loose *(Editorial, Fiction & Non-
Fiction)*
Lee Brackstone
David Tebbutt *(Finance)*
Nigel Marsh *(Production)*
Jason Cooper *(Rights)*
Will Atkinson *(Sales)*
Rachel Alexander *(Publicity)*
Belinda Matthews *(Music)*
Editorial: Paul Keegan *(Poetry)*
Julia Wells *(Children's)*
Dinah Wood *(Plays)*

*Biography & Autobiography; Children's
Books; Cinema, Video, TV & Radio;
Cookery, Wines & Spirits; Fiction; Literature
& Criticism; Music; Poetry; Politics & World
Affairs; Theatre, Drama & Dance*

ISBNs, Imprints & Series: 978 0 571

Associated Companies:
USA: Faber & Faber Inc

Distributor for:
De la Mare Publishing Ltd; Sanctuary
Publishing; Screenpress Publishing
USA: Faber & Faber Inc

Overseas Representation:
*Argentina, Bermuda, Bolivia, Brazil, Central
America, Chile, Columbia, Ecuador,
French West Indies, Jamaica, Mexico,
Paraguay, Peru, Uruguay & Venezuela:*
InterMedia Americana (IMA) Ltd,
London, UK
*Asia (including Japan, Korea, Taiwan &
Hong Kong):* Julian Ashton, Sevenoaks,
Kent, UK
Australia: Allen & Unwin Pty Ltd, Crows
Nest, NSW
Canada: Penguin Group Canada, Toronto,
Ont
*Central Europe, Netherlands, Belgium,
Luxembourg, Switzerland & Scandinavia:*
Bunmi Oke, Faber & Faber, London, UK
*Eastern Europe (excluding Russia & Baltic
States):* Csaba Lengyel de Bagota,
Budapest, Hungary
France, Germany & Austria: Patrick Keogh,
Faber & Faber, London, UK
India: Penguin Books India, New Delhi
Italy: Penguin Italia srl, Milan
*Middle East (including Israel & Iran), North
Africa, Malta & Turkey:* Peter Ward Book
Exports, London, UK
New Zealand: Allen & Unwin Pty Ltd,
Auckland
Pakistan: Faber & Faber, London, UK
Republic of Ireland: Gill Hess Ltd, Skerries,
Co Dublin
Singapore & Malaysia: Penguin Singapore,
Singapore
Southern Africa: Book Promotions Pty Ltd,
Cape Town, South Africa

Spain & Portugal: Penguin Spain, Madrid,
Spain
*Thailand, Cambodia, Laos, Vietnam &
Myanmar:* Keith Hardy, Hardy Bigfoss
International Co Ltd, Bangkok, Thailand
USA: Faber & Faber Inc, A Division of Farrer,
Strauss & Giroux, New York

Book Trade Association Membership:
Publishers Association

2265

*FABIAN SOCIETY
11 Dartmouth Street, London SW1H 9BN
Telephone: (020) 7227 4900
Fax: (020) 7976 7153
Email: info@fabian-society.org.uk
Web Site: www.fabian-society.org.uk

General Secretary: Sunder Katwala
Sales: Margaret McGillen
Editorial Director: Tom Hampson

*Academic & Scholarly; Economics;
Environment & Development Studies;
Philosophy; Politics & World Affairs*

ISBNs, Imprints & Series:
978 0 7163 Fabian Pamphlet

Associated Companies:
NCLC Publishers Ltd

Distributor for:
NCLC Publishers Ltd

Book Trade Association Membership:
BA

2266

FACET PUBLISHING
7 Ridgmount Street, London WC1E 7AE
Telephone: (020) 7255 0590
Fax: (020) 7255 0591
Email: info@facetpublishing.co.uk
Web Site: www.facetpublishing.co.uk

Warehouse:
Bookpoint Ltd, 130 Milton Park, Abingdon,
Oxon OX14 4SB
Telephone: 01235 827702
Fax: 01235 827703
Email: orders@bookpoint.co.uk

Managing Director: John Woolley
Managers: Kathryn Beecroft *(Production)*
Rohini Ramachandran *(Sales)*
Lena Stuart *(Marketing)*
Publisher: Helen Carley
Typesetter: June York
Editors: Louise Le Bas *(Commissioning)*
Lin Franklin *(Desk)*

*Academic & Scholarly; Bibliography &
Library Science; Educational & Textbooks;
Electronic (Professional & Academic);
Reference Books, Directories & Dictionaries*

New Titles: 26 (2008) , 35 (2009)

ISBNs, Imprints & Series:
978 0 85365, 978 1 85604 Clive Bingley;
Facet Publishing; Library Association
Publishing

Parent Company:
CILIP [Chartered Institute of Library and
Information Professionals]

Overseas Representation:
Australia & New Zealand: Inbooks, c/o
James Bennett Pty Ltd, Belrose, NSW,
Australia
Canada & USA: Neal-Schuman Publishers
Inc, New York, NY, USA
India: Book Marketing Services, Chennai
Japan: United Publishers Services Ltd, Tokyo
Middle East: International Publishing
Services (IPS) Middle East Ltd, Dubai, UAE

South East Asia: Taylor & Francis Asia
Pacific, Singapore
Spain & Portugal: Iberian Book Services,
Madrid, Spain

Book Trade Association Membership:
Publishers Association; CAPP; IPG

2267

FAMILY PUBLICATIONS
Denis Riches House, 66 Sandford Lane,
Kennington, Oxford OX1 5RP
Telephone: 0845 0500 879
Fax: 01865 321325
Email: sales@familypublications.co.uk
Web Site: www.familypublications.co.uk

Managing Director: Colin Mason

*Biography & Autobiography; History &
Antiquarian; Religion & Theology*

New Titles: 12 (2008) , 13 (2009)
No of Employees: 7
Annual Turnover: £400,000

ISBNs, Imprints & Series: 978 1 871217

Distributor for:
USA: Ascension Press; Bethlehem Books;
Ignatius Press; William H. Sadlier Inc

Overseas Representation:
Australia: Freedom Publishing, North
Melbourne, Vic

2268

A. & A. FARMAR
78 Ranelagh Village, Dublin 6,
Republic of Ireland
Telephone: +353 (01) 496 3625
Fax: +353 (01) 497 0107
Email: afarmar@iol.ie
Web Site: www.farmarbooks.com

Trade Orders (Republic of Ireland):
Columba Mercier Distribution Ltd,
55a Spruce Avenue,
Stillorgan Industrial Park, Blackrock,
Co Dublin, Republic of Ireland
Telephone: +353 (01) 294 2560
Fax: +353 (01) 294 2564

Editorial: Anna Farmar
Production: Tony Farmar

*Cookery, Wines & Spirits; History &
Antiquarian; Irish business & organisational
histories*

ISBNs, Imprints & Series:
978 1 899047, 978 1 906353

Overseas Representation:
UK (Trade Orders): Central Books Ltd,
London, UK

Book Trade Association Membership:
CLÉ (Irish PA)

2269

FEATHER BOOKS
P O Box 438, Shrewsbury SY3 0WN
Telephone: 01743 872177
Fax: 01743 872177
Email: john@waddysweb.freeuk.com
Web Site: www.waddysweb.freeuk.com

Director: Revd John Waddington-Feather
(Sales & Marketing)
Managers: Sheila Waddington-Feather
(Production)
Paul Evans *(Sub-Editor, Production)*
Tony Reavill *(Recording & Drama
Producer)*
David Grundy *(Music Director & Editor)*
Anna Waddington-Feather *(Public
Relations & Sub-Editor)*
Janet Evans *(Sub-Editor)*

Academic & Scholarly; Audio Books; Biography & Autobiography; Children's Books; Crime; Fiction; Humour; Literature & Criticism; Music; Poetry; Religion & Theology; Theatre, Drama & Dance

New Titles: 15 (2008) , 10 (2009)

ISBNs, Imprints & Series:
978 0 947718, 978 1 84175 Feather Books Drama Series
978 1 84175 Christianity & Literature Series; Feather Books Biography Series; Feather Books Music Series; Feather Books Poetry Series

Associated Companies:
Moorside Words & Music

2270 ━━━━━

*FHG GUIDES LTD
Abbey Mill Business Centre, Seedhill, Paisley PA1 1TJ
Telephone: 0141 887 0428
Fax: 0141 889 7204
Email: admin@fhguides.co.uk
Web Site: www.holidayguides.com

Book Trade Representative:
Christopher Halliday, Kuperard Publishers, 59 Hutton Grove, London N12 8DS
Telephone: (020) 8446 2440
Fax: (020) 8446 2441
Email: christopher@kuperard.co.uk

Publishing Director: G. Pratt

Guide Books; Sports & Games

ISBNs, Imprints & Series: 978 1 85055

Parent Company:
Kuperard Publishers

Book Trade Association Membership:
Periodical Publishers Association

2271 ━━━━━

FILAMENT PUBLISHING LTD
16 Croydon Road, Waddon, Croydon, Surrey CR0 4PA
Telephone: (020) 8688 2598
Fax: 0870 116 3530
Email: info@filamentpublishing.com
Web Site: www.filamentpublishing.com

Representation (UK):
Gardners Books, 1 Whittle Drive, Eastbourne, East Sussex BN23 6QH

Director: Christopher Day
Finance: Bernard Marchant
Editor: Zara Thatcher
Production: Andrew White

Biography & Autobiography; Educational & Textbooks; Electronic (Professional & Academic); Industry, Business & Management; Medical (incl. Self Help & Alternative Medicine); Sports & Games; Theatre, Drama & Dance; Vocational Training & Careers

New Titles: 10 (2008) , 10 (2009)
No of Employees: 4
Annual Turnover: £150,000

ISBNs, Imprints & Series: 978 1 905493

Book Trade Association Membership:
Publishers Association

2272 ━━━━━

FINDHORN PRESS LTD
305a The Park, Findhorn, Forres, Moray IV36 3TE
Telephone: 01309 690582
Fax: 01309 690036
Email: info@findhornpress.com

Web Site: www.findhornpress/

Publisher: Thierry Bogliolo
Managers: Carol Shaw *(Marketing & Publicity)*
Sabine Weeke *(Rights, Editorial)*

Animal Care & Breeding; Cookery, Wines & Spirits; Guide Books; Health & Beauty; Medical (incl. Self Help & Alternative Medicine); Religion & Theology; Ecology; Metaphysical; Mind, Body, Spirit; New Age

New Titles: 28 (2008) , 28 (2009)
No of Employees: 4
Annual Turnover: £600,000

ISBNs, Imprints & Series:
978 0 905249, 978 1 84409, 978 1 899171

Overseas Representation:
Australia: Brumby Books Holdings Pty Ltd, Kilsyth South, Vic
New Zealand: Ceres Books, Ellerslie
North America: Independent Publishers Group (IPG), Chicago, IL, USA
Republic of Ireland & Europe: Deep Books Ltd, London, UK
Singapore: Pen International Ltd, Singapore
South Africa: Faradawn CC, Saxonwold
USA: New Leaf Distributing Co, Lithia Springs, GA

Book Trade Association Membership:
IPG; Publishing Scotland

2273 ━━━━━

FIRST & BEST IN EDUCATION
Earlstrees Court, Earlstrees Road, Corby, Northants NN17 4HH
Telephone: 01536 399011 (Orders & Accounts), 399004 (Editorial)
Fax: 01536 399012
Email: sales@firstandbest.co.uk
Web Site: www.shop.firstandbest.co.uk

Finance Manager: Jane Edmonds
Managing Director: Tony Attwood
Senior Editor: Anne Cockburn

Educational & Textbooks; Electronic (Educational)

Book Trade Association Membership:
EPC

2274 ━━━━━

FIVE LEAVES PUBLICATIONS
PO Box 8786, Nottingham NG1 9AW
Telephone: 0115 969 3597
Email: info@fiveleaves.co.uk
Web Site: www.fiveleaves.co.uk

Publisher: Ross Bradshaw

Academic & Scholarly; Children's Books; Crime; Fiction; History & Antiquarian; Poetry; Theatre, Drama & Dance; Jewish

New Titles: 20 (2008) , 20 (2009)

ISBNs, Imprints & Series:
Crime Express
978 0 907123, 978 1 905512 Five Leaves Publications

Overseas Representation:
Spain & Portugal: Iberian Book Services, Madrid, Spain

2275 ━━━━━

FLAMBARD PRESS
Studio 16, Black Swan Court, 69 Westgate Road, Newcastle-upon-Tyne NE1 1SG
Telephone: 0191 222 1329
Email: flambardpress@btinternet.com
Web Site: www.flambardpress.co.uk

Company Secretary: Peter Lewis
Editor: Margaret Lewis
Managing Editor: Will Mackie

Biography & Autobiography; Crime; Fiction; Photography; Poetry

New Titles: 8 (2008) , 8 (2009)
No of Employees: 3

ISBNs, Imprints & Series:
978 1 873226, 978 1 906601

Book Trade Association Membership:
IPG

2276 ━━━━━

FLORAMEDIA UK LTD
Global House, Global Park, Moorside, Eastgates, Colchester CO1 2TW
Telephone: 01206 771040
Email: info@floramedia.co.uk
Web Site: www.floramedia.co.uk

Managing Director: N. Mathias

Gardening

New Titles: 1 (2009)
No of Employees: 28
Annual Turnover: £7M

ISBNs, Imprints & Series: 978 0 903001

Parent Company:
Netherlands: Floramedia Group BV

Overseas Representation:
Australia: Macbird Floraprint Pty Ltd, Scoresby, Vic
Austria: Floramedia GmbH, Vienna
Belgium: Floramedia NV, Antwerp
Canada: John Markham Associates, Sidney, BC
France: Floramedia, Lille
Germany: Verlagsgesellschaft Grun ist Leben mbH, Pinneberg
Liechtenstein: Floramedia Group AG, Vaduz
Netherlands: Floramedia Group BV, Zaandam
New Zealand: Floramedia New Zealand, Wellington
Republic of Ireland: Carleys Bridge Potteries Ltd, Enniscorthy
South Africa: Floramedia Southern Africa, Florida
Spain: Floramedia España, Valencia
Switzerland: Floramedia AG, Rapperswil-Jona

2277 ━━━━━

FLORIS BOOKS
15 Harrison Gardens, Edinburgh EH11 1SH
Telephone: 0131 337 2372
Fax: 0131 347 9919
Email: floris@florisbooks.co.uk
Web Site: www.florisbooks.co.uk

Warehouse & Orders:
BookSource, 50 Cambuslang Road, Glasgow G32 8NB
Telephone: 0845 370 0067
Fax: 0845 370 0068
Email: orders@booksource.net

Chief Executive: Christian Maclean
Marketing: Katy Lockwood-Holmes
Editorial: Sally Martin

Academic & Scholarly; Children's Books; Crafts & Hobbies; Gardening; Health & Beauty; Medical (incl. Self Help & Alternative Medicine); Philosophy; Religion & Theology

New Titles: 50 (2008) , 50 (2009)
No of Employees: 9

ISBNs, Imprints & Series:
978 0 86315, 978 0 903540, 978 0 906155

Distributor for:
Lindisfarne Press
USA: Biodynamic Farming & Gardening Association

Overseas Representation:
Australia: Footprint Books Pty Ltd, Warriewood, NSW
New Zealand: Ceres Books, Ellerslie
USA (34 Children's & Parents' titles): Gryphon House Inc, Beltsville, MD, USA
USA (all titles): Steiner Books Inc, Herndon, VA, USA

Book Trade Association Membership:
Publishing Scotland

2278 ━━━━━

FOLENS LTD
Waterslade House, Thame Road, Haddenham, Bucks HP17 8NT
Telephone: 0870 609 1235 (order hotline), 1237 (customer services)
Fax: 0870 609 1236 (order hotline)
Email: folens@folens.com
Web Site: www.folens.com

Chairman: David Moffatt
Directors: Adrian Cockell *(Managing)*
Peter Burton *(Publishing)*
Jacqui Dilley *(Marketing)*
John Cadell *(Group Managing)*

Atlases & Maps; Educational & Textbooks; Electronic (Educational); English as a Foreign Language; Reference Books, Directories & Dictionaries

New Titles: 74 (2008) , 68 (2009)
No of Employees: 40

ISBNs, Imprints & Series:
978 0 94788, 978 1 84163, 978 1 84191, 978 1 84303, 978 1 85008, 978 1 85276
Belair Publications
978 1 86202 Belair Publications

Overseas Representation:
Australia: Educational Supplies Pty Ltd
Bahrain: The Bookcase, Manama
Canada: Bacon & Hughes Ltd, Ottawa, Ont
Egypt: International Language Bookshop
Hong Kong: Transglobal Publishers Services Ltd
Jamaica: The Book Merchant Ltd, Kingston
Jordan: Al-Kashkool Bookshop, Amman; Philadelphia Book Gallery
Kuwait: Saeed & Samir Bookstore Co Ltd
Malaysia: Extrazeal; University Book Store (M) Sdn Bhd
Malta: Agius & Agius Ltd, Valletta
New Zealand: South Pacific Books (Imports) Ltd, Auckland
Oman: Al Manahil Educational Consultancy
Saudi Arabia: Elmia Bookstores, Al Khobar
Singapore: September 21 Enterprise Pte Ltd
South Africa: Everybody's Books, Durban
Spain: TEK Books (Bookworld Espana)
United Arab Emirates: All Prints Distributors & Publishers, UAE; Jashanmal National, UAE; Magrudy Enterprises, Dubai, UAE
USA: Social Studies School Service (USA)

Book Trade Association Membership:
Publishers Association; EPC

2279 ━━━━━

FOOD TRADE PRESS LTD
Station House, Hortons Way, Westerham, Kent TN16 1BZ
Telephone: 01959 563944
Fax: 01959 561285
Email: books@foodtradepress.com
Web Site: www.foodtradepress.com

Director: Adrian Binsted *(Publishing)*

Agriculture; Chemistry; Reference Books, Directories & Dictionaries; Food Science & Technology

ISBNs, Imprints & Series:
978 0 900379, 978 0 903962

Associated Companies:
Attwood & Binsted Ltd

Distributor for:
Campden & Chorleywood Research
Association; Leatherhead Food Research
Association
Denmark: Mercantila Publishing AS
Italy: Chiriotti Editori Srl
Spain: Montagud Editores SA
Switzerland: Binsted Frères SA
USA: American Association of Cereal
Chemists; American Institute of Baking;
Chemical Publishing Co Inc; CTI
Publications Inc; Food & Nutrition Press
Inc; Food Processors Institute; Edward E.
Judge & Sons

2280

FOOTPRINT HANDBOOKS
6 Riverside Court, Lower Bristol Road, Bath
BA2 3DZ
Telephone: 01225 469141
Fax: 01225 469461
Email: discover@footprintbooks.com
Web Site: www.footprintbooks.com

UK Trade Sales Agent:
GeoCenter International Ltd,
Meridian House, Churchill Way West,
Basingstoke, Hants RG21 6YR
Telephone: 01256 817987
Fax: 01256 817988
Email: sales@geocenter.co.uk
Web Site: www.geocenter.co.uk

Directors: Andy Riddle *(Managing)*
Patrick Dawson *(Commercial)*
Managers: Alan Murphy *(Publisher)*
Zoë Jackson *(Business Development)*
Liz Harper *(Marketing)*

*Guide Books; Sports & Games; Travel &
Topography*

New Titles: 35 (2008) , 37 (2009)
No of Employees: 20

ISBNs, Imprints & Series:
978 0 900751 Footprint Handbooks/Trade
& Travel Handbooks
978 1 900949, 978 1 903471, 978 1
904777, 978 1 906098 Footprint
Handbooks

Distributor for:
Authentik Guides; Insiders' Guides; Wexas
International
USA: Globe Pequot Press

Overseas Representation:
Australia & New Zealand: Woodslane Pty
Ltd, Warriewood, NSW, Australia
Belgium: Craenen bvba, Herent (Winksele)
Canada: Manda Group, Toronto, Ont
Europe: Bill Bailey Publishers
Representatives, Newton Abbot, UK
Israel: SKP, Tel Aviv
Latin America: InterMedia Americana (IMA)
Ltd, London, UK
Netherlands: Nilsson & Lamm BV, Weesp
Republic of Ireland: Fitzmull Books, Dublin
South Africa: Faradawn CC, Saxonwold
South East Asia: Pansing Distribution Pte
Ltd, Singapore
USA: Globe Pequot Press, Guilford, CT

2281

*FORENSIC SCIENCE SOCIETY
Clarke House, 18A Mount Parade,
Harrogate HG1 1BX
Telephone: 01423 506068
Fax: 01423 566391
Email: journal@forensic-science-
society.org.uk
Web Site: www.forensic-science-
society.org.uk

Hon. Editor: Niamh Nic Daéid

Scientific & Technical

2282

*THE FOSTERING NETWORK
87 Blackfriars Road, London SE1 8HA
Telephone: (020) 7620 6400
Fax: (020) 7620 6401

Director: Robert Tapsfield
Head of External Affairs: Lucy Peake
Publishing: David McConnell

*Children's Books; Educational & Textbooks;
Psychology & Psychiatry; Sociology &
Anthropology; Vocational Training &
Careers; Child Care*

ISBNs, Imprints & Series: 978 0 946015

2283

W. FOULSHAM & CO LTD
The Oriel, Thames Valley Court,
183–187 Bath Road, Slough, Berks
SL1 4AA
Telephone: 01753 526769
Fax: 01753 535003
Email: reception@foulsham.com
Web Site: www.foulsham.com

Distribution:
Macmillan Distribution (MDL), Houndmills,
Basingstoke RG21 2XS
Telephone: 01256 329242
Fax: 01256 812558
Email: mdl@macmillan.co.uk
Web Site: www.mdl.macmillan.co.uk

Directors: Barry Belasco *(Managing)*
Graham Kitchen *(Financial)*
Roy Mantel *(Production)*
Wendy Hobson *(Editorial)*

*Accountancy & Taxation; Antiques &
Collecting; Children's Books; Cookery,
Wines & Spirits; Crafts & Hobbies; Crime;
Educational & Textbooks; Gardening; Guide
Books; Health & Beauty; Humour; Industry,
Business & Management; Magic & the
Occult; Medical (incl. Self Help & Alternative
Medicine); Military & War; Poetry;
Reference Books, Directories &
Dictionaries; Religion & Theology; Travel &
Topography*

ISBNs, Imprints & Series:
978 0 572 Arcturus; Foulsham; Quantum

Overseas Representation:
Australia: Capricorn Link (Australia) Pty Ltd,
Windsor, NSW
*Belgium, Germany, Luxembourg,
Netherlands, Switzerland & Austria:*
Robbert J. Pleysier, Heerde, Netherlands
*Cambodia, Laos, Myanmar, Thailand,
Philippines & Vietnam:* Ashton
International Marketing Services,
Sevenoaks, Kent, UK
Canada: Codasat, Vancouver, BC
Caribbean: Macmillan Caribbean Ltd,
Oxford, UK
Central & Eastern Europe: Dr László Horváth
Publishers Representative, Budapest,
Hungary
Central & South America: InterMedia
Americana (IMA) Ltd, London, UK
Far East, Singapore & Malaysia: Ashton
International Marketing Services,
Sevenoaks, Kent, UK
*France, Gibraltar, Greece, Italy, Spain &
Portugal:* Sandro Salucci, Florence, Italy
India: Maya Publishers Pvt Ltd, New Delhi
Middle East: Richard Carman Associates,
Northwich, UK
New Zealand: Southern Publishers Group,
Auckland
South Africa: Alternative Books CC,
Ferndale

Sub Saharan Africa: InterMedia Africa Ltd
(IMA), London, UK
USA: Associated Publishers Group,
Nashville, TN

2284

FOUR COURTS PRESS
7 Malpas Street, Dublin 8,
Republic of Ireland
Telephone: +353 (01) 453 4668
Fax: +353 (01) 453 4672
Email: info@fourcourtspress.ie
Web Site: www.fourcourtspress.ie

Distribution:
Gill & Macmillan, Hume Avenue,
Park West, Dublin 12, Republic of Ireland
Telephone: +353 (01) 500 9555
Fax: +353 (01) 500 9599
Email: info@fourcourtspress.ie
Web Site: www.fourcourtspress.ie

Managing Director: Martin Healy
Marketing: Anthony Tierney
Editorial: Martin Fanning

*Academic & Scholarly; Archaeology; Fine
Art & Art History; History & Antiquarian;
Law; Literature & Criticism; Military & War;
Music; Philosophy; Religion & Theology*

New Titles: 53 (2008) , 50 (2009)
No of Employees: 4
Annual Turnover: £800,000

ISBNs, Imprints & Series:
Four Courts Press; Open Air
978 0 906127, 978 1 84682, 978 1 85182

Overseas Representation:
USA: International Specialized Book
Services Inc, Portland, OR

2285

SAMUEL FRENCH LTD
52 Fitzroy Street, London W1T 5JR
Telephone: (020) 7387 9373
Fax: (020) 7387 2161
Email: theatre@samuelfrench-
london.co.uk
Web Site: www.samuelfrench-
london.co.uk

Directors: Leon F. Embry *(Chairman)*
Vivien Goodwin *(Managing)*
Amanda Smith
Paul Taylor

Theatre, Drama & Dance

New Titles: 25 (2008) , 25 (2009)
No of Employees: 36

ISBNs, Imprints & Series: 978 0 573

Parent Company:
Samuel French Inc

Distributor for:
USA: Samuel French Inc

Overseas Representation:
Australia: The Dominie Group, Brookvale,
NSW
East Africa: Phoenix Players Ltd, Nairobi,
Kenya
Malta: Dingli Co International, Valletta
New Zealand: Play Bureau of New Zealand
Ltd, New Plymouth
Republic of Ireland: Drama League of
Ireland, Dublin
*South Africa, Namibia, Swaziland,
Botswana & Lesotho:* Dalro (Pty) Ltd,
Braamfontein, South Africa
Zimbabwe: National Theatre Organization,
Harare

Book Trade Association Membership:
Publishers Association; BA

2286

FRIENDS OF THE EARTH
26–28 Underwood Street, London N1 7JQ
Telephone: (020) 7490 1555
Fax: (020) 7490 0881
Web Site: www.foe.co.uk &
community.foe.co.uk

Manager: Adam Bradbury *(Publications)*

*Academic & Scholarly; Educational &
Textbooks; Environment & Development
Studies; Gardening; Reference Books,
Directories & Dictionaries; Transport*

ISBNs, Imprints & Series: 978 1 85750

2287

GADFLY ENTERTAINMENT LTD
15–19 Cavendish Square, London
W1G 0DD
Email: info@gadfly-ent.com
Web Site: www.gadfly-ent.com

2288

GALACTIC CENTRAL PUBLICATIONS
25a Copgrove Road, Leeds, West Yorkshire
LS8 2SP
Telephone: 0113 248 8124
Email: philsp@philsp.com
Web Site: www.philsp.com

Publisher: Phil Stephensen-Payne

Bibliography & Library Science

ISBNs, Imprints & Series: 978 1 871133

Overseas Representation:
USA: Chris Drumm, Polk City, IA

2289

THE GALLERY PRESS
Loughcrew, Oldcastle, Co Meath,
Republic of Ireland
Telephone: +353 (049) 854 1779
Fax: +353 (049) 854 1779
Email: gallery@indigo.ie
Web Site: www.gallerypress.com

Director: Peter Fallon *(Editorial, Production)*
Administration: Jean Barry
Suella Wynne
Sales & Accounts: Anne Duggan

Fiction; Poetry; Theatre, Drama & Dance

New Titles: 12 (2008) , 13 (2009)
No of Employees: 4

ISBNs, Imprints & Series:
978 0 902996, 978 0 904011, 978 1 85235

2290

GALORE PARK PUBLISHING LTD
19–21 Sayers Lane, Tenterden, Kent
TN30 6BW
Telephone: 01580 764242
Fax: 01580 764142
Email: info@galorepark.co.uk
Web Site: www.galorepark.co.uk

Directors: Nicholas Oulton *(Managing)*
Louise Martine
Aidan Gill *(Publishing)*
Marketing Manager / Public Relations:
Natalie Friend
Financial Controller: Steve Jones

Children's Books; Educational & Textbooks

New Titles: 32 (2008) , 24 (2009)
No of Employees: 14
Annual Turnover: £1.2M

ISBNs, Imprints & Series:
978 1 902984 Galore Park Publishing; Iseb
Publications

Book Trade Association Membership:
Publishers Association; BA; IPG

2291

GARNET PUBLISHING LTD
8 Southern Court, South Street, Reading
RG1 4QS
Telephone: 0118 959 7847
Fax: 0118 959 7356 (Trade Enquiries &
Orders)
Email: dan@garnetpublishing.co.uk
Web Site: www.garnetpublishing.co.uk

Managers: Dan Nunn *(Permissions, Rights
& Editorial)*
Nick Holroyd *(Office, Production &
Finance)*
Val Eve *(Sales)*

*Academic & Scholarly; Architecture &
Design; Cookery, Wines & Spirits;
Economics; Electronic (Professional &
Academic); Fiction; Gender Studies; Guide
Books; History & Antiquarian; Literature &
Criticism; Photography; Politics & World
Affairs; Religion & Theology; Sociology &
Anthropology; Travel & Topography*

New Titles: 20 (2008) , 20 (2009)

ISBNs, Imprints & Series:
978 1 85964, 978 1 873938, 978 1 902932
Garnet Publishing; Ithaca Press; South
Street Press

Associated Companies:
Garnet Education; Ithaca Press; South
Street Press

Overseas Representation:
Australia: InBooks, Frenchs Forest, NSW
Europe: Andrew Durnell Marketing Ltd,
Tunbridge Wells, UK
USA (Academic): International Specialized
Book Services Inc, Portland, OR, USA
USA (Trade): IPM, Dulles, VA, USA

Book Trade Association Membership:
IPG

2292

GATEHOUSE MEDIA LTD
PO Box 965, Warrington, Cheshire
WA4 9DE
Telephone: 01925 267778
Fax: 01925 267778
Email: info@gatehousebooks.com
Web Site: www.gatehousebooks.com

Directors: Catherine White *(Managing)*
Mark White

*Audio Books; Educational & Textbooks;
English as a Foreign Language*

ISBNs, Imprints & Series:
978 1 84231 Gatehouse Books

Overseas Representation:
Canada: Grass Roots Press, Edmonton, Alb
USA: Peppercorn Books Press, Snow Camp,
NC

Book Trade Association Membership:
Publishers Association

2293

GEDDES & GROSSET
David Dale House, New Lanark ML11 9DJ
Telephone: 01555 665000
Fax: 01555 665694
Email: info@gandg.sol.co.uk

Sales:
David Dale House, New Lanark ML11 9DJ

Telephone: 01555 665000
Fax: 01555 665694
Email: info@gandg.sol.co.uk

Warehouse:
Peter Haddock Ltd, Industrial Estate,
Pinfold Lane, Bridlington YO16 5BT
Telephone: 01262 678121
Fax: 01262 400043

Executives: Ron Grosset *(Publisher)*
Mike Miller *(Publisher)*
Manager: Liz Small *(Sales & Marketing)*

*Atlases & Maps; Children's Books; Cookery,
Wines & Spirits; History & Antiquarian;
Magic & the Occult; Medical (incl. Self Help
& Alternative Medicine); Reference Books,
Directories & Dictionaries*

New Titles: 29 (2008) , 42 (2009)
No of Employees: 8
Annual Turnover: £2.3M

ISBNs, Imprints & Series:
978 1 85534, 978 1 902407

Parent Company:
D. C. Thomson & Co Ltd

Associated Companies:
Waverley Books Ltd

Overseas Representation:
Africa & Caribbean: Kelvin van Hasselt
Publishing Services, Briningham, Norfolk,
UK
Central & South America: InterMedia
Americana Ltd (IMA), Gibraltar
Southern Africa: Book Promotions Pty Ltd,
Cape Town, South Africa

Book Trade Association Membership:
Publishing Scotland

2294

GEOCENTER INTERNATIONAL LTD
Meridian House, Churchill Way West,
Basingstoke, Hants RG21 6YR
Telephone: 01256 817987
Fax: 01256 817988
Email: sales@geocenter.co.uk
Web Site: www.geocenter.co.uk

Distribution:
Grantham Book Services, Trent Road,
Grantham, Lincs NG31 7XG
Telephone: 01476 541080
Fax: 01476 541061

Public Relations:
Julia Spence, 29 St Mary's Street,
Wallingford, Oxon OX10 0ET
Telephone: 01491 824524
Fax: 01491 824694
Email: juliaspence@ukonline.co.uk

Sales & Marketing Director: Ian
MacDonald
Managers: Andy Casey *(Sales)*
Petra Hourd *(Marketing – Insight)*
Donna Burridge *(Marketing –
Cartographic)*
Sam Bufton *(Marketing – Berlitz
Language)*
Diane McEntee *(Marketing – Berlitz
Travel)*
Hayley Whitlock *(Marketing – Ullmann)*

*Academic & Scholarly; Architecture &
Design; Atlases & Maps; Cookery, Wines &
Spirits; Gardening; Guide Books;
Languages & Linguistics; Music;
Photography; Reference Books, Directories
& Dictionaries; Transport; Travel &
Topography*

New Titles: 483 (2008) , 395 (2009)
No of Employees: 18
Annual Turnover: £7.8M

ISBNs, Imprints & Series:
978 0 84165 AMC Maps & Atlases
978 0 95428 Hg2 (Hedonist)
978 0 95490 Dinos Maps
978 1 84159 Everyman
978 1 84306 Landmark
978 2 8315, 978 981 246 Berlitz
978 3 468 Langenscheidt Dictionaries
978 3 575 GeoCenter Maps
978 3 82976 Baedeker
978 3 8331 Ullmann
978 3 88618 Nelles Maps
978 962 421, 978 981 234, 978 981 258
Insight Guides
978 962 593 Periplus Maps

Parent Company:
Germany: Langenscheidt KG

Distributor for:
AMC [AMC Maps & Atlases]; Apa Guides
[Insight Guides]; Langenscheidt
[Dictionaries]; Nelles Verlag [Nelles
Guides & Maps]; Periplus Editions
[Guides, Maps & Cookery Books]; RV
Verlag [GeoCenter Maps]; Ullmann [Art
& Architecture, Lifestyle, Reference]

Overseas Representation:
Europe: Bill Bailey Publishers
Representatives, Newton Abbot, UK
South America: InterMedia Americana Ltd
(IMA), Gibraltar

Book Trade Association Membership:
Book Data Subscriber

2295

THE GEOGRAPHICAL ASSOCIATION
160 Solly Street, Sheffield S1 4BF
Telephone: 0114 296 0088
Fax: 0114 296 7176
Email: info@geography.org.uk
Web Site: www.geography.org.uk

Chief Executive: David Lambert
Programme Director: John Lyon
Managers: Richard Gill *(Business)*
Ruth Totterdell *(Publications)*
Assistant Editor: Dorcas Turner

*Atlases & Maps; Educational & Textbooks;
Electronic (Educational); Geography &
Geology; Guide Books; Travel & Topography*

New Titles: 15 (2008) , 20 (2009)
No of Employees: 24

ISBNs, Imprints & Series:
978 0 900395, 978 0 948512, 978 1
84377, 978 1 899085, 978 1 903448

Book Trade Association Membership:
EPC

2296

GEOGRAPHY PUBLICATIONS
24 Kennington Road, Templeogue,
Dublin 6W, Republic of Ireland
Telephone: +353 (01) 456 6085
Fax: +353 (01) 456 6085
Email: books@geographypublications.com
Web Site:
www.geographypublications.com

Contact: William Nolan

*Academic & Scholarly; Archaeology; Atlases
& Maps; Biography & Autobiography;
Educational & Textbooks; Geography &
Geology; History & Antiquarian; Languages
& Linguistics; Reference Books, Directories
& Dictionaries*

New Titles: 4 (2008) , 3 (2009)

ISBNs, Imprints & Series:
978 0 906602 History & Society Series

2297

**GEOLOGICAL SOCIETY PUBLISHING
HOUSE**
Unit 7, Brassmill Enterprise Centre,
Brassmill Lane, Bath BA1 3JN
Telephone: 01225 445046
Fax: 01225 442836
Email: neal.marriott@geolsoc.org.uk &
dawn.angel@geolsoc.org.uk (sales
enquiries)
Web Site: www.geolsoc.org.uk/bookshop

Director of Publishing: Neal Marriott
Marketing Assistant: Sam Kaye
Editors: Angharad Hills *(Commissioning)*
Sarah Gibbs *(Senior Production)*
Sales & Customer Services Supervisor:
Dawn Angel

*Academic & Scholarly; Engineering;
Environment & Development Studies;
Geography & Geology; Scientific &
Technical*

New Titles: 25 (2008) , 25 (2009)
No of Employees: 13

ISBNs, Imprints & Series:
978 0 903317, 978 1 86239, 978 1 897799
Geological Society

Distributor for:
USA: American Association of Petroleum
Geologists; Geological Society of
America; SEPM

Overseas Representation:
India: EWP, New Delhi
Spain & Portugal: Iberian Book Services,
Madrid, Spain
USA: AAPG, Tulsa; Princeton Selling Group
Inc, Wayne, PA

Book Trade Association Membership:
Association of Learned & Professional
Society Publishers

2298

STANLEY GIBBONS
399 Strand, London WC2R 0LX
Telephone: (020) 7836 8444
Fax: (020) 7836 8444
Email: enquiries@stanleygibbons.co.uk
Web Site: stanleygibbons.com

Publishing, Mail Order:
7 Parkside, Christchurch Road, Ringwood,
Hants BH24 3SH
Telephone: 01425 472363
Fax: 01425 470247
Web Site: www.stanleygibbons.com

Chief Executive: Michael Hall
Directors: Mark Henley *(Finance)*
Ann-Marie Halligan *(Publishing)*
Chief Operating Officer: Donal Duff
Company Secretary: Richard Purkis
Marketing Manager: Alex Hanrahan

*Crafts & Hobbies; Reference Books,
Directories & Dictionaries*

New Titles: 26 (2008) , 30 (2009)
No of Employees: 120
Annual Turnover: £20M

ISBNs, Imprints & Series: 978 0 85259

Parent Company:
UK: Stanley

Associated Companies:
UK: Fraser's

Overseas Representation:
Australia: Renniks Publications Pty Ltd,
Banksmeadow, NSW
Belgium: N. V. deZittere (DZT)/Davo, Tielt
(Brabant)
Canada: Unitrade Associates, Toronto, Ont

Denmark: Samlerforum/Davo, Karup
Finland: Davo C/o Kapylan, Helsinki
France: ARPHI/Davo, Viroflay
Germany: Schaubek Verlag Leipzig,
  Markranstaedt
Italy: Ernesto Marini SRL, Genoa
Japan: Japan Philatelic, Tokyo
Netherlands: Uitgeverij Davo BV, Deventer
New Zealand: House of Stamps,
  Paraparaumu; Philatelic Distributors,
  New Plymouth
Norway: Skanfil A/S, Haugesund
Saudi Arabia: Arabian Stamp Centre,
  Riyadh
Singapore: C S Philatelic Agency
Sweden: Chr Winther Sorensen AB,
  Knaered
USA: Filatco, Appleton, WI

2299

GIBSON SQUARE
47 Lonsdale Square, London N1 1EW
Telephone: (020) 7096 1100
Fax: (020) 7993 2214
Email: info@gibsonsquare.com
Web Site: www.gibsonsquare.com

Warehouse:
Littlehampton Book Services,
Faraday Close, Durrington, Worthing,
West Sussex BN13 3RB
Telephone: 01903 828500
Fax: 01903 828802
Email: orders@lbsltd.co.uk
Web Site: www.lbsltd.co.uk

Publisher: Martin Rynja

*Biography & Autobiography; Cinema,
Video, TV & Radio; Fine Art & Art History;
Gay & Lesbian Studies; History &
Antiquarian; Humour; Philosophy; Politics &
World Affairs; Travel & Topography*

ISBNs, Imprints & Series:
978 1 903933, 978 1 906142

Overseas Representation:
Australia: Tower Books Pty Ltd, Frenchs
  Forest, NSW
Canada & USA: NBN, Blue Ridge Summit,
  PA, USA
New Zealand: Addenda Ltd, Grey Lynn

Book Trade Association Membership:
IPG

2300

GILL & MACMILLAN LTD
Hume Avenue, Park West, Dublin 12,
Republic of Ireland
Telephone: +353 (01) 500 9500
Fax: +353 (01) 500 9599
Email: ftobin@gillmacmillan.ie
Web Site: www.gillmacmillan.ie

Chairman: M. H. Gill
Directors: M. D. O'Dwyer *(Managing)*
  A. Murray *(Educational Publishing)*
  P. A. Thew *(Marketing & Sales)*
  B. D. Curtin *(Company Secretary/
    Financial)*
  M. O'Keeffe *(Production)*
  F. M. Tobin *(General Publishing)*
  J. Manning *(Distribution)*

*Academic & Scholarly; Biography &
Autobiography; Children's Books; Cookery,
Wines & Spirits; Economics; Educational &
Textbooks; Guide Books; History &
Antiquarian; Humour; Literature &
Criticism; Politics & World Affairs;
Psychology & Psychiatry; Reference Books,
Directories & Dictionaries; Travel &
Topography*

New Titles: 113 (2008) , 116 (2009)
No of Employees: 70
Annual Turnover: £9.5M

ISBNs, Imprints & Series:
978 0 7171 Newleaf; RíRá
978 0 946551, 978 1 858600 Gateway

Overseas Representation:
Australia: Brumby Books Holdings Pty Ltd,
  Kilsyth South, Vic
India, Pakistan & Sri Lanka: Pan Macmillan,
  New Delhi, India
Middle East, South East & North Asia: Pan
  Macmillan Asia, Hong Kong
New Zealand: New Holland Publishers (NZ)
  Ltd, Auckland
South Africa: Pan Macmillan SA Pty Ltd,
  Johannesburg
UK: Bounce! Sales & Marketing Ltd, London

Book Trade Association Membership:
CLÉ (Irish PA)

2301

GLASGOW MUSEUMS PUBLISHING
Glasgow Museums Resource Centre,
200 Woodhead Road, Glasgow G53 7NN
Telephone: 0141 276 9452
Fax: 0141 276 9305
Email: susan.pacitti@csglasgow.org
Web Site: www.glasgowmuseums.com

Managing Editor: Susan Pacitti

*Archaeology; Fashion & Costume; Fine Art
& Art History; History & Antiquarian;
Transport*

New Titles: 1 (2008) , 3 (2009)
No of Employees: 3

ISBNs, Imprints & Series: 978 0 902752

Parent Company:
Culture & Sport Glasgow

Book Trade Association Membership:
Publishing Scotland

2302

GLOBAL ORIENTAL LTD
PO Box 219, Folkestone CT20 2WP
Telephone: 01303 226799
Fax: 01303 243087
Email: info@globaloriental.co.uk
Web Site: www.globaloriental.co.uk

Distribution (UK):
Orca Book Services Ltd, Stanley House,
3 Fleets Lane, Poole, Dorset BH15 3AJ
Telephone: 01202 665432
Fax: 01202 666219

Managing Director & Publisher: Paul
  Norbury
Assistant Editor: David Blakeley

*Academic & Scholarly; Biography &
Autobiography; Fashion & Costume;
Gender Studies; Geography & Geology;
History & Antiquarian; Illustrated & Fine
Editions; Languages & Linguistics; Literature
& Criticism; Philosophy; Politics & World
Affairs; Psychology & Psychiatry; Religion &
Theology; Sociology & Anthropology; Travel
& Topography; Oriental*

New Titles: 22 (2008) , 32 (2009)

ISBNs, Imprints & Series:
978 1 86034 (selected)
978 1 874267 (selected)
978 1 901903, 978 1 905246
978 1 906876

Overseas Representation:
Australia: InBooks, Belrose, NSW
China: Access Asia Media Services,
  Shanghai, P. R. of China
India: Maya Publishers Pvt Ltd, New Delhi
Japan: United Publishers Services Ltd, Tokyo

Korea: Impact Korea, Seoul, Republic of
  Korea
Singapore & Malaysia: Taylor & Francis Asia
  Pacific, Singapore
Taiwan: Unifacmanu Trading Co Ltd, Taipei
USA: University of Hawai'i Press, Honolulu

2303

GLOBAL PROFESSIONAL
PUBLISHING
Random Acres, Slip Mill Lane, Hawkhurst,
Kent TN18 5AD
Telephone: 01580 753387
Fax: 01580 753201
Email: publishing@gppbooks.com
Web Site: www.gppbooks.com

Distribution:
Publishers Group UK, 8 The Arena,
Mollison Avenue, Enfield, Middx EN3 7NL
Telephone: (020) 8804 0400
Fax: (020) 8804 0044
Web Site: www.pguk.co.uk

Managing Director: Eric Dobby *(Sales &
  Rights)*
Executive: Nick Lockett

*Academic & Scholarly; Accountancy &
Taxation; Computer Science; Economics;
Educational & Textbooks; Electronic
(Educational); Electronic (Professional &
Academic); Industry, Business &
Management; Law; Mathematics &
Statistics; Reference Books, Directories &
Dictionaries*

New Titles: 40 (2008) , 50 (2009)
No of Employees: 2
Annual Turnover: £300,000

ISBNs, Imprints & Series:
978 0 85297, 978 1 906403

Parent Company:
Global Professional Publishing Holdings

Overseas Representation:
Australia: Woodslane, Mona Vale, NSW
Benelux: Jos de Jong, Just in Time
  Promotions, Heenstal, Netherlands
Eastern Europe: Dr László Horváth
  Publishers Representative, Budapest,
  Hungary
Italy, Greece & Cyprus: Charles Gibbes
  Associates, London, UK
Middle East & Malta: Avicenna Partnership,
  Oxford, UK
South Africa: Palgrave Macmillan,
  Johannesburg
South East Asia: Asia Publishers Services
  Ltd, Hong Kong
South West Asia: APD Singapore Pte Ltd,
  Singapore
Spain, Portugal & Gibraltar: Iberian Book
  Services, Madrid, Spain
USA & Canada: Stylus Publishing Inc,
  Sterling, VA, USA

2304

*GLOWWORM BOOKS & GIFTS LTD
Unit 4, Bishopsgate Business Park,
Broxburn EH52 5LH
Telephone: 01506 857570
Fax: 01506 858100
Web Site: www.glowwormbooks.co.uk

Directors: Katrena Allan *(Managing)*
  Gordon Allan *(Production)*

Children's Books

ISBNs, Imprints & Series:
978 0 955755, 978 1 871512

Book Trade Association Membership:
BSA

2305

*GLYNDWR PUBLISHING
PO Box 68, Cowbridge, Vale of Glamorgan
CF71 9AY
Telephone: 01446 775516
Email: breverton@hotmail.co.uk
Web Site: www.glyndwrpublishing.co.uk

Principal: T. Breverton

*Academic & Scholarly; Biography &
Autobiography; History & Antiquarian;
Military & War; Nautical; Reference Books,
Directories & Dictionaries*

ISBNs, Imprints & Series:
978 1 903529 Wales Books - Glyndwr
  Publishing

Associated Companies:
USA: Pelican Publishing Co

2306

ALAN GODFREY MAPS
Prospect Business Park, Leadgate, Consett
DH8 7PW
Telephone: 01207 583388
Fax: 01207 583399
Email: godfreyedition@btinternet.com
Web Site: www.alangodfreymaps.co.uk

Contact: Alan Godfrey

Atlases & Maps; History & Antiquarian

New Titles: 126 (2008) , 126 (2009)
No of Employees: 4

ISBNs, Imprints & Series:
978 0 85054, 978 0 907554, 978 1 84151,
  978 1 84784

Overseas Representation:
Australia: Mapworks, North Essendon, Vic
Germany: GeoCenter Touristik
  Medienservice GmbH, Stuttgart

Book Trade Association Membership:
British Cartographic Society

2307

GODSFIELD PRESS LTD
2–4 Heron Quays, London E14 4JP
Telephone: (020) 7531 8400
Fax: (020) 7531 8562
Email: publisher@godsfieldpress.com
Web Site: www.octopusbooks.co.uk/
  godsfield-press

Publisher: Jo Hemmings
UK Sales & Marketing: Steven Edney
Managing Editor: Clare Churly
Head of Foreign Rights: John Saunders-
  Griffiths

*Magic & the Occult; Medical (incl. Self Help
& Alternative Medicine); Religion &
Theology*

ISBNs, Imprints & Series:
978 1 84181, 978 1 899434

Parent Company:
Octopus Publishing Group

Associated Companies:
Bounty; Cassell Illustrated; Conran; Gaia;
  Hamlyn; Millers; Mitchell Beazley;
  Philip's; Spruce

2308

THE GOLDSMITH PRESS LTD
Newbridge, Co Kildare, Republic of Ireland
Telephone: +353 (045) 433613
Fax: +353 (045) 434648
Email: de@iol.ie

Director: Vivienne Abbott
Secretary: Breda Ennis

*Academic & Scholarly; Biography &
Autobiography; Cookery, Wines & Spirits;
English as a Foreign Language; Fine Art &
Art History; Literature & Criticism; Poetry*

No of Employees: 4

ISBNs, Imprints & Series: 978 1 870491

Book Trade Association Membership:
CLÉ (Irish PA)

2309 ━━━

VICTOR GOLLANCZ LTD
Orion House, 5 Upper St Martins Lane,
London WC2H 9EA
Telephone: (020) 7240 3444
Fax: (020) 7240 5822
Web Site: www.orionbooks.co.uk

Warehouse, Trade Enquiries & Orders:
see The Orion Publishing Group Ltd

Directors: Lisa Milton *(Managing)*
Dallas Manderson *(Group Sales)*
Mark Streatfeild *(Export Sales)*
Mark Prior *(Finance)*
Dominic Smith *(UK Sales)*
Simon Spanton *(Editorial)*
Jo Fletcher *(Editorial)*

Fiction; Science Fiction

ISBNs, Imprints & Series:
978 0 575 Victor Gollancz Ltd; VGSF

Parent Company:
The Orion Publishing Group Ltd

Overseas Representation:
see: The Orion Publishing Group Ltd,
London, UK

2310 ━━━

*GOMER
Llandysul, Ceredigion SA44 4JL
Telephone: 01559 363090
Fax: 01559 363758
Email: meinir@gomer.co.uk
Web Site: www.gomer.co.uk

Directors: J. H. Lewis *(Executive)*
Jonathan Lewis *(Managing)*
Mairwen Prys Jones *(Publishing)*
Accounts: Carol Bignell
Sales: Meinir James *(Head of Marketing)*

*Biography & Autobiography; Children's
Books; Fine Art & Art History; History &
Antiquarian; Languages & Linguistics;
Literature & Criticism; Photography;
Poetry; Reference Books, Directories &
Dictionaries; Sports & Games; Transport;
Welsh Language Publications*

ISBNs, Imprints & Series:
978 0 85088, 978 0 86383, 978 1 84323,
978 1 85902 Pont (English language
publications for children)

Parent Company:
J. D. Lewis & Sons Ltd

Book Trade Association Membership:
BA; IPG; Union of Welsh Publishers &
Booksellers

2311 ━━━

GOTHIC IMAGE PUBLICATIONS
PO Box 2568, Glastonbury, Somerset
BA6 8XR
Telephone: 01458 831281
Fax: 01458 833385
Email: publications@gothicimage.co.uk
Web Site: www.gothicimage.co.uk

Trade Orders:
PGUK, Mollison Avenue, Enfield, Middx
EN3 7NJ
Telephone: (020) 8804 0400
Fax: (020) 8804 0044

Directors: Frances Howard-Gordon *(All
titles - Editorial & Commissioning)*
Jamie George *(Export Sales)*
Diana Macleash *(Financial Controller)*

*Biography & Autobiography; Fine Art & Art
History; Guide Books; History &
Antiquarian; Humour; Illustrated & Fine
Editions; Magic & the Occult; Philosophy;
Photography; Politics & World Affairs;
Psychology & Psychiatry; Religion &
Theology; Travel & Topography*

New Titles: 3 (2008) , 2 (2009)
No of Employees: 3

ISBNs, Imprints & Series:
978 0 906362 Traveller's Guide Series

Overseas Representation:
Europe: PGUK, Enfield, UK
USA: SCB Distributors, Gardena, CA

2312 ━━━

GOWER PUBLISHING CO LTD
Wey Court East, Union Road, Farnham,
Surrey GU9 7PT
Telephone: 01252 331551
Fax: 01252 736736
Email: info@gowerpublishing.com
Web Site: www.gowerpublishing.com

**Customer Service Department/World
Distribution:**
Bookpoint Ltd, 39 Milton Park, Abingdon,
Oxon OX14 4TD
Telephone: 01235 400400
Fax: 01235 400454
Email: gower@bookpoint.co.uk
Web Site: www.gowerpub.com

Management: N. A. E. Farrow *(Chairman)*
Rachel Lynch *(Managing Director)*
Darren Wise *(Finance Director)*
Richard Dowling *(Sales Director)*
Josephine Burgess *(Director - Publishing
Systems)*
Jonathan Norman *(Publishing Director -
Training Resources & Business Books)*
Susan White *(Marketing Manager)*
Foreign Rights: K. Towndrow

*Accountancy & Taxation; Architecture &
Design; Educational & Textbooks;
Engineering; Industry, Business &
Management; Vocational Training & Careers*

ISBNs, Imprints & Series:
978 0 566 Gower
978 0 7546 Ashgate
978 0 85331 Lund Humphries

Parent Company:
Ashgate Publishing Co Ltd

Associated Companies:
USA: Ashgate Publishing Co

Overseas Representation:
*Africa (excluding South Africa & North
Africa):* InterMedia Africa Ltd (IMA),
London, UK
Central & Eastern Europe: Dr László Horváth
Publishers Representative, Budapest,
Hungary
India: Maya Publishers Pvt Ltd, New Delhi
Iran: Kowkab Publishers, Tehran
Japan: United Publishers Services Ltd, Tokyo
Korea: Information & Culture Korea (ICK),
Seoul, Republic of Korea
Middle East: Publishers International
Marketing, Burmarsh, UK
North & South America: Ashgate Publishing
Co, Burlington, VT, USA

Pakistan: Book Bird Publishers
Representatives, Lahore
*South East Asia, Myanmar (Burma), China,
Hong Kong, South Korea, Australia &
New Zealand:* Ashgate Publishing Asia-
Pacific, Newport, NSW, Australia

Book Trade Association Membership:
IPG

2313 ━━━

*GRACEWING PUBLISHING
Gracewing House, 2 Southern Avenue,
Leominster, Herefordshire HR6 0QF
Telephone: 01568 616835
Fax: 01568 613289
Email: gracewingx@aol.com
Web Site: www.gracewing.co.uk

Managing Director: Tom Longford *(Sales,
Editorial)*
Managers: Jo Ashworth *(Publishing)*
Adrian Hodnett *(Customer Service)*
Mary Clewer *(Accounts)*
Monica Manwaring *(Publicity)*

*Academic & Scholarly; Architecture &
Design; Biography & Autobiography; Guide
Books; History & Antiquarian; Philosophy;
Religion & Theology*

ISBNs, Imprints & Series: 978 0 85244

Distributor for:
Mercer University Press; Newman House;
OSV; Smyth & Helwys; St Bedes;
Templegate

Overseas Representation:
Australia: Freedom Publishing, North
Melbourne, Vic
Canada: Novalis Inc, Toronto, Ont
USA: Liturgy Training Publications, Chicago,
IL; Morehouse, Harrisburg, PA

2314 ━━━

GRAFFEG
2 Radnor Court, 256 Cowbridge Road East,
Cardiff CF5 1GZ
Telephone: (029) 2037 7312
Fax: (029) 2039 8101
Email: info@graffeg.com
Web Site: www.graffeg.com

Representation (Wales only):
Welsh Books Council, Castell Brychan,
Aberystwyth, Ceredigion SY23 2JB

Managing Director: Peter Gill
Marketing Manager: Vanessa Bufton

*Architecture & Design; Cookery, Wines &
Spirits; Gardening; Geography & Geology;
Guide Books; Natural History;
Photography; Travel & Topography*

New Titles: 9 (2008) , 2 (2009)

ISBNs, Imprints & Series:
978 0 9544334, 978 1 905582

Overseas Representation:
Worldwide: Antique Collectors' Club,
Woodbridge, Suffolk, UK

2315 ━━━

**W. F. GRAHAM (NORTHAMPTON)
LTD**
2 Pondwood Close, Moulton Park,
Northampton NN3 6RT
Telephone: 01604 645537
Fax: 01604 648414
Email: books@wfgraham.co.uk
Web Site: www.wfgraham.co.uk

Managing Director: Tim Graham
Manager: Ian Wilson *(General)*

Children's Books

No of Employees: 6

ISBNs, Imprints & Series: 978 1 85128

Overseas Representation:
West Indies: Humphrys Roberts Associates,
London, UK

2316 ━━━

*GRANADA LEARNING
The Chiswick Centre,
414 Chiswick High Road, London W4 5TF
Telephone: (020) 8996 3363
Fax: (020) 8742 8546
Email: mail@granadalearning.co.uk
Web Site: www.gl-assessment.co.uk

Educational & Textbooks

Book Trade Association Membership:
Publishers Association

2317 ━━━

GRANTA BOOKS
12 Addison Avenue, London W11 4QR
Telephone: (020) 7605 1360
Fax: (020) 7605 1361
Email: rights@granta.com
Web Site: www.granta.com

Trade Orders:
TBS Ltd, Distribution Centre,
Colchester Road, Frating Green, Colchester,
Essex CO7 7DW
Telephone: 01206 255678
Fax: 01206 255930
Email: mdl@macmillan.co.uk

Representation (UK):
Faber & Faber Ltd, Bloomsbury House,
74–77 Great Russell Street, London
WC1B 3DA
Telephone: (020) 7927 3800
Fax: (020) 7927 3801
Email: sales@faber.co.uk

Sales: Brigid Macleod
Publicity: Pru Rowlandson
Production: Sarah Wasley
Rights: Angela Rose
Editorial: Sara Holloway

*Biography & Autobiography; Fiction;
Politics & World Affairs; Travel &
Topography*

ISBNs, Imprints & Series:
978 0 90314 Granta Magazine
978 1 86207 Granta Books

Parent Company:
Granta Publications

Associated Companies:
Granta Magazine

Overseas Representation:
Australia & New Zealand: Allen & Unwin Pty
Ltd, Sydney, NSW, Australia
Canada: House of Anansi, Toronto, Ont
Europe: International Sales Director, Miles
Poynton, Faber & Faber, London, UK
Indian Subcontinent: Penguin Books India,
New Delhi, India
Northern Europe: Bridget Lane, Faber &
Faber, London, UK
Republic of Ireland: Repforce Ireland,
Irishtown, Dublin
South Africa: Penguin Books South Africa
(Pty) Ltd, Johannesburg
Southern Europe: Melissa Elders, Faber &
Faber, London, UK
*USA, Middle East, Eastern Europe, Africa
(excluding South Africa), Latin America &
Caribbean:* sales@granta.com, UK

2318 ■

GRANTA EDITIONS
25–27 High Street, Chesterton, Cambridge
CB4 1ND
Telephone: 01223 352790
Fax: 01223 460718
Email: bpc@bpccam.co.uk
Web Site: www.bpccam.co.uk

Warehouse:
CED, Over Industrial Park, 2 Norman Way,
Over, Cambridge CB24 5QE
Telephone: 01954 231957
Fax: 01954 230041

London Office:
The Baltic Exchange, St Mary Axe, London
EC3A 8EX
Telephone: (020) 7623 2308
Fax: (020) 7623 2309
Email: bpc@bpccam.co.uk
Web Site: www.bpccam.co.uk

Managing Director: Colin Walsh
Managers: Susan Buck (Accounts)
Jo Littlechild (Marketing)
Jo'e Coleby (Editorial Project)

Academic & Scholarly; Accountancy &
Taxation; Agriculture; Antiques &
Collecting; Aviation; Biography &
Autobiography; Cookery, Wines & Spirits;
Do-It-Yourself; Educational & Textbooks;
Environment & Development Studies;
Fashion & Costume; Fine Art & Art History;
Guide Books; Health & Beauty; Illustrated &
Fine Editions; Law; Medical (incl. Self Help &
Alternative Medicine); Music; Natural
History; Nautical; Reference Books,
Directories & Dictionaries; Scientific &
Technical; Sports & Games; Theatre, Drama
& Dance; Travel & Topography

ISBNs, Imprints & Series:
978 0 906782, 978 1 857570

Parent Company:
Book Production Consultants Ltd

Associated Companies:
Book Connections Ltd

2319 ■

GREEN BOOKS
Foxhole, Dartington, Totnes, Devon
TQ9 6EB
Telephone: 01803 863843 & 863260
Fax: 01803 863843
Email: sales@greenbooks.co.uk
Web Site: www.greenbooks.co.uk

UK Trade Distribution:
Central Books, 99 Wallis Road, London
E9 5LN
Telephone: 0845 458 9911
Fax: 0845 458 9912
Email: info@centralbooks.com
Web Site: www.centralbooks.com

Publisher: John Elford
Sales & Marketing: Bee West
Editorial: Amanda Cuthbert

Architecture & Design; Biography &
Autobiography; Cookery, Wines & Spirits;
Do-It-Yourself; Economics; Environment &
Development Studies; Fine Art & Art
History; Gardening; Guide Books; Health &
Beauty; Literature & Criticism; Natural
History; Philosophy; Poetry; Politics & World
Affairs; Reference Books, Directories &
Dictionaries; Travel & Topography

New Titles: 15 (2008) , 15 (2009)
No of Employees: 5
Annual Turnover: £700,000

ISBNs, Imprints & Series:
978 0 9527302 Themis Books

978 1 870098 Green Books & Resurgence
Books
978 1 900322 Green Earth Books
978 1 903998 Green Books

Distributor for:
USA: Chelsea Green Publishing Co [selected
titles]

Overseas Representation:
Australia: Brumby Books Holdings Pty Ltd,
Kilsyth South, Vic
New Zealand: Ceres Books, Ellerslie
USA: Chelsea Green Publishing Co, White
River Junction, VT

Book Trade Association Membership:
IPG

2320 ■

*GREEN MAGIC
The Long Barn, Sutton Mallet, Somerset
TA7 9AR
Telephone: 01278 722888
Fax: 01278 722565
Email: petergotto@aol.com
Web Site:
www.greenmagicpublishing.com

Representation (UK):
Counter Culture, (address as above)
Telephone: (as above)
Fax: (as above)

Representation:
Bookspeed, 16 Salamander Yards,
Edinburgh EH6 7DD

Owner: Pete Gotto

Archaeology; Magic & the Occult; Medical
(incl. Self Help & Alternative Medicine);
Religion & Theology; Travel & Topography

ISBNs, Imprints & Series:
978 0 9536631, 978 0 9542963, 978 0
9547230

Overseas Representation:
Australia: Brumby Books Holdings Pty Ltd,
Kilsyth South, Vic
Canada: Marginal Distribution,
Peterborough
New Zealand: Peaceful Living Publications,
Auckland
South Africa: Bacchus Books, Gauteng
USA: SCB Distributors, Gardena, CA

Book Trade Association Membership:
BA

2321 ■

***W. GREEN THE SCOTTISH LAW
PUBLISHER**
[a Thomson Company]
21 Alva Street, Edinburgh EH2 4PS
Telephone: 0131 225 4879
Fax: 0131 225 2104
Email: Alan.Bett@thomson.com
Web Site: www.wgreen.thomson.com

Director: Mrs Gilly Grant
Marketing Manager: Alan Bett
Publisher: Mrs Jill Hyslop

Law

ISBNs, Imprints & Series: 978 0 414

Parent Company:
International Thomson Corporation

Overseas Representation:
Australia: The Law Book Co Ltd, North Ryde
Bangladesh: Karim International, Dhaka
Botswana: Kerrison Book Services,
Gaborone
Canada: Carswell Publishing Ltd,
Scarborough, Ont

Ghana: J. A. Amoah, Accra
India: N. M. Tripathi Pte Ltd, Bombay
Israel: Steimatzky Ltd, Bnei Brak
Japan: Macmillan Shuppan KK, Tokyo
Kenya, Tanzania, Uganda & Mauritius:
Kelvin van Hasselt Publishing Services,
Briningham, Norfolk, UK
Malawi, Zambia & Zimbabwe: Barbie
Keene, Harare, Zimbabwe
Malaysia, Singapore & Brunei: Malayan Law
Journal Pte Ltd, Singapore
Pakistan: Pakistan Law House, Karachi

Book Trade Association Membership:
Publishing Scotland

2322 ■

**GREENHILL BOOKS / LIONEL
LEVENTHAL LTD**
3 Barham Avenue, Elstree, Herts WD6 3PW
Telephone: (020) 8953 4969
Fax: (020) 8953 4969
Email: l.leventhal@hotmail.co.uk
Web Site: www.greenhillbooks.com

Warehouse:
Bookpoint Ltd, 39 Milton Park, Abingdon,
Oxon OX14 4TD
Telephone: 01235 400400
Fax: 01235 832068

Director: Lionel Leventhal

Aviation; History & Antiquarian; Military &
War

Overseas Representation:
Australia & New Zealand: Peribo Pty Ltd,
Mount Kuring-Gai, NSW, Australia
Austria, Switzerland, Czech & Slovak
Republics, Hungary, Poland, Croatia,
Slovenia, Spain (including Gibraltar) &
Portugal: Sandro Salucci, Florence, Italy
Belgium: De Krijger, Erps
Canada: Vanwell Publishing Ltd, St
Catharines, Ont
France & Netherlands: Casemate Books,
Newbury, UK
Germany: Robbert J. Pleysier, Heerde,
Netherlands
India: Knowledge World International, Delhi
Middle East & Far East: Publishers
International Marketing, Burmarsh, UK
New Zealand: South Pacific Books (Imports)
Ltd, Auckland
South Africa: Peter Renew, Titles SA,
Johannesburg
USA: MBI Publishing Co, St Paul, MN

2323 ■

GREENLEAF PUBLISHING
Aizlewood's Mill, Nursery Street, Sheffield
S3 8GG
Telephone: 0114 282 3475
Fax: 0114 282 3476
Email: sales@greenleaf-publishing.com
Web Site: www.greenleaf-publishing.com

Office Manager: Jayney Bown
Directors: Dean Bargh (Editorial)
John Stuart (Managing)

Academic & Scholarly; Educational &
Textbooks; Environment & Development
Studies; Industry, Business & Management;
Scientific & Technical

No of Employees: 4

ISBNs, Imprints & Series:
978 1 874719, 978 1 906093

Overseas Representation:
Australia: DA Information Services Pty Ltd,
Mitcham, Vic
India: Viva Books, New Delhi
Taiwan: Unifacmanu Trading Co Ltd, Taipei
USA & Canada: Renouf Publishing Co Ltd,
Ottawa, Ont, Canada

2324 ■

*GREENLIGHT PUBLISHING
119 Newland Street, Witham, Essex
CM8 1WF
Telephone: 01376 521900
Fax: 01376 521901
Email: alan@acguk.com
Web Site: www.greenlightpublishing.co.uk

Managing Director: Alan Golbourn
IT Manager: Daniel Golbourn

Antiques & Collecting; Archaeology; Crafts
& Hobbies

ISBNs, Imprints & Series: 978 1 897738

Parent Company:
UK: Ace Publications Ltd

2325 ■

*GREENWOOD PUBLISHING GROUP
Wilkinson House, Jordan Hill, Oxford
OX2 8DP
Telephone: 01865 314201
Fax: 01865 314657
Email: suzanne.wheatley@harcourt.co.uk
Web Site: www.greenwood.com &
www.heineman.com

Customer Service:
Linacre House, Jordan Hill, Oxford OX2 8DP
Telephone: 01865 888181
Fax: 01865 314091
Email:
greenwood.enquiries@harcourt.co.uk

Representation:
Roundhouse Group, Millstone, Limers Lane,
Northam, Devon EX39 2RG
Telephone: 01237 474474
Fax: 01237 474774
Email: roundhouse.group@ukgateway.net

Director: Tony Sloggett
Marketing Manager: Suzanne Wheatley
Senior Acquisitions Editor: Simon Mason

Academic & Scholarly; Bibliography &
Library Science; Biography &
Autobiography; Cinema, Video, TV &
Radio; Economics; Educational &
Textbooks; Gender Studies; History &
Antiquarian; Industry, Business &
Management; Law; Literature & Criticism;
Medical (incl. Self Help & Alternative
Medicine); Military & War; Music;
Philosophy; Politics & World Affairs;
Psychology & Psychiatry; Reference Books,
Directories & Dictionaries; Religion &
Theology; Science Fiction; Sociology &
Anthropology; Sports & Games; Theatre,
Drama & Dance

ISBNs, Imprints & Series:
978 0 275 Praeger Publishers
978 0 313, 978 0 8371 Greenwood Press
978 0 325 Heinemann USA
978 0 86569 Auburn House
978 0 86709 Boynton/Cook
978 0 89789 Bergin & Garvey
978 0 89930, 978 1 56720 Quorum Books
978 1 56750 Ablex Publishing
978 1 57356 Oryx Press
978 1 84645 Greenwood World Publishing

Parent Company:
Houghton Mifflin Harcourt

Overseas Representation:
Africa: Kelvin van Hasselt Publishing
Services, Briningham, Norfolk, UK
Australia & New Zealand: DA Information
Services Pty Ltd, Mitcham, Vic, Australia
Canada (Institutional orders only): Edu
Reference Publishers Direct Inc, Toronto,
Ont, Canada
Cyprus, Malta, Turkey, Jordan, Palestine,

Morocco, Tunisia & Algeria: Claire de Gruchy, Avicenna Partnership, Oxford, UK
Egypt, Gulf States, Iran, Iraq, Lebanon, Libya & Syria: Bill Kennedy, Avicenna Partnership, Oxford, UK
Europe: Andrew Durnell Marketing Ltd, Tunbridge Wells, UK
Hong Kong, Taiwan, China & Korea: Asia Publishers Services Ltd, Hong Kong
India, Sri Lanka, Bangladesh & Pakistan: Overleaf, New Delhi, India
Israel: Franklins International, Tel Aviv
Japan: Yushodo Co Ltd, Tokyo
Mexico, Central & South America & Caribbean (including Puerto Rico): Cranbury International LLC, Montpelier, VT, USA
Singapore, Malaysia, Thailand, Indonesia, Philippines, Brunei, Vietnam, Camabodia & Laos: APD Singapore Pte Ltd, Singapore
South Africa: Heinemann International South Africa, Sandton

2326

GRESHAM BOOKS LTD
19–21 Sayers Lane, Tenterden, Kent TN30 6BW
Telephone: 01580 767596
Fax: 01580 764142
Email: info@gresham-books.co.uk
Web Site: www.gresham-books.co.uk

Directors: Nicholas Oulton *(Managing)*
Louise Martine

History & Antiquarian; Music; Religion & Theology

No of Employees: 3
Annual Turnover: £350,000

ISBNs, Imprints & Series:
978 0 905418, 978 0 946095, 978 0 9502121

Parent Company:
UK: Galore Park Publishing Ltd

2327

GRUB STREET
4 Rainham Close, London SW11 6SS
Telephone: (020) 7924 3966 & 7738 1008
Fax: (020) 7738 1009
Email: post@grubstreet.co.uk
Web Site: www.grubstreet.co.uk

Distribution:
Littlehampton Book Services Ltd, Faraday Close, Durrington, Worthing, West Sussex BN13 3RB
Telephone: 01903 828500
Fax: 01903 828802
Email: ...@lbsltd.co.uk
Web Site: www.lbsltd.co.uk

Director: John Davies
Sales & Marketing: Anne Dolamore

Aviation; Cookery, Wines & Spirits; Military & War

New Titles: 34 (2008) , 36 (2009)
No of Employees: 5
Annual Turnover: £940,000

ISBNs, Imprints & Series:
978 0 948817, 978 1 898697, 978 1 902304, 978 1 904010, 978 1 904943, 978 1 906502

Overseas Representation:
Asia & Middle East: Grub Street, London, UK
Australia: Capricorn Link (Australia) Pty Ltd, Windsor, NSW
Canada: Vanwell Publishing Ltd, St Catharines, Ont
New Zealand: Nationwide Book Distributors

North & West Europe: EMS (Anselm Robinson), London, UK
Republic of Ireland: Vivienne Lavery, Blackrock, Co Dublin
Scandinavia: Angell Eurosales, Berwick-on-Tweed, UK
South Africa: Penguin Books South Africa (Pty) Ltd, Johannesburg
Southern Europe: Jenny & Penny Padovani, London, UK
USA: Casemate Publishers & Book Distributors LLC, Havertown, PA

Book Trade Association Membership:
IPG; BA (Associate Member)

2328

GUILDHALL PRESS
Unit 15, Rath Mor Centre, Bligh's Lane, Derry BT48 0LZ
Telephone: (028) 7136 4413
Fax: (028) 7137 2949
Email: info@ghpress.com
Web Site: www.ghpress.com

Manager: Paul Hippsley *(Project & Managing Editor, Marketing)*

Academic & Scholarly; Biography & Autobiography; Children's Books; Crime; Educational & Textbooks; Fiction; Gay & Lesbian Studies; Guide Books; History & Antiquarian; Humour; Literature & Criticism; Music; Photography; Poetry; Politics & World Affairs; Theatre, Drama & Dance

ISBNs, Imprints & Series: 978 0 946451

Overseas Representation:
Australia: Irish Book Centre, Melbourne
USA: Irish Books & Media Inc, Minneapolis, MN

Book Trade Association Membership:
CLÉ (Irish PA)

2329

GULLANE CHILDREN'S BOOKS
See: Meadowside Children's Books

2330

GWASG CARREG GWALCH
12 Iard yr Orsaf, Llanrwst, Conwy LL26 0EH
Telephone: 01492 642031
Fax: 01492 641502
Email: llyfrau@carreg-gwalch.com
Web Site: www.carreg-gwalch.com

Manager: Myrddin ap Dafydd
Editor: Gordon Jones

Folklore; Welsh Interest

New Titles: 85 (2008) , 85 (2009)
No of Employees: 14
Annual Turnover: £700,000

ISBNs, Imprints & Series:
978 0 86381, 978 1 84524, 978 1 84527

Overseas Representation:
Worldwide: Welsh Book Centre, Aberystwyth, UK

Book Trade Association Membership:
Welsh PA

2331

GWASG GWENFFRWD
PO Box 21, Corwen LL21 9WZ
Telephone: 0845 330 6754

Director of Research: Dr H. G. A. Hughes

Academic & Scholarly; Bibliography & Library Science; Biography &

Autobiography; Children's Books; Educational & Textbooks; Electronic (Professional & Academic); History & Antiquarian; Languages & Linguistics; Literature & Criticism; Poetry; Politics & World Affairs; Reference Books, Directories & Dictionaries; Religion & Theology; Sociology & Anthropology; Travel & Topography

ISBNs, Imprints & Series:
978 0 9501861, 978 1 85651

2332

GWASG GWYNEDD
Hafryn, Llwyn Hudol, Pwllheli, Gwynedd LL53 5YE
Telephone: 01758 612483

Managing Director: Alwyn Elis
Editor: Nan Elis

Biography & Autobiography; Children's Books; Welsh Interest

New Titles: 12 (2008) , 12 (2009)
No of Employees: 4

ISBNs, Imprints & Series: 978 0 86074

2333

HACHETTE CHILDREN'S BOOKS
338 Euston Road, London NW1 3BH
Telephone: (020) 7873 6000
Fax: (020) 7873 6024
Email: gm@hachettechildrens.co.uk

Distribution Centre:
Bookpoint Ltd, 130 Milton Park, Abingdon, Oxon OX14 4SB
Telephone: 01235 400400
Fax: 01235 400445

Directors: Marlene Johnson *(Managing)*
Catherine Newman *(Chief Operating Officer)*
Les Phipps *(Group Sales)*
Andrew Sharp *(Group Rights)*
Charmian Allwright *(Group Production)*
Margaret Conroy *(Publishing (Audio & Licensed))*
Anne McNeil *(Publishing (Picture Books & Fiction))*
Susan Barry *(Marketing)*
Rachel Cooke *(Franklin Watts)*
Anne Marimuthu *(Finance)*
Paul Litherland *(Trade Sales)*
Penny Morris *(Orchard Books)*

Audio Books; Children's Books; Educational & Textbooks; Fiction; Fine Art & Art History; Poetry; Reference Books, Directories & Dictionaries; Books for Babies; Novelty Books

New Titles: 1452 (2008) , 1332 (2009)
No of Employees: 110

ISBNs, Imprints & Series:
Aladdin/Watts; Animal Ark Series; Felicity Wishes range; Franklin Watts; Hodder Home Learning Series; Orchard Books; Rainbow Magic
978 0 340 Hodder Children's Books; Kipper range
978 0 750 Hodder Wayland

Parent Company:
Hachette UK

Distributor for:
Aladdin

Overseas Representation:
Africa, West Indies, South & Central America: Tony Moggach, InterMedia Americana (IMA) Ltd, London, UK
Australia: Hachette Livre Australia, Sydney, NSW

Australia & New Zealand: Watts ANZ, Sydney, NSW, Australia
Brazil (paperbacks): Agencia Siciliano de Livros, São Paulo, Brazil
Canada (trade & paperbacks): McArthur & Co Publishers Ltd, Toronto, Ont, Canada
Eastern Europe: David Williams, InterMedia Americana (IMA) Ltd, London, UK
Germany, Switzerland & Austria: Gabriele Kern Publishers Services, Frankfurt-am-Main, Germany
Hong Kong: Publishers' Associates Ltd
India: Ajay Parmar, New Delhi
Israel: Steimatzky Ltd, Bnei Brak
Italy, Spain, Portugal & Gibraltar: Penny Padovani, London, UK
Japan & Korea: Yasy Murayama, Ageo, Japan
Netherlands (trade): Nilsson & Lamm BV, Weesp, Netherlands
New Zealand: Hachette Livre New Zealand, Auckland
Norway, Sweden, Finland, Denmark, Iceland, Netherlands & France: Angell Eurosales, Berwick-on-Tweed, UK
Pakistan (paperbacks): Liberty Books (Pvt) Ltd, Karachi, Pakistan
Republic of Ireland & Northern Ireland: Repforce Ireland Ltd, Monkstown, Republic of Ireland
Singapore & Malaysia: APD Singapore Pte Ltd, Singapore
South Africa: Jonathan Ball Publishers (Pty) Ltd, Jeppestown; Pan Macmillan SA Pty Ltd, Hyde Park
South Africa & Southern Africa (Wayland): Pan Macmillan SA Pty Ltd, Hyde Park, South Africa
Southern Africa (trade): Jonathan Ball Publishers (Pty) Ltd, Johannesburg, South Africa

Book Trade Association Membership:
Publishers Association; EPC

2334

*HACHETTE LIVRE UK LTD
338 Euston Road, London NW1 3BH
Telephone: (020) 7873 6000
Fax: (020) 7873 6024
Web Site: www.hachettelivre.co.uk

Academic & Scholarly; Children's Books; Educational & Textbooks; Electronic (Professional & Academic); Law; Medical (incl. Self Help & Alternative Medicine); Religion & Theology; Trade

Associated Companies:
UK: Philip Allan; Chambers Harrap Publishers Ltd; Hachette Children's Books; Hodder & Stoughton; Hodder Education Group; Little, Brown Group UK; John Murray; Octopus Publishing Group; Orion Publishing Group; Piatkus Books

Book Trade Association Membership:
Publishers Association

2335

HACHETTE SCOTLAND
2A Christie Street, Paisley PA1 1NB
Telephone: 0141 552 8082
Email:
bob.mcdevitt@hachettescotland.co.uk
Web Site: www.hachettescotland.co.uk

Publisher: Bob McDevitt
Editor: Wendy McCance
Regional Sales Manager: Gillian McKay

Biography & Autobiography; Cookery, Wines & Spirits; Crime; Fiction; Health & Beauty; History & Antiquarian; Humour; Military & War; Music; Sports & Games

New Titles: 1 (2008) , 10 (2009)
No of Employees: 3
Annual Turnover: £750,000

ISBNs, Imprints & Series: 978 0 7553

Parent Company:
UK: Hachette UK

Overseas Representation:
British Commonwealth of Nations (including Canada): Peter Newsom, Headline Export Sales, London, UK

Book Trade Association Membership:
Publishers Association; Publishing Scotland

2336 ▬

PETER HADDOCK PUBLISHING
Pinfold Lane, Bridlington, East Yorkshire YO16 6BT
Telephone: 01262 678121
Fax: 01262 400043
Email: sales@phpublishing.co.uk
Web Site: www.phpublishing.co.uk

Directors: Rodney Noon *(Managing)*
David Haddock
Pat Hornby
Managers: Peter Thornton *(Shipping)*
Brian Pannhausen *(Warehouse)*
Jason Hickey *(Customer Services)*

Children's Books; Reference Books, Directories & Dictionaries

ISBNs, Imprints & Series:
Big Time
978 0 7105

Parent Company:
D. C. Thomson & Co Ltd

Book Trade Association Membership:
BA

2337 ▬

HALBAN PUBLISHERS
22 Golden Square, Piccadilly, London W1F 9JW
Telephone: (020) 7437 9300
Fax: (020) 7437 9512
Email: books@halbanpublishers.com
Web Site: www.halbanpublishers.com

Distribution:
Littlehampton Book Services,
Faraday Close, Durrington, Worthing,
West Sussex BN13 3RB
Telephone: 01903 828842
Fax: 01903 828621
Email: rose.mellish@lbsltd.co.uk

Directors: Peter Halban
Martine Halban

Biography & Autobiography; Fiction; History & Antiquarian; Literature & Criticism; Philosophy; Politics & World Affairs; Religion & Theology

ISBNs, Imprints & Series:
978 1 870015, 978 1 905559

Overseas Representation:
Australia: Allen & Unwin Pty Ltd, Crows Nest, NSW
Canada: McArthur & Co Publishers Ltd, Toronto, Ont
Caribbean: Humphrys Roberts Associates, London, UK
East & West Africa: Richard Carman Associates, Northwich, UK
Europe (excluding Scandinavia & Netherlands): c/o Florence Chatelain, The Orion Publishing Group Ltd, London, UK
India, Sri Lanka & Bangladesh: Maya Publishers Pvt Ltd, New Delhi, India
Japan, South East Asia, Far East & Pakistan: Ralph & Sheila Summers, Woodford Green, Essex, UK
Middle East & North Africa: Peter Ward Book Exports, London, UK
Netherlands: Consul Books, Blaricum

New Zealand: Hodder Moa Beckett Publishers (NZ) Ltd, Auckland
Republic of Ireland: Gill Hess Ltd, Skerries, Co Dublin
Russia, Baltic States & former USSR: Tony Moggach, IMA, London, UK
Scandinavia: Pernille Larsen (Books for Europe), Roskilde, Denmark
South Africa: Jonathan Ball Publishers (Pty) Ltd, Johannesburg
South America: Humphrys Roberts Associates, Cotia SP, Brazil
USA & other territories: Export Department, The Orion Publishing Group Ltd, London, UK
Yugoslavia, Bosnia, Romania, Poland, Bulgaria, Hungary, Czech Republic, Slovakia, Slovenia & Croatia: Csaba & Jackie Lengyel de Bagota, Budapest, Hungary

Book Trade Association Membership:
IPG

2338 ▬

HALDANE MASON LTD
PO Box 34196, London NW10 3YB
Telephone: (020) 8459 2131
Fax: (020) 8728 1216
Email: info@haldanemason.com
Web Site: www.haldanemason.com

Warehouse, Trade Enquiries & Orders:
Vine House Distribution Ltd,
The Old Mill House, Mill Lane, Uckfield,
East Sussex TN22 5AA
Telephone: 01825 767396
Fax: 01825 765649
Email: sales@vinehouseuk.co.uk

Directors: Ron Samuel
Ms Sydney Francis

Children's Books; Cookery, Wines & Spirits; Crafts & Hobbies; Educational & Textbooks; Health & Beauty; Medical (incl. Self Help & Alternative Medicine); Natural History; Sports & Games

ISBNs, Imprints & Series:
Haldane Mason; Red Kite Books
978 1 902463
978 1 905339

Book Trade Association Membership:
IPG

2339 ▬

ROBERT HALE LTD
Clerkenwell House,
45–47 Clerkenwell Green, London
EC1R 0HT
Telephone: (020) 7251 2661
Fax: (020) 7490 4958
Email: enquire@halebooks.com
Web Site: www.halebooks.com

Warehouse & Returns:
Combined Book Services, Units I/K,
Paddock Wood Distribution Centre,
Paddock Wood, Tonbridge, Kent TN12 6UU
Telephone: 01892 837171
Fax: 01892 837272
Email: orders@combook.co.uk

Directors: John Hale *(Managing)*
Robert Kynaston *(Finance)*
Managers: Nick Chaytor *(Rights)*
Gill Jackson *(General)*
Robert Hale *(Production)*
Victoria Lyle *(Editorial)*

Animal Care & Breeding; Antiques & Collecting; Biography & Autobiography; Cinema, Video, TV & Radio; Crafts & Hobbies; Crime; Fiction; Humour; Magic & the Occult; Military & War; Music; Natural History; Photography; Politics & World Affairs; Reference Books, Directories & Dictionaries; Travel & Topography

ISBNs, Imprints & Series:
978 0 7090, 978 0 7091, 978 0 7198 NAG Press
978 0 85131 J. A. Allen

Distributor for:
Phoenix

Overseas Representation:
Australia: DLS Australia (Pty) Ltd, Braeside, Vic
France, Germany, Netherlands, Austria & Switzerland: Ted Dougherty, London, UK
Italy, Spain, Portugal, Greece & Gibraltar: Penny Padovani, London, UK
New Zealand: South Pacific Books (Imports) Ltd, Auckland
South Africa: Trinity Books CC, Randburg
USA: Trafalgar Square Publishing, North Pomfret, VT

2340 ▬

HALSGROVE
Halsgrove House, Ryelands Estate,
Bagley Road, Wellington, Somerset
TA21 9PZ
Telephone: 01823 653777
Fax: 01823 665294
Email: sales@halsgrove.com
Web Site: www.halsgrove.com

Managing Director: Julian Davidson
Chairman: Steven Pugsley
Publisher: Simon Butler

Archaeology; Aviation; Biography & Autobiography; Fine Art & Art History; Guide Books; History & Antiquarian; Illustrated & Fine Editions; Military & War; Natural History; Travel & Topography

New Titles: 180 (2008) , 200 (2009)
No of Employees: 15
Annual Turnover: £1.8M

ISBNs, Imprints & Series:
978 0 906551 Rylands
978 0 906690 Halstar
978 1 84114 Halsgrove

Parent Company:
UK: D. A. A. Halsgrove Ltd

Associated Companies:
UK: Halstar Ltd

Distributor for:
UK: Halsgrove; Halstar; Ryelands

2341 ▬

HAMBLEDON CONTINUUM LTD
see: Continuum International Publishing Group

2342 ▬

HAMMERSMITH PRESS LTD
496 Fulham Palace Road, London SW6 6JD
Telephone: (020) 7736 9132
Fax: (020) 7348 7521
Email: gmb@hammersmithpress.co.uk
Web Site: www.hammersmithpress.co.uk

Distribution:
Combined Book Services, Unit Y,
Paddock Wood Distribution Centre,
Paddock Wood, Tonbridge, Kent TN12 6UU
Telephone: 01892 837171
Fax: 01892 837272
Email: orders@combook.co.uk
Web Site: www.combook.co.uk

Director: Georgina Bentliff

Biography & Autobiography; Health & Beauty; Medical (incl. Self Help & Alternative Medicine)

New Titles: 5 (2008) , 8 (2009)
Annual Turnover: £85,000

ISBNs, Imprints & Series: 978 1 905140

Book Trade Association Membership:
IPG

2343 ▬

HANBURY PLAYS
Keeper's Lodge, Broughton Green,
Droitwich, Worcs WR9 7EE
Telephone: 01527 821564
Email: hanburyplays@tiscali.co.uk
Web Site: www.hanburyplays.co.uk

Proprietor: Brian J. Burton

Theatre, Drama & Dance; Plays

New Titles: 6 (2008) , 14 (2009)

ISBNs, Imprints & Series:
978 0 85197, 978 0 907926, 978 1 85205

Distributor for:
USA: Contemporary Drama Service; Pioneer Drama Service

Overseas Representation:
Australia: The Dominie Group, Brookvale, NSW
Malta: Dingli Co International, Valletta
New Zealand: Play Bureau of New Zealand Ltd, New Plymouth

2344 ▬

HARDEN'S LTD
14 Buckingham Street, London WC2N 6DF
Telephone: (020) 7839 4763
Fax: (020) 7839 7561
Email: rh@hardens.com
Web Site: www.hardens.com

Directors: Richard Harden
Peter Harden

Guide Books; Reference Books, Directories & Dictionaries

ISBNs, Imprints & Series: 978 1 873721

2345 ▬

HARLEQUIN MILLS & BOON LTD
Eton House, 18–24 Paradise Road,
Richmond, Surrey TW9 1SR
Telephone: (020) 8288 2800
Fax: (020) 8288 2899
Web Site: www.millsandboon.co.uk

Directors: Guy Hallowes *(Managing)*
Stuart Barber *(Finance & IS, Company Secretary)*
Karin Stoecker *(Editorial)*
Jackie McGee *(Human Resources)*
Clare Somerville *(Retail Sales & Marketing)*
Angela Meredith *(Retail Operations & Production)*
Tim Cooper *(Direct Marketing)*
Ian Roberts *(Sales)*

Fiction; Trade

No of Employees: 99
Annual Turnover: £19.8M

Book Trade Association Membership:
Publishers Association

2346 ▬

HARPERCOLLINS PUBLISHERS LTD
77–85 Fulham Palace Road, London
W6 8JB
Telephone: (020) 8741 7070
Fax: (020) 8307 4440
Email: enquiries@harpercollins.co.uk
Web Site: www.harpercollins.co.uk

Registered Office (Warehouse, Trade Orders & Distribution, Finance):
Westerhill Road, Bishopbriggs, Glasgow
G64 2QR
Telephone: 0141 772 3200
Fax: 0141 772 3200 x3119

Chief Executive Officer: Victoria Barnsley
(*Publisher*)
Chief Operating Officer: Keith Mullock
(*Executive*)
Managing Directors: Robert Scriven
(*Languages*)
Mario Santos (*Children's*)
Belinda Budge (*Publisher, HarperCollins*)
John Bond (*Press Books*)
David Swarbrick (*Group Sales & Marketing*)
Nigel Ward (*Education*)
Katie Fulford (*Special Projects*)
Directors: James Graves (*Group Production*)
Lucy Vanderbilt (*Rights, General Books*)
Sylvia May (*International Sales, General Books*)
Myles Archibald (*Rights & Associate Publisher - Collins Reference*)
Helen Ellis (*Publicity*)
Executive Directors: Julian Thomas
(*Business Systems & Services*)
Sean Plunkett (*Supply Chain*)
Ed Kielbasiewicz (*Finance*)
Siobhan Kenny (*Communications*)
Publishing Directors: Denise Bates
(*Illustrated Reference*)
Julia Wisdom (*Harper Fiction, Crime*)
Susan Watt (*Harper Fiction*)
Jonathan Taylor (*Harper Sport*)
Jane Johnson (*Harper Fiction, Voyager*)
Gillie Russell (*Children's Fiction*)
Sally Potter (*Harper Thorsons/Harper Element*)
Nick Pearson (*Fourth Estate*)
David Brawn (*Tolkien & Estates*)
Sue Buswell (*Children's Picture Books*)
Clare Smith (*Harper Press Fiction*)
Arabella Pike (*Harper Press Non-Fiction*)
Lynne Drew (*Harper Fiction*)

Animal Care & Breeding; Antiques & Collecting; Architecture & Design; Atlases & Maps; Audio Books; Biography & Autobiography; Biology & Zoology; Chemistry; Children's Books; Cinema, Video, TV & Radio; Cookery, Wines & Spirits; Crafts & Hobbies; Crime; Do-It-Yourself; Economics; Educational & Textbooks; Electronic (Educational); Electronic (Entertainment); Electronic (Professional & Academic); English as a Foreign Language; Environment & Development Studies; Fiction; Fine Art & Art History; Gardening; Gender Studies; Geography & Geology; Guide Books; Health & Beauty; History & Antiquarian; Humour; Illustrated & Fine Editions; Industry, Business & Management; Languages & Linguistics; Literature & Criticism; Magic & the Occult; Medical (incl. Self Help & Alternative Medicine); Military & War; Music; Natural History; Photography; Physics; Poetry; Politics & World Affairs; Psychology & Psychiatry; Reference Books, Directories & Dictionaries; Religion & Theology; Science Fiction; Scientific & Technical; Sports & Games; Travel & Topography

ISBNs, Imprints & Series:
Collins; Collins Classics; Collins Crime;
Collins Dictionaries COBUILD; Collins
New Naturalist Library; Collins Teacher;
Collins/Times Maps & Atlases;
CollinsEducation; CollinsGems; Fourth
Estate; Harper Perennial; Harper Sport;
HarperCollins; HarperCollins Audio;
HarperCollins Children's Books;
HarperCollins Entertainment;
HarperCollins Non-Fiction; Janes; Times
Books; Tolkien; Voyager

Parent Company:
News Corporation

Overseas Representation:
Australia: HarperCollins Publishers, Pymble, NSW
Canada: HarperCollins Publishers, Toronto & Scarborough, Ont
India: HarperCollins Publishers India Pvt Ltd, New Delhi
New Zealand: HarperCollins (NZ) Ltd, Glenfield, Auckland
USA: HarperCollins Publishers, New York
Worldwide (except countries listed): HarperCollins Publishers Ltd, Glasgow & London, UK

Book Trade Association Membership:
Publishers Association

2347

HARRIMAN HOUSE
3A Penns Road, Petersfield, Hants
GU32 2EW
Telephone: 01730 233870
Fax: 01730 233880
Email: info@harriman-house.com
Web Site: www.harriman-house.com

Managing Director: Myles Hunt
Publisher: Suzanne Anderson
Publicity & Marketing: Louise Hinchen
Head of Production: Nick Read
Editor: Craig Pearce
Sales: Chris Parker

Accountancy & Taxation; Economics; Industry, Business & Management

New Titles: 25 (2008) , 35 (2009)
No of Employees: 12

ISBNs, Imprints & Series:
978 1 897597, 978 1 905641, 978 1
906659

Overseas Representation:
Central & Eastern Europe: Tony Moggach, Publishers Sales Representation, London, UK
Spain, Portugal & Gibraltar: Peter Prout, Iberian Book Services, Madrid, Spain
Western Europe (including Austria, Belgium, France, Germany, Greece, Italy, Luxembourg, Malta, Netherlands & Switzerland): Ted Dougherty, London, UK

2348

HART PUBLISHING
16C Worcester Place, Oxford OX1 2JW
Telephone: 01865 517530
Fax: 01865 510710
Email: mail@hartpub.co.uk
Web Site: www.hartpub.co.uk

Warehouse:
Hoddle, Doyle, Meadows, Station Road, Linton, Cambridge CB1 6UX

Joint Owners/Directors: Richard Hart
(*Managing*)
Jane Parker (*Sales & Marketing*)

Academic & Scholarly; Law

New Titles: 91 (2008) , 120 (2009)

ISBNs, Imprints & Series:
978 1 84113, 978 1 84946, 978 1 901362

Distributor for:
Belgium: Intersentia

Overseas Representation:
Benelux: Intersentia, Antwerp, Belgium
Canada: Codasat, c/o University Toronto Press Distribution, Downsview, Ont
Central & Eastern Europe: Dr László Horváth Publishers Representative, Budapest, Hungary

Greece, Turkey, Arab Middle East & North Africa: James & Lorin Watt Ltd, Publishing Consultants, Oxford, UK
India: Ravindra Saxena, Sara Books Pvt Ltd, New Delhi
Italy & France: Mare Nostrum Publishing Consultants, Rome, Italy
Scandinavia: Colin Flint Ltd, Harlow, UK
South East Asia: STM Publisher Services Pte Ltd, Singapore
Spain & Portugal: Peter Prout Iberian Book Services, Madrid, Spain
USA: International Specialized Book Services Inc, Portland, OR

Book Trade Association Membership:
IPG

2349

HARVARD UNIVERSITY PRESS
Fitzroy House, Chenies Street, London
WC1E 7EY
Telephone: (020) 7306 0603
Fax: (020) 7306 0604
Email: info@HUP-MITpress.co.uk
Web Site: www.hup.harvard.edu

Orders & Warehouse:
c/o John Wiley & Sons,
Southern Cross Trading Estate,
1 Oldlands Way, Bognor Regis, West Sussex
PO22 9SA
Telephone: 01243 779777
Fax: 01243 829121
Email: cs-books@wiley.co.uk

Managing Director: Ann Sexsmith
Publicity & Promotion Manager:
Rebekah White

Academic & Scholarly; Biography & Autobiography; Biology & Zoology; Cinema, Video, TV & Radio; Economics; Fine Art & Art History; Gender Studies; Health & Beauty; History & Antiquarian; Law; Literature & Criticism; Military & War; Music; Natural History; Philosophy; Politics & World Affairs; Psychology & Psychiatry; Reference Books, Directories & Dictionaries; Religion & Theology; Sociology & Anthropology

New Titles: 200 (2008) , 200 (2009)

ISBNs, Imprints & Series:
978 0 674 Belknap; Harvard University Press
978 0 67499 Loeb Classical Library

Parent Company:
USA: Harvard University Press

Overseas Representation:
China: Everest International Publishing Services, Beijing, P. R. of China
Germany, Austria, Switzerland & Italy: Uwe Lüdemann, Berlin, Germany
Hong Kong: Jane Lam, Aromix Books
India: Mediamatics, Calcutta
Israel: Rodney Franklin Agency, Tel Aviv
Japan: Rockbook, Tokyo
Malaysia: Simon Tay, Apex Knowledge, Selangor
Middle East (excluding Greece & Israel): Avicenna Partnership, Oxford, UK
North America, Mexico & Central America: Harvard University Press, Cambridge, MA, USA
Poland, Hungary, Croatia, Slovenia, Slovakia, Czech Republic, Russia, Lithuania, Latvia, Estonia, Romania, Serbia, Albania & Bosnia Herzegovina: Ewa Ledóchowicz, Konstancin-Jeziorna, Poland
Scandinavia, Netherlands, Luxembourg, Belgium & France: Fred Hermans, Bovenkarspel, Netherlands
South Africa: Cory Voigt Associates, Johannesburg
South East Asia: Joseph Goh, IGP Services, Singapore

South Korea: Se-Yung Jun & Min-Hwa Yoo, Seoul, Republic of Korea
Spain & Portugal: Chris Humphrys, Gaucin, Spain
Taiwan: B. K. Norton, Taipei

Book Trade Association Membership:
IPG

2350

HARVEY MAP SERVICES LTD
12–22 Main Street, Doune, Perthshire
FK16 6BJ
Telephone: 01786 841202
Fax: 01786 841098
Email: sh@harveymaps.co.uk
Web Site: www.harveymaps.co.uk

Managing Director: Susan Harvey
Office Manager: Jacci Cameron

Atlases & Maps; Sports & Games

New Titles: 9 (2008) , 7 (2009)
No of Employees: 7
Annual Turnover: £560,000

ISBNs, Imprints & Series: 978 1 85137

Distributor for:
Canada: Chrismar Inc
Denmark: Compukort
South Africa: Jacana Media [Maps]

Book Trade Association Membership:
International Map Trade Association

2351

HAWKER PUBLICATIONS
Culvert House, Culvert Road, London
SW11 5DH
Telephone: (020) 7720 2108
Fax: (020) 7498 3023
Email: kate@hawkerpublications.com
Web Site: www.careinfo.com

Distribution:
NBN Plymbridge Ltd, Estover Road, Plymouth, Devon PL6 7PZ
Telephone: 01752 202300

Directors: Dr R. Hawkins (*Managing*)
P. Petker (*Sales*)

Health & Beauty; Medical (incl. Self Help & Alternative Medicine); Vocational Training & Careers

ISBNs, Imprints & Series:
978 1 874790 Better Care Guides; Hawker Publications

Overseas Representation:
Australia: Basing House Books, Hammondville, NSW

2352

HAWTHORN PRESS
Hawthorn House, 1 Lansdown Lane, Stroud, Glos GL5 1BJ
Telephone: 01453 757040
Fax: 01453 751138
Email: info@hawthornpress.com
Web Site: www.hawthornpress.com

Distribution & Sales:
BookSource, 50 Cambuslang Road, Glasgow G32 8NB
Telephone: 0845 370 0063
Fax: 0845 370 0064
Email: orders@booksource.net

Directors: Martin Large
Judy Large
Managers: Alan Lord (*Finance*)
Claire Percival (*Administrator*)

Academic & Scholarly; Children's Books; Crafts & Hobbies; Educational & Textbooks; Gardening; Gender Studies; Industry, Business & Management; Medical (incl. Self Help & Alternative Medicine); Music; Psychology & Psychiatry; Religion & Theology

New Titles: 7 (2008) , 9 (2009)
Annual Turnover: £300,000

ISBNs, Imprints & Series:
978 0 950706, 978 1 903458
978 1 869890 Conflict & Peace Building; Early Years Education; Family Activities & Crafts; Parenting & Child Health; Psychology & Self Help; Rudolf Steiner Education

Overseas Representation:
Australia: Footprint Books Pty Ltd, Warriewood, NSW
Canada: Tri-fold Books, Guelph, Ont
New Zealand: Ceres Books, Ellerslie
South Africa: Peter Hyde Associates (Pty) Ltd, Cape Town; Rudolf Steiner Publications, Bryanston
USA (All titles): Steiner Books Inc, Herndon, VA, USA

Book Trade Association Membership:
IPG

2353 ▬

HAYNES PUBLISHING
Sparkford, Nr Yeovil, Somerset BA22 7JJ
Telephone: 01963 440635 & 442080 (Customer Services – Trade)
Fax: 01963 440825 & 440001 (Customer Services)
Email: sales@haynes.co.uk
Web Site: www.haynes.co.uk

Directors: J. Haynes *(Managing)*
James Bunkum *(Finance)*
Jeremy Yates-Round *(Sales & Marketing, UK & Europe)*
Nigel Clements *(Production)*
Matthew Minter *(Motor Trade, Editorial)*
Mark Hughes *(Book Division, Editorial)*
Graham Cook *(Overseas Sales & Rights)*

Animal Care & Breeding; Architecture & Design; Atlases & Maps; Aviation; Biography & Autobiography; Children's Books; Computer Science; Crafts & Hobbies; Crime; Do-It-Yourself; Electronic (Professional & Academic); Gardening; Guide Books; Health & Beauty; History & Antiquarian; Medical (incl. Self Help & Alternative Medicine); Military & War; Music; Nautical; Photography; Reference Books, Directories & Dictionaries; Scientific & Technical; Sports & Games; Transport; Travel & Topography

New Titles: 91 (2008) , 99 (2009)
No of Employees: 88
Annual Turnover: £31.1M

ISBNs, Imprints & Series:
978 0 85059, 978 1 85260 Patrick Stephens Ltd
978 0 85429 G. T. Foulis
978 0 85696, 978 0 900550 J. H. Haynes & Co Ltd
978 0 902280, 978 0 946609, 978 1 85509 Oxford Illustrated Press
978 1 84425, 978 1 85010, 978 1 85960 Haynes

Parent Company:
UK: Haynes Publishing Group Plc

Distributor for:
USA: David Bull Publishing

Overseas Representation:
Australia: Haynes Manuals Inc, Padstow, NSW
New Zealand: Pace Publications, Wanganui

Sweden: Haynes Publishing Nordiska AB, Uppsala
USA: Haynes Manuals Inc, Newbury Park, CA
USA (non-Manual titles only): MBI Publishing Co, St Paul, MN, USA

Book Trade Association Membership:
BA

2354 ▬

HAYWARD PUBLISHING
Southbank Centre, Belvedere Road, London SE1 8XX
Telephone: (020) 7921 0826
Fax: (020) 7921 0700
Email: deborah.power@southbankcentre.co.uk
Web Site: www.southbankcentre.co.uk

Sales Manager: Deborah C. Power
Publications Co-ordinator: Giselle Osborne
Art Publisher: Mary Richards

Architecture & Design; Fine Art & Art History; Photography

New Titles: 9 (2008) , 8 (2009)

ISBNs, Imprints & Series: 978 1 85332

Book Trade Association Membership:
BA

2355 ▬

HEART OF ALBION PRESS
62 Wartnaby Street, Market Harborough, Leics LE16 9BE
Telephone: 01858 431717
Email: albion@indigogroup.co.uk
Web Site: www.hoap.co.uk

Owner: R. N. Trubshaw

Archaeology; Electronic (Educational); Guide Books; History & Antiquarian; Magic & the Occult; Philosophy; Psychology & Psychiatry; Religion & Theology; Sociology & Anthropology

ISBNs, Imprints & Series:
978 1 872883, 978 1 905646 Alternative Albion; Explore Books; Heart of Albion

2356 ▬

ROGER HEAVENS
2 Lowfields, Little Eversden, Cambridge CB23 1HJ
Telephone: 01223 262839
Fax: 01223 262033
Email: roger.heavens@btinternet.co.uk
Web Site: www.booksoncricket.net

Proprietor: Roger Heavens
Editors: Sally Heavens
Roger Packham

Academic & Scholarly; Sports & Games

New Titles: 4 (2008) , 5 (2009)

ISBNs, Imprints & Series:
978 1 900592 Roger Heavens; RH Business Books

Overseas Representation:
Australia: Roger Page, Yallambe, Vic

2357 ▬

HELION & CO LTD
26 Willow Road, Solihull, West Midlands B91 1UE
Telephone: 0121 705 3393
Fax: 0121 711 4075
Email: info@helion.co.uk
Web Site: www.helion.co.uk

Managing Director: Duncan Rogers
General Manager: Wilfrid Rogers

Academic & Scholarly; History & Antiquarian; Military & War

New Titles: 10 (2008) , 15 (2009)
No of Employees: 4

ISBNs, Imprints & Series:
978 1 874622, 978 1 906033 Helion & Co Ltd
978 1 905756 Unveiled Publishing

Distributor for:
Aegis Consulting/Aberjona Press; Eagle Editions; Reid Air Publishing; Vanwell Publishing

Overseas Representation:
Australia & New Zealand: Crusader Trading Pty Ltd, Weston, ACT, Australia
Austria, France, Switzerland, Benelux, Germany, Eastern Europe, Greece, Italy, Portugal, Spain, Gibraltar, Slovenia & Croatia: Casemate Publishing UK, Newbury, UK
Canada: Vanwell Publishing Ltd, St Catharines, Ont
USA: Casemate Publishers & Book Distributors LLC, Havertown, PA

2358 ▬

HEMMING INFORMATION SERVICES
32 Vauxhall Bridge Road, London SW1V 2SS
Telephone: (020) 7973 6604
Fax: (020) 7233 5053
Email: l.alderson@hgluk.com
Web Site: www.hgluk.com

Also at:
8 The Old Yarn Mills, Sherborne, Dorset DT9 3RQ
Telephone: 01935 816030
Fax: 01935 817200
Email: info@hisdorset.com

Also at:
Hereford House, Bridle Path, Croydon, Surrey CR9 4NL
Telephone: (020) 8680 4200
Fax: (020) 8680 8400

Directors: Graham Bond *(Managing)*
Linda Alderson *(Production)*
Mike Burton *(Editorial (Local Government titles))*
Emma Sabin *(Sales)*
Senior Editor: Dean Wanless

Reference Books, Directories & Dictionaries

No of Employees: 150

ISBNs, Imprints & Series: 978 0 7079

Parent Company:
Hemming Group Ltd

Book Trade Association Membership:
Data Publishers Association; European Directory Publishers Association

2359 ▬

IAN HENRY PUBLICATIONS LTD
20 Park Drive, Romford, Essex RM1 4LH
Telephone: 01708 749119
Fax: 01708 736213
Email: info@ian-henry.com
Web Site: www.ian-henry.com

Managing Director: Ian Wilkes *(Publisher)*

Cookery, Wines & Spirits; Educational & Textbooks; Fiction; History & Antiquarian; Humour; Medical (incl. Self Help & Alternative Medicine); Theatre, Drama & Dance; Transport

New Titles: 8 (2008) , 11 (2009)

ISBNs, Imprints & Series: 978 0 86025

Distributor for:
UK: Havering Museum

2360 ▬

***THE HERBERT PRESS**
[an imprint of A. & C. Black]
38 Soho Square, London W1D 3HB
Telephone: (020) 7758 0320
Fax: (020) 7758 0222
Email: llambert@acblack.com

Chairman: Nigel Newton
Managing Director: Jill Coleman
Publisher: Linda Lambert

Architecture & Design; Crafts & Hobbies; Fashion & Costume; Fine Art & Art History; Illustrated & Fine Editions

ISBNs, Imprints & Series:
978 0 7136, 978 0 906969, 978 1 871569 Design Handbooks; The Herbert History of Art & Architecture

Parent Company:
A. C. Black Plc

Associated Companies:
Bloomsbury

Overseas Representation:
Australia: Allen & Unwin Pty Ltd, Sydney, NSW
Europe: Penguin Group, London, UK

2361 ▬

NICK HERN BOOKS
The Glasshouse, 49a Goldhawk Road, London W12 8QP
Telephone: (020) 8749 4953
Fax: (020) 8735 0250
Email: info@nickhernbooks.demon.co.uk
Web Site: www.nickhernbooks.co.uk

Distribution:
Grantham Book Services Ltd, Trent Road, Grantham, Lincs NG31 7XQ
Telephone: 01476 541000
Fax: 01476 541060
Email: orders@gbs.tbs-ltd.co.uk

Managing Director: Nick Hern
Production Editor: Matt Applewhite
Managers: Robin Booth *(Marketing & Publicity)*
Ian Higham *(Sales)*

Cinema, Video, TV & Radio; Theatre, Drama & Dance

New Titles: 51 (2008) , 55 (2009)

ISBNs, Imprints & Series:
978 1 84842, 978 1 85459

Distributor for:
Canada: Playwrights Press Canada
USA: Drama Book Publishers; Theatre Communications Group

Overseas Representation:
Australia: Currency Press, Sydney
Canada: Playwrights Press Canada, Toronto, Ont
USA: Theatre Communications Group, New York

Book Trade Association Membership:
IPG

2362 ▬

***HIGHLAND BOOKS**
Two High Pines, Knoll Road, Godalming, Surrey GU7 2EP
Telephone: 01483 424560

Fax: 01483 424388
Email: info@highlandbks.com
Web Site: www.highlandbks.com

Distribution / Trade Orders:
STL, PO Box 300, Kingstown Broadway, Carlisle, Cumbria CA3 0QS
Telephone: 01228 512512
Fax: 01228 514949
Web Site: www.stl.org

Director: Philip Ralli

Biography & Autobiography; Children's Books; Religion & Theology

ISBNs, Imprints & Series:
978 0 946616, 978 1 897913 Highland
978 1 905496 Usharp

Overseas Representation:
New Zealand: Scripture Union Wholesale, Wellington
South Africa: Methodist Wholesale, Cape Town

2363 ━━━━━

HINTON HOUSE PUBLISHERS LTD
Newman House, 4 High Street, Buckingham MK18 1NT
Telephone: 01280 822557
Fax: 0560 313 5274
Email: info@hintonpublishers.com
Web Site: www.hintonpublishers.com

Publisher: Sarah Miles

Educational & Textbooks; Medical (incl. Self Help & Alternative Medicine); Psychology & Psychiatry

New Titles: 5 (2008) , 10 (2009)

ISBNs, Imprints & Series: 978 1 906531

Distributor for:
Canada: Pembroke Publishers Ltd
USA: Stenhouse Publishers

Book Trade Association Membership:
Publishers Association

2364 ━━━━━

HIPPOPOTAMUS PRESS
22 Whitewell Road, Frome, Somerset BA11 4EL
Telephone: 01373 466653
Fax: 01373 466653
Email: rjhippopress@aol.com

Publisher: R. John
Editor: M. Pargitter
Editorial Assistant: Anna Martin

Literature & Criticism; Poetry

ISBNs, Imprints & Series: 978 0 904179

Distributor for:
Austria: University of Salzburg Press

2365 ━━━━━

HISTORICAL PUBLICATIONS LTD
32 Ellington Street, London N7 8PL
Telephone: (020) 7607 1628
Fax: (020) 7609 6451
Email:
richardson@historicalpublications.co.uk

Distribution:
Countryside Books, 2 Highfield Avenue, Newbury, Berks RG14 5DS
Telephone: 01635 43816
Fax: 01635 551004
Email: info@countrysidebooks.co.uk
Web Site: www.countrysidebooks.co.uk

Managing Director: John Richardson
Secretary: Helen English

Architecture & Design; History & Antiquarian; Travel & Topography

No of Employees: 3

ISBNs, Imprints & Series:
978 0 948667, 978 1 905286

2366 ━━━━━

HOBNOB PRESS
PO Box 1838, East Knoyle, Salisbury SP3 6FA
Telephone: 01747 830015
Email: john@hobnobpress.co.uk
Web Site: www.hobnobpress.co.uk

Sole Trader: John Chandler

Academic & Scholarly; Archaeology; Guide Books; History & Antiquarian; Literature & Criticism; Travel & Topography

New Titles: 9 (2008) , 12 (2009)

ISBNs, Imprints & Series: 978 0 946418

Distributor for:
Ex Libris Press; Wiltshire Buildings Record; Wiltshire Record Society

2367 ━━━━━

HODDER EDUCATION
338 Euston Road, London NW1 3BH
Telephone: (020) 7873 6000
Fax: (020) 7873 6299 & 6325
Web Site: www.hoddereducation.co.uk

Distribution Centre:
Bookpoint Ltd, 130 Milton Park, Abingdon, Oxon OX14 4SB
Telephone: 01235 400400
Fax: 01235 400445

Directors: Thomas Webster *(Chief Executive)*
Elisabeth Tribe *(Managing, Schools)*
C. P. Shaw *(Tertiary)*
Alyssum Ross *(Business Operations)*
Katie Roden *(Consumer Education)*
John Mitchell *(Scotland – Hodder Gibson)*
Robert Sulley *(International)*
Tim Mahar *(Consumer Education Sales & Marketing, HE)*
Janice Tolan *(School Sales & Marketing, FE)*
Jim Belben *(Schools (Humanities & Modern Languages))*
Steve Connolly *(Editorial Digital Publishing)*
Patrick White *(Managing, Chambers Harrap)*

Academic & Scholarly; Accountancy & Taxation; Animal Care & Breeding; Antiques & Collecting; Archaeology; Atlases & Maps; Audio Books; Aviation; Biology & Zoology; Chemistry; Cinema, Video, TV & Radio; Computer Science; Cookery, Wines & Spirits; Crafts & Hobbies; Do-It-Yourself; Economics; Educational & Textbooks; Electronic (Educational); Electronic (Professional & Academic); English as a Foreign Language; Environment & Development Studies; Gardening; Gender Studies; Geography & Geology; Health & Beauty; History & Antiquarian; Industry, Business & Management; Languages & Linguistics; Law; Literature & Criticism; Mathematics & Statistics; Medical (incl. Self Help & Alternative Medicine); Natural History; Philosophy; Physics; Politics & World Affairs; Psychology & Psychiatry; Reference Books, Directories & Dictionaries; Religion & Theology; Scientific & Technical; Sociology & Anthropology; Sports & Games; Vocational Training & Careers

ISBNs, Imprints & Series:
978 0 245 Harrap

978 0 340 Hodder & Stoughton; Hodder & Stoughton Educational; Hodder Arnold; Hodder Murray; Teach Yourself
978 0 550 Chambers
978 0 7131 Arnold
978 0 7169 Hodder Gibson
978 0 7195 John Murray
978 0 86003, 978 1 84489 Philip Allan

Parent Company:
Hodder Headline Plc/Hachette Livre

Associated Companies:
Headline Book Publishing Ltd; Hodder & Stoughton

Overseas Representation:
All other international queries: Rebecca Duprey, International Sales Manager, Hodder, London, UK
Antigua (School FE Medical Trade): The Best of Books, St John's, Antigua
Argentina: Kel Ediciones SA (Agents), Buenos Aires
Australia (FE/Medical/Trade): Hachette Livre Australia, Sydney, NSW, Australia
Australia (Livewires): Cambridge University Press, Australia
Australia (School – excluding Livewires): Cengage (Australia), NSW, Australia
Bangladesh (School/FE/Medical/Trade): Ansania Mission Book Distribution House, Bangladesh
Barbados (School/FE/Medical/Trade): Julie White, Barbados
Benelux, Italy & Scandinavia (FE Medical Trade): Ben Doming, Hodder, London, UK
Cameroon (School/FE/Medical/Trade): Macmillan Publishers Cameroon Ltd, Limbe, Cameroon
Canada (FE/Medical/Trade, excluding Teach Yourself): Oxford University Press Canadian Branch, Don Mills, Ont, Canada
Canada (School – excluding Modern Languages): Bacon & Hughes Ltd, Ottawa, Ont, Canada
Canada (School – Modern Languages only): The Resource Centre, Waterloo, Canada
Canada (Teach Yourself): McGraw-Hill, Canada
Caribbean (Trade) & South America (School/FE/Medical/Trade): Humphrys Roberts Associates, London, UK
China (School/FE/Medical/Trade): Ian Taylor Associates Ltd, London, UK
Egypt (School): Macmillan Publishers Egypt Ltd, Cairo, Egypt
Ethiopia (School/FE/Medical/Trade): Etcon Ltd, Ethiopia
Europe (School): Gill Dee, International Schools Sales Manager, Hodder, London, UK
France, Spain & Portugal (FE/Medical/Trade): Anne Kelsall, Hodder, London, UK
Germany, Austria & Switzerland (School/FE/Medical/Trade): Giana Elyea, Hodder, London, UK
Ghana (School/FE/Medical/Trade): EPP Book Services Ltd, Accra, Ghana
Greece & Cyprus (FE/Medical/Trade): Zitsa Seraphimidi, J & L Watt, Paleo Faliro, Greece
Hong Kong (School/FE/Medical/Trade) & Taiwan (School): Asia Publishers Services Ltd, Hong Kong
Hong Kong (School): Pilot Publishers Services Ltd, Kowloon, Hong Kong
India (School/FE/Trade, excluding Teach Yourself): Viva Group, New Delhi, India
India (Medical): Jaypee Brothers Medical Publishers (Pte) Ltd, New Delhi, India
India (Teach Yourself): Hachette India, New Delhi, India
Iran (FE/Medical/Trade): Farhad Maftoon, Tehran, Iran
Israel (FE/Medical/Trade): Rodney Franklin Agency, Tel Aviv, Israel
Jamaica (School/FE/Medical/Trade): Kingston Bookshop, Kingston, Jamaica
Japan (School/FE/Trade): United Publishers Services Ltd, Tokyo, Japan

Japan (Medical): Nankodo Co Ltd, Tokyo, Japan
Korea (School/FE/Medical/Trade): Information & Culture Korea (ICK), Seoul, Republic of Korea
Malawi (School/FE/Medical/Trade): Bookland International, Malawi
Maldives (School/FE/Medical/Trade): Asrafee Bookshop, Maldives
Mauritius (School/FE/Medical/Trade): Editions le Printemps, Vacoas, Mauritius
Middle East (FE/Medical/Trade): James & Lorin Watt Ltd, Publishing Consultants, Oxford, UK
Middle East (School): Gill Dee, Hodder, London, UK
Namibia, Swaziland, Botswana, Lesotho & South Africa (School/FE/Medical): Macmillan South Africa Publishers (Pty) Ltd, Braamfontein, South Africa
Namibia, Swaziland, Botswana, Lesotho, South Africa & Zimbabwe (Trade): Pan Macmillan SA Pty Ltd, Hyde Park, South Africa
New Zealand (School/FE/Medical/Trade): Hachette Livre New Zealand, Auckland, New Zealand
Nigeria (School/FE/Medical/Trade): Bounty Press Ltd, Ibadan, Nigeria
Pakistan (School/FE/Medical/Trade): Andrew White, The White Partnership, Tunbridge Wells, UK
Republic of Ireland (School/FE/Medical/Trade): Vivienne Lavery, Blackrock, Co Dublin, Republic of Ireland
Scandinavia, Benelux & Eastern Europe (FE/Medical/Trade): Jacek Lewinson, Warsaw, Poland
Singapore, Indonesia, Brunei, Malaysia, Thailand & Philippines (School/FE/Medical): APD Malaysia, Malaysia; APD Singapore Pte Ltd, Singapore
Singapore, Indonesia, Brunei, Malaysia, Thailand & Philippines (Trade): Pansing Distribution Pte Ltd, Singapore
St Lucia (School FE Medical Trade): Nathaniel's Books, St Lucia
Tanzania (School/FE/Medical/Trade): Macmillan Aidan Ltd, Dar es Salaam, Tanzania
Trinidad & Tobago (School/FE/Medical/Trade): RIK Services Ltd, San Fernando, Trinidad
Turkey (Medical): Nobel Tip Kitabevlen, Turkey
Uganda (School/FE/Medical/Trade): Macmillan Uganda Ltd, Kampala, Uganda
USA (FE/Medical): Oxford University Press Inc USA, New York, NY, USA
USA (Teach Yourself): McGraw-Hill, Chicago, IL, USA
USA (Trade – excluding Teach Yourself): Trafalgar Square Publishing / IPG, Chicago, IL, USA
Zambia (School/FE/Medical/Trade): Macmillan Zambia, Lusaka, Zambia

Book Trade Association Membership:
EPC; IGSMTP; CAPP

2368 ━━━━━

HODDER GIBSON
2A Christie Street, Paisley PA1 1NB
Telephone: 0141 848 1609
Fax: 0141 889 6315
Email: hoddergibson@hodder.co.uk
Web Site: www.hoddereducation.co.uk

Distribution:
Bookpoint, 130 Milton Park, Abingdon, Oxon OX14 4SB
Telephone: 01235 400400

Managing Director: John Mitchell
Sales Manager: Jim Donnelly

Academic & Scholarly; Educational & Textbooks

New Titles: 30 (2008) , 15 (2009)

No of Employees: 4

ISBNs, Imprints & Series:
978 0 340 Hodder
978 0 7169 formerly Robert Gibson & Sons

Parent Company:
Hachette UK

Book Trade Association Membership:
EPC; Publishing Scotland

2369 ▬

HODDER & STOUGHTON FAITH
338 Euston Road, London NW1 3BH
Telephone: (020) 7873 6000
Fax: (020) 7873 6059
Email: hodderfaith-sales@hodder.co.uk
Web Site: www.hodder.co.uk

Distribution Centre:
Bookpoint Ltd, 130 Milton Park, Abingdon, Oxon OX14 4SB
Telephone: 01235 400400
Fax: 01235 400445

Directors: Wendy Grisham (Publishing)
Jean Whitnall (Sales)
Publisher, Bibles & Digital Media: Ian Metcalfe

Biography & Autobiography; Fiction; History & Antiquarian; Humour; Medical (incl. Self Help & Alternative Medicine); Religion & Theology

New Titles: 20 (2008) , 25 (2009)

ISBNs, Imprints & Series:
978 0 340 Hodder & Stoughton; New International Version

Parent Company:
Hachette Livre UK Ltd

Associated Companies:
Edward Arnold Ltd; Hachette Livre; Headline Book Publishing Ltd

Overseas Representation:
Australia: Hachette Livre Australia, Sydney, NSW
Canada (Christian trade): R. G. Mitchell Family Books Inc, Kitchener, Ont, Canada
Canada (General trade): McArthur & Co Publishers Ltd, Toronto, Ont, Canada
India: Hachette India, Mumbai
New Zealand: Hachette Livre New Zealand, Auckland
Singapore: Pansing Distribution Sdn Bhd
Southern Africa: Jonathan Ball Publishers (Pty) Ltd, Johannesburg, South Africa
USA: Trafalgar Square Publishing, North Pomfret, VT

2370 ▬

HODDER & STOUGHTON GENERAL
338 Euston Road, London NW1 3BH
Telephone: (020) 7873 6000
Fax: (020) 7873 6195

Distribution Centre:
Bookpoint Ltd, 130 Milton Park, Abingdon, Oxon OX14 4SB
Telephone: 01235 400400
Fax: 01235 400445

Directors: Jamie Hodder-Williams (Managing)
Lisa Highton (Deputy Managing)
Lucy Hale (Sales)
Karen Geary (Publicity)
Auriol Bishop (Creative)
Helen Dance (Chief Operating Officer)
Carolyn Mays (Fiction)
Rowena Webb (Non-Fiction)
Rupert Lancaster (Audio)
Carole Welch (Sceptre)
Subsidiary Rights: Jason Bartholomew (Rights)

Audio Books; Biography & Autobiography; Cinema, Video, TV & Radio; Cookery, Wines & Spirits; Crime; Fiction; History & Antiquarian; Humour; Military & War; Politics & World Affairs; Science Fiction; Sports & Games

ISBNs, Imprints & Series:
978 0 340 Hodder & Stoughton; Mobius; Sceptre

Parent Company:
Hachette UK Ltd

Associated Companies:
Headline Book Publishing Ltd
France: Hachette Livre

Overseas Representation:
Australia: Hachette Livre Australia, Sydney, NSW
Canada (trade & paperbacks): McArthur & Co Publishers Ltd, Toronto, Ont, Canada
New Zealand: Hachette Livre New Zealand, Auckland
Pakistan (paperbacks): Liberty Books (Pvt) Ltd, Karachi, Pakistan
Singapore: Pansing Distribution Sdn Bhd
Southern Africa (trade): Jonathan Ball Publishers (Pty) Ltd, Jeppestown, South Africa

2371 ▬

ALISON HODGE PUBLISHERS
2 Clarence Place, Penzance, Cornwall TR20 8XA
Telephone: 01736 368093
Email: info@alison-hodge.co.uk
Web Site: www.alison-hodge.co.uk

Distribution:
Tormark, Redruth, Cornwall TR16 5HY
Telephone: 01209 822101
Fax: 01209 822035
Email: sales@tormark.co.uk

Publisher: Alison Hodge

Biography & Autobiography; Cookery, Wines & Spirits; Fine Art & Art History; Gardening; Natural History; Photography; Sports & Games; Travel & Topography

New Titles: 5 (2008) , 5 (2009)

ISBNs, Imprints & Series:
The County Gardens Guides Inspirations Series; Pocket Cornwall
978 0 906720

Overseas Representation:
Europe: Bill Bailey Publishers Representatives, Newton Abbot, UK

2372 ▬

HOLLAND PUBLISHING PLC
18 Bourne Court, Southend Road, Woodford Green, Essex IG8 8HD
Telephone: (020) 8551 7711
Fax: (020) 8551 1266
Email: sales@holland-publishing.co.uk
Web Site: www.holland-publishing.co.uk

Managing Director: J. W. Holland
Company Secretary: Mrs S. M. Holland

Children's Books; Educational & Textbooks

ISBNs, Imprints & Series:
Christmas is Fun; Colouring is Fun; Creative Colouring; Doodle Design; Halloween is Fun; Learning is Fun; Little Star Creations; Phonics is Fun; Puzzle Zone
978 1 85038

2373 ▬

HOLO BOOKS
Clarendon House, 52 Cornmarket, Oxford OX1 3HJ
Telephone: 01865 513681
Fax: 01865 554199
Email: holobooks@yahoo.co.uk
Web Site: www.holobooks.co.uk

Orders:
Central Books, 99 Wallis Road, London E9 5LN
Telephone: (020) 8986 4854
Fax: (020) 8533 5821
Email: orders@centralbooks.com
Web Site: www.centralbooks.co.uk

Partners: Susanna Hoe
Derek Roebuck
Manager: Leonie Harries

Academic & Scholarly; Archaeology; Biography & Autobiography; Gender Studies; Guide Books; History & Antiquarian; Humour; Law; Travel & Topography

ISBNs, Imprints & Series:
The Arbitration Press; Of Islands and Women Series; The Women's History Press

Distributor for:
Hong Kong: Roundhouse Publications (Asia)
USA: Bear Creek Books

Overseas Representation:
Hong Kong: Far East Media
USA: Wm. W. Gaunt & Sons Inc, Holmes Beach, FL

2374 ▬

HONNO (WELSH WOMEN'S PRESS)
Unit 14, Creative Units,
Aberystwyth Arts Centre, Penglais Campus, Aberystwyth, Ceredigion SY23 3GL
Telephone: 01970 623150
Fax: 01970 623150
Email: post@honno.co.uk
Web Site: www.honno.co.uk

Secretary (Honorary):
Ailsa Craig, Heol y Cawl, Dinas Powys, Vale of Glamorgan CF6 4AH
Telephone: (029) 2051 5014
Fax: (029) 2051 5014
Email: (as above)
Web Site: (as above)

Marketing Manager: Helena Earnshaw
Editor: Caroline Oakley
Production & Administration: Lesley Rice
Finance: Fran Lewis

Biography & Autobiography; Crime; Fiction

New Titles: 8 (2008) , 7 (2009)
No of Employees: 4

ISBNs, Imprints & Series:
978 1 870206, 978 1 906784 Honno Classic Fiction; Honno Modern Fiction; Honno Voices

Book Trade Association Membership:
IPG; Union of Welsh Booksellers & Publishers

2375 ▬

HOPSCOTCH EDUCATIONAL PUBLISHING
St Jude's Church, Dulwich Road, Herne Hill, London SE24 0PB
Telephone: (020) 7738 5454
Fax: (020) 7778 8317
Email: angela.s@markallengroup.com
Web Site: www.hopscotchbooks.com

Sales & Distribution:
Telephone: 01722 717022
Email: sales@hopscotchbooks.com

Manager: Angela Shaw (Publishing)
Assistant: Rebecca Haworth (Publishing)

Educational & Textbooks

New Titles: 5 (2008) , 12 (2009)
Annual Turnover: £240,000

ISBNs, Imprints & Series:
978 1 902239, 978 1 904307, 978 1 905390

Parent Company:
UK: Mark Allen Group

Book Trade Association Membership:
BESA

2376 ▬

HOW TO BOOKS LTD
Spring Hill House, Spring Hill Road, Begbroke, Oxford OX5 1RX
Telephone: 01865 375794
Fax: 01865 379162
Email: info@howtobooks.co.uk
Web Site: www.howtobooks.co.uk

Customer Services:
Grantham Book Services, Trent Road, Grantham, Lincs NG31 7XG
Telephone: 01476 541080
Fax: 01476 541061
Email: orders@gbs.tbs-ltd.co.uk
Web Site: www.howtobooks.co.uk

Sales Representation (UK & Ireland):
Compass DSA Ltd,
13 Progress Business Centre,
Whittle Parkway, Slough SL1 6DQ
Telephone: 01628 559500
Fax: 01628 663876
Email: sales@compass-dsa.co.uk

Managing Director: Giles Lewis
Editorial: Nikki Read
Rights: Ros Loten
Production: Bill Antrobus
Finance: Martin Wilkinson

Accountancy & Taxation; Antiques & Collecting; Cookery, Wines & Spirits; Educational & Textbooks; Gardening; Guide Books; Industry, Business & Management; Literature & Criticism; Medical (incl. Self Help & Alternative Medicine); Reference Books, Directories & Dictionaries; Travel & Topography; Vocational Training & Careers; Creative Writing; Home & Family; Living & Working Abroad; Property

New Titles: 80 (2008) , 65 (2009)

ISBNs, Imprints & Series:
978 1 84528, 978 1 85703, 978 1 905862
How To Books; Spring Hill

Parent Company:
UK: How To Ltd

Overseas Representation:
Africa: Kelvin van Hasselt Publishing Services, Briningham, Norfolk, UK
Australia & New Zealand: Footprint Books Pty Ltd, Sydney, NSW, Australia
Austria, Germany & Benelux: Robbert J. Pleysier, Heerde, Netherlands
China & Japan: Chris Ashdown, Ferndown, UK
East Asia: Pansing Distribution Pte Ltd, Singapore
Eastern Europe & Greece: Tony Moggach, InterMedia Americana (IMA) Ltd, London, UK
France, Switzerland, Italy & Malta: Ted Dougherty, ESA, London, UK
Latin America & West Indies: InterMedia Americana (IMA) Ltd, London, UK
Middle East & Turkey: Publishers International Marketing, Polfages, France
South Africa: Phambili CC, Kensington

Spain & Portugal: Peter Prout Iberian Book Services, Madrid, Spain
USA: Parkwest Publications Inc, Miami, FL

Book Trade Association Membership:
IPG

2377

HUMAN KINETICS EUROPE LTD
107 Bradford Road, Stanningley, Leeds LS28 6AT
Telephone: 0113 255 5665
Fax: 0113 255 5885
Email: hk@hkeurope.com
Web Site: www.humankinetics.com/

Managing Director: Sara Cooper
Managers: Sian Partridge *(Sales)*
Graham Wilson *(Finance)*
Karen Ingram *(Customer Services)*
Rory Aspell *(Marketing)*
John Dickinson *(Editorial)*

Academic & Scholarly; Educational & Textbooks; Electronic (Educational); Electronic (Professional & Academic); Health & Beauty; Medical (incl. Self Help & Alternative Medicine); Psychology & Psychiatry; Scientific & Technical; Sports & Games; Theatre, Drama & Dance

New Titles: 150 (2008) , 150 (2009)
No of Employees: 16
Annual Turnover: £1.9M

ISBNs, Imprints & Series:
978 0 73600, 978 0 87322, 978 0 88011, 978 0 918438, 978 0 931250

Parent Company:
USA: Human Kinetics Inc

Associated Companies:
Australia: Human Kinetics
Canada: Human Kinetics
New Zealand: Human Kinetics

Overseas Representation:
Australia: Human Kinetics (Australia), Torrens Park, SA
Brazil (academic): Tecmedd, São Paulo, Brazil
Canada: Human Kinetics (Canada), Windsor, Ont
China (including Hong Kong): AA Media Services, Shanghai, P. R. of China
India: Disvan Enterprises, New Delhi
Iran: Kowkab Publishers, Tehran
Japan: Eureka Press, Kyoto
Korea: Daehan Media Co Ltd, Seoul, Republic of Korea
New Zealand: Human Kinetics (New Zealand), Auckland
Singapore & Malaysia: Icon Books Singapore Pte Ltd, Singapore
South Africa (academic): Academic & Professional Book Distributor, Johannesburg, South Africa
South Africa (trade): Real Books CC, Johannesburg, South Africa
Taiwan: Unifacmanu Trading Co Ltd, Taipei
Thailand, Indonesia, Bangladesh, Brunei & Philippines: Alkem Co (S) Pte Ltd, Singapore
USA: Human Kinetics, Champaign, IL

Book Trade Association Membership:
IPG

2378

JOHN HUNT PUBLISHING LTD
c/o O Books, The Bothy, Deershot Lodge, Park Lane, Ropley, Hants SO24 0BE
Fax: 01962 773769
Email: john.hunt@0-books.net
Web Site: www.johnhunt-publishing.com & www.o-books.net

Directors: John Hunt *(Editorial)*

Kate Rowlandson *(Sales)*
Manager: Ros Baynes *(Accounts)*

Children's Books; Fiction; Magic & the Occult; Philosophy; Psychology & Psychiatry; Religion & Theology

New Titles: 80 (2008) , 100 (2009)
No of Employees: 6
Annual Turnover: £1M

ISBNs, Imprints & Series:
978 1 84298 John Hunt
978 1 903816 O-Books

Overseas Representation:
Australia: Brumby Books Holdings Pty Ltd, Kilsyth South, Vic
New Zealand: Peaceful Living Publications, Auckland
Singapore: STP Distributors Pte Ltd
South Africa: Alternative Books CC, Ferndale
USA & Canada: NBN, Blue Ridge Summit, PA, USA

Book Trade Association Membership:
IPG

2379

C. HURST & CO (PUBLISHERS) LTD
41 Great Russell Street, London WC1B 3PL
Telephone: (020) 7255 2201
Email: michael@hurstpub.co.uk
Web Site: www.hurstpub.co.uk

Distribution:
Marston Book Services, PO Box 269, Abingdon, Oxon OX14 4YN
Telephone: 01235 465500
Fax: 01235 465555

Directors: Michael Dwyer *(Managing, Publisher)*
Kathleen May *(Marketing)*
Managing Editor: Daisy Leitch

Academic & Scholarly; Gender Studies; Military & War; Politics & World Affairs; Religion & Theology; Sociology & Anthropology

New Titles: 35 (2008) , 40 (2009)
No of Employees: 3
Annual Turnover: £600,000

ISBNs, Imprints & Series:
978 0 903983, 978 0 905838, 978 1 85065

Distributor for:
Signal Books

Overseas Representation:
Australia: UNIREPS University and Reference Publishers' Services, Sydney, NSW
Benelux, France & Suisse Romande: Michael Geoghegan, London, UK
China & Hong Kong: Access Asia Media Services, Beijing, P. R. of China
Eastern Europe: Ewa Ledóchowicz, Konstancin-Jeziorna, Poland
Greece, Malta, Italy & Cyprus: Charles Gibbes Associates, Louslitges, France
Japan: United Publishers Services Ltd, Tokyo
Middle East: Avicenna Partnership, Oxford, UK
Nordic countries: Colin Flint Ltd, Harlow, UK
Republic of Ireland: Geoff Bryan, Dublin
South East Asia: Horizon Books Pte Ltd, Singapore
Southern Africa: Bacchus Books, Johannesburg, South Africa
Spain & Portugal: Iberian Book Services, Madrid, Spain

Book Trade Association Membership:
IPG

2380

HYPATIA PUBLICATIONS
[including Patten Press]
Trevelyan House, 16 Chapel Street, Penzance, Cornwall TR18 4AW
Telephone: 01736 366597
Fax: 01736 333307
Email: info@hypatia-trust.org.uk
Web Site: www.hypatia-trust.org.uk

Warehouse:
Jamieson Library, Old Post Office, Newmill, Penzance, Cornwall TR20 8XN
Telephone: 01736 360549
Email: budden@lineone.net

Directors: Dr Melissa Hardie
Dr Phil Budden *(Finance)*
Donna Anton *(IT)*
P/A: Peter Waverly

Academic & Scholarly; Bibliography & Library Science; Biography & Autobiography; Educational & Textbooks; Fine Art & Art History

New Titles: 3 (2008) , 3 (2009)
Annual Turnover: £25,000

ISBNs, Imprints & Series: 978 1 872229

Parent Company:
UK: The Hypatia Trust

Associated Companies:
UK: Jamieson Library; Patten Press

Overseas Representation:
USA: Malcolm Summers, VT

2381

ICHEME
165–189 Railway Terrace, Rugby CV21 3HQ
Telephone: 01788 578214
Fax: 01788 560833
Email: jcressey@icheme.org
Web Site: www.icheme.org

Marketing Executive: Jo Cheshire
Marketing Manager: Jacqueline Cressey

Engineering; Scientific & Technical

Annual Turnover: £500,000

ISBNs, Imprints & Series: 978 0 85295

Distributor for:
USA: Princeton Selling Group Inc

Overseas Representation:
Asia: Clarke Associates Ltd, Bristol, UK
Australia & New Zealand: DA Information Services Pty Ltd, Mitcham, Vic, Australia
Europe: Momenta Publishing Ltd, Hindhead, Surrey, UK
USA & Canada: Princeton Selling Group Inc, Wayne, PA, USA

2382

ICON BOOKS LTD
Omnibus Business Centre, 39–41 North Road, London N7 9DP
Telephone: (020) 7700 9964
Fax: (020) 7697 9501
Email: info@iconbooks.co.uk
Web Site: www.iconbooks.co.uk

Distribution:
TBS Distribution Centre, Colchester Road, Frating Green, Colchester, Essex CO7 7DW
Telephone: 01206 255678 (UK trade) & 255644 (Export)
Fax: 01206 255930 (UK trade) & 255916 (Export)
Email: sales@tbs-ltd.co.uk & export@tbs-ltd.co.uk

UK Rights (Icon & Wizard titles):
The Marsh Agency, 50 Albemarle Street, London W1S 4BD
Telephone: (020) 7493 4361
Fax: (020) 7495 8961
Email: steph@patersonmarsh.co.uk

Sales Representation (UK):
Faber & Faber, 3 Queen Square, London WC1N 3AU
Telephone: (020) 7465 0045
Fax: (020) 7465 0034
Email: sales@faber.co.uk

Directors: Peter Pugh *(Managing)*
Simon Flynn *(Publishing)*
Duncan Heath *(Editorial)*
Andrew Furlow *(Marketing)*
Najma Finlay *(Publicity)*

Academic & Scholarly; Aviation; Biography & Autobiography; Chemistry; Children's Books; Crime; Economics; Educational & Textbooks; Fiction; Gender Studies; Geography & Geology; Health & Beauty; History & Antiquarian; Humour; Languages & Linguistics; Literature & Criticism; Mathematics & Statistics; Military & War; Natural History; Philosophy; Physics; Poetry; Politics & World Affairs; Psychology & Psychiatry; Reference Books, Directories & Dictionaries; Religion & Theology; Science Fiction; Scientific & Technical; Sociology & Anthropology; Sports & Games

ISBNs, Imprints & Series:
978 1 84046, 978 1 84831

Associated Companies:
Wizard Books

Overseas Representation:
Australasia: Allen & Unwin Pty Ltd, Sydney, NSW, Australia
Canada: Penguin Group Canada, Toronto, Ont
Singapore & Malaysia: Penguin Books Singapore, Jurong, Singapore
South Africa: Book Promotions Ltd, Johannesburg
USA (Rights - Icon & Wizard titles): Carol Mann Agency, New York, NY, USA
USA (Totem Books): National Book Network Inc, Blue Ridge Summit, PA, USA

2383

ICSA INFORMATION & TRAINING LTD
16 Park Crescent, London W1B 1AH
Telephone: (020) 7612 7020
Fax: (020) 7323 1132
Email: publishing@icsa.co.uk
Web Site: www.icsabookshop.co.uk

Distribution, Orders, Customer Service & Accounts:
Marston Book Services Ltd, PO Box 269, Abingdon, Oxon OX14 4YN
Telephone: 01235 465500
Fax: 01235 465555
Email: direct.order@marston.co.uk

Joint Managing Directors: Clare Grist Taylor
Susan Richards
Sales & Marketing: Kate Murphy
New Business Development: Isabel Gillies

Industry, Business & Management

ISBNs, Imprints & Series:
978 0 902197, 978 1 85418, 978 1 86072, 978 1 87286

Book Trade Association Membership:
IPG

2384

IHS BRE PRESS
Garston, Watford, Herts WD25 9XX

Telephone: 01923 664761
Fax: 01923 662477
Email: brepress@ihs.com
Web Site: www.brebookshop.com

Sales & Customer Service:
IHS BRE Press, Willoughby Road, Bracknell,
Berks RG12 8FB
Telephone: 01344 328038
Fax: 01344 328005
Email: brepress@ihs.com
Web Site: www.brebookshop.com

Publisher: Nick Clarke

*Architecture & Design; Environment &
Development Studies; Scientific & Technical*

New Titles: 50 (2008) , 50 (2009)

ISBNs, Imprints & Series:
978 1 84806 IHS BRE Press
978 1 86081 BRE Press

Parent Company:
UK: IHS

2385 ▬▬▬▬▬▬▬▬▬▬▬▬▬

THE ILEX PRESS LTD
210 High Street, Lewes, East Sussex
BN7 2NS
Telephone: 01273 487440
Fax: 01273 487441
Web Site: www.ilex-press.com

**Sales & Distribution, Trade Enquiries &
Orders:**
Trade Distribution & Accounts,
Thames & Hudson (Distributors),
44 Clockhouse Road, Farnborough, Hants
GU14 7QZ
Telephone: 01252 541602
Fax: 01252 541602
Email:
customerservices@thameshudson.co.uk

Directors: Alastair Campbell *(Publisher)*
Stephen Paul *(Managing)*
Peter Bridgewater *(Creative)*

*Crafts & Hobbies; Electronic
(Entertainment); Fine Art & Art History;
Industry, Business & Management;
Photography*

ISBNs, Imprints & Series: 978 1 904705

2386 ▬▬▬▬▬▬▬▬▬▬▬▬▬

IMPERIAL COLLEGE PRESS
57 Shelton Street, Covent Garden, London
WC2H 9HE
Telephone: (020) 7836 3954
Fax: (020) 7836 2020
Email: edit@icpress.co.uk
Web Site: www.icpress.co.uk

Trade Enquiries & Orders:
World Scientific Publishing,
57 Shelton Street, Covent Garden, London
WC2H 9HE
Telephone: (020) 7836 0888
Fax: (020) 7836 2020
Email: sales@wspc.co.uk
Web Site: www.wspc.co.uk

Chairman: Prof K. K. Phua
Publisher: Laurent Chaminade
Editors: Lance Sucharov *(Senior
Commissioning)*
Lizzie Bennett *(Senior)*

*Academic & Scholarly; Biology & Zoology;
Chemistry; Computer Science; Economics;
Electronic (Educational); Electronic
(Professional & Academic); Engineering;
Environment & Development Studies;
Industry, Business & Management;
Mathematics & Statistics; Medical (incl. Self
Help & Alternative Medicine); Physics;
Scientific & Technical*

ISBNs, Imprints & Series: 978 1 86094

Parent Company:
Singapore: World Scientific

Overseas Representation:
Hong Kong: World Scientific Publishing
(HK) Co Ltd
India: World Scientific Publishing Co Pte Ltd,
Bangalore
Singapore: World Scientific Publishing Co
Pte Ltd
Taiwan: World Scientific Publishing Co Pte
Ltd, Taipei
USA: World Scientific Publishing Co Inc,
River Edge, NJ

2387 ▬▬▬▬▬▬▬▬▬▬▬▬▬

IMPRINT ACADEMIC
PO Box 200, Exeter, Devon EX5 5HY
Telephone: 01392 851550
Fax: 01392 851178
Email: sandra@imprint.co.uk
Web Site: www.imprint.co.uk

Partners: J. K. B. Sutherland
K. A. Sutherland
Managing Editor: A. Freeman
Administrator: S. Good
Print Manager: D. Hall

*Academic & Scholarly; Philosophy; Politics &
World Affairs; Psychology & Psychiatry;
Religion & Theology; Scientific & Technical;
Sociology & Anthropology*

ISBNs, Imprints & Series:
978 0 907845, 978 1 84540 Idealist
Studies; Imprint Art; Societas

Overseas Representation:
USA: Ingram Publisher Services Inc,
Chambersburg, PA; Philosophy
Documentation Center, Charlottesville,
VA

2388 ▬▬▬▬▬▬▬▬▬▬▬▬▬

**IMRAY LAURIE NORIE & WILSON
LTD**
Wych House, The Broadway, St Ives,
Huntingdon PE27 5BT
Telephone: 01480 462114
Fax: 01480 496109
Email: ilnw@imray.com
Web Site: www.imray.com

Directors: William Wilson *(Managing)*
Mrs E. N. Wilson
Ian Rippington *(Sales)*
Accountant: Emma Woodfield

*Geography & Geology; Nautical; Sports &
Games; Transport; Travel & Topography*

New Titles: 10 (2008) , 10 (2009)
No of Employees: 20

ISBNs, Imprints & Series:
978 0 85288, 978 1 84623

Associated Companies:
Stanfords Charts

Distributor for:
Ordnance Survey; J. M. Pearson & Sons;
RCC Pilotage Foundation; RYA Royal
Yachting Association; United Kingdom
Hydrographic Office
France: Editions du Briel; Editions Vagnon;
Euromapping; Grafocarte
Netherlands: ANWB; Hydrographic Office
Norway: Hydrographic Office
Republic of Ireland: Irish Cruising Club
USA: Cruising Guide Publications;
Seaworthy Publications; University of
Hawaii Press

Overseas Representation:
Australia: Boat Books (Australia) Pty Ltd,

Sydney, NSW; Boat Books (Australia) Pty
Ltd, Melbourne, Vic
Belgium: The Boathouse, Nieuwpoort
France: Accastillage Diffusion, St-Martin de
Crau; Groupe Calade Diffusion, Aix-en-
Provence
Greece: AP Marine, Thessaloniki; Contract
Yacht Services, Levkas; Lalizas, Piraeus
PC; Tecrep Marine SA, Piraeus
Italy: Edizioni Il Frangente, Verona
Netherlands: Vrolijk Watersport BV,
Scheveningen
New Zealand: Trans-Pacific Marine Ltd,
Auckland
Republic of Ireland: Viking Marine, Dublin
Spain: Flint Suministros SL, Barcelona
Switzerland: Iten Yachttechnik, Arbon
USA: Bluewater Books and Charts, Fort
Lauderdale, FL; Seaworthy Publications
Inc, Port Washington, WI; Weems &
Plath, Annapolis, MD

Book Trade Association Membership:
International Map Trade Association

2389 ▬▬▬▬▬▬▬▬▬▬▬▬▬

IN EASY STEPS LTD
5C Southfield Road, Southam, Warks
CV47 0FB
Telephone: 01926 817999
Fax: 01926 817005
Email: sevanti@ineasysteps.com
Web Site: www.ineasysteps.com

Distribution:
Bookpoint Ltd, 130 Milton Park, Abingdon,
Oxon OX14 4SB
Telephone: 01235 400400
Fax: 01235 832068

Directors: Sevanti Kotecha *(Business
Development)*
Harshad Kotecha *(Publishing)*

*Accountancy & Taxation; Computer
Science; Crafts & Hobbies; Educational &
Textbooks; Electronic (Professional &
Academic); Industry, Business &
Management; Photography; Reference
Books, Directories & Dictionaries; Scientific
& Technical; Vocational Training & Careers*

ISBNs, Imprints & Series:
978 1 84078 In easy steps
978 1 874029 Complete Guides; In easy
steps

Overseas Representation:
Australia & New Zealand: Woodslane Pty
Ltd, Warriewood, NSW, Australia
South Africa: Intersoft Simon (Pty) Ltd,
Johannesburg
South East Asia: STP Distributors Pte Ltd,
Singapore
USA: Publishers Group West, Berkeley, CA

Book Trade Association Membership:
IPG

2390 ▬▬▬▬▬▬▬▬▬▬▬▬▬

**INCORPORATED COUNCIL OF LAW
REPORTING FOR ENGLAND AND
WALES**
Megarry House, 119 Chancery Lane,
London WC2A 1PP
Telephone: (020) 7242 6471
Fax: (020) 7831 5247
Email: postmaster@iclr.co.uk
Web Site: www.lawreports.co.uk

Binding Dept & Warehouse:
3 Star Yard, London WC2A 2JL
Telephone: (020) 7242 8632
Fax: (020) 7405 4898
Email: postmaster@iclr.co.uk
Web Site: www.lawreports.co.uk

Secretary: Kevin Laws
Managers: Graham Chapman *(Office)*
Stephen Mitchell *(Binding)*

Editor: Clive Scowen
Permissions Secretary: Helen Yates
(Assistant to Secretary)
Administrators: Louise Carlin *(Marketing)*
Claire Honey *(Subscription)*

Law

New Titles: 1 (2009)
No of Employees: 60
Annual Turnover: £5M

Overseas Representation:
Australia: LBC Information Services, Rozelle,
NSW
Canada: Carswell Publishing Ltd,
Scarborough, Ont

2391 ▬▬▬▬▬▬▬▬▬▬▬▬▬

INDEPENDENT MUSIC PRESS
PO Box 69, Church Stretton, Shropshire
SY6 6WZ
Telephone: 07954 135773
Fax: 01694 720049
Email: martin@impbooks.com
Web Site: www.impbooks.com

*Biography & Autobiography; Fashion &
Costume; Music*

New Titles: 8 (2008) , 8 (2009)
No of Employees: 2

2392 ▬▬▬▬▬▬▬▬▬▬▬▬▬

INSTANT-BOOKS UK LTD
10 Tennyson Close, Dallington,
Northampton NN5 7HJ
Email: instant.books@ntlworld.com
Web Site: www.instant-books.org

Directors: David Brawn *(Company
Secretary)*
Ros Brawn
P. Tomlinson
J. Cawley
N. Robbins-Cherry
G. Robbins-Cherry

*Atlases & Maps; Guide Books; Travel &
Topography*

New Titles: 20 (2008) , 40 (2009)

ISBNs, Imprints & Series:
978 1 84834 Instant-Book Editions; Tour &
Trail Maps; Walk! Guidebooks

2393 ▬▬▬▬▬▬▬▬▬▬▬▬▬

***INSTITUTE FOR EMPLOYMENT
STUDIES**
Mantell Building, University of Sussex,
Brighton BN1 9RF
Telephone: 01273 873694
Fax: 01273 690430
Email: iesbooks@employment-
studies.co.uk
Web Site: www.employment-studies.co.uk

Distributors:
Gardners Books Ltd, 1 Whittle Drive,
Eastbourne BN23 6QH
Telephone: 01323 521555
Fax: 01323 521666
Email: sales@gardners.com
Web Site: www.gardners.com

Publications & Marketing Manager:
Richard James

Industry, Business & Management

ISBNs, Imprints & Series:
978 1 85184 IES Report Series

2394 ▬▬▬▬▬▬▬▬▬▬▬▬▬

***INSTITUTE FOR FISCAL STUDIES**
Third Floor, 7 Ridgmount Street, London
WC1E 7AE

Telephone: (020) 7291 4800
Fax: (020) 7323 4780
Email: mailbox@ifs.org.uk
Web Site: www.ifs.org.uk/

Director: Robert Chote
Executive Administrator: Robert Markless
Research Director: Richard Blundell
External Relations Manager: Emma
  Hyman

*Academic & Scholarly; Accountancy &
Taxation; Economics; Law*

ISBNs, Imprints & Series:
978 0 902992, 978 1 873357
Commentary; Report; Working Paper

2395 ▬

INSTITUTE OF ACOUSTICS
77A St Peter's Street, St Albans, Herts
AL1 3BN
Telephone: 01727 848195
Fax: 01727 850553
Email: ioa@ioa.org.uk
Web Site: www.ioa.org.uk

Chief Executive: Kevin Macan-Lind
Editor: Ian Bennett
Advertising Manager: Dennis Baylis

Academic & Scholarly; Scientific & Technical

No of Employees: 10
Annual Turnover: £1M

2396 ▬

**INSTITUTE OF DEVELOPMENT
STUDIES**
University of Sussex, Brighton, Sussex
BN1 9RE
Telephone: 01273 915637
Fax: 01273 621202
Email: bookshop@ids.ac.uk &
  g.edwards@ids.ac.uk (Subscription
  enquiries)
Web Site: www.ids.ac.uk/go/bookshop/

Communications Manager: Nick Perkins
Co-ordinators: Alison Norwood
  (Production)
  Gary Edwards *(Marketing & Database)*

*Academic & Scholarly; Agriculture;
Bibliography & Library Science; Economics;
Educational & Textbooks; Environment &
Development Studies; Gender Studies;
Industry, Business & Management; Politics
& World Affairs; Sociology & Anthropology*

ISBNs, Imprints & Series:
978 0 903354, 978 1 85864 Institute of
  Development Studies
978 0 903715 Bridge Reports; Bulletin;
  Development Bibliographies; Discussion
  Papers; IDS Commisioned Studies;
  Research Reports; Working Papers

2397 ▬

**INSTITUTE OF EDUCATION
(PUBLICATIONS), UNIVERSITY OF
LONDON**
20 Bedford Way, London WC1H 0AL
Telephone: (020) 7612 6000
Email: ioepublications@ioe.ac.uk
Web Site: www.ioe.ac.uk/publications

Trade Enquiries, Orders & Distribution:
Central Books Ltd, 99 Wallis Road, London
E9 5LN
Telephone: 0845 458 9911
Fax: 0845 458 9912
Email: info@centralbooks.com
Web Site: www.centralbooks.com

Publisher: Jim Collins

Academic & Scholarly; Educational &

*Textbooks; Sociology & Anthropology;
Vocational Training & Careers*

New Titles: 15 (2009)
No of Employees: 4

ISBNs, Imprints & Series:
978 0 85473 Bedford Way Papers (series);
  Inaugural Professorial Lectures (series);
  Issues in Practice (series); Viewpoints
  (series)

Overseas Representation:
North America: Stylus Publishing Inc,
  Sterling, VA, USA

Book Trade Association Membership:
IPG

2398 ▬

***INSTITUTE OF EMPLOYMENT
RIGHTS**
The People's Centre,
50–54 Mount Pleasant, Liverpool L3 5SD
Telephone: 0151 702 6925
Fax: 0151 702 6935
Email: office@ier.org.uk
Web Site: www.ier.org.uk

Brighton Office:
Phelim MacCafferty,
Projects & Events Officer,
179 Preston Road, Brighton BN1 6AG
Telephone: 01273 330819
Email: phelim@ier.org.uk

Director: Carolyn Jones
Administration & Publications Officer:
  Treena Johnson
Projects & Events Officer: Phelim
  MacCafferty

*Academic & Scholarly; Economics; Law;
Politics & World Affairs*

ISBNs, Imprints & Series:
978 0 9543781, 978 0 9551795, 978 1
  873271

2399 ▬

**INSTITUTE OF FOOD SCIENCE &
TECHNOLOGY**
5 Cambridge Court,
210 Shepherds Bush Road, London W6 7NJ
Telephone: (020) 7603 6316
Fax: (020) 7602 9936
Email: info@ifst.org
Web Site: www.ifst.org

Chief Executive: Helen Wild
Team Executive: Angela Winchester

Scientific & Technical

ISBNs, Imprints & Series: 978 0 905367

Book Trade Association Membership:
Association of Learned Society Publishers

2400 ▬

**THE INSTITUTE OF MATHEMATICS
AND ITS APPLICATIONS**
Catherine Richards House,
16 Nelson Street, Southend-on-Sea, Essex
SS1 1EF
Telephone: 01702 354020
Fax: 01702 354111
Email: post@ima.org.uk
Web Site: www.ima.org.uk

Director: David Youdan *(Executive)*

Mathematics & Statistics

No of Employees: 13

ISBNs, Imprints & Series: 978 0 905091

Book Trade Association Membership:
Association of Learned & Professional
Society Publishers

2401 ▬

**INSTITUTE OF PHYSICS &
ENGINEERING IN MEDICINE**
Fairmount House, 230 Tadcaster Road, York
YO24 1ES
Telephone: 01904 610821
Fax: 01904 612279
Email: office@ipem.ac.uk
Web Site: www.ipem.ac.uk

General Secretary: R. W. Neilson
Publications Co-ordinator: M. Goodall

*Engineering; Medical (incl. Self Help &
Alternative Medicine); Physics; Scientific &
Technical*

New Titles: 2 (2008) , 4 (2009)
No of Employees: 10

ISBNs, Imprints & Series:
978 1 903613 IPEM Report Series

Book Trade Association Membership:
Association of Learned & Professional
Society Publishers

2402 ▬

**INSTITUTION OF ENGINEERING AND
TECHNOLOGY (IET)**
Michael Faraday House, Six Hills Way,
Stevenage, Herts SG1 2AY
Telephone: 01438 767328
Fax: 01438 765515
Email: books@theiet.org
Web Site: www.theiet.org

Trade Enquiries & Orders:
PO Box 96, Stevenage, Herts SG1 2SD
Telephone: 01438 767328
Fax: 01438 767375
Email: sales@theiet.org
Web Site: www.theiet.org

Warehouse:
7 Fulton Close, Argyle Way, Stevenage,
Herts
Telephone: 01438 355029
Fax: 01438 355034

Directors: Steven Mair *(Managing)*
  Amanda Weaver *(Publishing)*
Sales Manager: Bianca Campbell

*Academic & Scholarly; Computer Science;
Educational & Textbooks; Electronic
(Professional & Academic); Engineering;
Industry, Business & Management;
Scientific & Technical*

New Titles: 17 (2008) , 20 (2009)

ISBNs, Imprints & Series:
978 0 85296, 978 0 86341, 978 0 901223,
  978 0 906048, 978 1 84919

Associated Companies:
Peter Peregrinus Ltd
USA: INSPEC Inc

Overseas Representation:
Far East: Clarke Associates Ltd, Bristol, UK
USA & Canada: Princeton Selling Group Inc,
  Wayne, PA, USA

Book Trade Association Membership:
BA; IGSMTP; Association of Learned &
Professional Society Publishers

2403 ▬

INTELLECT LTD
The Mill, Parnall Road, Fishponds, Bristol
BS16 3JG
Telephone: 0117 958 9910
Fax: 0117 958 9911

Email: info@intellectbooks.com
Web Site: www.intellectbooks.com/

Distribution:
Gardners Books, 1 Whittle Drive,
Eastbourne BN23 6QH
Telephone: 01323 521777
Fax: 01323 521666
Email: custcare@gardners.com
Web Site: www.gardners.com

Chairman: Masoud Yazdani *(Editor-in-
  Chief)*
Associate Publisher: May Yao

*Academic & Scholarly; Architecture &
Design; Cinema, Video, TV & Radio;
Computer Science; Educational &
Textbooks; Electronic (Educational);
Electronic (Professional & Academic);
Environment & Development Studies;
Gender Studies; History & Antiquarian;
Languages & Linguistics; Literature &
Criticism; Philosophy; Scientific & Technical;
Sociology & Anthropology; Theatre, Drama
& Dance*

New Titles: 42 (2008) , 52 (2009)
No of Employees: 17
Annual Turnover: £800,000

ISBNs, Imprints & Series:
Advances in Art & Urban Futures; Advances
  in Human Computer Interaction; Bahá'í
  Books (series); Changing Media,
  Changing Europe (series); Computer and
  the History of Art (series); Decode Books
  (series); ECREA (series); Elm Bank
  Publications; European Studies Series;
  Intellect Play Series; Progress in Neural
  Networks; Readings in Art and Design
  Education (series); Studies in Popular
  Culture (series); Theatre & Consciousness
  (series); Trends in Functional
  Programming; Venton
978 0 89391, 978 1 56750, 978 1 84150,
  978 1 871516

Overseas Representation:
Australasia: Inbooks, Sydney, NSW,
  Australia
North America: University of Chicago Press,
  Chicago, IL, USA
Singapore: Book Editions

Book Trade Association Membership:
IPG

2404 ▬

***INTERACTYX**
[formerly The Enterprise Library]
2 Aboyne Castle Business Centre, Aboyne,
Aberdeenshire AB34 5LP
Telephone: 01339 386282
Fax: 01339 887787
Email: info@ent-lib.co.uk
Web Site: www.livecon.com

Academic & Scholarly

Book Trade Association Membership:
Publishers Association

2405 ▬

INTERNATIONAL MEDICAL PRESS
36 St Mary at Hill, London EC3R 8DU
Telephone: (020) 7398 0700
Fax: (020) 7398 0701
Email: info@intmedpress.com
Web Site: www.intmedpress.com

*Academic & Scholarly; Electronic
(Professional & Academic); Medical (incl.
Self Help & Alternative Medicine)*

ISBNs, Imprints & Series: 978 1 901769

Book Trade Association Membership:
Publishers Association

2406 ━━━━

**INTERNATIONAL NETWORK FOR
THE AVAILABILITY OF SCIENTIFIC
PUBLICATIONS (INASP)**
58 St Aldates, Oxford OX1 1ST
Telephone: 01865 249909
Fax: 01865 251060
Email: inasp@inasp.info
Web Site: www.inasp.info/

Director: Tag McEntegart *(Executive)*
Senior Programme Manager: Julie
  Walker *(Head of Publishing Support)*
Programme Officer: Sioux Cumming
  (Publishing Support)

*Academic & Scholarly; Bibliography &
Library Science; Electronic (Professional &
Academic); Reference Books, Directories &
Dictionaries*

ISBNs, Imprints & Series: 978 1 902928

Book Trade Association Membership:
Association of Learned & Professional
Society Publishers

2407 ━━━━

IOP PUBLISHING
Dirac House, Temple Back, Bristol BS1 6BE
Telephone: 0117 929 7481
Fax: 0117 929 4318
Email: custserv@iop.org
Web Site: www.iop.org

Directors: Jerry Cowhig *(Managing)*
  Michael Bray *(Financial)*
  Ken Lillywhite *(Business Development &
    Journals Sales & Marketing)*
  Karen O'Flaherty *(Group Human
    Resources)*
  Nicola Gulley *(Editorial)*
  James Walker *(Group IT)*

*Computer Science; Electronic (Professional
& Academic); Mathematics & Statistics;
Physics; Scientific & Technical*

New Titles: 3 (2008) , 6 (2009)
No of Employees: 262
Annual Turnover: £33.83M

Parent Company:
The Institute of Physics

Associated Companies:
USA: IOP Publishing Inc

Overseas Representation:
Japan (books): Eastern Book Service Inc,
  Tokyo, Japan
Japan (journals): Maruzen Co Ltd, Tokyo,
  Japan
Other Territories (books): Enquiries, Institute
  of Physics Publishing, Bristol, UK
Pakistan (books): Pak Book Corporation,
  Lahore, Pakistan
*South East Asia, New Zealand & Australia
  (books):* Hemisphere Publication Services,
  Singapore
USA & Canada (books): IOP Publishing,
  Williston, VT, USA
USA, Canada & Mexico (journals):
  American Institute of Physics, Melville,
  NY, USA

Book Trade Association Membership:
IGSMTP; Association of Learned &
Professional Society Publishers

2408 ━━━━

IRWELL PRESS LTD
59A High Street, Clophill, Beds MK45 4BE
Telephone: 01525 861888
Fax: 01525 862044
Email: George@irwellpress.co.uk
Web Site: www.irwellpress.co.uk

Directors: George Reeve
  Chris Hawkins

Transport

New Titles: 9 (2008) , 8 (2009)

ISBNs, Imprints & Series:
978 1 871608, 978 1 903266, 978 1
  906919

Overseas Representation:
Australia: Train World Property, East
  Brighton, Vic

2409 ━━━━

*ISIS PUBLISHING LTD
Unit 7, Centremead, Osney Mead, Oxford
OX2 0ES
Telephone: 01865 250333
Fax: 01865 790358
Email: pauline.horne@isis-publishing.co.uk
Web Site: www.isis-publishing.co.uk

Distribution:
Ulverscroft Large Print Books Ltd,
The Green, Bradgate Road, Anstey,
Leicester LE7 7FU
Telephone: 0116 236 4325
Fax: 0116 234 0205
Email: sales@ulverscroft.co.uk
Web Site: www.ulverscroft.co.uk

Director: Robert Thirlby *(Chief Executive)*
Managers: Pauline Horne *(Distribution,
  General, Sales & Marketing)*
  Lorna Dubose *(Finance)*
  Becky Curtis *(Editorial – General Books)*

*Audio Books; Biography & Autobiography;
Crime; Fiction; Humour; Poetry; Science
Fiction; Large Print Publications*

ISBNs, Imprints & Series:
978 0 7531, 978 1 84559, 978 1 85089,
  978 1 85695

Parent Company:
Ulverscroft Group Ltd

Overseas Representation:
Australia: Ulverscroft Large Print Books
  (Australia) Pty Ltd, Crows Nest, NSW
Canada: Stricker Books, Toronto, Ont
Denmark: Bierman & Bierman A/S,
  Grindsted
Japan: PIC, Tokyo
New Zealand: Ulverscroft Large Print Books
  Ltd, Fielding
Norway: Lydlitteratur, Nesoya
Republic of Ireland: Ulverscroft Large Print
  Books Ltd, Dublin
South Africa (Audio): Book Talk Pty Ltd,
  Parkhurst, South Africa
Sweden: Bibliotekstjanst AB, Lund
USA (Audio & Large print): Ulverscroft
  Large Print Books (USA) Inc, West
  Seneca, NY, USA

2410 ━━━━

THE ISLAMIC TEXTS SOCIETY
Botanic House, 100 Hills Road, Cambridge
CB2 1JZ
Telephone: 01223 314387
Fax: 01223 324342
Email: mail@its.org.uk
Web Site: www.its.org.uk

Distribution:
Orca Book Services Ltd, Unit A3,
Fleets Corner, Poole, Dorset BH17 0HL
Telephone: 01202 665432
Fax: 01202 666219
Email: orders@orcabookservices.co.uk

Trust Secretary: Fatima Azzam

*Academic & Scholarly; Law; Religion &
Theology; Islam*

ISBNs, Imprints & Series:
Al-Ghazali Series
978 0 946621, 978 1 903682 Fundamental
  Rights & Liberties Series: Principles &
  Applications

Overseas Representation:
USA: Independent Publishers Group (IPG),
  Chicago, IL

Book Trade Association Membership:
Publishers Association

2411 ━━━━

*ISTE LTD
6 Fitzroy Square, London W1T 5DX
Telephone: (020) 7387 7333
Fax: (020) 7380 1051
Email: info@iste.co.uk
Web Site: www.iste.co.uk

Book Trade Association Membership:
Publishers Association

2412 ━━━━

ITHACA PRESS
[Books on The Middle East]
8 Southern Court, South Street, Reading
RG1 4QS
Telephone: 0118 959 7847
Fax: 0118 959 7356 (Trade Enquiries &
  Orders)
Email: dan@garnetpublishing.co.uk
Web Site: www.garnetpublishing.co.uk

Representation (UK):
Compass Academic,
The Barley Mow Centre,
10 Barley Mow Passage, Chiswick, London
W4 4PH
Telephone: (020) 8994 6477

Managing Director: Khalil Abu Shawareb
Managers: Dan Nunn *(Editorial, Rights &
  Permissions)*
  Nick Holroyd *(Production Controller)*

*Academic & Scholarly; Economics; Fiction;
Gender Studies; History & Antiquarian;
Languages & Linguistics; Law; Literature &
Criticism; Politics & World Affairs; Religion
& Theology; Sociology & Anthropology*

New Titles: 12 (2008) , 12 (2009)

ISBNs, Imprints & Series:
978 0 86372, 978 0 903729

Parent Company:
Garnet Publishing Ltd

Overseas Representation:
Australia: InBooks, Frenchs Forest, NSW
Europe: Andrew Durnell Marketing Ltd,
  Tunbridge Wells, UK
USA (academic): International Specialized
  Book Services Inc, Portland, OR, USA
USA (trade): International Publishers
  Marketing Inc, Sterling, VA, USA

Book Trade Association Membership:
IPG

2413 ━━━━

IVP
IVP Book Centre, Norton Street,
Nottingham NG7 3HR
Telephone: 0115 978 1054
Fax: 0115 942 2694
Email: ivp@ivpbooks.com
Web Site: www.ivpbooks.com

Chief Executive Officer: Brian Wilson
Finance & Operations: George Russell

*Academic & Scholarly; Reference Books,
Directories & Dictionaries; Religion &
Theology*

New Titles: 48 (2008) , 44 (2009)

ISBNs, Imprints & Series:
978 0 85110, 978 0 85111, 978 1 84474
  Apollos; IVP
978 0 85684 Crossway Books

Distributor for:
Bible Society; Christian Medical Fellowship;
  Dorling Kindersley Religious; Eagle
  Publishing; Good Book Company;
  Piquant
Australia: Matthias Media; Youthworks
USA: Crossway Books; IVP

Overseas Representation:
East Africa: Keswick Book Society, Nairobi,
  Kenya
Netherlands: ASAF Import 3, Westervoort
New Zealand: Soul Distributors, Auckland
Philippines: Evangelical Outreach Inc,
  Quezon City; Overseas Missionary
  Fellowship, Manila
Singapore: Bethesda Book Centre
South Africa: Protestant Book Centre, Cape
  Town
Sweden: Din Bok -
  Formsamlingsbokhandeln, Goteborg
USA: InterVarsity Press, Downers Grove, IL

Book Trade Association Membership:
Christian Suppliers' Group; Evangelical
Christian Publishers Association

2414 ━━━━

IWA PUBLISHING
Alliance House, 12 Caxton Street, London
SW1H 0QS
Telephone: (020) 7654 5500
Fax: (020) 7654 5555
Email: publications@iwap.co.uk
Web Site: www.iwapublishing.com

Orders:
Portland Customer Services,
Commerce Way, Whitehall Industrial Estate,
Colchester CO2 8HP
Telephone: 01206 796351
Fax: 01206 799331
Email: sales@portland-services.com

**Publisher, Managing Director &
  Commissioning Editor:** Michael Dunn
Managers: Michelle Jones *(Publications)*
  Ian Morgan *(Marketing)*

*Academic & Scholarly; Electronic
(Professional & Academic); Engineering;
Industry, Business & Management;
Reference Books, Directories &
Dictionaries; Scientific & Technical*

No of Employees: 10

ISBNs, Imprints & Series:
978 1 84339, 978 1 900222

Parent Company:
International Water Association

Overseas Representation:
Australia & New Zealand: Australian Water
  Association, Artarmon, NSW, Australia;
  DA Information Services Pty Ltd,
  Mitcham, Vic, Australia
India: Surinder K. Lijhara, Overseas Media,
  Faridabad
Japan: Kay Kato Associates, Kanagawa
Malaysia: Tony Poh, STM Publisher Services
  Pte Ltd, Singapore
North America: Martin P. Hill Consulting,
  New York, NY, USA
Taiwan: Ta Tong Book Co Ltd, Taipei

Book Trade Association Membership:
Association of Learned & Professional
Society Publishers

2415

*JAMES & JAMES (PUBLISHERS) LTD
2–5 Benjamin Street, London E1M 5QL
Email: mj@tmiltd.com
Web Site: www.tmiltd.com

Chairman: Hamish MacGibbon

*Academic & Scholarly; History &
Antiquarian; Industry, Business &
Management*

ISBNs, Imprints & Series: 978 0 907383

Parent Company:
Third Millennium Information Ltd

2416

JANE'S INFORMATION GROUP LTD
163 Brighton Road, Coulsdon, Surrey
CR5 2YH
Telephone: (020) 8700 3745
Fax: (020) 8763 1006
Email: info.uk@janes.com
Web Site: www.janes.com

Directors: Ian Kay *(Reference)*
Steve Cannon *(Finance)*
Michael Dell
Public Relations: Amanda Castle

*Aviation; Electronic (Professional &
Academic); Industry, Business &
Management; Military & War; Nautical;
Politics & World Affairs; Reference Books,
Directories & Dictionaries; Transport*

ISBNs, Imprints & Series: 978 0 7106

Parent Company:
IHS

Overseas Representation:
Australia & New Zealand: Jane's
Information Group Australia, Rozelle,
NSW, Australia
Egypt: Middle East Agency, Cairo
India: Jane's Information Group, New Delhi
*Indonesia, Korea, Malaysia, Singapore &
Taiwan:* Jane's Information Group Asia,
Singapore
Japan: Jane's Information Group, Tokyo
Kuwait & Saudi Arabia: Jane's Information
Group, Dubai, UAE
North & South America: Jane's Information
Group Inc, Alexandria, VA, USA
Worldwide (excluding countries listed):
Jane's Information Group, UK

Book Trade Association Membership:
Data Publishers Association

2417

JANUS PUBLISHING CO LTD
105–107 Gloucester Place, London
W1U 6BY
Telephone: (020) 7486 6633
Fax: (020) 7486 6090
Email: publisher@januspublishing.co.uk
Web Site: www.januspublishing.co.uk

Distribution/Sales:
25 Winnock Road, Colchester, Essex
CO1 2BG
Telephone: 01206 578856
Fax: 01206 573221
Email: sales@januspublishing.co.uk

Directors: J. A. Leung *(Managing, Rights &
Permissions)*
Tina Brand *(Sales)*

*Academic & Scholarly; Biography &
Autobiography; Children's Books; Crime;
Do-It-Yourself; Economics; Educational &
Textbooks; Fashion & Costume; Fiction; Fine
Art & Art History; History & Antiquarian;
Humour; Literature & Criticism; Magic & the
Occult; Medical (incl. Self Help & Alternative*

*Medicine); Military & War; Nautical;
Philosophy; Poetry; Politics & World Affairs;
Religion & Theology; Science Fiction;
Sociology & Anthropology; Sports &
Games; Theatre, Drama & Dance*

New Titles: 18 (2008) , 20 (2009)
No of Employees: 5
Annual Turnover: £130,000

ISBNs, Imprints & Series:
978 1 85756 Janus Books
978 1 90283 Empiricus Books

Parent Company:
Junction Books Ltd

Overseas Representation:
Malaysia, Singapore & Brunei: Proof Line
(M) Sdn Bhd, Petaling Jaya, Malaysia
Scandinavia: Richard Bowen c/o Janus
Publishing Co Ltd, London, UK
USA & Canada: IPG, Concord, MA, USA

Book Trade Association Membership:
BA; IPG

2418

JARNDYCE BOOKSELLERS
46 Great Russell Street, London WC1B 3PA
Telephone: (020) 7631 4220
Fax: (020) 7631 1882
Email: books@jarndyce.co.uk
Web Site: www.jarndyce.co.uk

Partners: Brian Lake
Janet Nassau

*Academic & Scholarly; Bibliography &
Library Science; Economics; Fiction;
Languages & Linguistics; Literature &
Criticism; Poetry; Reference Books,
Directories & Dictionaries; Sociology &
Anthropology*

ISBNs, Imprints & Series: 978 1 900718

Book Trade Association Membership:
Antiquarian Booksellers' Association;
Provincial Booksellers' Fairs Association

2419

JOLLY LEARNING LTD
Tailours House, High Road, Chigwell, Essex
IG7 6DL
Telephone: (020) 8501 0405
Fax: (020) 8500 1696
Email: chris@jollylearning.co.uk
Web Site: www.jollylearning.co.uk

Managing Director: Christopher Jolly
Managers: Diane Harding *(Accounts)*
Androula Stratton *(Marketing)*
Angela Hockley *(Editorial)*

*Educational & Textbooks; Electronic
(Educational)*

No of Employees: 10
Annual Turnover: £3M

ISBNs, Imprints & Series:
978 1 84414, 978 1 870946, 978 1 903619

Overseas Representation:
USA: Jolly Learning Ltd, c/o American
International Distribution Corporation,
Williston, VT

Book Trade Association Membership:
IPG

2420

***JONES & BARTLETT
INTERNATIONAL**
Barb House, Barb Mews, London W6 7PA
Telephone: 01278 723553
Fax: 01278 723554
Email: ldowning@jbpub.com

Web Site: www.jbpub.com

Warehouse, Trade Enquiries & Orders:
Macmillan Distribution (MDL), Brunel Road,
Houndmills, Basingstoke RG21 6XS
Telephone: 01256 329242
Fax: 01256 331413
Email: mdl@macmillan.co.uk
Web Site: www.macmillan-mdl.co.uk

Managers: Richard Warner
Lorna Downing *(Product)*
Chris Gribble *(Sales)*

*Biology & Zoology; Chemistry; Computer
Science; Educational & Textbooks;
Geography & Geology; Law; Mathematics
& Statistics; Medical (incl. Self Help &
Alternative Medicine); Physics; Psychology
& Psychiatry; Scientific & Technical; Sports &
Games; Vocational Training & Careers*

ISBNs, Imprints & Series:
978 0 7637, 978 0 86729

Parent Company:
USA: Jones & Bartlett Inc

2421

JORDAN PUBLISHING LTD
21 St Thomas Street, Bristol BS1 6JS
Telephone: 0117 918 1530
Fax: 0117 925 0486
Email: leah-
woolcock@jordanpublishing.co.uk
Web Site: www.jordanpublishing.co.uk

Managing Director: Caroline Vandridge-
Ames
Head of Marketing & Sales: Ann-Marie
Vowles
Editorial Manager: Achim Bosse

*Accountancy & Taxation; Crime; Electronic
(Professional & Academic); Industry,
Business & Management; Law*

ISBNs, Imprints & Series:
978 0 85308, 978 1 84661 Family Law;
Jordans

Parent Company:
West of England Trust

2422

*RICHARD JOSEPH PUBLISHERS LTD
PO Box 15, Torrington, Devon EX38 8ZJ
Telephone: 01805 625750
Fax: 01805 625376
Email: office@sheppardsworld.co.uk
Web Site: www.sheppardsworld.co.uk

Managing Director: Richard Joseph
Compiler: (to be appointed)
Production Manager: Claire Brumham

Reference Books, Directories & Dictionaries

ISBNs, Imprints & Series:
978 1 872699 Sheppard

2423

S. KARGER AG
c/o London Liaison Office, 4 Rickett Street,
London SW6 1RU
Telephone: (020) 7386 0500
Fax: (020) 7610 3337
Email: uk@karger.ch
Web Site: www.karger.com

President: Dr Thomas Karger
Chief Executive Officer: Gabriella Karger
Finance: Rolf Zurlinden
Sales & Marketing: Moritz Thommen
Production: Hermann Vonlanthen
Editorial & Rights: Thomas Nold

Mathematics & Statistics; Medical (incl. Self

*Help & Alternative Medicine); Psychology &
Psychiatry*

New Titles: 60 (2008) , 60 (2009)
No of Employees: 250

ISBNs, Imprints & Series: 978 3 8055

Parent Company:
Switzerland: S. Karger AG

Overseas Representation:
Australia: DA Information Services Pty Ltd,
Mitcham, Vic
Baltic States: Bookshop Krisostomus, Tartu,
Estonia
*China, Hong Kong, Taiwan, Malaysia &
Indonesia:* Karger China, Shanghai, P. R.
of China
France: Librairie Médi-Sciences SARL, Paris
Germany: S. Karger GmbH, Freiburg
*Gulf Council countries, Iran, Middle East,
North Africa & Turkey:* Trans Middle East
International Distribution Co Ltd,
Amman, Jordan
India, Bangladesh & Sri Lanka: Karger India,
New Delhi, India; Panther Publishers
Private Ltd, Bangalore, India
Japan: Karger Japan Inc, Tokyo
Pakistan: Tahir M. Lodhi, Lahore
Republic of Ireland: S. Karger AG, London,
UK
Singapore: APAC Publishers Services Pte Ltd
South & Central America: Cranbury
International LLC, Montpelier, VT, USA
South Africa: Academic Marketing Services
(Pty) Ltd, Craighall
Switzerland (Head Office): S. Karger AG,
Basel, Switzerland
Thailand: Karger Libri International
Subscription Agency, Bangkok
USA: S. Karger Publishers Inc, Unionville

2424

KARNAC BOOKS LTD
118 Finchley Road, London NW3 5HT
Telephone: (020) 7431 1075
Fax: (020) 7435 9076
Email: shop@karnacbooks.com
Web Site: www.karnacbooks.com

Directors: Oliver Rathbone *(Managing)*
Alex Massey *(Sales)*

Gender Studies; Psychology & Psychiatry

New Titles: 70 (2008) , 90 (2009)
No of Employees: 11

ISBNs, Imprints & Series:
978 0 946439, 978 1 85575 Clunie Press;
Institute of Psycho-Analysis, London;
Karnac Books; Library of Analytical
Psychology; Maresfield Library; Systemic
Thinking Theory & Practice Series;
Tavistock Institute of Marital Studies
(TIMS); Winnicott Studies (Series)
978 1 85575 Harris Meltzer Trust;
International Psychoanalytical
Association; Tavistock Clinic Series;
UKCP Series

Distributor for:
Apex One; Carl Auer International; Rebus
Press; Tavistock Institute of Marital
Studies; Zeig Tucker & Co

Overseas Representation:
Europe: Andrew Durnell Marketing Ltd,
Tunbridge Wells, UK

Book Trade Association Membership:
BA; IPG

2425

*RICHARD KAY PUBLICATIONS
80 Sleaford Road, Boston, Lincs PE21 8EU
Telephone: 01205 353231
Email: rebecca@richardkay.freeserve.co.uk

Proprietor: Richard K. Allday

Academic & Scholarly; Biography & Autobiography; History & Antiquarian; Medical (incl. Self Help & Alternative Medicine); Military & War; Politics & World Affairs; Reference Books, Directories & Dictionaries

ISBNs, Imprints & Series:
978 0 902662, 978 1 902882

Distributor for:
History of Boston Project

2426

KENYON-DEANE
10 Station Road Industrial Estate, Colwall, Malvern, Herefordshire WR13 6RN
Telephone: 01684 540154
Fax: 01684 540154
Email: simon@cressrelles.co.uk
Web Site: www.cressrelles.co.uk

Managers: Leslie Smith *(Finance, Production, Editorial & Rights)*
Simon Smith *(Sales & Marketing)*

Theatre, Drama & Dance

New Titles: 6 (2008) , 8 (2009)

ISBNs, Imprints & Series: 978 0 7155

Parent Company:
Cressrelles Publishing Co Ltd

Distributor for:
USA: Anchorage Press

Overseas Representation:
Australia: Origin Theatrical, Sydney, NSW
New Zealand: Play Bureau of New Zealand Ltd, New Plymouth
Republic of Ireland: Drama League of Ireland, Dublin
South Africa: Dalro (Pty) Ltd, Braamfontein
USA: Bakers Plays, Quincy, MA

2427

KEW PUBLISHING
Sir Joseph Banks Building, Royal Botanic Gardens, Kew, Richmond, Surrey TW9 3AE
Telephone: (020) 8332 5751 & 5219 (trade enquiries)
Fax: (020) 8332 5646
Email: publishing@kew.org & kewbooks@kew.org
Web Site: www.kew.org & www.kewbooks.org

Head of Publishing: Gina Fullerlove
Sales, Marketing & Business Development: John Harris
Production Controller: Lloyd Kirton

Academic & Scholarly; Biology & Zoology; Fine Art & Art History; Scientific & Technical

New Titles: 20 (2008) , 30 (2009)
No of Employees: 12
Annual Turnover: £700,000

ISBNs, Imprints & Series: 978 1 84246

Parent Company:
UK: Royal Botanic Gardens

Book Trade Association Membership:
IPG

2428

HILDA KING EDUCATIONAL
Ashwells Manor Drive, Penn, Bucks HP10 8EU
Telephone: 01494 813947 & 817947
Fax: 01494 813947
Email: rkinged@aol.com

Web Site: www.hildaking.co.uk

Director: Hilda King
Executive: R. E. King

Educational & Textbooks

ISBNs, Imprints & Series: 978 1 873533

2429

LAURENCE KING PUBLISHING LTD
361–373 City Road, London EC1V 1LR
Telephone: (020) 7841 6900
Fax: (020) 7841 6939
Email: enquiries@laurenceking.com
Web Site: www.laurenceking.com

Chairman: Nick Perren
Directors: Laurence King *(Managing)*
John Stoddart *(Financial)*
Felicity Awdry *(Production)*
Philip Cooper *(Editorial)*
Lee Ripley *(Editorial–College & Fine Art)*
Managers: Janet Pilch *(Rights)*
Lewis Gill *(Marketing)*
Katy Dunningham *(Sales)*

Architecture & Design; Fashion & Costume; Fine Art & Art History

New Titles: 40 (2008) , 50 (2009)
No of Employees: 35

ISBNs, Imprints & Series:
Portfolio (series)

Book Trade Association Membership:
Publishers Association

2430

THE KING'S ENGLAND PRESS
Cambertown House, Commercial Road, Goldthorpe, Rotherham S63 9BL
Telephone: 01484 663790
Fax: 01484 663790
Email: steve@kingsengland.com
Web Site: www.kingsengland.com & www.pottypoets.com

Managing Director: Steve Rudd
Company Secretary: Debbie Nunn

Archaeology; Children's Books; History & Antiquarian; Poetry; Travel & Topography

ISBNs, Imprints & Series: 978 1 872438

2431

JESSICA KINGSLEY PUBLISHERS
116 Pentonville Road, London N1 9JB
Telephone: (020) 7833 2307
Fax: (020) 7837 2917
Email: post@jkp.com
Web Site: www.jkp.com

Trade Enquiries & Orders:
Macmillan Distribution (MDL), Brunel Road, Houndmills, Basingstoke, Hants RG21 6XS
Telephone: 01256 302985
Fax: 01256 841426
Email: trade@macmillan.co.uk
Web Site: www.macmillandistribution.co.uk

Managing Director: Jessica Kingsley
Finance: Dee Brigham
Marketing: Helen Longmate
Electronic Media: Jemima Kingsley
Sales: Robert Ertle
Managers: Helen Longmate *(Rights)*
Octavia Kingsley *(Production)*

Academic & Scholarly; Children's Books; Educational & Textbooks; Health & Beauty; Law; Medical (incl. Self Help & Alternative Medicine); Psychology & Psychiatry; Religion & Theology; Sociology & Anthropology; Sports & Games; Vocational Training & Careers

New Titles: 148 (2008) , 140 (2009)
No of Employees: 30

ISBNs, Imprints & Series:
978 1 84310 Community, Culture and Change
978 1 84310, 978 1 85302 Jessica Kingsley Publishers
978 1 84819 Singing Dragon
978 1 85302 Children in Charge; Forensic Focus; Research Highlights in Social Work

Associated Companies:
USA: Jessica Kingsley Publishers Inc

Overseas Representation:
Australia & New Zealand: Footprint Books Pty, Mona Vale, NSW, Australia
Canada: University of British Columbia Press, Vancouver, BC
Europe: Andrew Durnell Marketing Ltd, Tunbridge Wells, UK
Hong Kong, Taiwan, China, Philippines & Korea: Asia Publishers Services Ltd, Hong Kong
Japan: United Publishers Services Ltd, Tokyo
USA: Jessica Kingsley Publishers Inc, Philadelphia

Book Trade Association Membership:
Publishers Association; EPC; CAPP

2432

KINGSWAY PUBLICATIONS
[a division of Kingsway Communications Ltd]
Lottbridge Drove, Eastbourne, East Sussex BN23 6NT
Telephone: 01323 437751
Fax: 01323 411970
Email: books@kingsway.co.uk
Web Site: www.kingsway.co.uk

Distribution & Warehouse:
STL Wholesale, PO Box 300, Kingstown Broadway, Carlisle, Cumbria CA3 0QS
Telephone: 01228 512512
Fax: 01228 514949

Chief Executive Officer: John Paculabo
Managers: Richard Herkes *(Publishing)*
Bill Owen *(Finance & Administration)*
Miriam Doherty *(Trade Books)*

Biography & Autobiography; Religion & Theology

New Titles: 13 (2008) , 10 (2009)

ISBNs, Imprints & Series:
Great Ideas; Honor; Life Journey; Nexgen; Riveroak; Survivor; Victor
978 0 85476, 978 0 85491, 978 0 86065, 978 0 86239, 978 0 902088, 978 1 84291 Kingsway

Parent Company:
David C. Cook

Distributor for:
Barbour; Charisma House; Harrison House; Lifeway, Broodman & Holmon; New Leaf Press; Regal

Overseas Representation:
Australia: Kennedy International, NSW
Canada: David C. Cook Distribution Canada, Paris, Ont
South Africa: Struik Christian Books Pty Ltd, Maitland, Cape Town

2433

*CHRIS KINGTON PUBLISHING
33–41 Dallington Street, London EC1V 0BB
Telephone: (020) 7954 3474
Fax: 0845 450 6410
Email: enquiries@chriskingtonpublishing.co.uk

Web Site: www.chriskingtonpublishing.co.uk

Educational & Textbooks; Electronic (Professional & Academic)

Book Trade Association Membership:
Publishers Association

2434

KNOW THE SCORE BOOKS
118 Alcester Road, Studley, Warwickshire B80 7NT
Telephone: 01527 454482
Fax: 01527 452183
Email: info@knowthescorebooks.com
Web Site: www.knowthescorebooks.com

Warehouse:
Frating Green, Colchester, Essex CO7 7DW
Telephone: 01206 255678
Fax: 01206 255930
Email: sales@tbs-ltd.co.uk

Managing Director: Simon Lowe
Marketing Manager: Tony Lyons

Sports & Games; Travel & Topography

New Titles: 30 (2008) , 30 (2009)
No of Employees: 3
Annual Turnover: £420,000

ISBNs, Imprints & Series:
978 1 84818, 978 1 905449

Book Trade Association Membership:
IPG

2435

KOGAN PAGE LTD
120 Pentonville Road, London N1 9JN
Telephone: (020) 7278 0433
Fax: (020) 7837 6348
Email: kpinfo@koganpage.com or kpsales@koganpage.com
Web Site: www.koganpage.com

Warehouse:
Littlehampton Book Services, Faraday Close, Durrington, Worthing, West Sussex BN13 3RB
Telephone: 01903 828800
Fax: 01903 828802

Directors: Philip Kogan *(Chairman)*
Helen Kogan *(Managing)*
Gordon Watts *(Financial)*
Louise Cameron *(Publishing Services)*
Ben Glover *(Sales)*
Cathy Frazer *(Marketing)*

Academic & Scholarly; Accountancy & Taxation; Educational & Textbooks; Electronic (Educational); Electronic (Professional & Academic); Industry, Business & Management; Reference Books, Directories & Dictionaries; Transport; Vocational Training & Careers

ISBNs, Imprints & Series: 978 0 7494

Distributor for:
Bloomberg Press [excluding Americas]; GMB Publishing

Overseas Representation:
Australia & New Zealand: Woodslane Pty Ltd, Warriewood, NSW, Australia
Burma, China, Vietnam, Hong Kong, Taiwan, Middle East & Thailand: Publishers International Marketing, London, UK
Canada: Renouf Publishing Co Ltd, Ottawa, Ont
Caribbean: InterMedia Americana (IMA) Ltd, London, UK
India: Viva Books, New Delhi
Singapore, Malaysia & Brunei: Penguin Books Singapore, Jurong, Singapore

South Africa: Book Promotions Pty Ltd, Diep River
USA: Ingram Publisher Services, La Vergne, TN

Book Trade Association Membership:
Publishers Association; Data Publishers Association

2436

KUBE PUBLISHING LTD
Ratby Lane, Markfield, Leicester LE67 9SY
Telephone: 01530 249230
Fax: 01530 249656
Email: info@kubepublishing.com
Web Site: www.kubepublishing.com

Director: Haris Ahmad
Executives: Anwar Cara *(Production)*
Khalid Manzoor *(Distribution & Sales)*
Administration: Miss Rufeedah Cara
Commissioning Editor: Yahya Birt

Academic & Scholarly; Audio Books; Children's Books; Economics; Educational & Textbooks; Law; Religion & Theology

New Titles: 10 (2008) , 19 (2009)

ISBNs, Imprints & Series:
978 0 86037 Islamic Foundation
978 0 9536768 Revival
978 1 84774 Kube

Distributor for:
Pakistan: Institute of Policy Studies; Islamic Book Publishers
USA: Foundation for Islamic Knowledge; Institute of Islamic Thought

Overseas Representation:
USA & Canada: Consortium Sales & Distribution, Minneapolis, MN, USA

2437

KYLE CATHIE LTD
122 Arlington Road, London NW1 7HP
Telephone: (020) 7692 7215
Fax: (020) 7692 7260
Email: general.enquiries@kyle-cathie.com
Web Site: www.kylecathie.com

Distribution:
Littlehampton Book Services Ltd,
Faraday Close, Durrington, West Sussex BN13 3RB
Telephone: 01903 828800
Fax: 01903 828801
Email: orders@lbsltd.co.uk
Web Site: www.lbsltd.co.uk

Directors: Kyle Cathie *(Managing)*
Paul Game *(Financial)*
Julia Barder *(Sales & Marketing)*
Catherine Heygate *(Rights)*
Production Controller: Gemma John
Senior Commissioning Editor: Judith Hannam

Cookery, Wines & Spirits; Crafts & Hobbies; Gardening; Health & Beauty; Reference Books, Directories & Dictionaries; Sports & Games

New Titles: 50 (2008) , 60 (2009)
No of Employees: 18
Annual Turnover: £5.5M

ISBNs, Imprints & Series: 978 1 85626

Distributor for:
UK: Duncan Petersen Publishing Ltd

Overseas Representation:
Australia: Simon & Schuster (Australia) Pty Ltd, Pymble, NSW
India: Penguin Books India, New Delhi
New Zealand: New Holland Publishers (NZ) Ltd, Auckland

South Africa: Penguin Books South Africa (Pty) Ltd, Johannesburg
USA & Canada: National Book Network, Lanham, MD, USA

2438

LANDMARK PUBLISHING LTD
The Oaks, Moor Farm Road West,
Ashbourne, Derbyshire DE6 1HD
Telephone: 01335 347349
Fax: 01335 347303
Email: office@landmarkpublishing.co.uk
Web Site: www.landmarkpublishing.co.uk

Trade Enquiries:
Grantham Book Services, Trent Road,
Grantham, Lincs NG31 7XQ
Telephone: 01476 541080

Trade Enquiries (alternative):
Tiptree Book Services

Managing Director: C. L. M. Porter
Managers: C. Gilbert *(Sales & Marketing)*
S. Porter *(Office)*

Antiques & Collecting; Aviation; Guide Books; History & Antiquarian; Nautical; Transport; Travel & Topography

New Titles: 35 (2008) , 25 (2009)
No of Employees: 6

ISBNs, Imprints & Series:
978 1 84306 Landmark Collectors Library; Landmark Countryside Collection; Landmark Visitors Guides

2439

PETER LANG LTD
Evenlode Court, Main Road,
Long Hanborough, Witney, Oxon OX29 8SZ
Telephone: 01993 880088
Fax: 01993 882040
Email: oxford@peterlang.com
Web Site: www.peterlang.net

Publishing Director: Graham Speake
Commissioning Editors: Hannah Godfrey
Nick Reynolds
Production Manager: Mette Bundgaard

Academic & Scholarly

New Titles: 120 (2008) , 140 (2009)
No of Employees: 7
Annual Turnover: £500,000

ISBNs, Imprints & Series: 978 3 03911

Parent Company:
Switzerland: Peter Lang

Associated Companies:
Belgium: P. I. E. – Peter Lang SA
Germany: Peter Lang GmbH
USA: Peter Lang Publishing Inc

Overseas Representation:
Worldwide: Peter Lang, Pieterlen, Switzerland

Book Trade Association Membership:
IPG

2440

LAW SOCIETY PUBLISHING
113 Chancery Lane, London WC2A 1PL
Telephone: (020) 7841 5472
Fax: (020) 7320 5853
Email: publishing@lawsociety.org.uk
Web Site: www.lawsociety.org.uk/bookshop

Distribution:
Prolog, PO Box 99, Sudbury, Suffolk CO10 2SN
Telephone: 0870 850 1422
Fax: 01787 313995

Financial Controller: Dotum Begboaji
Managers: Stephen Honey *(Publishing)*
Sarah Foulkes *(Production)*
Millie Patel *(Marketing)*
Commissioning Editors: Janet Noble
Ben Mullane
Simon Blackett

Law

New Titles: 26 (2008) , 26 (2009)

ISBNs, Imprints & Series:
978 1 85328 The Law Society

Parent Company:
The Law Society

Book Trade Association Membership:
Data Publishers Association

2441

*LAWPACK PUBLISHING LTD
76–89 Alscot Road, London SE1 3AW
Telephone: (020) 7394 4040
Fax: (020) 7394 4041
Email: enquiries@lawpack.co.uk
Web Site: www.lawpack.co.uk

Managing Director: Thomas Coles
Editor: Jamie Ross
Sales Manager: Russell Roworth

Computer Science; Do-It-Yourself; Law; Reference Books, Directories & Dictionaries; Vocational Training & Careers

ISBNs, Imprints & Series:
978 1 898217, 978 1 902646, 978 1 904053, 978 1 905261

2442

*LDA
Hyde Buildings, Ashton Road, Hyde,
Cheshire SK14 4SH
Telephone: 0161 367 2000
Fax: 0161 367 2094
Email: katy.james@findel-education.co.uk
Web Site: www.idalearning.com

Managing Director: Emma Markey *(Brand)*
Marketing Manager: Katy James

Children's Books; Educational & Textbooks

ISBNs, Imprints & Series:
978 0 905114, 978 1 85503

Parent Company:
Findel Education

Overseas Representation:
Australia: The Educational Experience Pty Ltd, Newcastle, NSW
Austria: Der Spielzeugmacher, St Georgen
Barbados: Quest, Christ Church
Belgium: Baert Sprl, Brussels
Canada: Louise Kool & Galt Ltd, Scarborough, Ont; Louise Kool & Galt Ltd, Scarborough, Ont
Denmark: Gonge, Egå
Finland: Early Learning OY, Helsinki
France: Mot a Mot, Paris
Germany: Verlag An Der Ruhr, Mülheim
Greece: Ed Toys, Athens; Andreas Leon, Athens
Hong Kong: Artsberg Enterprises Ltd
Iceland: Namsgagnastofnun, Reykjavik
Israel: Shaked Education Games & Learning Materials, Holon
Italy: Edizioni Centro Studio Erickson, Trento; La Favelliana, Milan
Malaysia: Young Learners Educational Centre, Kuala Lumpur
Malta: Royal Trading Agency, Valletta
Netherlands: Dalcomtext, Paterswolde; Pro Special, Zutphen; Swets & Zeitlinger BV, Lisse
Norway: Okani Laermidler, Bergen

Portugal: ABACO, Lisbon; PSICO, Lisbon
Republic of Ireland: Carrol Educational Supplies, Dublin; K. & M. Evans, Dublin; Surgisales Teaching Aids, Dublin
Singapore: International Quality Toys
South Africa: Educational Toy Centre, Johannesburg; Play & Schoolroom Pty, Parklands
Spain: Eductrade, Madrid
Sweden: Beta Pedagog, Skällinge; Playing & Learning, Danderyd
Thailand: Productivity Corp Ltd, Bangkok
USA: Living & Learning Inc, Bethlehem, PA

Book Trade Association Membership:
IPG; BESA

2443

LEARNING MATTERS LTD
33 Southernhay East, Exeter EX1 1NX
Telephone: 01392 215560
Fax: 01392 215561
Email: info@learningmatters.co.uk
Web Site: www.learningmatters.co.uk

Distribution:
BEBC Distribution, Albion Close, Parkstone, Poole BH12 3LL
Telephone: 0845 230 9000
Fax: 01202 715556
Email: learningmatters@bebc.co.uk
Web Site: www.bebc.co.uk

Managing Director: Jonathan Harris
Sales & Marketing Manager: Zoe Engert

Academic & Scholarly; Educational & Textbooks; Sociology & Anthropology

New Titles: 50 (2008) , 60 (2009)
No of Employees: 12

ISBNs, Imprints & Series:
978 1 84445, 978 1 903300

Overseas Representation:
Barbados: Days Bookstore, Bridgetown
Ghana: EPP Books Services Ltd, Accra
Hong Kong: Asia Publishers Services Ltd
Jamaica: The Book Merchant Ltd, Kingston
Malaysia: APD Kuala Lumpur Pte Ltd, Selangor
Singapore: APD Singapore Pte Ltd

Book Trade Association Membership:
IPG

2444

LEARNING TOGETHER
18 Shandon Park, Belfast BT5 6NW
Telephone: (028) 9040 2086
Fax: (028) 9040 2086
Email: info@learningtogether.co.uk
Web Site: www.learningtogether.co.uk

Distribution:
Orca Book Services, Unit A3, Fleets Corner, Poole, Dorset BH17 0HL
Telephone: 01202 665432
Fax: 01202 666219
Email: mail@orcabookservices.co.uk

Representation:
c/o Alan Goodworth, Roundhouse Group, Millstone, Limers Lane, Northam, North Devon EX39 2RG
Telephone: 01237 474474
Fax: 01237 474774
Email: roundhouse.group@ukgateway.net

Managing Director: Janet McConkey
Author/Publisher: Stephen McConkey

Educational & Textbooks

ISBNs, Imprints & Series:
978 1 873385 Practice Tests In Series

Book Trade Association Membership:
Publishers Association; EPC

2445

LEATHERHEAD FOOD INTERNATIONAL
Randalls Road, Leatherhead, Surrey KT22 7RY
Telephone: 01372 822556 & 822241 (Sales)
Fax: 01372 822272
Email: publications@leatherheadfood.com
Web Site: www.leatherheadfood.com

Chief Executive Officer: Dr Paul Berryman
Business Manager, Market & Technical Services: Victoria Emerton

Law; Scientific & Technical

New Titles: 2 (2008) , 5 (2009)
No of Employees: 210

ISBNs, Imprints & Series:
978 0 905748, 978 1 904007, 978 1 905224

Overseas Representation:
Australia & New Zealand: DA Information Services Pty Ltd, Mitcham, Vic, Australia
North America: Publications Resource Group, North Adams, MA, USA

2446

LEGAL ACTION GROUP
242 Pentonville Road, London N1 9UN
Telephone: (020) 7833 2931
Fax: (020) 7837 6094
Email: lag@lag.org.uk
Web Site: www.lag.org.uk

Director: Steve Hynes
Managers: Esther Pilger *(Publisher)*
Nim Moorlhy *(Marketing)*
Customer Services Executives: Adam Wilson
Andrew Troszok

Law

ISBNs, Imprints & Series:
978 0 905099, 978 1 903307

Book Trade Association Membership:
IPG

2447

***LEGEND PRESS**
Unit 11, 63 Clerkenwell Road, London EC1M 5NP
Telephone: (020) 7253 7019
Email: info@legendpress.co.uk
Web Site: www.legendpress.co.uk

Managing Director: Tom Chalmers

Fiction

ISBNs, Imprints & Series:
978 0 9551032, 978 1 906558

Book Trade Association Membership:
IPG

2448

LETTERLAND INTERNATIONAL LTD
33 New Road, Barton, Cambridge CB23 7AY
Telephone: 0870 766 2629
Fax: 01223 264126
Email: info@letterland.com
Web Site: www.letterland.com

Distribution:
Grantham Book Services, Trent Road, Grantham, Lincs NG31 7XQ
Telephone: 01476 541080
Fax: 01476 541061
Email: orders@letterland.com
Web Site:
www.granthambookservices.co.uk

Directors: Mark Wendon
Jenny Cant *(Marketing)*
Production Manager: Jonathan Wendon

Children's Books; Educational & Textbooks; Electronic (Educational); English as a Foreign Language

New Titles: 5 (2008) , 5 (2009)
No of Employees: 10

ISBNs, Imprints & Series:
978 0 907345, 978 1 86209

Overseas Representation:
Australia: Ed Source, Bassendean, WA
Canada: Educan, Weston, Ont
China: Ian Taylor & Associates, Beijing, P. R. of China
Hong Kong: ETC Educational Technology Connection (HK) Ltd, Tai Koo Shing
Japan: J & N English Club, Shizuoka-ken
Korea: Infobooks, Seoul, Republic of Korea
Middle East & North Africa: International Publishers Representatives (IPR) Ltd, Nicosia, Cyprus
New Zealand: Wakelin Educational Services, Ashburton
Nigeria: Kcxploits, Lagos
Singapore: Tumble Tots (Asia) Pty Ltd, Singapore
South Africa: Educational Ideas, Johannesburg
Taiwan: Hello! Book Club, Taipei County
USA: Letterland International, Enfield, NH

Book Trade Association Membership:
Publishers Association; EPC; IPG; International Reading Association

2449

LETTS AND LONSDALE
4 Grosvenor Place, London SW1X 7DL
Telephone: (020) 7096 2900
Fax: (020) 7096 2945
Email: orders@lettsandlonsdale.co.uk
Web Site: www.lettsandlonsdale.com

Warehouse, Distribution:
HarperCollins, Campsie View, Westerhill Road, Bishopbriggs, Glasgow G64 2QT

Directors: Andrew Ware *(Managing)*
Helen Jacobs *(Publishing)*

Biology & Zoology; Chemistry; Children's Books; Educational & Textbooks; Geography & Geology; History & Antiquarian; Languages & Linguistics; Mathematics & Statistics; Philosophy; Physics; Psychology & Psychiatry; Reference Books, Directories & Dictionaries; Scientific & Technical; Sociology & Anthropology; Sports & Games; Vocational Training & Careers

ISBNs, Imprints & Series:
978 1 84085, 978 1 84315, 978 1 85758, 978 1 85805, 978 1 90589, 978 1 90641

Associated Companies:
Leckie & Leckie

Overseas Representation:
Argentina: Edytex, Buenos Aires
Botswana: Book Promotions Pty Ltd, Diep River, South Africa
Caribbean: The Book Merchant Ltd, Kingston, Jamaica
India: Overleaf, New Delhi
Malaysia: APD Kuala Lumpur Pte Ltd, Selangor
Middle East: Peter Ward Book Exports, London, UK
New Zealand: Addenda, Auckland
Pakistan: Publishers Marketing Associates, Karachi
Philippines: CRW Books, Rizal
Singapore: APD Singapore Pte Ltd

Tanzania, Uganda & Seychelles: A–Z Africa Book Services, Rotterdam, Netherlands

Book Trade Association Membership:
EPC

2450

DEWI LEWIS PUBLISHING
8 Broomfield Road, Heaton Moor, Stockport SK4 4ND
Telephone: 0161 442 9450
Fax: 0161 442 9450
Email: mail@dewilewispublishing.com
Web Site: www.dewilewispublishing.com

Trade Enquiries & Orders:
Turnaround, Unit 3 Olympia Trading Estate, Coburg Road, London N22 6TZ
Telephone: (020) 8829 3000
Fax: (020) 8881 5088
Email: orders@turnaround-uk.com
Web Site: www.turnaround-uk.com

Publisher: Dewi Lewis
Sales & Marketing Director: Caroline Warhurst

Architecture & Design; Fine Art & Art History; Illustrated & Fine Editions; Photography; Reference Books, Directories & Dictionaries; Sports & Games

ISBNs, Imprints & Series:
978 1 899235, 978 1 904587

Overseas Representation:
Germany: Visual Books Sales Agency, Berlin
New Zealand: Southern Publishers Group, Auckland
North America: Consortium Book Sales & Distribution Inc, St Paul, MN, USA

2451

***LEXUS LTD**
60 Brook Street, Glasgow G40 2AB
Telephone: 0141 556 0440
Fax: 0141 556 2202
Email:
peterterrell@lexusforlanguages.co.uk
Web Site: www.lexusforlanguages.co.uk

Publisher: Peter Terrell
Typesetter & Designer: Elfreda Crehan

Educational & Textbooks; Languages & Linguistics; Reference Books, Directories & Dictionaries

ISBNs, Imprints & Series:
978 1 904737 Chinese Classroom; Travelmates

2452

LIBERTIES PRESS
Guinness Enterprise Centre, Taylor's Lane, Dublin 8, Republic of Ireland
Telephone: +353 (01) 402 0805
Email: sean@libertiespress.com
Web Site: www.libertiespress.com

Directors: Sean O'Keeffe
Peter O'Connell

Architecture & Design; Cookery, Wines & Spirits; Health & Beauty; History & Antiquarian; Literature & Criticism; Politics & World Affairs; Religion & Theology; Sports & Games

ISBNs, Imprints & Series:
978 0 9545335, 978 1 905483

Parent Company:
Republic of Ireland: Liberties Media Ltd

Book Trade Association Membership:
CLÉ (Irish PA)

2453

LIBRIS LTD
26 Lady Margaret Road, London NW5 2XL
Telephone: (020) 7482 2390
Email: libris@onetel.com
Web Site: www.librislondon.co.uk

Orders:
Central Books Ltd, 99 Wallis Road, London E9 5LN
Telephone: (020) 8986 4854
Fax: (020) 8533 5821
Email: orders@centralbooks.com

Directors: N. M. Jacobs
S. A. Kitzinger

Academic & Scholarly; Biography & Autobiography; Fiction; Languages & Linguistics; Literature & Criticism; Music; Photography; Poetry; Travel & Topography

New Titles: 2 (2009)

ISBNs, Imprints & Series:
978 1 870352, 978 1 870352

2454

THE LILLIPUT PRESS LTD
62–63 Sitric Road, Arbour Hill, Dublin 7, Republic of Ireland
Telephone: +353 (01) 671 1647
Fax: +353 (01) 671 1233
Email: info@lilliputpress.ie
Web Site: www.lilliputpress.ie

Distributors (Trade Orders):
Gill & Macmillan, Hume Avenue, Park West, Dublin 12, Republic of Ireland
Telephone: +353 (01) 500 9500
Fax: +353 (01) 500 9599

Directors: Antony Farrell *(Managing & Publisher)*
David Dickson
Vincent Hurley
Terence Brown
Vivienne Guinness
Kathy Gilfillan
Daniel Caffrey

Academic & Scholarly; Architecture & Design; Biography & Autobiography; Fiction; Fine Art & Art History; History & Antiquarian; Illustrated & Fine Editions; Literature & Criticism; Music; Photography; Reference Books, Directories & Dictionaries

New Titles: 21 (2008) , 18 (2009)
No of Employees: 3
Annual Turnover: £300,000

ISBNs, Imprints & Series:
978 0 946640, 978 1 84351, 978 1 874675, 978 1 901866

Overseas Representation:
France: Lora Fountain Literary Agent, Paris
UK: Central Books Ltd, London

Book Trade Association Membership:
CLÉ (Irish PA)

2455

FRANCES LINCOLN LTD
4 Torriano Mews, Torriano Avenue, London NW5 2RZ
Telephone: (020) 7284 4009
Fax: (020) 7485 0490
Email: reception@frances-lincoln.com
Web Site: www.franceslincoln.com

Warehouse, Trade Enquiries & Orders:
Bookpoint Ltd, 130 Milton Park, Abingdon, Oxon OX14 4SB
Telephone: 01235 400400
Fax: 01235 400500

Directors: John Nicoll *(Managing)*

Jon Rippon (Finance)
Managers: Sara Borthwick (Business)
Jo Christian (Editorial – Adult Books)
Andrew Dunn (Editorial – Adult Books)
Maurice Lyon (Editorial – Children's
Books)
Laura Grandi (Production)
Gail Lynch (Sales & Marketing)

Architecture & Design; Children's Books;
Cookery, Wines & Spirits; Fine Art & Art
History; Gardening; Guide Books; Health &
Beauty; Illustrated & Fine Editions; Religion
& Theology; Sports & Games; Travel &
Topography; Art & Mythology; Design &
Decoration; Mind Body Spirit; Parenting

New Titles: 150 (2008) , 150 (2009)
No of Employees: 40
Annual Turnover: £7M

ISBNs, Imprints & Series:
978 0 7112, 978 1 84507

Distributor for:
Allen & Unwin [Children's Books]; Barn Owl
Books Ltd; Boxer Books; Natural History
Museum; Tara Publishing
USA: New York Review of Books

Overseas Representation:
All countries other than those listed:
Frances Lincoln, London, UK
Australia (Adult Books) & New Zealand:
Bookwise International, Adelaide, SA,
Australia
Australia (Children's Books): Walker Books
Australia, Newtown, NSW, Australia
South Africa: Pan Macmillan SA Pty Ltd,
Hyde Park
USA (Children's Books): Publishers Group
West, Berkeley, CA, USA

Book Trade Association Membership:
IPG

2456

LION HUDSON PLC
Wilkinson House, Jordan Hill Road, Oxford
OX2 7DR
Telephone: 01865 302750
Fax: 01865 302757
Email: info@lionhudson.com
Web Site: www.lionhudson.com

Directors: Denis Cole (Chairman)
Paul Clifford (Managing)
Nicholas Jones (Deputy Managing)
John O'Nions (Sales & Marketing)
Roy McCloughry
Stephen Price (Production)
Sales Manager: Robert Wendover (Export)
International & Subsidiary Rights: Paul
Whitton
Financial Controller: Vicky Pulley

Biography & Autobiography; Children's
Books; Educational & Textbooks; Religion &
Theology

New Titles: 170 (2008) , 160 (2009)
No of Employees: 53
Annual Turnover: £8.7M

ISBNs, Imprints & Series:
978 0 7459, 978 0 85648 Aslan; Lion; Lion
Children's
978 1 85424 Monarch
978 1 85985 Candle

Overseas Representation:
Australia: Bookwise International, Adelaide,
SA
New Zealand: New Holland Publishers (NZ)
Ltd, Auckland
South Africa: Pearson Education, Cape
Town

Book Trade Association Membership:
Publishers Association; EPC

2457

LISU
Loughborough University, Loughborough,
Leics LE11 3TU
Telephone: 01509 635680
Fax: 01509 635699
Email: lisu@lboro.ac.uk
Web Site: www.lboro.ac.uk/departments/
dis/lisu

Director: Claire Creaser

Bibliography & Library Science; Reference
Books, Directories & Dictionaries

New Titles: 7 (2008) , 6 (2009)

ISBNs, Imprints & Series:
978 0 948848, 978 1 905499
978 1 901786 LISU Reports

Parent Company:
Loughborough University

2458

LITTLE, BROWN BOOK GROUP
100 Victoria Embankment, London
EC4Y 0DY
Telephone: (020) 7911 8000
Fax: (020) 7911 8100
Email: info@littlebrown.co.uk
Web Site: www.littlebrown.co.uk,
www.orbitbooks.co.uk &
www.virago.co.uk

Distribution Centre:
TBS Ltd, Colchester Road, Frating Green,
Colchester, Essex CO7 7DW
Telephone: 01206 255678 (orders)
Fax: 01206 255930 (orders)
Email: exportmanagement@tbs-ltd.co.uk

Directors: Ursula Mackenzie (Chief
Executive Officer & Publisher)
David Kent (Chief Operating Officer)
Diane Spivey (Rights)
Roger Cazalet (Publishing Strategy)
Duncan Spilling (Art)
Robert Manser (Group Sales &
Marketing)
Richard Beswick (Managing – Little
Brown & Abacus)
Tim Holman (Publisher – Orbit)
Lennie Goodings (Publisher – Virago)
Antonia Hodgson (Publisher – Sphere &
Piatkus)
Nick Ross (Production)
Siobhan Hughes (Legal)
Julian Shaw (Finance)

Audio Books; Biography & Autobiography;
Crime; Fiction; History & Antiquarian;
Humour; Literature & Criticism; Military &
War; Music; Politics & World Affairs;
Psychology & Psychiatry; Science Fiction;
Sports & Games; Travel & Topography

New Titles: 350 (2008)
No of Employees: 140

ISBNs, Imprints & Series:
978 0 316, 978 1 4087 Little, Brown
978 0 349 Abacus
978 0 7499 Piatkus
978 0 7515 Sphere Paperbacks
978 0 8212 Bulfinch
978 1 4055 Audio Books
978 1 84149, 978 1 85723 Orbit
978 1 84408, 978 1 85381, 978 1 86049
Virago
978 1 84744 Sphere Hardbacks
978 1 904233 Atom

Parent Company:
Hachette Livre Group of Companies

Overseas Representation:
Africa: A–Z Africa Book Services,
Rotterdam, Netherlands

Australia: Hachette Livre Australia, Sydney,
NSW
Canada: Penguin Group Canada, Toronto,
Ont
Caribbean, Central & South America: Jerry
Carrillo Inc, USA
China: Wei Zhao, New York, NY, USA
France & Scandinavia: Melanie Boesen,
Hachette US, Denmark
Germany, Sweden & Middle East: Simon
McArt, Little, Brown Book Group,
London, UK
India: Penguin Books India, New Delhi
Italy: Penguin Italia srl, Milan
Japan, Thailand, Indonesia, Hong Kong,
Korea & Taiwan: Gilles Fauveau, Japan
New Zealand: Hachette Livre New Zealand,
Auckland
Singapore & Malaysia: Penguin Books
Singapore, Jurong, Singapore
South Africa: Penguin Books SA (Pty) Ltd,
Denver Ext 4
Spain & Portugal: Penguin Books SA,
Madrid, Spain
Switzerland, Belgium, Netherlands,
Gibraltar, Malta & Cyprus: Sarah
Humphreys, Little, Brown Book Group,
London, UK

Book Trade Association Membership:
BA; Book Marketing Ltd

2459

LITTLE TIGER PRESS
[an imprint of Magi Publications]
1 The Coda Centre, 189 Munster Road,
London SW6 6AW
Telephone: (020) 7385 6333
Fax: (020) 7385 7333
Email: info@littletiger.co.uk
Web Site: www.littletigerpress.com

Distribution:
Macmillan Distribution (MDL), Brunel Road,
Houndmills, Basingstoke, Hants RG21 6XS
Telephone: 01256 302692
Fax: 01256 812521
Email: mdl@macmillan.co.uk

Proprietor: Monty Bhatia
Directors: David Bucknor (Sales)
Aude Lavielle (Rights)
Yolande Denny (Production)
Publisher: Jude Evans

Children's Books

ISBNs, Imprints & Series:
978 1 84506, 978 1 85430 Little Tiger Press
978 1 84715 Stripes Publishing

Parent Company:
Magi Publications

Overseas Representation:
Australia: Global Language Books,
Toongabbie, NSW
Hong Kong: Publishers' Associates Ltd
Malaysia: Pansing Distributors (M) Sdn Bhd,
Shah Alam
Singapore & Brunei: STP Distributors Pte
Ltd, Singapore
Southern Africa: Titles SA, Johannesburg,
South Africa

2460

**THE LITTMAN LIBRARY OF JEWISH
CIVILIZATION**
PO Box 645, Oxford OX2 0UJ
Telephone: 01865 790740
Fax: 01865 722964
Email: info@littman.co.uk
Web Site: www.littman.co.uk

Distribution:
NBN International, Estover Road, Plymouth
PL6 7PY
Telephone: 01752 202300
Fax: 01752 202333

Email: orders@nbninternational.com
Web Site: www.nbninternational.com

Managing Editor: Connie Webber
Chief Executive Officer: Ludo Craddock
Directors: Colette Littman
Robert Littman

Academic & Scholarly; Biography &
Autobiography; Educational & Textbooks;
Fine Art & Art History; History &
Antiquarian; Literature & Criticism; Music;
Philosophy; Politics & World Affairs;
Religion & Theology; Sociology &
Anthropology; Theatre, Drama & Dance

ISBNs, Imprints & Series:
978 1 874774, 978 1 904113, 978 1
906764

Overseas Representation:
Australia & New Zealand: Peribo Pty Ltd,
Mount Kuring-Gai, NSW, Australia
USA & Canada: International Specialized
Book Services Inc, Portland, OR, USA

Book Trade Association Membership:
IPG

2461

LIVERPOOL UNIVERSITY PRESS
4 Cambridge Street, Liverpool L69 7ZU
Telephone: 0151 794 2233
Fax: 0151 794 2235
Email: lup@liv.ac.uk
Web Site: http://www.liverpool-
unipress.co.uk

Sales & Distribution:
Marston Book Services, PO Box 269,
Abingdon, Oxon OX14 4YN
Telephone: 01235 465500
Fax: 01235 465555
Email: trade.order@marston.co.uk
Web Site: www.marston.co.uk

Publisher: Anthony Cond
Managers: Simon Bell (Sales & Marketing)
Tracey Mooney (Finance)
Andrew Kirk (Production)
Editor: Helen Tookey (Journals Production)
Journals Publishing Executive: Clare
Hooper
Sales & Marketing Assistant: Janet Smith

Academic & Scholarly; Architecture &
Design; Educational & Textbooks; Fine Art &
Art History; History & Antiquarian;
Languages & Linguistics; Literature &
Criticism; Politics & World Affairs; Science
Fiction; Sociology & Anthropology

ISBNs, Imprints & Series:
978 0 85323, 978 1 84631

Overseas Representation:
Africa & Middle East: International
Publishing Services (IPS) Middle East Ltd,
Dubai, UAE
Benelux & Germany: Roy de Boo, Hooge
Mierde, Netherlands
Central & Latin America: InterMedia
Americana (IMA) Ltd, London, UK
Far East (excluding Japan): STM Publisher
Services Pte Ltd, Singapore
France & Italy: Flavio Marcello Publishers'
Agents & Consultants, Padua, Italy
India: Viva Group, New Delhi
Malaysia: Yuha Associates, Selangor Darul
Ehsan
North America: International Specialized
Book Services Inc, Portland, OR, USA
Republic of Ireland: John Fitzpatrick, Dublin
Scandinavia: Jan Norbye, Ølstykke,
Denmark
Spain & Portugal: Iberian Book Services,
Madrid, Spain

Book Trade Association Membership:
CAPP; IPG

2462

LIVING TIME® MEDIA INTERNATIONAL
Units 18c–19c, Wem Business Park,
New Street, Wem, Shropshire SY4 5JX
Telephone: 01939 236623
Fax: 01939 234873
Email: info@livingtime.co.uk
Web Site: www.livingtime.co.uk

Global Rights:
5 Tite Street, Chelsea, London SW3 4JU
Telephone: 07877 851410
Fax: 01939 234873 (rights)
Email: rights@livingtime.co.uk
Web Site: www.livingtime.co.uk

Head of Publishing/Chief Executive:
Alderson Smith
Editor-in-Chief: Edouard d'Araille
International Sales Executive: John
Hargreaves
Rights Executives: James Hartley (Foreign
& Subsidiary)
Anthony Nevill (Film)
Carolyn Eden (Children's Book)

Academic & Scholarly; Biography &
Autobiography; Children's Books; Cinema,
Video, TV & Radio; Crime; Educational &
Textbooks; Electronic (Educational);
Electronic (Entertainment); English as a
Foreign Language; Fiction; History &
Antiquarian; Literature & Criticism;
Philosophy; Poetry; Psychology &
Psychiatry; Science Fiction

New Titles: 24 (2008) , 80 (2009)
No of Employees: 8
Annual Turnover: £500,000

ISBNs, Imprints & Series:
978 1 903331 Living Time® Press
978 1 905820 Living Time® Media
International
978 1 906904 Living Time® Digital

Parent Company:
Living Time®

Associated Companies:
The Academy of the 3rd Millennium™;
Fortune Street®; Living Time Vision
(LTV); Living Time® Design; Living Time®
Docufilms; Living Time® Films Ltd; Living
Time® Legal; Living Time® Music

Overseas Representation:
Worldwide: Hubert Janssen, Living Time®
Europe, Amsterdam, Netherlands

Book Trade Association Membership:
Publishers Association

2463

LOGASTON PRESS
Little Logaston, Woonton, Almeley,
Herefordshire HR3 6QH
Telephone: 01544 327344
Email: logastonpress@btinternet.com
Web Site: www.logastonpress.co.uk

Proprietors: Andy Johnson
Karen Stout

Archaeology; Architecture & Design; Fine
Art & Art History; Guide Books; History &
Antiquarian; Natural History; Reference
Books, Directories & Dictionaries; Rural
Interest

New Titles: 16 (2008) , 20 (2009)

ISBNs, Imprints & Series:
978 0 9510242, 978 1 873827, 978 1
904396, 978 1 906663 Monuments in
the Landscape Series

2464

LOMOND BOOKS LTD
14 Freskyn Place,
East Mains Industrial Estate, Broxburn
EH52 5NF
Telephone: 01506 855955
Fax: 01506 855965
Email: sales@lomondbooks.co.uk

Directors: Trevor Maher
Duncan Baxter (Sales)
Jackie Brown (Operations)
Michael Burke

Children's Books; Cookery, Wines & Spirits;
Crafts & Hobbies; Guide Books; History &
Antiquarian; Humour; Illustrated & Fine
Editions; Natural History; Reference Books,
Directories & Dictionaries

ISBNs, Imprints & Series:
978 0 94778, 978 1 84204

Book Trade Association Membership:
BA

2465

LUATH PRESS LTD
543/2 Castlehill, The Royal Mile, Edinburgh
EH1 2ND
Telephone: 0131 225 4326
Fax: 0131 225 4324
Email: gavin.macdougall@luath.co.uk
Web Site: www.luath.co.uk

Distribution:
HarperCollins, Westerhill Road,
Bishopbriggs, Glasgow G64 2QR
Telephone: 0870 787 1722
Fax: 0870 787 1723
Email: enquiries@harpercollins.co.uk
Web Site: b2b.harpercollins.co.uk

Director, Rights & Overseas
Distribution: Gavin MacDougall
Production & Editorial: Leila Cruickshank
Sales & Marketing: Chani McDain
Press & Events: Alice Jacobs

Biography & Autobiography; Children's
Books; Cinema, Video, TV & Radio;
Cookery, Wines & Spirits; Crime; Fiction;
Gardening; Geography & Geology; Guide
Books; History & Antiquarian; Humour;
Languages & Linguistics; Literature &
Criticism; Magic & the Occult; Medical (incl.
Self Help & Alternative Medicine); Military
& War; Music; Natural History;
Photography; Poetry; Politics & World
Affairs; Sports & Games; Theatre, Drama &
Dance; Travel & Topography; Veterinary
Science; Walking

New Titles: 40 (2009)

ISBNs, Imprints & Series:
Scots in; Viewpoints
978 0 946487 Luath Guides to Scotland;
Walk with Luath; Wild Lives
978 0 946487, 978 1 84282 Let's Explore
978 0 946487, 978 1 84282, 978 1 906307
Luath
978 0 946487, 978 1 84282 On the Trail
of; The Quest for
978 1 84282, 978 1 905222 Luath
Storyteller

Overseas Representation:
Australia & New Zealand: Luath Press Ltd,
Edinburgh, UK
USA & Canada: Ingram Publisher Services,
Nashville, TN, USA

Book Trade Association Membership:
Publishing Scotland

2466

LUND HUMPHRIES
Ashgate Publishing Group, Wey Court East,
Union Road, Farnham, Surrey GU9 7PT
Telephone: 01252 331551
Fax: 01252 736736
Email: info@lundhumphries.com
Web Site: www.lundhumphries.com

Trade Distribution:
Bookpoint Ltd, 39 Milton Park, Abingdon,
Oxon OX14 4TD
Telephone: 01235 400400
Fax: 01235 400413
Email: orders@bookpoint.co.uk

Directors: Nigel Farrow (Chairman,
Ashgate Publishing)
Lucy Myers (Managing)

Academic & Scholarly; Antiques &
Collecting; Architecture & Design; Fine Art
& Art History; Photography

ISBNs, Imprints & Series: 978 1 84822

Parent Company:
Ashgate Publishing

Overseas Representation:
Australia & Far East: Ashgate Publishing
Asia-Pacific, Newport, NSW, Australia
Central & Eastern Europe: Dr László Horváth
Publishers Representative, Budapest,
Hungary
Finland, Sweden, Norway, Denmark &
Iceland: Andrew Durnell Marketing Ltd,
Tunbridge Wells, UK
France & Netherlands: Casemate Books,
Newbury, UK
Germany, Austria, Switzerland, Italy,
Greece, Luxembourg & Belgium: Ted
Dougherty, London, UK
India: Maya Publishers Pvt Ltd, New Delhi
Japan (stockholding agents): United
Publishers Services Ltd, Tokyo, Japan
Korea: Information & Culture Korea (ICK),
Seoul, Republic of Korea
Middle East: Publishers International
Marketing, Sutton St Nicholas,
Herefordshire, UK
New Zealand: South Pacific Books (Imports)
Ltd, Auckland
South Africa: Peter Hyde Associates (Pty)
Ltd, Cape Town
South America & Africa (excluding South
Africa): InterMedia Americana (IMA) Ltd,
London, UK
Spain & Portugal: Penny Padovani, London,
UK
USA & Canada: Lund Humphries,
Burlington, VT, USA

2467

THE LUTTERWORTH PRESS
PO Box 60, Cambridge CB1 2NT
Telephone: 01223 350865
Fax: 01223 366951
Email: publishing@lutterworth.com
Web Site: www.lutterworth.com

Trade Enquiries & Orders:
James Clarke & Co, PO Box 60, Cambridge
CB1 2NT
Telephone: (as above)
Fax: (as above)
Email: orders@jamesclarke.co.uk
Web Site: (as above)

Managing Director: Adrian Brink
Customer Service: Anna Januszkiewicz
Accounts Department: Penny Bull
Sales & Publicity: Antoaneta Ouzounova
Megan Waddington
Editorial: Aidan van de Weyer
Ian Bignall

Academic & Scholarly; Antiques &
Collecting; Architecture & Design;
Biography & Autobiography; Children's

Books; Crafts & Hobbies; Educational &
Textbooks; Fine Art & Art History; History &
Antiquarian; Illustrated & Fine Editions;
Literature & Criticism; Military & War;
Natural History; Philosophy; Politics & World
Affairs; Reference Books, Directories &
Dictionaries; Religion & Theology; Sports &
Games

New Titles: 22 (2008) , 35 (2009)
No of Employees: 9

ISBNs, Imprints & Series:
978 0 7188 The Lutterworth Press
978 0 7444 Patrick Hardy
978 0 906554 Acorn Editions

Parent Company:
James Clarke & Co Ltd

Overseas Representation:
China & Asia: AA Media Services, Shanghai,
P. R. of China
Philippines: Edwin Makabenta, Quezon City
USA: Ingram Publisher Services Inc,
Chambersburg, PA

Book Trade Association Membership:
EPC; CAPP; IPG

2468

McCRIMMON PUBLISHING CO LTD
10–12 High Street, Great Wakering, Essex
SS3 0EQ
Telephone: 01702 218956
Fax: 01702 216082
Email: info@mccrimmons.com
Web Site: www.mccrimmons.com

Bookshop:
All Saints Pastoral Centre, London Colney,
St Albans, Herts
Telephone: 01727 827612
Fax: 01727 827612
Email: (as above)
Web Site: (as above)

Secretary: Joan McCrimmon
Director: Don McCrimmon (Sales)
Graphic Designer: Nick Snode
Accounts: Sue Anderson
Bookshop Manager: Louise Madden
Sales Ledger: Caroline Lee
Warehouse: Robert Mossop

Children's Books; Educational & Textbooks;
Electronic (Educational); Music; Religion &
Theology

No of Employees: 9
Annual Turnover: £785,000

ISBNs, Imprints & Series: 978 0 85597

Distributor for:
USA: Harcourt Brace & Co; Harcourt
Religion Publishers (RE division); LTP
Publications; Printery House Inc

Overseas Representation:
Australia: John Garrett Publishing,
Mulgrave, Vic
Hong Kong: Catholic Truth Society
New Zealand: Pleroma Christian Supplies,
Otane, Central Hawkes Bay
South Africa: The Catholic Bookshop, Cape
Town

2469

McGRAW-HILL EDUCATION
Shoppenhangers Road, Maidenhead, Berks
SL6 2QL
Telephone: 01628 502500
Fax: 01628 770224
Web Site: www.mcgraw-hill.co.uk

**Senior Vice-President, Europe, MEA &
Asia Pac:** Simon Allen (Senior
International, English Language
Publishing)

Managing Directors: John Donovan *(UK/ Northern & Central Europe)*
Thanos Blintzios *(MEA)*
Directors: Alan Martin *(Operations/ Finance, EMEA)*
Lefteris Souris *(Sales & Marketing, MEA)*
Derek Moseley *(Sales HE, UK & South Africa)*
Alice Duijser *(Marketing HE & OUP)*
Emma Gibson *(Professional/Medical Division UK/NE)*
General Managers: Shona Mullen *(Content & Digital Development EMEA)*
Rob Ince *(UK Schools)*

Academic & Scholarly; Accountancy & Taxation; Architecture & Design; Aviation; Biology & Zoology; Chemistry; Computer Science; Economics; Educational & Textbooks; Electronic (Educational); Electronic (Professional & Academic); Engineering; English as a Foreign Language; Geography & Geology; Industry, Business & Management; Law; Mathematics & Statistics; Medical (incl. Self Help & Alternative Medicine); Philosophy; Physics; Politics & World Affairs; Psychology & Psychiatry; Reference Books, Directories & Dictionaries; Scientific & Technical; Sociology & Anthropology; Transport; Vocational Training & Careers

ISBNs, Imprints & Series: 978 0 07

Parent Company:
USA: McGraw-Hill Inc

Associated Companies:
Open University Press
Australia: McGraw-Hill Education
Canada: McGraw-Hill Ryerson Ltd
Colombia: McGraw-Hill/InterAmericana (Colombia) SA
India: McGraw-Hill Education (India) Pvt Ltd
Italy: McGraw-Hill Libri Italia srl
Japan: McGraw-Hill Book Co
Mexico: Libros McGraw-Hill de Mexico SA de CV
Portugal: McGraw-Hill/Interamericana de Portugal Ltda
Singapore: McGraw-Hill International Book Co
Spain: McGraw-Hill Interamericana de España SAU
USA: Wm. C. Brown; Brown & Benchmark; Irwin; Irwin Professional; Osborne/ McGraw-Hill
Venezuela: McGraw-Hill/InterAmericana (Venezuela) SA

Distributor for:
USA: Amacom; Berrett-Koehler; Harvard Business School Press; R & D Books

Book Trade Association Membership:
Publishers Association; BA

2470

MACMILLAN CHILDREN'S BOOKS LTD
20 New Wharf Road, London N1 9RR
Telephone: (020) 7014 6000
Fax: (020) 7014 6001
Web Site: www.panmacmillan.com

Trade Enquiries:
Macmillan Distribution (MDL), Houndmills, Basingstoke, Hants RG21 6XS
Telephone: 01256 329242
Fax: 01256 840154
Email: mdl@macmillan.co.uk

Directors: Emma Hopkin *(Managing)*
Ian Mitchell *(Production)*
Kate Mackenzie *(Rights)*
Anne Glenn *(Art)*
Rebecca McNally *(Publishing, Fiction)*
Suzanne Carnell *(Editorial, Picture & Gift Books)*
Gaby Morgan *(Editorial, Poetry & Non-Fiction)*

Martin Challis *(Publishing, Kingfisher)*
Ed Ripley *(Sales)*
Hilary Downie *(Rights, Kingfisher)*

Audio Books; Children's Books; Poetry

ISBNs, Imprints & Series:
978 0 330, 978 0 333 Campbell Books; Macmillan Children's Books; Young Picador
978 0 7534 Kingfisher

Parent Company:
Macmillan Ltd

Associated Companies:
Macmillan Education Ltd; Macmillan Publishers Ltd; Palgrave Macmillan Ltd; Pan Macmillan Ltd

Book Trade Association Membership:
Publishers Association; Children's Book Circle; PA Children's Book Group

2471

MACMILLAN EDUCATION
Macmillan Oxford, Between Towns Road, Oxford OX4 3PP
Telephone: 01865 405700
Fax: 01865 405701
Web Site: www.macmillaneducation.com

Distribution:
Macmillan Distribution (MDL), Houndmills, Basingstoke, Hants RG21 6XS
Telephone: 01256 329242
Fax: 01256 840154
Email: mdl@macmillan.co.uk

Chairman: Julian Drinkall *(Chief Executive)*
Directors: Jeremy Dieguez *(Managing, Europe)*
Paul Emmett *(Finance)*
Mark Chalmers *(Group Finance, Mac Ed)*
John Peacock *(Technology, Digital & Operations)*
Flavio Centofanti *(Regional, Middle East)*
Steven Tweed *(Regional Sales, Africa)*
Cathy Smith *(International ELT Sales & Marketing)*
Steven Maginn *(Regional, East Asia)*
Alison Hubert *(Africa & Caribbean, International Curriculum)*
Angela Lilley *(International ELT Publishing)*
Sue Bale *(Dictionary Publishing)*
Publisher, Latin America: Sharon Servis
Company Secretary: Martin Powter

Atlases & Maps; Biology & Zoology; Chemistry; Children's Books; Educational & Textbooks; English as a Foreign Language; Environment & Development Studies; Geography & Geology; History & Antiquarian; Languages & Linguistics; Mathematics & Statistics; Physics; Reference Books, Directories & Dictionaries; Vocational Training & Careers

ISBNs, Imprints & Series:
Macmillan Education; Macmillan Heinemann ELT
978 0 333, 978 1 405

Parent Company:
Macmillan Ltd

Associated Companies:
Macmillan Children's Books; Macmillan Publishers Ltd; Palgrave Macmillan; Pan Macmillan

Overseas Representation:
See: Macmillan Publishers Ltd, Basingstoke, UK

Book Trade Association Membership:
Publishers Association

2472

MACMILLAN PRESS LTD
see: Palgrave Macmillan

2473

MACMILLAN PUBLISHERS LTD
Brunel Road, Houndmills, Basingstoke, Hants RG21 6XS
Telephone: 01256 329242
Fax: 01256 842754
Web Site: www.macmillan.co.uk

Directors: Dr A. Thomas *(Chief Executive)*
D. J. G. Knight *(Managing, Palgrave)*
W. H. Farries *(Group Central Finance, Macmillan)*
S. C. Inchcombe *(Managing, Nature Publishing Group)*
J. Drinkall *(Managing, Macmillan Education)*
A. Forbes Watson *(Managing, Pan Macmillan)*
R. Nathan *(Strategy)*
Company Secretary: C. E. Fleming
Chief Finance Officer: J. M. Wheeldon

Academic & Scholarly; Architecture & Design; Audio Books; Biography & Autobiography; Biology & Zoology; Chemistry; Children's Books; Cinema, Video, TV & Radio; Computer Science; Cookery, Wines & Spirits; Crafts & Hobbies; Crime; Economics; Educational & Textbooks; Electronic (Professional & Academic); Engineering; English as a Foreign Language; Environment & Development Studies; Fiction; Fine Art & Art History; Gardening; Gender Studies; Guide Books; Health & Beauty; History & Antiquarian; Humour; Languages & Linguistics; Law; Literature & Criticism; Mathematics & Statistics; Medical (incl. Self Help & Alternative Medicine); Military & War; Music; Natural History; Philosophy; Physics; Poetry; Politics & World Affairs; Psychology & Psychiatry; Reference Books, Directories & Dictionaries; Religion & Theology; Science Fiction; Scientific & Technical; Sociology & Anthropology; Sports & Games; Theatre, Drama & Dance; Travel & Topography

No of Employees: 1500
Annual Turnover: £233M

ISBNs, Imprints & Series:
Boxtree; Campbell Books; Kingfisher; Macmillan; Macmillan Children's Books; Macmillan Digital Audio; Macmillan New Writing; Nature; Nature Publishing Group; Palgrave Macmillan; Pan Macmillan; Papermac; Picador; Priddy Books; Sidgwick & Jackson

Parent Company:
Germany: Georg von Holtzbrinck GmbH

Associated Companies:
Argentina: Editorial Estrada SA; Editorial Puerto de Palos SA; Macmillan Publishers SA
Armenia: Macmillan Armenia CJS
Australia: Macmillan Distribution Services Pty Ltd; Macmillan Publishers Australia Pty Ltd; Macquarie Library Pty Ltd; Macquarie Online Pty Ltd; Pan Macmillan Australia Pty Ltd
Botswana: Macmillan Botswana Publishing Co (Pty) Ltd
Brazil: Macmillan do Brasil
Cameroon: Macmillan Publishers Cameroon Ltd
Egypt: Macmillan Publishers Egypt Ltd
Ghana: Unimax Macmillan Ltd
Greece: Macmillan Hellas SA
Hong Kong: Macmillan Production (Asia) Ltd Ltd; Macmillan Publishers (China) Ltd
India: Cosmic Graphic & Designs Pvt Ltd; Frank Brothers & Co (Publishers) Ltd; ICC

India Pvt Ltd; Macmillan India Ltd; Macmillan Publishers india Ltd; MPS Technologies Ltd
Japan: Macmillan Language House Ltd; Nature Japan KK
Kenya: Macmillan Kenya (Publishers) Ltd
Malawi: Macmillan Malawi Ltd
Mexico: Ediciones Castillo SA de CV; Editorial Macmillan de Mexico SA de CV
Mozambique: Macmillan Mozambique Lda
Namibia: Gamsberg Macmillan Publishers (Pty) Ltd
New Zealand: Macmillan Publishers New Zealand Ltd
Nigeria: Macmillan Nigeria Publishers Ltd; Northern Nigerian Publishing Co Ltd
Peru: Macmillan Publishers SA
Poland: Macmillan Polska Sp.Z.O.O.
Republic of Ireland: Gill & Macmillan Ltd
Republic of Korea: Macmillan Korea Publishers Ltd
Romania: Macmillan Romania SRL
Rwanda: Macmillan Rwanda Publishers Ltd
South Africa: Clever Books (Pty) Ltd; Hodder & Stoughton Ed SA (Pty) Ltd; Macmillan South Africa Publishers (Pty) Ltd; Pan Macmillan South Africa Publishers (Pty) Ltd
Spain: Macmillan Iberia SA
Swaziland: Macmillan Boleswa Publishers Pty Ltd; Macmillan Swaziland National Publishing Co (Pty) Ltd
Tanzania: Macmillan Aidan Ltd
Uganda: Macmillan Uganda Ltd
UK: Boxtree Ltd; Campbell Books Ltd; Kingfisher Publications Ltd; Macmillan Children's Books; Macmillan Distribution Ltd; Macmillan Education; Macmillan English Campus; Macmillan New Writing; Nature Publishing Group Ltd; Palgrave Macmillan; Pan Macmillan; Picador; Rodale; Sidgwick & Jackson Ltd; Stockton Press Ltd; Think Books
USA: Bedford, Freeman & Worth Publishing Group LLC; Tom Doherty Associates LLC; Farrar, Straus & Giroux LLC; Henry Holt and Co LLC; Holtzbrinck Publishers LLC; ICC Inc; Macmillan Academic Publishing Inc; Macmillan Publishers Inc; Nature America Inc; St Martin's Press LLC; Stockton Press Inc
Zambia: Macmillan Publishers (Zambia) Ltd
Zimbabwe: College Press Publishers (Pvt) Ltd
Hong Kong: Macmillan New Asia Publishers Ltd

Distributor for:
see: Macmillan Children's Books; Macmillan Education; Palgrave Macmillan; Pan Macmillan

Overseas Representation:
Armenia: Macmillan Armenia JV CJSC, Yerevan
Australia: Macmillan Education Australia, South Yarra, Vic; Pan Macmillan (Australia) Pty Ltd, Sydney, NSW
Botswana: Macmillan Botswana Publishing Co Ltd, Gaborone
Brazil: Macmillan do Brasil, São Paulo
Cameroon: Macmillan Publishers Cameroon Ltd, Limbe
China: Macmillan Publishers (China) Ltd, Hong Kong; Pan Macmillan Asia, Hong Kong; Macmillan Ltd, Beijing Office, Beijing, P. R. of China
Cyprus: Char. J. Philippides & Son Ltd, Nicosia
Dubai: Macmillan Education Dubai, Dubai, UAE
East & Central Africa: Macmillan Kenya (Publishers) Ltd, Nairobi, Kenya
Egypt: Macmillan Publishers Egypt Ltd, Cairo
Ethiopia: Macmillan Publishers Ltd, Addis Ababa
France: Laila Belyazid, Paris
France & Netherlands: Anne Georges, Brussels, Belgium
Gambia: Macmillan Publishers Ltd, Banjul
Ghana: Unimax Macmillan Ltd, Accra
Greece: Macmillan Hellas LLC, Athens

Hong Kong: Macmillan Education, East Asia; Macmillan Production Asia
Hungary: Edit Szabo, Budapest
India: Books India Pvt Ltd, New Delhi; Macmillan Publishers India Ltd, Bangalore; Macmillan Publishers India Ltd, Bangalore; Palgrave Macmillan, New Delhi
Italy: Macmillan Publishers Ltd, Milan
Japan: Macmillan Language House, Tokyo; Nature Japan, Tokyo
Kenya: Macmillan Kenya (Publishers) Ltd, Nairobi
Korea: Macmillan Korea Publishers Ltd, Seoul, Republic of Korea
Malawi: Macmillan Malawi Ltd, Blantyre
Mexico & Central America: Editorial Macmillan de Mexico SA de CV, Mexico DF, Mexico
Mozambique: Macmillan Mozambique Lda
Namibia: Gamsberg Macmillan Publishers (Pty) Ltd, Windhoek
New Zealand: Macmillan Publishers New Zealand Ltd, Auckland
Nigeria: Macmillan Nigeria Publishers Ltd, Yaba - Lagos
Pakistan: Book Bird Publishers Representatives, Lahore
Peru: Macmillan Publishers SA, Lima
Poland: Macmillan Polska, Warsaw
Republic of Ireland: Gill & Macmillan Ltd, Dublin
Romania: Macmillan Romania SRL, Bucharest
Rwanda: Macmillan Publishers Rwanda Ltd, Kigali
Sierra Leone: Macmillan Publishers Ltd, Freetown
Singapore: Pansing Distribution Sdn Bhd
South Africa: Macmillan South Africa Publishers (Pty) Ltd, Braamfontein; Pan Macmillan SA Pty Ltd, Hyde Park
Swaziland: Macmillan Boleswa Publishers (Pty) Ltd, Manzini
Taiwan: Macmillan Education, Taipei
Tanzania: Macmillan Aidan Ltd, Dar es Salaam
Turkey: Macmillan Publishers Ltd, Istanbul
Uganda: Macmillan Uganda Ltd, Kampala
Zambia: Macmillan Zambia, Lusaka
Zimbabwe: College Press Publishers (Pvt) Ltd, Harare

Book Trade Association Membership:
Publishers Association; IPG

2474

MAGNA LARGE PRINT BOOKS
Magna House, Long Preston, Skipton, North Yorks BD23 4ND
Telephone: 01729 840225 & 840526
Fax: 01729 840683
Email: dallen@magnaprint.co.uk

Director: Robert Thirlby *(Chairman)*
General Manager: Diane Allen
Accounts: David Mellin

Audio Books; Fiction; Large Print Books; Story Sound Audio Cassettes & CDs

New Titles: 336 (2008) , 336 (2009)

ISBNs, Imprints & Series:
978 0 7505, 978 1 84262 Large Print
978 1 85903 Audio

Parent Company:
Ulverscroft Large Print Books

Distributor for:
Mills & Boon Large Print

Overseas Representation:
Worldwide: Ulverscroft Large Print Books, UK

2475

*THE MAIA PRESS LTD
82 Forest Road, London E8 3BH

Telephone: (020) 7683 8141
Fax: (020) 7683 8141
Email: maggie@maiapress.com
Web Site: www.maiapress.com

Trade Enquiries, Distributor:
Central Books, 99 Wallis Road, London E9 5LN
Telephone: (020) 8986 4854
Fax: (020) 8533 5821
Email: bill@centralbooks.com
Web Site: www.centralbooks.com

Representation (UK):
Turnaround Publisher Services Ltd, Unit 3, Olympia Trading Estate, Coburg Road, London N22 6TZ
Telephone: (020) 8829 3000
Fax: (020) 8881 5088
Email: andy@turnaround-uk.com
Web Site: www.turnaround-uk.com

Directors: Maggie Hamand
Jane Havell

Fiction

ISBNs, Imprints & Series: 978 1 904559

Overseas Representation:
Australia: Tower Books Pty Ltd, Frenchs Forest, NSW
Far East: Ashton International Marketing Services, Sevenoaks, Kent, UK
France, Belgium, Netherlands, Germany, Austria, Switzerland, Croatia, Slovenia, Hungary, Czech Republic, Slovakia & Poland: Michael Geoghegan, London, UK
Scandinavia: Angell Eurosales, Berwick-on-Tweed, UK
Singapore & Malaysia: Pansing Distribution Pte Ltd, Singapore
Southern Europe: Padovani Books Ltd, London, UK
USA: Dufour Editions Inc, Chester Springs, PA

Book Trade Association Membership:
IPG

2476

MAINSTREAM PUBLISHING CO (EDINBURGH) LTD
7 Albany Street, Edinburgh EH1 3UG
Telephone: 0131 557 2959
Fax: 0131 556 8720
Email:
enquiries@mainstreampublishing.com
Web Site:
www.mainstreampublishing.com

Distribution, Trade Enquiries & Orders:
TBS Ltd, Colchester Road, Frating Green, Colchester, Essex CO7 7DW
Telephone: 01206 255600
Fax: 01206 255930

Directors: Bill Campbell *(Joint Managing, Editorial)*
Peter MacKenzie *(Joint Managing, Sales)*
Fiona Brownlee *(Marketing & Rights, Publicity)*
Ailsa Bathgate *(Editorial)*
Company Accountant: Douglas Nicoll
Production Manager: Neil Graham *(Production & Design)*

Biography & Autobiography; Cinema, Video, TV & Radio; Cookery, Wines & Spirits; Crime; Fine Art & Art History; Guide Books; Health & Beauty; History & Antiquarian; Humour; Illustrated & Fine Editions; Literature & Criticism; Medical (incl. Self Help & Alternative Medicine); Military & War; Music; Photography; Politics & World Affairs; Sports & Games

New Titles: 80 (2008) , 80 (2009)
No of Employees: 18

ISBNs, Imprints & Series:
978 0 906391, 978 1 84018, 978 1 84596, 978 1 85158

Associated Companies:
Random House UK [Partner]

Overseas Representation:
Australia: Random House Australia Pty Ltd, Sydney, NSW
Canada: Random House of Canada Ltd, Mississauga, Ont
Caribbean & Latin America: Random House Inc, New York, NY, USA
Germany, Switzerland, Austria, Belgium, Denmark, Finland & Luxembourg: Jörg Riekenbrauk, Cologne, Germany
Hong Kong, Taiwan, South Korea & China: Stanson Yeung, Random House of Canada Ltd, Toronto, Ont, Canada
India, Sri Lanka & Bangladesh: N. S. Krishna, Random House Publishers India Pte Ltd, New Delhi, India
New Zealand: Random House New Zealand Ltd, Auckland
Norway, Sweden, Spain, France, Italy, Portugal, Cyprus, Greece, Malta, Middle East, Pakistan & Africa (excluding South Africa): Random House Group Ltd, London, UK
South Africa: Random House (SA) Pty Ltd, Parktown
USA: Trafalgar Square Publishing / IPG, Chicago, IL

Book Trade Association Membership:
BA; Publishing Scotland

2477

MANAGEMENT POCKETBOOKS LTD
Laurel House, Station Approach, Alresford, Hants SO24 9JH
Telephone: 01962 735573
Fax: 01962 733637
Email: sales@pocketbook.co.uk
Web Site: www.pocketbook.co.uk

Directors: Ros Baynes *(Managing)*
Adrian Hunt

Educational & Textbooks; Industry, Business & Management

New Titles: 9 (2008) , 12 (2009)
No of Employees: 8

ISBNs, Imprints & Series:

978 1 870471, 978 1 903776
Management Pocketbooks; Teachers' Pocketbooks

Overseas Representation:
Australia: Training Solutions Group, Mudgeeraba, Qld
Caribbean: InterMedia Americana (IMA) Ltd, London, UK
Far East: Publishers International Marketing, Ferndown, Dorset, UK
India: Research Press, New Delhi
South Africa: Learning Resources Pty Ltd, Johannesburg

Book Trade Association Membership:
IPG

2478

MANCHESTER UNIVERSITY PRESS
Oxford Road, Manchester M13 9NR
Telephone: 0161 275 2310
Fax: 0161 274 3346
Email: mup@manchester.ac.uk
Web Site: manchesteruniversitypress.co.uk

Distribution (Trade Enquiries, Orders & Warehouse):
NBN International, Plymbridge House, Estover Road, Plymouth, Devon PL6 7PY
Telephone: 01752 202301
Fax: 01752 202333

Email: enquiries@nbninternational.com
Web Site: www.nbninternational.com

Sales Representation (UK):
Yale University Press, 47 Bedford Square, London WC1B 3DP
Telephone: (020) 7079 4900
Fax: (020) 7079 4901
Email: sales@yaleup.co.uk

Chief Executive Officer & Production Director: David Rodgers
Head of Sales & Marketing: Ben Stebbing
Head of Editorial: Matthew Frost

Academic & Scholarly; Architecture & Design; Cinema, Video, TV & Radio; Economics; Educational & Textbooks; Gay & Lesbian Studies; Gender Studies; History & Antiquarian; Illustrated & Fine Editions; Languages & Linguistics; Law; Literature & Criticism; Politics & World Affairs; Reference Books, Directories & Dictionaries; Sociology & Anthropology; Theatre, Drama & Dance; Transport

New Titles: 140 (2008) , 140 (2009)
No of Employees: 18
Annual Turnover: £1.8M

ISBNs, Imprints & Series:
978 0 7190 Manchester University Press
978 1 901341 Mandolin

Parent Company:
UK: The University of Manchester

Distributor for:
Netherlands: Amsterdam University Press

Overseas Representation:
Asia & Middle East: Publishers International Marketing, Sutton St Nicholas, Herefordshire, UK
Australia & New Zealand: Footprint Books Pty Ltd, Warriewood, NSW, Australia
Canada: University of British Columbia Press, Vancouver, BC
Canada (Orders & Customer Service): cUPT Distribution, Toronto, Ont, Canada
Europe: Andrew Durnell Marketing Ltd, Tunbridge Wells, UK
India (Representation): Andrew White, The White Partnership, Tunbridge Wells, UK
India (Sales): Viva Books, New Delhi, India
Japan: United Publishers Services Ltd, Tokyo
Malaysia: Publishers Marketing Services, Petaling Jaya
Republic of Ireland: Robert Towers, Monkstown, Co Dublin
Singapore: Publishers Marketing Services Pte Ltd
USA: Palgrave, New York, NY

Book Trade Association Membership:
IPG; Association of Learned & Professional Society Publishers

2479

MANDRAKE OF OXFORD
PO Box 250, Oxford OX1 1AP
Telephone: 01865 243671
Fax: 01865 432929
Email: mandrake@mandrake.uk.net
Web Site: www.mandrake.uk.net

Directors: Mogg Morgan
Kim Morgan

Children's Books; Crime; Fiction; Fine Art & Art History; Literature & Criticism; Magic & the Occult; Medical (incl. Self Help & Alternative Medicine); Philosophy; Poetry; Religion & Theology; Sociology & Anthropology; New Science

ISBNs, Imprints & Series:
978 1 869928 Golden Dawn
978 1 869928, 978 1 906958 Mandrake of Oxford

Overseas Representation:
USA: Ingram Publisher Services, Nashville, TN; New Leaf Distributing Co, Lithia Springs, GA

Book Trade Association Membership:
IPG

2480

MANEY PUBLISHING
Suite 1C, Joseph's Well, Hanover Walk, Leeds LS3 1AB
Telephone: 0113 386 8154
Fax: 0113 386 8178
Email: maney@maney.co.uk
Web Site: www.maney.co.uk

Also at:
1 Carlton House Terrace, London SW1Y 5AF
Telephone: (020) 7451 7300
Fax: (020) 7451 7307

Directors: Michael Gallico *(Managing)*
Mark Simon *(Publishing)*
Shelly Lynds *(Sales & Marketing)*
Managers: Liz Rosindale *(Managing Editor)*
Mark Hull *(Managing Editor)*
Lynne Medhurst *(Head of Corporate Marketing)*
Emily Simpson *(Head of Direct Marketing)*
Gaynor Redvers-Mutton *(Business Development)*
US Executive Publisher: Kim Martin

Academic & Scholarly; Archaeology; Architecture & Design; Atlases & Maps; Bibliography & Library Science; Biography & Autobiography; Electronic (Professional & Academic); Engineering; Environment & Development Studies; Fashion & Costume; Fine Art & Art History; Geography & Geology; History & Antiquarian; Illustrated & Fine Editions; Languages & Linguistics; Literature & Criticism; Medical (incl. Self Help & Alternative Medicine); Military & War; Religion & Theology; Scientific & Technical; Transport

ISBNs, Imprints & Series:
Legenda
978 0 901286 Northern Universities Press
978 0 901286, 978 1 902653 Maney Publishing

Distributor for:
European Respiratory Society; Modern Humanities Research Association; Pasold Research Fund; Society for Italian Studies; Society for Medieval Archaeology

Overseas Representation:
USA: Publishers Communication Group, Boston, MA

Book Trade Association Membership:
IGSMTP; Association of Learned & Professional Society Publishers

2481

MANSON PUBLISHING LTD
73 Corringham Road, London NW11 7DL
Telephone: (020) 8905 5150
Fax: (020) 8201 9233
Email: manson@mansonpublishing.com
Web Site: www.mansonpublishing.com

Distribution:
John Wiley & Sons Ltd,
Customer Services Dept, 1 Oldlands Way, Bognor Regis, West Sussex PO22 9SA
Telephone: 01243 843294
Fax: 01243 843303
Email: cs-books@wiley.com
Web Site: www.wiley.co.uk

Managing Director: Michael Manson

Agriculture; Animal Care & Breeding; Biology & Zoology; Geography & Geology; Medical (incl. Self Help & Alternative Medicine); Scientific & Technical; Veterinary Science

ISBNs, Imprints & Series:
978 1 84076, 978 1 874545

Associated Companies:
The Veterinary Press Ltd

Overseas Representation:
All other areas: Wiley-Blackwell, Oxford, UK
Australia & New Zealand (Medical & Veterinary titles): All things Medical, Sydney University, Sydney, NSW, Australia
Australia & New Zealand (Science titles): CSIRO Publishing, Collingwood, Vic, Australia
Japan (Medical & Veterinary titles): Nankodo Co Ltd, Tokyo, Japan

Book Trade Association Membership:
Publishers Association; IPG

2482

MARITIME BOOKS
Lodge Hill, Liskeard, Cornwall PL14 4EL
Telephone: 01579 343663
Fax: 01579 346747
Email: sales@navybooks.com
Web Site: www.navybooks.com

Managing Director: M. Critchley
Editor: S. Bush
Manager: P. Garnett

Military & War; Transport

ISBNs, Imprints & Series:
978 0 907771, 978 1 904459

2483

MAVERICK HOUSE PUBLISHERS
Office 19, Dunboyne Business Park, Dunboyne, Co Meath, Republic of Ireland
Telephone: +353 (01) 825 5717
Fax: +353 (01) 686 5036
Email: info@maverickhouse.com
Web Site: www.maverickhouse.com

Managing Director: Jean Harrington

Biography & Autobiography; Crime; Humour; Military & War; Politics & World Affairs; Sports & Games

ISBNs, Imprints & Series:
978 0 9542945, 978 0 9548707, 978 0 9548708, 978 1 905379

Overseas Representation:
Australia: Tower Books Pty Ltd, Frenchs Forest, NSW
Singapore & Malaysia: Paperclip, Singapore
UK: Turnaround Publisher Services Ltd, London

Book Trade Association Membership:
CLÉ (Irish PA)

2484

MEADOWSIDE CHILDREN'S BOOKS & GULLANE CHILDREN'S BOOKS
185 Fleet Street, London EC4A 2HS
Telephone: (020) 7400 1092
Fax: (020) 7400 1037
Email: info@meadowsidebooks.com & info@gullanebooks.com
Web Site: www.meadowsidebooks.com & www.gullanebooks.com

Publisher: Simon Rosenheim
Directors: Rupert Harbour *(Sales)*
Katherine Judge *(Rights)*
Marketing & Publicity Manager: Clare Simms

Children's Books

ISBNs, Imprints & Series:
978 1 84539 Meadowside
978 1 86233 Gullane

Parent Company:
UK: D. C. Thomson

Overseas Representation:
Australia & New Zealand: Bookwise International, Wingfield, SA, Australia

2485

MEHRING BOOKS
PO Box 3978, Sheffield S1 2BS
Telephone: 0114 213 0191
Email: sales@mehringbooks.co.uk
Web Site: www.mehringbooks.co.uk

Contact: Richard Turner

Economics; History & Antiquarian; Literature & Criticism; Politics & World Affairs

New Titles: 2 (2008), 4 (2009)

ISBNs, Imprints & Series:
978 0 929087, 978 1 873045

Distributor for:
Australia: Mehring Books
Germany: Arbeiterpresse Verlag
USA: Mehring Books

Overseas Representation:
Australia: Mehring Books, Marrickville, NSW
Germany: Arbeiterpresse Verlag, Essen
USA: Mehring Books, Oak Park, MI

Book Trade Association Membership:
IPG

2486

MELISENDE
Pennine Way Office, 87–89 Saffron Hill, London EC1N 8QU
Telephone: (020) 7269 9870
Email: melisende@btinternet.com
Web Site: www.melisende.com

Editorial: Leonard Harrow
Sales & Marketing: Alan Ball

Academic & Scholarly; Archaeology; Architecture & Design; Crafts & Hobbies; Fine Art & Art History; History & Antiquarian; Illustrated & Fine Editions; Politics & World Affairs; Religion & Theology; Travel & Topography

New Titles: 6 (2008), 10 (2009)

ISBNs, Imprints & Series: 978 1 901764

Distributor for:
Altajir World of Islam Trust; Sangam Books Ltd
Cyprus: Rimal Publications
India: East & West Publishing; Orientblackswan; UBSPD

Overseas Representation:
Middle East: Rimal Publications, Cyprus

2487

MENTOR BOOKS
43 Furze Road, Sandyford Industrial Estate, Dublin 18, Republic of Ireland
Telephone: +353 (01) 295 2112/3
Fax: +353 (01) 295 2114
Email: all@mentorbooks.ie
Web Site: www.mentorbooks.ie

General Manager: Daniel C. McCarthy

Academic & Scholarly; Biography & Autobiography; Biology & Zoology; Cinema, Video, TV & Radio; Crime; Economics; Educational & Textbooks; Fiction; Geography & Geology; Guide Books; Health & Beauty; History & Antiquarian; Humour; Industry, Business & Management; Languages & Linguistics; Mathematics & Statistics; Photography; Poetry; Politics & World Affairs; Reference Books, Directories & Dictionaries; Scientific & Technical; Sports & Games; Travel & Topography

ISBNs, Imprints & Series:
978 0 947548, 978 1 902586, 978 1 84210

Book Trade Association Membership:
CLÉ (Irish PA)

2488

MERCIER PRESS LTD
Unit 3, Oak House, Riverview Business Park, Bessboro Road, Blackrock, Cork, Republic of Ireland
Telephone: +353 (021) 461 4700
Fax: +353 (021) 461 4802
Email: info@mercierpress.ie
Web Site: www.mercierpress.ie

Managing Director: Clodagh Feehan
Commissioning Editors: Mary Feehan
Eoin Purcell
Rights & Permissions: Sharon O'Donovan
Managing Editor: Wendy Logue
Sales Executive: Niamh Hatton
Marketing Co-ordinator: Patrick Crowley
Design: Catherine Twibill

Academic & Scholarly; Archaeology; Biography & Autobiography; Children's Books; Fiction; History & Antiquarian; Humour; Literature & Criticism; Poetry; Politics & World Affairs; Religion & Theology; Theatre, Drama & Dance

ISBNs, Imprints & Series:
978 0 85342, 978 1 85635 Mercier Press
978 1 86023 Marino Books

Overseas Representation:
Australia: Tower Books Pty Ltd, Frenchs Forest, NSW
USA: James Trading Group, Nanuet, NY

Book Trade Association Membership:
CLÉ (Irish PA); Independent Publishers Guild

2489

MERCURY BOOKS
20 Bloomsbury Street, London WC1B 3JH
Telephone: (020) 7636 7171
Fax: (020) 7636 1922

Director: Finbarr McCabe *(Sales)*

Archaeology; Atlases & Maps; Geography & Geology; History & Antiquarian; Literature & Criticism; Military & War; Reference Books, Directories & Dictionaries

ISBNs, Imprints & Series:
978 1 84560, 978 1 904668

Parent Company:
Caxton Publishing Group

Overseas Representation:
Australia & New Zealand: Bookwise International, Wingfield, SA, Australia
Europe: Bill Bailey Publishers Representatives, Newton Abbot, UK
Far East: Bookwise Asia, Singapore, Singapore
South Africa: Peter Matthews Agencies, Alberton
USA & Canada: International Publishers Marketing Inc, Herndon, VA, USA

2490 ▪

MERCURY JUNIOR
20 Bloomsbury Street, London WC1B 3JH
Telephone: (020) 7636 7171
Fax: (020) 7636 1922

Director: Finbarr McCabe (*Sales & Marketing*)

Children's Books

ISBNs, Imprints & Series:
978 1 84560, 978 1 904668

Parent Company:
Caxton Publishing Group

Overseas Representation:
Australia & New Zealand: Bookwise
 International, Wingfield, SA, Australia
Europe: Bill Bailey Publishers
 Representatives, Newton Abbot, UK
Far East: Bookwise Asia, Singapore,
 Singapore
South Africa: Peter Matthews Agencies,
 Alberton
USA & Canada: International Publishers
 Marketing Inc, Herndon, VA, USA

2491 ▪

THE MERLIN PRESS LTD
99b Wallis Road, London E9 5LN
Telephone: (020) 8533 5800
Email: info@merlinpress.co.uk
Web Site: www.merlinpress.co.uk

Distribution:
Central Books Ltd, 99 Wallis Road, London
E9 5LN
Telephone: (020) 8986 4854
Fax: (020) 8533 5821
Email: orders@centralbooks.com

Managing Director: Anthony Zurbrugg
Manager: Adrian Howe

Academic & Scholarly; Biography & Autobiography; Economics; Gender Studies; History & Antiquarian; Politics & World Affairs; Sociology & Anthropology

ISBNs, Imprints & Series:
978 0 85036 The Merlin Press Ltd
978 1 85284 Green Print

Parent Company:
Africa Book Centre Ltd

Overseas Representation:
Australia: Eleanor Brasch Enterprises,
 Artarmon, NSW
Canada: Fernwood Books, Black Point, NS
South Africa: Blue Weaver Marketing, Tokai
USA: Independent Publishers Group (IPG),
 Chicago, IL

2492 ▪

MERLIN PUBLISHING/WOLFHOUND PRESS
Newmarket Hall, Cork Street, Dublin 8,
Republic of Ireland
Telephone: +353 (01) 453 5866
Fax: +353 (01) 453 5930
Email: publishing@merlin.ie
Web Site: www.merlinwolfhound.com

Distribution:
Gill & Macmillan, Hume Avenue,
Park West, Dublin 12, Republic of Ireland
Telephone: +353 (01) 500 9500
Fax: +353 (01) 500 9599
Email: info@gillmacmillan.ie
Web Site: www.gillmacmillan.ie

Managing Director: Chenile Keogh
 (*Publisher*)
Sales Representative: Robert Doran

Academic & Scholarly; Biography &

Autobiography; Children's Books; Cinema, Video, TV & Radio; Cookery, Wines & Spirits; Crime; Educational & Textbooks; Fiction; Fine Art & Art History; Gender Studies; Guide Books; Health & Beauty; History & Antiquarian; Humour; Law; Literature & Criticism; Music; Photography; Poetry; Politics & World Affairs; Reference Books, Directories & Dictionaries; Religion & Theology; Sports & Games; Travel & Topography

New Titles: 8 (2008) , 8 (2009)
No of Employees: 2

ISBNs, Imprints & Series:
Wolfhound Press
978 0 86327
978 1 903582, 978 1 907162 Merlin
 Publishing

Parent Company:
Republic of Ireland: Merlin Media Ltd

Overseas Representation:
UK: Bounce! Sales & Marketing Ltd, London
USA (Wolfhound & Merlin): Interlink
 Publishing Group Inc, Northampton, MA,
 USA

Book Trade Association Membership:
CLÉ (Irish PA)

2493 ▪

MERRELL PUBLISHERS LTD
81 Southwark Street, London SE1 0HX
Telephone: (020) 7928 8880
Fax: (020) 7928 1199
Email: mail@merrellpublishers.com
Web Site: www.merrellpublishers.com

Trade & Credit Orders, Returns:
Marston Book Services, PO Box 269,
Abingdon, Oxon OX14 4YN
Telephone: 01235 465500
Fax: 01235 465555
Email: trade.order@marston.co.uk

Directors: Hugh Merrell (*Rights*)
 Claire Chandler (*Editorial*)
 Nicola Bailey (*Art*)
 Lulu Cane (*Sales & Marketing*)
Production Manager: Alenka Oblak

Academic & Scholarly; Architecture & Design; Fashion & Costume; Fine Art & Art History; Illustrated & Fine Editions; Photography; Transport

New Titles: 36 (2008) , 25 (2009)
No of Employees: 14

ISBNs, Imprints & Series: 978 1 85894

Overseas Representation:
All other territories: Lulu Cane, Merrell
 Publishers, London, UK
Australia & New Zealand: Bookwise
 International, Wingfield, SA, Australia
Canada: Canadian Manda Group, Toronto,
 Ont
Central America & Caribbean: Chris
 Humphrys, Humphrys Roberts
 Associates, London, UK
Eastern Europe: Csaba & Jackie Lengyel de
 Bagota, CLB Marketing Services,
 Budapest, Hungary
Estonia, Latvia & Lithuania: Tony Moggach,
 InterMedia Americana (IMA) Ltd,
 London, UK
France: Critiques Livres Distribution,
 Bagnolet
Germany, Austria & Switzerland: Gabriele
 Kern Publishers Services, Frankfurt-am-
 Main, Germany
*Hong Kong, Taiwan, China, Korea, Japan,
 Indonesia, Philippines & Thailand:* Julian
 Ashton, Ashton International Marketing
 Services, Sevenoaks, Kent, UK
India, Bangladesh, Nepal, Bhutan & Sri

Lanka: Surit Mitra, Maya Publishers Pvt
 Ltd, New Delhi, India
Italy, Greece, Spain & Portugal: Padovani
 Books Ltd, Montanare di Cortona, Italy;
 Padovani Books Ltd, London, UK
Malaysia, Singapore & Brunei: Pansing
 Distribution Pte Ltd, Singapore
Middle East, Turkey, Israel, Cyprus & Malta:
 Peter Ward Book Exports, London, UK
Netherlands, Belgium & Luxembourg:
 Nilsson & Lamm BV, Weesp, Netherlands
Republic of Ireland & Northern Ireland:
 Robert Towers, Monkstown, Co Dublin,
 Republic of Ireland
Scandinavia: Elisabeth Harder-Kreimann,
 Hamburg, Germany
South America: Terry Roberts, Humphrys
 Roberts Associates, Cotia SP, Brazil
Southern Africa: Shirley Cooksley, Quartet
 Books, Sunningdale, South Africa
USA: Perseus Group, Jackson, TN

2494 ▪

*MERTON PRIORY PRESS LTD
9 Owen Falls Avenue, Chesterfield S41 0FR
Telephone: 01246 554026
Email: mertonpriory@btinternet.com
Web Site: www.merton.dircon.co.uk

Owner: Philip Riden

Academic & Scholarly; Archaeology; Biography & Autobiography; History & Antiquarian; Transport

ISBNs, Imprints & Series: 978 1 898937

2495 ▪

METHODIST PUBLISHING
17 Tresham Road, Orton Southgate,
Peterborough PE2 6SG
Telephone: 01733 235962
Fax: 01733 390325
Web Site:
 www.methodistpublishing.org.uk

Chair: Eric Jarvis
Heads of Department: Jane McClean
 (*Accounts*)
 Karen Kendall (*Customer Services*)

Academic & Scholarly; Educational & Textbooks; Electronic (Professional & Academic); Poetry; Religion & Theology

ISBNs, Imprints & Series:
978 0 716204 Epworth
978 1 85852 Inspire; Methodist Publishing
 House

Parent Company:
The Methodist Church

Overseas Representation:
USA (Epworth titles only): Westminster
 John Knox Press, Louisville, KY, USA

Book Trade Association Membership:
BA

2496 ▪

*MEYRICK MARKETING LTD
[trading as The Francis Frith Collection]
Frith's Barn, Teffont, Salisbury, Wilts
SP3 5QP
Telephone: 01722 716376
Fax: 01722 716881
Email: sales@francisfrith.co.uk
Web Site: www.francisfrith.co.uk

Directors: John Buck (*Managing*)
 Jason Buck (*Development*)
 John Brewer (*Finance*)
Managing Editor: Julia Skinner
IP Rights Manager: Isobel Hall

History & Antiquarian; Photography; Travel & Topography

ISBNs, Imprints & Series:
978 1 84589, 978 1 85937

Book Trade Association Membership:
IPG

2497 ▪

MICHELIN MAPS & GUIDES
Hannay House, 39 Clarendon Road,
Watford WD17 1JA
Telephone: 01923 205240
Fax: 01923 205241
Web Site: www.michelin.co.uk/travel

Warehouse/Returns:
Michelin Tyre Plc, Maps & Guides,
Building 82 Campbell Road,
Stoke on Trent, Staffs ST4 4EY
Telephone: 01923 205242
Fax: 01923 205241

**Commercial Director, Head of Travel
 Publications:** I. Murray
Trade Marketing Manager: J. Khawam

Atlases & Maps; Guide Books; Travel & Topography

ISBNs, Imprints & Series:
978 1 90626 The Green Guide Series
978 2 06 710, 978 2 06 713 Regional Map
 Series
978 2 06 710, 978 2 06 714 Zoom Map
 Series
978 2 06 711, 978 2 06 714 National Map
 Series
978 2 06 713 Local Map Series
978 2 06 713, 978 2 06 714 The Red Guide
 Series

Parent Company:
France: Manufacture Française des
 Pneumatiques Michelin

Overseas Representation:
Belgium & Luxembourg: Michelin Belux,
 Brussels, Belgium
Italy: Michelin Italiana SPA, Milan
Spain: Michelin Espana Portugal SA, Madrid
USA: Michelin Travel Publications,
 Greenville, SC

Book Trade Association Membership:
BA

2498 ▪

MICROFORM ACADEMIC PUBLISHERS
Main Street, East Ardsley, Wakefield,
West Yorkshire WF3 2AP
Telephone: 01924 825700
Fax: 01924 871005
Email: map@microform.co.uk
Web Site: www.britishonlinearchives.co.uk

Managing Director: Nigel Le Page
Head of Publishing: Roderick Vassie

Academic & Scholarly; Biography & Autobiography; Economics; Electronic (Professional & Academic); History & Antiquarian; Literature & Criticism; Military & War; Politics & World Affairs; Religion & Theology; Sociology & Anthropology

New Titles: 30 (2008) , 35 (2009)

ISBNs, Imprints & Series:
British Records Relating to America in
 Microform (BRRAM) (series); Records of
 the Raj (series)
978 1 85117 British Records on the Atlantic
 World, 1700-1850

Associated Companies:
UK: Microform Imaging Ltd

Overseas Representation:
Japan: Far Eastern Booksellers, Tokyo
USA & Canada: PraXess, New York, NY, USA

2499

MIDDLETON PRESS
Easebourne Lane, Midhurst, Sussex
GU29 9AZ
Telephone: 01730 813169
Fax: 01730 812601
Web Site: www.middletonpress.co.uk

Author & Proprietor: Dr J. C. V. Mitchell

Military & War; Nautical; Transport

ISBNs, Imprints & Series:
978 0 906520, 978 1 873793, 978 1
901706, 978 1 904474, 978 1 906008

2500

MILESTONE PUBLICATIONS
62 Murray Road, Horndean, Waterlooville,
Hants PO8 9JL
Telephone: 023 9259 7440
Fax: 023 9259 1975
Email: info@gosschinaclub.co.uk
Web Site: www.gosschinaclub.co.uk

Managing Director: Lynda Pine
(Publishing)
Manageress: Debbie Webb

Antiques & Collecting

No of Employees: 5

ISBNs, Imprints & Series:
978 1 85265, 978 1 903852

Parent Company:
Goss & Crested China Ltd

2501

*MILET PUBLISHING LTD
c/o Turnaround Publisher Services Ltd,
Unit 3, Olympia Trading Estate,
Coburg Road, Wood Green, London
N22 6TZ
Telephone: (020) 8829 3000
Fax: (020) 8881 5088
Email: info@milet.com
Web Site: www.milet.com

Directors: Patricia A. Billings
Sedat Turhan

*Children's Books; English as a Foreign
Language; Fiction; Languages & Linguistics;
Reference Books, Directories & Dictionaries*

ISBNs, Imprints & Series: 978 1 84059

Distributor for:
Turkey: Engin; Fono; Net; Redhouse/Sev; A.
Turizm

Overseas Representation:
Australia & New Zealand (Distributors):
Global Language Books, Toongabbie,
NSW, Australia; Tower Books Pty Ltd,
Frenchs Forest, NSW, Australia
USA & Canada (Distributors): Tuttle
Publishing, North Clarendon, VT, USA

2502

J. GARNET MILLER
10 Station Road Industrial Estate, Colwall,
Malvern, Worcs WR13 6RN
Telephone: 01684 540154
Fax: 01684 540154
Email: simon@cressrelles.co.uk
Web Site: www.cressrelles.co.uk

Managers: Leslie Smith
Simon Smith

Theatre, Drama & Dance

New Titles: 10 (2008) , 12 (2009)

Parent Company:
Cressrelles Publishing Co Ltd

Overseas Representation:
Australia: Origin Theatrical, Sydney, NSW
New Zealand: Play Bureau of New Zealand
Ltd, New Plymouth
Republic of Ireland: Drama League of
Ireland, Dublin
South Africa: Dalro (Pty) Ltd, Braamfontein
USA: Bakers Plays, Quincy, MA

2503

MILLER'S
2–4 Heron Quays, London E14 4JP
Telephone: (020) 7531 8400
Fax: (020) 7531 8650
Email: info-mb@mitchell-beazley.co.uk
Web Site: www.octopusbooks.co.uk

Distributor:
Littlehampton Book Services Ltd,
Faraday Close, Durrington, Worthing,
West Sussex BN13 3RB
Telephone: 01903 828500
Fax: 01903 828625

Director: Judith Miller *(Publisher/
Managing)*
Publishing Manager: Julie Brooke

Antiques & Collecting

Parent Company:
Hachette

Associated Companies:
Mitchell Beazley; Octopus Publishing Group

Overseas Representation:
See: Octopus Publishing Group, London, UK

Book Trade Association Membership:
BA

2504

THE MIT PRESS LTD
Fitzroy House, 11 Chenies Street, London
WC1E 7EY
Telephone: (020) 7306 0603
Fax: (020) 7306 0604
Email: info@HUP-MITpress.co.uk
Web Site: www-mitpress.mit.edu

Trade & Warehouse:
John Wiley & Sons Ltd, Distribution Centre,
Southern Cross Trading Estate,
1 Oldlands Way, Bognor Regis, West Sussex
PO22 9SA
Telephone: 01243 779777
Fax: 01243 820250
Email: cs-books@wiley.co.uk

Managers: Ann Sexsmith *(General)*
Ann Twiselton *(Publicity)*
Judith Bullent *(Texts/Exhibitions)*

*Academic & Scholarly; Architecture &
Design; Bibliography & Library Science;
Biography & Autobiography; Biology &
Zoology; Computer Science; Economics;
Environment & Development Studies; Fine
Art & Art History; Gay & Lesbian Studies;
Gender Studies; Industry, Business &
Management; Languages & Linguistics;
Music; Natural History; Philosophy;
Photography; Politics & World Affairs;
Psychology & Psychiatry; Reference Books,
Directories & Dictionaries; Scientific &
Technical*

New Titles: 225 (2008) , 225 (2009)

ISBNs, Imprints & Series:
978 0 262 American Association for
Artificial Intelligence Press; Bradford
Books; MIT Press
978 0 936756, 978 1 57027, 978 1 58435
Semiotext(e)
978 0 942299, 978 1 890951 Zone Books

Parent Company:
USA: MIT Press

Distributor for:
Afterall; Semiotext(e); Zone Books (Urzone
Publishing Ltd)

Overseas Representation:
Australia & New Zealand: Footprint Books
Pty Ltd, Warriewood, NSW, Australia
*Belgium, France, Iceland, Netherlands,
Norway, Sweden, Finland & Denmark:*
Fred Hermans, Bovenkarspel,
Netherlands
Canada & Australia: David Stimpson,
Toronto, Ont, Canada
Caribbean: John Atkin, Norwalk, CT, USA
Central America: Jose Rios, Guatemala
China: Wei Zhao, Everest International
Publishing Services, Beijing, P. R. of China
Germany, Austria, Switzerland & Italy: Uwe
Lüdemann, Berlin, Germany
Hong Kong: Jane Lam, Kowloon
India: Mediamatics, Calcutta
Iran: Farhad Maftoon, Tehran
Israel: Rodney Franklin Agency, Tel Aviv
Japan: Rockbook, Tokyo
Malaysia & Brunei: Simon Tay, Apex
Knowledge, Selangor, Malaysia
Mexico: Cynthia Zimpfer, Morelos
*Middle East (excluding Greece, Iran &
Israel):* Avicenna Partnership, Oxford, UK
Pakistan: Saleem Malik, World Press, Lahore
Philippines: Jean Lim, Megatexts Phil,
Makati City
*Poland, Hungary, Croatia, Slovenia,
Slovakia, Czech Republic, Russia, Serbia,
Romania, Albania, Bosnia & Herzegovina,
Latvia, Lithuania & Estonia:* Ewa
Ledóchowicz, Konstancin-Jeziorna,
Poland
*Singapore, Indonesia, Vietnam, Laos,
Cambodia & Myanmar:* Susanne Patrick,
IGP Services, Singapore
South Africa: Cory Voigt Associates,
Johannesburg
South Korea: Se-Yung Jun & Min-Hwa Yoo,
Seoul, Republic of Korea
Spain & Portugal: Chris Humphrys, Gaucin,
Spain
Taiwan: B. K. Norton, Taipei

2505

MITCHELL BEAZLEY
2–4 Heron Quays, London E14 4JP
Telephone: (020) 7531 8400
Fax: (020) 7537 0773
Web Site: www.octopusbooks.co.uk

Distribution:
Littlehampton Book Services,
Faraday Close, Durrington, Worthing,
West Sussex BN13 3RB
Telephone: 01903 828801
Fax: 01903 828802
Web Site:
www.pubeasy.books.lbsltd.co.uk

Directors: David Lamb *(Publisher)*
Tracey Smith *(Editorial)*

*Antiques & Collecting; Archaeology;
Architecture & Design; Cookery, Wines &
Spirits; Crafts & Hobbies; Fashion &
Costume; Fine Art & Art History;
Gardening; Health & Beauty; History &
Antiquarian; Illustrated & Fine Editions;
Medical (incl. Self Help & Alternative
Medicine); Music; Natural History;
Photography; Reference Books, Directories
& Dictionaries; Sports & Games; Travel &
Topography*

Parent Company:
Hachette UK Ltd

Overseas Representation:
See: Octopus Publishing Group, London, UK

Book Trade Association Membership:
BA

2506

M&K PUBLISHING
[an imprint of M&K Update Ltd]
The Old Bakery, St John's Street, Keswick,
Cumbria CA12 5AS
Telephone: 01768 773030
Fax: 01768 781099
Email: enquiries@mkupdate.co.uk
Web Site: www.mkupdate.co.uk

Co-Directors: Mike Roberts
Ken Russell

*Academic & Scholarly; Medical (incl. Self
Help & Alternative Medicine); Psychology &
Psychiatry*

New Titles: 10 (2008) , 12 (2009)
No of Employees: 7
Annual Turnover: £150,000

ISBNs, Imprints & Series: 978 1 905539

Parent Company:
UK: M&K Update Ltd

Overseas Representation:
Worldwide: IMR Agency Ltd, Lancaster, UK

Book Trade Association Membership:
Publishers Association

2507

MOONLIGHT PUBLISHING LTD
The King's Manor, East Hendred, Oxon
OX12 8JY
Telephone: 01235 821821
Fax: 01235 821155
Email: johnclement@btconnect.com
Web Site:
www.moonlightpublishing.co.uk

Warehouse, Trade Enquiries & Orders:
BookSource, 50 Cambuslang Road,
Glasgow G32 8NB
Telephone: 0845 370 0067
Fax: 0845 370 0068
Email: moonlight@booksource.net
Web Site: www.booksource.net

Managing Director: John Clement

*Atlases & Maps; Children's Books; English
as a Foreign Language; Fine Art & Art
History; Music; Natural History*

New Titles: 3 (2008) , 14 (2009)
No of Employees: 2
Annual Turnover: £196,000

ISBNs, Imprints & Series:
978 1 85103 Close-Ups; First Discovery; My
First Discoveries; Torchlight

Overseas Representation:
Australia: Era, Brooklyn Park, SA
Canada: Rainbow Books, Vancouver, BC
India: Rupa, New Delhi
Japan: First Discovery Japan, Tokyo
Korea: JY Books, Gyeonnggi-Do, Republic
of Korea
Malaysia: BR Group, Kuching, Sarawak
South Africa: Wild Dog Press, Johannesburg
Spain: Distribuidora Vicens Vives, Barcelona
Taiwan: Children's Publications Co Ltd,
Taipei

Book Trade Association Membership:
Publishers Association; Publishing Scotland

2508

**MOORLEY'S PRINT & PUBLISHING
LTD**
23 Park Road, Ilkeston, Derbyshire DE7 5DA
Telephone: 0115 932 0643
Fax: 0115 932 0643
Email: info@moorleys.co.uk
Web Site: www.moorleys.co.uk

Directors: Peter R. Newberry *(Joint Managing, Financial)*
Patrick Mancini *(Joint Managing, Production)*

History & Antiquarian; Music; Poetry; Religion & Theology; Theatre, Drama & Dance

New Titles: 9 (2008) , 6 (2009)
No of Employees: 6

ISBNs, Imprints & Series:
978 0 86071, 978 0 901495

Associated Companies:
Truedata Computer Services

Distributor for:
Cliff College Publishing; Darby Publications; Mainstream Baptists for Life & Growth; Met Specials; Nimbus Press; Social Work Christian Fellowship
Malaysia: Pustaka Sufes SDN BHD

Book Trade Association Membership:
Christian Booksellers Association; Publishing Licensing Society

2509 ▬▬▬▬▬

MOTOR RACING PUBLICATIONS LTD
PO Box 1318, Croydon, Surrey CR9 5YP
Telephone: (020) 8654 2711
Fax: (020) 8407 0339
Email: john@mrpbooks.co.uk
Web Site: www.mrpbooks.co.uk

Orders:
Vine House Distribution Ltd,
The Old Mill House, Mill Lane, Uckfield,
East Sussex TN22 5AA
Telephone: 01825 767396
Fax: 01825 765649
Email: sales@vinehouseuk.co.uk
Web Site: www.vinehouseuk.co.uk

Managing Director: John Blunsden

Biography & Autobiography; Sports & Games; Transport

New Titles: 2 (2008) , 1 (2009)
Annual Turnover: £115,000

ISBNs, Imprints & Series:
978 0 900549, 978 0 947981, 978 1 899870 Motor Racing Publications; MRP Publishing
978 0 948358 The Fitzjames Press

Associated Companies:
The Fitzjames Press

Overseas Representation:
All territories (excluding Australia, New Zealand, USA, Canada & Republic of Ireland): Gunnar Lie Associates, London, UK
USA & Canada: MBI Distribution Services, Osceola, WI, USA

2510 ▬▬▬▬▬

*MULTI SCIENCE PUBLISHING CO LTD
5 Wates Way, Brentwood, Essex CM15 9TB
Telephone: 01277 224632
Fax: 01277 223453
Email: mscience@globalnet.co.uk
Web Site: www.multi-science.co.uk

Academic & Scholarly; Architecture & Design; Aviation; Computer Science; Electronic (Professional & Academic); Engineering; Environment & Development Studies; Physics; Reference Books, Directories & Dictionaries; Scientific & Technical; Sports & Games

ISBNs, Imprints & Series: 978 0 906522

Book Trade Association Membership:
IGSMTP

2511 ▬▬▬▬▬

MURDOCH BOOKS UK LTD
6th Floor, Erico House,
93–99 Upper Richmond Road, London
SW15 2TG
Telephone: (020) 8785 5995
Fax: (020) 8785 5985

Distribution & Invoicing:
Macmillan Distribution Ltd, Brunel Road,
Houndmills, Basingstoke, Hants RG21 2XS
Telephone: 01256 329242
Fax: 01256 327961

Group Chief Executive: Juliet Rogers
International Rights & Export: Cathy Slater
UK Sales & Marketing: Carrie Boyes
UK Finance Director: John Sprinks

Biography & Autobiography; Cookery, Wines & Spirits; Crafts & Hobbies; Do-It-Yourself; Gardening; Health & Beauty; History & Antiquarian; Travel & Topography

ISBNs, Imprints & Series:
978 1 74045 Murdoch Books
978 1 74045, 978 1 74196, 978 1 92120, 978 1 92125 Pier 9

Parent Company:
Australia: Murdoch Books Pty Ltd

Overseas Representation:
Asia: Pan Macmillan Asia, Hong Kong
Australia & New Zealand: Murdoch Books Pty Ltd, Sydney, NSW, Australia
Europe: Gabriele Kern Publishers Services, Frankfurt-am-Main, Germany; Angell Eurosales, Berwick-on-Tweed, UK; Penny Padovani, London, UK
Middle East: Peter Ward Book Exports, London, UK

2512 ▬▬▬▬▬

JOHN MURRAY PUBLISHERS
[a division of Hachette UK]
338 Euston Road, London NW1 3BH
Telephone: (020) 7873 6000
Fax: (020) 7873 6446
Web Site: www.johnmurray.co.uk

UK Orders & Invoicing, Payments & Credit Control & Warehouse:
Bookpoint, 130 Milton Park, Abingdon,
Oxon OX14 4SB
Telephone: 01235 400400
Fax: 01235 821511

Directors: Roland Philipps *(Managing)*
James Spackman *(Sales & Marketing)*
Nikki Barrow *(Publicity)*
Jason Bartholomew *(Rights)*
Eleanor Birne *(Publishing)*

Biography & Autobiography; Fiction; Fine Art & Art History; History & Antiquarian; Humour; Military & War; Travel & Topography

ISBNs, Imprints & Series: 978 0 7195

Parent Company:
Hachette UK

Overseas Representation:
Australia: Alliance Distribution Services Pty Ltd, Tuggerah, NSW; Hachette Livre Australia, Sydney, NSW
Canada: McArthur & Co Publishers Ltd, Toronto, Ont
Hong Kong: Asia Publishers Services Ltd
India: Hachette Book Publishing India Pvt Ltd, Gurgaon
Netherlands (Hardbacks and Trade Paperbacks): Nilsson & Lamm BV, Weesp, Netherlands

Netherlands (Paperbacks): Van Ditmar BV, Amsterdam, Netherlands
New Zealand: Hachette Livre New Zealand, Auckland
Pakistan: Oxford University Press Pakistan Branch, Karachi
Singapore & Malaysia: Pansing Distribution Sdn Bhd, Singapore
South Africa: Jonathan Ball Publishers (Pty) Ltd, Johannesburg
USA: Trafalgar Square Publishing, North Pomfret, VT

Book Trade Association Membership:
IPG

2513 ▬▬▬▬▬

MW EDUCATIONAL
Westcliff Drive, Leigh-on-Sea, Essex SS9 2LB
Telephone: 01702 715282
Fax: 01702 715172
Email: mweducational@yahoo.co.uk
Web Site: www.mweducational.co.uk

Distribution:
Gardners Books Ltd, 1 Whittle Drive,
Eastbourne, East Sussex BN23 6QH
Telephone: 01323 521555

Chief Executive Officer: Mark Chatterton

Children's Books; Educational & Textbooks

New Titles: 2 (2009)

ISBNs, Imprints & Series:
978 1 901146 The A Plus Series of 11+ Practice Papers; The Advantage Series of SATs Practice Papers

2514 ▬▬▬▬▬

MYRIAD EDITIONS
59 Lansdowne Place, Brighton BN3 1FL
Telephone: 01273 720000
Email: candida@MyriadEditions.com
Web Site: www.MyriadEditions.com

Directors: Candida Lacey *(Managing)*
Robert Benewick
Judith Mackay
Design: Corinne Pearlman
Production: Isabelle Lewis
Editorial: Jannet King
Rights: Sadie Mayne
Fiction: Vicky Blunden

Academic & Scholarly; Atlases & Maps; Electronic (Professional & Academic); Environment & Development Studies; Fiction; Gender Studies; Military & War; Politics & World Affairs

Overseas Representation:
China & Taiwan: Big Apple Tuttle-Mori Agency Inc, Taipei, Taiwan
Japan: Tuttle-Mori Agency Inc, Tokyo
Spain, Portugal & South America: Ilustrata Empresariale SL, Barcelona, Spain

Book Trade Association Membership:
IPG

2515 ▬▬▬▬▬

MYRMIDON BOOKS LTD
Rotterdam House, 116 Quayside,
Newcastle upon Tyne NE1 3DY
Telephone: 0191 206 4005
Email: enquiries@myrmidonbooks.com
Web Site: www.myrmidonbooks.com

Distribution:
Littlehampton Book Services,
Faraday Close, Durrington, Worthing,
West Sussex TN13 3RB
Telephone: 01903 828500
Email: enquiries@lbsltd.co.uk
Web Site: www.lbsltd.co.uk

Director: Edward Handyside *(Publishing)*

Fiction

ISBNs, Imprints & Series: 978 1 905802

Overseas Representation:
Australia & New Zealand: Bookwise International, Wingfield, SA, Australia
Singapore, Malaysia & neighbouring territories: Pansing Distribution Pte Ltd, Singapore
South Africa & neighbouring territories: Zytek Publishing (Pty) Ltd, Bedfordview, South Africa

Book Trade Association Membership:
Publishers Association; IPG

2516 ▬▬▬▬▬

NATE (NATIONAL ASSOCIATION FOR THE TEACHING OF ENGLISH)
50 Broadfield Road, Sheffield S8 0XJ
Telephone: 01142 555419
Fax: 01142 555296
Email: info@nate.org.uk
Web Site: www.nate.org.uk

Publications Manager: A. Fairhall
Company Secretary: L. Fairfax
Communications Director: I. McNeilly

Academic & Scholarly; Educational & Textbooks; Literature & Criticism; Theatre, Drama & Dance

No of Employees: 8
Annual Turnover: £250,000

ISBNs, Imprints & Series:
Cracking KS3 Scripts; Critical Reading at post 16; Guided Reading Packs; NATE Drama Packs
978 0 901291 Classic Reading
978 0 904709 Perspectives in Education

Distributor for:
Australia: Phoenix Books

Book Trade Association Membership:
EPC

2517 ▬▬▬▬▬

THE NATIONAL ACADEMIES PRESS
5 Victoria House, 138 Watling Street East,
Towcester NN12 6BT
Telephone: 01327 357770
Fax: 01327 359572
Email: nap@oppuk.co.uk
Web Site: www.nap.edu

Warehouse & Distribution:
Marston Book Services, 160 Milton Park,
PO Box 169, Abingdon, Oxon OX14 4YN
Telephone: 01235 465521
Email: direct.orders@marston.co.uk
Web Site: www.marston.co.uk

Marketing Manager: Gary Hall

Academic & Scholarly; Agriculture; Animal Care & Breeding; Biology & Zoology; Chemistry; Educational & Textbooks; Engineering; Environment & Development Studies; Geography & Geology; Industry, Business & Management; Mathematics & Statistics; Medical (incl. Self Help & Alternative Medicine); Natural History; Nautical; Physics; Psychology & Psychiatry; Scientific & Technical; Veterinary Science

ISBNs, Imprints & Series:
978 0 309 Joseph Henry Press; National Academies Press

Parent Company:
USA: National Academies Press

2518

NATIONAL ARCHIVES OF SCOTLAND
HM General Register House, Edinburgh EH1 3YY
Telephone: 0131 535 1314
Fax: 0131 535 1360
Email: enquiries@nas.gov.uk
Web Site: www.nas.gov.uk

Keeper of the Records of Scotland:
George P. MacKenzie
Head of Collection Development: David Brown

History & Antiquarian

New Titles: 1 (2009)

ISBNs, Imprints & Series: 978 1 870874

Book Trade Association Membership:
Publishing Scotland

2519

THE NATIONAL AUTISTIC SOCIETY (NAS)
393 City Road, London EC1V 1NG
Telephone: (020) 7833 2299
Fax: (020) 7833 9666
Email: nas@nas.org.uk
Web Site: www.autism.org.uk

Trade Enquiries & Orders:
Central Books, 99 Wallis Road, London E9 5LN
Telephone: 0845 458 9911
Fax: 0845 458 9912
Email: nas@centralbooks.com
Web Site: www.autism.org.uk/pubs

Publications Sales: Cathy Mercer
Publications Marketing: Alex Tyla
Communications: Kathryn Quinton

Children's Books; Educational & Textbooks; Psychology & Psychiatry

New Titles: 5 (2008) , 10 (2009)

ISBNs, Imprints & Series:
978 1 899280
978 1 905722

Book Trade Association Membership:
Publishers Form, NCVO

2520

NATIONAL CHILDREN'S BUREAU
Book Sales, 8 Wakley Street, London EC1V 7QE
Telephone: (020) 7843 6049
Fax: (020) 7843 6087
Email: publications@ncb.org.uk
Web Site: www.ncb.org.uk/books

Publishing Manager: Paula McMahon
Publishing Officer: Rebecca Mason

Academic & Scholarly; Educational & Textbooks; Electronic (Professional & Academic); Reference Books, Directories & Dictionaries

New Titles: 5 (2008) , 5 (2009)
No of Employees: 2
Annual Turnover: £200,000

ISBNs, Imprints & Series:
978 0 902817, 978 1 870985, 978 1 874579, 978 1 900990, 978 1 904787, 978 1 905818

Book Trade Association Membership:
IPG

2521

NATIONAL EXTENSION COLLEGE TRUST LTD
The Michael Young Centre, Purbeck Road, Cambridge CB2 8HN
Telephone: 01223 400200r2528
Fax: 01223 400399
Email: info@nec.ac.uk
Web Site: www.nec.ac.uk

Directors: Gavin Teasdale (Chief Executive)
Jorgen Clausen (Finance)
Tim Burton (Education)
Tony Hopwood (Business Development)

Economics; Educational & Textbooks; Electronic (Educational); Fine Art & Art History; Languages & Linguistics; Law; Mathematics & Statistics; Medical (incl. Self Help & Alternative Medicine); Physics; Psychology & Psychiatry; Religion & Theology; Sociology & Anthropology; Vocational Training & Careers

New Titles: 7 (2008) , 13 (2009)
No of Employees: 44
Annual Turnover: £3M

ISBNs, Imprints & Series:
978 0 86082, 978 1 85356

Book Trade Association Membership:
IPG

2522

NATIONAL GALLERIES OF SCOTLAND
Belford Road, Edinburgh EH4 3DS
Telephone: 0131 624 6257 & 6261
Fax: 0131 623 7135
Email: publications@nationalgalleries.org
Web Site: www.nationalgalleries.org

Head of Publishing: Janis Adams
Publishing Manager: Christine Thompson
Editorial Assistant: Olivia Sheppard

Fine Art & Art History; Photography

New Titles: 20 (2008) , 18 (2009)

ISBNs, Imprints & Series:
978 0 903148, 978 0 903598, 978 1 903278

Overseas Representation:
North America: Antique Collectors Club Ltd, Easthampton, MA, USA

2523

*NATIONAL GALLERY CO LTD
St Vincent House, 30 Orange Street, London WC2H 7HH
Telephone: (020) 7747 5950
Fax: (020) 7747 5951
Email: admin@nationalgallery.co.uk
Web Site: www.nationalgallery.co.uk

Distribution:
Yale University Press, 47 Bedford Square, London WC1B 3DP
Telephone: (020) 7079 4900
Fax: (020) 7079 4901
Email: sales@yaleup.co.uk
Web Site: www.yalebooks.co.uk

Publisher: Louise Rice (Publishing & Logistics Director)
Editors: J. Green (Senior Project)
Tom Windross (Project)
Claire Young (Project)
Publishing Administrator: Davida Saunders
Production Manager: Jane Hyne
Production Controller: Penny Le Tissier
Picture Researchers: Suzanne Bosman (Senior)
Maria Ranauro

Academic & Scholarly; Children's Books; Cookery, Wines & Spirits; Electronic (Educational); Electronic (Professional & Academic); Fine Art & Art History; Guide Books

ISBNs, Imprints & Series:
978 0 901791, 978 0 947645, 978 1 85709

Parent Company:
The National Gallery Trust

Overseas Representation:
Africa (excluding Southern Africa & Nigeria): Kelvin van Hasselt Publishing Services, Briningham, Norfolk, UK
Austria, Germany, Italy & Switzerland: Uwe Lüdemann, Berlin, Germany
Benelux, Denmark, Finland, France, Iceland, Norway & Sweden: Fred Hermans, Bovenkarspel, Netherlands
Hong Kong, China & Philippines: Ed Summerson, Asia Publishers Services Ltd, Hong Kong
India: S. Janakiraman, Book Marketing Services, Chennai
Iran: Farhad Maftoon, Tehran
Middle East: International Publishers Representatives (IPR) Ltd, Nicosia, Cyprus
Nigeria: Bounty Press Ltd, Ibadan
Pakistan: Anwer Iqbal, Book Bird Publishers Representatives, Lahore
Poland, Czech Republic, Hungary & Slovenia: Ewa Ledóchowicz, Konstancin-Jeziorna, Poland
Republic of Ireland & Northern Ireland: Robert Towers, Monkstown, Co Dublin, Republic of Ireland
Singapore, Malaysia, Brunei & Indonesia: APD Singapore Pte Ltd, Singapore
Southern Africa: Book Promotions Pty Ltd, Diep River, South Africa
Spain & Portugal: Chris Humphrys, Provincia de Malaga, Spain
USA, Canada, Mexico, Central & South America, Australia, New Zealand, Japan, Korea & Taiwan: Yale University Press, New Haven, CT, USA

2524

NATIONAL GALLERY OF IRELAND
National Gallery Bookshop, Merrion Square, Dublin 2, Republic of Ireland
Telephone: +353 (01) 663 3518
Fax: +353 (01) 661 9898
Email: bookshop@ngi.ie
Web Site: www.nationalgallery.ie

Bookshop Accounts: Kate Brown
Manager: Lydia Furlong
Rights & Reproduction: Marie McFeely

Fine Art & Art History

New Titles: 4 (2008)
No of Employees: 9
Annual Turnover: €1.3M

ISBNs, Imprints & Series: 978 0 903162

Overseas Representation:
Worldwide: Art Books International Ltd, London, UK; Paul Holberton Ltd, UK

Book Trade Association Membership:
Booksellers Association; CLÉ (Irish PA)

2525

NATIONAL HOUSING FEDERATION
Lion Court, 25 Procter Street, Holborn, London WC1V 6NY
Telephone: (020) 7067 1010
Fax: (020) 7067 1011
Email: info@housing.org.uk
Web Site: www.housing.co.uk

Publishing Manager: Bev Markham
Production Editor: Fiona Shand
Publishing Co-ordinator: Rick Lloyd

Accountancy & Taxation; Educational & Textbooks; Law; Reference Books, Directories & Dictionaries; Vocational Training & Careers

ISBNs, Imprints & Series: 978 0 86297

2526

NATIONAL PORTRAIT GALLERY PUBLICATIONS
National Portrait Gallery, St Martin's Place, London WC2H 0HE
Telephone: (020) 7306 0055 ext 266 & (020) 7312 2482 (direct line)
Fax: (020) 7321 6657
Email: pvadhia@npg.org.uk
Web Site: www.npg.org.uk/publications

Distribution:
Grantham Book Services, Trent Road, Grantham, Lincs NG31 7XG
Telephone: 01476 541080
Fax: 01476 541061
Email: orders@gbs.tbs_ltd.co.uk (UK only)
Web Site: www.granthambookservices.co.uk

Representation (UK):
Casemate Books, 17 Cheap Street, Newbury, Berks RG14 5DD
Telephone: 01635 231091
Fax: 01635 41619
Web Site: www.casematepublishing.co.uk

Head of Trading: Robert Carr-Archer
Head of Rights & Reproductions: Tom Morgan
Managers: Celia Joicey (Publishing)
Ruth Müller-Wirth (Production)
Pallavi Vadhia (Sales & Marketing)
Editors: Beka Cohen (Project)
Claudia Bloch
Christopher Tinker (Managing)
Sales & Marketing Assistant: Victoria Jones

Academic & Scholarly; Biography & Autobiography; Fashion & Costume; Fine Art & Art History; Gender Studies; History & Antiquarian; Illustrated & Fine Editions; Literature & Criticism; Photography

ISBNs, Imprints & Series:
978 0 904017, 978 1 85514

Overseas Representation:
Australia: Peribo Pty Ltd, Mount Kuring-Gai, NSW
France: Casemate Books, Newbury, UK
Germany, Austria, Switzerland, Belgium & Luxembourg: Exhibitions International, Leuven, Belgium
Italy, Spain, Portugal & Greece: Penny Padovani, London, UK
Netherlands: Amsterdam University Press, Amsterdam
Republic of Ireland & Northern Ireland: Robert Towers, Monkstown, Co Dublin, Republic of Ireland
South America: David Williams, InterMedia Americana (IMA) Ltd, London, UK
USA: Antique Collectors Club Ltd, Easthampton, MA

Book Trade Association Membership:
BA; IPG

2527

THE NATIONAL TRUST
Heelis, Kemble Drive, Swindon, Wilts SN2 2NA
Telephone: 01793 817400
Fax: 01793 817401
Email: grant.berry@nationaltrust.org.uk
Web Site: www.nationaltrust.org.uk

Also at:
Anova Books, 10 Southcombe Street, London W14 0RA

Telephone: (020) 7605 1400
Web Site: www.anovabooks.com

Managers: John Stachiewicz (*Commercial & Publisher*)
Grant Berry (*Publishing*)
Property Publisher: Oliver Garrett
Editors: Anna Groves
Claire Forbes (*Assistant, Guidebook*)

Academic & Scholarly; Agriculture; Antiques & Collecting; Archaeology; Architecture & Design; Biography & Autobiography; Children's Books; Cookery, Wines & Spirits; Fashion & Costume; Fine Art & Art History; Gardening; Guide Books; History & Antiquarian; Humour; Natural History; Reference Books, Directories & Dictionaries; Travel & Topography

New Titles: 13 (2008) , 12 (2009)
No of Employees: 5

ISBNs, Imprints & Series:
978 0 7078, 978 1 8435

Parent Company:
Anova Books [books]; The History Press [guide books]

2528 ▬▬▬

THE NATIONAL YOUTH AGENCY
Eastgate House,
19–23 Humberstone Road, Leicester
LE5 3GJ
Telephone: 0116 242 7350
Fax: 0116 242 7444
Email: nya@nya.org.uk
Web Site: www.nya.org.uk

Media Services Manager: Andy
Hopkinson

Academic & Scholarly; Educational & Textbooks

New Titles: 12 (2008) , 6 (2009)
No of Employees: 4
Annual Turnover: £100,000

ISBNs, Imprints & Series: 978 0 86155

2529 ▬▬▬

NATURAL HISTORY MUSEUM PUBLISHING
The Natural History Museum,
Cromwell Road, London SW7 5BD
Telephone: (020) 7942 5060
Fax: (020) 7942 5291
Email: publishing@nhm.ac.uk
Web Site: www.nhm.ac.uk/publishing

Warehouse & Distribution:
Bookpoint Ltd, 130 Milton Park, Abingdon,
Oxon OX14 4SB
Telephone: 01235 400400
Fax: 01235 400500
Email: mailorder@bookpoint.co.uk

Managers: Lynn Millhouse (*Production*)
Trudy Brannan (*Editorial*)
Colin Ziegler (*Head of Publishing*)
Sales & Marketing Executive: Howard
Trent

Academic & Scholarly; Archaeology; Biography & Autobiography; Biology & Zoology; Children's Books; Educational & Textbooks; Fine Art & Art History; Geography & Geology; Natural History; Reference Books, Directories & Dictionaries; Scientific & Technical

New Titles: 10 (2008) , 10 (2009)
No of Employees: 5
Annual Turnover: £550,000

ISBNs, Imprints & Series: 978 0 565

2530 ▬▬▬

NAXOS AUDIOBOOKS
40A High Street, Welwyn, Herts AL6 9EQ
Telephone: 01438 717808
Fax: 01438 717809
Email:
naxos_audiobooks@compuserve.com
Web Site: www.naxos.co.uk/audiobooks/

Distribution:
Select Music & Video,
34A Holmethorpe Avenue, Redhill, Surrey
RH1 2NN
Telephone: 01737 645600
Fax: 01737 766316

Director: Nicolas Soames
Sales Manager: Mark Scott

Audio Books

ISBNs, Imprints & Series: 978 962634

Parent Company:
Hong Kong: HNH International

Associated Companies:
Naxos Classical Music
Hong Kong: Naxos Classical Music

Overseas Representation:
Australia: Select, Sydney
Austria: Gramola Co, Vienna, Australia
Brazil: RKR Musical, Sao Paulo
Canada: Naxos of Canada Ltd,
Scarborough, Ont
Czech Republic: Classic Music Distribution,
Prague
Denmark: Olga Musik, Ry
Finland: FG Distribution, Helsinki
France: Naxos of France, Paris
Germany: MVD, Munich; Naxos
Deutschland, Münster
Greece: Greek Record Club, Athens
Hungary: Phoenix Studio, Budapest
Iceland: JAPIS, Reykjavik
Israel: MCI Records, Tel Aviv
Japan: Naxos Japan, Nagoya & Tokyo
Korea: Hae Dong Co Ltd, Seoul, Republic of
Korea
Malaysia: AV Masters Sdn Bhd, Kuala
Lumpur
Netherlands: Vanguard Classics,
Nieuwegein
New Zealand: Triton Music Ltd, Auckland
Norway: Musikkdistribusjon AS, Oslo
Philippines: Universal Records, Kalookan
City
Republic of Ireland: Cosmic Sounds Ltd,
Dublin
Singapore: Naxos Pte Ltd
Slovak Republic: Slovart Music, Bratislava,
Slovakia
South Africa: Booktalk (Pty) Ltd, Craighall
Spain: FERYSA, Madrid
Sri Lanka: Titus Stores, Columbo
Sweden: Naxos Sweden, Orebro
Switzerland: FAME, Meggen (Lucerne)
Taiwan: Rock Records & Tapes, Taipei
Thailand: Media Plus & Broadcasting
Network Ltd, Bangkok
Turkey: Haci Emin Elendi Sokak, Istanbul
USA: Naxos of America Inc, Pennsauken, NJ

Book Trade Association Membership:
Spoken Word Publishers' Association

2531 ▬▬▬

NEED2KNOW
Remus House, Coltsfoot Drive, Woodston,
Peterborough PE2 9JX
Telephone: 01733 898103
Fax: 01733 313524
Email: sales@n2kbooks.com
Web Site: www.need2knowbooks.co.uk

Imprint Manager: Kate Gibbard

Cookery, Wines & Spirits; Health & Beauty; Medical (incl. Self Help & Alternative

Medicine); Vocational Training & Careers

New Titles: 19 (2008) , 16 (2009)

ISBNs, Imprints & Series:
afterschoolclub.net; Anchor Books; New
Fiction; Poetry Now; Pond View; Triumph
House; Writers' Bookshop; Young
Writers
978 1 86144 Need2Know

Parent Company:
Forward Press Ltd

Book Trade Association Membership:
BA

2532 ▬▬▬

NELSON THORNES LTD
[formerly Stanley Thornes Ltd & Thomas
Nelson & Sons Ltd]
Delta Place, 27 Bath Road, Cheltenham
GL53 7TH
Telephone: 01242 267100
Fax: 01242 221914 (General) & 253695
(Orders)
Email: info@nelsonthornes.com
Web Site: www.nelsonthornes.com

Distribution:
Alexandra Way, Ashchurch, Tewkesbury,
Glos GL20 8PE

Directors: Mary O'Connor (*Managing*)
Clive Rushton (*Finance*)
Jim Green (*Sales & Marketing*)
Hitel Patel (*Operations*)
Emma Bourne (*International/Primary/
NTOL/BEAM*)
**Head of Customer Services &
Distribution:** Margot van de Weijer

Accountancy & Taxation; Biology & Zoology; Chemistry; Children's Books; Computer Science; Economics; Educational & Textbooks; Electronic (Educational); Engineering; Environment & Development Studies; Fashion & Costume; Geography & Geology; Health & Beauty; History & Antiquarian; Industry, Business & Management; Languages & Linguistics; Law; Literature & Criticism; Mathematics & Statistics; Medical (incl. Self Help & Alternative Medicine); Physics; Politics & World Affairs; Psychology & Psychiatry; Religion & Theology; Scientific & Technical; Sociology & Anthropology; Sports & Games; Theatre, Drama & Dance; Vocational Training & Careers

No of Employees: 357

ISBNs, Imprints & Series:
978 0 17, 978 0 7487, 978 1 4085

Parent Company:
UK: Infinitas Learning

Distributor for:
Australia: Cengage; Macmillan Library

Overseas Representation:
Antigua & Montserrat: The Best of Books,
St John's, Antigua
Argentina: Kel Ediciones SA (Agents),
Buenos Aires
Australia (Primary & Secondary): Cengage
(Australia), NSW, Australia
Bahamas: Media Enterprises Ltd, Nassau
Barbados: Days Bookstore, Bridgetown
Belize: The Book Center, Belize City
*Botswana, South Africa, Lesotho,
Swaziland, Mozambique & Namibia:*
Macmillan Education Ltd, Oxford, UK
*Canada (Primary & Secondary, excluding
Modern Languages, & Further
Education):* Bacon & Hughes Ltd,
Ottawa, Ont, Canada
*Canada (Secondary Modern Languages
only):* The Resource Centre, Waterloo,
Canada

Chile: Books and Bits, Santiago
Colombia: The English Book Centre, Bogota
Dominica: Jays Ltd, Roseau
Egypt: Galaxy Trade, Giza
Fiji & Pacific Islands: Premier Book Centre,
Ba, Fiji
Ghana: EPP Book Services Ltd, Accra
Greece: Compendium, Athens
Grenada: Grenada Teachers School
Supplies, St George's
*Gulf States, Iran, Syria, Libya, Jordan,
Lebanon, Cyprus, Yemen, Tunis, Turkey,
Morocco & Algeria (Further & Higher
Education only):* International Publishing
Services (IPS) Middle East Ltd, Dubai, UAE
Guyana: Austin's Book Services,
Georgetown
Hong Kong & Macao: Transglobal
Publishers Services Ltd, Hong Kong
*India, Bangladesh, Sri Lanka, Nepal &
Bhutan:* Overleaf, New Delhi, India
Jamaica: Kingston Bookshop, Kingston
Kenya: Savani's Book Centre, Nairobi
Malawi & Zambia: Anglia Book Distributors
Ltd, Blantyre, Malawi
Malaysia: APD Kuala Lumpur Pte Ltd,
Selangor
Malta: Miller Distributors Ltd, Luqa
Mauritius: Editions le Printemps, Vacoas
New Zealand: Opus Textbooks, Auckland
Nigeria: Chelis Bookazine, Lagos
*North America & Canada (Higher Education
titles only):* International Specialized
Book Services Inc, Portland, OR, USA
Pakistan: Publishers Marketing Associates,
Karachi
Philippines: M. V. Mojica, Manila
*Republic of Ireland (Modern Languages
only):* Modern Languages, Dublin,
Republic of Ireland
*Republic of Ireland (Primary, Secondary &
Further Education):* Carrol Educational
Supplies, Dublin, Republic of Ireland
Singapore & Brunei: APD Singapore Pte Ltd,
Singapore
St Vincent & The Grenadines: Gaymes Book
Centre, St Vincent
*Sweden, Denmark, Norway, Finland,
Iceland, Estonia, Latvia & Lithuania
(Health Science & Science & Engineering
titles only):* David Towle International,
Stockholm, Sweden
*Tajikistan, Uzbekistan, Kazakhstan,
Kyrgyzstan & Turkmenistan:* Silk Road
Media, London, UK
Trinidad & Tobago: Books Etc, San
Fernando, Trinidad
Uruguay: Opiciones en Educacion
Vietnam: Fahasa Companie, Ho Chi Minh
City

Book Trade Association Membership:
Publishers Association

2533 ▬▬▬

**NETWORK CONTINUUM
EDUCATION LTD**
see: Continuum International Publishing
Group

2534 ▬▬▬

**NEW HOLLAND PUBLISHERS (UK)
LTD**
Garfield House, 86–88 Edgware Road,
London W2 2EA
Telephone: (020) 7724 7773
Fax: (020) 7724 6184
Email: enquiries@nhpub.co.uk
Web Site:
www.newhollandpublishers.com

Distribution:
Grantham Book Services, Trent Road,
Grantham, Lincs NG31 7XQ
Telephone: 01476 541080
Fax: 01476 541061
Email: orders@gbs.tbs-ltd.co.uk
Web Site:
www.granthambookservices.co.uk

Directors: Steve Connolly *(Managing)*
Sandy Caven *(Finance)*
Rosemary Wilkinson *(Publishing)*
Monica Meehan *(Rights)*
Terry Shaughnessy *(UK Sales & Marketing)*
Production Manager: Joan Woodruffe

Animal Care & Breeding; Cookery, Wines & Spirits; Crafts & Hobbies; Crime; Do-It-Yourself; Gardening; Guide Books; Health & Beauty; Humour; Natural History; Politics & World Affairs; Reference Books, Directories & Dictionaries; Sports & Games; Travel & Topography

New Titles: 80 (2008) , 75 (2009)
No of Employees: 47
Annual Turnover: £6M

ISBNs, Imprints & Series:
978 1 84537 Globetrotters
978 1 86011 Cadogan Guides

Parent Company:
South Africa: Struik Group SA

Associated Companies:
Australia: New Holland Australia
New Zealand: New Holland Publishers (NZ) Ltd
South Africa: Random House Struik

Distributor for:
USA: Thomas Nelson Inc

Overseas Representation:
Australia: New Holland Publishers, Chatswood, NSW
Caribbean & Central America: Christopher Humphrys, Humphrys Roberts Associates, London, UK
China & Hong Kong: United Century Book Services Ltd, Hong Kong
Eastern Europe & Russia: Tony Moggach, InterMedia Americana (IMA) Ltd, London, UK
India: India Book Distributors (Bombay) Ltd, Mumbai
Japan: Yohan, Tokyo
Malaysia & Singapore: Pansing Distribution Pte Ltd, Singapore
Mexico: Arturo Gutierrez Hernandez, Mexico
New Zealand: New Holland Publishers (NZ) Ltd, Auckland
Pakistan: Tahir M. Lodhi, Lahore
Republic of Ireland & Northern Ireland: Alasdair Verschoyle, Compass Independent Book Sales Ltd, Naas, Co Kildare, Republic of Ireland
Scandinavia: Katie McNeish, McNeish Publishing International, East Sussex, UK
South America: Terry Roberts, Humphrys Roberts Associates, Cotia SP, Brazil
Southern, Central & East Africa: Struik New Holland Publishing (Pty) Ltd, Cape Town, South Africa
Spain, Portugal & Gibraltar: Peter Prout, Iberian Book Services, Madrid, Spain
Thailand, Cambodia, Vietnam, Laos & Myanmar: Keith Hardy, Hardy Bigfoss International Co Ltd, Bangkok, Thailand
USA (Globetrotters & Cadogan): Globe Pequot Press, Guilford, CT, USA
USA (Lifestyle Books): Sterling Publishing Co Inc, New York, NY, USA
Western Europe: Ted Dougherty, London, UK

2535 ▬▬▬▬▬

NEW INTERNATIONALIST PUBLICATIONS LTD
55 Rectory Road, Oxford OX4 1BW
Telephone: 01865 811400
Fax: 01865 793152
Email: ni@newint.org
Web Site: www.newint.org

Representation (UK):
Turnaround Publisher Services Ltd, Unit 3, Olympia Trading Estate, Coburg Road, London N22 6TZ
Telephone: (020) 8829 3000
Fax: (020) 8881 5088

Company Accountant: Frank Syratt
Managers: Fran Harvey *(Production)*
Dan Raymond-Barker *(Publications Marketing)*
Publications Editor: Troth Wells
Magazine Marketing: Amanda Synnott

Atlases & Maps; Cookery, Wines & Spirits; Electronic (Educational); Environment & Development Studies; Fiction; Photography; Politics & World Affairs; Reference Books, Directories & Dictionaries

New Titles: 20 (2008) , 20 (2009)
No of Employees: 19
Annual Turnover: £3M

ISBNs, Imprints & Series:
; World Changing
978 0 9540499, 978 1 869847, 978 1 904456, 978 1 906523 No-Nonsense Series

Parent Company:
New Internationalist Trust Ltd

Overseas Representation:
Australia: Palgrave Macmillan, South Yarra, Vic
Australia & Papua New Guinea: New Internationalist Publications Ltd, Adelaide, SA, Australia
Canada: New Internationalist Publications Ltd, Toronto, Ont
New Zealand & Aotearoa: New Internationalist Publications Ltd, Christchurch, New Zealand
South Africa: Stephan Phillips (Pty) Ltd, Cape Town
USA: Consortium Book Sales & Distribution Inc, St Paul, MN

Book Trade Association Membership:
IPG; Periodical Publishers Association

2536 ▬▬▬▬▬

NEW ISLAND BOOKS LTD
2 Brookside, Dundrum Road, Dublin 14, Republic of Ireland
Telephone: +353 (01) 298 3411
Fax: +353 (01) 298 7912
Email: sales@newisland.ie & editor@newisland.ie
Web Site: www.newisland.ie

Distribution:
Gill & Macmillan, Hume Avenue, Park West, Dublin 12, Republic of Ireland
Telephone: +353 (01) 500 9555
Fax: +353 (01) 500 9599

Representation (Republic of Ireland & Northern Ireland):
Compass Ireland, 39 Craddockstown Way, Naas, Co Kildare, Republic of Ireland
Telephone: +353 (045) 880805
Fax: +353 (045) 880806
Email: alasdair@compassireland.ie

Publisher: Edwin Higel
Managers: Deirdre O'Neill *(Editorial)*
Inka Hagen *(Production & Design)*
Aisling Glynn *(Accounts)*
Mariel Deegan *(Marketing, Publicity & Sales)*
Maria White *(Rights)*

Biography & Autobiography; English as a Foreign Language; Fiction; Gender Studies; Guide Books; History & Antiquarian; Humour; Literature & Criticism; Poetry; Politics & World Affairs; Theatre, Drama & Dance

New Titles: 25 (2008) , 30 (2009)

ISBNs, Imprints & Series:
978 1 848400, 978 1 874597, 978 1 902602, 978 1 904301, 978 1 905494

Overseas Representation:
UK: Compass DSA, Slough
USA & Canada: Dufour Editions Inc, Chester Springs, PA, USA

Book Trade Association Membership:
CLÉ (Irish PA)

2537 ▬▬▬▬▬

NEW PLAYWRIGHTS' NETWORK
10 Station Road Industrial Estate, Colwall, Malvern, Worcs WR13 6RN
Telephone: 01684 540154
Fax: 01684 540154
Email: simon@cressrelles.co.uk
Web Site: www.cressrelles.co.uk

Contact: L. G. Smith

Theatre, Drama & Dance

New Titles: 8 (2008) , 10 (2009)

ISBNs, Imprints & Series: 978 0 86319

Overseas Representation:
Australia: Origin Theatrical, Sydney, NSW
New Zealand: Play Bureau of New Zealand Ltd, New Plymouth
Republic of Ireland: Drama League of Ireland, Dublin
South Africa: Dalro (Pty) Ltd, Braamfontein
USA: Bakers Plays, Quincy, MA

2538 ▬▬▬▬▬

NEWPRO UK LTD
Old Sawmills Road, Faringdon, Oxon SN7 7DS
Telephone: 01367 242411
Fax: 01367 241124
Email: sales@newprouk.co.uk
Web Site: www.newprouk.co.uk

Managing Director & Publisher:
Christopher J. Coleman
Company Secretary: Beryl L. Coleman

Antiques & Collecting; Natural History; Photography

ISBNs, Imprints & Series:
Fountain Press; Hove Foto Books
978 0 86343, 978 0 906447, 978 1 87403

Distributor for:
Classic Collection; Fountain Press; Hove Foto Books; Van Hasbroeck
Italy: Editrice Reflex
USA: Centennial Photo Service; Marling Menu Masters; McKeown's Price Guides

Overseas Representation:
Far East, Near East & Middle East: Publishers International Marketing, Storrington, UK
South Africa: Zytek Publishing (Pty) Ltd, Bedfordview

2539 ▬▬▬▬▬

NHS IMMUNISATION INFORMATION
Department of Health, Wellington House, 133–155 Waterloo Road, London SE1 8UG
Telephone: (020) 7972 4973
Fax: (020) 7972 3989
Email: chris.owen@dh.gsi.gov.uk
Web Site: www.immunisation.nhs.uk

Academic & Scholarly; Educational & Textbooks; Medical (incl. Self Help & Alternative Medicine)

New Titles: 10 (2008) , 10 (2009)

Book Trade Association Membership:
Publishers Association

2540 ▬▬▬▬▬

NIELSEN BOOK
3rd Floor, Midas House, 62 Goldsworth Road, Woking, Surrey GU21 6LQ
Telephone: 01483 712200
Fax: 01483 712201
Email: info.book@nielsen.com
Web Site: www.nielsenbook.co.uk

Editorial:
89–95 Queensway, Stevenage, Herts SG1 1EA
Telephone: 0845 450 0016
Fax: 01438 745578
Email: newtitles.book@nielsen.com & pubhelp.book@nielsen.com
Web Site: www.nielsenbook.co.uk

President: Jonathan Nowell
Directors: Richard Knight *(Operations)*
Ann Betts *(Commercial)*
Jon Windus *(Product Development)*
Andrew Sugden *(Financial)*
Leonie Dorkins *(Human Resources)*
Simon Skinner *(Sales)*
Julie Meynink *(Business Development)*
Head of Marketing: Mo Siewcharran
Senior Managers: Peter Mathews *(Publishing Services)*
Howard Willows *(Data Development)*
Gwyneth Morgan *(Editorial Systems)*
Samantha Watson *(Quality Assurance)*
Manager: Vesna Nall *(Publisher Subscriptions)*
Head of Data Sales: Paul Dibble
Head of BookNet Sales: Stephen Long

Bibliography & Library Science; Information Services

Associated Companies:
BDS; Bookseller Publications; ISTC Agency; Nielsen BookData; Nielsen BookData Asia Pacific; Nielsen BookNet; Nielsen BookScan; The Nielsen Company; UK ISBN Agency; UK SAN Agency

Overseas Representation:
South Africa: Publications Network (Pty) Ltd (trading as SAPNet)

Book Trade Association Membership:
BA; IPG; Data Publishers Association

2541 ▬▬▬▬▬

NIGHTINGALE PRESS
6 The Old Dairy, Melcombe Road, Bath BA2 3LR
Telephone: 01225 478444
Fax: 01225 478440
Email: sales@manning-partnership.co.uk
Web Site: www.manning-partnership.co.uk

Distribution:
Central Books, 99 Wallis Road, London E9 5LN
Telephone: 0845 458 9911
Fax: 0845 458 9912
Email: info@centralbooks.com
Web Site: www.centralbooks.com

Directors: Garry Manning *(Managing)*
Roger Hibbert *(Sales)*
Finance Manager: Julie Pearson

Humour

New Titles: 4 (2008) , 3 (2009)
No of Employees: 5
Annual Turnover: £1.08M

ISBNs, Imprints & Series: 978 1 903056

Parent Company:
UK: The Manning Partnership

Distributor for:
Australia: Brimax; Five Mile Press
UK: Brown Dog Books; Carrol & Brown; Fanahan Books; Interpet Publishing; Lorenz Books; Search Press; Southwater Books
USA: Falcon; GPP; Sourcebooks

Overseas Representation:
USA: Richard Gay, Shepperton, Middlesex, UK

2542

NMS ENTERPRISES LIMITED - PUBLISHING
National Museums Scotland, Chambers Street, Edinburgh EH1 1JF
Telephone: 0131 247 4026
Fax: 0131 247 4012
Email: publishing@nms.ac.uk
Web Site: www.nms.ac.uk/books

Representation:
CPR, SPCK Head Office, 36 Causton Street, London SW1P 4ST
Telephone: (020) 7592 3900
Email: sales@spck.org.uk

Distribution (UK):
BookSource, 50 Cambuslang Road, Glasgow G32 8NB
Telephone: 0845 370 0067
Fax: 0845 370 0068
Email: orders@booksource.net

Director of Publishing: Lesley A. Taylor
Marketing Manager: Kate Blackadder
Administration & Sales: Maggie Wilson

Academic & Scholarly; Antiques & Collecting; Archaeology; Architecture & Design; Biography & Autobiography; Biology & Zoology; Children's Books; Cookery, Wines & Spirits; Educational & Textbooks; Fine Art & Art History; Geography & Geology; Guide Books; History & Antiquarian; Military & War; Natural History; Poetry; Scientific & Technical; Sociology & Anthropology; Transport

New Titles: 10 (2008) , 17 (2009)
No of Employees: 3

ISBNs, Imprints & Series:
978 0 948636, 978 1 901663, 978 1 905267

Parent Company:
National Museums Scotland

Overseas Representation:
USA: Antique Collectors Club Ltd, Easthampton, MA

Book Trade Association Membership:
Publishing Scotland

2543

NORTH YORK MOORS NATIONAL PARK
The Old Vicarage, Bondgate, Helmsley, Yorks YO62 5BP
Telephone: 01439 770657
Fax: 01439 770691
Email: J.Renney@northyorkmoors-npa.gov.uk
Web Site: www.moors.uk.net

Head of Information Services: Julie Lawrence
Finance Officer: Pat Waters-Marsh
Sales & Marketing Assistant: Darren Sims
Information & Interpretation Manager: Jill Renney
Interpretation Officer: Mark Lewis

Archaeology; Biology & Zoology; Children's

Books; Educational & Textbooks; Environment & Development Studies; Geography & Geology; Guide Books; History & Antiquarian; Natural History

ISBNs, Imprints & Series:
978 0 907480, 978 1 904622

2544

NORTHCOTE HOUSE PUBLISHERS LTD
Horndon House, Horndon, Tavistock, Devon PL19 9NQ
Telephone: 01822 810066
Fax: 01822 810034
Email: northcote.house@virgin.net
Web Site: www.northcotehouse.co.uk

Distributors:
Combined Book Services, Unit Y, Paddock Wood Distribution Centre, Paddock Wood, Tonbridge, Kent TN12 6UU
Telephone: 01892 837171
Fax: 01892 837372
Email: orders@combook.co.uk
Web Site: www.combook.co.uk

Managing Director: Brian Hulme (Publisher)
Marketing Manager: Sarah Piper

Educational & Textbooks; Literature & Criticism; Theatre, Drama & Dance

New Titles: 25 (2008) , 30 (2009)
No of Employees: 3

ISBNs, Imprints & Series:
978 0 7463 Northcote House; Resources in Education; Starting Out....; Writers and Their Work

Overseas Representation:
Africa (excluding South Africa) & Eastern Europe: Tony Moggach, IMA, London, UK
Australia & New Zealand: Book & Volume, Birregurra, Vic, Australia
Caribbean: Hugh Dunphy, Kingston, Jamaica
Germany, Austria, Switzerland, France, Italy & Benelux: Ted Dougherty, London, UK
India: Maya Publishers Pvt Ltd, New Delhi
Middle East: Hani Kreidieh, Beirut, Lebanon
Pakistan: Book Bird Publishers Representatives, Lahore
Scandinavia: David Towle International, Stockholm, Sweden
Spain & Portugal: Peter Prout Iberian Book Services, Madrid, Spain
USA & Canada: Ashgate Publishing Co, Burlington, VT, USA

Book Trade Association Membership:
IPG

2545

W. W. NORTON & COMPANY LTD
Castle House, 75–76 Wells Street, London W1T 3QT
Telephone: (020) 7323 1579
Fax: (020) 7436 4553
Email: office@wwnorton.co.uk
Web Site: www.wwnorton.co.uk

Distribution:
John Wiley & Sons Ltd, 1 Oldlands Way, Shripney, Bognor Regis, Sussex PO22 9SA
Telephone: 01243 779777
Fax: 01243 820250
Email: cs-books@wiley.co.uk

Directors: R. A. Cameron (Managing & Chairman)
S. King
W. D. McFeely (USA)
S. R. Lawrence (USA)
G. Luciano (USA)
Patrick Wright

R. Harrington (USA)
A. J. Llewellyn

Architecture & Design; Biology & Zoology; Chemistry; Cinema, Video, TV & Radio; Computer Science; Cookery, Wines & Spirits; Economics; Fine Art & Art History; Gardening; Gender Studies; Geography & Geology; History & Antiquarian; Literature & Criticism; Mathematics & Statistics; Military & War; Music; Natural History; Nautical; Philosophy; Physics; Poetry; Politics & World Affairs; Psychology & Psychiatry; Sports & Games; Theatre, Drama & Dance

ISBNs, Imprints & Series:
978 0 393 Norton
978 0 87140 Liveright
978 0 88150 Countryman Press

Parent Company:
USA: W. W. Norton & Company

Distributor for:
USA: Dalkey Archive Press; New Directions Publishing Corporation

Overseas Representation:
Africa & Caribbean: Kelvin van Hasselt Publishing Services, Briningham, Norfolk, UK
India: Viva Group, New Delhi
Middle East & North Africa: International Publishers Representatives (IPR) Ltd, Nicosia, Cyprus
Pakistan: World Press, Lahore
Republic of Ireland: Andrew Russell Book Representation, Co Cork
South Africa: Chris Reinders, The African Moon Press, Kelvin

2546

NORWOOD PUBLISHERS LTD
3 Chapel Street, Norwood Green, Halifax, West Yorkshire HR3 8QU
Telephone: 01274 602454
Fax: 01274 676665
Email: enquiries@norwoodpublishers.co.uk

Partners: M. H. Wolfenden
Mrs A. M. Wolfenden

Educational & Textbooks

ISBNs, Imprints & Series: 978 1 873784

2547

THE NOSTALGIA COLLECTION
Silver Link Publishing Ltd, The Trundle, Ringstead Road, Great Addington, Kettering, Northants NN14 4BW
Telephone: 01536 330543 & 330588
Fax: 01536 330588
Email: sales@nostalgiacollection.com
Web Site: www.nostalgiacollection.com

Directors: Peter Townsend (Managing, Publisher)
Frances Townsend (Company Secretary)
Managers: Michael Sanders (Production)
David Walshaw (Mail Order & Advertising)

History & Antiquarian; Military & War; Nautical; Transport; Nostalgia

ISBNs, Imprints & Series:
978 0 947971, 978 1 85794 Silver Link Publishing Ltd
978 1 85895 Past & Present Publishing Ltd

Associated Companies:
Past & Present Publishing Ltd; Silver Link Publishing Ltd

Distributor for:
Past & Present Publishing Ltd; Silver Link Publishing Ltd

Book Trade Association Membership:
BA

2548

OAK TREE PRESS
19 Rutland Street, Cork, Republic of Ireland
Telephone: +353 (021) 431 3855
Fax: +353 (021) 431 3496
Email: info@oaktreepress.com
Web Site: www.oaktreepress.com

Directors: Brian O'Kane (Managing)
Rita O'Kane (Sales)

Academic & Scholarly; Accountancy & Taxation; Educational & Textbooks; Industry, Business & Management; Law

ISBNs, Imprints & Series:
978 1 84621 Oak Tree eWare
978 1 86076, 978 1 872853, 978 1 904887 Oak Tree Press

Parent Company:
Republic of Ireland: Cork Publishing Ltd

2549

THE O'BRIEN PRESS LTD
12 Terenure Road East, Rathgar, Dublin 6, Republic of Ireland
Telephone: +353 (01) 492 3333
Fax: +353 (01) 492 2777
Email: books@obrien.ie
Web Site: www.obrien.ie

Publisher: Michael O'Brien
Directors: Ivan O'Brien (Managing)
Mary Web (Editorial)
Managers: Ciara O'Hara (Rights)
Erika McGann (Production)
Ruth Heneghan (Marketing)

Architecture & Design; Biography & Autobiography; Children's Books; Cookery, Wines & Spirits; Guide Books; Humour; Politics & World Affairs; Sports & Games; Travel & Topography

New Titles: 49 (2008) , 39 (2009)
No of Employees: 15
Annual Turnover: £2.2M

ISBNs, Imprints & Series:
978 0 86278, 978 0 905140, 978 1 84717

Associated Companies:
Republic of Ireland: O'Brien Educational

Overseas Representation:
Britain: Compass DSA, Slough, UK
USA & Canada: James Trading Group, Nanuet, NY, USA

Book Trade Association Membership:
IPG

2550

OCTOPUS PUBLISHING GROUP
2–4 Heron Quays, London E14 4JP
Telephone: (020) 7531 8400
Fax: (020) 7531 8650
Email: info@octopus-publishing.co.uk
Web Site: www.octopusbooks.co.uk

Distribution:
Littlehampton Book Services Ltd, Faraday Close, Durrington, Worthing, West Sussex BN13 3PB
Telephone: 01903 828500
Fax: 01903 828625
Email: orders@lbsltd.co.uk
Web Site: www.lbsltd.co.uk

Directors: Alison Goff (Chief Executive Officer)
Andrew Welham (Deputy Chief Executive Officer)
Angela Luxton (Commercial)
Steven Edney (UK Sales & Marketing)

Fiona Smith *(Publicity)*
Frances Johnson *(Group Head of Operations)*
Henri Masurel *(Group Finance)*

Animal Care & Breeding; Antiques & Collecting; Architecture & Design; Atlases & Maps; Cookery, Wines & Spirits; Crafts & Hobbies; Do-It-Yourself; Fine Art & Art History; Gardening; Health & Beauty; History & Antiquarian; Natural History; Sports & Games

No of Employees: 140

ISBNs, Imprints & Series:
978 0 600 Cassell Illustrated; Conran Octopus; Gaia; Godsfield Press; Hamlyn; Mitchell Beazley; Philips; Spruce

Parent Company:
Hachette UK

Overseas Representation:
All Other Territories: Octopus Export Sales, Octopus Publishing Group, London, UK
Australia: Hachette Livre Australia, Sydney, NSW
Canada: Canadian Manda Group, Toronto, Ont
Caribbean: Chris Humphrys & Linda Hopkins, London, UK
Caribbean (for Philip's): David Williams, InterMedia Americana (IMA) Ltd, London, UK
Central America: Arturo Gutierrez Hernandez, Mexico, Mexico
China, Hong Kong & Taiwan: Edward Summerson, Asia Publishers Services Ltd, Hong Kong
France, Belgium, Netherlands, Scandinavia, Iceland, Baltics, Eastern Europe & Russia: Bill Bailey Publishers Representatives, Newton Abbot, UK
Germany, Switzerland & Austria: Gabriele Kern Publishers Services, Frankfurt-am-Main, Germany
India, Bangladesh & Sri Lanka: Hachette Book Publishing India Pvt Ltd, Gurgaon, India
Italy & Greece: Penny Padovani, London, UK
Malaysia: APD Kuala Lumpur Pte Ltd, Selangor
Middle East, North Africa, Cyprus, Malta & Israel: Ray Potts, Publishers International Marketing, Polfages, France
New Zealand: Hachette Livre New Zealand, Auckland
Philippines & Korea: Benjie Ocampo, Pasig City, Philippines
Singapore, Thailand, Indonesia, Vietnam, Brunei, Laos & Cambodia: APD Singapore Pte Ltd, Singapore
South Africa: Penguin Books South Africa (Pty) Ltd, Johannesburg
South America: Terry Roberts, Humphrys Roberts Associates, Cotia SP, Brazil
Spain, Portugal & Gibraltar: Jenny Padovani, Barcelona, Spain
Sub-Saharan Africa: Anita Zih- De Haan, Rotterdam, Netherlands
USA: Octopus Books USA, c/o Hachette Book Group USA, Boston, MA

Book Trade Association Membership:
Publishers Association

2551 ▬▬▬

OLD HOUSE BOOKS
The Old Police Station,
Moretonhampstead, Devon TQ13 8PA
Telephone: 01647 440707
Fax: 01647 440202
Email: edward@allhusen.co.uk
Web Site: www.oldhousebooks.co.uk

Managing Director: Edward Allhusen

Atlases & Maps; Crafts & Hobbies; Geography & Geology; Guide Books; History & Antiquarian; Natural History; Reference Books, Directories & Dictionaries; Sports & Games; Transport; Travel & Topography

ISBNs, Imprints & Series: 978 1 873590

Overseas Representation:
USA: Parkwest Publications Inc, Miami, FL

2552 ▬▬▬

OLD POND PUBLISHING LTD
Dencora Business Centre,
36 White House Road, Ipswich IP1 5LT
Telephone: 01473 238200
Fax: 01473 238201
Email: sales@oldpond.com
Web Site: www.oldpond.com

Director: Roger Smith *(Publisher)*
Marketing Manager: Heather Jarrold

Agriculture; Transport; Veterinary Science

New Titles: 10 (2008) , 12 (2009)
No of Employees: 4

ISBNs, Imprints & Series:
978 0 9533651, 978 1 903366, 978 1 905523, 978 1 906853

Book Trade Association Membership:
IPG

2553 ▬▬▬

THE OLD STILE PRESS
Catchmays Court, Llandogo,
Monmouthshire NP25 4TN
Telephone: 01291 689226
Email: oldstile@dircon.co.uk
Web Site: www.oldstilepress.com

Partners: Nicolas McDowall
Frances McDowall

Illustrated & Fine Editions; Literature & Criticism; Poetry; Theatre, Drama & Dance

New Titles: 2 (2008) , 2 (2009)

ISBNs, Imprints & Series: 978 0 907664

Book Trade Association Membership:
Fine Press Book Association

2554 ▬▬▬

*THE OLEANDER PRESS
16 Orchard Street, Cambridge CB1 1JT
Telephone: 01223 350898
Email: editor@oleanderpress.com
Web Site: www.oleanderpress.com

Managing Director: Jon Gifford *(Publisher)*
Managers: Jane Doyle *(Sales)*
Will Marston *(Rights)*

Biography & Autobiography; History & Antiquarian; Humour; Languages & Linguistics; Literature & Criticism; Poetry; Reference Books, Directories & Dictionaries; Sports & Games; Travel & Topography

ISBNs, Imprints & Series:
978 0 900891, 978 0 902675, 978 0 906672

2555 ▬▬▬

OMNIBUS PRESS
14–15 Berners Street, London W1T 3LJ
Telephone: (020) 7612 7400
Fax: (020) 7612 7545
Email: richard.hudson@musicsales.co.uk
Web Site: www.omnibuspress.co.uk

Warehouse:
Book Sales Ltd, Newmarket Road,
Bury St Edmunds, Suffolk IP33 3YB
Telephone: 01284 702600
Fax: 01284 768301
Email: music@musicsales.co.uk
Web Site: www.musicsales.co.uk

Directors: Robert Wise *(Managing)*
Tony Latham *(Financial)*
Richard Hudson *(Sales)*
Production Manager: Susan Currie
Editor: Chris Charlesworth

Biography & Autobiography; Music

ISBNs, Imprints & Series:
Sanctuary
978 0 7119 Music Sales; Wise Publications
978 0 7119, 978 1 84609, 978 1 84772
Omnibus Press
978 1 8444 Omnibus Press

Parent Company:
Music Sales Ltd

Associated Companies:
Australia: Music Sales (Pty) Ltd
USA: Music Sales Corp

Distributor for:
Dover Books; IMP; Parker Mead Ltd; Rogan House; Schirmer Books

Overseas Representation:
Australia: Macmillan Distribution, South Yarra, Vic
Australia (for Music Shops): Music Sales (Australia), Rosebery, NSW, Australia
Belgium: Exhibitions International, Leuven
Central America, Mexico & Caribbean: Humphrys Roberts Associates, London, UK
Eastern Europe: Tony Moggach, InterMedia Americana (IMA) Ltd, London, UK
France: Music Sales Ltd, UK
Germany, Austria & Switzerland: Gabriele Kern Publishers Services, Frankfurt-am-Main, Germany
Greece, Turkey, Cyprus, Malta & Middle East: Peter Ward Book Exports, London, UK
Indian Sub Continent: Publishers International Marketing, Storrington, UK
Netherlands & Luxembourg: Nilsson & Lamm BV, Weesp, Netherlands
New Zealand: Macmillan Publishers New Zealand Ltd, Auckland
Scandinavia: McNeish Publishing International, East Sussex, UK
South Africa: Trinity Books CC, Randburg
South America: Humphrys Roberts Associates, Cotia SP, Brazil
South East & North Asia: Chris Ashdown Publishers International Marketing, London, UK
Spain, Portugal, Gibraltar & Italy: Penny Padovani, London, UK
USA & Canada: Music Sales Corporation, Chester, NY, USA

Book Trade Association Membership:
BA (Associate Member)

2556 ▬▬▬

ON STREAM PUBLICATIONS LTD
Currabaha, Cloghroe, Co Cork,
Republic of Ireland
Telephone: +353 (021) 438 5798
Email: info@onstream.ie
Web Site: www.onstream.ie

Managing Director & Editor: Roz Crowley

Academic & Scholarly; Biography & Autobiography; Cookery, Wines & Spirits; Environment & Development Studies; Health & Beauty; Reference Books, Directories & Dictionaries

ISBNs, Imprints & Series: 978 1 897685

Book Trade Association Membership:
CLÉ (Irish PA)

2557 ▬▬▬

ONEWORLD CLASSICS
London House,
243–253 Lower Mortlake Road, Richmond, Surrey TW9 2LL
Telephone: (020) 8948 9550
Fax: (020) 8948 5599
Email: info@oneworldclassics.com
Web Site: www.oneworldclassics.com

Publishing Director: Alessandro Gallenzi
Associate Publisher: Elisabetta Minervini

Fiction; Literature & Criticism; Poetry

New Titles: 50 (2008) , 50 (2009)

ISBNs, Imprints & Series:
978 0 7145 Calder Publications
978 1 84749 One World Classics

Associated Companies:
UK: Calder Publications Ltd

Overseas Representation:
Australia: Tower Books Pty Ltd, Frenchs Forest, NSW
South Africa: Penguin Books South Africa (Pty) Ltd, Johannesburg
USA & Canada: Trafalgar Square Publishing / IPG, Chicago, IL, USA

2558 ▬▬▬

ONLYWOMEN PRESS LTD
40 St Lawrence Terrace, London W10 5ST
Telephone: (020) 8354 0796
Fax: (020) 8960 2817
Email: onlywomenpress@btconnect.com
Web Site: www.onlywomenpress.com

Trade Distribution:
Central Books Ltd, 99 Wallis Road, London E9 5LN
Telephone: 0845 458 9911
Fax: 0845 458 9912
Web Site: www.centralbooks.com

Directors: L. Mohin *(Managing)*
V. J. Lee

Academic & Scholarly; Biography & Autobiography; Children's Books; Crime; Fiction; Gay & Lesbian Studies; Gender Studies; Literature & Criticism

New Titles: 4 (2008) , 5 (2009)

ISBNs, Imprints & Series: 978 0 906500

Overseas Representation:
Australia: Bulldog Books, Beaconsfield, NSW
North America: Alamo Square Distribution, USA

Book Trade Association Membership:
IPG

2559 ▬▬▬

THE OPEN BIBLE TRUST
Fordland Mount, Upper Basildon, Reading RG8 8LU
Telephone: 01491 671357
Email: admin@obt.org.uk
Web Site: www.obt.org.uk

Editor: Michael Penny *(Administrator)*
Treasurer: Sylvia Penny

Religion & Theology

New Titles: 7 (2008) , 6 (2009)
No of Employees: 2
Annual Turnover: £32,000

ISBNs, Imprints & Series:
978 0 947778, 978 1 902859

Associated Companies:
USA: Bible Search Publications Inc

Overseas Representation:
Australia: Benean Bible Fellowship of Australia, Glendale, NSW
Canada: Lloyd Allen, Scarborough, Ont
New Zealand: Graeme Abbott, Hamilton
USA: Bible Search Publications, Brookfield, WI

2560

OPEN GATE PRESS
[incorporating Centaur Press (1954)]
51 Achilles Road, London NW6 1DZ
Telephone: (020) 7431 4391
Fax: (020) 7431 5129
Email: books@opengatepress.co.uk
Web Site: www.opengatepress.co.uk

Trade Enquiries & Orders:
Central Books Ltd, 99 Wallis Road, London E9 5LN
Telephone: 0845 458 9911
Fax: 0845 458 9912
Email: sales@centralbooks.com
Web Site: www.centralbooks.com

Editorial: Jeannie Cohen
Production: Elisabeth Petersdorff

Academic & Scholarly; Environment & Development Studies; Philosophy; Politics & World Affairs; Psychology & Psychiatry; Religion & Theology

New Titles: 4 (2008) , 4 (2009)
No of Employees: 3

ISBNs, Imprints & Series:
978 0 900001, 978 1 871871

Associated Companies:
Centaur Press; Linden Press [imprint of Centaur Press]

Book Trade Association Membership:
Publishers Association; IPG

2561

OPEN UNIVERSITY WORLDWIDE
Michael Young Building, Walton Hall, Milton Keynes, Bucks MK7 6AA
Telephone: 01604 858785
Web Site: www.ouw.co.uk

Academic & Scholarly; Biology & Zoology; Chemistry; Computer Science; Economics; Educational & Textbooks; Electronic (Educational); Engineering; English as a Foreign Language; Environment & Development Studies; Fine Art & Art History; Geography & Geology; History & Antiquarian; Industry, Business & Management; Languages & Linguistics; Literature & Criticism; Mathematics & Statistics; Medical (incl. Self Help & Alternative Medicine); Natural History; Physics; Politics & World Affairs; Psychology & Psychiatry; Religion & Theology; Scientific & Technical; Sociology & Anthropology; Theatre, Drama & Dance

New Titles: 132 (2008) , 150 (2009)

ISBNs, Imprints & Series:
978 0 7492, 978 1 84873

2562

OPTIMUS PROFESSIONAL PUBLISHING
33–41 Dallington Street, London EC1V 0BB
Telephone: 0845 450 6404
Fax: 0845 450 6410
Email: info@teachingexpertise.com
Web Site: www.teachingexpertise.com

Managing Director: Emma Rogers

Educational & Textbooks; Electronic (Educational); Geography & Geology; History & Antiquarian; Natural History; Vocational Training & Careers

New Titles: 28 (2008) , 30 (2009)
No of Employees: 40
Annual Turnover: £6M

ISBNs, Imprints & Series:
Chris Kington Publishing; Optimus Education; Teach to Inspire
978 1 899857, 978 1 904677, 978 1 905538, 978 1 906517

Parent Company:
Electric Word PLC

Book Trade Association Membership:
EPC

2563

*ORCHARD PUBLISHING
43–47 Mill Way, Grantchester, Cambs CB3 9ND
Telephone: 01223 845788
Fax: 01223 845862
Email: opl@callan.co.uk
Web Site: www.callan.co.uk

Academic & Scholarly; Educational & Textbooks

Book Trade Association Membership:
Publishers Association

2564

O'REILLY UK LTD
4 Castle Street, Farnham, Surrey GU9 7HS
Telephone: 01252 711776
Fax: 01252 734211
Email: information@oreilly.co.uk
Web Site: www.oreilly.com

Distributors:
John Wiley, 1 Oldlands Way, Bognor Regis PO22 9SA
Telephone: 01243 779777
Fax: 01243 843303
Email: cs-books@wiley.co.uk

Managing Director: Graham Cameron
Managers: Josette Garcia *(Public Relations)*
Simon Chappell *(Sales)*

Computer Science

ISBNs, Imprints & Series:
978 0 59600, 978 1 56592, 978 1 93395, 978 1 93435

Parent Company:
USA: O'Reilly Media Inc

Book Trade Association Membership:
IPG

2565

ORION BOOKS LTD
Orion House, 5 Upper St Martins Lane, London WC2H 9EA
Telephone: (020) 7240 3444
Fax: (020) 7240 4822

Trade Counter & Warehouse:
Littlehampton Book Services Ltd, Faraday Close, Durrington, Worthing, West Sussex BN13 3RB
Telephone: 01903 828500
Fax: 01903 828625
Web Site: www.orionbooks.co.uk

Managing Directors: Lisa Milton *(Orion Books)*
Susan Lamb *(Orion Paperbacks)*

Publishing Director: Jon Wood *(Orion Fiction)*
Publisher: Fiona Kennedy *(Orion Children's)*

Biography & Autobiography; Children's Books; Fiction; Science Fiction; Fantasy

ISBNs, Imprints & Series:
978 1 84255, 978 1 85881 Orion Children's
978 1 85797 Orion; Orion Paperbacks
978 1 85798 Gollancz
978 1 85799 Phoenix
978 1 89758 Phoenix House

Parent Company:
The Orion Publishing Group Ltd

Overseas Representation:
see: The Orion Publishing Group Ltd, London, UK

2566

THE ORION PUBLISHING GROUP LTD
Orion House, 5 Upper St Martins Lane, London WC2H 9EA
Telephone: (020) 7240 3444
Fax: (020) 7240 4822

Trade Counter & Warehouse:
Littlehampton Book Services Ltd, Faraday Close, Durrington, Worthing, West Sussex BN13 3RB
Telephone: 01903 828500
Fax: 01903 828625
Email: ...@lbsltd.co.uk
Web Site: www.lbsltd.co.uk

Chairman: Arnaud Nourry
Chief Executives: Peter Roche
Malcolm Edwards *(Deputy & Publisher)*
Directors: Susan Lamb *(Managing – Mass Market)*
Lisa Milton *(Managing – Orion Books)*
Dallas Manderson *(Group Sales)*
Dominic Smith *(Home Sales)*
Mark Streatfeild *(Export Sales)*
Fiona McIntosh *(Production)*
Mark Prior *(Finance)*
Chris Emerson *(Distribution)*
Lord Weidenfeld
Susan Howe *(Group Rights)*

Antiques & Collecting; Archaeology; Audio Books; Biography & Autobiography; Children's Books; Cinema, Video, TV & Radio; Cookery, Wines & Spirits; Crafts & Hobbies; Crime; Fashion & Costume; Fiction; Fine Art & Art History; Gardening; Guide Books; Health & Beauty; History & Antiquarian; Humour; Illustrated & Fine Editions; Military & War; Natural History; Nautical; Philosophy; Politics & World Affairs; Reference Books, Directories & Dictionaries; Science Fiction; Sports & Games; Travel & Topography

ISBNs, Imprints & Series:
978 0 297 W & N Illustrated; Weidenfeld & Nicolson
978 0 304 Cassell
978 0 460 J M Dent; Everyman Paperbacks
978 0 460, 978 0 7528, 978 1 85797 Orion Paperbacks
978 0 575, 978 1 85797, 978 1 85798 Gollancz
978 0 752 First Time Authors Fiction; Oriel
978 0 7528 Orion Fiction; Orion Media
978 0 7538 Phoenix Mass Market
978 1 84212 Phoenix Press
978 1 84255, 978 1 85881 Orion Children's
978 1 85797 Orion
978 1 89758 Phoenix House

Parent Company:
France: Hachette Livre

Associated Companies:
Cassell plc; J M Dent Ltd; Victor Gollancz; Littlehampton Book Services Ltd; Orion Books Ltd; George Weidenfeld and Nicolson Ltd

Distributor for:
Peter Halban Publishers

Overseas Representation:
Australia: Hachette Livre Australia (Orion Division), Sydney, NSW
Austria, Belgium, Cyprus, France, Germany, Greece, Italy, Luxembourg, Netherlands, Portugal, Spain & Switzerland: Kim Tyler, The Orion Publishing Group Ltd, London, UK
Canada: Hachette Book Group, Toronto, Ont
Caribbean: Chris Humphrys, Humphrys Roberts Associates, London, UK
Eastern Europe: Csaba & Jackie Lengyel de Bagota, Budapest, Hungary
India: Hachette India, New Delhi
India, Pakistan, South America, Singapore, Hong Kong, Thailand, Japan, Indonesia & Malaysia: Michael Goff, The Orion Publishing Group Ltd, London, UK
New Zealand: Hachette New Zealand (Orion Division), Auckland
Philippines, Korea & Taiwan: Ralph & Sheila Summers, Woodford Green, Essex, UK
Scandinavia, Middle East, Turkey, Malta, Russia, North Africa & Baltic States: Jennie McCann, The Orion Publishing Group Ltd, London, UK
South Africa: Jonathan Ball Publishers (Pty) Ltd, Johannesburg

2567

OSPREY PUBLISHING LTD
Midland House, West Way, Botley, Oxford OX2 0PH
Telephone: 01865 727022
Fax: 01865 727017
Email: info@ospreypublishing.com
Web Site: www.ospreypublishing.com

Distribution:
Grantham Book Services,
Isaac Newton Way,
Alma Park Industrial Estate, Grantham, Lincs NG31 9SD
Telephone: 01476 541080
Fax: 01476 541061
Email: orders@gbs-tbs-ltd.co.uk

Directors: Rebecca Smart *(Managing)*
Chris Tinsley *(Finance)*
Joanna Sharland *(Rights)*

Aviation; History & Antiquarian; Military & War

New Titles: 128 (2008) , 140 (2009)
No of Employees: 38
Annual Turnover: £6M

ISBNs, Imprints & Series:
978 0 85045, 978 1 84176, 978 1 84603, 978 1 84908, 978 1 85532

Overseas Representation:
Australia: Capricorn Link (Australia) Pty Ltd, Windsor, NSW
Benelux, Austria, Germany & Switzerland: Robbert J. Pleysier, Heerde, Netherlands
Eastern Europe: Tony Moggach, London, UK
Far East: Ashton International Marketing Services, Sevenoaks, Kent, UK
France: Guillaume Etasse, Paris
Greece & Italy: Sandro Salucci, Florence, Italy
Middle East: Peter Ward Book Exports, London, UK
New Zealand: David Bateman Ltd, Auckland
Scandinavia: Katie McNeish, East Sussex, UK
Spain, Portugal & Gibraltar: Iberian Book Services, Madrid, Spain

USA, Caribbean & Latin America: Random House Publishing Services, New York, NY, USA

2568

*OUTSELL INC / EPS
[formerly Electronic Publishing Services]
26 Rosebery Avenue, London EC1R 4SX
Telephone: (020) 7837 3345
Fax: (020) 7837 8901
Email: dworlock@outsellinc.com
Web Site: www.outsellinc.com

Electronic (Professional & Academic)

Book Trade Association Membership:
Publishers Association

2569

*OVOLO PUBLISHING LTD
1 The Granary, Brook Farm, Ellington, Huntingdon, Cambs PE28 0AE
Telephone: 01480 891777
Fax: 01480 893836
Email: info@ovolobooks.co.uk
Web Site: www.ovolobooks.co.uk

Managing Director: Mark Neeter
Marketing Manager: Michelle Thorn

Architecture & Design; Do-It-Yourself; Music

Distributor for:
UK: Centaur Books; Waterways World Books

Book Trade Association Membership:
IPG

2570

PETER OWEN PUBLISHERS
73 Kenway Road, London SW5 0RE
Telephone: (020) 7373 5628 & 7370 6093
Fax: (020) 7373 6760
Email: admin@peterowen.com
Web Site: www.peterowen.com

Trade Counter & Warehouse:
Central Books, 99 Wallis Road, London E9 5LN
Telephone: (020) 8986 4854
Fax: (020) 8533 5821
Email: orders@centralbooks.com
Web Site: www.centralbooks.com

Directors: Peter Owen *(Managing)*
Antonia Owen *(Editorial)*
Managers: Nick Pearson *(Production)*
Michael O'Connell *(Sales & Publicity)*
Simon Smith *(Rights & Editorial)*

Biography & Autobiography; Cinema, Video, TV & Radio; Fashion & Costume; Fiction; Gay & Lesbian Studies; History & Antiquarian; Literature & Criticism; Music; Theatre, Drama & Dance

New Titles: 25 (2008) , 25 (2009)

ISBNs, Imprints & Series:
978 0 7206 Peter Owen Modern Classics

Overseas Representation:
Australia: Peribo Pty Ltd, Mount Kuring-Gai, NSW
Canada: Scholarly Book Services Inc, Toronto
Europe, Scandinavia & Iceland: Books for Europe, Massagno, Switzerland
New Zealand: Addenda Ltd, Grey Lynn
South Africa: Stephan Phillips (Pty) Ltd, Cape Town
USA: Dufour Editions Inc, Chester Springs, PA

Book Trade Association Membership:
IPG

2571

OXBOW BOOKS
10 Hythe Bridge Street, Oxford OX1 2EW
Telephone: 01865 241249
Fax: 01865 794449
Email: oxbow@oxbowbooks.com
Web Site: www.oxbowbooks.com

Managing Director: David Brown
Finance: Jane Lovell
Editorial: Clare Litt
Marketing: Hilary Schan
Sales: James Dickson
Production: Val Lamb

Academic & Scholarly; Archaeology; Biography & Autobiography; Fashion & Costume; History & Antiquarian; Literature & Criticism; Natural History; Nautical; Sociology & Anthropology; Classical Studies; Egyptology; Medieval Studies

New Titles: 43 (2008) , 50 (2009)

ISBNs, Imprints & Series:
978 0 85668 Aris & Phillips
978 0 946897, 978 1 84217, 978 1 900188 Oxbow Books
978 0 9545575, 978 1 905119 Windgather Press
978 1 905223 Heritage Publications

Distributor for:
American Numismatic Society; American School of Classical Studies in Athens; American School of Prehistoric Research; American Schools of Oriental Research; American Society of Papyrologists; Antiquity Publications; Archaeological Institute of America; Aris and Phillips; Armatura Press; Association for Study of Travel in Egypt & the Near East; Australian Centre for Egyptology; British Academy [Backlist titles]; British Institute in East Africa; The British Institute of Archaeology at Ankara; British Museum Press Scholarly Titles; The British School at Rome; British School of Archaeology in Iraq; Francis Cairns Publications; Cambridge Philological Society; Canterbury Archaeological Trust; Celtic Studies Publications; Center for Old World Archaeology & Art; Classical Press of Wales; Cotsen Institute of Archaeology at UCLA; Council for British Research in the Levant; Czech Institute of Archaeology; East Anglian Archaeology; Edinburgh University, Dept of Archaeology; Egypt Exploration Society; Gibb Memorial Trust; Griffith Institute of Oxford University; Halgo; Illuminata Publishers; Institute for Aegean Prehistory Academic Press; Institute for Mesoamerican Studies; Institute of Classical Archaeology; International Monographs in Prehistory; Journal of Juristic Papyrology; Kelsey Museum of Archaeology; The Khalili Collections; Legenda; Maney Publishing [heritage titles]; McDonald Institute for Archaeological Research; Museum of Fine Arts, Boston; Museum of London Archaeology Service; National Heritage Board of Sweden; Ocarina Books; Orcadian Books [archaeology titles]; Oriental Institute Chicago; Oxford Archaeology; Oxford Centre for Maritime Archaeology; Oxford University School of Archaeology; Society of Antiquaries of London; Spire Books; St George's Chapel, Windsor; University of Iceland Press; Wessex Archaeology; Western Academic & Specialist Press; Windgather Press; Yale Egyptological Seminar; York University, Dept of Archaeology
Albania: Centre for Albanian Archaeology
Australia: Macmillan Art Publishers
Belgium: Citeaux
Colombia: Pro Calima Foundation
Denmark: Viking Ship Museum, Roskilde
Germany: Vandenhoeck & Ruprecht

Greece: Ekdotike Athenon; Institute for Philosophical Research
Israel: Israel Antiquities Authority
Netherlands: Sidestone Press
Poland: Akanthina
Sweden: Riksantikvarieambetet; Societas Archaeologica Upsaliensis
Turkey: Homer Kitabevi
USA: Eliot Werner Publications; Gorgias Press; Regatta Press

Overseas Representation:
Far East (excluding Japan) & South East Asia: Chris Ashdown, Publishers International Marketing, Los Angeles, CA, USA
Germany, Netherlands & Belgium: Roy de Boo, Continental Contacts, Hooge Mierde, Netherlands
Italy & Greece: Flavio Marcello Publishers' Agents & Consultants, Padua, Italy
Middle East: Ray Potts, Publishers International Marketing, Sutton St Nicholas, Herefordshire, UK
Scandinavia: Jan Norbye, Ølstykke, Denmark
Spain, Portugal & Gibraltar: Peter Prout, Iberian Book Services, Madrid, Spain
USA & Canada: The David Brown Book Co, Oakville, CT, USA

Book Trade Association Membership:
IPG; American Booksellers Association

2572

*OXFAM PUBLISHING
Oxfam House, John Smith Drive, Cowley, Oxford OX4 2JY
Telephone: 01865 473727
Fax: 01865 472393
Email: publish@oxfam.org.uk
Web Site: www.oxfam.org.uk/ publications.html

Warehouse:
BEBC Distribution, PO Box 1496, Parkstone, Dorset BH12 3YD
Telephone: 01202 712933
Fax: 01202 712930
Email: oxfam@bebc.co.uk

Sales & Marketing Manager: Robert Cornford
Promotions Executive: Jennie Morant
Managing Editor: Claire Harvey

Academic & Scholarly; Agriculture; Children's Books; Economics; Educational & Textbooks; Electronic (Educational); Environment & Development Studies; Gender Studies; Politics & World Affairs

ISBNs, Imprints & Series:
978 0 85598 Oxfam Publications
978 1 870727 Oxfam Education

Overseas Representation:
All other territories: BEBC Distribution, Parkstone, UK
Australia & New Zealand: InBooks, Frenchs Forest, NSW, Australia
Bangladesh: Midas, Dhaka
Canada: Renouf Publishing Co Ltd, Ottawa, Ont
Caribbean: Ian Randle Publishers Ltd, Kingston, Jamaica
Egypt: The Middle East Readers Information Center, Cairo
Eritrea: The Red Sea Press Inc, Asmara
Ethiopia: T.G.B. Roman Trading Enterprise, Addis Ababa
Germany: Missing Link International Booksellers, Bremen; Triops - Tropical Scientific Books, Darmstadt
Ghana: EPP Books Services Ltd, Accra
India: Maya Publishers Pvt Ltd, New Delhi
Kenya: Legacy Books & Distributors, Nairobi
Lebanon: Co-operative for Research & Training on Development, Beirut
Malawi: Anglia Book Distributors Ltd, Blantyre

Malaysia: MDC Book Distribution, Kuala Lumpur
Mongolia: Nomin House Co Ltd, Ulaanbaatar
Nepal: Everest Media International, Kathmandu
Nigeria: EPP Books, Lagos
Rwanda: Bookshop Ikirezi, Kigali
Singapore: Select Books Pte Ltd
South Africa, Botswana, Swaziland, Lesotho, Mozambique & Namibia: Anglia Book & Freight Consolidator, Knysna, South Africa
Switzerland: Münstergass-Buchhandlung, Berne
Tanzania: Mkuki na Nyota Publishers, Dar es Salaam
Thailand: Booknet Co Ltd, Bangkok
Uganda: Fountain Publishers Ltd, Kampala
USA: Stylus Publishing LLC, Herndon, VA
Zambia: Prestige Books, Lusaka
Zimbabwe: Prestige Books, Harare

Book Trade Association Membership:
IPG

2573

OXFORD UNIVERSITY PRESS
Great Clarendon Street, Oxford OX2 6DP
Telephone: 01865 556767
Fax: 01865 557746
Email: webenquiry@oup.com
Web Site: www.oup.com

Chief Executive: Nigel Portwood
Finance Director: David Gillard
Managing Directors: Kate Harris
(Educational Division)
Peter Marshall *(ELT)*
Martin Richardson *(Academic & Journals)*
Neil Tomkins *(International Division)*
Jesus Lezcano *(OUP Spain)*
President OUP USA: Tim Barton

Academic & Scholarly; Biology & Zoology; Children's Books; Economics; Educational & Textbooks; Electronic (Professional & Academic); English as a Foreign Language; Industry, Business & Management; Languages & Linguistics; Law; Mathematics & Statistics; Medical (incl. Self Help & Alternative Medicine); Music; Philosophy; Physics; Politics & World Affairs; Psychology & Psychiatry; Reference Books, Directories & Dictionaries; Religion & Theology; Trade

Annual Turnover: £578M

Book Trade Association Membership:
Publishers Association

2574

PACKARD PUBLISHING LTD
Forum House, Stirling Road, Chichester, West Sussex PO19 7DN
Telephone: 01243 537977
Fax: 01243 537977
Email: info@packardpublishing.co.uk
Web Site: www.packardpublishing.com

Director: Michael Packard *(Managing, Sales, Rights & Permissions)*

Academic & Scholarly; Agriculture; Architecture & Design; Biology & Zoology; Educational & Textbooks; Environment & Development Studies; Gardening; Geography & Geology; Languages & Linguistics; Music; Natural History; Reference Books, Directories & Dictionaries; Scientific & Technical; Sports & Games

New Titles: 2 (2008) , 6 (2009)

ISBNs, Imprints & Series:
978 0 906527, 978 1 85341 Packard
978 0 948690 Packard (Arabic titles)

Distributor for:
Lebanon: Librairie du Liban
USA: Carolina Biological Supply Co Inc
(Biology Readers only); Stipes Publishing
LLC

Overseas Representation:
North America: Stipes Publishing LLC,
Champaign, IL, USA

2575

PALGRAVE MACMILLAN
Houndmills, Basingstoke, Hants RG21 6XS
Telephone: 01256 329242
Fax: 01256 479476
Web Site: www.palgrave.com

Warehouse, Trade Enquiries & Orders:
Macmillan Distribution (MDL), Brunel Road,
Houndmills, Basingstoke, Hants RG21 6XS
Telephone: 01256 329242
Fax: 01256 840154
Email: mdl@macmillan.co.uk

Chairman: Annette Thomas
Directors: D. J. G. Knight *(Managing)*
S. Burridge *(Publishing, Scholarly &
Reference)*
M. Hewinson *(Publishing, College)*
D. Bull *(Publishing, Journals)*
L. Keelan *(Sales)*
V. Capstick *(Marketing)*
A. J. Jones *(Digital Development)*
Finance: R. H. Hartgill
Operations: J. W. Peacock

*Academic & Scholarly; Accountancy &
Taxation; Biology & Zoology; Chemistry;
Computer Science; Economics; Educational
& Textbooks; Electronic (Educational);
Engineering; Environment & Development
Studies; Gender Studies; Geography &
Geology; History & Antiquarian; Industry,
Business & Management; Languages &
Linguistics; Law; Literature & Criticism;
Mathematics & Statistics; Medical (incl. Self
Help & Alternative Medicine); Philosophy;
Physics; Politics & World Affairs; Psychology
& Psychiatry; Reference Books, Directories &
Dictionaries; Religion & Theology; Scientific
& Technical; Sociology & Anthropology;
Theatre, Drama & Dance; Vocational
Training & Careers*

New Titles: 1163 (2008) , 1182 (2009)

ISBNs, Imprints & Series:
978 0 333, 978 1 4039

Parent Company:
Macmillan Ltd

Associated Companies:
Macmillan Children's Books; Macmillan
Education; Macmillan Publishers Ltd; Pan
Macmillan Ltd; Stockton Press Ltd
USA: Stockton Press Inc

Distributor for:
Bedford; W. H. Freeman; Sinauer
Associates; Spectrum; University Science
Books; Worth Publishers

Overseas Representation:
Africa (excluding areas listed): Africa Dept,
Palgrave Macmillan Ltd, Basingstoke,
Hants, UK
Australia: Palgrave Macmillan, South Yarra,
Vic
Austria & Germany: Katrin Lilienthal,
Frankfurt-am-Main, Germany
China: Frank Xu, Macmillan c/o FLTRP,
Beijing, P. R. of China
Colombia: Grupo K-T-Dra Ltda, Santa Fe de
Bogota
*Denmark, Norway, Finland, Sweden &
Iceland:* Steve Haslemere, Colin Flint Ltd,
Publishers Scandinavian Consultancy,
Cambridge, UK
East Asia (including Hong Kong, Philippines,

Thailand, Vietnam & Indonesia): Steve
Maginn, Palgrave Macmillan, Macmillan
Publishers (China) Ltd, Hong Kong
Eastern Europe: Janet Levinson, Warsaw,
Poland
Egypt: Ali Abdul Wahab, Macmillan
Publishers Egypt Ltd, Cairo
Ethiopia: Meskerem Demeke, Addis Ababa
Europe (excluding areas listed): European
Dept, Palgrave Macmillan Ltd,
Basingstoke, Hants, UK
Ghana: Unimax Publishers Ltd, Accra-North
Greece & Cyprus: Zitsa Seraphimidi, Faliro,
Greece
India: Ajit De, Calcutta; Kalpana Shukla,
Palgrave Macmillan, New Delhi; V. Ravi,
Palgrave Macmillan, Chennai; Sunil
Sharma, New Delhi; Anand Vithalkar,
Mumbai
Iran: Sepehr Bookshop, Tehran
Italy & France: David Pickering, Mare
Nostrum Publishing Consultants, Rome,
Italy
Japan: Palgrave Macmillan Ltd, Basingstoke,
Hants, UK
Jordan: Jaqueline Sabri, Amman
Kenya: Macmillan Kenya (Publishers) Ltd,
Nairobi
Korea: Jinsoo Yoon, Macmillan Publishers,
Jongro-Gu, Seoul, Republic of Korea
Latin America, Caribbean & all other areas:
Palgrave Macmillan Ltd, Basingstoke,
Hants, UK
Lebanon: Faisal Mreish, Beirut
Malaysia: UBSD Distribution Sdn Bhd,
Selangor
Middle East (excluding areas listed): Middle
Eastern Dept, Palgrave Macmillan Ltd,
Basingstoke, Hants, UK
*Netherlands, Belgium, Luxembourg, France
& Switzerland:* Daan Timmermans,
Brussels, Belgium
New Zealand: Vicki Johnson, Macmillan
Publishers New Zealand Ltd, Auckland
Nigeria: Macmillan Nigeria Publishers Ltd,
Yaba - Lagos
Pakistan: Book Bird Publishers
Representatives, Lahore
Singapore & Brunei: Pansing Distribution
Sdn Bhd, Singapore
*Southern Africa (including Botswana,
Lesotho & Swaziland):* Cory Voigt,
Palgrave Macmillan, Johannesburg,
South Africa
Spain: Trinidad Lopez, Madrid
Taiwan: Wendy Wu, Macmillan Education,
Taipei
Tanzania: Macmillan Aidan Ltd, Dar es
Salaam
Uganda: Macmillan Uganda Ltd, Kampala
United Arab Emirates: Ali Basim, Macmillan
Education Dubai, Dubai, UAE
USA: Palgrave Macmillan, New York, NY

Book Trade Association Membership:
Publishers Association; CAPP; BDPA; STM

2576

PAN MACMILLAN
20 New Wharf Road, London N1 9RR
Telephone: (020) 7014 6000
Fax: (020) 7014 6001
Email: books@macmillan.co.uk
Web Site: www.panmacmillan.com

Warehouse, Trade Enquiries & Orders:
Macmillan Distribution (MDL), Houndmills,
Basingstoke, Hants RG21 6XS
Telephone: 01256 329242
Fax: 01256 840154
Email: mdl@macmillan.co.uk

Directors: Anthony Forbes Watson
(Managing)
Annette Thomas *(Chief Executive Officer,
Macmillan Publishers Ltd)*
Emma Hopkin *(Managing, Macmillan
Children's Books)*
Ian Metcalfe *(Financial)*
Anna Bond *(UK Sales)*

Aimee Roche *(International Sales)*
Ian Mitchell *(Production)*
Geoff Duffield *(Sales & Marketing)*
Camilla Elworthy *(Publicity)*
Fiona Carpenter *(Art & Design)*
Imogen Taylor *(Editorial, Fiction)*
Paul Baggaley *(Publisher – Picador)*
Maria Rejt *(Publishing – Macmillan, Pan,
Picador)*
Jeremy Trevathan *(Publishing –
Macmillan, Pan)*
Georgina Morley *(Editorial, Non-Fiction)*
Margaret Halton *(Rights)*

*Biography & Autobiography; Children's
Books; Cinema, Video, TV & Radio; Fiction;
Gardening; Guide Books; Health & Beauty;
History & Antiquarian; Literature &
Criticism; Science Fiction; Sports & Games;
Travel & Topography*

ISBNs, Imprints & Series:
978 0 230 Macmillan Children's Books;
Tor; Macmillan
978 0 283 Sidgwick & Jackson
978 0 330 Pan; Picador
978 0 333 Campbell
978 0 752 Boxtree

Parent Company:
Macmillan Ltd

Associated Companies:
Boxtree Ltd; Macmillan Children's Books;
Macmillan Education; Macmillan
Publishers Ltd; Palgrave Macmillan; Pan
Books Ltd; Sidgwick & Jackson Ltd

Overseas Representation:
All other areas - send orders to:
International Department, Pan
Macmillan, Basingstoke, UK
Australia: Pan Macmillan (Australia) Pty Ltd,
Sydney, NSW
Canada: H. B. Fenn & Co Ltd, Bolton, Ont
Hong Kong: Publishers' Associates Ltd
India: Pan Macmillan, New Delhi
Japan: Shino Yasuda, Tokyo
New Zealand: Macmillan Publishers New
Zealand Ltd, Auckland
Republic of Ireland: David Adamson, Dublin
*South Africa, Botswana, Lesotho,
Swaziland, Namibia & Zimbabwe:* Pan
Macmillan SA Pty Ltd, Hyde Park, South
Africa
South East Asia: Pansing Distribution Sdn
Bhd, Singapore
West Indies & Caribbean: Macmillan
Education Ltd, Oxford, UK

Book Trade Association Membership:
Publishers Association

2577

PANAF BOOKS
19 Muirfield, Biddenham, Bedford
MK40 4FB
Telephone: 01234 340430
Fax: 0870 333 1196
Email: zakakembo@yahoo.co.uk
Web Site: www.panafbooks.com

Distribution:
W & G Foyles Ltd, Dept No 19,
113–119 Charing Cross Road, London
WC2H 0EB
Telephone: (020) 7440 3245 & (020) 7437
5660

Distribution & Stockist:
Gardners Books, 1 Whittle Drive,
Eastbourne BN23 6QH
Telephone: 01323 521555
Fax: 01323 525502 & 521666
Email: customercare@gardners.com

Publisher: S. S. Kakembo
Group Financial Adviser: C. W. Little
Director: E. R. Kakembo

Sales: E. Nani-Kofi
Consultant: J. Milne

*Academic & Scholarly; Biography &
Autobiography; Politics & World Affairs;
Sociology & Anthropology*

ISBNs, Imprints & Series:
978 0 901787 Panaf; PGL –
Autobiographies & Biographies Series

Parent Company:
Panaf Ltd

Overseas Representation:
*East Africa (including Uganda, Kenya &
Tanzania):* Crane Publishers Ltd,
Kampala, Uganda
Ghana: Hensteve Publications Ltd, Accra
USA: Lightning Source Inc (US), Lavergne,
TN

2578

PAPADAKIS PUBLISHER
Kimber Studio, Winterbourne, Newbury,
Berks RG20 8AN
Telephone: 01635 248833
Email: alex@papadakis.net
Web Site: www.papadakis.net

Studio/Retail:
11 Shepherd Market, Mayfair, London
W1J 7PG

Publishing Director: Alexandra Papadakis

*Architecture & Design; Cookery, Wines &
Spirits; Fashion & Costume; Gardening;
Natural History; Photography*

New Titles: 10 (2008) , 10 (2009)

ISBNs, Imprints & Series:
978 1 901092 New Architecture
978 1 901092, 978 1 906506 Papadakis

Parent Company:
New Architecture Group Ltd

Overseas Representation:
Rest of World: John Rule Sales & Marketing,
London, UK
USA: Antique Collectors Club, Wappinger
Falls, NY

Book Trade Association Membership:
Publishers Association

2579

*PATHFINDER BOOKS
120 Bethnal Green Road, London E2 6DG
Telephone: (020) 7613 3855
Fax: (020) 7613 3855
Email: admin@pathfinderbooks.co.uk
Web Site: www.pathfinderpress.com

Manager: J. Silberman

*Academic & Scholarly; Economics; Gender
Studies; History & Antiquarian; Military &
War; Philosophy; Politics & World Affairs;
Sociology & Anthropology*

ISBNs, Imprints & Series:
978 0 87348 Pathfinder

Distributor for:
USA: Pathfinder Press

Overseas Representation:
Australia, Asia & Pacific: Pathfinder Press,
Haymarket, NSW, Australia
Canada: Pathfinder Press Distribution,
Toronto, Ont
Iceland: Pathfinder, Reykjavik
New Zealand: Pathfinder, Auckland
Sweden: Pathfinder, Hägersten
USA, Caribbean & Latin America:
Pathfinder Press, New York, USA

2580

PAVILION
Anova Books, 10 Southcombe Street,
London W14 0RA
Telephone: (020) 7605 1400
Fax: (020) 7605 1401
Email: rleeds@anovabooks.com
Web Site: www.anovabooks.com

Warehouse, Trade Orders & Enquiries:
HarperCollins, Glasgow
Telephone: 0141 306 3100
Fax: 0141 306 3767

Associate Publisher: Anna Cheifetz
Head of Marketing & Publicity: Jane Ellis

*Architecture & Design; Biography &
Autobiography; Children's Books; Cinema,
Video, TV & Radio; Cookery, Wines &
Spirits; Fashion & Costume; Gardening;
Health & Beauty; Music; Photography;
Theatre, Drama & Dance; Travel &
Topography*

ISBNs, Imprints & Series: 978 1 86205

Parent Company:
Anova Books

Overseas Representation:
Australia: HarperCollins Publishers, Pymble,
NSW
*Belgium, France, Netherlands &
Luxembourg:* Anova Books, London, UK
Canada: Raincoast Books, Vancouver, BC
Caribbean, Mexico & Central America:
Christopher Humphrys, Humphrys
Roberts Associates, London, UK
Eastern Europe: Csaba Lengyel de Bagota,
CLB Marketing Services, Budapest,
Hungary
Far East: Julian Ashton, Ashton
International Marketing Services,
Sevenoaks, Kent, UK
Germany, Switzerland & Austria: Gabriele
Kern Publishers Services, Frankfurt-am-
Main, Germany
India: Mr Seshadri, Overleaf, New Delhi
Italy, Spain, Portugal & Greece: Penny
Padovani, London, UK
New Zealand: HarperCollins (NZ) Ltd,
Glenfield, Auckland
Pakistan: Tahir M. Lodhi, Lahore
Russia & Baltic States: Tony Moggach,
InterMedia Americana (IMA) Ltd,
London, UK
Scandinavia: Katie McNeish, McNeish
Publishing International, East Sussex, UK
Singapore & Malaysia: Pansing Distribution
Sdn Bhd, Singapore
South Africa: Quartet Sales & Marketing,
Northcliffe
South America: Terry Roberts, Humphrys
Roberts Associates, Cotia SP, Brazil
USA: Independent Publishers Group (IPG),
Chicago, IL

Book Trade Association Membership:
IPG

2581

PAVILION CHILDREN'S BOOKS
Anova Books Ltd, 10 Southcombe Street,
London W1Y 0RA
Telephone: (020) 7605 1400
Fax: (020) 7605 1401
Email: childrens@anovabooks.com
Web Site: www.anovabooks.com

Trade Enquiries:
HarperCollins Distribution, Campsie View,
Westerhill Road, Bishopbriggs, Glasgow
G64 2QT
Telephone: 0141 772 3200
Email: orders@harpercollins.co.uk

Publisher: Ben Cameron
Sales Director: Jonathan White
Rights Manager: Sinead Hurley

Children's Books

New Titles: 15 (2008) , 20 (2009)

ISBNs, Imprints & Series:
978 1 84138, 978 1 85561 Belitha Press
978 1 84347, 978 1 903174 Big Fish
978 1 84365, 978 1 85145, 978 1 85793,
978 1 86205 Pavilion Children's Books
978 1 84458 Chrysalis Children's Books
978 1 85602 David Bennett Books
978 1 903370 Learning World
978 1 903954, 978 1 904516 Zigzag

Parent Company:
Anova Books Ltd

Associated Companies:
Belitha Press; David Bennett Books; Big
Fish; Learning World; Pavilion Books;
Zigzag

2582

**PAVILION JOURNALS (BRIGHTON)
LTD**
Suite N4, The Old Market,
Upper Market Street, Hove BN3 1AS
Telephone: 01273 783720
Fax: 01273 783723
Email: info@pavilionjournals.com
Web Site: www.pavilionjournals.com

Managers: Jo Sharrocks *(Publishing)*
Paul Somerville *(Marketing)*

*Academic & Scholarly; Electronic
(Professional & Academic); Medical (incl.
Self Help & Alternative Medicine);
Psychology & Psychiatry; Sociology &
Anthropology; Health & Social Care*

2583

PC PUBLISHING
Keeper's House, Merton, Thetford, Norfolk
IP25 6QH
Telephone: 01953 889900
Email: info@pc-publishing.com
Web Site: www.pc-publishing.com

Distribution:
Littlehampton Book Services,
Faraday Close, Durrington, Worthing,
West Sussex BN13 3RB
Telephone: 01903 828500
Fax: 01903 828625

Director: Philip Chapman *(Publisher)*

Music; Scientific & Technical; Computers

ISBNs, Imprints & Series:
978 1 870775, 978 1 906005

Parent Company:
UK: Music Technology Books Ltd

Overseas Representation:
Australia: Woodslane Pty Ltd, Warriewood,
NSW
USA: O'Reilly Associates, Sebastopol, CA

2584

PCCS BOOKS LTD
2 Cropper Row, Alton Road, Ross-on-Wye
HR9 5LA
Telephone: 01989 763900
Fax: 01989 763901
Email: contact@pccs-books.co.uk
Web Site: www.pccs-books.co.uk

Editorial:
The Old Police House, Llangarron,
Ross-on-Wye HR9 6PT
Telephone: 01989 770270
Fax: 01989 770700
Email: pete@pccs-books.co.uk
Web Site: www.pccs-books.co.uk

Directors: Maggie Taylor-Sanders
Peter J. Sanders

*Academic & Scholarly; Gender Studies;
Medical (incl. Self Help & Alternative
Medicine); Psychology & Psychiatry;
Religion & Theology*

New Titles: 11 (2008) , 17 (2009)
No of Employees: 7

ISBNs, Imprints & Series:
978 1 898059 Critical Psychology Division
(Series); PCCS Books; Person-Centred
Approach & Client-Centred Therapy
Essential Readers (Series); Primers Series;
Rogers' Therapeutic Conditions Series
(Vols 1–4); Steps in Counselling Series
978 1 906254 Straight Talking
Introductions Series

Book Trade Association Membership:
IPG

2585

PEARSON EDUCATION
Edinburgh Gate, Harlow, Essex CM20 2JE
Telephone: 01279 623623
Fax: 01279 431059
Web Site: www.pearson.com

*Academic & Scholarly; Educational &
Textbooks; Electronic (Professional &
Academic); Law*

Parent Company:
UK: Pearson Group

Book Trade Association Membership:
Publishers Association

2586

PEARSON EDUCATION
[formerly Harcourt Education]
Halley Court, Jordan Hill, Oxford OX2 8EJ
Telephone: 01865 311366
Fax: 01865 314641
Email: enquiries@pearson.com
Web Site: www.heinemann.co.uk

*Educational & Textbooks; Electronic
(Professional & Academic)*

Parent Company:
UK: Pearson Group

Associated Companies:
UK: Ginn; Heinemann; Payne-Gallway;
Raintree; Rigby

Book Trade Association Membership:
Publishers Association

2587

PEN PRESS
25 Eastern Place, Brighton BN2 1GJ
Telephone: 0845 108 0530
Fax: 01273 261434
Email: info@penpress.co.uk
Web Site: www.penpress.co.uk &
www.pulppress.co.uk

Directors: Lynn Ashman
Grace Rafael
Arts Design: Jacqueline Abromet
Senior Editor: Linda Lloyd
Rights: Danny Bowman *(Pulp Press)*

*Biography & Autobiography; Children's
Books; Cookery, Wines & Spirits; Crime; Do-
It-Yourself; Educational & Textbooks;
Fiction; Gay & Lesbian Studies; Health &
Beauty; Humour; Industry, Business &
Management; Literature & Criticism; Magic
& the Occult; Medical (incl. Self Help &
Alternative Medicine); Military & War;
Music; Philosophy; Poetry; Politics & World
Affairs; Reference Books, Directories &
Dictionaries; Religion & Theology; Science*

*Fiction; Sports & Games; Theatre, Drama &
Dance; Travel & Topography*

New Titles: 75 (2008) , 100 (2009)

ISBNs, Imprints & Series:
Pen Press; Pulp Press
978 1 900796, 978 1 904018, 978 1
904754, 978 1 905203, 978 1 906206,
978 1 906710
978 1 907172

Parent Company:
UK: Indepenpress Publishing Ltd

Book Trade Association Membership:
BA; IPG; The Guild of Master Craftsmen

2588

*THE PENGUIN GROUP (UK) LTD
80 Strand, London WC2R 0RL
Telephone: (020) 7010 3000
Fax: (020) 7010 6060
Email: ...@uk.penguingroup.com
Web Site: www.penguin.co.uk

Distribution Centre:
Penguin UK, Central Park, Rugby,
Warwickshire CV23 0WB
Telephone: 01788 514300

Also at:
Pearson Shared Services/Pearson Education,
Edinburgh Gate, Harlow, Essex CM20 2JE
Telephone: 01279 623102
Fax: 0870 850 5255
Email: veronica.reeve@pearsontc.co.uk

Chief Executive: John Makinson
Managing Directors: Helen Fraser
(Penguin)
Gary June *(Dorling Kindersley)*
Francesca Dow *(Puffin)*
Sally Floyer *(Frederick Warne)*
Tom Weldon *(Penguin General)*
Directors: Brian Landers *(Finance)*
Susan Taylor *(Human Resources)*
Peter Bowron *(Group Sales &
Distribution)*
Helena Peacock *(Legal)*
Simon Prosser *(Publishing – Hamish
Hamilton)*
Liz Allen *(Production)*
Tony Lacey *(Publishing – Viking)*
Juliet Annan *(Publishing – Fig Tree)*
Louise Moore *(Publishing – Michael
Joseph)*
Chantal Noel *(Rights – Penguin)*

*Academic & Scholarly; Antiques &
Collecting; Archaeology; Atlases & Maps;
Audio Books; Biography & Autobiography;
Children's Books; Cinema, Video, TV &
Radio; Cookery, Wines & Spirits; Crafts &
Hobbies; Crime; Do-It-Yourself; Fiction;
Gardening; Guide Books; Health & Beauty;
History & Antiquarian; Humour; Industry,
Business & Management; Literature &
Criticism; Medical (incl. Self Help &
Alternative Medicine); Military & War;
Music; Natural History; Philosophy;
Photography; Poetry; Politics & World
Affairs; Psychology & Psychiatry; Reference
Books, Directories & Dictionaries; Religion &
Theology; Travel & Topography*

ISBNs, Imprints & Series:
Joint ventures with BBC Paperbacks
978 0 14 Arkana; Ladybird; Penguin;
Penguin Audiobooks; Puffin
978 0 140 Allen Lane; Penguin Classics;
Penguin Music Classics; The Penguin
Press; Frederick Warne
978 0 241 Hamish Hamilton
978 0 670 Viking
978 0 7181 Michael Joseph

Associated Companies:
Dorling Kindersley Ltd; Hamish Hamilton
Ltd; Michael Joseph Ltd; Ladybird Books
Ltd [subsidiary of Penguin]; Rough

Guides; Ventura Publishing Ltd; Viking
Ltd; Frederick Warne (& Co) Ltd
Australia: Penguin Books Australia Ltd
Canada: Penguin Books Canada Ltd
New Zealand: Penguin Books (NZ) Ltd
USA: Penguin Putnam Inc

Distributor for:
Which; Wisden

Overseas Representation:
All other areas: Penguin International Sales,
London, UK
Australia: Penguin Books Australia Ltd,
Camberwell, Vic
Canada: Penguin Group Canada, Toronto,
Ont
France: Penguin France SA, Blagnac
Germany & Austria: Penguin Books
Deutschland GmbH, Frankfurt am Main,
Germany
India, Bangladesh, Sri Lanka & Nepal:
Penguin Books India, New Delhi, India
Italy: Penguin Italia srl, Milan
Netherlands: Penguin Books BV, Amsterdam
New Zealand: Penguin Books (New
Zealand) Ltd, Auckland
*Poland, Baltic States, Slovenia, Slovakia &
Ukraine:* Grazyna Soszynska, Poznan-
Baranowo, Poland
Singapore & Malaysia: Penguin Books
Singapore & Malaysia, Singapore
South Africa: Penguin Group SA, Rosebank
Spain & Portugal: Penguin Books SA,
Madrid, Spain
USA: Penguin Group USA, New York, NY

2589 ■

PENNANT BOOKS LTD
PO Box 5675, London W1A 3FB
Telephone: (020) 7387 6400
Email: info@pennantbooks.com
Web Site: www.pennantbooks.com

Distribution, Trade Enquiries & Orders:
Littlehampton Book Services,
Faraday Close, Worthing, West Sussex
BN13 3RB
Telephone: 01903 828500
Fax: 01903 828801
Email: enquiries@lbsltd.co.uk
Web Site: www.lbsltd.co.uk

Directors: Cass Pennant *(Managing)*
Paul Boon *(Marketing)*
Caxley Pennant
Editor: Paul A. Woods
PR – Events & Publicity: Philomena
Muinzer

*Academic & Scholarly; Biography &
Autobiography; Crime; Humour; Music;
Sociology & Anthropology; Sports & Games*

New Titles: 15 (2008) , 20 (2009)
No of Employees: 2

ISBNs, Imprints & Series: 978 1 906015

Associated Companies:
UK: Pennant Publishing Ltd

Overseas Representation:
Republic of Ireland: Compass Independent
Book Sales Ltd, Naas, Co Kildare

Book Trade Association Membership:
IPG

2590 ■

PENTATHOL PUBLISHING
40 Gibson Street, Wrexham,
Wrexham County LL13 7NS

Owner/Chief Executive: Athol E. Cowen

Poetry

ISBNs, Imprints & Series: 978 1 8730

Book Trade Association Membership:
Publishers Association; BA

2591 ■

PHAIDON PRESS LTD
18 Regent's Wharf, All Saints Street,
London N1 9PA
Telephone: (020) 7843 1000
Fax: (020) 7843 1010
Web Site: www.phaidon.com

Orders:
Phaidon Customer Services
Telephone: (020) 7843 1234
Fax: (020) 7843 1111
Email: sales@phaidon.com
Web Site: www.phaidon.com

Warehouse:
Grove Lane, Marston Trading Estate, Frome,
Somerset BA11 4AT
Telephone: 01373 474710
Fax: 01373 474711
Web Site: www.phaidon.com

Directors: Andrew Price *(Chairman)*
James Booth-Clibborn *(International
Sales & Marketing)*
Amanda Renshaw *(Editorial)*
Emilia Terragni *(Editorial)*
Jonathan Feinmesser *(Financial)*
Simon Gwynn *(UK Sales)*
Paul Hammond *(Production)*

*Academic & Scholarly; Architecture &
Design; Children's Books; Cinema, Video,
TV & Radio; Cookery, Wines & Spirits;
Fashion & Costume; Fine Art & Art History;
Illustrated & Fine Editions; Music;
Photography*

ISBNs, Imprints & Series: 978 0 7148

Associated Companies:
France: Phaidon Sarl
Germany: Phaidon Verlag
Japan: Phaidon KK
USA: Phaidon Press Inc

Overseas Representation:
Australia: United Book Distributors,
Scoresby, Vic
France: Phaidon SARL, Paris
Germany: Phaidon Verlag GmbH, Berlin
Italy: Messagerie Libri, Assago
New Zealand: Pearson New Zealand,
Auckland
Other Territories: Phaidon Press Ltd,
London, UK
South Africa: Book Promotions Pty Ltd,
Cape Town
Spain: Logista Librodis, Madrid
USA: Phaidon Press Inc, New York, NY

2592 ■

THE PHARMACEUTICAL PRESS
1 Lambeth High Street, London SE1 7JN
Telephone: (020) 7735 9141
Fax: (020) 7572 2509
Email: pharmpress@rpsgb.org
Web Site: www.pharmpress.com

Orders:
The Pharmaceutical Press, c/
o Turpin Distribution,
Stratton Business Park, Pegasus Drive,
Biggleswade, Beds SG18 8TQ
Telephone: 01767 604971
Fax: 01767 601640
Email: rps@turpin-distribution.com
Web Site: www.pharmpress.com

Representation (UK):
Compass Academic Ltd,
Barley Mow Centre,
10 Barley Mow Passage, London W4 4PH
Telephone: (020) 8994 6477
Fax: (020) 8400 6132
Email: ca@compass-academic.co.uk

Directors: R. Bolick *(Managing,
Publications)*
P. J. Weller *(Development)*
Managers: J. Wilson *(Production)*
J. Mulholland *(Licensing)*
J. Dargan *(Marketing)*
C. Watling *(Sales)*

*Academic & Scholarly; Electronic
(Professional & Academic); Medical (incl.
Self Help & Alternative Medicine); Scientific
& Technical; Veterinary Science*

New Titles: 25 (2008) , 30 (2009)
No of Employees: 130
Annual Turnover: £22M

ISBNs, Imprints & Series: 978 0 85369

Parent Company:
The Royal Pharmaceutical Society of Great
Britain

Overseas Representation:
Australia: Australian Pharmaceutical
Publishing Co Ltd, Hawthorn;
Pharmaceutical Society of Australia,
Curtin
Canada: Login Bros Canada, Winnipeg,
Man
Germany, Austria & Switzerland: Deutscher
Apotheker Verlag, Stuttgart, Germany
Greece: J & L Watt, Paleo Faliro
Israel: Probook, Tel Aviv
Italy: David Pickering, Rome
Japan: Maruzen Co Ltd, Tokyo
Middle East: James & Lorin Watt Ltd,
Publishing Consultants, Oxford, UK
New Zealand: Pharmaceutical Society of
New Zealand, Wellington
Republic of Ireland: Brookside Publishing
Services, Dublin
Scandinavia, Finland, Iceland & Baltic States:
David Towle International, Stockholm,
Sweden
South Africa: Pharmaceutical Society of
South Africa, Pretoria
Spain & Portugal: Christina de Lara Ruiz,
Madrid, Spain
USA: Pharmaceutical Press, Grayslake, IL

Book Trade Association Membership:
IGSMTP; Association of Learned &
Professional Society Publishers

2593 ■

PHILIP'S
2–4 Heron Quays, London E14 4JP
Telephone: (020) 7531 8427
Fax: (020) 7531 8474
Web Site: www.octopusbooks.co.uk

Distribution:
Littlehampton Book Services,
Faraday Close, Durrington, West Sussex
BN13 3RP
Telephone: 01903 828500
Fax: 01903 828625
Email: orders@lbsltd.co.uk
Web Site: www.lbsltd.co.uk

Directors: Victoria Dawbarn *(Rights &
Contract Sales)*
David Gaylard *(Mapping)*

*Atlases & Maps; Educational & Textbooks;
Natural History; Reference Books,
Directories & Dictionaries; Astronomy;
Globes*

ISBNs, Imprints & Series: 978 0 540

Parent Company:
Octopus Publishing Group [part of Hachette
Livre, France]

Overseas Representation:
See: Octopus Publishing Group, London, UK

Book Trade Association Membership:
International Map Traders Association

2594 ■

PIATKUS BOOKS
Little, Brown Book Group,
100 Victoria Embankment, London
EC4Y 0DY
Telephone: (020) 7911 8030
Fax: (020) 7911 8100
Email: info@littlebrown.co.uk
Web Site: www.littlebrown.co.uk &
www.piatkus.co.uk

Distribution:
Grantham Book Services,
Isaac Newton Way, Alma Industrial Estate,
Grantham, Lincs NG31 9SD
Telephone: 01476 541000
Fax: 01476 541060

Directors: Ursula Mackenzie *(Chief
Executive Officer & Publisher)*
Gill Bailey *(Non-Fiction Editorial)*
Robert Manser *(UK Sales & Marketing)*
Nick Ross *(Production)*
Emma Beswetherick *(Fiction)*
Julian Shaw *(Finance)*
Diane Spivey *(Rights)*

*Biography & Autobiography; Cookery,
Wines & Spirits; Crime; Fiction; Gender
Studies; Health & Beauty; History &
Antiquarian; Humour; Industry, Business &
Management; Magic & the Occult; Medical
(incl. Self Help & Alternative Medicine);
Military & War; Music; Psychology &
Psychiatry; Sociology & Anthropology*

New Titles: 200 (2008) , 180 (2009)

ISBNs, Imprints & Series:
978 0 7499 Portrait Books
978 0 7499, 978 0 86188 Piatkus Books

Parent Company:
France: Hachette Livre
UK: Little, Brown Book Group

Overseas Representation:
Australia: Hachette Livre Australia, Sydney,
NSW
Canada: Georgetown Warehouse, Toronto,
Ont
New Zealand: Hachette Livre New Zealand,
Auckland
Singapore & Malaysia: Pansing Distribution
Sdn Bhd, Singapore
South Africa: Penguin Books SA (Pty) Ltd,
Denver Ext 4

2595 ■

PICCADILLY PRESS
5 Castle Road, London NW1 8PR
Telephone: (020) 7267 4492
Fax: (020) 7267 4493
Email: books@piccadillypress.co.uk
Web Site: www.piccadillypress.co.uk

Warehouse & Distribution:
Grantham Book Services, Trent Road,
Grantham, Lincs NG31 7XQ
Telephone: 01476 541080
Fax: 01476 541061

Publisher & Managing Director: Brenda
Gardner
UK Rights & Book Clubs: Lea Garton
Editorial/Commissioning: Ruth Williams
Anne Clark
Rights: Margot Edwards
Financial Controller: Geoffrey Lill
Publicity: Mary Byrne
Managers: Geoff Barlow *(Production)*
Robert Snuggs *(Sales)*
Assistant Editor: Melissa Hyder
Publishing Assistant: Vivien Tesseras

Children's Books; Books for Parents

New Titles: 35 (2008) , 35 (2009)
No of Employees: 4

ISBNs, Imprints & Series:
978 1 84812, 978 1 85340

Overseas Representation:
Australia: Peribo Pty Ltd, Mount Kuring-Gai, NSW
Malaysia & Singapore: Bounce! Sales & Marketing Ltd, London, UK
New Zealand: South Pacific Book Distributors, Auckland
Southern Africa: Trinity Books CC, Randburg, South Africa

Book Trade Association Membership:
IPG

2596

PICKERING & CHATTO (PUBLISHERS) LTD
21 Bloomsbury Way, London WC1A 2TH
Telephone: (020) 7405 1005
Fax: (020) 7405 6216
Email: info@pickeringchatto.co.uk
Web Site: www.pickeringchatto.com

Distribution & Orders:
Turpin Distribution Ltd,
Stratton Business Park, Pegasus Drive, Biggleswade, Beds SG18 8QT
Telephone: 01767 604800
Fax: 01767 601640
Web Site: www.turpin-distribution.com

Directors: James Powell
Lord Rees-Mogg *(Chairman)*
Editorial & Rights: Mark Pollard
David Heaton *(Production)*
Finance: Stephen Warren

Academic & Scholarly; Economics; History & Antiquarian; Literature & Criticism; Religion & Theology; Scientific & Technical

New Titles: 60 (2008) , 70 (2009)
No of Employees: 11
Annual Turnover: £1.1M

ISBNs, Imprints & Series: 978 1 85196

Overseas Representation:
India: Applied Media, New Delhi
Japan: Japan Book Associates, Kyoto
Spain & Portugal: Iberian Book Services, Madrid, Spain
Taiwan: Unifacmanu Trading Co Ltd, Taipei
USA: Ashgate Publishing Co, Burlington, VT

Book Trade Association Membership:
IPG

2597

PIPERS' ASH LTD
Church Road, Christian Malford, Chippenham, Wiltshire SN15 4BW
Telephone: 01249 720563
Fax: 0870 056 8916
Email: pipersash@supamasu.com
Web Site: www.supamasu.com

Managing Director: A. Tyson
Secretary: Mrs A. M. Tyson

Biography & Autobiography; Children's Books; Fiction; Literature & Criticism; Philosophy; Poetry; Psychology & Psychiatry; Religion & Theology; Science Fiction; Sports & Games; Theatre, Drama & Dance

New Titles: 12 (2008) , 12 (2009)

ISBNs, Imprints & Series:
978 1 902628, 978 1 904494, 978 1 906928 Biographies; Children's Libraries; Cornucopia; Kickstarters; Stagecraft; Trinity Collections

Overseas Representation:
Australia: Stephen Tyson, Sydney

New Zealand: Dr Yvonne Eve Walus, Auckland

2598

PIQUANT EDITIONS
4 Thornton Road, Carlisle, Cumbria CA3 9HZ
Telephone: 01228 525075
Fax: 01228 501051
Email: info@piquant.net
Web Site: www.piquant.net

Representation (UK):
IVP, Norton Street, Nottingham NG7 3HR
Telephone: 0115 978 1054
Email: sales@ivpbooks.com

Director: Pieter Kwant
Publisher & Editor: Elria Kwant
Sales & Operations Manager: Luke Lewis

Biography & Autobiography; Fiction; Fine Art & Art History; Illustrated & Fine Editions; Reference Books, Directories & Dictionaries; Religion & Theology

New Titles: 4 (2008) , 6 (2009)

ISBNs, Imprints & Series:
978 1 903689 Fire and Blood series; Piquant Editions; Visibilia series

Overseas Representation:
USA: STL Inc, Waynesboro, GA

Book Trade Association Membership:
Publishers Association

2599

THE PLAYWRIGHTS PUBLISHING CO
70 Nottingham Road, Burton Joyce, Notts NG14 5AL
Telephone: 01159 313356
Email: playwrightspublishing@yahoo.com
Web Site: www.geocities.com/playwrightspublishingco

Proprietor: Liz Breeze
Consultant: Tony Breeze

Theatre, Drama & Dance

New Titles: 6 (2008) , 6 (2009)
No of Employees: 2

ISBNs, Imprints & Series:
978 1 872758 Ventus Books
978 1 873130 Playwrights Publishing Co

Associated Companies:
Ventus Books

Distributor for:
Ventus Books

2600

PLOWRIGHT PRESS
PO Box 66, Warwick CV34 4XE
Telephone: 01926 499433
Fax: 01926 499433
Web Site: www.plowrightpress.co.uk

Director: Ruth Johns

Biography & Autobiography; Environment & Development Studies; Gender Studies; History & Antiquarian; Sociology & Anthropology

ISBNs, Imprints & Series:
978 0 907895, 978 0 951696, 978 0 954312, 978 0 955094 'Ordinary' Lives Series

Distributor for:
Family First Ltd; Ruth's Archive

Book Trade Association Membership:
IPG; Society of Authors

2601

PLUTO BOOKS LTD
345 Archway Road, London N6 5AA
Telephone: (020) 8374 2193
Fax: (020) 8348 9133
Email: pluto@plutobooks.com
Web Site: www.plutobooks.com

Trade Enquiries & Orders:
Marston Book Services,
Unit 160 Milton Park, Abingdon, Oxon OX14 4SD
Telephone: 01235 465500
Fax: 01235 465555
Email: trade.orders@marston.co.uk
Web Site: www.marston.co.uk

Directors: Anne Beech *(Managing)*
Roger Van Zwanenberg *(Chair)*
Simon Liebesny *(Sales)*
Rights & Permissions: Gilly Duff
Managing Editor: Robert Webb
Marketing Manager: Alec Gregory

Academic & Scholarly; Cinema, Video, TV & Radio; Economics; Environment & Development Studies; Gender Studies; Law; Literature & Criticism; Philosophy; Politics & World Affairs; Sociology & Anthropology

New Titles: 50 (2008) , 55 (2009)

ISBNs, Imprints & Series:
978 0 7453, 978 0 86104 Pluto Press
978 1 85172 Journeyman Press

Distributor for:
Paradigm Publishers

Overseas Representation:
Australia: Palgrave Macmillan, Melbourne, Vic
Canada (stock-holding distributor): Fernwood Books, Toronto, Ont
Germany: Missing Link International Booksellers, Bremen, Germany
Germany, Austria, Switzerland, Scandinavia, Benelux, France, Italy, Greece, Malta, Central Europe & Baltic States: Andrew Durnell Marketing Ltd, Tunbridge Wells, UK
India: Maya Publishers Pvt Ltd, New Delhi
Japan: United Publishers Services Ltd, Tokyo
Middle East: International Publishers Representatives (IPR) Ltd, Nicosia, Cyprus
Republic of Ireland & Northern Ireland: Brookside Publishing Services, Dublin, Republic of Ireland
South Africa: Horizon Books, Plumstead
South East Asia: Taylor & Francis Asia Pacific, Kowloon, Hong Kong; Taylor & Francis Asia Pacific, Petaling Jaya, Malaysia; Taylor & Francis, Beijing, P. R. of China; Taylor & Francis Asia Pacific, Singapore
Spain & Portugal: Iberian Book Services, Madrid, Spain
USA: Palgrave Macmillan, New York, NY
USA (Orders): MPS Distribution Center, Gordonsville, VA, USA

Book Trade Association Membership:
IPG

2602

THE POLICY PRESS
University of Bristol, Fourth Floor, Beacon House, Queen's Road, Bristol BS8 1QU
Telephone: 0117 331 4054
Fax: 0117 331 4093
Email: tpp-info@bris.ac.uk
Web Site: www.policypress.org.uk

Distribution:
Marston Book Services, PO Box 269, Abingdon, Oxon OX14 4YN
Telephone: 01235 465500
Fax: 01235 465556

Email: direct.orders@marston.co.uk
Web Site: www.marston.co.uk/

UK Representation:
Compass Academic Ltd,
13 Progress Business Centre, Whittle Parkway, Slough SL1 6DQ
Telephone: 01628 559500
Fax: 01628 663876
Email: ca@compass-academic.co.uk
Web Site: www.academic.compass-booksales.co.uk

Directors: Alison Shaw
Julia Mortimer *(Assistant)*

Academic & Scholarly; Economics; Educational & Textbooks; Gender Studies; Politics & World Affairs; Sociology & Anthropology

ISBNs, Imprints & Series:
978 1 84742, 978 1 86134

Parent Company:
University of Bristol

Overseas Representation:
Australia, New Zealand & Papua New Guinea: DA Information Services Pty Ltd, Mitcham, Vic, Australia
Europe (excluding UK): Durnell Marketing Ltd, Tunbridge Wells, UK
India, Sri Lanka, Nepal, Bangladesh & Bhutan: Surit Mitra, Maya Publishers Pvt Ltd, New Delhi, India
Japan: Kinokuniya Co Ltd, Tokyo; Maruzen Co Ltd, Tokyo
Malaysia & Brunei: UBSD Distribution Sdn Bhd, Selangor, Malaysia
Middle East & North Africa: Dar Kreidieh, Beirut, Lebanon
Pakistan: Tahir M. Lodhi, Lahore
South Africa: Blue Weaver Marketing, Tokai
Taiwan: Unifacmanu Trading Co Ltd, Taipei
Thailand, Taiwan, Hong Kong, Korea, China, Singapore, Malaysia, Philippines & Vietnam: Tony Poh Leong Wah, Singapore, Singapore
USA & Canada: International Specialized Book Services Inc, Portland, OR, USA

Book Trade Association Membership:
IPG

2603

POLITY PRESS
65 Bridge Street, Cambridge CB2 1UR
Telephone: 01223 324315
Fax: 01223 461385
Email: editorial@polity.co.uk
Web Site: www.polity.co.uk

Distribution Warehouse:
John Wiley & Sons Ltd, 1 Oldlands Way, Bognor Regis, West Sussex PO22 9SA
Telephone: 01243 843294
Fax: 01243 843303
Email: cs-books@wiley.co.uk

Publicity:
Polity Press, 9600 Garsington Road, Oxford OX4 2DQ
Telephone: 01865 476711
Fax: 01865 471711
Email: boconnor@wiley.com
Web Site: www.polity.co.uk

Directors: Anthony Giddens *(Editorial)*
David Held *(Editorial)*
John Thompson *(Editorial)*

Academic & Scholarly; Cinema, Video, TV & Radio; Educational & Textbooks; Gender Studies; History & Antiquarian; Literature & Criticism; Philosophy; Politics & World Affairs; Sociology & Anthropology

New Titles: 77 (2008) , 116 (2009)
No of Employees: 22

ISBNs, Imprints & Series: 978 0 7456

Overseas Representation:
Australia: John Wiley & Sons Australia Ltd,
Milton, Qld
Canada: John Wiley & Sons Canada Ltd,
Etobicoke, Ont
Europe, Middle East & Africa: Karen
Wootton, John Wiley & Sons Ltd,
Chichester, UK
Germany: Wiley-VCH, Weinheim
Japan: Wiley Japan, Tokyo
Singapore: John Wiley & Sons (Asia) Pte Ltd
USA: John Wiley & Sons Inc, Hoboken, NJ

Book Trade Association Membership:
IPG

2604 ■■■■■■■■

PORTHILL PUBLISHERS
PO Box 311, Edgware, Middx HA9 9EA
Telephone: (020) 8958 6783
Fax: (020) 8905 4516

Director: Radomir Putnikovich
Secretary: Penelope Putnikovich

Children's Books; Fine Art & Art History;
Humour

ISBNs, Imprints & Series: 978 1 870732

2605 ■■■■■■■■

PORTICO
10 Southcombe Street, London W14 0RA
Telephone: (020) 7605 1400
Fax: (020) 7605 1401
Web Site: www.anovabooks.com

Warehouse, Trade Orders & Enquiries:
HarperCollins, Glasgow G64 2QT
Telephone: 0141 306 3100
Fax: 0141 306 3767

Head of Marketing & Publicity: Jane Ellis

Humour; Languages & Linguistics; Music;
Reference Books, Directories &
Dictionaries; Sports & Games

ISBNs, Imprints & Series: 978 1 9063

Parent Company:
Anova Books

Overseas Representation:
Australia: HarperCollins Publishers, Pymble,
NSW
Belgium, France, Netherlands &
Luxembourg: Ted Dougherty, London,
UK
Caribbean, Mexico & Central America:
Christopher Humphrys, Lynda Hopkins,
Humphrys Roberts Associates, London,
UK
Eastern Europe: Csaba Lengyel de Bagota,
Jackie Lengyel de Bagota, CLB Marketing
Services, Budapest, Hungary
Far East: Julian Ashton, Ashton
International Marketing Services,
Sevenoaks, Kent, UK
Germany, Switzerland & Austria: Gabriele
Kern Publishers Services, Frankfurt-am-
Main, Germany
India: Anova Books, London, UK
Italy, Spain, Portugal & Greece: Penny
Padovani, Padovani Books Ltd, London,
UK
Middle East: Peter Ward Book Exports,
London, UK
New Zealand: HarperCollins (NZ) Ltd,
Glenfield, Auckland
Pakistan: Tahir M. Lodhi, Lahore
Russia, Baltic States, Israel & Sub-Saharan
Africa: Tony Moggach, InterMedia
Americana IMA Ltd, London, UK
Scandinavia: Katie McNeish, McNeish
Publishing International, East Sussex, UK
Singapore: Pansing Distribution Sdn Bhd

South Africa: Quartet Sales & Marketing,
Northcliffe
South America: Terry Roberts, Humphrys
Roberts Associates, Cotia SP, Brazil
USA & Canada: Trafalgar Square Publishing,
distributed by Independent Publishers
Group, Chicago, IL, USA

Book Trade Association Membership:
IPG

2606 ■■■■■■■■

PORTLAND PRESS LTD
Commerce Way, Colchester CO2 8HP
Telephone: 01206 796351
Fax: 01206 799331
Email: editorial@portlandpress.com &
sales@portland-services.com
Web Site: www.portlandpress.com &
www.portland-services.com

Directors: Rhonda Oliver *(Managing)*
John Misselbrook *(Financial)*
Adam Marshall *(Marketing & Sales)*
John Day *(IT)*

Academic & Scholarly; Biology & Zoology;
Educational & Textbooks; Electronic
(Professional & Academic); Medical (incl.
Self Help & Alternative Medicine);
Reference Books, Directories &
Dictionaries; Scientific & Technical

New Titles: 3 (2008), 3 (2009)
No of Employees: 90
Annual Turnover: £4.5M

ISBNs, Imprints & Series:
978 0 904498 Biochemical Society
978 1 85578, 978 1 85578 Portland Press

Parent Company:
The Biochemical Society

Distributor for:
Antiquity Publications Ltd; Bioscientifica
Ltd; Earthscan; Energy Institute; Expert
Information; International Water
Association Publishing; The Policy Press;
Practical Action Publishing; Professional
Engineering Publishing; The Royal
Society; Royal Society of Chemistry;
Royal Society of Medicine; SCR
Publishing; The Society for
Endocrinology; Vathek Publishing; WEF
Publishing

Overseas Representation:
Australia: DA Information Services Pty Ltd,
Mitcham, Vic
India: Affiliated East-West Press Pvt Ltd,
New Delhi
Japan: USACO Corporation, Tokyo

Book Trade Association Membership:
IGSMTP; IPG; Association of Learned &
Professional Society Publishers; UK Serials
Group

2607 ■■■■■■■■

PORTOBELLO BOOKS LTD
12 Addison Avenue, Holland Park, London
W11 4QR
Telephone: (020) 7605 1380
Fax: (020) 7605 1361
Email: mail@portobellobooks.com
Web Site: www.portobellobooks.com

Directors: David Graham *(Managing)*
Laura Barber *(Editorial)*
Angela Rose *(Rights)*
Pru Rowlandson *(Publicity)*
Brigid Macleod *(Sales)*
Publisher: Philip Gwyn Jones

Biography & Autobiography; Fiction;
History & Antiquarian; Politics & World
Affairs; Travel & Topography

New Titles: 28 (2008), 22 (2009)

Annual Turnover: £1.1M

ISBNs, Imprints & Series: 978 1 84627

Associated Companies:
UK: Granta

Overseas Representation:
Australia & New Zealand: Allen & Unwin Pty
Ltd, Sydney, NSW, Australia
Canada: House of Anansi, Toronto, Ont
European Union: Faber & Faber, London,
UK
Far East: Julian Ashton, Sevenoaks, Kent,
UK
Netherlands: Nilsson & Lamm BV, Weesp
South Africa: Penguin Books South Africa
(Pty) Ltd, Johannesburg

Book Trade Association Membership:
IPG; Independent Alliance

2608 ■■■■■■■■

POSITIVE PRESS LTD
28a Gloucester Road, Trowbridge, Wilts
BA14 0AA
Telephone: 01225 719204
Fax: 01225 712187
Email: dankat@jennymosley.co.uk
Web Site: www.circle-time.co.uk

Managing Director: Jenny Mosley
Sales Account Manager: Danka Tadd

Children's Books; Educational & Textbooks

New Titles: 4 (2008)
No of Employees: 8

ISBNs, Imprints & Series:
978 0 09540, 978 0 09545, 978 0 95301,
978 1 90460, 978 1 90486

Book Trade Association Membership:
BA

2609 ■■■■■■■■

PRACTICAL PRE-SCHOOL BOOKS
St Jude's Church, Dulwich Road, Herne Hill,
London SE24 0PB
Telephone: (020) 7738 5454
Fax: (020) 7733 2325
Email:
orders@practicalpreschoolbooks.com
Web Site:
www.practicalpreschoolbooks.com

Directors: Rebecca Linssen *(Group*
Editorial)
Mark Allen *(Managing)*
Associate Publisher: Angela Shaw
(Publishing)
Publishing Manager: Rebecca Haworth
(Publishing)

Educational & Textbooks

New Titles: 12 (2008), 12 (2009)

ISBNs, Imprints & Series:
978 1 902438, 978 1 904575

Parent Company:
UK: Mark Allen Group

Book Trade Association Membership:
EPC; IPG

2610 ■■■■■■■■

PRESTEL PUBLISHING LTD
4 Bloomsbury Place, London WC1A 2QA
Telephone: (020) 7323 5004
Fax: (020) 7636 8004
Email: sales@prestel-uk.co.uk
Web Site: www.prestel.com

Warehouse, Trade Enquiries & Orders:
Macmillan Distribution Ltd, Brunel Road,
Houndmills, Basingstoke, Hants RG21 6XS

Telephone: 01256 302692
Fax: 01256 812588
Email: orders@macmillan.co.uk

Managing Director: Andrew Hansen
Commissioning Editor (London): Philippa
Hurd
Sales, Marketing & Publicity Executive:
Anna Kenning
Key Accounts Manager: Oliver Barter

Antiques & Collecting; Archaeology;
Architecture & Design; Children's Books;
Cinema, Video, TV & Radio; Fashion &
Costume; Fine Art & Art History; Guide
Books; Photography; Travel & Topography

ISBNs, Imprints & Series:
978 0 9542079, 978 1 904563 Trolley
978 1 934772 Periscope Publishing Ltd
978 3 7913 Adventures in Art Series;
Pegasus Series

Parent Company:
Germany: Prestel Verlag GmbH & Co KG
[part of Verlagsgruppe Random House
GmbH]

Associated Companies:
USA: Prestel Publishing

Overseas Representation:
Africa (excluding South Africa): Tony
Moggach, InterMedia Americana (IMA)
Ltd, London, UK
Asia (including China, Hong Kong, Korea,
Philippines & Taiwan): Ed Summerson,
Asia Publishers Services Ltd, Hong Kong
Australia: Peribo Pty Ltd, Mount Kuring-Gai,
NSW
Canada: Canadian Manda Group, Toronto,
Ont
France: Interart SARL, Paris
Iran: Book City, Tehran
Israel: Lonnie Kahn & Co Ltd, Rishon Lezion
Japan: Andrew Hansen, Prestel, London, UK
Malta, Cyprus, Turkey, Middle East & North
Africa: Peter Ward Book Exports, London,
UK
Netherlands & Belgium: Nilsson & Lamm BV,
Weesp, Netherlands
Scandinavia: Elisabeth Harder-Kreimann,
Hamburg, Germany
South & Central America: David Williams,
InterMedia Americana (IMA) Ltd,
London, UK
South Africa: Zytek Publishing, Gardenview
South East Asia: Peter Couzens, Sales East,
Bangkok, Thailand
Southern Europe: Books for Europe,
Massagno, Switzerland
Switzerland: Buchzentrum AG, Hägendorf
USA: Prestel Publishing, New York, NY

2611 ■■■■■■■■

PRINCETON UNIVERSITY PRESS
6 Oxford Street, Woodstock, Oxon
OX20 1TW
Telephone: 01993 814500
Fax: 01993 814504
Email: admin@pupress.co.uk
Web Site: www.pup.princeton.edu

Publishing Director - Europe: Richard
Baggaley
Publicity & Marketing Manager: Caroline
Priday
Senior Editor: Ian Malcolm
Director of Subsidiary Rights: Benjamin
Tate

Academic & Scholarly; Biology & Zoology;
Economics; Educational & Textbooks;
Electronic (Professional & Academic);
Environment & Development Studies;
History & Antiquarian; Industry, Business &
Management; Law; Mathematics &
Statistics; Natural History; Philosophy;
Politics & World Affairs; Reference Books,
Directories & Dictionaries; Scientific &
Technical; Sociology & Anthropology

ISBNs, Imprints & Series: 978 0 691

Parent Company:
USA: Princeton University Press

Overseas Representation:
All other countries: Export Department, Princeton University Press, Ewing, NJ, USA
Continental Europe & Israel: Customer Service Operations, Princeton University Press, c/o John Wiley & Sons Ltd, Bognor Regis, UK

Book Trade Association Membership:
IPG

2612 ▬▬▬▬

PROFESSIONAL ENGINEERING PUBLISHING
1 Birdcage Walk, London SW1H 9JJ
Telephone: (020) 7304 6852
Fax: (020) 7304 6852
Email: peterw@pepublishing.com
Web Site: www.pepublishing.com

Directors: Peter Williams *(Academic)*
Paul Williams *(Commercial)*
John Pullin *(Editorial)*
Managers: D. Fidler *(Systems Finance)*
M. Spencer *(Production)*
M. Lord *(Marketing & Development)*
R. Grimes *(Journals Publisher)*

Academic & Scholarly; Aviation; Computer Science; Engineering; Medical (incl. Self Help & Alternative Medicine); Nautical; Scientific & Technical; Transport

Annual Turnover: £7M

Parent Company:
Institution of Mechanical Engineers

Overseas Representation:
India: Allied Publishers Ltd, New Delhi

Book Trade Association Membership:
Association of Learned & Professional Society Publishers; UK Serials Group (UKSG)

2613 ▬▬▬▬

PROFILE BOOKS
3A Exmouth House, Pine Street, London EC1R 0JH
Telephone: (020) 7841 6300
Fax: (020) 7841 3969
Email: info@profilebooks.com
Web Site: www.profilebooks.com

Directors: Andrew Franklin *(Managing)*
Stephen Brough *(Editorial)*
Kate Griffin *(Marketing)*
Claire Beaumont *(Sales)*
Ruth Killick *(Publicity)*
Rights Manager: Penny Daniel *(Editorial & Rights)*
Publishers: Pete Ayrton
Daniel Crewe *(Associate)*
Mark Ellingham
Publicity: Rebecca Gray

Biography & Autobiography; Crime; Fiction; History & Antiquarian; Industry, Business & Management; Politics & World Affairs

New Titles: 65 (2008) , 75 (2009)
No of Employees: 23
Annual Turnover: £9M

ISBNs, Imprints & Series:
The Economist Books; Profile Books; Serpent's Tail

Overseas Representation:
Australia & New Zealand: Allen & Unwin Pty Ltd, Sydney, NSW, Australia
Europe: Faber & Faber, London, UK

Hong Kong, China, Taiwan & Philippines: Asia Publishers Services Ltd, Hong Kong
India & Pakistan: Viva Books, New Delhi, India
Middle East, North Africa & Turkey: Peter Ward Book Exports, London, UK
Singapore, Malaysia, Thailand & Vietnam: APD Singapore Pte Ltd, Singapore
South Africa: Book Promotions Pty Ltd, Cape Town
USA & Canada: Consortium Book Sales & Distribution, Minneapolis, MN, USA

Book Trade Association Membership:
IPG

2614 ▬▬▬▬

PROQUEST
International Office, The Quorum, Barnwell Road, Cambridge CB5 8SW
Telephone: 01223 215512
Fax: 01223 215514
Email: marketing@proquest.co.uk
Web Site: www.proquest.co.uk

Sales: T. Robinson
General Manager & Vice-President Technology & Operations: J. Taylor
Marketing: S. Tilley

Academic & Scholarly; Accountancy & Taxation; Agriculture; Bibliography & Library Science; Biology & Zoology; Economics; Electronic (Educational); Electronic (Professional & Academic); History & Antiquarian; Literature & Criticism; Mathematics & Statistics; Medical (incl. Self Help & Alternative Medicine); Music; Physics; Poetry; Politics & World Affairs; Psychology & Psychiatry; Reference Books, Directories & Dictionaries; Religion & Theology; Scientific & Technical; Theatre, Drama & Dance

ISBNs, Imprints & Series: 978 0 85964

Parent Company:
USA: ProQuest

Overseas Representation:
Australia & New Zealand: ProQuest, Melbourne, Vic, Australia
China: ProQuest, Beijing, P. R. of China
Dubai: ProQuest, Dubai Media City, UAE
Europe: ProQuest, Cambridge, UK
Germany: ProQuest, Friedberg
Hong Kong: ProQuest, Wanchai
Italy: ProQuest, Florence
Japan: ProQuest, Yokohama
Korea, Taiwan, Philippines & Vietnam: ProQuest, Seoul, Republic of Korea
Latin America: ProQuest, Rio de Janeiro, Brazil
North America: ProQuest, Ann Arbor, MI, USA
South East Asia & Far East: ProQuest, Petaling Jaya, Malaysia
Spain: ProQuest España, Madrid

Book Trade Association Membership:
Publishers Association

2615 ▬▬▬▬

PROSPECT BOOKS
Allaleigh House, Blackawton, Totnes, Devon TQ9 7DL
Telephone: 01803 712269
Fax: 01803 712311
Email: tom.jaine@prospectbooks.co.uk
Web Site: www.prospectbooks.co.uk

Distribution:
Central Books, 99 Wallis Road, London E9 5LN
Telephone: (020) 8986 4854

Owner: Tom Jaine

Cookery, Wines & Spirits

New Titles: 6 (2008) , 10 (2009)

2616 ▬▬▬▬

PUBLISHING HOUSE
Trinity Place, Barnstaple EX32 9HG
Telephone: 01271 328892
Fax: 01271 328768
Email: mail@vernoncoleman.com
Web Site: www.vernoncoleman.com

Publishing Director: Sue Ward

Fiction; Medical (incl. Self Help & Alternative Medicine); Politics & World Affairs

ISBNs, Imprints & Series:
978 0 9503527, 978 1 898146 Chilton Designs
978 0 9521492, 978 1 898947 European Medical Journal
978 1 899726 Blue Books
978 1 904001 Great Fiction

2617 ▬▬▬▬

PUNK PUBLISHING LTD
3 The Yard, Pegasus Place, London SE11 5SD
Telephone: (020) 7820 9333
Email: sophie@punkpublishing.co.uk
Web Site: www.punkpublishing.com

Publisher: Jonathan Knight
Editor: Keith Didcock

Travel & Topography

New Titles: 3 (2008) , 5 (2009)
No of Employees: 3

ISBNs, Imprints & Series:
978 0 9552036, 978 1 9068890

Book Trade Association Membership:
IPG

2618 ▬▬▬▬

PUSHKIN PRESS
12 Chester Terrace, London NW1 4ND
Telephone: (020) 7730 0750
Email: books@pushkinpress.com
Web Site: www.pushkinpress.com

Executive: Melissa Ulfane

Fiction

New Titles: 14 (2008) , 16 (2009)

ISBNs, Imprints & Series:
978 1 901285, 978 1 906548

2619 ▬▬▬▬

QUADRILLE PUBLISHING LTD
5th Floor, Alhambra House, 27–31 Charing Cross Road, London WC2H 0LS
Telephone: (020) 7839 7117
Fax: (020) 7839 7118
Email: enquiries@quadrille.co.uk

Directors: Alison Cathie *(Managing)*
Jane O'Shea *(Publishing)*
Vincent Smith *(Deputy Managing)*
Helen Lewis *(Creative)*
Ian West *(Sales)*
Melanie Gray *(International Sales)*
Manager: Clare Lattin *(Publicity)*

Architecture & Design; Cookery, Wines & Spirits; Crafts & Hobbies; Do-It-Yourself; Fashion & Costume; Gardening; Health & Beauty; Humour; Magic & the Occult; Medical (incl. Self Help & Alternative Medicine); Photography

New Titles: 35 (2008) , 39 (2009)
No of Employees: 31

ISBNs, Imprints & Series:
978 1 844000, 978 1 899988, 978 1 902757, 978 1 903845

Book Trade Association Membership:
BA

2620 ▬▬▬▬

QUARTET BOOKS
27 Goodge Street, London W1T 2LD
Telephone: (020) 7636 3992
Fax: (020) 7637 1866
Email: info@quartetbooks.co.uk
Web Site: www.quartetbooks.co.uk

Warehouse:
NBN International, Estover Road, Plymouth PL6 7PZ
Telephone: 01752 202300
Fax: 01752 202330
Web Site: www.nbninternational.com

Director: David Elliott

Biography & Autobiography; Fiction; History & Antiquarian; Music

New Titles: 21 (2008) , 18 (2009)
No of Employees: 5

ISBNs, Imprints & Series:
978 0 86072 Robin Clark

Parent Company:
Namara Group

Associated Companies:
Robin Clark; The Women's Press

Overseas Representation:
Australia: Tower Books Pty Ltd, Frenchs Forest, NSW
Caribbean & South America: InterMedia Americana (IMA) Ltd, London, UK
France, Belgium, Germany, Austria, Switzerland, Italy & Greece: Ted Dougherty, London, UK
India, Denmark, Finland, Norway & Sweden: Quartet Books Ltd, London, UK
Japan: Japan/English Service Inc, Chiba-ken
Middle East: Peter Ward Book Exports, London, UK
Netherlands: Nilsson & Lamm BV, Weesp
New Zealand: Southern Publishers Group, Auckland
South Africa: Trinity Books CC, Randburg
Spain & Portugal: Iberian Book Services, Madrid, Spain
Sub-Saharan Africa (excluding South Africa) & Eastern Europe: InterMedia Americana (IMA) Ltd, London, UK
USA: Interlink Publishing Group Inc, Northampton, MA

2621 ▬▬▬▬

QUILLER PUBLISHING LTD
Wykey House, Wykey, Shrewsbury SY4 1JA
Telephone: 01939 261616
Fax: 01939 261606
Email: info@quillerbooks.com
Web Site: www.countrybooksdirect.com

Warehouse, Distribution, Orders & Sales Enquiries:
Grantham Book Services, Trent Road, Grantham, Lincolnshire NG31 7XQ
Telephone: 01476 541080
Fax: 01476 541061
Email: orders@gbs.tbs-ltd.co.uk

Directors: Andrew Johnston *(Managing)*
John Beaton *(Editorial)*
Managers: Julie Ward *(Marketing)*
Jonathan Heath *(Sales)*
Rob Dixon *(Production)*

Animal Care & Breeding; Antiques &

Collecting; Biography & Autobiography; Cookery, Wines & Spirits; Crafts & Hobbies; Fine Art & Art History; Gardening; Humour; Illustrated & Fine Editions; Military & War; Natural History; Nautical; Reference Books, Directories & Dictionaries; Sports & Games; Transport; Travel & Topography; Veterinary Science

New Titles: 35 (2008) , 35 (2009)
No of Employees: 10

ISBNs, Imprints & Series:
978 0 901366, 978 1 872082, 978 1 872119, 978 1 905693 Kenilworth Press
978 0 907621, 978 1 84689, 978 1 904057 Quiller Press
978 0 948253 The Sportsman's Press
978 1 84037, 978 1 85310 Swan Hill Press

Distributor for:
South Africa: Rowland Ward
UK: The Pony Club
USA: Half Halt Press; Stackpole Books [Hunting & Fishing Titles only]

Overseas Representation:
Australia: Peribo Pty Ltd, Mount Kuring-Gai, NSW
Europe & Scandinavia: Books for Europe, London, UK
South Africa: Trinity Books CC, Randburg
USA & Canada: Half Halt Press, Boonsboro, MD, USA; Stackpole Books Inc, Mechanicsburg, PA, USA

Book Trade Association Membership:
IPG

2622 ▬▬▬

*QUINTESSENCE PUBLISHING CO LTD
Quintessence House, Grafton Road, New Malden, Surrey KT3 3AB
Telephone: (020) 8949 6087
Fax: (020) 8336 1484
Email: info@quintpub.co.uk
Web Site: www.quintpub.co.uk

Finance Manager: Mrs Susan Newbury

Medical (incl. Self Help & Alternative Medicine)

ISBNs, Imprints & Series:
978 0 86715, 978 1 85097, 978 3 87632, 978 4 87417

Parent Company:
Germany: Quintessenz Verlag

Associated Companies:
Japan: Quintessence Publishing Co Ltd
USA: Quintessence Publishing Co Inc

Distributor for:
Germany: Quintessenz Verlags GmbH
Japan: Quintessence Publishing Co Ltd
USA: Quintessence Publishing Co Inc

Overseas Representation:
Australia: Martin Halas Dental Co Pty Ltd, Sydney
Brazil: Quintessence Editora Ltda, São Paulo

Book Trade Association Membership:
BA

2623 ▬▬▬

RACEFORM LTD
RFM House, Compton, Newbury, Berks RG20 6NL
Telephone: 01635 578080
Fax: 01635 578101
Email: julian.brown@racingpost.com
Web Site: www.racingpost.com/shop

Book Publishing Manager: Julian Brown

Sports & Games

New Titles: 45 (2008) , 50 (2009)
No of Employees: 18

ISBNs, Imprints & Series:
978 1 904317, 978 1 905153, 978 1 906820 Raceform
978 1 905156 Highdown Books / Racing Post

Parent Company:
Racing Post

2624 ▬▬▬

THE RADCLIFFE PRESS
6 Salem Road, London W2 4BU
Telephone: (020) 7243 1225
Fax: (020) 7243 1226

Distributor:
Macmillan Distribution Ltd, Brunel Road, Houndmills, Basingstoke, Hants RG21 6XS

Publisher: Lester Crook
Managers: Liz Stuckey *(Finance)*
Stuart Weir *(Production)*
Isabella Steer *(Rights)*
Martin Ashworth *(Sales)*
Paul Davighi *(Marketing)*
Elizabeth Spaulding *(Publicity)*
Liz Friend Smith *(Editor)*

Biography & Autobiography; History & Antiquarian; Military & War; Politics & World Affairs; Travel & Topography

ISBNs, Imprints & Series:
978 1 84511, 978 1 85043, 978 1 86064

Overseas Representation:
Australia: Palgrave Macmillan, South Yarra, Vic
USA: Palgrave Macmillan, New York, NY

2625 ▬▬▬

RADCLIFFE PUBLISHING LTD
18 Marcham Road, Abingdon, Oxon OX14 1AA
Telephone: 01235 528820
Fax: 01235 528830
Email: contact.us@radcliffemed.com
Web Site: www.radcliffe-oxford.com

Directors: Gregory Moxon *(Managing)*
Gillian Nineham *(Editorial)*
Margaret McKeown *(Financial)*
Managers: Jamie Etherington *(Editorial)*
Steve Bonner *(Production)*
Executives: Dan Allen *(Marketing)*
Carlos Sejournant *(Sales)*

Educational & Textbooks; Electronic (Educational); Electronic (Professional & Academic); Industry, Business & Management; Medical (incl. Self Help & Alternative Medicine); Reference Books, Directories & Dictionaries; Scientific & Technical; Vocational Training & Careers

ISBNs, Imprints & Series:
978 1 84619, 978 1 85775, 978 1 870905

Overseas Representation:
Australia: Elsevier Australia, Marrickville, NSW
India, Bangladesh, Sri Lanka, Nepal & Pakistan: Jaypee Brothers Medical Publishers (Pte) Ltd, New Delhi, India
Middle East: International Publishing Services (IPS) Middle East Ltd, Dubai, UAE
Scandinavia: David Towle International, Stockholm, Sweden
Singapore, Malaysia, Thailand, Vietnam, Cambodia, Laos, Myanmar, Brunei, Indonesia, Philippines & Taiwan: Alkem Co (S) Pte Ltd, Singapore
USA: Martin P. Hill Consulting, New York, NY

Book Trade Association Membership:
IPG

2626 ▬▬▬

RAND PUBLICATIONS
5 Victoria House, 138 Watling Street East, Towcester NN12 6BT
Telephone: 01327 357770
Fax: 01327 359572
Email: rand@oppuk.co.uk
Web Site: www.rand.org

Warehouse & Distribution:
NBN International, Estover Road, Plymouth PL6 7PY
Telephone: 01752 202301
Fax: 01752 202331
Email: orders@nbninternational.com
Web Site: www.nbninternational.com

Manager: Gary Hall

Academic & Scholarly; Economics; Educational & Textbooks; Military & War; Politics & World Affairs

ISBNs, Imprints & Series: 978 0 8330

Parent Company:
USA: Rand Publications

2627 ▬▬▬

RANDOM HOUSE CHILDREN'S BOOKS
61–63 Uxbridge Road, London W5 5SA
Telephone: (020) 8579 2652
Fax: (020) 8231 6767
Web Site: www.kidsatrandomhouse.co.uk

Directors: Philippa Dickinson *(Managing)*
Helen Randles *(Sales)*
Barry O'Donovan *(Marketing)*
Jane Seery *(Production)*
Bronwen Bennie *(Rights)*
Publishers: Annie Eaton *(Fiction)*
Fiona Macmillan *(Colour & Custom Publishing)*

Children's Books

Parent Company:
UK: Random House Group Ltd

Associated Companies:
UK: Bodley Head; Jonathan Cape; Corgi; Doubleday; David Fickling Books; Hutchinson; Red Fox; Tamarind

Book Trade Association Membership:
Publishers Association

2628 ▬▬▬

RANDOM HOUSE UK LTD
20 Vauxhall Bridge Road, London SW1V 2SA
Telephone: (020) 7840 8400
Fax: (020) 7233 8791
Web Site: www.randomhouse.co.uk

Chair & Chief Executive Officer: Gail Rebuck
Deputy Chief Executive Officer: Ian Hudson
Directors: Mark Gardiner *(Group Finance)*
Garry Prior *(Group Sales)*
Stephen Esson *(Group Production)*
Maureen Corish *(Group Communications)*

Architecture & Design; Children's Books; Cookery, Wines & Spirits; Crafts & Hobbies; Crime; Do-It-Yourself; Economics; Fiction; Fine Art & Art History; Gardening; Guide Books; Health & Beauty; History & Antiquarian; Humour; Illustrated & Fine Editions; Literature & Criticism; Military & War; Music; Natural History; Philosophy; Photography; Poetry; Politics & World Affairs; Science Fiction; Sports & Games; Transport; Trade

Parent Company:
UK: Random House Group Ltd

Associated Companies:
UK: Arrow; BBC Books; Black Lace; Bodley Head; Jonathan Cape; Century; Chatto & Windus; Ebury; Everyman; Fodor; Harvill Secker; William Heinemann; Hutchinson; Mainstream; Pimlico; Preface; Random House Books; Rider; Time Out; Vermilion; Vintage; Virgin Books; Yellow Jersey

Book Trade Association Membership:
Publishers Association

2629 ▬▬▬

RANSOM PUBLISHING LTD
51 Southgate Street, Winchester S023 9EH
Telephone: 01962 862307
Email: ransom@ransom.co.uk
Web Site: www.ransom.co.uk

Directors: Jenny Ertle *(Managing)*
Stephen Rickard *(Publishing)*
Marketing Manager: Rebecca Pash

Children's Books; Educational & Textbooks; Electronic (Educational)

New Titles: 100 (2008) , 100 (2009)
No of Employees: 5

ISBNs, Imprints & Series:
978 1 84167, 978 1 900127 321 Go!; Backstreet; Boffin Boy; Cutting Edge; Dark Man; Goal!; Siti's Sisters; Starchasers; Trailblazers

Book Trade Association Membership:
IPG

2630 ▬▬▬

RAVETTE PUBLISHING LTD
PO Box 876, Horsham, West Sussex RH12 9GH
Telephone: 01403 711443
Fax: 01403 711554
Email: ravettepub@aol.com

Warehouse, Invoicing & Accounts:
Orca Book Services, Stanley House, 3 Fleets Lane, Poole, Dorset BH15 3AJ
Telephone: 01202 665432
Fax: 01202 666219
Email: mail@orcabookservices.co.uk
Web Site: www.orcabookservices.co.uk

Managing Director: Mrs M. Lamb
Production Manager: R. Lamb
Company Secretary: Miss I. Parris

Children's Books; Humour; Music

No of Employees: 3

ISBNs, Imprints & Series:
978 1 84161 Born to Shop; Juicy Lucy; Odd Streak; Peanuts; Garfield; Hackman
978 1 84161, 978 1 85304 The Odd Squad

Overseas Representation:
Australia: Peribo Pty Ltd, Mount Kuring-Gai, NSW
Japan: Yasmy International Marketing, Ageo
Middle East: Peter Ward Book Exports, London, UK
Philippines, Korea, Taiwan, Thailand & Indonesia: Ashton International Marketing Services, Sevenoaks, Kent, UK
Singapore & Malaysia: Pansing Distribution Sdn Bhd, Singapore
South Africa: Bag of Books, Park Town
Spain, Gibraltar & Portugal: Humphrys Roberts Associates, Malaga, Spain

Book Trade Association Membership:
IPG; Bookdata

2631

REARDON PUBLISHING
[also known as Reardon and Son Publishers]
PO Box 919, Cheltenham, Glos GL50 9AN
Telephone: 01242 231800
Email: reardon@bigfoot.com
Web Site: www.reardon.co.uk &
www.cotswoldbookshop.com

Director: Nicholas Reardon

*Archaeology; Atlases & Maps; Audio
Books; Children's Books; Cinema, Video, TV
& Radio; Guide Books; History &
Antiquarian; Humour; Magic & the Occult;
Military & War; Natural History; Nautical;
Travel & Topography*

ISBNs, Imprints & Series:
Walkcards (series)
978 0 9508674 Rideabout Series
978 1 873877 Walkabout Series
978 1 874192 Driveabout Series

Distributor for:
Cheltenham Tourism; Cicerone Press;
Cordee; Corinium Publications; Estate
Publications; Flukes UK; Harvey Maps;
OS Maps; Philips Maps; Rambler
Association; Video Ex

Book Trade Association Membership:
Outdoor Writers Guild

2632

REDCLIFFE PRESS LTD
81g Pembroke Road, Bristol BS8 3EA
Telephone: 0117 973 7207
Fax: 0117 923 8991
Email: info@redcliffepress.co.uk
Web Site: www.redcliffepress.co.uk

Trade Orders:
Orca Book Services Ltd, Unit A3,
Fleets Corner, Poole, Dorset BH17 0HL
Telephone: 01202 665432
Fax: 01202 666219
Email: orders@orcabookservices.co.uk

Directors: A. N. Sansom *(Sales)*
John Sansom *(Publishing)*
Clara Sansom *(Production)*

*Architecture & Design; Fine Art & Art
History; History & Antiquarian; Literature &
Criticism; Poetry; West Country History*

New Titles: 25 (2009)
No of Employees: 3

ISBNs, Imprints & Series:
978 1 900178, 978 1 904537, 978 1
906593

Associated Companies:
Art Dictionaries Ltd; Sansom & Co Ltd;
Westcliffe Books

Overseas Representation:
USA: Antique Collectors Club Ltd,
Easthampton, MA

2633

REDEMPTORIST PUBLICATIONS
Alphonsus House, Chawton, Hants
GU34 3HQ
Telephone: 01420 88222
Fax: 01420 88805
Email: rp@rpbooks.co.uk
Web Site: www.rpbooks.co.uk

Director: Rev Denis McBride *(Publishing)*
Head of Operations: Andrew Lane
Managers: Michael Roberts *(Sales &
Service)*
Christine Thirkell *(Financial Controller)*
Patricia Wilson *(Marketing)*
Andrew Lyon *(Editorial)*

Religion & Theology

New Titles: 15 (2009)
No of Employees: 27

ISBNs, Imprints & Series: 978 0 85231

Distributor for:
USA: Abbey Press; Creative
Communications; Dimension Books;
HarperCollins; ICS Publications; Liguori/
Triumph; Loyola Press; Peter Pauper
Press; RCL (Resources for Christian
Living); Regina Press (Malhame);
Resurrection Press; Servant Publications;
Sophia Institute; St Anthony Messenger
Press/Franciscan Catholic Book
Publishing Co

Book Trade Association Membership:
BA

2634

REFLECTIONS OF A BYGONE AGE
15 Debdale Lane, Keyworth, Notts
NG12 5HT
Telephone: 0115 937 4079
Fax: 0115 937 6197
Email:
reflections@postcardcollecting.co.uk

Contacts: Brian Lund
F. Mary Lund

History & Antiquarian; Transport

New Titles: 2 (2008) , 7 (2009)

ISBNs, Imprints & Series:
978 0 946245, 978 1 900138, 978 1
905408

2635

THE RICHMOND PUBLISHING CO
[Ltd]
PO Box 963, Slough SL2 3RS
Telephone: 01753 643104
Fax: 01753 646553

Managing Director: Mrs S. J. Davie

*Academic & Scholarly; Biology & Zoology;
Educational & Textbooks; Natural History;
Scientific & Technical*

Annual Turnover: £40,000

ISBNs, Imprints & Series:
978 0 85546 Richmond Publishing
978 1 85153 Field Studies Council

Distributor for:
Field Studies Council; WWF United
Kingdom

2636

RIPLEY PUBLISHING LTD
2nd Floor, 22 The Causeway,
Bishop's Stortford, Herts CM23 2EJ
Email: marshall@ripleys.com
Web Site: www.ripleys.com

Publisher: Anne Marshall
Managing Editor: Becky Miles
Foreign Rights Manager: Amanda Dula

Children's Books; Fiction

Parent Company:
Canada: The Jim Pattison Group

2637

RIPPING YARNS.COM
5 Old Inn Road, Findon, Aberdeenshire
AB12 3RT
Telephone: 01224 783197
Email: admin@rippingyarns.com

Web Site: www.rippingyarns.com

Director: Ian Robertson

*Military & War; Sports & Games; Travel &
Topography*

Annual Turnover: £20,000

ISBNs, Imprints & Series:
978 0 9541794, 978 1 904466

Parent Company:
Rockbuy Ltd

Overseas Representation:
Europe: Cordee, Leicester, UK

2638

RISING STARS UK LTD
22 Grafton Street, London W1S 4EX
Telephone: (020) 7495 6793
Fax: (020) 7495 6796
Email: info@risingstars-uk.com
Web Site: www.risingstars-uk.com

**Customer Service, Trade Enquiries &
Warehouse:**
Macmillan Distribution (MDL), Brunel Road,
Houndmills, Basingstoke, Hants RG21 6XS

Directors: Andrea Carr *(Managing)*
Tim Pearce *(Production)*
Camilla Erskine *(Publishing)*

*Children's Books; Educational & Textbooks;
Electronic (Educational); Fiction*

ISBNs, Imprints & Series:
978 1 84680, 978 1 905056

Overseas Representation:
Contact: English Language International,
Dunstable, UK

Book Trade Association Membership:
Publishers Association; EPC; IPG

2639

ROADMASTER PUBLISHING
PO Box 176, Chatham, Kent ME5 9AQ
Telephone: 01634 862843
Fax: 01634 201555
Email: info@roadmasterpublishing.co.uk

Sales Manager: Malcolm Wright

*Geography & Geology; Guide Books;
Nautical; Transport; Travel & Topography*

ISBNs, Imprints & Series: 978 1 871814

Distributor for:
Nostalgia Road Publications; Trans-Pennine
Publishing

2640

ROBINSWOOD PRESS LTD
30 South Avenue, Stourbridge,
West Midlands DY8 3XY
Telephone: 01384 397475
Fax: 01384 440443
Email: cjm@robinswoodpress.com
Web Site: www.robinswoodpress.com

Managing Director: C. J. Marshall
Company Secretary: S. M. Marshall
**Editor & Personal Assistant to
Managing Director:** S. Connolly

*Academic & Scholarly; Children's Books;
Educational & Textbooks; Electronic
(Educational); English as a Foreign
Language; Fiction*

New Titles: 15 (2009)
No of Employees: 4
Annual Turnover: £100,000

ISBNs, Imprints & Series:
978 1 869981, 978 1 906053

Associated Companies:
Republic of Ireland: Robinswood Press
(Dublin) Ltd

Overseas Representation:
Republic of Ireland: STA Ltd, Dublin

2641

ROBSON BOOKS
The Old Magistrates Court,
10 Southcombe Street, London W14 0RA
Telephone: (020) 7605 1400
Fax: (020) 7605 1401
Email: mcroft@anovabooks.com
Web Site: www.anovabooks.com

Distributors:
HarperCollins Distribution, Campsie View,
Westerhill Road, Bishopbriggs, Glasgow
G64 2QT
Telephone: 0141 306 3100
Fax: 0141 306 3767

Publisher: Malcolm Croft
Publicity & Marketing Manager: Jane
Ellis

*Biography & Autobiography; Cinema,
Video, TV & Radio; Cookery, Wines &
Spirits; Crime; Health & Beauty; Humour;
Music; Sports & Games; Theatre, Drama &
Dance; Travel & Topography*

ISBNs, Imprints & Series: 978 1 86105

Parent Company:
Anova Books Group Ltd

Overseas Representation:
Asia: Ashton International Marketing
Services, Sevenoaks, Kent, UK
Australia: HarperCollins Publishers, Pymble,
NSW
Canada: Raincoast Books, Vancouver, BC
France & Benelux: Ted Dougherty, London,
UK
Germany, Switzerland & Austria: Gabriele
Kern Publishers Services, Frankfurt-am-
Main, Germany
Italy, Spain & Portugal: Penny Padovani,
Padovani Books Ltd, London, UK
New Zealand: HarperCollins (NZ) Ltd,
Glenfield, Auckland
Scandinavia: McNeish Publishing
International, East Sussex, UK
Singapore & Malaysia: Pansing Distribution
Sdn Bhd, Singapore
South Africa: Trinity Books CC, Randburg
USA: Trafalgar Square Publishing,
distributed by Independent Publishers
Group, Chicago, IL

Book Trade Association Membership:
IPG

2642

ALAN ROGERS GUIDES LTD
Spelmonden Old Oast, Goudhurst,
Cranbrook, Kent TN17 1HE
Telephone: 01580 214000
Email: susie@alanrogers.com
Web Site: www.alanrogers.com

Publishing Manager: Susie Smart

Travel & Topography

ISBNs, Imprints & Series:
978 0 954527, 978 0 955048, 978 1
906215

Parent Company:
Mark Hammerton Group

Book Trade Association Membership:
BA

2643

ROTOVISION SA
Sheridan House, 114 Western Road, Hove,
East Sussex BN3 1DD
Telephone: 01273 727268 & 716010/11/
12 (Customer Services)
Fax: 01273 727269
Email: sales@rotovision.com
Web Site: www.rotovision.com

Directors: Piers Spence *(Managing)*
Nicole Kemble *(Rights)*
Financial Controller: Mari Ahlfeld-Smith
Publisher: April Sankey

*Architecture & Design; Cinema, Video, TV &
Radio; Fashion & Costume; Fine Art & Art
History; Music; Photography; Reference
Books, Directories & Dictionaries; Theatre,
Drama & Dance*

ISBNs, Imprints & Series: 978 2 88046

Parent Company:
Quarto Group

Overseas Representation:
Australia: Thames & Hudson (Australia) Pty
Ltd, Fishermans Bend, Vic
France: Interart SARL, Paris
Germany, Switzerland & Austria: Michael
Klein, Vilsbiburg, Germany
Middle East: International Publishing
Services (IPS) Middle East Ltd, Dubai, UAE
South East Asia: APD Singapore Pte Ltd,
Singapore

Book Trade Association Membership:
BA

2644

ROUND HALL LTD
43 Fitzwilliam Place, Dublin 2,
Republic of Ireland
Telephone: +353 (01) 662 5301
Fax: +353 (01) 662 5302
Email: roundhall.info@thomson.com
Web Site: www.roundhall.thomson.com

Distribution:
Gill & Macmillan, Hume Avenue,
Park West, Dublin 12, Republic of Ireland
Telephone: +353 (01) 500 9500

Director: Julie Clarke
Managers: Anne Waters *(Finance)*
Terri McDonnell *(Production)*
Martin McCann *(Editorial)*
Catherine Dolan *(Commercial)*
Brendan Reid *(Sales)*
Pauline Ward *(Sales)*
Maura Smyth *(Marketing)*

*Academic & Scholarly; Accountancy &
Taxation; Educational & Textbooks;
Electronic (Professional & Academic);
Industry, Business & Management; Law;
Medical (incl. Self Help & Alternative
Medicine); Reference Books, Directories &
Dictionaries*

ISBNs, Imprints & Series:
978 1 85800, 978 1 899738 Round Hall
978 1 86089 Round Hall Professional

Parent Company:
USA: Thomson Reuters Corp

Associated Companies:
Australia: LBC
Canada: Carswell
New Zealand: Brookers
UK: Sweet & Maxwell
USA: West Group

2645

ROUNDHOUSE PUBLISHING LTD
Roundhouse Group, Maritime House,
Basin Road North, Hove, East Sussex
BN41 1WR
Telephone: 01273 704962
Fax: 01273 704963
Email: sales@roundhousegroup.co.uk
Web Site: www.roundhousegroup.co.uk

Warehouse & Distribution:
Orca Book Services, Stanley House,
Fleets Lane, Poole, Dorset BH15 3AJ
Telephone: 01202 665432
Fax: 01202 666219
Email: orders@orca-book-services.co.uk

Managing Director: Alan Goodworth
(Publisher)
Marketing Manager: Matt Goodworth

*Academic & Scholarly; Architecture &
Design; Biography & Autobiography;
Children's Books; Cinema, Video, TV &
Radio; Cookery, Wines & Spirits; Crafts &
Hobbies; Fine Art & Art History; Guide
Books; Health & Beauty; History &
Antiquarian; Industry, Business &
Management; Literature & Criticism;
Medical (incl. Self Help & Alternative
Medicine); Military & War; Music; Natural
History; Philosophy; Photography; Politics &
World Affairs; Reference Books, Directories
& Dictionaries; Sports & Games; Theatre,
Drama & Dance; Travel & Topography*

ISBNs, Imprints & Series:
978 1 85710 Roundabout - Books for
Young Readers; Roundhouse Publishing

Associated Companies:
Roundabout Books; Roundhouse Reference
Books; Roundtrip Travel; Windsor Books
International

Distributor for:
Australia: Allen & Unwin; Hale &
Iremonger; Health Directions; National
Gallery of Victoria; University of
Queensland Press; Watermark Press
Austria: Strokes International
Belgium: Editions l'Octogone
Canada: Crabtree; Key Porter Books; Self-
Counsel Press; Ulysses Travel Guides
France: Petit Futé Guides; Sisyphe Editions
Germany: Feierabend Unique Books
Hong Kong: PPP Co
India: Marg Publications; Vadhera Art
Gallery
Italy: Arkivia Books; Charta Art Books;
Drago Publishing; Giunti Editore
Netherlands: New in Chess
New Zealand: Awa Press
Republic of Ireland: Irish Museum of
Modern Art
Singapore: Archipelago Press
Spain: Ebiz Guides; Ediciones Poligrafa;
Monsa Publications; Parramon
Ediciones; Santana Books
UK: Burke Publishing; Cameron & Hollis;
Georgina Campbell; Learning Together;
Northern Bee Books; Angela Patchell
Books; Sea Squirt Books; Sinclair-
Stevenson; Thalamus Publishing; Michael
Wilcox School of Colour; WRTH Books
USA: Allworth Press; AM Editores; Black
Sparrow Press; Boyds Mills Press;
Breckling Press; C & T Publications;
Capstone; Classroom Complete;
Creative Homeowner; Cumberland
House; Design Studio Press; Fairview
Press; Free Spirit; Getty Publications;
David R. Godine; Greenwood
Publishing; Gryphon House; Hunter
Publishing; Interlink Publishing; Knock
Knock Books; Landauer; Martingale &
Co; One Peace Books; Open Road;
Paragon House; Pelican Publishing;
Portland Press; Praeger Publishing;
Quality Medical Pub.; RDR Books; Robins
Lane Press; J Ross Publishing; Seven

Locks Press; Soundprints; Star Bright
Books; Triumph Books; University Press
of Mississippi; Vanguard Press; Weigl
Publishers; Westholme; Writings of Mary
Baker Eddy

Overseas Representation:
Europe (East) & Scandinavia: Bill Bailey
Publishers Representatives, Totnes, UK
Europe (South): Bookport Associates,
Milan, Italy
Europe (Spain & Portugal only): Iberian
Book Services, Madrid, Spain
Europe (West) (excluding Scandinavia): Ted
Dougherty, London, UK
Middle East: Richard Ward, London, UK

2646

ROUTE PUBLISHING LTD
PO Box 167, Pontefract WF8 4WW
Telephone: 01977 797695
Email: info@route-online.com
Web Site: www.route-online.com

Distribution:
Central Books, 99 Wallis Road, London
E9 5LN
Telephone: (020) 8986 4854
Fax: (020) 8533 5821
Email: bill@centralbooks.com
Web Site: www.centralbooks.com

Directors: Ian Daley *(Artistic)*
Isabel Galan *(Public Relations)*

Biography & Autobiography; Fiction; Poetry

ISBNs, Imprints & Series: 978 1 901927

Overseas Representation:
USA: Dufour Editions Inc, Chester Springs,
PA

2647

*ROUTLEDGE-CAVENDISH
2 Park Square, Milton Park, Abingdon,
Oxon OX14 4RN
Telephone: (020) 7017 6000
Fax: (020) 7017 6336
Email: law@routledge.com
Web Site: www.routledgecavendish.com

Publisher: Fiona Kinnear

*Academic & Scholarly; Educational &
Textbooks; Electronic (Professional &
Academic); Environment & Development
Studies; Gay & Lesbian Studies; Gender
Studies; Law; Medical (incl. Self Help &
Alternative Medicine); Philosophy; Politics &
World Affairs*

ISBNs, Imprints & Series:
Birkbeck Law Press; The Glasshouse Press;
UCL Press
978 1 85941, 978 1 874241, 978 1 876213

Parent Company:
Taylor & Francis Group

Book Trade Association Membership:
BA; IGSMTP; CAPP; IPG

2648

JOSEPH ROWNTREE FOUNDATION
The Homestead, 40 Water End, York
YO30 6WP
Telephone: 01904 629241
Fax: 01904 620072
Email: julia.lewis@jrf.org.uk
Web Site: www.jrf.org.uk

Distribution:
York Publishing Services, 64 Hallfield Road,
Layerthorpe, York YO31 7ZQ
Telephone: 01904 430033
Fax: 01904 430868
Email: orders@yps.ymn.co.uk

Directors: Julia Unwin CBE
Julia Lewis *(Communications)*
Paul Dack *(Finance)*

*Academic & Scholarly; Architecture &
Design; Economics; Politics & World Affairs;
Sociology & Anthropology*

2649

ROYAL COLLECTION PUBLICATIONS
Stable Yard House, St James's Palace,
London SW1A 1JR
Telephone: (020) 7024 5584
Fax: (020) 7839 8168
Email:
jacky.collissharvey@royalcollection.org.u
k
Web Site: www.royalcollection.org.uk

Distribution:
Thames & Hudson Ltd, 181a High Holborn,
London WC1V 7QX
Telephone: (020) 7845 5000
Fax: (020) 7845 5055
Web Site: www.thamesandhudson.com

Publisher: Jacky Colliss Harvey
Commissioning Editor: Kate Owen
Publishing Assistants: Debbie Bogard
Sabrina MacKenzie

*Academic & Scholarly; Antiques &
Collecting; Architecture & Design;
Biography & Autobiography; Fashion &
Costume; Fine Art & Art History; Guide
Books; History & Antiquarian; Illustrated &
Fine Editions; Natural History; Photography*

New Titles: 9 (2008) , 6 (2009)
No of Employees: 4

ISBNs, Imprints & Series:
978 1 902163, 978 1 902163, 978 1
905686, 978 1 905686

Overseas Representation:
Rest of World: Thames & Hudson Ltd,
London, UK
USA & Canada: Antique Collectors Club
Ltd, Easthampton, MA, USA

2650

**ROYAL COLLEGE OF GENERAL
PRACTITIONERS**
14 Princes Gate, Hyde Park, London
SW7 1PU
Telephone: (020) 7581 3232
Fax: (020) 7225 3047
Email: hfarrelly@rcgp.org.uk
Web Site: www.rcgp.org.uk

Publishing Manager: Ms Helen Farrelly

*Academic & Scholarly; Medical (incl. Self
Help & Alternative Medicine)*

ISBNs, Imprints & Series: 978 0 85084

Book Trade Association Membership:
Association of Learned & Professional
Society Publishers

2651

ROYAL COLLEGE OF PSYCHIATRISTS
17 Belgrave Square, London SW1X 8PG
Telephone: (020) 7235 2351
Fax: (020) 7259 6507
Email: publications@rcpsych.ac.uk
Web Site: www.rcpsych.ac.uk

Warehouse:
Turpin Distribution, Customer Services,
Pegasus Drive, Stratton Business Park,
Biggleswade, Beds SG18 8TQ
Telephone: 01767 604951
Fax: 01767 601640
Email: custserv@turpin-distribution.com
Web Site: www.turpin-distribution.com

Head of Publications: Dave Jago
Sales & Marketing Manager: Daniel
 Tomkins

*Academic & Scholarly; Medical (incl. Self
Help & Alternative Medicine); Psychology &
Psychiatry*

New Titles: 7 (2008) , 12 (2009)

ISBNs, Imprints & Series:
978 0 902241, 978 1 901242 Gaskell;
RCPsych Publications

Overseas Representation:
Australia & New Zealand: All things
 Medical, Sydney University, Sydney, NSW,
 Australia
Republic of Ireland: Compass Academic,
 London, UK
Scandinavia (including Iceland & Estonia):
 David Towle International, Stockholm,
 Sweden
USA & Canada: Princeton Selling Group Inc,
 Wayne, PA, USA

Book Trade Association Membership:
IPG; Association of Learned & Professional
Society Publishers

2652

**ROYAL GEOGRAPHICAL SOCIETY
(WITH INSTITUTE OF BRITISH
GEOGRAPHERS)**
1 Kensington Gore, London SW7 2AR
Telephone: (020) 7591 3022
Fax: (020) 7591 3001
Email: rhed@rgs.org
Web Site: www.rgs.org

Head of Finance & Services: David Riviere
Managing Editor: Journals: Amy Swann

*Academic & Scholarly; Electronic
(Educational); Electronic (Professional &
Academic); Environment & Development
Studies; Geography & Geology*

ISBNs, Imprints & Series:
RGS-IBG Book Series (academic/scholarly
 texts only)

2653

ROYAL IRISH ACADEMY
Academy House, 19 Dawson Street,
Dublin 2, Republic of Ireland
Telephone: +353 (01) 676 2570 & 676
 4222
Fax: +353 (01) 676 2346
Email: publications@ria.ie
Web Site: www.ria.ie

Executive Secretary: Patrick Buckley
 (Rights & Permissions)
Managing Editor: Ruth Hegarty
 (Production & Sales)

*Academic & Scholarly; Archaeology; Atlases
& Maps; Biology & Zoology; History &
Antiquarian; Languages & Linguistics;
Reference Books, Directories & Dictionaries*

New Titles: 9 (2008) , 7 (2009)
No of Employees: 6

ISBNs, Imprints & Series:
978 0 901714, 978 0 9543855, 978 1
 874045

Overseas Representation:
North America: International Specialized
 Book Services Inc, Portland, OR, USA

Book Trade Association Membership:
CLÉ (Irish PA); Association of Learned &
Professional Society Publishers

2654

**THE ROYAL SOCIETY OF
CHEMISTRY**
Sales & Customer Care,
Thomas Graham House, Science Park,
Milton Road, Cambridge CB4 0WF
Telephone: 01223 420066
Fax: 01223 426017
Email: sales@rsc.org
Web Site: www.rsc.org

Warehouse:
Portland Customer Services, Portland Press,
Commerce Way, Colchester CO2 8HP
Telephone: 01206 226050
Fax: 01206 799331
Email: sales@portland-services.com
Web Site: www.portlandpress.com

Director: Robert Parker *(Publishing)*
Managers: Barry Anderson *(Home & Export
 Sales & Customer Care)*
 Nichole Gibson *(Production Operations)*

*Academic & Scholarly; Chemistry;
Educational & Textbooks; Electronic
(Educational); Electronic (Professional &
Academic); Reference Books, Directories &
Dictionaries; Scientific & Technical*

ISBNs, Imprints & Series:
978 0 85186, 978 0 85404

Overseas Representation:
Asia, Australia & New Zealand: Clarke
 Associates Ltd, Bristol, UK
*Australia, New Zealand & Papua New
 Guinea:* DA Information Services Pty Ltd,
 Mitcham, Vic, Australia
Hungary: Dr László Horváth Publishers
 Representative, Budapest
India: S. Janakiraman, Book Marketing
 Services, Chennai
Italy: Flavio Marcello Publishers' Agents &
 Consultants, Padua
Japan: Aiko Hoyosa, Tokyo
*Middle East, Malta, Greece, Turkey, Cyprus
 & Iran:* Farhad Maftoon, Tehran, Iran;
 Anthony Rudkin Associates, Oxford, UK
Nigeria: Olu Anulopo, Bounty Books,
 Ibadan
North America & Mexico: Springer-Verlag
 New York Inc, Secaucus, NJ, USA
Scandinavia & Iceland: Colin Flint Ltd,
 Harlow, UK
South America: Terry Roberts, Humphrys
 Roberts Associates, Cotia SP, Brazil
Spain & Portugal: Arie Ruitenbeek, Madrid,
 Spain

Book Trade Association Membership:
Association of Learned Society Publishers;
STM (European Group)

2655

**ROYAL SOCIETY OF MEDICINE
PRESS LTD**
1 Wimpole Street, London W1G 0AE
Telephone: (020) 7290 3945
Fax: (020) 7290 2929
Email: ian.jones@rsm.ac.uk
Web Site: www.rsmpress.co.uk

Warehousing & Distribution:
Marston Book Services, PO Box 269,
Abingdon, Oxon OX14 4YN
Telephone: 01235 465500
Fax: 01235 465555

Managing Director: Peter Richardson
Head of Sales & Marketing: Ian Jones
Finance: Mark Johnstone
Managers: Mark Sanderson *(Production)*
 Lucy McIvor *(Journals Development)*
Editors: Alison Campbell *(Managing)*
 Sarah Ogden *(Commissioning)*

*Medical (incl. Self Help & Alternative
Medicine)*

New Titles: 20 (2008) , 20 (2009)
No of Employees: 18
Annual Turnover: £2.3M

ISBNs, Imprints & Series:
978 1 85315 Controversies and Dilemmas
 Series; Eponymists in Medicine Series;
 Get Through Series; In Practice Series;
 International Congress and Symposium
 Series; Key Advances Series; Key Paper
 Conferences Series; Recent Advances
 Series; Round Table Series

Parent Company:
Royal Society of Medicine

Overseas Representation:
USA: Bookmasters Inc, Ashland, OH

Book Trade Association Membership:
Association of Learned & Professional
Society Publishers

2656

RUSSELL HOUSE PUBLISHING LTD
4 St George's House,
Uplyme Road Business Park, Lyme Regis
DT7 3LS
Telephone: 01297 443948
Fax: 01297 442722
Email: help@russellhouse.co.uk
Web Site: www.russellhouse.co.uk

Directors: Geoffrey Mann *(Managing)*
 Martin Jones
 Terry Nemko

*Academic & Scholarly; Educational &
Textbooks; Electronic (Educational);
Electronic (Professional & Academic);
Gender Studies; Industry, Business &
Management; Law; Medical (incl. Self Help
& Alternative Medicine); Psychology &
Psychiatry; Sociology & Anthropology;
Sports & Games; Theatre, Drama & Dance;
Vocational Training & Careers*

New Titles: 19 (2008) , 20 (2009)
No of Employees: 7
Annual Turnover: £400,000

ISBNs, Imprints & Series:
978 1 898924, 978 1 903855, 978 1
 905541

Overseas Representation:
Australia: Psychoz, Vic
North America: International Specialized
 Book Services Inc, Portland, OR, USA

2657

SAGE PUBLICATIONS LTD
1 Oliver's Yard, 55 City Road, London
EC1Y 1SP
Telephone: (020) 7324 8500
Fax: (020) 7324 8600
Email: info@sagepub.co.uk
Web Site: www.sagepub.co.uk

Warehouse:
Unit 11, Keirbeck Business Centre,
North Woolwich Road, Silvertown, London
E16 2BG

Directors: Stephen Barr *(Managing)*
 Katherine Jackson *(Financial & Deputy
 Managing)*
 Ziyad Marar *(Deputy Managing)*
 Clive Parry *(Marketing & Sales)*
 Phil Denvir *(IT)*
 Richard Fidczuk *(Production)*
 Sara Miller McCune
 Blaise Simqu
 Paul Chapman
 Tony Histed *(Associate, Sales)*
 Anne Farlow *(Non-Executive)*
 Brenda Gowley *(Non-Executive)*
Managers: Alison Browne *(Customer
 Service (Books))*
 Huw Alexander *(Rights & Permissions)*

*Academic & Scholarly; Bibliography &
Library Science; Economics; Educational &
Textbooks; Electronic (Educational); Gender
Studies; Industry, Business & Management;
Mathematics & Statistics; Politics & World
Affairs; Psychology & Psychiatry; Reference
Books, Directories & Dictionaries; Religion &
Theology; Scientific & Technical; Sociology
& Anthropology*

ISBNs, Imprints & Series:
978 0 7619, 978 0 8039, 978 1 4129

Parent Company:
USA: SAGE Publications Inc

Associated Companies:
Paul Chapman Publishing Ltd
India: SAGE Publications Pvt Ltd
USA: Corwin Press Inc; Pine Forge Press Inc;
 Sage Publications Inc

Overseas Representation:
Australia & New Zealand: Footprint Books
 Pty Ltd, Sydney, NSW, Australia
South Africa: Academic Marketing Services
 (Pty) Ltd, Craighall

Book Trade Association Membership:
Publishers Association; IPG

2658

SAINT ALBERT'S PRESS
[British Province of Carmelites]
Carmelite Projects & Publications Office,
More House, Heslington, York YO10 5DX
Telephone: 01904 411521
Email: projects@carmelites.org.uk
Web Site: www.carmelite.org/sap/

Orders & Book Deposit:
Saint Albert's Press Book Distribution,
Carmelite Friars, 34 Tanners Street,
Faversham, Kent ME13 7JN
Telephone: 01795 537038
Fax: 01795 539511
Email: saintalbertspress@carmelites.org.uk
Web Site: www.carmelite.org/sap/

Director: Johan Bergström-Allen
Sales: Julie Ann Davies
Bursar: Richard Copsey

*Academic & Scholarly; History &
Antiquarian; Poetry; Religion & Theology*

New Titles: 2 (2008) , 5 (2009)

ISBNs, Imprints & Series: 978 0 904849

Parent Company:
UK: Carmelite Charitable Trust

Associated Companies:
UK: The Carmelite Press; Whitefriars Press

Distributor for:
Italy: Edizioni Carmelitane
USA: Carmelite Institute

Book Trade Association Membership:
IPG

2659

ST JEROME PUBLISHING LTD
2 Maple Road West, Brooklands,
Manchester M23 9HH
Telephone: 0161 973 9856
Fax: 0161 905 3498
Email: stjerome@compuserve.com
Web Site: www.stjerome.co.uk

Managing Director: Ken Baker

*Academic & Scholarly; Electronic
(Professional & Academic)*

New Titles: 12 (2008) , 11 (2009)

ISBNs, Imprints & Series:
978 1 900650, 978 1 905763

Book Trade Association Membership:
Publishers Association; IPG

2660

ST PAULS PUBLISHING
187 Battersea Bridge Road, London
SW11 3AS
Telephone: (020) 7978 4300
Fax: (020) 7978 4370
Email: editorial@stpaulspublishing.com
Web Site: www.stpaulspublishing.com

Director: Celso Godilano
Commissioning Editor: Annabel Robson
Sales & Marketing: Paul Tennant
Permissions & Foreign Rights: Pamela
Tamburini

*Biography & Autobiography; Children's
Books; Philosophy; Psychology &
Psychiatry; Religion & Theology*

New Titles: 8 (2008) , 17 (2009)

ISBNs, Imprints & Series: 978 0 85439

Associated Companies:
Argentina: Ediciones San Pablo
Australia: St Pauls Publications
Brazil: Edições San Pablo
Canada: Medias Paul
Colombia: Ediciones San Pablo
France: Editions Mediaspaul
India: Better Yourself Books; St Pauls
Italy: Edizioni San Paolo
Japan: Chuoshuppan-Sha
Kenya: St Pauls Publications
Mexico: Ediciones San Pablo
Philippines: St Pauls
Portugal: Edições San Pablo
Republic of Ireland: St Pauls
Republic of Korea: St Pauls
Spain: Ediciones San Pablo
USA: Alba House
Venezuela: Ediciones San Pablo

Distributor for:
St Pauls

Overseas Representation:
Australia: St Pauls Publications, Homebush
Kenya: St Paul Book Centre, Nairobi
Nigeria: St Paul Book Centre, Oke-Padi
Tanzania: St Paul Book Centre, Dar-es-
Salaam
Uganda: St Paul Book Centre, Kampala

Book Trade Association Membership:
BA

2661

SALT PUBLISHING LTD
14A High Street, Fulbourn, Cambridge
CB21 5DH
Telephone: 01223 882220
Fax: 01223 882260
Email: enquiries@saltpublishing.com
Web Site: www.saltpublishing.com

Editor: Chris Hamilton-Emery
General Manager: Jennifer Hamilton-
Emery
Publishing Assistant: Charlotte Prince

*Biography & Autobiography; Fiction;
Literature & Criticism; Poetry*

New Titles: 50 (2008) , 50 (2009)
No of Employees: 3
Annual Turnover: £120,000

ISBNs, Imprints & Series:
978 0 646 Folio (Salt)
978 1 84471, 978 1 876857 Salt Publishing

Overseas Representation:
Australia: Inbooks, c/o James Bennett Pty
Ltd, Belrose, NSW
USA: Small Press Distribution Inc, Berkeley,
CA

Book Trade Association Membership:
IPG

2662

*SANDSTONE PRESS LTD
PO Box 5725, 1 High Street, Dingwall,
Ross-shire IV15 9WJ
Telephone: 01349 862583
Fax: 01349 862583
Email: info@sandstonepress.com
Web Site: www.sandstonepress.com

Directors: Robert Davidson *(Managing)*
Iain Gordon *(Company Secretary)*
Moira Forsyth

*Academic & Scholarly; Biography &
Autobiography; Crime; English as a Foreign
Language; Environment & Development
Studies; Fiction; Humour; Illustrated & Fine
Editions; Literature & Criticism; Politics &
World Affairs; Science Fiction; Sports &
Games*

ISBNs, Imprints & Series:
978 1 905207 Sandstone Highliner Series;
Sandstone Meanmnach Series;
Sandstone Vista Series

Book Trade Association Membership:
Publishing Scotland

2663

SANSOM & CO LTD
81g Pembroke Road, Clifton, Bristol
BS8 3EA
Telephone: 0117 973 7207
Fax: 0117 923 8991
Email: johnsansom@aol.com &
info@sansomandcompany.co.uk
Web Site: www.sansomandcompany.co.uk

Trade Orders:
Orca Book Services, Unit A3, Fleets Corner,
Poole, Dorset BH17 0HL
Telephone: 01202 665432
Fax: 01202 666219
Email: orders@orcabookservices.co.uk
Web Site: www.orcabookservices.co.uk

Directors: A. N. Sansom *(Sales)*
John Sansom *(Publishing)*
Clara Sansom *(Production)*

*Architecture & Design; Fine Art & Art
History; Literature & Criticism*

New Titles: 10 (2008) , 18 (2009)

ISBNs, Imprints & Series:
978 1 900178, 978 1 904537, 978 1
906593

Associated Companies:
Art Dictionaries Ltd; Redcliffe Press Ltd

Overseas Representation:
USA: Antique Collectors' Club,
Woodbridge, Suffolk, UK

2664

SAQI BOOKS
26 Westbourne Grove, London W2 5RH
Telephone: (020) 7221 9347
Fax: (020) 7229 7492
Email: enquiries@saqibooks.com
Web Site: www.saqibooks.com

Distribution:
Gazelle Book Services, White Cross Mills,
Hightown, South Road, Lancaster LA1 4XS
Telephone: 01524 68765

Fax: 01524 63232
Email: ian@gazellebooks.co.uk

Publisher/Director: André Gaspard
Marketing: Ashley Biles
Rights: Lynn Gaspard

*Academic & Scholarly; Architecture &
Design; Biography & Autobiography;
Cookery, Wines & Spirits; Fiction; Fine Art &
Art History; Gender Studies; History &
Antiquarian; Humour; Literature &
Criticism; Philosophy; Photography; Poetry;
Politics & World Affairs; Religion &
Theology; Sociology & Anthropology; Arab
World; Islam; Middle East*

ISBNs, Imprints & Series:
Saqi Essentials; Brief Introduction (series)
978 0 86356

Associated Companies:
Lebanon: Dar Al Saqi Sarl

Overseas Representation:
Australia: Palgrave Macmillan, South Yarra,
Vic
USA: Consortium Publishers, St Paul, MN

Book Trade Association Membership:
BA; CAPP; IPG

2665

*SAVE THE CHILDREN
1 St John's Lane, London EC1M 4AR
Telephone: (020) 7012 6400
Fax: (020) 7012 6963
Email: f.ellery@savethechildren.org.uk
Web Site: www.savethechildren.org.uk

Distributor:
NBN International, Estover Road, Estover,
Plymouth PL6 7PY
Telephone: 01752 202301
Fax: 01752 202333
Email: orders@nbninternational.com
Web Site: www.nbninternational.com

Managers: Frances Ellery *(Publications,
Editorial)*
Sue Macpherson *(Planning & Production)*

*Academic & Scholarly; Children's Books;
Educational & Textbooks; Politics & World
Affairs; Sociology & Anthropology*

ISBNs, Imprints & Series:
978 1 841870, 978 1 870322, 978 1
899120

Book Trade Association Membership:
IPG

2666

ALASTAIR SAWDAY PUBLISHING
The Old Farmyard, Yanley Lane,
Long Ashton, Bristol BS41 9LR
Telephone: 01275 395430
Fax: 01275 393388
Email: info@sawdays.co.uk
Web Site: www.sawdays.co.uk/bookshop

Distribution & Sales:
Penguin (UK), 80 The Strand, London
WC2R 0RL
Telephone: (020) 7010 3000
Fax: (020) 7010 3198
Email: sales@penguin.co.uk

Publisher/Chairman: Alastair Sawday
Directors: Annie Shillito *(Editorial)*
Toby Sawday *(Business Development)*
Managers: Julia Richardson *(Production,
Web/IT)*
Bridget Bishop *(Finance)*
Rob Richardson *(Sales & Marketing)*
Sue Bourner *(Editorial, Web/IT)*
Joe Green *(Web/IT)*

*Environment & Development Studies;
Guide Books; Travel & Topography*

New Titles: 5 (2008) , 5 (2009)
No of Employees: 21
Annual Turnover: £2.1M

ISBNs, Imprints & Series:
978 1 901970, 978 1 906136 Alastair
Sawday's Special Places to Stay; Fragile
Earth

Overseas Representation:
USA & Canada: Globe Pequot Press,
Guilford, CT, USA
Worldwide (excluding USA & Canada):
Penguin Books Ltd, London, UK

Book Trade Association Membership:
IPG

2667

S. B. PUBLICATIONS
14 Bishopstone Road, Seaford, East Sussex
BN25 2UB
Telephone: 01323 893498
Fax: 01323 893860
Email: sbpublications@tiscali.co.uk
Web Site: www.sbpublications.co.uk

Owner/Manager: Mrs L. S. Woods
Finance: Mrs D. Quick
Sales Manager: Lindsay Woods
Editorial: Ms E. Howe
Proofreader: C. Howden
Sales & Administration: Miss C. Gillett

*Guide Books; History & Antiquarian;
Natural History; Travel & Topography; Local
History (S. E. England); Walking (S. E.
England)*

New Titles: 10 (2008) , 10 (2009)

ISBNs, Imprints & Series: 978 1 85770

2668

SCALA PUBLISHERS LTD
Northburgh House, 10 Northburgh Street,
London EC1V 0AT
Telephone: (020) 7490 9900
Fax: (020) 7336 6870
Email: jmckinley@scalapublishers.com
Web Site: www.scalapublishers.com

Directors: David Campbell *(Chairman)*
Jennifer Wright *(Museum Publications
(USA))*
Jenny McKinley *(Marketing &
Publications (excl. USA))*
Oliver Craske *(Editorial)*
Tim Clarke *(Production)*
Mark Bicknell *(Finance)*

*Antiques & Collecting; Architecture &
Design; Children's Books; Fine Art & Art
History; Guide Books; Illustrated & Fine
Editions; Sports & Games; Travel &
Topography*

New Titles: 30 (2008) , 30 (2009)
No of Employees: 12

ISBNs, Imprints & Series: 978 1 85759

Associated Companies:
France: Editions Scala

Overseas Representation:
Australia (Sales): Bookwise International,
Adelaide, SA, Australia
Worldwide: ACC Distribution, Woodbridge,
Suffolk, UK

Book Trade Association Membership:
IPG

2669

SCHOLASTIC UK LTD
Euston House, 24 Eversholt Street, London
NW1 1DB
Telephone: (020) 7756 7756
Web Site: www.scholastic.co.uk

School Book Clubs:
(as above)

Scholastic Children's Books:
(as above)

School Book Fairs:
(as above)

Scholastic Education:
Villiers House, Clarendon Avenue,
Leamington Spa, Warks CV32 5PR

Directors: Elaine McQuade *(Scholastic
Children's Books – Managing)*
Alan Hurcombe *(Group Managing)*
Denise Cripps *(Education – Managing)*
Alan Hurcombe *(Finance)*

Children's Books; Educational & Textbooks

Parent Company:
USA: Scholastic Inc

Associated Companies:
Australia: Scholastic Australia Pty Ltd
Canada: Scholastic Canada Ltd
New Zealand: Scholastic New Zealand Ltd
UK: Chicken House Publishing

Overseas Representation:
Australia: Scholastic Australia Ltd, Gosford,
NSW
Canada: Scholastic Canada Ltd, Markham,
Ont
*Far East (excluding Singapore, Malaysia &
Indonesia):* Scholastic Hong Kong, Hong
Kong
New Zealand: Scholastic NZ, Auckland

Book Trade Association Membership:
Publishers Association; EPC; Periodical
Publishers Association

2670

SCHOOLPLAY PRODUCTIONS LTD
15 Inglis Road, Colchester, Essex CO3 3HU
Telephone: 01206 540111
Fax: 01206 766944
Email: schoolplay@inglis-
house.demon.co.uk
Web Site:
www.schoolplayproductions.co.uk

Directors: J. R. Lucas *(Managing)*
W. Baker
Administrators: Mrs C. S. Wenden
Mrs B. M. Sparkes

*Educational & Textbooks; Music; Theatre,
Drama & Dance*

New Titles: 5 (2009)
No of Employees: 3

ISBNs, Imprints & Series:
978 1 872475, 978 1 902472

Book Trade Association Membership:
Publishers Association

2671

SCHOTT MUSIC LTD
48 Great Marlborough Street, London
W1F 7BB
Telephone: (020) 7534 0700
Fax: (020) 7534 0719
Email: info@schott-music.com
Web Site: www.schott-music.com

Trade Enquiries & Orders:
MDS Service Centre,
5–6 Raywood Office Complex,
Leacon Lane, Charing, Ashford, Kent
TN27 0EN
Telephone: 01233 712233
Fax: 01233 714948
Email: orders.uk@mds-partner.com
Web Site: www.smdextranet.schott-
extranet.de

Directors: Judith Webb *(Joint Managing)*
Roberto Garcia *(Sales & Marketing)*
Manager: Guy Thomas *(Buying)*
Head of International Publishing:
Wendy Lampa

Academic & Scholarly; Music

New Titles: 40 (2008) , 20 (2009)

ISBNs, Imprints & Series:
978 0 85162 Boosey & Hawkes Music
Publishers Ltd
978 0 901938, 978 0 946535, 978 1
902455 Schott London
978 0 930448 Schott USA
978 3 254 Atlantis Musikbuch-Verlag AG
978 3 7931, 978 3 87090 Bote & Bock
GmbH & Co KG
978 3 7957 Schott Music GmbH & Co KG
978 3 901974 Richard Strauss GmbH & Co
KG
978 3 920030 Apollo-Verlag Paul Lincke
GmbH
978 3 920045 Ars-Viva-Verlag
978 3 920201 Cranz GmbH
978 3 920468, 978 3 937315 Matth.
Hohner AG
978 3 923051 Anton J. Benjamin GmbH
978 3 932398 Schott Music & Media GmbH
(Intuition)

Parent Company:
Germany: Schott Music GmbH & Co KG

Associated Companies:
Ernst Eulenburg Ltd

Distributor for:
A piacere; Ars viva; Bardic Edition; Boosey &
Hawkes Music Publishers Ltd; Delius
Trust; Edition HH; Finzi Trust; Hyperion;
Itchy Fingers Publications; Universal
Edition Ltd
Austria: Amadeus; Apollo-Verlag Paul
Lincke GmbH; Ars-Viva-Verlag; Atlantis-
Musikbuch-Verlag; Anton J. Benjamin
GmbH; Boosey & Hawkes GmbH; Bote &
Bock GmbH & Co KG; Cranz GmbH; G.
Henle Verlag; Matth. Hohner AG;
Möseler Verlag; Musikverlag Doblinger;
Musikverlag Zimmermann; Ries & Erler;
Schott Music GmbH & Co KG; Sikorski;
Richard Strauss GmbH & Co KG
Canada: Bartok Records; European
American Music Distributors LLC; Carl
Fischer Music; Hal Leonard Corporation;
Musica Russica; Theodore Presser
Company; Schott Music Corporation
Czech Republic: Panton
Finland: Fennica Gehrmann
Germany: Amadeus; Apollo-Verlag Paul
Lincke GmbH; Ars-Viva-Verlag; Atlantis-
Musikbuch-Verlag; Anton J. Benjamin
GmbH; Boosey & Hawkes GmbH; Bote &
Bock GmbH & Co KG; Cranz GmbH; G.
Henle Verlag; Matth. Hohner AG;
Möseler Verlag; Musikverlag Doblinger;
Musikverlag Zimmermann; Ries & Erler;
Schott Music GmbH & Co KG; Sikorski;
Richard Strauss GmbH & Co KG
Japan: Zen On Music Company
Poland: PWM
Russia: DSCH; Russian Music Publishing
Singapore: Classical Spectrum
Slovakia: Panton
USA: Bartok Records; European American
Music Distributors LLC; Carl Fischer
Music; Hal Leonard Corporation; Musica
Russica; Theodore Presser Company;
Schott Music Corporation

Overseas Representation:
Europe: Schott Music GmbH & Co KG,
Mainz, Germany
Japan: Schott Japan Co Ltd, Tokyo
USA: Hal Leonard Corporation, Milwaukee,
WI

2672

SCION PUBLISHING LTD
Bloxham Mill, Barford Road, Bloxham, Oxon
OX15 4FF
Telephone: 01295 722873
Fax: 01295 722875
Web Site: www.scionpublishing.com

Distribution:
NBN International, Estover Road, Plymouth
PL6 7PZ

Directors: Dr Jonathan Ray *(Managing)*
Simon Watkins *(Sales & Marketing)*

*Academic & Scholarly; Biology & Zoology;
Chemistry; Medical (incl. Self Help &
Alternative Medicine); Scientific & Technical*

New Titles: 10 (2008) , 10 (2009)
No of Employees: 4
Annual Turnover: £650,000

ISBNs, Imprints & Series: 978 1 904842

Distributor for:
Brazil: Artes Medicas
UK: Medical Partners Publishing; The Ray
Society
USA: Cold Spring Harbor Laboratory Press;
DNA Press; Roberts & Co

Overseas Representation:
Americas (North & South): Cold Spring
Harbor Laboratory Press, Woodbury, NY,
USA
Australia & New Zealand: Macmillan
Education Australia, South Yarra, Vic,
Australia
*Europe (excluding France, Italy, Spain &
Portugal):* Andrew Durnell Marketing
Ltd, Tunbridge Wells, UK
Far East: The White Partnership, Tunbridge
Wells, UK
France, Italy, Spain & Portugal: Flavio
Marcello Publishers' Agents &
Consultants, Padua, Italy
South Africa: Mike Brightmore, Academic
Marketing Services, Johannesburg

2673

SCM-CANTERBURY PRESS LTD
13–17 Long Lane, London EC1A 9PN
Telephone: (020) 7776 7551
Fax: (020) 7776 7556
Email: office@hymnsam.co.uk
Web Site: www.hymnsam.co.uk

Warehouse & Distribution:
St Mary's Works, St Mary's Plain, Norwich
NR3 3BH
Telephone: 01603 612914
Fax: 01603 624483
Email:
admin@norwichbooksandmusic.co.uk

Directors: Dominic Vaughan *(Group Chief
Executive Officer)*
Michael Addison *(Sales & Marketing)*
Christine Smith *(Commissioning)*
Managers: Stephen Rogers *(Production)*
Brenda Medhurst *(Financial Controller)*
Kevin Allard *(UK Sales)*
Administrator: Rebecca Hills *(Rights)*
Commissioning Editors: Natalie Watson
(SCM Press)
Valerie Bingham *(RMEP)*

*Academic & Scholarly; Biography &
Autobiography; Educational & Textbooks;
Gay & Lesbian Studies; Gender Studies;
Music; Philosophy; Reference Books,
Directories & Dictionaries; Religion &*

Theology; Travel & Topography

ISBNs, Imprints & Series:
978 0 334 SCM Press
978 0 900274, 978 1 85175 Religious and
Moral Education Press
978 0 907547 Hymns Ancient & Modern
978 1 85311 Canterbury Press, Norwich

Parent Company:
Hymns Ancient and Modern Ltd

Distributor for:
Acora [Canterbury Press]; Cairns; Church
House Publishing; Churches Together in
Britain & Ireland; Concilium; Darton,
Longman & Todd; Epworth Press; Joint
Liturgical Studies; RSCM; SLG Press
[Canterbury Press]

Overseas Representation:
Australia (Canterbury Press, Norwich):
Rainbow Books, Fairfield, Vic, Australia
*Canada (SCM Press & Canterbury Press,
Norwich):* Novalis Inc, Toronto, Ont,
Canada
*Continental Europe (Canterbury Press &
SCM Press):* Durnell Marketing Ltd,
Tunbridge Wells, UK
New Zealand (Canterbury Press, Norwich):
Church Book Stores, Auckland, New
Zealand
*Republic of Ireland (Canterbury Press & SCM
Press):* Columba Book Service, Blackrock,
Co Dublin, Republic of Ireland
South Africa (SCM Press): Pearson, South
Africa
*USA (SCM Press & Canterbury Press,
Norwich):* Westminster John Knox Press,
Louisville, KY, USA

Book Trade Association Membership:
Publishers Association; IPG

2674

SCOTTISH CHILDREN'S PRESS
Unit 6, Newbattle Abbey Business Park,
Newbattle Road, Dalkeith EH22 3LJ
Telephone: 0131 660 4757 (editorial) &
4666 (orders)
Fax: 0870 285 4846 & 0131 660 4666
(orders)
Email: info@scottishbooks.com &
orders@scottishbooks.com
Web Site: www.scottishbooks.com

Directors: Brian Pugh *(Company Secretary)*
Avril Gray

*Archaeology; Biography & Autobiography;
Children's Books; Cookery, Wines & Spirits;
Fiction; History & Antiquarian; Languages &
Linguistics; Natural History; Poetry; Religion
& Theology; Sports & Games*

ISBNs, Imprints & Series: 978 1 899827

Associated Companies:
S.C.P. Publishers Ltd [trading as Scottish
Cultural Press]

2675

SCOTTISH CULTURAL PRESS
Unit 6, Newbattle Abbey Business Park,
Newbattle Road, Dalkeith EH22 3LJ
Telephone: 0131 660 6366 (editorial) &
4666 (orders)
Fax: 0870 285 4846
Email: info@scottishbooks.com &
orders@scottishbooks.com
Web Site: www.scottishbooks.com

Directors: Brian Pugh *(Company Secretary)*
Avril Gray

*Archaeology; Audio Books; Biography &
Autobiography; Cookery, Wines & Spirits;
Environment & Development Studies;
Geography & Geology; History &*

Antiquarian; Languages & Linguistics; Literature & Criticism; Military & War; Natural History; Nautical; Poetry; Reference Books, Directories & Dictionaries; Religion & Theology; Sociology & Anthropology; Theatre, Drama & Dance; Scottish Culture

ISBNs, Imprints & Series:
978 1 84017, 978 1 898218 Scottish
   Cultural Press (S.C.P. Publishers Ltd)
978 1 899827 Scottish Children's Press
   (S.C.P. Childrens Ltd)

Associated Companies:
S.C.P. Childrens Ltd [trading as Scottish
   Children's Press]

2676 ■

SCOTTISH TEXT SOCIETY
School of English Studies,
University of Nottingham, Nottingham
NG7 2RD
Telephone: 0115 951 5922
Fax: 0115 951 5924
Email:
   editorialsecretary@scottishtextsociety.org
Web Site: www.scottishtextsociety.org

Registered Office:
Basement Flat, 25 Buccleuch Place,
Edinburgh EH8 9LN

President: Sally Mapstone
Editorial Secretary: Nicola Royan

Academic & Scholarly; History & Antiquarian; Literature & Criticism; Poetry

New Titles: 3 (2008) , 1 (2009)

ISBNs, Imprints & Series: 978 1 897976

Overseas Representation:
Worldwide: Boydell & Brewer Ltd,
   Woodbridge, Suffolk, UK

Book Trade Association Membership:
Publishing Scotland

2677 ■

SCRIPTURE UNION PUBLISHING
Scripture Union, 207–209 Queensway,
Bletchley, Milton Keynes, Bucks MK2 2EB
Telephone: 01908 856000
Fax: 01908 856111
Email: info@scriptureunion.org.uk
Web Site: www.scripture.org.uk/

Warehouse:
STL, Carlisle

Mail Order:
PO Box 5148, Milton Keynes MLO
MK2 2YX
Telephone: 01908 856006
Fax: 01908 856020
Email: subs@scriptureunion.org.uk

Directors: Terry Clutterham *(Publishing)*
   Jim Thody *(Ministry Promotion)*
Managers: Dave Parsons *(Publishing
   Accounts)*
   Rosemary North *(Rights)*
   Clive Cornelius *(Production)*

Children's Books; Educational & Textbooks; Music; Religion & Theology

New Titles: 52 (2008) , 29 (2009)
No of Employees: 24
Annual Turnover: £2.7M

ISBNs, Imprints & Series:
978 0 85421, 978 0 86201 Scripture Union

Overseas Representation:
Australasia, East Asia & Pacific: Resources
   for Ministry, Gosford, NSW, Australia
Canada: Scripture Union, Pickering

New Zealand: Scripture Union Wholesale,
   Wellington
USA: Scripture Union, Wayne, PA

Book Trade Association Membership:
BA; EPC

2678 ■

***SEARCH PRESS LTD**
Wellwood, North Farm Road,
Tunbridge Wells, Kent TN2 3DR
Telephone: 01892 510850
Fax: 01892 515903
Email: sales@searchpress.com
Web Site: www.searchpress.com

Directors: Martin de la Bédoyère
   (Managing)
   Caroline de la Bédoyère
   Rosalind Dace *(Editorial)*
Editors: Katie Chester
   Heather Scott
   Sophie Kersey
Designer: Juan Hayward
Production Manager: Inger Arthur

Children's Books; Crafts & Hobbies; Do-It-Yourself; Gardening

ISBNs, Imprints & Series:
978 0 85532 Beginner's Guide to
   Needlecrafts; Children's Crafts; Design
   Source Books; Leisure Arts; Search Press
978 1 84448, 978 1 903975

Distributor for:
Akacia; Ashby & Woolsey; Country
Bumpkins; Forté Uitgevers; Interweave
Press; Kangaroo Press; Sally Milner
Publishing; Peel Productions; David
Porteous Editions; School of Colour
Publishing; Scrapbook Storytelling;
Traplet Publications; XRX Books

Overseas Representation:
Africa & Caribbean: Kelvin van Hasselt
   Publishing Services, Briningham, Norfolk,
   UK
Asia, Japan & Pacific Islands: Publishers
   International Marketing, Dulles, VA, USA
Australia: Keith Ainsworth (Pty) Ltd, Penrith,
   NSW
Canada: Fitzhenry & Whiteside Ltd,
   Markham, Ont
Eastern Europe: Tony Moggach, InterMedia
   Americana (IMA) Ltd, London, UK
Germany, Austria & Switzerland: PS
   Publishers' Services, Frankfurt, Germany
India: Maya Publishers Pvt Ltd, New Delhi
Iran: Samin Far Qeshm Co, Tehran
Italy, Spain, Portugal, Gibraltar & Greece:
   Penny Padovani, London, UK
Malta: Hobbyworld, Mosta, UK
New Zealand: David Bateman Ltd, Auckland
Pakistan: Tahir M. Lodhi, Lahore
Scandinavia: Angell Eurosales, Berwick-on-
   Tweed, UK
Singapore & Malaysia: Mark Kuo, Selangor
   Darul Ehsan, Malaysia
Southern Africa: Trinity Books CC,
   Randburg, South Africa
Turkey: Belsu Ic Ve Dis Tic Ltd, STI, Istanbul
USA & Canada (book trade): Independent
   Publishers Group (IPG), Chicago, IL, USA
USA (craft industry): Search Press USA,
   Petaluma, CA, USA

2679 ■

SEASQUIRT PUBLICATIONS
18d Church Gate, Loughborough, Leics
LE11 1UD
Telephone: 01509 219633
Fax: 01509 264441
Email: info@seasquirtbooks.com
Web Site: www.jimjazzmouse.com &
   www.infestedwaters.co.uk

Executive: David Hughes

Children's Books; Trade

Book Trade Association Membership:
Publishers Association; BA; IPG

2680 ■

SEDA PUBLICATIONS
[Staff & Educational Development
Association]
Woburn House, 20–24 Tavistock Square,
London WC1H 9HF
Telephone: (020) 7380 6767
Fax: (020) 7387 2655
Email: office@seda.ac.uk
Web Site: www.seda.ac.uk

Co-chair of SEDA: Lawrie Phipps

Academic & Scholarly

New Titles: 6 (2008) , 6 (2009)

Book Trade Association Membership:
Association of Learned & Professional
Society Publishers

2681 ■

SEREN
57 Nolton Street, Bridgend CF31 3AE
Telephone: 01656 663018
Email: seren@seren-books.com
Web Site: www.seren-books.com

Distribution:
Central Books, 99 Wallis Road, London
E9 5LN
Telephone: (020) 8986 4854
Fax: (020) 8533 5821
Email: orders@centralbooks.com
Web Site: www.centralbooks.com

Managing Director: Mick Felton
Marketing Officers: Simon Hicks
   Tori Kirwan-Taylor
Editors: Amy Wack *(Poetry)*
   Penny Thomas *(Fiction)*

Biography & Autobiography; Fiction; Fine Art & Art History; Literature & Criticism; Poetry; Politics & World Affairs; Theatre, Drama & Dance

New Titles: 21 (2008) , 25 (2009)
No of Employees: 6
Annual Turnover: £200,000

ISBNs, Imprints & Series:
978 0 907476, 978 1 85411

Parent Company:
Poetry Wales Press Ltd

Overseas Representation:
Australia: Eleanor Brasch Enterprises,
   Artarmon, NSW
USA & Canada: Independent Publishers
   Group (IPG), Chicago, IL, USA

2682 ■

SESSIONS OF YORK
The Ebor Press, Huntington Road, York
YO31 9HS
Telephone: 01904 659224
Fax: 01904 637068
Email: ebor.info@sessionsofyork.co.uk
Web Site: www.sessionsofyork.co.uk

Chairman & Managing Director: W. Mark
   Sessions
Publishing Manager: Bob Jarrett

Archaeology; Biography & Autobiography; Children's Books; History & Antiquarian; Industry, Business & Management; Natural History; Poetry; Politics & World Affairs; Religion & Theology

New Titles: 19 (2008) , 20 (2009)

ISBNs, Imprints & Series: 978 1 85072

Parent Company:
William Sessions Holdings Ltd

Book Trade Association Membership:
Quakers Uniting in Publishing

2683 ■

***SEVERN HOUSE PUBLISHERS LTD**
9–15 High Street, Sutton, Surrey SM1 1DF
Telephone: (020) 8770 3930
Fax: (020) 8770 3850
Email: editorial@severnhouse.com
Web Site: www.severnhouse.com

Distribution:
Grantham Book Services Ltd,
Isaac Newton Way,
Alma Park Industrial Estate, Grantham,
Lincs NG31 9SD
Telephone: 01476 541080
Fax: 01476 541061

Chairman: Edwin Buckhalter
Publishing Director: Amanda Stewart
Sales Manager: Michelle Duff

Crime; Fiction; Science Fiction

ISBNs, Imprints & Series:
978 0 7278 Severn House Large Print
978 1 84751 Trade Paperbacks

Parent Company:
Severn House Books (Holdings) Ltd

Associated Companies:
USA: Severn House Publishers

Overseas Representation:
Australia: DLS Australia (Pty) Ltd, Braeside,
   Vic
USA: Ingram Publisher Services, Nashville,
   TN

Book Trade Association Membership:
Crime Writers Association; Romantic
Novelists Association

2684 ■

SGC BOOKS
PO Box 49, Spalding, Lincs PE11 1NZ
Telephone: 01775 712424
Fax: 01775 762618
Email: chalksoft@clara.co.uk
Web Site: www.chalksoft.clara.co.uk

Directors: David Baldwin *(Managing)*
   Gillian Baldwin *(Home Sales, Rights)*

Children's Books; Gardening; Health & Beauty; Natural History

ISBNs, Imprints & Series: 978 1 85116

Parent Company:
Chalksoft Ltd

Associated Companies:
Nene Valley Publishing

Book Trade Association Membership:
IPG

2685 ■

SHARON HOUSE PUBLISHING
152 Wakefield Road, Ossett,
West Yorkshire WF5 9AQ
Telephone: 01924 279966
Fax: 01924 279966
Email: books@sharonhousepublishing.com
Web Site:
   www.sharonhousepublishing.com

Directors: Anna McKann
   Tim Wicks

Children's Books; Trade

New Titles: 2 (2008) , 2 (2009)

No of Employees: 3

ISBNs, Imprints & Series: 978 0 9554438

Book Trade Association Membership:
Publishers Association

2686

SHAW & SONS LTD
21 Bourne Park, Bourne Road, Crayford,
Kent DA1 4BZ
Telephone: 01322 621100
Fax: 01322 550553
Email: sales@shaws.co.uk
Web Site: www.shaws.co.uk

Directors: R. H. Smith *(Finance)*
Crispin Williams *(Publications)*

*Academic & Scholarly; Educational &
Textbooks; Law; Reference Books,
Directories & Dictionaries*

New Titles: 10 (2008) , 10 (2009)

ISBNs, Imprints & Series:
978 0 7219 R. Hazell & Co; Shaw & Sons
978 0 9045 Owen Wells Publishing

Parent Company:
Shaw & Sons Group Ltd

Book Trade Association Membership:
Law Services Association

2687

SHEAF PUBLISHING
Beehive Works, Milton Street, Sheffield
S3 7WL
Telephone: 0114 273 9067
Fax: 0114 270 6888

Manager: T. Cooper

History & Antiquarian; Transport

No of Employees: 4

ISBNs, Imprints & Series:
978 0 9505458, 978 1 85048

2688

SHELDON PRESS
36 Causton Street, London SW1P 4ST
Telephone: (020) 7592 3900
Fax: (020) 7592 3939
Email: jmoriarty@spck.org.uk
Web Site: www.sheldonpress.co.uk

Directors: Joanna Moriarty *(Publishing)*
Alan Mordue *(Sales & Marketing)*
Editor: Fiona Marshall
Rights Manager: Sophie Dean

*Gender Studies; Health & Beauty; Medical
(incl. Self Help & Alternative Medicine);
Psychology & Psychiatry*

New Titles: 25 (2008) , 25 (2009)

ISBNs, Imprints & Series:
978 0 85969 Sheldon Press
978 1 902694 Azure Books

Parent Company:
The Society for Promoting Christian
Knowledge (SPCK)

Overseas Representation:
Australia: Willow Connection Pty Ltd,
Brookvale, NSW
India: ISPCK, Delhi

2689

SHELDRAKE PRESS
188 Cavendish Road, London SW12 0DA
Telephone: (020) 8675 1767
Fax: (020) 8675 7736

Email: enquiries@sheldrakepress.co.uk
Web Site: www.sheldrakepress.co.uk

Distribution:
NBN International Ltd, Estover Road,
Plymouth PL6 7PY
Telephone: 01752 202300
Fax: 01752 202330
Email: enquiries@nbninternational.com
Web Site: www.nbninternational.com

Director: Simon Rigge *(Publisher)*
Company Secretary: Roger Rigge

*Architecture & Design; Children's Books;
Cookery, Wines & Spirits; Guide Books;
History & Antiquarian; Humour; Transport;
Travel & Topography*

New Titles: 3 (2009)

ISBNs, Imprints & Series: 978 1 873329

Parent Company:
Sheldrake Holdings Ltd

Overseas Representation:
USA: Interlink Publishing Group Inc,
Northampton, MA

2690

**SHEPHEARD-WALWYN
(PUBLISHERS) LTD**
15 Alder Road, London SW14 8ER
Telephone: (020) 8241 5927
Email: books@shepheard-walwyn.co.uk
Web Site: www.shepheard-walwyn.co.uk

Orders:
NBN International, Plymbridge House,
Estover Road, Plymouth PL6 7PY
Telephone: 01752 202301
Fax: 01752 202330
Email: orders@nbninternational.com
Web Site: www.nbninternational.com

Managing Director: Anthony R. A. Werner

*Academic & Scholarly; Biography &
Autobiography; Economics; History &
Antiquarian; Illustrated & Fine Editions;
Philosophy; Politics & World Affairs;
Religion & Theology; Scottish Interest*

New Titles: 7 (2008) , 7 (2009)
No of Employees: 2
Annual Turnover: £90,000

ISBNs, Imprints & Series:
The Letters of Marsilio Ficino; Marsilio
Ficino's Commentaries on Plato's
Writings; Who's Who in British History
series
978 0 85683

Overseas Representation:
Australia & New Zealand: John Reed Book
Distribution, Brookvale, NSW, Australia
USA & Canada: Independent Publishers
Group (IPG), Chicago, IL, USA

2691

SHERWOOD PUBLISHING
Wildhill, Broadoak End, Hertford SG14 2JA
Telephone: 01992 550246
Fax: 01992 535283
Email: sherwood@adinternational.com
Web Site: www.sherwoodpublishing.com

Chief Executive: Mrs Julie Hay

*Industry, Business & Management;
Psychology & Psychiatry*

New Titles: 4 (2009)

ISBNs, Imprints & Series:
978 0 9521964, 978 0 9539852

Overseas Representation:
India: Creative Communication and
Management Center, Bombay

Book Trade Association Membership:
IPG

2692

*THE SHETLAND TIMES LTD
Gremista, Lerwick, Shetland ZE1 0PX
Telephone: 01595 693622
Fax: 01595 694637
Email: publishing@shetland-times.co.uk
Web Site: www.shetland-books.co.uk

Scottish Agent:
BookSource, 50 Cambuslang Road,
Glasgow G32 8NB

Publications Manager: Charlotte Black

*Biography & Autobiography; Guide Books;
Music; Natural History*

ISBNs, Imprints & Series:
978 0 900662, 978 1 898852, 978 1
904746

Book Trade Association Membership:
BA; Publishing Scotland

2693

SHIRE PUBLICATIONS LTD
Midland House, West Way, Botley, Oxford
OX2 0PH
Email: shire@shirebooks.co.uk
Web Site: www.shirebooks.co.uk

Director: Rebecca Smart *(Managing)*
Managers: Sue Ross *(Home & Export Sales)*
Nicholas Wright *(Publisher)*

*Antiques & Collecting; Archaeology;
Architecture & Design; Biography &
Autobiography; Gardening; Guide Books;
History & Antiquarian; Military & War;
Natural History; Sociology & Anthropology;
Transport; Travel & Topography*

New Titles: 33 (2008) , 59 (2009)
No of Employees: 5
Annual Turnover: £500,000

ISBNs, Imprints & Series:
978 0 7478, 978 0 85263

Parent Company:
UK: Osprey Publishing Group

2694

SHORT BOOKS LTD
3A Exmouth House, Pine Street, London
EC1R 0JH
Telephone: (020) 7833 9429
Fax: (020) 7833 9500
Email: Rebecca@shortbooks.biz
Web Site: www.theshortbookco.com

Distribution:
TBS, Colchester Road, Frating Green,
Colchester CO7 7DW
Telephone: 01206 255678
Fax: 01206 255930

Publisher: Rebecca Nicolson
Managing Director: Catherine Gibbs
Editor: Aurea Carpenter

*Biography & Autobiography; Children's
Books; Fiction; History & Antiquarian;
Humour; Philosophy; Sports & Games*

New Titles: 11 (2008) , 16 (2009)

ISBNs, Imprints & Series:
978 1 904095, 978 1 904977, 978 1
906021

Book Trade Association Membership:
IPG

2695

SIGEL PRESS
51A Victoria Road, Cambridge CB4 3BW
Telephone: 01223 303303
Fax: 01223 303303
Email: info@sigelpress.com
Web Site: www.sigelpress.com

Directors: Thomas Sigel *(Managing &
Publisher)*
Andrew Hogbin *(Operations)*

*Academic & Scholarly; Accountancy &
Taxation; Audio Books; Children's Books;
Educational & Textbooks; Environment &
Development Studies; Fiction; Industry,
Business & Management; Military & War;
Science Fiction*

New Titles: 2 (2008) , 4 (2009)
No of Employees: 3

ISBNs, Imprints & Series: 978 1 905941

Associated Companies:
USA: Sigel Press

Book Trade Association Membership:
IPG

2696

SIGMA PRESS
Stobart House, Pontyclerc, Penybanc Road,
Ammanford, Carmarthenshire SA18 3HP
Telephone: 01269 593100
Fax: 01269 596116
Email: info@sigmapress.co.uk
Web Site: www.sigmapress.co.uk

Managing Director: Nigel Evans
Managing Editor: Jane Evans

*Crafts & Hobbies; Guide Books; Sports &
Games; Travel & Topography*

New Titles: 10 (2009)
No of Employees: 5

ISBNs, Imprints & Series:
978 0 905104, 978 1 85058 Sigma
Leisure; Sigma Press

Parent Company:
UK: Stobart Davies Ltd

Overseas Representation:
USA: Barnes & Noble Distribution,
Jamesburg, NJ

Book Trade Association Membership:
BA; IPG

2697

SILVER MOON BOOKS
108c Goldhurst Terrace, London NW6 3HR
Telephone: (020) 7625 7592

Trade Enquiries & Orders:
Turnaround Publisher Services, Unit 3,
Olympia Trading Estate, Coburg Road,
London N22 6TZ
Telephone: (020) 8829 3000
Fax: (020) 8881 5088

Director: Jane Cholmeley

Fiction; Gay & Lesbian Studies

ISBNs, Imprints & Series: 978 1 872642

2698

SIMON & SCHUSTER (UK) LTD
1st Floor, 222 Gray's Inn Road, London
WC1X 8HB
Telephone: (020) 7316 1900

Fax: (020) 7316 0331
Email: @simonandschuster.co.uk
Web Site: www.simonsays.co.uk

**Customer Services & Distribution
Centre:**
HarperCollins, Customer Service Centre,
Westerhill Road, Bishopbriggs, Glasgow
G64 2QT
Telephone: 0141 306 3100
Fax: 0141 306 3767

Directors: Ian Stewart Chapman
(Managing)
Suzanne Baboneau (Adult Publishing)
Julie Wright (Pocket Books Publisher)
Mike Jones (Editorial – Non-Fiction)
Ingrid Selberg (Children's Publishing)
Charlotte Robertson (Group Sales)
Hannah Corbett (Publicity – Adult Trade)
David Hyde (Production)
Sarah Birdsey (Rights)
Nick Hayward (Export Sales)
Stuart Mullin (Finance & Operations)
Dawn Burnett (Marketing)

Audio Books; Biography & Autobiography;
Children's Books; Cookery, Wines & Spirits;
Crime; Fiction; Guide Books; Health &
Beauty; Humour; Industry, Business &
Management; Medical (incl. Self Help &
Alternative Medicine); Music; Politics &
World Affairs; Science Fiction; Sports &
Games; Travel & Topography

ISBNs, Imprints & Series:
978 0 671, 978 0 684, 978 0 7432, 978 1
4165 Free Press; Scribner
978 0 671, 978 0 684, 978 0 7432, 978 1
4165, 978 1 84737 Simon & Schuster
978 0 671, 978 0 7434, 978 1 4165, 978 1
84739 Pocket
978 0 6898, 978 1 4169, 978 1 84738
Simon & Schuster Children's
978 0 7435 Simon & Schuster Audio

Parent Company:
USA: Simon & Schuster Inc

Distributor for:
UK: Duncan Baird; BL Publishing; Long Barn
Books
USA: Andrews McMeel; Atria; Fireside; Free
Press; Pocket; Scribner; Simon & Schuster
Inc; Simon & Schuster Audio;
Touchstone; VIZ Media; Zagat

Overseas Representation:
Australia: Simon & Schuster (Australia) Pty
Ltd, Pymble, NSW
Canada: Simon & Schuster (Canada),
Markham, Ont
New Zealand: HarperCollins (NZ) Ltd,
Glenfield, Auckland
Singapore: Penguin Books Singapore,
Jurong
South Africa: Jonathan Ball Publishers (Pty)
Ltd, Johannesburg
USA: Trafalgar Square Publishing / IPG,
Chicago, IL

Book Trade Association Membership:
Publishers Association

2699

CHARLES SKILTON LTD
2 Caversham Street, London SW3 4AH
Telephone: (020) 7351 4995
Fax: (020) 7351 4995
Email: leonard.holdsworth@btinternet.com

Directors: James Hughes (Managing)
Margaret Fletcher (Sales)
Editor: Leonard Holdsworth

Cinema, Video, TV & Radio; Cookery, Wines
& Spirits; Fashion & Costume; Fiction; Fine

Art & Art History; Gay & Lesbian Studies;
Guide Books; Illustrated & Fine Editions;
Literature & Criticism; Military & War;
Poetry; Theatre, Drama & Dance;
Transport; Travel & Topography

New Titles: 12 (2008), 15 (2009)
No of Employees: 6

ISBNs, Imprints & Series:
978 0 284 Skilton
978 1 901846 Christchurch

Parent Company:
Christchurch Publishers Ltd

Associated Companies:
Caversham Communications Ltd;
Christchurch Publishers Ltd; Luxor Press

Book Trade Association Membership:
IPG

2700

SLIGHTLY FOXED
67 Dickinson Court, 15 Brewhouse Yard,
London EC1V 4JX
Telephone: (020) 7549 2121
Fax: 0870 199 1245
Email: all@foxedquarterly.com
Web Site: www.foxedquarterly.com

Managing Director: Gail Pirkis
Co-Editor: Hazel Wood
Marketing Manager: Stephanie Allen
Administrator: Jennie Paterson

Academic & Scholarly; Biography &
Autobiography; Children's Books; Fiction;
Gardening; History & Antiquarian;
Illustrated & Fine Editions; Travel &
Topography

New Titles: 8 (2008), 8 (2009)

ISBNs, Imprints & Series: 978 1 906562

Book Trade Association Membership:
IPG

2701

SLS LEGAL PUBLICATIONS (NI)
Lansdowne House, 50 Malone Road,
Belfast BT9 5BS
Telephone: (028) 9066 7711
Fax: (028) 9066 7733
Email: s.gamble@qub.ac.uk
Web Site: www.sls.qub.ac.uk

Director: Miss M. Dudley
Publications Editor: Mrs S. Gamble

Academic & Scholarly; Law

No of Employees: 5
Annual Turnover: £76,000

ISBNs, Imprints & Series: 978 0 85389

Book Trade Association Membership:
Publishers Association; CAPP

2702

**SMITH SETTLE PRINTING &
BOOKBINDING LTD**
Gateway Drive, Yeadon, West Yorkshire
LS19 7XY
Telephone: 0113 250 9201
Fax: 0113 250 9223
Email: sales@smithsettle.com
Web Site: www.smithsettle.com

Directors: Donald Waters (Managing)
Tracey Daly (Finance)

Academic & Scholarly; Agriculture;
Archaeology; Biography & Autobiography;
History & Antiquarian; Illustrated & Fine

Editions; Sports & Games; Travel &
Topography

No of Employees: 2

ISBNs, Imprints & Series: 978 1 84103

Associated Companies:
Westbury

Distributor for:
Ken Smith Publishing Ltd; Woodstock
Books Ltd

Book Trade Association Membership:
IPG

2703

*ADAM SMITH INSTITUTE
23 Great Smith Street, London SW1P 3BL
Telephone: (020) 7222 4995
Fax: (020) 7222 1436
Email: info@adamsmith.org.uk
Web Site: www.adamsmith.org.uk

Director: Dr Eamonn Butler
President: Dr Madsen Pirie

Accountancy & Taxation; Economics;
Politics & World Affairs

ISBNs, Imprints & Series:
978 0 906517, 978 1 870109, 978 1
873712, 978 1 902737

Parent Company:
ASI (Research) Ltd

2704

COLIN SMYTHE LTD
PO Box 6, Gerrards Cross, Bucks SL9 8XA
Telephone: 01753 886000
Fax: 01753 886469
Email: sales@colinsmythe.co.uk
Web Site: www.colinsmythe.co.uk

Warehouse & Despatch only:
Print on Demand, 9 Culley Court,
Bakewell Road, Orton Southgate,
Peterborough PE2 6WA
Telephone: 01733 237867
Fax: 01733 234309

Managing Director: Colin Smythe (Sales,
Editorial, Rights & Production)

Academic & Scholarly; Bibliography &
Library Science; Biography &
Autobiography; Literature & Criticism;
Theatre, Drama & Dance; Heraldry; Orders
of Knighthood

New Titles: 3 (2008), 5 (2009)
No of Employees: 2
Annual Turnover: £60,000

ISBNs, Imprints & Series:
978 0 85105 Dolmen Press
978 0 86140, 978 0 900675, 978 0 901072
978 0 905715 Van Duren

Distributor for:
Republic of Ireland: Tir Eolas
USA: ELT Press

Overseas Representation:
Ireland: Hibernian Book Services, Dublin,
Republic of Ireland
USA & Canada: Dufour Editions Inc, Chester
Springs, PA, USA
USA & Canada (recent academic titles):
Oxford University Press Inc USA, New
York, NY, USA

Book Trade Association Membership:
Publishers Association; IPG; Booksellers'
Association Associate Member

2705

*SNOWBOOKS
120 Pentonville Road, London N1 9JN
Telephone: 0790 406 2414
Email: emma@snowbooks.com
Web Site: www.snowbooks.com

Distribution:
Littlehampton Book Services,
Faraday Close, Durrington, Worthing,
West Sussex BN13 3RB
Telephone: 01903 828511
Fax: 01903 828801
Email: orders@lbsltd.co.uk
Web Site: www.lbsltd.co.uk

Managing Director: Emma Barnes
Chairman: Rob Jones
Publisher: Anna Torborg

Cookery, Wines & Spirits; Crafts & Hobbies;
Crime; Fiction; Humour; Illustrated & Fine
Editions; Science Fiction; Sports & Games;
Transport

ISBNs, Imprints & Series:
978 0 954575, 978 1 905005, 978 1
906727

Overseas Representation:
Australia: Julie Pinkham, Hardie Grant
Books, Prahran, Vic
Europe & Ireland: Andrew Durnell, Durnell
Marketing Ltd, Tunbridge Wells, UK
Far East: Peter Couzens, Sales East,
Bangkok, Thailand
USA & Canada: Consortium Publishers, St
Paul, MN, USA

Book Trade Association Membership:
IPG

2706

SOCCER BOOKS LTD
72 St Peter's Avenue, Cleethorpes, Lincs
DN35 8HU
Telephone: 01472 696226
Fax: 01472 698546
Email: info@soccer-books.co.uk
Web Site: www.soccer-books.co.uk

Directors: John Robinson (Managing)
Michael Robinson

Sports & Games; Transport

New Titles: 10 (2008), 13 (2009)
No of Employees: 4

ISBNs, Imprints & Series:
978 1 86223 Complete Results & Line-ups
(Series); Football In (Series); Supporters'
Guide (Series)

2707

SOCIAL AFFAIRS UNIT
10/11 Morley House,
314–322 Regent Street, London W1B 5SA
Telephone: (020) 7637 4356
Fax: (020) 7436 8530
Email: mosbacher@socialaffairsunit.org.uk
Web Site: www.socialaffairsunit.org.uk

Director: Michael Mosbacher

Academic & Scholarly; Crime; Economics;
Educational & Textbooks; Environment &
Development Studies; Industry, Business &
Management; Medical (incl. Self Help &
Alternative Medicine); Politics & World
Affairs; Reference Books, Directories &
Dictionaries; Sociology & Anthropology

New Titles: 10 (2008), 11 (2009)
No of Employees: 3
Annual Turnover: £350,000

ISBNs, Imprints & Series:
978 0 907631, 978 1 904863

2708

THE SOCIETY FOR PROMOTING CHRISTIAN KNOWLEDGE (SPCK)
36 Causton Street, London SW1P 4ST
Telephone: (020) 7592 3900
Fax: (020) 7592 3939
Email: publishing@spck.org.uk
Web Site: www.spck.org.uk

Warehouse & Distribution:
Marston Book Services, Unit 160,
Milton Park, Abingdon, Oxon OX14 4SD
Telephone: 01235 465500
Fax: 01235 465555

Directors: Simon Kingston (*Chief Executive Officer*)
Joanna Moriarty (*Publishing*)
Alan Mordue (*Sales & Marketing*)
Barry Finch (*Production*)
Editors: Alison Barr
Fiona Marshall
Ruth McCurry
Rights: Sophie Dean (*Sales Co-ordinator*)

Academic & Scholarly; Illustrated & Fine Editions; Medical (incl. Self Help & Alternative Medicine); Psychology & Psychiatry; Religion & Theology

ISBNs, Imprints & Series:
978 0 281 SPCK; Triangle Books
978 0 7459 Lynx Communication
978 0 85969, 978 1 84709 Sheldon Press
978 1 902694 Azure Books

Overseas Representation:
Australia: Willow Connection Pty Ltd,
Brookvale, NSW
Canada: Bayard Distribution, Toronto, Ont
Far East (Sheldon): CKK Ltd, Northwood,
Middx, UK
Far East (SPCK, Triangle, Azure): Publishers
International Marketing, London, UK
India: ISPCK, Delhi
Middle East (Sheldon): Family Bookshop
Group Co Ltd, Limassol, Cyprus
New Zealand (SPCK, Triangle, Azure):
Omega Distributors Ltd, Auckland, New
Zealand
Northern Europe: Ted Dougherty, London,
UK
South Africa (Sheldon): Alternative Books
CC, Ferndale, South Africa
USA (SPCK, Triangle, Azure): Westminster
John Knox Press, Louisville, KY, USA

Book Trade Association Membership:
Publishers Association

2709

SOCIETY OF ANTIQUARIES OF SCOTLAND
NMS, Chambers Street, Edinburgh EH1 1JF
Telephone: 0131 247 4145
Fax: 0131 247 4163
Email: publications@socantscot.org
Web Site: www.socantscot.org

Director: Dr Simon Gilmour
Sales & Publicity Manager: Erin Osborne-
Martin (*Managing Editor*)

*Academic & Scholarly; Archaeology; History
& Antiquarian*

New Titles: 3 (2008) , 5 (2009)
No of Employees: 6
Annual Turnover: £200,000

ISBNs, Imprints & Series: 978 0 903903

2710

SOCIETY OF GENEALOGISTS ENTERPRISES LTD
14 Charterhouse Buildings, London
EC1M 7BA
Telephone: (020) 7251 8799
Fax: (020) 7250 1800

Email: sales@sog.org.uk
Web Site: www.sog.org.uk/

Chief Executiver: June Perrin
Retail Manager: Anthony Mortimer

History & Antiquarian

New Titles: 1 (2008) , 5 (2009)

ISBNs, Imprints & Series: 978 1 903462

Parent Company:
Society of Genealogists

Book Trade Association Membership:
BA

2711

THE SOCIETY OF METAPHYSICIANS LTD
Archers' Court, Stonestile Lane, The Ridge,
Hastings, East Sussex TN35 4PG
Telephone: 01424 751577
Fax: 01424 751577
Email: newmeta@btinternet.com
Web Site: www.metaphysicians.org.uk

Managing Director: Dr J. J. Williamson
Secretary: Ms C. Yuen
Research: D. Cumberland (*Scientific &
Literary*)
Miss D. Harris (*Paranormal*)
Tutor: Mervin Gould
Web: David Servera-Williamon

*Academic & Scholarly; Educational &
Textbooks; Electronic (Educational);
Environment & Development Studies;
Magic & the Occult; Medical (incl. Self Help
& Alternative Medicine); Philosophy;
Scientific & Technical; Esoteric;
Neometaphysics; Paraphysics;
Parapsychology*

New Titles: 6 (2008) , 12 (2009)
No of Employees: 4

ISBNs, Imprints & Series:
978 0 900680, 978 1 85228, 978 1 85810

Associated Companies:
Metaphysical Research Group
Argentina: Sociedad de Metafisica Inglesa
Belgium: Society of Metaphysicians
Italy: Istituto Italiano di Ricerche Metafisiche
Nigeria: Society of Metaphysicians (Nigeria)
Ltd

Distributor for:
USA: Ars Obscura [Archival Reproductions];
Health Research [Rare reprints]

Overseas Representation:
Australia: Magic Circle Bookshop, Perth
Belgium: Ignoramus, As; L' Univers
Particulier, Brussels
Netherlands: Boekhandel Synthese, 's
Gravenhage
New Zealand: Bennet's Bookshop,
Palmerston North
Spain: Eyras Editorial, Madrid
Tenerife: Soluciones, Spain
USA: H.R., Pomeroy, WA

2712

SOLIDUS
Hope Springs, Far End, Sheepscombe,
Stroud, Glos GL6 7RL
Telephone: 01452 758940
Email: info@soliduspress.com
Web Site: www.soliduspress.com

Manager: Helen Miles

Children's Books; Fiction

ISBNs, Imprints & Series:
978 0 954337 Solidus

978 1 904529 Back to Front

2713

SOUTHGATE PUBLISHERS
The Square, Sandford, Crediton, Devon
EX17 4LW
Telephone: 01363 776888
Fax: 01363 776889
Email: info@southgatepublishers.co.uk
Web Site: www.southgatepublishers.co.uk

Managing Director: Drummond
Johnstone
Production Manager: Marlene Buckland

*Educational & Textbooks; Environment &
Development Studies; Vocational Training &
Careers*

ISBNs, Imprints & Series: 978 1 85741

Associated Companies:
Mosaic Educational Publications

Distributor for:
Campaign for Learning; Learning Through
Landscapes Trust

Overseas Representation:
Canada: Bacon & Hughes Ltd, Ottawa, Ont

Book Trade Association Membership:
IPG

2714

SOUVENIR PRESS LTD
43 Great Russell Street, London WC1B 3PD
Telephone: (020) 7580 9307/8 & 7637
5711/2/3
Fax: (020) 7580 5064
Email: souvenirpress@ukonline.co.uk

Distributors & Warehouse:
Bookpoint Ltd, 130 Milton Trading Estate,
Abingdon, Oxon OX14 4SB
Telephone: 01235 400400
Fax: 01235 400413

Managing Director & Chairman: Ernest
Hecht

*Academic & Scholarly; Animal Care &
Breeding; Antiques & Collecting;
Archaeology; Biography & Autobiography;
Crafts & Hobbies; Gardening; Gender
Studies; Health & Beauty; Humour;
Industry, Business & Management;
Literature & Criticism; Magic & the Occult;
Medical (incl. Self Help & Alternative
Medicine); Military & War; Music; Natural
History; Philosophy; Psychology &
Psychiatry; Religion & Theology; Sociology
& Anthropology; Sports & Games; Theatre,
Drama & Dance; Travel & Topography;
Veterinary Science*

New Titles: 45 (2008) , 40 (2009)

ISBNs, Imprints & Series:
978 0 285 Condor Books; Human
Horizons; Souvenir Press (Educational &
Academic) Ltd; Souvenir Press Ltd

Associated Companies:
Pictorial Presentations Ltd; Pop Universal
Ltd; Souvenir Press (Educational &
Academic) Ltd

Overseas Representation:
Australia: Tower Books Pty Ltd, Brookvale,
NSW
*Austria, Benelux, France, Germany,
Switzerland, Greece & Italy:* Ted
Dougherty, London, UK
India: Rupa, New Delhi
Middle East: Peter Ward Book Exports,
London, UK
New Zealand: Addenda, Auckland
Scandinavia: John Edgeler, London, UK
South Africa: Trinity Books CC, Randburg

2715

SPARTAN PRESS MUSIC PUBLISHERS LTD
Strathmashie House, Laggan,
Inverness-shire PH20 1BU
Telephone: 01528 544770
Fax: 01528 544771
Email: sales@spartanpress.co.uk
Web Site: www.spartanpress.co.uk

Directors: Mark Goddard (*Managing*)
Pat Goddard
Managers: Sandra Grant (*Sales*)
Ian Stevenson (*IT*)

Music

ISBNs, Imprints & Series:
ISMN: 57 999

Distributor for:
Netherlands: European Music Centre
UK: Camden Music; Colne Edition; G. S.
Music; Hunt Edition; Múzicas Editions;
Nova Music; Pan Educational Music;
Queen's Temple Publications; Sunshine
Music Co; Useful Music; Yorke Edition

Overseas Representation:
Netherlands: European Music Centre,
Huizen
USA & Canada: Theodore Presser Co, King
of Prussia, PA, USA

2716

SPECIAL INTEREST MODEL BOOKS LTD
50a Willis Way, Poole, Dorset BH15 3SY
Telephone: 01202 649930
Fax: 01202 649950
Email: chrlloyd@globalnet.co.uk
Web Site:
www.specialinterestmodelbooks.co.uk

Managing Director: Chris Lloyd

*Aviation; Cookery, Wines & Spirits; Crafts &
Hobbies; Engineering; Nautical; Transport*

New Titles: 6 (2008) , 6 (2009)

ISBNs, Imprints & Series:
978 0 85242 Workshop Practice Series
978 0 900841 Amateur Winemaker Books
978 1 85486 formerly Argus Books;
formerly MAP (Model & Allied
Publications); formerly Nexus Special
Interest Books

Overseas Representation:
Australia: Capricorn Link (Australia) Pty Ltd,
Windsor, NSW
Eastern Europe, East & West Africa:
Anthony Moggach, InterMedia
Americana (IMA) Ltd, London, UK
New Zealand: South Pacific Books (Imports)
Ltd, Auckland
*Scandinavia (including Denmark, Sweden,
Norway, Finland & Iceland) &
Netherlands:* Angell Eurosales, Berwick-
on-Tweed, UK
South Africa: Everybody's Books, Kwa Zulu
Natal, South Africa
South & Central America & Caribbean:
David Williams, InterMedia Americana
(IMA) Ltd, London, UK
*South East Asia (including Singapore,
Malaysia, Brunei, Indonesia, Hong Kong,
Taiwan, China, Philippines, Thailand &
Japan):* Ashton International Marketing
Services, Sevenoaks, Kent, UK
*Southern Europe (including Spain, Portugal,
Italy, Malta & Greece):* Joe Portelli,
Bookport Associates, Corsico (MI), Italy
*Western Europe (including France, Belgium,
Germany, Switzerland & Austria):*
Anselm Robinson, European Marketing
Services, London, UK

2717

SPEECHMARK PUBLISHING LTD
70 Alston Drive, Bradwell Abbey,
Milton Keynes MK13 9HG
Telephone: 0845 034 4610
Fax: 0845 034 4649
Email: info@speechmark.net
Web Site: www.speechmark.net

Customer Service:
(as above)
Telephone: 0800 243755 & 0845 034
4610
Fax: 0845 034 4649
Email: sales@speechmark.net
Web Site: www.speechmark.net

Managing Director: Liz Lane
Marketing Manager: Su Wheeler
Publishing: Tanya Dean

*Children's Books; Educational & Textbooks;
English as a Foreign Language; Health &
Beauty; Languages & Linguistics; Medical
(incl. Self Help & Alternative Medicine);
Psychology & Psychiatry; Care of the
Elderly; Occupational Therapy; Speech
Therapy*

ISBNs, Imprints & Series:
ColorCards; Helping Children with
Feelings; Speechmark Editions
978 0 86388

Parent Company:
UK: Electric Word Plc

2718

SPOKESMAN
Russell House, Bulwell Lane, Nottingham
NG6 0BT
Telephone: 0115 978 4504 & 970 8318
Fax: 0115 942 0433
Email: elfeuro@compuserve.com
Web Site: www.spokesmanbooks.com

Managers: Ken Fleet *(General)*
Tony Simpson *(Publications)*
Editor: Ken Coates

*Economics; Fiction; History & Antiquarian;
Military & War; Philosophy; Poetry; Politics
& World Affairs; Sociology &
Anthropology; Theatre, Drama & Dance;
Europe; Works of Bertrand Russell*

New Titles: 10 (2008) , 11 (2009)
No of Employees: 4
Annual Turnover: £50,000

ISBNs, Imprints & Series:
978 0 85124 Socialist Renewal; The
Spokesman

Associated Companies:
Bertrand Russell Peace Foundation Ltd

2719

SPORTSBOOKS LTD
1 Evelyn Court, Malvern Road, Cheltenham
GL50 2JR
Telephone: 01242 256755
Fax: 01242 254694
Email: randall@sportsbooks.ltd.uk
Web Site: www.sportsbooks.ltd.uk

Distribution:
Turnaround Publisher Services Ltd, Unit 3,
Olympia Industrial Estate, Coburg Road,
London N22 6TZ
Telephone: (020) 8829 3000
Fax: (020) 8881 5088
Email: orders@turnaround-uk.com
Web Site: www.turnaround-psl.com

Chairman: Randall Northam
Director: Veronica Northam

*Fiction; History & Antiquarian; Sports &
Games*

ISBNs, Imprints & Series:
978 0 9541544, 978 1 899807 BMM;
Sportsbooks

Overseas Representation:
Australia & New Zealand: Landmark Press,
Drovin, Vic, Australia
South Africa: Zytek Publishing (Pty) Ltd,
Bedfordview

2720

SPRINGER LONDON
Ashbourne House, The Guildway,
Old Portsmouth Road, Guildford GU3 1LP
Telephone: 01483 734646
Fax: 01483 734411
Email: jean.lovell-butt@springer.com
Web Site: www.springer.com

Managers: Beverley Ford *(General)*
Gabrielle Bunning *(Finance)*

*Academic & Scholarly; Chemistry;
Computer Science; Engineering;
Mathematics & Statistics; Medical (incl. Self
Help & Alternative Medicine)*

No of Employees: 35

Book Trade Association Membership:
Publishers Association

2721

STACEY INTERNATIONAL
128 Kensington Church Street, London
W8 4BH
Telephone: (020) 7221 7166
Fax: (020) 7792 9288
Email: info@stacey-international.co.uk
Web Site: www.stacey-international.co.uk

Distribution:
Central Books, 99 Wallis Road,
Hackney Wick, London E9 5LN
Telephone: 0845 458 9911
Fax: 0845 458 9912
Email: orders@centralbooks.com
Web Site: www.centralbooks.com

Chairman: T. C. G. Stacey
Director: Max Scott

*Academic & Scholarly; Archaeology;
Architecture & Design; Biography &
Autobiography; Children's Books;
Educational & Textbooks; Fine Art & Art
History; Geography & Geology; Guide
Books; History & Antiquarian; Illustrated &
Fine Editions; Languages & Linguistics;
Military & War; Natural History;
Photography; Politics & World Affairs;
Reference Books, Directories &
Dictionaries; Religion & Theology; Travel &
Topography*

New Titles: 30 (2008) , 30 (2009)
No of Employees: 8

ISBNs, Imprints & Series:
978 0 905743, 978 0 9559447, 978 0
9559602, 978 1 900988, 978 1 903185,
978 1 905299
978 1 906768

Parent Company:
Stacey Arts Ltd

Associated Companies:
Capuchin Classics; Gorilla Guides; Rubicon
Press

Overseas Representation:
Australia: Peribo Pty Ltd, Mount Kuring-Gai,
NSW
Europe: Durnell Marketing Ltd, Tunbridge
Wells, UK
USA: The David Brown Book Co, Oakville,

CT; Interlink Publishing Group Inc,
Northampton, MA; IPG, Concord, MA

Book Trade Association Membership:
IPG

2722

STAINER & BELL LTD
PO Box 110, 23 Gruneisen Road, London
N3 1DZ
Telephone: (020) 8343 3303
Fax: (020) 8343 3024
Email: post@stainer.co.uk
Web Site: www.stainer.co.uk

Directors: Keith Wakefield *(Joint
Managing, Marketing, Permissions,
Accounts & Distribution)*
Carol Wakefield *(Joint Managing)*
Antony Kearns *(Deputy Managing)*
Nicholas Williams *(Publishing)*
Amanda Aknai *(Production)*

*Academic & Scholarly; Biography &
Autobiography; History & Antiquarian;
Music; Reference Books, Directories &
Dictionaries; Religion & Theology; Theatre,
Drama & Dance*

New Titles: 25 (2008) , 25 (2009)
No of Employees: 10
Annual Turnover: £888,221

ISBNs, Imprints & Series:
978 0 85249 Augener; Early English Church
Music; Galliard; Music for London
Entertainment; Musica Britannica;
Stainer & Bell; Weekes; Joseph Williams

Associated Companies:
Galliard Ltd

Distributor for:
USA: ECS Publishing Co [Rental Library]

Overseas Representation:
USA (hymn copyrights & selected titles):
Hope Publishing, Carol Stream, IL, USA
USA (Rental Library): ECS Publishing Co,
Boston, MA, USA

Book Trade Association Membership:
The Music Publishers Association Ltd

2723

RUDOLF STEINER PRESS
Hillside House, The Square, Forest Row,
East Sussex RH18 5ES
Telephone: 01342 824433
Fax: 01342 826437
Email: office@rudolfsteinerpress.com
Web Site: www.rudolfsteinerpress.com

Trade Enquiries & Orders:
BookSource, 50 Cambuslang Road,
Glasgow G32 8NB
Telephone: 0845 370 0063
Fax: 0845 370 0064
Email: orders@booksource.net
Web Site: www.booksource.net

Manager: Sevak Gulbekian *(Chief Editor)*

*Biography & Autobiography; Educational &
Textbooks; Fine Art & Art History; Magic &
the Occult; Medical (incl. Self Help &
Alternative Medicine); Music; Philosophy;
Politics & World Affairs; Religion &
Theology; Sociology & Anthropology;
Theatre, Drama & Dance*

New Titles: 20 (2008) , 20 (2009)
No of Employees: 2
Annual Turnover: £175,000

ISBNs, Imprints & Series:
978 0 85440, 978 1 85584 Mercury Arts
Publications; New Knowledge Books;
Sophia Books; Rudolf Steiner Press
978 0 88010, 978 0 091014 Steiner Books

978 0 88010, 978 0 91014
Anthroposophic Press

Distributor for:
Mercury Arts Publications; New Knowledge
Books
Australia: Completion Press
USA: Steinerbooks

Overseas Representation:
Australia: Rudolf Steiner Book Centre,
Sydney, NSW
Canada: Tri-fold Books, Guelph, Ont
New Zealand: Ceres Books, Ellerslie
South Africa: Rudolf Steiner Publications,
Bryanston
USA: Steiner Books Inc, Herndon, VA

Book Trade Association Membership:
IPG

2724

STENLAKE PUBLISHING LTD
54–58 Mill Square, Catrine, Ayrshire
KA5 6RD
Telephone: 01290 551122
Fax: 01290 551122
Email: enquiries@stenlake.co.uk
Web Site: www.stenlake.co.uk

Editorial: David Pettigrew
Managing Director: Richard Stenlake
Sales: Alex F. Young

*Aviation; Crafts & Hobbies; History &
Antiquarian; Literature & Criticism;
Nautical; Poetry; Transport*

ISBNs, Imprints & Series:
978 0 907526 Alloway Publishing
978 1 84033, 978 1 872074 Stenlake
Publishing

2725

STOBART DAVIES LTD
Stobart House, Pontyclerc, Penybanc Road,
Ammanford, Carmarthenshire SA18 3HP
Telephone: 01269 593100
Fax: 01269 596116
Email: sales@stobartdavies.com
Web Site: www.stobartdavies.com

Directors: Jane Evans
Nigel Evans

*Crafts & Hobbies; Do-It-Yourself; Natural
History; Scientific & Technical*

New Titles: 7 (2008) , 6 (2009)
No of Employees: 5
Annual Turnover: £202,500

ISBNs, Imprints & Series:
978 0 85442 Stobart Davies Ltd
978 1 85058 Sigma Leisure / Sigma Press

Parent Company:
Stobart Davis (2002) Ltd

Overseas Representation:
Australia & New Zealand: Footprint Books
Pty Ltd, Warriewood, NSW, Australia
Europe: Ted Dougherty, London, UK
Far East: Sales East, Bangkok, Thailand
New Zealand: David Bateman Ltd, Auckland
South Africa: Peter Hyde Associates (Pty)
Ltd, Cape Town

Book Trade Association Membership:
BA; IPG

2726

*STOKESBY HOUSE PUBLICATIONS
Stokesby, Norfolk NR29 3ET
Telephone: 01493 750645
Email: pamela.minett@waitrose.com
Web Site: www.stokesbyhouse.co.uk

Publisher & Marketing: Pamela Minett

Educational & Textbooks; Environment & Development Studies; Medical (incl. Self Help & Alternative Medicine)

ISBNs, Imprints & Series:
978 0 9514490, 978 1 873600

2727 ▬

STOTT'S CORRESPONDENCE COLLEGE
PO Box 35488, St John's Wood, London
NW8 6WD
Telephone: (020) 7586 4499
Email: microworld@ndirect.co.uk
Web Site: www.microworld.uk.com

Director: S. C. Albert

Academic & Scholarly; Crafts & Hobbies; Fashion & Costume; Health & Beauty

Distributor for:
Australia: Stott's Correspondence College

2728 ▬

STRI (SPORTS TURF RESEARCH INSTITUTE)
St Ives Estate, Bingley, West Yorks
BD16 1AU
Telephone: 01274 565131
Fax: 01274 561891
Email: info@stri.co.uk
Web Site: www.stri.co.uk/bookshop

Chief Executive: Dr Gordon McKillop
Financial Director: Mark Godfrey
Head of External Affairs: Anne Wilson

Educational & Textbooks; Environment & Development Studies; Reference Books, Directories & Dictionaries; Scientific & Technical; Sports & Games

New Titles: 2 (2008) , 3 (2009)
No of Employees: 70
Annual Turnover: £3.5M

ISBNs, Imprints & Series:
978 0 9503647, 978 1 873431

Overseas Representation:
Australia & New Zealand: Johima Pty Ltd,
Parramatta, NSW, Australia

2729 ▬

STRONG OAK PRESS
PO Box 728, Crawley, West Sussex
RH10 7WD
Telephone: 01293 552727
Email: strongoakpress@hotmail.com

Managing Director: Steven Apps

Biography & Autobiography; Fine Art & Art History; History & Antiquarian; Military & War; Travel & Topography; List of Books on Scotland (History, Art)

ISBNs, Imprints & Series:
978 0 907590, 978 1 871048 Spa Books

Distributor for:
The Strong Oak Press Ltd
South Africa: William Waterman
Publications [including Ashanti
Publishing & Justified Press]

2730 ▬

STUDYMATES LTD
Studymates House, PO Box 225, Abergele,
Conwy County LL18 9AY
Telephone: 01745 832863
Fax: 01745 826606
Email: manager@studymates.co.uk
Web Site: www.studymates.co.uk

Warehouse, Trade Enquiries & Orders:
Central Books Ltd, 99 Wallis Road, London
E9 5LN
Telephone: 0845 458 9911
Email: sales@centralbooks.com

Representation (UK):
Compass Academic Ltd,
The Barley Mow Centre,
10 Barley Mow Passage, Chiswick, London
W4 4PH
Telephone: (020) 8994 6477
Fax: (020) 8400 6132

Directors: Graham Lawler *(Managing)*
Judith Lawler *(Finance)*

Academic & Scholarly; Audio Books; Biology & Zoology; Chemistry; Educational & Textbooks; Electronic (Educational); English as a Foreign Language; History & Antiquarian; Industry, Business & Management; Languages & Linguistics; Law; Literature & Criticism; Mathematics & Statistics; Medical (incl. Self Help & Alternative Medicine); Military & War; Physics; Poetry; Politics & World Affairs; Religion & Theology; Scientific & Technical; Sociology & Anthropology; Theatre, Drama & Dance

ISBNs, Imprints & Series:
978 1 84285 Aber-Torchlight Books;
Studymates Professional

Overseas Representation:
Australia & New Zealand: Footprint Books
Pty Ltd, Sydney, NSW, Australia
Caribbean: Humphrys Roberts Associates,
London, UK

Book Trade Association Membership:
IPG

2731 ▬

SUBBUTEO NATURAL HISTORY BOOKS
The Rea, Upton Magna, Shrewsbury
SY4 4UR
Telephone: 01743 708017
Fax: 01743 709504
Email: joy.enston@birdfood.co.uk
Web Site: www.wildlifebooks.com

Senior Executive: Tony Cordery
Finance: Paul Humber
Marketing Manager: Claire Smith

Natural History

New Titles: 2 (2009)
No of Employees: 164
Annual Turnover: £19.9M

Parent Company:
UK: C J Wild Bird Foods Ltd

Distributor for:
Rainforest Expeditions SAC Publications;
Vazquez Mazzini Editores SLR; Thomas
Velqui
South Africa: Avian Demography Unit
Spain: Arts Grafiques Delmau; Nayade
Editorial
UK: Arlequin Press; Dizzy Daisy Books;
Hobby Publications; Osmia Publications;
Wings Plants & Paws
USA: American Birding Association

Book Trade Association Membership:
BA

2732 ▬

SUMMER PALACE PRESS
31 Stranmillis Park, Belfast BT9 5AU
Telephone: (028) 9066 7759
Email: cladnageeragh@eircom.net

Co-Directors: Joan Newmann
Kate Newmann

Poetry

New Titles: 8 (2009)

ISBNs, Imprints & Series:
978 0 9535912, 978 0 9544752, 978 0
9552122, 978 0 9560995

Book Trade Association Membership:
CLÉ (Irish PA)

2733 ▬

SUMMERSDALE PUBLISHERS LTD
46 West Street, Chichester, West Sussex
PO19 1RP
Telephone: 01243 771107
Fax: 01243 786300
Email: enquiries@summersdale.com
Web Site: www.summersdale.com

Warehouse, Trade Enquiries & Orders:
Littlehampton Book Services,
Faraday Close, Durrington, Worthing,
West Sussex BN13 3RB
Telephone: 01903 828500
Fax: 01903 828625
Email: orders@lbsltd.co.uk
Web Site: www.lbsltd.co.uk

Directors: Alastair Williams *(Joint
Managing)*
Stewart Ferris *(Joint Managing)*
Nicky Douglas *(Sales)*
Jennifer Barclay *(Editorial)*

Audio Books; Cookery, Wines & Spirits; Crafts & Hobbies; Electronic (Educational); Electronic (Entertainment); Electronic (Professional & Academic); Guide Books; History & Antiquarian; Humour; Sports & Games; Travel & Topography

New Titles: 76 (2008) , 90 (2009)
No of Employees: 14
Annual Turnover: £3M

ISBNs, Imprints & Series:
978 1 84024, 978 1 84953, 978 1 873475

Distributor for:
Protection Publications

Overseas Representation:
Australia & New Zealand: Peribo Pty Ltd,
Mount Kuring-Gai, NSW, Australia
India: Surit Mitra, New Delhi
Northern Europe: Michael Geoghegan,
London, UK
Scandinavia: McNeish Publishing
International, East Sussex, UK
*South East & North East Asia, Middle East &
Africa:* Chris Ashdown, Publishers
International Marketing, Ferndown,
Dorset, UK
Southern Africa: Zytek Publishing (Pty) Ltd,
Bedfordview, South Africa
Southern Europe: Bookport Associates,
Milan, Italy

Book Trade Association Membership:
IPG

2734 ▬

SUNFLOWER BOOKS
PO Box 36160, London SW7 3WS
Telephone: (020) 7589 2377
Fax: (020) 7589 2377
Email: mail@sunflowerbooks.co.uk
Web Site: www.sunflowerbooks.co.uk

Distribution:
Portfolio Books Ltd, 2nd Floor,
Westminster House, Kew Road, Richmond,
Surrey TW9 2ND
Telephone: (020) 8326 5620
Fax: (020) 8326 5621

Joint Managing Directors: Pat
Underwood
John Seccombe

Travel & Topography

New Titles: 4 (2008) , 2 (2009)

ISBNs, Imprints & Series:
978 0 948513, 978 1 85691 Landscapes
Series
978 1 85691 Sunflower Complete Guides;
Walk & Eat Series

Parent Company:
P. A. Underwood Ltd

2735 ▬

SUPPORTIVE LEARNING PUBLICATIONS (SLP)
23 West View, Chirk, Wrexham LL14 5HL
Telephone: 01691 774778
Fax: 01691 774849
Web Site: www.slpeducation.co.uk

Marketing Director: Phil Roberts

Educational & Textbooks; Geography & Geology; History & Antiquarian; Humour; Mathematics & Statistics; Sports & Games; Theatre, Drama & Dance

Annual Turnover: £100,000

ISBNs, Imprints & Series: 978 1 871585

Overseas Representation:
All other areas: Blackwell Publishing Ltd,
Oxford, UK
USA, Canada & Puerto Rico: Blackwell
Publishing Inc, Malden, MA, USA;
Blackwell Publishing Professional, Ames,
IA, USA

Book Trade Association Membership:
EPC

2736 ▬

SUSSEX ACADEMIC PRESS
PO Box 139, Eastbourne, East Sussex
BN24 9BP
Telephone: 01323 479220
Fax: 01323 478185
Email: edit@sussex-academic.co.uk
Web Site: www.sussex-academic.co.uk

Warehouse, Trade Enquiries & Orders:
Gazelle Book Services, White Cross Mills,
Hightown, Lancaster LA1 4XS
Telephone: 01524 68765
Fax: 01524 63232

Directors: Anthony Grahame *(Editorial)*
Anita Grahame *(Finance)*

Academic & Scholarly; Archaeology; Bibliography & Library Science; Biography & Autobiography; Economics; Educational & Textbooks; Environment & Development Studies; Fine Art & Art History; Gender Studies; Geography & Geology; History & Antiquarian; Industry, Business & Management; Law; Literature & Criticism; Military & War; Music; Philosophy; Politics & World Affairs; Psychology & Psychiatry; Religion & Theology; Sociology & Anthropology; Sports & Games; Theatre, Drama & Dance

New Titles: 45 (2008) , 45 (2009)
No of Employees: 4
Annual Turnover: £170,000

ISBNs, Imprints & Series:
978 1 84519, 978 1 898723, 978 1
902210, 978 1 903900 Sussex Academic
978 1 898595 The Alpha Press

Parent Company:
The Alpha Press

Overseas Representation:
North America: International Specialized
Book Services Inc, Portland, OR, USA

Rest of the World: Gazelle Book Services Ltd, Lancaster, UK

2737

SUSSEX PUBLICATIONS
World Microfilms, PO Box 35488, St John's Wood, London NW8 6WD
Telephone: (020) 7586 4499
Email: microworld@ndirect.co.uk
Web Site: www.microworld.uk.com

Director: S. C. Albert

Academic & Scholarly; Audio Books; Cinema, Video, TV & Radio; Fine Art & Art History; History & Antiquarian; Literature & Criticism; Music

ISBNs, Imprints & Series:
978 0 905272, 978 1 86013

2738

THE SWEDENBORG SOCIETY
20–21 Bloomsbury Way, London WC1A 2TH
Telephone: (020) 7405 7986
Fax: (020) 7831 5848
Email: richard@swedenborg.org.uk
Web Site: www.swedenborg.org.uk

Company Secretary: Richard Lines
Publications Manager: Stephen McNeilly

Academic & Scholarly; Literature & Criticism; Religion & Theology

New Titles: 2 (2008) , 2 (2009)
No of Employees: 5
Annual Turnover: £250,000

ISBNs, Imprints & Series: 978 0 85448

2739

SYMPOSIUM PUBLICATIONS LITERARY & ART
37 Chepstow Road, London W2 5BP
Telephone: (020) 7792 3762
Email: sympo@sympo.fsworld.co.uk
Web Site: www.sympo.co.uk

Director: Mrs L. A. Melech
Editorial Consultant: J. Wheeler-Melech

Academic & Scholarly; Children's Books; Educational & Textbooks; English as a Foreign Language; Fine Art & Art History; Literature & Criticism; Poetry

ISBNs, Imprints & Series:
978 0 9524749 Symposium Brush-Up Shakespeare Series; Symposium Gem Art Series
978 0 9547757 Sympo Sunrise (Children's Stories)

Overseas Representation:
Spain: Débora Vázquez Padín, Pontevedra

2740

TA HA PUBLISHERS LTD
Unit 4, The Windsor Centre, Windsor Grove, West Norwood, London SE27 9NT
Telephone: (020) 8670 1888
Fax: (020) 8670 1998
Email: sales@taha.co.uk
Web Site: www.taha.co.uk

Directors: A. Siddiqui
Dr Abia A. Siddiqui *(Editor)*
Rights: Dr J. U. N. Rafai

Children's Books; Languages & Linguistics; Religion & Theology

ISBNs, Imprints & Series:
978 0 907461, 978 1 842000, 978 1 897940

Associated Companies:
Diwan Press Ltd

Overseas Representation:
USA: Islamic Bookstore.com, Baltimore, MD

2741

*TABB HOUSE
7 Church Street, Padstow, Cornwall PL28 8BG
Telephone: 01841 532316
Fax: 01841 532316

Distributor (for West Country titles in Cornwall, Devon & Somerset):
Tor Mark Press, PO Box 4, Redruth, Cornwall TR16 5YX
Telephone: 01209 822101
Fax: 01209 822035
Email: sales@tormarkpress.prestel.co.uk
Web Site: www.willowbooks.co.uk

Wholesaler (for all titles for Waterstone's):
Gardners Books Ltd, 1 Whittle Drive, Willingdon Drove, Eastbourne, Sussex BN23 6QH
Telephone: 01323 521555
Fax: 01323 521666
Email: sales@gardners.com
Web Site: www.gardners.com

Director: Caroline White *(Editorial)*
Promotion & Marketing Manager: K. Bickmore

Biography & Autobiography; Children's Books; Fiction; Literature & Criticism; Poetry; Local History & Factual

ISBNs, Imprints & Series:
978 0 907018, 978 1 873951
978 0 953951 Tabb House Originals

Book Trade Association Membership:
IPG

2742

TAIGH NA TEUD MUSIC PUBLISHERS
13 Upper Breakish, Isle of Skye IV42 8PY
Telephone: 01471 822528
Fax: 01471 822811
Email: sales@scotlandsmusic.com
Web Site: www.scotlandsmusic.com & www.playscottishmusic.com

Sales Manager: Alasdair Martin
Music Editor: Christine Martin

Languages & Linguistics; Music

New Titles: 18 (2008) , 5 (2009)
No of Employees: 2
Annual Turnover: £80,000

ISBNs, Imprints & Series:
978 1 871931 Taigh na Teud

Overseas Representation:
Australia: Celtic Southern Cross, Bracknell, Tasmania
North America: Music Sales Corporation, Chester, NY, USA

2743

TANGERINE DESIGNS LTD
1 Limpley Mill, Lower Stoke, Bath BA2 7EJ
Telephone: 01225 720001
Email: enquiries@tangerinedesigns.co.uk
Web Site: www.tangerinedesigns.co.uk

Managing Director: Christine Swift

Children's Books

Distributor for:
UK: Alligator Books [foreign rights agent]; Funkkia [publishing licensor]

Book Trade Association Membership:
Publishers Association

2744

TANGO BOOKS LTD
PO Box 32595, London W4 5YD
Telephone: (020) 8996 9970
Fax: (020) 8996 9977
Email: info@tangobooks.co.uk
Web Site: www.tangobooks.co.uk

Sales & Marketing:
Bounce!, 14 Greville Street, London EC1N 8SB
Telephone: (020) 7138 3650
Fax: (020) 7138 3658
Email: sales@bouncemarketing.co.uk
Web Site: www.bouncemarketing.co.uk

Directors/Publishers: Sheri Safran
David Fielder

Children's Books; Educational & Textbooks

New Titles: 20 (2008) , 20 (2009)
No of Employees: 5
Annual Turnover: £1M

2745

TARQUIN PUBLICATIONS
99 Hatfield Road, St Albans, Herts AL1 4JL
Telephone: 0870 143 2568
Fax: 0845 456 6385
Email: sales@tarquinbooks.com
Web Site: www.tarquinbooks.com

Editorial: Andrew Griffin
Sales & Promotion: Peter Watson

Atlases & Maps; Children's Books; Crafts & Hobbies; Educational & Textbooks; Mathematics & Statistics; Do-it-Yourself Pop-up Books

ISBNs, Imprints & Series:
978 0 906212, 978 1 899618

Parent Company:
Richard Griffin (1820) Ltd

Overseas Representation:
Australia: W & G Education Pty Ltd, Berwick, Vic; H. E. Wootton & Sons, Toorak, Vic
New Zealand: Eton Press (Auckland) Ltd, Auckland; Mahobe Resources (NZ), Newmarket
Portugal: Editôra Replicação, Lisbon
Singapore: Nature Craft Pte Ltd
USA: Parkwest Publications Inc, Jersey City, NJ

Book Trade Association Membership:
IPG

2746

*TARTARUS PRESS
Coverley House, Carlton-in-Coverdale, Leyburn, North Yorks DL8 4AY
Telephone: 01969 640399
Fax: 01969 640399
Email: tartarus@pavilion.co.uk
Web Site: www.tartaruspress.com

Co-Proprietors: R. B. Russell
Rosalie Parker

Antiques & Collecting; Fiction; Illustrated & Fine Editions; Literature & Criticism; Reference Books, Directories & Dictionaries

ISBNs, Imprints & Series: 978 1 872621

2747

TATE PUBLISHING
[a division of Tate Enterprises Ltd]
Millbank, London SW1P 4RG
Telephone: (020) 7887 8869/70/71

Fax: (020) 7887 8878
Email: tgpl@tate.org.uk

Warehouse, Trade Enquiries & Orders:
Telephone: (020) 7887 8869 (5 lines)
Fax: (020) 7887 8878
Email: tgpl@tate.org.uk
Web Site: www.tate.org.uk

Managers: Celia Clear *(Chief Executive)*
James Attlee *(Sales & Marketing)*
Sarah Rogers *(Finance)*
Sarah Tucker *(Production)*
Roger Thorp *(Publishing)*

Children's Books; Fine Art & Art History; Photography

New Titles: 35 (2008) , 36 (2009)

ISBNs, Imprints & Series:
British Artists Series; Movements in Modern Art Series; St Ives Artists Series
978 0 905005, 978 0 946590, 978 1 85437 Essential Artists Series
978 1 85437 Modern Artists Series

Parent Company:
Tate Enterprises Ltd

Overseas Representation:
Asia (including Hong Kong, Taiwan, China, Korea & Philippines): Asia Publishers Services Ltd, Hong Kong
Australia: Thames & Hudson (Australia) Pty Ltd, Fishermans Bend, Vic
Austria, Belgium, Germany, Netherlands & Switzerland: Exhibitions International, Leuven, Belgium
Denmark, Finland, Iceland, Norway & Sweden: Elisabeth Harder-Kreimann, Hamburg, Germany
Eastern Europe: Phil Tyers, Athens, Greece
Far East (including Japan, Vietnam, Singapore, Malaysia, Indonesia & Thailand): Andrew Hansen, London, UK
France: Interart SARL, Paris
Italy, Greece, Spain & Portugal: Penny Padovani, London, UK
Mexico, Central America & Caribbean: Chris Humphrys, Humphrys Roberts Associates, London, UK
Middle East: Ray Potts, Villanton, France
North & South America & Canada: Harry N. Abrams Inc, New York, NY, USA
Republic of Ireland & Northern Ireland: Gabrielle Redmond, Dublin, Republic of Ireland
South Africa: David Krut Publishing, Johannesburg
South America: David Williams, InterMedia Americana (IMA) Ltd, London, UK

Book Trade Association Membership:
BA

2748

I. B. TAURIS & CO LTD
6 Salem Road, London W2 4BU
Telephone: (020) 7243 1225
Fax: (020) 7243 1226
Email: mail@ibtauris.com
Web Site: www.ibtauris.com

Distribution:
Macmillan Distribution Ltd, Brunel Road, Houndmills, Basingstoke, Hants RG21 6XS

Directors: Iradj Bagherzade *(Chairman & Publisher)*
Jonathan McDonnell *(Managing)*
Isabella Steer *(Rights)*
Managers: Stuart Weir *(Production)*
Liz Stuckey *(Financial)*
Martin Ashworth *(Sales)*
Paul Davighi *(Marketing)*
Elizabeth Spaulding *(Publicity)*

Academic & Scholarly; Archaeology; Architecture & Design; Biography & Autobiography; Cinema, Video, TV &

Radio; Fine Art & Art History; Gender Studies; Geography & Geology; Guide Books; History & Antiquarian; Military & War; Politics & World Affairs; Reference Books, Directories & Dictionaries; Religion & Theology; Sociology & Anthropology

New Titles: 190 (2008) , 220 (2009)
No of Employees: 25

ISBNs, Imprints & Series:
978 1 84511, 978 1 85043, 978 1 86064
International Library of African Studies; International Library of Historical Studies; International Library of Human Geography; International Library of Political Studies; Isma'ili Heritage Series; Library of International Relations; Library of Middle East History; Library of Modern Middle East Studies; Library of Ottoman Studies; Tauris Parke Paperbacks

Associated Companies:
British Academic Press; Tauris Academic Studies; Tauris Parke Books

Distributor for:
UAE: The Emirates Center for Strategic Studies & Research
Federal Trust; Libri Publications; The Radcliffe Press; Philip Wilson Publishers

Overseas Representation:
Africa (excluding South Africa & Zimbabwe): InterMedia Americana (IMA) Ltd, London, UK
Australia: Palgrave Macmillan, South Yarra, Vic
India: Viva Group, New Delhi
Iran: Behruz Neirami, Tehran
Japan: United Publishers Services Ltd, Tokyo
Korea, China, Hong Kong & Taiwan: Taylor & Francis Asia Pacific, Singapore
Middle East & North Africa: International Publishers Representatives (IPR) Ltd, Nicosia, Cyprus
New Zealand: Macmillan Publishers New Zealand Ltd, Auckland
Northern Europe: Andrew Durnell Marketing Ltd, Tunbridge Wells, UK
South America & Caribbean: InterMedia Americana (IMA) Ltd, London, UK
USA & Canada: Palgrave Macmillan, New York, NY, USA

Book Trade Association Membership:
IPG

2749 ▬▬▬▬▬▬▬

TAYLOR & FRANCIS
2 & 4 Park Square, Milton Park, Abingdon, Oxford OX14 4RN
Telephone: (020) 7017 6000
Fax: (020) 7017 6336
Email: jackie.benoist@tandf.co.uk
Web Site: www.taylorandfrancis.com

Warehouse, Trade Enquiries & Orders:
Bookpoint, 130 Milton Park, Abingdon, Oxon OX14 4SB
Telephone: 01235 400400

Chief Executive: Roger Horton
Directors: Jeremy North (Managing – Books)
Christoph Chesher (Sales)
Stuart Dawson (Finance)
Ian Bannerman (Managing – Journals)
Mark Majurey (Digital Development – Books)
David Green (Publishing – Journals)
Beverley Acreman (Marketing – Journals)
Matt Howells (Production – Journals)
Claire L'Infant (Humanities – Books)
Alan Jarvis (Social Sciences – Books)
Nigel Eyre (Production – Books)
Jackie Harbor (Marketing – Books)
Rights Managers: Adele Parker (Books)
Paulette Dooler (Journals)

Academic & Scholarly; Archaeology; Architecture & Design; Biology & Zoology; Chemistry; Economics; Educational & Textbooks; Electronic (Professional & Academic); Engineering; Environment & Development Studies; Gay & Lesbian Studies; Gender Studies; Geography & Geology; History & Antiquarian; Industry, Business & Management; Languages & Linguistics; Law; Literature & Criticism; Mathematics & Statistics; Medical (incl. Self Help & Alternative Medicine); Military & War; Music; Philosophy; Physics; Politics & World Affairs; Psychology & Psychiatry; Reference Books, Directories & Dictionaries; Religion & Theology; Scientific & Technical; Sociology & Anthropology; Sports & Games; Theatre, Drama & Dance

New Titles: 2700 (2008) , 3000 (2009)
No of Employees: 800

ISBNs, Imprints & Series:
978 0 415 Psychology Press; Routledge; Routledge-Cavendish; Taylor & Francis
978 0 8058 Lawrence Erlbaum Associates
978 0 8247 Dekker
978 0 8493 CRC

Parent Company:
Informa Plc

Associated Companies:
India: Routledge India Office
Norway: Taylor & Francis AS
Singapore: Taylor & Francis Asia Pacific
Sweden: Taylor & Francis AB
USA: Garland Science; Taylor & Francis Books Inc

Distributor for:
Guildford Press; Swedish Pharmaceutical Press

Overseas Representation:
Australia: Palgrave Macmillan, South Yarra, Vic
Austria, Switzerland & Germany: Gabriela Mauch, Area Sales Manager, Central Europe, Stuttgart, Germany
Belgium, Netherlands, France & Luxembourg: Liza Walraven, Sales Representative, Amsterdam, Netherlands
Botswana: Arthur Oageng, Book Promotions/Horizon Books
China: Taylor & Francis, Beijing, P. R. of China
Eastern Europe: Marek Lewinson, Warsaw, Poland
Greece: Ryan Cooper, Taylor & Francis Group, Abingdon, UK
India: Taylor & Francis Books India Pvt Ltd, New Delhi
Israel: Franklins International, Tel Aviv
Japan: Hans Van Ess, Sales & Marketing Executive, Tokyo
Korea: Information & Culture Korea (ICK), Seoul, Republic of Korea
Malaysia & Brunei: David Yeong, General Manager, Petaling Jaya, Malaysia
Mexico, Central & South America: Cranbury International LLC, Montpelier, VT, USA
Middle East & North Africa: International Publishing Services (IPS) Middle East Ltd, Dubai, UAE
New Zealand: Victoria Johnson, Macmillan Publishers New Zealand Ltd, Auckland
Nigeria: Publisher Support Services Ltd, Ikeja
North America: Taylor & Francis Inc, Boca Raton, FL, USA
Norway, Denmark, Faroe Islands, Sweden, Finland & Iceland: Keith Gray, Sales Representative, Copenhagen, Denmark
Pakistan: M. Anwer Iqbal, Book Bird Publishers Representatives, Lahore
Republic of Ireland: Brookside Publishing Services, Dublin
Singapore, Hong Kong, Vietnam, Philippines, Indonesia, Taiwan & Thailand: Taylor & Francis Asia Pacific, Singapore

South Africa, Namibia, Lesotho & Swaziland: Book Promotions Pty Ltd, Diep River, South Africa
Spain, Portugal & Italy: Philip Veysey, Area Sales Manager, Madrid, Spain
West Indies & Caribbean: Jasmina Basic, Taylor & Francis Group, Abingdon, UK

Book Trade Association Membership:
IGSMTP; CAPP

2750 ▬▬▬▬▬▬▬

TAYLOR GRAHAM PUBLISHING
29 Church Street, Southport PR9 0QT
Web Site: www.taylorgraham.com

Director: Peter J. Taylor

Academic & Scholarly; Bibliography & Library Science; Computer Science; Scientific & Technical

ISBNs, Imprints & Series: 978 0 947568

Overseas Representation:
USA & Canada: Taylor Graham Publishing, Los Angeles, CA, USA

Book Trade Association Membership:
UK Serials Group

2751 ▬▬▬▬▬▬▬

*TEACHIT (UK) LTD
1 Widsombe Parade, Bath BA2 4JT
Telephone: 01225 788850
Email: mail@teachit.co.uk
Web Site: www.teachit.co.uk

Educational & Textbooks; Electronic (Professional & Academic)

Book Trade Association Membership:
Publishers Association

2752 ▬▬▬▬▬▬▬

TELEGRAM
26 Westbourne Grove, London W2 5RH
Telephone: (020) 7229 2911
Fax: (020) 7229 7492
Email: lynn@telegrambooks.com
Web Site: www.telegrambooks.com

Distribution (UK):
Marston Book Services Ltd, 160 Milton Park, Abingdon, Oxon OX14 4SD
Telephone: 01235 465500
Fax: 01235 465555
Web Site: www.marston.co.uk

Sales (UK):
Compass, The Barley Mow Centre, 10 Barley Mow Passage, Chiswick W4 4PH
Telephone: (020) 8994 6477
Fax: (020) 8400 6132
Web Site: www.compass-booksales.co.uk

Director: André Gaspard
Commissioning Editor: Lara Frankena
Managers: Lynn Gaspard (Rights)
Ashley Biles (Sales)
Kelly Pike (Publicity)
Production Editor: Shikha Sethi

Biography & Autobiography; Fiction

New Titles: 14 (2008) , 18 (2009)

ISBNs, Imprints & Series: 978 1 84659

Parent Company:
Saqi Books

Overseas Representation:
Australia & New Zealand: Palgrave Macmillan, South Yarra, Vic, Australia
Europe: Andrew Durnell, Andrew Durnell Marketing Ltd, Tunbridge Wells, UK

India: Pradeep Kumar, Viva Marketing, New Delhi
Italy: Agnese Incisa, Letteraria Agnese Incisa, Turin
Middle East: Dar al Saqi SARL, Beirut, Lebanon
Netherlands & Scandinavia: Jan Michael, Amsterdam, Netherlands
Pakistan: Mohammad Eusoph, Mr Books, Islamabad
Singapore: Nelson Koh, Horizon Books Pte Ltd
South Africa: Stephan Phillips (Pty) Ltd, Cape Town
Spain, Portugal & Germany: Anna Soler-Pont, Pontas Literary & Film Agency, Barcelona, Spain
USA & Canada: Consortium Publishers, St Paul, MN, USA

Book Trade Association Membership:
IPG

2753 ▬▬▬▬▬▬▬

THOMAS TELFORD LTD
40 Marsh Wall, London E14 9TP
Telephone: (020) 7987 6999
Fax: (020) 7538 4101
Email: leon.heward-mills@thomastelford.com
Web Site: www.thomastelford.com

Warehouse:
c/o Combined Book Services, Unit 1/K, Paddock Wood Distribution Centre, Paddock Wood, Kent TN12 6UU
Telephone: 01892 837171
Fax: 01892 837272

Retail Bookshop:
1 Great George Street, London SW1P 3AA
Telephone: (020) 7665 2464
Fax: (020) 7665 2245

Representation (UK & Northern Ireland):
Momenta Publishing Ltd, 2 Moorlands Close, Hindhead, Surrey GU26 6SY

Managers: Leon Heward-Mills (Publisher)
David Atkins (Editorial & Production)
Richard Oldershaw (Sales)

Architecture & Design; Engineering; Scientific & Technical

ISBNs, Imprints & Series: 978 0 7277

Parent Company:
Institution of Civil Engineers

Distributor for:
British Geotechnical Society

Overseas Representation:
Australia & New Zealand: DA Information Services Pty Ltd, Mitcham, Vic, Australia
Germany: Bernd Feldmann, Oranienburg
Italy, France, Spain, Portugal & Greece: AMS Europe Ltd, Farnham, UK
Japan: Maruzen Co Ltd, Tokyo
Republic of Ireland, Netherlands & Belgium: Momenta Publishing Ltd, Hindhead, Surrey, UK
South Africa: South African Institution of Civil Engineers, Midrand
USA: American Society of Civil Engineers, Reston, VA

Book Trade Association Membership:
Association of Learned & Professional Society Publishers

2754 ▬▬▬▬▬▬▬

TELOS PUBLISHING LTD
61 Elgar Avenue, Tolworth, Surrey KT5 9SP
Telephone: (020) 8399 1921
Email: david@telos.co.uk
Web Site: www.telos.co.uk

Business/Accounts:
5a Church Road, Shortlands, Bromley, Kent
BR2 0HP
Telephone: (020) 8466 1115
Email: stephen@telos.co.uk

Publishers: David J. Howe
Stephen James Walker

Cinema, Video, TV & Radio; Crime; Fiction

New Titles: 5 (2008) , 4 (2009)

ISBNs, Imprints & Series:
978 1 84583, 978 1 903889

Overseas Representation:
Australia & New Zealand: Bookwise
International, Wingfield, SA, Australia
USA & Canada: Fitzhenry & Whiteside Ltd,
Markham, Ont, Canada

2755

TEMPLAR PUBLISHING
The Granary, North Street, Dorking, Surrey
RH4 1DN
Telephone: 01306 876361
Fax: 01306 889097
Email: info@templarco.co.uk
Web Site: www.templarco.co.uk

Sales & Marketing:
Bounce Sales & Marketing,
14 Greville Street, London EC1N 8SB

Distribution:
Grantham Book Services, Trent Road,
Grantham, Lincs NG31 7XG

Directors: Amanda Wood *(Managing)*
Richard Johnson *(Financial)*
Ruth Huddleston *(Sales & Marketing)*
Karen Ellison *(Production)*
Odile Louis-Sidney *(Rights)*

Children's Books; Fiction

New Titles: 119 (2008) , 76 (2009)
No of Employees: 42
Annual Turnover: £15M

ISBNs, Imprints & Series:
978 1 84011, 978 1 898784
978 1 904513 Amazing Baby

Parent Company:
Bonnier Publishing Ltd

Book Trade Association Membership:
BA; IPG

2756

TEMPLE LODGE PUBLISHING
Hillside House, The Square, Forest Row,
East Sussex RH18 5ES
Telephone: 01342 824000
Fax: 01342 826437
Email: office@templelodge.com
Web Site: www.templelodge.com

Distribution:
BookSource, 50 Cambuslang Road,
Glasgow G32 8NB
Telephone: 0141 643 3955
Fax: 0845 370 0068
Email: orders@booksource.net
Web Site: www.booksource.net

Chief Editor: S.E. Gulbekian

*Health & Beauty; Magic & the Occult;
Medical (incl. Self Help & Alternative
Medicine); Philosophy; Politics & World
Affairs; Religion & Theology*

New Titles: 10 (2008) , 10 (2009)
Annual Turnover: £62,000

ISBNs, Imprints & Series:
978 0 904693, 978 1 902636, 978 1
906999

Overseas Representation:
Australia: Rudolf Steiner Book Centre,
Sydney, NSW
Canada: Tri-fold Books, Guelph, Ont
New Zealand: Steinerbooks, Auckland
South Africa: Rudolf Steiner Publications,
Bryanston
USA: Steiner Books Inc, Herndon, VA

Book Trade Association Membership:
IPG

2757

TENEUES PUBLISHING UK LTD
York Villa, York Road, Byfleet, Surrey
KT14 7HX
Telephone: 01932 403509
Fax: 01932 403514
Email: amcdonald@teneues.co.uk
Web Site: www.teneues.com

Trade Enquiries & Orders:
Combined Book Services, Unit Y,
Paddock Wood Distribution Centre,
Tonbridge, Kent TN12 6UU
Telephone: 01892 835599
Fax: 01892 837272
Email: orders@combook.co.uk

Chairman: Hendrik Teneues
Managers: Alexandra McDonald *(Sales &
Marketing)*
Bridget Clark *(Sales)*
Administrator: Elaine Hyde

*Architecture & Design; Photography; Travel
& Topography*

New Titles: 60 (2008) , 80 (2009)
No of Employees: 3
Annual Turnover: £2M

ISBNs, Imprints & Series:
978 1 60160, 978 3 8238, 978 3 8327
Teneues
978 3 57091 Stern Portfolios

2758

THAMES & HUDSON LTD
181A High Holborn, London WC1V 7QX
Telephone: (020) 7845 5000
Fax: (020) 7845 5050
Email: l.willis@thameshudson.co.uk
Web Site: www.thamesandhudson.com

Warehouse, Accounts & Returns:
Thames & Hudson (Distributors) Ltd,
44 Clockhouse Road, Farnborough, Hants
GU14 7QZ
Telephone: 01252 541602
Fax: 01252 377380
Email:
customerservices@thameshudson.co.uk

Directors: Thomas Neurath *(Chairman)*
Constance Kaine *(Deputy Chairman)*
Jamie Camplin *(Managing)*
Trevor Naylor *(Sales & Marketing)*
Peter Meades *(Financial)*
Christopher Ferguson *(Operations)*
Neil Palfreyman *(Production)*
Brian Meek *(Company Secretary)*
Johanna Neurath *(Design)*
Christian Frederking *(Rights)*
Export Area Managers: Stephen Embrey
Sara Ticci
Scipio Stringer
Managers: Laura Willis *(Marketing)*
Melanie Stacey *(UK Sales)*
Media: Collette Hutchinson
Sales: Jonathan Earl
Export Sales: Ian Bartley

*Academic & Scholarly; Antiques &
Collecting; Archaeology; Architecture &*

*Design; Biography & Autobiography; Crafts
& Hobbies; Educational & Textbooks;
Environment & Development Studies;
Fashion & Costume; Fine Art & Art History;
Gardening; Gay & Lesbian Studies; Guide
Books; History & Antiquarian; Illustrated &
Fine Editions; Literature & Criticism; Magic
& the Occult; Military & War; Music;
Natural History; Philosophy; Photography;
Reference Books, Directories &
Dictionaries; Religion & Theology; Sociology
& Anthropology; Theatre, Drama & Dance;
Travel & Topography*

ISBNs, Imprints & Series:
978 0 500 Thames & Hudson
978 0 642 National Gallery of Australia
978 0 7141 British Museum Press
978 0 784763 Art Gallery of NSW
978 0 86565 Vendome
978 0 87070 Museum of Modern Art, New
York
978 0 89207 Guggenheim Museum
Publications
978 0 89381, 978 1 597110, 978 1 931788
Aperture
978 0 900946, 978 1 903973 The Royal
Academy of Arts
978 0 906183 Institute for Archaeo-
Metallurgical Studies
978 0 952741 Frieze
978 0 952766, 978 1 900826, 978 1
902686 Scriptum
978 0 953703 Dakini
978 0 9542813, 978 0 9546894, 978 1
9057120 Chris Boot
978 0 977985, 978 0 979048 Mark Batty
Publisher
978 1 85669 Laurence King
978 1 86154 Booth-Clibborn
978 1 900828 Violette Editions
978 1 902163 The Royal Collection
978 1 904705 Ilex Press
978 2 0801, 978 2 08030 Flammarion SA,
France
978 2 884790, 978 2 940373 Ava
Publishing
978 3 86521, 978 3 88243, 978 3 905509,
978 3 931141 Steidl
978 3 87624, 978 8 88118, 978 8 88491
Skira Editore
978 3 938780 Braun Verlagshaus
978 9 748225, 978 9 749863 River Books

Parent Company:
T & H Holdings Ltd

Associated Companies:
Thames & Hudson (Distributors) Ltd
Australia: Thames & Hudson (Australia) Pty
Ltd
France: Editions Thames & Hudson sarl
P. R. of China: Thames & Hudson China Ltd
Singapore: Thames & Hudson (S) Pte Ltd
USA: Thames & Hudson Inc

Distributor for:
British Museum Press; Laurence King
Australia: National Gallery of Australia
France: Flammarion SA
Germany: Braun Verlagshaus
Israel: Institute for Archaeo-Metallurgical
Studies
Italy: Skira Editore
USA: Mark Batty Publisher; Museum of
Modern Art, New York

Overseas Representation:
*Africa, Caribbean, Central America, Eastern
Europe, Eastern Mediterranean, India,
Italy, Japan, Mexico, Middle East,
Pakistan, Portugal & Spain:* Export Sales
Department, Thames & Hudson Ltd,
London, UK
*Australia, New Zealand, Papua New Guinea
& Pacific Islands:* Thames & Hudson
(Australia) Pty Ltd, Fishermans Bend, Vic,
Australia
*Austria, Switzerland & Germany (excluding
South):* Michael Klein, Vilsbiburg,
Germany

Bangladesh: Zeenat Book Supply Ltd, Dhaka
Brazil & South America: Terry Roberts, Cotia
SP, Brazil
China, Hong Kong & Macau: Thames &
Hudson China Ltd, Aberdeen, Hong
Kong
France: Interart SARL, Paris
Germany (South): Wolfgang Willmann &
Susanne Sieger, Frankfurt, Germany
Iran: Book City, Tehran
Israel: Lonnie Kahn & Co Ltd, Rishon Lezion
Korea & Taiwan: Asia Publishers Services
Ltd, Hong Kong
Lebanon: Levant Distributors, Beirut
Malaysia: Thames & Hudson (S) Pte Ltd,
Petaling Jaya
Netherlands: Menno Visser, Utrecht
Republic of Ireland: UK Sales Department,
Thames & Hudson Ltd, London, UK
Scandinavia & Baltic States: Per Burell,
Stocksund, Sweden
Singapore & South East Asia: Thames &
Hudson (S) Pte Ltd, Singapore
*South Africa, Swaziland, Lesotho, Namibia,
Botswana & Zimbabwe:* Peter Hyde
Associates (Pty) Ltd, Cape Town, South
Africa
Thailand: Asia Book Co Ltd, Bangkok

Book Trade Association Membership:
Publishers Association

2759

THARPA PUBLICATIONS
Conishead Priory, Ulverston, Cumbria
LA12 9QQ
Telephone: 01229 588599
Fax: 01229 483919
Email: sales.uk@tharpa.com
Web Site: www.tharpa.com

Director: Sue Jenkins
Managers: Murdo McNab *(Distribution)*
Manuel Rivero-Demartine *(Production)*
Steph Atkinson *(Sales & Marketing)*

Religion & Theology; Mind Body Spirit

ISBNs, Imprints & Series:
978 0 948006, 978 0 9548790

Parent Company:
New Kadampa Tradition

Overseas Representation:
Australia: Gary Allen Pty Ltd, Smithfield,
NSW
Canada: Tharpa Canada, Toronto, Ont
Singapore & Malaysia: MPH Distributors,
Singapore
South Africa: Bacchus Books, Gauteng
USA (Office): Tharpa Publications, New
York, NY, USA

Book Trade Association Membership:
IPG

2760

*THIRD MILLENNIUM PUBLISHING
LTD
2–5 Benjamin Street, London EC1M 5QL
Telephone: (020) 7336 0144
Fax: (020) 7608 1188
Email: info@tmiltd.com
Web Site: www.tmiltd.com

Chairman: Julian Platt
Publisher: Christopher Fagg
Directors: Joel Burden *(Business
Development)*
David Burt
Managers: Michael D. Jackson *(Marketing)*
Bonnie Murray *(Production)*

*Antiques & Collecting; Educational &
Textbooks; Fine Art & Art History; Guide
Books; Military & War; Photography*

ISBNs, Imprints & Series: 978 1 903942

Distributor for:
UK: Pardoe Blacker Design

Overseas Representation:
USA & Canada: Dan Farrell, Antique
Collectors Club Ltd, Easthampton, MA,
USA

2761

SWEET & MAXWELL THOMSON REUTERS (LEGAL)
(*formerly* THOMSON INTERNATIONAL
LEGAL & REGULATORY)
100 Avenue Road, Swiss Cottage, London
NW3 3PF
Telephone: (020) 7393 7000
Fax: (020) 7393 7010
Web Site: www.thomson.com/solutions/
legal

Law

Associated Companies:
UK: Current Law Publishers; ESC
Publishing; Gee Publishing; W. Green &
Son; Information for Industry; Legal
Information Resources; Morgan Hill;
Pensions Research; Professional
Publishing; Steven & Sons; Sweet &
Maxwell; Thomson Tax; Westlaw UK

Book Trade Association Membership:
Publishers Association

2762

THOROGOOD PUBLISHING LTD
10–12 Rivington Street, London EC2A 3DU
Telephone: (020) 7749 4748
Fax: (020) 7720 6110
Email: info@thorogoodpublishing.co.uk
Web Site:
www.thorogoodpublishing.co.uk

Trade Orders:
Marston Book Services, 160 Milton Park,
Abingdon, Oxon OX14 4SD
Telephone: 01235 465500
Fax: 01235 465655
Email: trade.enq@marston.co.uk
Web Site: www.marston.co.uk

Directors: Neil Thomas *(Chairman)*
Nina Rossey *(Finance)*
Managers: Angela Spall *(General, Editorial,
Production)*
Matthew Harris *(Marketing)*
Marketing Executive: Twaambo Munjanja

*Accountancy & Taxation; Biography &
Autobiography; Fiction; Industry, Business &
Management; Law; Military & War; Travel &
Topography*

New Titles: 20 (2009)

ISBNs, Imprints & Series: 978 1 85418

Associated Companies:
UK: Falconbury Ltd

Overseas Representation:
Australia & New Zealand: Woodslane Pty
Ltd, Warriewood, NSW, Australia
Europe: Andrew Durnell Marketing Ltd,
Tunbridge Wells, UK
Hong Kong, Taiwan, China & Korea: Asia
Publishers Services Ltd, Hong Kong
India: Viva Group, New Delhi
Latin America: InterMedia Americana (IMA)
Ltd, London, UK
Middle East, Greece & Cyprus: Ray Potts,
Publishers International Marketing,
Polfages, France
Singapore, Malaysia & South East Asia: APD
Singapore Pte Ltd, Singapore

2763

F. A. THORPE PUBLISHING
The Green, Bradgate Road, Anstey,
Leicester LE7 7FU
Telephone: 0116 236 4325
Fax: 0116 234 0205
Email: enquiries@ulverscroft.co.uk
Web Site: dspace.dial.pipex.com/town/
plaza/hf33/

Chief Executive: Robert Thirlby

*Biography & Autobiography; Fiction; Travel
& Topography; Large Print Leisure*

New Titles: 456 (2008) , 456 (2009)

ISBNs, Imprints & Series:
978 0 7089, 978 1 84395, 978 1 84617,
978 1 84782 Charnwood Hardback
Series; Linford Softcover Series;
Ulverscroft Hardcover Series

Associated Companies:
Isis Publishing; Magna Large Print Books;
Ulverscroft Large Print Books Ltd

Distributor for:
Soundings Audio Books

Overseas Representation:
Australia: Sandra Lavender, Crows Nest
Canada: Mrs Diane Van Veen, Burlington,
Ont
New Zealand: John Gregory, Feilding
USA: Ulverscroft Large Print Books (USA)
Inc, West Seneca, NY

2764

THOTH PUBLICATIONS
64 Leopold Street, Loughborough, Leics
LE11 5DN
Telephone: 01509 210626
Fax: 01509 238034
Email: enquiries@thoth.co.uk
Web Site: www.thoth.co.uk

Senior Partner: Tom Clarke
Partner: Susan Attwood

*Biography & Autobiography; Magic & the
Occult; Religion & Theology*

New Titles: 2 (2008) , 6 (2009)

ISBNs, Imprints & Series: 978 1 870450

Distributor for:
Sun Chalice

Book Trade Association Membership:
BA

2765

THRASS (UK) LTD
Units 1–3 Tarvin Sands, Barrow Lane,
Tarvin, Chester CH3 8JF
Telephone: 01829 741413
Fax: 01829 741419
Email: enquiries@thrass.demon.co.uk
Web Site: www.thrass.co.uk

Director: Alan Davies
Consultant: Hilary Davies
Office Manager: Rachel Woodward

*Educational & Textbooks; Electronic
(Educational)*

New Titles: 4 (2008) , 4 (2009)

ISBNs, Imprints & Series:
978 1 904912, 978 1 906295

2766

TINDAL STREET PRESS
217 The Custard Factory, Gibb Street,
Birmingham B9 4AA
Telephone: 0121 773 8157
Email: alan@tindalstreet.co.uk
Web Site: www.tindalstreet.co.uk

Distribution (UK):
Turnaround, Unit 3, Olympia Trading Estate,
Coburg Road, London N22 6TZ
Telephone: (020) 8829 3000
Email: orders@turnaround-uk.com
Web Site: www.turnaround-uk.com

Publishing Director: Alan Mahar
Editor/Marketing Manager: Luke Brown

Fiction

New Titles: 6 (2008) , 8 (2009)
No of Employees: 5

ISBNs, Imprints & Series:
978 0 9535895, 978 0 9541303, 978 0
9547913, 978 0 9551384, 978 0
9556476

Overseas Representation:
Australia: Tower Books Pty Ltd, Frenchs
Forest, NSW; Tower Books Pty Ltd,
Brookvale, NSW
New Zealand: Addenda, Auckland
USA & Canada: Dufour Editions Inc, Chester
Springs, PA, USA

Book Trade Association Membership:
IPG

2767

TITAN PUBLISHING GROUP
144 Southwark Street, London SE1 0UP
Telephone: (020) 7620 0200
Fax: (020) 7803 1990
Email: editorial@titanemail.com
Web Site: www.titanbooks.com

Trade Enquiries & Orders:
Grantham Book Services, Trent Road,
Grantham, Lincs NG31 7XG
Telephone: 01476 541080
Fax: 01476 541061
Email: orders@gbs.tbs-ltd.co.uk

Directors: Nick Landau *(Managing)*
Vivian Cheung *(Executive)*
Tim Whale *(Global Sales)*
Katy Wild *(Editorial)*
Head of Finance: Chris Horn
Marketing Manager: Chris McLane
Print & Paper Buyer: Kevin Wooff
Rights Executive: Jenny Boyce

*Children's Books; Cinema, Video, TV &
Radio; Graphic Novels*

ISBNs, Imprints & Series: 978 1 84576

Overseas Representation:
All other countries: Titan Books, Sales &
Marketing Department, London, UK
Central & Eastern Europe (including Poland):
Csaba Lengyel de Bagota, Budapest,
Hungary
Far East: Ralph & Sheila Summers, Formtone
Ltd, London, UK
*France, Belgium, Netherlands, Greece,
Malta, Israel & South Africa:* Paul
Walton, Chislehurst, UK
Germany, Switzerland & Austria: Gabriele
Kern Publishers Services, Frankfurt-am-
Main, Germany
Middle East: Peter Ward Book Exports,
London, UK
Republic of Ireland: Gill Hess Ltd, Skerries,
Co Dublin
Scandinavia & Italy: Katie McNeish,
McNeish Publishing International, East
Sussex, UK
Spain, Portugal & Gibraltar: Peter Prout,
Iberian Book Services, Madrid, Spain

2768

TOP THAT! PUBLISHING PLC
Marine House, Tide Mill Way, Woodbridge,
Suffolk IP12 1AP
Telephone: 01394 386651
Fax: 01394 386011
Email: barrie@topthatpublishing.com
Web Site: www.topthatpublishing.com

Directors: Barrie Henderson *(Managing)*
Dave Greggor *(Sales)*
Simon Couchman *(Creative)*
Douglas Eadie *(Finance)*
Daniel Graham *(Editorial)*
Stuart Buck *(Production)*
Head of European Sales: Georgina Eade
International Sales Manager: Sean
Buckley

*Children's Books; Cookery, Wines & Spirits;
Crafts & Hobbies; Gardening; Guide Books;
Health & Beauty; Humour; Natural History;
Reference Books, Directories & Dictionaries*

No of Employees: 25
Annual Turnover: £8.5M

ISBNs, Imprints & Series:
Pocket Money Press; Tide Mill Press
978 1 84229 Kudos
978 1 902973 Art Rom; Art Tricks; Cool
Kits; Explorasaws; file-online.com; Fun
Kits; I-Quiz; Know How Know Why;
Magic Bookshop Bears; Megatastic; Mini
Maestro; Paper Magic; Play Pals; Puzzle
Zone; Stickertastic; Teachers Pets; Top
That!

Overseas Representation:
USA: Top That! Publishing, Valencia, CA

Book Trade Association Membership:
IPG

2769

TOPICAL RESOURCES
Jumps Farm, Durton Lane, Broughton,
Preston, Lancs PR3 5LE
Telephone: 01772 863158
Fax: 01772 866153
Email: sales@topical-resources.co.uk
Web Site: www.topical-resources.co.uk

Partners: Peter Bell
Heather Bell
Sales Assistants: Kath Cope
Sue Concill

*Audio Books; Children's Books; Educational
& Textbooks*

ISBNs, Imprints & Series:
978 1 872977, 978 1 905509

Overseas Representation:
Republic of Ireland: Martin Pender, Primary
Educational Resources, Enniscorthy, Co
Wexford

2770

TRANSWORLD PUBLISHERS LTD
[a company of the Random House Group
Ltd]
61–63 Uxbridge Road, London W5 5SA
Telephone: (020) 8579 2652
Fax: (020) 8579 5479
Email: info@transworld-publishers.co.uk
Web Site: www.booksattransworld.co.uk

Warehouse & Distribution:
PO Box 17, Wellingborough, Northants
NN8 4BU
Telephone: 01933 225761
Fax: 01933 271235
Email: warehouse@transworld-
publishers.co.uk

Directors: Larry Finlay *(Managing)*
Bill Scott-Kerr *(Publisher)*

Sally Gaminara (*Publishing – Bantam Press*)
Marianne Velmans (*Publishing – Doubleday*)
Tom Fussell (*Finance*)
Ed Christie (*Sales & Marketing*)
Martin Higgins (*UK Sales*)
Janine Giovanni (*UK Marketing*)
Diana Jones (*International Sales*)
Alison Martin (*Production*)
Patsy Irwin (*Publicity*)
Andy Lay (*Operations Manager*)
Claire Ward (*Art*)
Helen Edwards (*Rights*)

Audio Books; Biography & Autobiography; Cinema, Video, TV & Radio; Cookery, Wines & Spirits; Crime; Fiction; Gardening; Health & Beauty; History & Antiquarian; Humour; Military & War; Music; Politics & World Affairs; Science Fiction; Sports & Games; Travel & Topography; New Age

No of Employees: 140

ISBNs, Imprints & Series:
Channel 4 Books
978 0 385 Doubleday
978 0 552 Black Swan; Corgi
978 0 553 Bantam
978 0 593 Bantam Press; Eden Project
978 0 903 Expert Gardening Books
978 1 848 Transworld Ireland

Parent Company:
USA: Random House Inc

Associated Companies:
Random House Children's Books; Random House UK Ltd
Australia: Random House Australia Pty Ltd
Canada: Random House of Canada Ltd
New Zealand: Random House New Zealand Ltd
South Africa: Random House (Pty) Ltd

Overseas Representation:
Australia: Random House Australia Pty Ltd, Sydney, NSW
Canada: Random House of Canada Ltd, Toronto, Ont
New Zealand: Random House New Zealand Ltd, Auckland
South Africa: Random House Struik Pty Ltd, Parktown

Book Trade Association Membership:
BA (Associate Member)

2771

TRAVEL PUBLISHING LTD
Airport Business Centre,
10 Thornbury Road, Estover, Plymouth
PL6 7PP
Telephone: 01752 697280
Fax: 01752 697299
Email: info@travelpublishing.co.uk
Web Site: www.travelpublishing.co.uk

Sales & Distribution:
Portfolio, Suite 3 & 4, Great West House,
Great West Road, Brentford, Middx
TW8 9DF
Telephone: (020) 8326 5620
Fax: (020) 8326 5621
Email: e-mail@portfoliobooks.com

Directors: Peter Robinson (*Chairman*)
Chris Day (*Company Secretary*)

Guide Books; Travel & Topography

New Titles: 8 (2008) , 10 (2009)

ISBNs, Imprints & Series:
978 1 902007, 978 1 904434 Country Living Rural Guides; Golfers Guides; Hidden Inns; Hidden Places; Off the Motorway
978 1 904434 Country Living Garden

Centres & Nurseries of Britain; Country Pubs & Inns

Overseas Representation:
USA & Canada: Casemate Publishers & Book Distributors LLC, Havertown, PA, USA

Book Trade Association Membership:
IPG

2772

TRENTHAM BOOKS
Westview House, 734 London Road,
Oakhill, Stoke on Trent ST4 5NP
Telephone: 01782 745567 & 844699
Fax: 01782 745553
Email: tb@trentham-books.co.uk
Web Site: www.trentham-books.co.uk

Editorial:
28 Hillside Gardens, Highgate, London
N6 5ST
Telephone: (020) 8348 2174
Email: gillian@trentham-books.co.uk

Directors: Gillian Klein (*Chairman, Rights & Permissions, Editor*)
Barbara Wiggins (*Business Manager*)

Academic & Scholarly; Educational & Textbooks; Gender Studies; Law; Politics & World Affairs; Theatre, Drama & Dance

New Titles: 22 (2008) , 30 (2009)
No of Employees: 5

ISBNs, Imprints & Series:
978 0 948080, 978 0 9507735, 978 1 85856

Associated Companies:
Trentham Print Design Ltd

Distributor for:
Arts Council [selected titles]; Commission for Racial Equality [selected titles]; Design and Technology Association [selected titles]; Open University [selected titles]
France: European Institute of Education & Social Policy [selected titles]; UNESCO Institute for Educational Planning [selected titles]

Overseas Representation:
Australia, New Zealand & South East Asia: DA Information Services Pty Ltd, Mitcham, Vic, Australia
Canada: Bacon & Hughes Ltd, Ottawa, Ont
China, Taiwan, Hong Kong & South East Asia: Tony Poh Leong Wah, Singapore, Singapore
Malaysia: UBSD Distribution Sdn Bhd, Selangor
Philippines: Megatexts Phil Inc, Cebu City
Spain & Portugal: Iberian Book Services, Madrid, Spain
Taiwan: Unifacmanu Trading Co Ltd, Taipei
USA: Stylus Publishing Inc, Sterling, VA

Book Trade Association Membership:
IPG

2773

TRINITARIAN BIBLE SOCIETY
Tyndale House, Dorset Road, London
SW19 3NN
Telephone: (020) 8543 7857
Fax: (020) 8543 6370
Email: TBS@trinitarianbiblesociety.org
Web Site: www.trinitarianbiblesociety.org

Online Sales:
Web Site: www.TBS-sales.org

General Secretary: D. P. Rowland
Assistant General Secretary: D. Larlham
Office Manager: M. Wilson

Religion & Theology

No of Employees: 25

ISBNs, Imprints & Series:
978 0 907861, 978 1 86228

Overseas Representation:
Australia: Trinitarian Bible Society (Australia), Grafton, NSW
Brazil: Sociedade Bíblica Trinitariana do Brasil, São Paulo
Canada: Trinitarian Bible Society, Chilliwack, BC
New Zealand: Trinitarian Bible Society (New Zealand), Gisborne
USA: Trinitarian Bible Society (USA), Grand Rapids, MI

2774

*TRIUMPH HOUSE
Remus House, Coltsfoot Drive, Woodston,
Peterborough PE2 9JX
Telephone: 01733 898102
Fax: 01733 313524
Email: triumphhouse@forwardpress.co.uk
Web Site: www.forwardpress.co.uk

Communications Assistant: Sharon Spencer (*Marketing*)

Poetry; Religion & Theology

ISBNs, Imprints & Series:
afterschoolclub.net; Anchor Books; Need2Know; New Fiction; Poetry Now; Pond View; Spotlight Poets; Writers' Bookshop; Young Writers
978 1 86161, 978 1 90422 Triumph House

Parent Company:
Forward Press

Book Trade Association Membership:
BA

2775

TROG ASSOCIATES LTD
PO Box 243, South Croydon, Surrey
CR2 6NZ
Telephone: (020) 8681 3301
Email: eric.sutherland@tesco.net
Web Site: www.trogassesltd.biz

Contact: Eric Sutherland

Accountancy & Taxation; Health & Beauty; Industry, Business & Management; Literature & Criticism

New Titles: 2 (2008) , 5 (2009)
Annual Turnover: £46,000

ISBNs, Imprints & Series: 978 1 906440

Associated Companies:
UK: www.lulu.com/uk

2776

TROTMAN PUBLISHING
[an imprint of Crimson Publishing Ltd]
Crimson Publishing Ltd,
Westminster House, Kew Road, Richmond
TW9 2ND
Telephone: (020) 8334 1786
Fax: (020) 8334 1601
Email: jessicas@crimsonpublishing.co.uk
Web Site: www.trotman.co.uk

Warehouse:
NBN International Ltd, Estover Road,
Plymouth PL6 7PY
Telephone: 01752 202301
Fax: 01752 202333

Directors: David Lester (*Managing*)
Thomas Lee (*Commercial*)
Commissioning Editor: Jessica Spencer

Educational & Textbooks; Industry, Business & Management; Reference Books, Directories & Dictionaries; Travel & Topography; Vocational Training & Careers

New Titles: 17 (2009)

ISBNs, Imprints & Series:
978 0 85660, 978 1 84455 Trotman; Trotman Education

Parent Company:
UK: Crimson Publishing Ltd

Book Trade Association Membership:
IPG; Data Publishers Association

2777

TROUBADOR PUBLISHING LTD
5 Weir Road, Kibworth Beauchamp, Leics
LE8 0LQ
Telephone: 0116 279 2299
Fax: 0116 279 2277
Email: books@troubador.co.uk
Web Site: www.troubador.co.uk

Directors: Jeremy Thompson (*Managing*)
Jane Rowland (*Academic Publishing*)
Managers: Julia Fuller (*Marketing*)
Terry Compton (*Production*)

Academic & Scholarly; Biography & Autobiography; Children's Books; Cookery, Wines & Spirits; Crime; Economics; Fiction; Guide Books; History & Antiquarian; Humour; Industry, Business & Management; Languages & Linguistics; Literature & Criticism; Magic & the Occult; Medical (incl. Self Help & Alternative Medicine); Military & War; Natural History; Philosophy; Poetry; Politics & World Affairs; Psychology & Psychiatry; Science Fiction; Theatre, Drama & Dance; Transport; Travel & Topography

New Titles: 134 (2008) , 150 (2009)
No of Employees: 5
Annual Turnover: £700,000

ISBNs, Imprints & Series:
978 1 848761, 978 1 899293, 978 1 905886, 978 1 906221, 978 1 906510 Matador
978 1 904744 T2
978 1 905237 Italian Studies

Book Trade Association Membership:
IPG

2778

TRURAN
Goonance, Water Lane, St Agnes, Cornwall
TR5 0RA
Telephone: 01872 553821
Email: info@truranbooks.co.uk
Web Site: www.truranbooks.co.uk

Trade Enquiries:
Tor Mark Press,
United Downs Industrial Estate, St Day,
Redruth, Cornwall TR16 5HY
Telephone: 01209 822101
Fax: 01209 822035
Email: sales@tormarkpress.prestel.co.uk

Directors: Ivan Corbett
Heather Corbett

Aviation; Biography & Autobiography; Cookery, Wines & Spirits; Fiction; Fine Art & Art History; Gardening; Geography & Geology; Guide Books; History & Antiquarian; Languages & Linguistics; Military & War; Natural History; Nautical; Photography; Reference Books, Directories & Dictionaries

New Titles: 4 (2008) , 4 (2009)

ISBNs, Imprints & Series:
Cornish Classics; Truran
978 0 9506431, 978 0 907566, 978 1
85022

Book Trade Association Membership:
IPG

2779

TSO (THE STATIONERY OFFICE LTD)
St Crispins, Duke Street, Norwich NR3 1PD
Telephone: 01603 622211
Fax: 01603 696506
Email: tsoservices@tso.co.uk
Web Site: www.tso.co.uk

Press & Offices:
Mandela Way, London SE1 5SS
Telephone: (020) 7394 4200
Email: tsoservices@tso.co.uk
Web Site: www.tso.co.uk

Directors: Richard South (Official
Publishing)
Richard Dell (Chief Executive Officer)
Richard Coward (Finance)
Gordon Samson (Operations)
Lisa Mallett (Head of Marketing)
Ashley Dampier (Head of Sales)

Academic & Scholarly; Accountancy &
Taxation; Aviation; Computer Science;
Economics; Educational & Textbooks;
Electronic (Professional & Academic);
Engineering; Geography & Geology;
Industry, Business & Management; Law;
Mathematics & Statistics; Medical (incl. Self
Help & Alternative Medicine); Nautical;
Politics & World Affairs; Reference Books,
Directories & Dictionaries; Scientific &
Technical; Transport; Veterinary Science

New Titles: 9100 (2008) , 9000 (2009)
No of Employees: 405
Annual Turnover: £70M

ISBNs, Imprints & Series:
International Organisations
978 0 10 Parliamentary Publications
978 0 11 Non-Parliamentary Publications
978 0 337 Northern Ireland Publications
978 0 8213 World Bank
978 1 55 International Monetary Fund

Distributor for:
Construction Industry Publications; English
Heritage [selected back-list titles only];
International Labour Organisation
France: Council of Europe; European
Pharmacopoeia Commission;
Organisation for Economic Co-operation
and Development; United Nations
Educational, Scientific and Cultural
Organisation
Germany: Deutscher Apotheker Verlag
Italy: Food and Agriculture Organisation of
the United Nations
Japan: Japanese Pharmacopoeia
Luxembourg: European Communities/
Union
Spain: World Tourism Organisation
Switzerland: United Nations; World Health
Organisation; World Trade Organisation
USA: Bernan Press; International Monetary
Fund; United Nations; US
Pharmacopoeia Convention; World Bank

Overseas Representation:
Australia: DA Information Services Pty Ltd,
Mitcham, Vic
Belgium & Luxembourg: Jean de Lannoy,
Brussels, Belgium
Brazil: Livraria Cultura Editora Ltda, São
Paulo
Canada: Renouf Publishing Co Ltd, Ottawa,
Ont
Croatia: VBZ d.o.o., Zagreb
Denmark: Arnold Busck, Copenhagen
Egypt: MERIC, Cairo
Finland: Akateeminen Kirjakauppa, Helsinki
Germany: Alexander Horn, Wiesbaden

Greece: Athenian Science, Athens
Hong Kong: Swindon Book Co Ltd
Hungary: SpeedUp Ltd, Budapest
Iceland: Boksala Studenta, Reykjavik
India: Apple Books, New Delhi
Italy: LEDWeb srl, Turin; Licosa SPA,
Florence
Japan: Maruzen Co Ltd, Tokyo
Jordan: Jordan Book Centre, Amman
Kuwait: The Kuwait Bookshop Co Ltd, Safat
Malaysia: Yuha Associates, Selangor Darul
Ehsan
Mexico: Libreria Arroyave, Mexico
Netherlands: Kooyker Ginsberg, Leiden;
Technische Boekhandel Waltman, Delft
Norway: Academic Book Centre, Oslo
Pakistan: Pak Book Corporation, Lahore;
Progressive International, Karachi
Peru: Concentra Business SAC, Lima
Poland: Ars Polona JSC, Warsaw
Singapore: Alkem Co (S) Pte Ltd
Slovenia: Mladinska Knjiga Trgovina Inc,
Ljubljana
South Africa: Alluvion Consulting, Benoni;
Pharma Books cc, Pretoria; The Tyneside,
Durban
Spain: Cymit Quimica SL, Barcelona; Diaz
de Santos SA, Madrid
Sweden: Longus Book Imports, Stockholm
Switzerland: Buchhandlung Hans Huber,
Berne; Stheli International Booksellers,
Zurich; Wepf & Co, Basel
United Arab Emirates: Al Mutanabbi
Bookshop, Abu Dhabi, UAE
USA: Balogh International Inc, Champaign,
IL; Bernan Associates, Lanham, MD;
InterProm USA, Houston, TX

Book Trade Association Membership:
BA; EPC; CAPP; Data Publishers Association

2780

*TTS GROUP
Nunn Brook Road, Huthwaite,
Sutton-in-Ashfield, Notts NG17 2HU
Telephone: 01623 447878
Fax: 01623 440543
Web Site: www.tts-group.co.uk

Book Trade Association Membership:
Publishers Association

2781

TWELVEHEADS PRESS
PO Box 59, Chacewater, Truro, Cornwall
TR4 8ZJ
Email: enquiries@twelveheads.com
Web Site: www.twelveheads.com

Partners: Alan Kittridge
Michael Messenger
John Stengelhofen

Archaeology; Guide Books; History &
Antiquarian; Nautical; Transport

New Titles: 4 (2008) , 3 (2009)

ISBNs, Imprints & Series: 978 0 906294

2782

TYNE BRIDGE PUBLISHING
Newcastle Libraries, PO Box 88,
Newcastle upon Tyne NE99 1DX
Telephone: 0191 277 4174
Fax: 0191 277 4137
Email: anna.flowers@newcastle.gov.uk
Web Site: www.newcastle.gov.uk/
tynebridgepublishing

Publications Manager: Anna Flowers
Marketing Officer: Vanessa Histon

Architecture & Design; Biography &
Autobiography; Engineering; Fine Art & Art
History; History & Antiquarian; Military &
War; Nautical

New Titles: 4 (2008) , 4 (2009)

No of Employees: 2
Annual Turnover: £60,000

ISBNs, Imprints & Series:
978 0 902653 Newcastle City Libraries
978 1 85795 Newcastle Libraries and
Information Service; Tyne Bridge
Publishing

Parent Company:
City & Council of Newcastle upon Tyne

2783

UCAS
Rosehill, New Barn Lane, Cheltenham, Glos
GL52 3LZ
Telephone: 01242 222444
Fax: 01242 544960
Email: publicationservices@ucas.ac.uk
Web Site: www.ucas.com

Trade Enquiries & Orders:
Publication Services, UCAS, PO Box 130,
Cheltenham, Glos GL52 3ZF
Telephone: 01242 544610
Fax: 01242 544806
Email: publicationservices@ucas.ac.uk
Web Site: www.ucasbooks.com

Head of Communications: Chris Dry
Publications Co-ordinator: Steven
Matthews
Senior Management Accountant:
Amruta Hiremath
Publication Services Manager: Joanne
Voysey

Academic & Scholarly; Educational &
Textbooks; Reference Books, Directories &
Dictionaries; Vocational Training & Careers

New Titles: 2 (2008) , 1 (2009)

ISBNs, Imprints & Series: 978 1 84361

2784

**ULVERSCROFT LARGE PRINT BOOKS
LTD**
The Green, Bradgate Road, Anstey, Leics
LE7 7FU
Telephone: 0116 236 4325
Fax: 0116 236 5522
Email: sales@ulverscroft.co.uk
Web Site: www.ulverscroft.co.uk

Trade

Book Trade Association Membership:
Publishers Association

2785

UNICORN PRESS
47 Earlham Road, Norwich NR2 3AD
Telephone: 01603 886151
Email: unicornpress@btinternet.com
Web Site: www.unicornpress.org

Trade Distributor:
Marston Book Services, 160 Milton Park,
PO Box 269, Abingdon, Oxford OX14 4YN
Telephone: 01235 465604
Fax: 01235 465655
Email: nichola.kidd@marston.co.uk

Proprietor: Hugh Tempest-Radford
Sales & Marketing: Lucy Hulme

Antiques & Collecting; Architecture &
Design; Biography & Autobiography; Crafts
& Hobbies; Fashion & Costume; Fine Art &
Art History; History & Antiquarian; Military
& War; Nautical; Photography; Reference
Books, Directories & Dictionaries

ISBNs, Imprints & Series:
978 0 906290, 978 1 906509

Overseas Representation:
All other areas: Unicorn Press, London, UK

Germany, France, Benelux, Italy, Austria,
Switzerland, Malta & Greece: Ted
Dougherty, London, UK
Spain, Portugal & Gibraltar: Chris
Humphrys, London, UK
USA: Antique Collectors Club Ltd,
Easthampton, MA

2786

**UNITED WRITERS PUBLICATIONS
LTD**
Ailsa, Castle Gate, Penzance, Cornwall
TR20 8BG
Telephone: 01736 365954
Fax: 01736 365954
Email: sales@unitedwriters.co.uk
Web Site: www.unitedwriters.co.uk

Editorial & Sales: M. Sheppard
Production: T. Sully

Biography & Autobiography; Children's
Books; Cinema, Video, TV & Radio;
Educational & Textbooks; Fiction; Humour;
Industry, Business & Management; Military
& War; Nautical; Psychology & Psychiatry;
Science Fiction; Sports & Games; Travel &
Topography

New Titles: 7 (2008) , 7 (2009)

ISBNs, Imprints & Series:
978 0 901976, 978 1 85200

2787

**UNIVERSITY COLLEGE DUBLIN
PRESS**
Newman House, 86 St Stephen's Green,
Dublin 2, Republic of Ireland
Telephone: +353 (01) 477 9812 & 9813
Fax: +353 (01) 477 9821
Email: ucdpress@ucd.ie
Web Site: www.ucdpress.ie

Distribution (Republic of Ireland):
Columba Mercier Distribution,
55A Spruce Avenue,
Stillorgan Industrial Park, Blackrock,
Co Dublin, Republic of Ireland
Fax: +353 (01) 294 2564

Representation (Republic of Ireland):
Hibernian Book Services,
93 Longwood Park, Rathfarnham,
Dublin 14, Republic of Ireland
Telephone: +353 (01) 493 6043
Fax: +353 (01) 493 7833

Executive Editor: Barbara Mennell
Assistant Editor: Noelle Moran

Academic & Scholarly

New Titles: 17 (2008) , 18 (2009)
No of Employees: 2

ISBNs, Imprints & Series:
978 1 900621, 978 1 904558, 978 1
906359

Overseas Representation:
Australia & New Zealand: Eleanor Brasch
Enterprises, Artarmon, NSW, Australia
Germany, Austria & Switzerland: SHS
Publishers' Consultants and
Representatives, Oranienberg, Germany
North America: Dufour Editions Inc, Chester
Springs, PA, USA
Spain & Portugal: Iberian Book Services,
Madrid, Spain
UK & Benelux countries: Theo Van de Bilt
Sales and Marketing, Sawbridgeworth,
UK
UK, Europe & all other countries
(distribution): Central Books Ltd, London,
UK

Book Trade Association Membership:
CLÉ (Irish PA)

2788

UNIVERSITY OF EXETER PRESS
Reed Hall, Streatham Drive, Exeter EX4 4QR
Telephone: 01392 263066
Fax: 01392 263064
Email: uep@exeter.ac.uk
Web Site: www.exeterpress.co.uk

Distribution:
NBN International, Estover Road, Plymouth
PL6 7PY
Telephone: 01752 202301
Fax: 01752 202331
Email: cservs@nbninternational.com
Web Site: www.nbninternational.com

Publisher: Simon Baker
Sales: Helen Gannon

*Academic & Scholarly; Archaeology;
Cinema, Video, TV & Radio; History &
Antiquarian; Literature & Criticism; Theatre,
Drama & Dance; Classical Studies; Film
History; Maritime History; Medieval English
Texts & Studies; Performance Studies*

New Titles: 25 (2008) , 25 (2009)

ISBNs, Imprints & Series:
978 0 85989 University of Exeter Press
978 1 904675 Bristol Phoenix Press
978 1 905816 The Exeter Press

Parent Company:
The Exeter Press Ltd

Overseas Representation:
Australia & New Zealand: Footprint Books
Pty, Mona Vale, NSW, Australia
Benelux: Roy de Boo, Hooge Mierde,
Netherlands
*China, Hong Kong, Taiwan & South East
Asia:* Tony Poh, Singapore
France & Italy: Flavio Marcello Publishers'
Agents & Consultants, Padua, Italy
Germany, Austria & Switzerland: SHS
Publishers' Consultants and
Representatives, Oranienberg, Germany
Greece & Cyprus: Charles Gibbes
Associates, Louslitges, France
Japan: United Publishers Services Ltd, Tokyo
Republic of Ireland: Quantum Publishing
Solutions Ltd, Paisley, UK
Scandinavia: Jan Norbye, Ølstykke,
Denmark
Spain & Portugal: Iberian Book Services,
Madrid, Spain
USA & Canada: University of Chicago Press,
Chicago, IL, USA

Book Trade Association Membership:
IPG

2789

**UNIVERSITY OF HERTFORDSHIRE
PRESS**
De Havilland LRC, College Lane, Hatfield
AL10 9AB
Telephone: 01707 284681
Fax: 01707 284666
Email: UHPress@herts.ac.uk
Web Site: www.herts.ac.uk/UHPress

Trade Enquiries & Orders:
Central Books Ltd, 99 Wallis Road, London
E9 5LN
Telephone: 0845 458 9911
Fax: 0845 458 9912
Email: info@centralbooks.com
Web Site: www.centralbooks.com

Press Manager: Jane Housham
Assistant: Sue Mariscal *(Administration)*
Production Editor: Sarah Elvins

*Academic & Scholarly; Educational &
Textbooks; Geography & Geology; History
& Antiquarian; Literature & Criticism; Magic
& the Occult; Mathematics & Statistics;
Psychology & Psychiatry; Sociology &*

Anthropology; Theatre, Drama & Dance

New Titles: 12 (2008) , 10 (2009)
No of Employees: 2

ISBNs, Imprints & Series:
978 0 900458, 978 1 905313 Guidelines
for Research in Parapsychology; The
Interface Collection; Regional and Local
History
978 0 9542189, 978 1 905313
Hertfordshire Publications
978 1 898543, 978 1 905313 University of
Hertfordshire (Faculties)
978 1 902806, 978 1 905313 University of
Hertfordshire Press

Parent Company:
University of Hertfordshire

Overseas Representation:
Spain & Portugal: Iberian Book Services,
Madrid, Spain
USA: Independent Publishers Group (IPG),
Chicago, IL

Book Trade Association Membership:
IPG

2790

UNIVERSITY OF WALES PRESS
10 Columbus Walk, Brigantine Place,
Cardiff CF10 4UP
Telephone: (029) 2049 6899
Fax: (029) 2049 6108
Email: press@press.wales.ac.uk
Web Site: uwp.co.uk

Distribution (UK):
NBN International Ltd, Estover Road,
Plymouth PL6 7PY
Telephone: 01752 202300
Fax: 01752 202330

Managers: Sîan Chapman *(Production)*
Bethan James *(Sales & Marketing)*
Commissioning Editor: Sarah Lewis
Finance: Paul Folland

*Academic & Scholarly; Archaeology;
Biography & Autobiography; Educational &
Textbooks; Gender Studies; History &
Antiquarian; Illustrated & Fine Editions;
Languages & Linguistics; Literature &
Criticism; Military & War; Music;
Philosophy; Poetry; Politics & World Affairs;
Reference Books, Directories &
Dictionaries; Religion & Theology; Sociology
& Anthropology; Sports & Games*

New Titles: 60 (2008) , 80 (2009)
No of Employees: 12

ISBNs, Imprints & Series:
978 0 7083, 978 0 900768 GPC Books;
Gwasg Prifysgol Cymru; University of
Wales Press

Parent Company:
University of Wales

Distributor for:
The Glamorgan County History Trust; Zena
Publications [one title]

Overseas Representation:
India: Maya Publishers Pvt Ltd, New Delhi
Japan: United Publishers Services Ltd, Tokyo
South East Asia: STM Publisher Services Pte
Ltd, Singapore
USA, Canada & Australia: Chicago
University Press, Chicago, IL, USA

Book Trade Association Membership:
IPG; Literary Publishers (Wales) Ltd

2791

MERLIN UNWIN BOOKS LTD
7 Corve Street, Ludlow, Shropshire SY8 1DB
Telephone: 01584 877456

Fax: 01584 877457
Email: books@merlinunwin.co.uk
Web Site: www.merlinunwin.co.uk

Warehouse & Returns:
Merlin Unwin Books Warehouse, c/
o Wow Distribution, The Yard,
Woofferton Grange, Brimfield, Ludlow
SY8 4NP

Directors: Merlin Unwin *(Management,
Design)*
Karen McCall *(Managing, Editorial)*
Finance: Gillian Bissell
Marketing & Production: Joanne Potter

*Agriculture; Biography & Autobiography;
Cookery, Wines & Spirits; Humour;
Illustrated & Fine Editions; Medical (incl. Self
Help & Alternative Medicine); Military &
War; Natural History; Philosophy;
Photography; Reference Books, Directories
& Dictionaries; Sports & Games*

New Titles: 6 (2008) , 9 (2009)
No of Employees: 4
Annual Turnover: £330,000

ISBNs, Imprints & Series:
978 1 873674, 978 1 90612

Distributor for:
LPPHA (London Police Pensioner Housing
Association)

Book Trade Association Membership:
IPG

2792

UPFRONT PUBLISHING
9 Culley Court, Bakewell Road,
Orton Southgate, Peterborough PE2 6XP
Telephone: 01733 311124
Fax: 01733 352933
Email: info@upfrontpublishing.com
Web Site: www.upfrontpublishing.com

Managing Director: Andy Cork
Publishing Manager: Simon Potter

Biography & Autobiography; Fiction; Poetry

New Titles: 80 (2008) , 120 (2009)
No of Employees: 22

ISBNs, Imprints & Series: 978 1 84426

Parent Company:
Print on Demand – Worldwide [formerly
Copytech Digital]

2793

USBORNE PUBLISHING LTD
Usborne House, 83–85 Saffron Hill, London
EC1N 8RT
Telephone: (020) 7430 2800
Fax: (020) 7242 0974 & 7430 1562
Email: mail@usborne.co.uk
Web Site: www.usborne.com

Warehouse:
HarperCollins, Westerhill Road,
Bishopsbriggs, Glasgow G64 2QT
Telephone: 0141 306 3100
Fax: 0141 306 3767

Directors: T. P. Usborne *(Managing)*
R. Jones *(General Manager)*
J. Tyler *(Editorial)*
D. Harte
L. Hunt
K. M. Ball *(Company Secretary)*
Rights Controller: E. Wright
UK Marketing: C. Herisson
Editorial: M. Larkin *(Fiction)*
G. Lewis

*Children's Books; Computer Science; Crafts
& Hobbies; Fiction; Languages &*

*Linguistics; Music; Natural History;
Reference Books, Directories &
Dictionaries; Scientific & Technical; Sports &
Games*

New Titles: 348 (2008) , 324 (2009)
No of Employees: 180
Annual Turnover: £35M

ISBNs, Imprints & Series:
978 0 7460, 978 0 86020

2794

VALLENTINE MITCHELL PUBLISHERS
Suite 314, Premier House,
112–114 Station Road, Edgware, Middx
HA8 7BJ
Telephone: (020) 8952 9526
Fax: (020) 8952 9242
Email: info@vmbooks.com
Web Site: www.vmbooks.com

Managing Director: Stewart Cass
Editor & Production: Jenni Tinson
Sales & Marketing, Publicity: Toby Harris

*Academic & Scholarly; Biography &
Autobiography; History & Antiquarian;
Politics & World Affairs; Religion &
Theology*

ISBNs, Imprints & Series: 978 0 85303

Book Trade Association Membership:
IPG

2795

*VELOCE PUBLISHING LTD
33 Trinity Street, Dorchester, Dorset
DT1 1TT
Telephone: 01305 260068
Fax: 01305 268864
Email: veloce@veloce.co.uk
Web Site: www.veloce.co.uk

Directors: Rod Grainger *(Publisher)*
Judith Brooks *(Company Secretary)*

*Biography & Autobiography; Illustrated &
Fine Editions; Reference Books, Directories
& Dictionaries; Sports & Games; Transport*

ISBNs, Imprints & Series:
978 1 84584, 978 1 874105, 978 1
901295, 978 1 903706, 978 1 904788

Overseas Representation:
Australia & New Zealand: Capricorn Link
(Australia) Pty Ltd, Windsor, NSW,
Australia
France: Editions du Palmier, Nîmes; Librairie
du Collectionneur, Paris
Germany: Heel-Verlag, Konigswinter
Germany, Austria & Benelux: Anselm
Robinson, London, UK
Japan: Shimada & Co Inc, Tokyo; Takahara
Bookstore Co Ltd, Aichi-ken
New Zealand: South Pacific Books (Imports)
Ltd, Auckland; TechBooks, Auckland
Scandinavia: MarGie Bookshop, Stockholm,
Sweden; Angell Eurosales, Berwick-on-
Tweed, UK
South Africa: Motor Books, Johannesburg
South East Asia: Ashton International
Marketing Services, Sevenoaks, Kent, UK
Spain & Italy: Bookport Associates, Corsico
(MI), Italy; Libro Motor SI, Madrid, Spain
USA: Motorbooks International Inc,
Osceola, WI

2796

*VERITAS PUBLICATIONS
Veritas House, 7–8 Lower Abbey Street,
Dublin 1, Republic of Ireland
Telephone: +353 (01) 878 8177
Fax: +353 (01) 878 6507
Email: publications@veritas.ie
Web Site: www.veritas.ie

Editors: Ruth Kennedy *(Managing)*
Donna Doherty *(Commissioning)*
Commercial Manager: Maureen Sanders
Publicity & Marketing: Amanda Conlon-McKenna
Director: Maura Hyland
Sales Representatives: Ann O'Neill
Sheila McMacken
Financial Controller: Eamonn Connelly

Academic & Scholarly; Biography & Autobiography; Children's Books; Educational & Textbooks; Philosophy; Religion & Theology; Social Issues

ISBNs, Imprints & Series:
978 0 85390, 978 0 86217, 978 1 84730, 978 1 85390

Parent Company:
Republic of Ireland: Veritas Communications

Overseas Representation:
Australia: John Garrett Publishing, Mulgrave, Vic
Malta: Libreria Taghlim Nisrani, Sliema
New Zealand: Catholic Supplies (NZ) Ltd, Wellington
South Africa: The Catholic Bookshop, Cape Town; St Augustine's Catholic Bookshop, Port Elizabeth
USA: Acta, Chicago, IL; Dufour Editions Inc, Chester Springs, PA; Ignatius Press, San Francisco, CA

Book Trade Association Membership:
CLÉ (Irish PA)

2797

VERTICAL EDITIONS
Unit 4a, Snaygill Industrial Estate, Skipton, North Yorkshire BD23 2QR
Telephone: 01756 790362
Fax: 01756 798618
Email: custserv@verticaleditions.com
Web Site: www.verticaleditions.com

Publisher: Karl Waddicor
Editor: Diane Evans

Biography & Autobiography; Sports & Games

New Titles: 6 (2008) , 7 (2009)

ISBNs, Imprints & Series: 978 1 904091

Book Trade Association Membership:
IPG

2798

VICTORIA & ALBERT MUSEUM PUBLISHING
Victoria & Albert Museum, South Kensington, London SW7 2RL
Telephone: (020) 7942 2966
Fax: (020) 7942 2967
Email: vapubs.info@vam.ac.uk
Web Site: www.vandabooks.com

Distribution:
Macmillan Distribution (MDL), Houndmills, Basingstoke RG21 6XS
Telephone: 01256 302692
Fax: 01256 812558 (UK orders) & 842084 (Export orders)
Email: mdl@macmillan.co.uk
Web Site:
www.macmillandistribution.co.uk

Head of Publishing: Mark Eastnent
Editors: Anjali Bulley *(Managing)*
Tom Windross *(Senior)*
Frances Ambler
Managers: Clare Davis *(Production)*
Clare Faulkner *(Marketing)*
Nina Jacobson *(Rights)*

Academic & Scholarly; Antiques & Collecting; Architecture & Design; Biography & Autobiography; Fashion & Costume; Fine Art & Art History; Photography; Theatre, Drama & Dance

New Titles: 26 (2008) , 30 (2009)
No of Employees: 10
Annual Turnover: £1.5M

ISBNs, Imprints & Series:
978 0 905209, 978 0 948107, 978 1 85177

Parent Company:
Victoria & Albert Museum

Overseas Representation:
Australia & New Zealand: Allen & Unwin Pty Ltd, Sydney, NSW, Australia
Central & Eastern Europe: Grazyna Soszynska, Poznan-Baranowo, Poland
France: Critiques Livres Distribution, Bagnolet
Germany & Austria: Penguin Books Deutschland GmbH, Frankfurt am Main, Germany
India: Maya Publishers Pvt Ltd, New Delhi
Italy: Penguin Italia srl, Milan
Netherlands, Belgium & Luxembourg: Penguin Books BV, Amsterdam, Netherlands
Singapore, Indonesia & Thailand: APD Singapore Pte Ltd, Singapore
South America & Central America: David Williams, InterMedia Americana (IMA) Ltd, London, UK
Southern Africa: Book Promotions Pty Ltd, Cape Town, South Africa
Spain & Portugal: Penguin Books SA, Madrid, Spain
Turkey, Africa, Middle East, Japan, Hong Kong, Taiwan, Korea, Scandinavia, Switzerland, Malta, Greece, Cyprus, Israel, China & Philippines: International Sales Department, Penguin Books Ltd, London, UK
USA: Harry N. Abrams Inc, New York, NY

Book Trade Association Membership:
IPG; International Association of Museum Publishers

2799

VIRGIN BOOKS LTD
20 Vauxhall bridge Road, London SW1V 2SA
Telephone: (020) 7840 8400
Email: info@virgin-books.co.uk
Web Site: www.virginbooks.com

Directors: John Sadler *(Managing)*
Clare Pierotti *(Publicity)*
Vickie Boff *(Marketing)*
Han Ismail *(Home Sales)*
Phil Brown *(Production)*
Editors: Ed Faulkner *(Editorial Director – Non-Fiction)*
Adam Nevill *(Commissioning – Erotic Fiction, Horror)*
Louisa Joyner *(Editorial Director – non-fiction)*

Audio Books; Biography & Autobiography; Cinema, Video, TV & Radio; Cookery, Wines & Spirits; Economics; Gay & Lesbian Studies; Health & Beauty; Humour; Illustrated & Fine Editions; Military & War; Music; Politics & World Affairs; Reference Books, Directories & Dictionaries; Sports & Games

ISBNs, Imprints & Series:
978 0 352 Black Lace (heteroerotic fiction by women); Nexus (heteroerotic fiction)
978 0 86369 Virgin (paperback)
978 1 85227 Virgin (hardback)

Parent Company:
Virgin Group Ltd

Overseas Representation:
Australia: Random House Australia Pty Ltd, Sydney, NSW
Canada: H. B. Fenn & Co Ltd, Bolton, Ont
Caribbean, South & Central America, Middle East, Pakistan & Africa (excluding South Africa): Felicity Smith, Random House Group Ltd, London, UK
Eastern Europe, Baltic States, Israel, Belarus, Russia, Turkey & Ukraine: Mariann Kenedi, Budapest, Hungary
Germany, Austria, Norway, Denmark, Finland: Jörg Riekenbrauk, Cologne, Germany
India: Random House Publishers India Pte Ltd, New Delhi
Japan: Akiko Iwamoto, Tokyo
Netherlands, Belgium, Luxembourg, France, Switzerland: Pauline Konink, Hilversum, Netherlands
New Zealand: Random House New Zealand Ltd, Auckland
Philippines, Guam, Thailand, Indonesia, Singapore, Malaysia, Hong Kong, Taiwan, South Korea & China: Transworld Publishers Ltd, London, UK
South Africa: Random House South Africa Pty Ltd, Houghton
Sweden, Iceland, Spain, Portugal, Gibraltar, Italy, Malta, Cyprus, Greece: Andrew Wyman, Random House Group Ltd, London, UK
USA: Macmillan, New York, NY

Book Trade Association Membership:
BA

2800

*VISION
101 Southwark Street, London SE1 0JF
Telephone: (020) 7928 5599
Fax: (020) 7928 8822
Email: info@visionpaperbacks.co.uk
Web Site: www.visionpaperbacks.co.uk

Warehouse:
Littlehampton Book Services, Faraday Close, Durrington, Worthing, West Sussex BN13 3RB
Telephone: 01903 828500
Fax: 01903 828625

Directors: Sheena Dewan *(Managing)*
Paul Swallow *(Sales)*

Biography & Autobiography; Crime; Gay & Lesbian Studies; Gender Studies; Military & War; Politics & World Affairs; Sociology & Anthropology

ISBNs, Imprints & Series:
978 1 901250, 978 1 904132, 978 1 905745 Fusion Press; Vision Paperbacks 978 1 904132, 978 1 905745 Vision

Parent Company:
Satin Publications Ltd

Overseas Representation:
All other export territories: Vision, London, UK
Australia: Bookwise International, Adelaide, SA
Singapore, Malaysia & Brunei: Horizon Books Pte Ltd, Singapore
South Africa: Quartet Sales & Marketing, Johannesburg
USA & Canada: Independent Publishers Group (IPG), Chicago, IL, USA

Book Trade Association Membership:
IPG

2801

VOLTAIRE FOUNDATION LTD
University of Oxford, 99 Banbury Road, Oxford OX2 6JX
Telephone: 01865 284600
Fax: 01865 284610
Email: email@voltaire.ox.ac.uk

Web Site: www.voltaire.ox.ac.uk

Distribution:
Marston Book Services, 160 Milton Park, Abingdon, Oxon OX14 4YN
Telephone: 01235 465521 (Trade) & 465500 (Direct Sales)
Fax: 01235 465555 (Trade) & 465556 (Direct Sales)
Email: trade.orders@marston.co.uk & direct.orders@marston.co.uk
Web Site: www.marston.co.uk

Director: Prof Nicholas Cronk
Publisher: Clare Fletcher *(Sales, Marketing)*
Managers: Janet Godden *(Editorial)*
Lyn Roberts *(Senior Publishing, SVEC)*
Administrator: Liz Hancock *(Sales, Marketing, Rights & Permissions, Admin Support)*

Academic & Scholarly; Bibliography & Library Science; Biography & Autobiography; Electronic (Professional & Academic); Fiction; History & Antiquarian; Languages & Linguistics; Literature & Criticism; Philosophy; Reference Books, Directories & Dictionaries; Religion & Theology

New Titles: 24 (2008) , 24 (2009)

ISBNs, Imprints & Series:
978 0 7294 Correspondance complète de Françoise de Graffigny; Correspondance complète de Jean Jacques Rousseau; Correspondance complète de Pierre Bayle; Correspondance générale de La Beaumelle; Œuvres complètes de Montesquieu; Œuvres complètes de Voltaire; SVEC (Studies on Voltaire and the Eighteenth Century); Vif Une nouvelle collection en livre de poche

Parent Company:
University of Oxford

Overseas Representation:
France: Aux Amateurs de Livres, Paris

2802

WALLFLOWER PRESS
6 Market Place, London W1W 8AF
Telephone: (020) 7436 9494
Email: yoram@wallflowerpress.co.uk
Web Site: www.wallflowerpress.co.uk

Representation (UK):
Signature Book Representation, PO Box 12, York YO1 7WD
Telephone: 01904 631320
Fax: 01904 675445
Email: admin@signaturebooks.co.uk

Commissioning Editor: Yoram Allon
Managers: Amanda O'Boyle *(Sales & Marketing)*
Tom Cabot *(Production)*
Jackie Downs *(Editorial)*
Lucy Hurst *(Publicity & Marketing)*

Academic & Scholarly; Cinema, Video, TV & Radio; Educational & Textbooks

New Titles: 22 (2008) , 31 (2009)
No of Employees: 5
Annual Turnover: £321,000

ISBNs, Imprints & Series:
978 1 903364, 978 1 904764, 978 1 905674, 978 1 906660

Overseas Representation:
Australia & New Zealand: Woodslane Pty Ltd, Warriewood, NSW, Australia
Europe: Andrew Durnell Marketing Ltd, Tunbridge Wells, UK
Middle East: Avicenna Partnership, Oxford, UK
South East Asia: Taylor & Francis, Singapore

USA & Canada: Columbia University Press, Irvington, NY, USA

2803

WARBURG INSTITUTE
University of London, Woburn Square, London WC1H 0AB
Telephone: (020) 7862 8949
Fax: (020) 7862 8955
Email: warburg.books@sas.ac.uk
Web Site: warburg.sas.ac.uk

Administrative Assistant: E. Witchell

Academic & Scholarly; Archaeology; Architecture & Design; Bibliography & Library Science; Biography & Autobiography; Fine Art & Art History; History & Antiquarian; Magic & the Occult; Philosophy; Religion & Theology

New Titles: 4 (2008) , 3 (2009)

ISBNs, Imprints & Series:
978 0 85481 Special Publications (Warburg); Studies of the Warburg Institute; Warburg Institute Colloquia; Warburg Institute Surveys and Texts; Warburg Studies and Texts

Overseas Representation:
Italy: Nino Aragno Editore, Savigliano

2804

WARD LOCK EDUCATIONAL CO LTD
Bic Ling Kee House, 1 Christopher Road, East Grinstead, West Sussex RH19 3BT
Telephone: 01342 318980
Fax: 01342 410980
Email: wle@lingkee.com
Web Site: www.wardlockeducational.com

Director: Au Bak Ling *(Chairman - Hong Kong)*
Sales, Rights & Permissions: Eileen Parsons *(Company Secretary)*

Biology & Zoology; Chemistry; Educational & Textbooks; Geography & Geology; Mathematics & Statistics; Music; Physics; Religion & Theology; English

ISBNs, Imprints & Series: 978 0 7062

Parent Company:
Ling Kee (UK) Ltd

Associated Companies:
BLA Publishing Ltd

Overseas Representation:
Australia (KMP only): Concept Mathematics Pty Ltd, Frankston, Vic, Australia
Canada: Bacon & Hughes Ltd, Ottawa, Ont
Republic of Ireland: International Educational Services, Leixlip

2805

WATERSIDE PRESS
Sherfield Gables, Reading Road, Sherfield-on-Loddon, Hook, Hants RG27 0JG
Telephone: 01256 882250
Fax: 0845 230 0744
Email: enquiries@watersidepress.co.uk
Web Site: www.watersidepress.co.uk

Proprietor: Bryan Gibson
Editor: Jane Green
Administrator: Alex Gibson

Academic & Scholarly; Biography & Autobiography; Crime; Educational & Textbooks; History & Antiquarian; Law; Reference Books, Directories & Dictionaries; Sociology & Anthropology; Theatre, Drama & Dance

New Titles: 9 (2008) , 9 (2009)

ISBNs, Imprints & Series:
978 1 872870, 978 1 904380, 978 1 906534

Overseas Representation:
USA: International Specialized Book Services Inc, Portland, OR

2806

PAUL WATKINS PUBLISHING
1 High Street, Donington, Lincs PE11 4TA
Telephone: 01775 821542
Email: pwatkins@pwatkinspublishing.fsnet.co.uk

Proprietor: Shaun Tyas

Academic & Scholarly; Architecture & Design; Fine Art & Art History; History & Antiquarian; Languages & Linguistics; Nautical

New Titles: 6 (2008) , 8 (2009)

ISBNs, Imprints & Series:
978 1 871615 Paul Watkins
978 1 900289 Shaun Tyas

Distributor for:
Caedmon of Whitby; English Place-Name Society; Richard III and Yorkist History Trust; Society for Name Studies in Britain and Ireland

Book Trade Association Membership:
Small Press Centre

2807

WEIDENFELD & NICOLSON
[Imprint of The Orion Publishing Group Ltd]
Orion House, 5 Upper St Martin's Lane, London WC2H 9EA
Telephone: (020) 7240 3444
Fax: (020) 7240 4822

Trade Counter & Warehouse:
Littlehampton Book Services Ltd, Faraday Close, Durrington, Worthing, West Sussex BN13 3RB
Telephone: 01903 828500
Fax: 01903 828802

Managing Director: Malcolm Edwards
Publishing: Alan Samson
Kirsty Dunseath
Editor-in-Chief: Michael Dover

Biography & Autobiography; Fiction; Humour; Illustrated & Fine Editions; Industry, Business & Management; Law; Philosophy; Photography; Politics & World Affairs; Sports & Games; Travel & Topography

ISBNs, Imprints & Series: 978 0 297

Parent Company:
The Orion Publishing Group Ltd

Overseas Representation:
see: The Orion Publishing Group Ltd, London, UK

2808

JOSEPH WEINBERGER LTD
12–14 Mortimer Street, London W1T 3JJ
Telephone: (020) 7580 2827
Fax: (020) 7436 9616
Email: general.info@jwmail.co.uk
Web Site: www.josef-weinberger.com

Directors: John Schofield *(Managing)*
Robert Heath *(Financial)*
Plays Division Manager: Michael Callahan

Theatre, Drama & Dance

ISBNs, Imprints & Series:
978 0 8222 Dramatists Play Service Inc
978 0 85676 Josef Weinberger Plays

Distributor for:
USA: Dramatists Play Service Inc

Overseas Representation:
Australia: Hal Leonard (Australia), Melbourne, Vic
New Zealand: Play Bureau of New Zealand Ltd, New Plymouth
Republic of Ireland & Northern Ireland: Drama League of Ireland, Dublin, Republic of Ireland
South Africa: Dalro (Pty) Ltd, Braamfontein
USA: Dramatists Play Service Inc, New York, NY

2809

WHICH? BOOKS
2 Marylebone Road, London NW1 4DF
Telephone: (020) 7770 7000
Fax: (020) 7770 7660
Email: books@which.co.uk
Web Site: www.which.co.uk

Head of Book Publishing: Angela Newton

Accountancy & Taxation; Guide Books; Law; Reference Books, Directories & Dictionaries; Vocational Training & Careers; Legal, Financial & Practical Advice; Personal Finance

ISBNs, Imprints & Series:
978 1 84490 The Good Food Guide; Which? Essential Guides

Parent Company:
Which? Ltd [part of Consumers' Association]

2810

WHITING & BIRCH LTD
90 Dartmouth Road, London SE23 3HZ
Telephone: (020) 8244 2421
Fax: (020) 8244 2448
Email: enquiries@whitingbirch.net
Web Site: www.whitingbirch.net

Directors: David Whiting
Diana Birch

Academic & Scholarly; Medical (incl. Self Help & Alternative Medicine); Psychology & Psychiatry; Sociology & Anthropology

New Titles: 5 (2008) , 15 (2009)
No of Employees: 3

ISBNs, Imprints & Series:
978 1 86177, 978 1 871177

Overseas Representation:
USA: Ingram Publisher Services Inc, Chambersburg, PA; Lightning Source Inc (US), Lavergne, TN

2811

*WHITTET BOOKS LTD
South House, Yatesbury Manor, Yatesbury, Wilts SN11 8YE
Telephone: 01672 539004
Fax: 01672 555555
Email: annabel@whittet.dircon.co.uk
Web Site: www.whittetbooks.com

Warehouse:
BSP, BSP House, Station Road, Linton, Cambs CB1 6NW
Telephone: 01223 894870
Fax: 01223 894871

Managing Director: Annabel Whittet

Agriculture; Animal Care & Breeding; Biology & Zoology; Gardening; Illustrated &

Fine Editions; Natural History; Veterinary Science

ISBNs, Imprints & Series:
978 0 905483, 978 1 873580

Parent Company:
A. Whittet & Co Ltd

Overseas Representation:
USA & Canada: Diamond Farm Book Publishers, Brighton, Canada

2812

WHITTLES PUBLISHING
Dunbeath Mains Cottages, Dunbeath, Caithness KW6 6EY
Telephone: 01593 731333
Fax: 01593 731400
Email: info@whittlespublishing.com
Web Site: www.whittlespublishing.com

Warehouse/Distributor:
BookSource, 50 Cambuslang Road, Glasgow G32 8NB
Telephone: 0845 370 0063
Fax: 0845 370 0064
Email: customerservice@booksource.net
Web Site: www.booksource.net

Publisher: Dr Keith Whittles
Sales & Promotions Manager: Mrs Sue Steven
Production Editor: Linsey Gullon

Academic & Scholarly; Biography & Autobiography; Educational & Textbooks; Engineering; Fiction; Geography & Geology; Military & War; Natural History; Nautical; Reference Books, Directories & Dictionaries; Scientific & Technical; General

New Titles: 20 (2008) , 25 (2009)
No of Employees: 6

ISBNs, Imprints & Series:
978 1 870325, 978 1 904445

Overseas Representation:
Australia, New Zealand & Papua New Guinea: James Bennett Pty Ltd, Belrose, NSW, Australia
Germany, Austria & Switzerland: Missing Link International Booksellers, Bremen, Germany
Hong Kong, China, Taiwan & Korea: Asia Publishers Services Ltd, Hong Kong
India: Sara Books Pvt Ltd, New Delhi
Italy, Spain, Portugal & France: Flavio Marcello Publishers' Agents & Consultants, Padua, Italy
Latin America, Caribbean & Sub-Saharan Africa: InterMedia Americana (IMA) Ltd, London, UK
Middle East (including Greece, Turkey & Iran): Avicenna Partnership, Dumfries, UK
Singapore, Malaysia, Brunei, Philippines, Indonesia, Thailand, Laos, Cambodia & Vietnam: APD Singapore Pte Ltd, Singapore
South Africa: Book Promotions (Pty) Ltd, Plumstead

Book Trade Association Membership:
Publishing Scotland

2813

WILD GOOSE PUBLICATIONS
4th Floor, Savoy House, 140 Sauchiehall Street, Glasgow G2 3DH
Telephone: 0141 332 6292
Fax: 0141 332 1090
Email: admin@ionabooks.com
Web Site: www.ionabooks.com

Trade Orders:
BookSource, 50 Cambuslang Road, Glasgow G32 8NB
Email: orders@booksource.net
Web Site: www.booksource.net

Publishing Managers: Sandra Kramer
Alex O'Neill *(Assistant & Marketing Officer)*
Production: Jane Riley
Office Administrator: Lorna Rae Sutton
Project Editor: Neil Paynter

Music; Religion & Theology

No of Employees: 5
Annual Turnover: £285,000

ISBNs, Imprints & Series:
978 0 947988, 978 1 901557, 978 1 905010

Parent Company:
The Iona Community

Overseas Representation:
Australia & New Zealand: Willow Connection Pty Ltd, Brookvale, NSW, Australia
Canada: Novalis Inc, Toronto, Ont
New Zealand: Pleroma Christian Supplies, Otane, Central Hawkes Bay
USA: GIA Publications, Chicago, IL

Book Trade Association Membership:
IPG

2814

JOHN WILEY & SONS LTD
The Atrium, Southern Gate, Chichester, West Sussex PO19 8SQ
Telephone: 01243 779777
Fax: 01243 775878
Email: europe@wiley.com
Web Site: www.wiley.com

European Distribution Centre:
Southern Cross Trading Estate,
1 Oldlands Way, Bognor Regis, West Sussex PO22 9SA
Telephone: 01243 779777
Fax: 01243 820250
Email: csbooks@wiley.co.uk

Directors: C. J. Dicks *(Chief Financial & Operations Officer)*
P. Kisray *(Vice-President Sales, Professional/Trade & Higher Education Publishing)*
C. Nobbs *(Vice-President Distribution, Europe, Middle East & Africa)*

Academic & Scholarly; Accountancy & Taxation; Agriculture; Animal Care & Breeding; Antiques & Collecting; Archaeology; Architecture & Design; Atlases & Maps; Aviation; Biography & Autobiography; Biology & Zoology; Chemistry; Children's Books; Computer Science; Cookery, Wines & Spirits; Do-It-Yourself; Economics; Educational & Textbooks; Electronic (Educational); Electronic (Professional & Academic); Engineering; Environment & Development Studies; Gardening; Geography & Geology; Guide Books; Health & Beauty; History & Antiquarian; Humour; Industry, Business & Management; Languages & Linguistics; Literature & Criticism; Magic & the Occult; Mathematics & Statistics; Medical (incl. Self Help & Alternative Medicine); Military & War; Music; Natural History; Philosophy; Photography; Physics; Poetry; Politics & World Affairs; Psychology & Psychiatry; Reference Books, Directories & Dictionaries; Religion & Theology; Scientific & Technical; Sociology & Anthropology; Sports & Games; Travel & Topography; Veterinary Science; Vocational Training & Careers

ISBNs, Imprints & Series:
978 0 470, 978 0 471

Parent Company:
USA: John Wiley & Sons Inc

Associated Companies:
Capstone Publishing Ltd; Whurr Publishers Ltd; Wiley Distribution Services Ltd; Wiley Heyden Ltd; Wiley-Blackwell Ltd
Germany: Wiley-VCH Verlag GmbH
Inpharm-Internet Services Ltd; Wiley Interface Ltd; Wiley Pharmafile Ltd

Distributor for:
USA: California University Press; Columbia University Press; Harvard University Press; Johns Hopkins University Press; Loeb Classical Library; The MIT Press; W. W. Norton & Co Ltd; O'Reilly UK Ltd; Princeton University Press; Sybex International Corp; The University of Chicago Press; Yale University Press

Overseas Representation:
Australia: John Wiley & Sons Australia Ltd, Milton, Qld
Canada: John Wiley & Sons Canada Ltd, Etobicoke, Ont
Japan: John Wiley & Sons Ltd, Tokyo
Mexico & Latin America, Pakistan & North Africa: John Wiley & Sons Inc, Hoboken, NJ, USA
Singapore & Asia: John Wiley & Sons (Asia) Pte Ltd, Singapore

Book Trade Association Membership:
Publishers Association; BA; EPC; IGSMTP; CAPP; IEPRC

2815

WILLOW ISLAND EDITIONS
41 Water Lane, Middlestown, Wakefield, West Yorkshire WF4 4PX
Telephone: 01924 270723
Email: richard@willowisland.co.uk
Web Site: www.willowisland.co.uk

Contact: Richard Bell

Crafts & Hobbies; Gardening; Guide Books; Natural History; Travel & Topography

New Titles: 1 (2008) , 2 (2009)

ISBNs, Imprints & Series: 978 1 902467

2816

NEIL WILSON PUBLISHING LTD
O/2 19 Netherton Avenue, Glasgow G13 1BQ
Telephone: 0141 954 8007
Fax: 0560 150 4806
Email: info@nwp.co.uk
Web Site: www.nwp.co.uk

Distribution, Sales Ledger & Trade Orders:
BookSource, 50 Cambuslang Road, Glasgow G32 5NB
Telephone: 0845 370 0067
Fax: 0845 370 0068
Email: orders@booksource.net
Web Site: www.booksource.net

Managing Director: Neil Wilson *(Sales, Rights & Permissions)*

Biography & Autobiography; Cookery, Wines & Spirits; Crime; Guide Books; History & Antiquarian; Humour; Military & War; Music; Nautical; Travel & Topography; Irish Interest; Scottish Interest

New Titles: 5 (2008) , 7 (2009)
Annual Turnover: £130,000

ISBNs, Imprints & Series:
11:9; The Angel's Share; The In Pinn; The Vital Spark
978 1 897784, 978 1 903238, 978 1 906476

Overseas Representation:
Republic of Ireland: Geoff Bryan, Dublin

USA: Interlink Publishing Group Inc, Northampton, MA

Book Trade Association Membership:
Publishing Scotland

2817

PHILIP WILSON PUBLISHERS
109 Drysdale Street, The Timber Yard, London N1 6ND
Telephone: (020) 7033 9900
Fax: (020) 7033 9922
Email: sales@philip-wilson.co.uk
Web Site: www.philip-wilson.co.uk

Directors: Philip Wilson
Slobodan Prohaska *(Finance)*

Antiques & Collecting; Architecture & Design; Fine Art & Art History; History & Antiquarian

New Titles: 16 (2009)

ISBNs, Imprints & Series: 978 0 85667

Distributor for:
India: Niyogi Books

Overseas Representation:
USA: Palgrave Macmillan, New York, NY
Worldwide: I. B. Tauris & Co Ltd, London, UK

2818

WINDHORSE PUBLICATIONS
38 Newmarket Road, Cambridge CB5 8DT
Telephone: (020) 7617 7514
Email: info@windhorsepublications.com
Web Site:
www.windhorsepublications.com

UK Trade Orders:
Wisdom Books, 25 Stanley Road, Ilford, Essex IG1 1RW
Telephone: (020) 8553 5020
Fax: (020) 8553 5122
Email: sales@wisdom-books.com
Web Site: www.wisdom-books.com

General Manager: Caroline Jestaz *(Editorial & Rights)*
Publishing Assistant: Sarah Ryan *(Sales & Marketing, Production)*

Biography & Autobiography; Medical (incl. Self Help & Alternative Medicine); Philosophy; Religion & Theology

New Titles: 3 (2008) , 6 (2009)
No of Employees: 2

ISBNs, Imprints & Series:
978 0 904766, 978 1 899579

Overseas Representation:
Asia: Horizon Books Pte Ltd, Singapore
Australia & New Zealand: Windhorse Books, Newtown, NSW, Australia
South Africa: Stephan Phillips (Pty) Ltd, Cape Town
USA: Consortium Book Sales & Distribution Inc, St Paul, MN

Book Trade Association Membership:
IPG

2819

WIT PRESS
Ashurst Lodge, Ashurst, Southampton, Hampshire SO40 7AA
Telephone: (023) 8029 3223
Fax: (023) 8029 2853
Email: witpress@witpress.com
Web Site: www.witpress.com

Chairman: Prof. C. A. Brebbia
Chief Executive Officer: David Anderson

Production Manager: B. Privett
Sales Co-ordinator: Ms Lorraine Carter

Academic & Scholarly; Archaeology; Architecture & Design; Biology & Zoology; Computer Science; Electronic (Professional & Academic); Engineering; Environment & Development Studies; Geography & Geology; Industry, Business & Management; Mathematics & Statistics; Medical (incl. Self Help & Alternative Medicine); Scientific & Technical; Transport

New Titles: 46 (2008) , 50 (2009)
No of Employees: 11
Annual Turnover: £500,000

ISBNs, Imprints & Series:
978 0 905451, 978 1 84564, 978 1 85312

Parent Company:
USA: Computational Mechanics International Ltd

Book Trade Association Membership:
LAPSLD

2820

WITHERBY SEAMANSHIP INTERNATIONAL
4 Dunlop Square, Deans, Livingston, West Lothian EH54 8SB
Telephone: 01506 463227
Fax: 01506 468999
Email: kat@emailws.com
Web Site: www.witherbyseamanship.com & www.witherbyinsurance.com

Directors: Iain Macneil *(Managing)*
Kat Heathcote
General Manager: Stewart Heney
Personal Assistant to Directors: Alison Hunter Gordon

Audio Books; Educational & Textbooks; Electronic (Professional & Academic); Industry, Business & Management; Law; Nautical; Reference Books, Directories & Dictionaries; Scientific & Technical; Transport

ISBNs, Imprints & Series:
978 0 900886, 978 0 948691, 978 1 85609

Distributor for:
Chartered Institute of Loss Adjustors; Institute of Chartered Shipbrokers; Institute of Risk Management; Intercargo; International Association of Classification Societies; International Chamber of Shipping; International Tanker Owners' Pollution Federation; INTERTANKO; Oil Companies International Marine Forum; The Society of Consulting Marine Engineers and Ship Surveyors; Society of International Gas Tanker & Terminal Operators; Tanker Structure Co-operative Forum

Overseas Representation:
Australia: Boat Books, St Kilda, Vic
Hong Kong: Hong Kong Ships Supplies Co
Japan: Cornes & Co, Tokyo
Singapore: Motion Smith
USA: New York Nautical, New York

Book Trade Association Membership:
BA; IPG

2821

WOLTERS KLUWER HEALTH (P & E) LTD
250 Waterloo Road, London SE1 8RD
Telephone: (020) 7981 0500
Fax: (020) 7981 0501
Email: enquiry@lww.co.uk
Web Site: www.lww.co.uk

Directors: Linda Albin *(Regional, Europe)*
Andrew Davis *(Marketing Services)*

Carlos Davis (*Vice-President, International*)
Cathy Peck (*Global Publishing*)
John Youens (*Sales: Middle East, Africa & Latin America*)

Academic & Scholarly; Electronic (Professional & Academic); Medical (incl. Self Help & Alternative Medicine)

New Titles: 411 (2008) , 349 (2009)
No of Employees: 16

ISBNs, Imprints & Series:
978 0 397 Lippincott
978 0 632, 978 1 405 Blackwells
978 0 683 Williams & Wilkins
978 0 781, 978 1 605 LWW
978 0 874, 978 1 582 Springhouse
978 1 574 Facts & Co
978 1 587 ACC
978 1 880 ASAM
978 1 901 WKH UK Editions
978 1 931 Amirsys

Associated Companies:
USA: Wolters Kluwer Health

Book Trade Association Membership:
Publishers Association

2822 ▬▬

THE WOMEN'S PRESS
27 Goodge Street, London W1T 2LD
Telephone: (020) 7636 3992
Fax: (020) 7637 1866
Email: david@the-womens-press.com
Web Site: www.the-womens-press.com

Warehouse:
NBN International Ltd, Estover Road, Plymouth PL6 7PY
Telephone: 01752 202300
Fax: 01752 202330
Email: control@nbninternational.com
Web Site: www.nbninternational.com

Director: David Elliott

Biography & Autobiography; Crime; Fiction; Gay & Lesbian Studies; Gender Studies; Health & Beauty; Literature & Criticism; Politics & World Affairs; Psychology & Psychiatry; Reference Books, Directories & Dictionaries; Teenage

ISBNs, Imprints & Series:
Livewire Books for Young Adults
978 0 7043

Overseas Representation:
Africa, Eastern Europe, Caribbean & South America: InterMedia Americana (IMA) Ltd, London, UK
Australia: Tower Books Pty Ltd, Frenchs Forest, NSW
Europe: Ted Dougherty, London, UK
New Zealand: Southern Publishers Group, Auckland
Republic of Ireland: Fergus Corcoran, Ennisherry
South Africa: Quartet Sales & Marketing, Johannesburg
Spain & Portugal: Iberian Book Services, Madrid, Spain
USA: Interlink Publishing Group Inc, Northampton, MA

Book Trade Association Membership:
IPG

2823 ▬▬

WOODHEAD PUBLISHING LTD
Abington Hall, Granta Park,
Great Abington, Cambridge CB21 6AH
Telephone: 01223 891358
Fax: 01223 893694
Email: custserv@woodhead-publishing.com
Web Site: www.woodheadpublishing.com

Warehouse & Distribution:
Combined Book Services, Units I/K, Paddock Wood Distribution Centre, Paddock Wood, Tonbridge, Kent TN12 6UU
Telephone: 01892 837171
Fax: 01892 837272
Email: (as above)

Directors: Martin Woodhead (*Managing*)
R. Burleigh (*Finance*)
Francis Dodds (*Editorial*)
Managers: Neil MacLeod (*Marketing*)
Mary Campbell (*Production*)
Commissioning Editors: Sarah Whitworth
Kathryn Wickett
Rob Sitton
Sheril Leich
Cliff Elwell
Laura Bunney
Ian Borthwick

Bibliography & Library Science; Electronic (Professional & Academic); Engineering; Environment & Development Studies; Industry, Business & Management; Law; Scientific & Technical

New Titles: 60 (2008) , 100 (2009)
No of Employees: 32
Annual Turnover: £3M

ISBNs, Imprints & Series:
978 1 84334 Chandos Publishing
978 1 84569, 978 1 85573 Woodhead Publishing
978 1 85573 Abington Publishing; Gresham Books

Distributor for:
Germany: Beuth (The German Standards Institute); Stahleisen (The German Iron & Steel Institute); VDI (The Association of German Engineers)
USA: CRC LLC Press Ltd

Overseas Representation:
China: Ian Taylor & Associates, Beijing, P. R. of China
Eastern Europe & Russia: Dr László Horváth Publishers Representative, Budapest, Hungary
Germany, Austria & Switzerland: Bernd Feldmann, Oranienburg, Germany
Greece, Middle East, Turkey, Cyprus & Malta: Avicenna Partnership, Oxford, UK
India: Sara Books Pvt Ltd, New Delhi
Iran: Farhad Maftoon, Tehran
Italy, Spain, Portugal & France: Flavio Marcello Publishers' Agents & Consultants, Padua, Italy
Japan: Ben Kato, Tokyo; United Publishers Services Ltd, Tokyo
Korea: Information & Culture Korea (ICK), Seoul, Republic of Korea
Mexico, Central & South America: Cranbury International LLC, Montpelier, VT, USA
Netherlands, Belgium & Luxembourg: Netwerk Academic Book Agency, Rotterdam, Netherlands
Nigeria: Bounty Books, Ibadan
Pakistan: Tahir M. Lodhi, Lahore
Scandinavia: Jan Norbye, Ølstykke, Denmark
South Africa: Academic Marketing Services, Johannesburg
South East Asia: APAC Publishers Services Pte Ltd, Singapore

Book Trade Association Membership:
IGSMTP; IPG

2824 ▬▬

WORDSWORTH EDITIONS LTD
8b East Street, Ware, Herts SG12 9HJ
Telephone: 01920 465167
Fax: 01920 462267
Email: enquiries@wordsworth-editions.com
Web Site: www.wordsworth-editions.com

Directors: Helen Trayler (*Managing*)
Derek Wright (*Finance*)

Children's Books; Fiction; Literature & Criticism; Poetry; Reference Books, Directories & Dictionaries

New Titles: 36 (2008) , 15 (2009)

ISBNs, Imprints & Series:
978 1 84022, 978 1 85326

Overseas Representation:
Australia & Papua New Guinea: Peribo Pty Ltd, Mount Kuring-Gai, NSW, Australia
Czech Republic: Bohemian Ventures sro, Prague
Germany & Austria: Buchvertrieb Blank GmbH, Vierkirchen, Germany
India: OM Book Services, Delhi
Malta & Gozo: Audio Visual Centre Ltd, Sliema, Malta
New Zealand & South Pacific: Allphy Book Distributors Ltd, Auckland, New Zealand
Poland: Top Mark Centre, Warsaw
Romania: Depositol De Carte Distribute, Bucharest; Noi Distribuție SA, Bucharest
Slovak Republic: Slovak Ventures sro, Nitra, Slovakia
Spain: Ribera Libros, SL, Arrigorriaga
USA: L. B. May & Associates, Knoxville, TN

2825 ▬▬

WORLD MICROFILMS
PO Box 35488, St John's Wood, London NW8 6WD
Telephone: (020) 7586 4499
Email: microworld@ndirect.co.uk
Web Site: www.microworld.uk.com, www.pidgeondigital.com

Director: S. C. Albert

Academic & Scholarly; Architecture & Design; Cinema, Video, TV & Radio; History & Antiquarian

ISBNs, Imprints & Series: 978 1 85035

Distributor for:
USA: Norman Ross Publishing Inc

2826 ▬▬

WORTH PRESS LTD
34 South End, Bassingbourn, Herts SG8 5NJ
Telephone: 01763 248075
Fax: 01763 248155
Email: info@worthpress.co.uk
Web Site: www.worthpress.co.uk

Warehouse:
Antony Rowe Ltd, Units 3 & 4, Pegasus Way, Bowerhill, Melksham SN12 6TR
Telephone: 01225 703691
Fax: 01225 704518

Contacts: Ken Webb
Rupert Webb

Architecture & Design; Aviation; Fiction; Military & War; Religion & Theology

ISBNs, Imprints & Series:
978 1 84931, 978 1 903025

Overseas Representation:
Asia: John Beaufoy, Oxford, UK
Europe: Cristina Galimberti, Bristol, UK
Scandinavia: Anglo-Nordic Books, Godalming, UK

2827 ▬▬

XPL PUBLISHING
99 Hatfield Road, St Albans, Herts AL1 4EG
Telephone: 0870 143 2569
Fax: 0845 456 6385
Email: sales@xplpublishing.com

Web Site: www.xplpublishing.com

Managing Director: Andrew Griffin

Academic & Scholarly; Accountancy & Taxation; Industry, Business & Management; Law; Medical (incl. Self Help & Alternative Medicine)

ISBNs, Imprints & Series: 978 1 85811

Parent Company:
Richard Griffin (1820) Ltd

Overseas Representation:
Hong Kong: Bloomsbury Books Ltd
Republic of Ireland: Brookside Publishing Services, Dublin
USA: International Specialized Book Services Inc, Portland, OR

Book Trade Association Membership:
IPG

2828 ▬▬

Y LOLFA CYF
Hen Swyddfa'r Heddlu, Talybont, Ceredigion SY24 5HE
Telephone: 01970 832304
Fax: 01970 832782
Email: ylolfa@ylolfa.com
Web Site: www.ylolfa.com

Director: Garmon Gruffudd
Administrator: Sonia Hughes
Editor: Lefi Gruffudd
Marketing: Morgan Tomos
Production: Paul Williams

Biography & Autobiography; Children's Books; Cookery, Wines & Spirits; Crafts & Hobbies; Fiction; Guide Books; Humour; Languages & Linguistics; Music; Poetry; Politics & World Affairs; Sports & Games; Welsh Language Books

New Titles: 80 (2008) , 80 (2009)
No of Employees: 20

ISBNs, Imprints & Series:
Alcemi; Dinas
978 0 86243, 978 0 904864 Y Lolfa

Book Trade Association Membership:
Union of Welsh Publishers & Booksellers

2829 ▬▬

YALE UNIVERSITY PRESS LONDON
47 Bedford Square, London WC1B 3DP
Telephone: (020) 7079 4900
Fax: (020) 7079 4901
Email: firstname.lastname@yaleup.co.uk
Web Site: www.yalebooks.co.uk

Warehouse & Fulfilment:
John Wiley & Sons Ltd, Distribution Centre, Shripney Road, Bognor Regis, West Sussex PO22 9SA
Telephone: 01243 829121
Fax: 01243 82050

Directors: Robert Baldock (*Managing*)
Kate Pocock (*Sales & Marketing*)
Publishers: Gillian Malpass (*Art & Architecture*)
Sally Salvesen (*Decorative Arts*)
Heather McCallum (*Trade Books*)
Managers: Katie Harris (*Publicity*)
Charlotte Stafford (*Promotion & Direct Mail*)
Anne Bihan (*Rights*)
Andrew Jarmain (*Sales*)
Stephen Kent (*Production & Design*)
Accountant: Donal Burke

Academic & Scholarly; Archaeology; Architecture & Design; Biography & Autobiography; Economics; Fashion & Costume; Fine Art & Art History; Gender Studies; History & Antiquarian; Illustrated &

Fine Editions; Languages & Linguistics; Military & War; Music; Natural History; Philosophy; Photography; Politics & World Affairs; Religion & Theology; Theatre, Drama & Dance

ISBNs, Imprints & Series: 978 0 300

Parent Company:
USA: Yale University Press

Associated Companies:
Yale Representation Ltd

Overseas Representation:
Africa (excluding Southern Africa & Nigeria): Kelvin van Hasselt Publishing Services, Briningham, Norfolk, UK
Austria, Germany, Italy & Switzerland: Uwe Lüdemann, Berlin, Germany
Benelux, Denmark, Finland, France, Iceland, Norway & Sweden: Fred Hermans, Bovenkarspel, Netherlands
Hong Kong, China & Philippines: Asia Publishers Services Ltd, Hong Kong
India: S. Janakiraman, Book Marketing Services, Chennai
Iran: Farhad Maftoon, Tehran
Middle East: International Publishers Representatives (IPR) Ltd, Nicosia, Cyprus
Nigeria: Bounty Books, Ibadan
Pakistan: Anwer Iqbal, Book Bird Publishers Representatives, Lahore
Poland, Czech Republic, Croatia, Hungary, Slovakia & Slovenia: Ewa Ledóchowicz, Konstancin-Jeziorna, Poland
Republic of Ireland & Northern Ireland: Robert Towers, Monkstown, Co Dublin, Republic of Ireland
Singapore, Malaysia, Brunei & Indonesia: APD Singapore Pte Ltd, Singapore
Southern Africa: Book Promotions Pty Ltd, Diep River, South Africa
Spain & Portugal: Chris Humphrys, Gaucin, Spain
USA, Central & South America, Mexico, Canada, Australia, New Zealand, Japan, Korea & Taiwan: Yale University Press, New Haven, CT, USA

Book Trade Association Membership:
Publishers Association; CAPP; IPG

2830

YORE PUBLICATIONS
12 The Furrows, Harefield, Middx UB9 6AT
Telephone: 01895 823404
Fax: 01895 823404r2865
Email: fay.twydell@blueyonder.co.uk
Web Site: www.yore.demon.co.uk/index.html

Partners: Dave Twydell
Fay Twydell
Typist/Secretary: Kara Matthews

Sports & Games

New Titles: 5 (2008) , 4 (2009)

ISBNs, Imprints & Series:
978 0 954163, 978 0 954783, 978 0 955788, 978 1 874427

2831

ZAMBEZI PUBLISHING LTD
22 Second Avenue, Camels Head, Plymouth, Devon PL2 2EQ
Telephone: 01752 367300
Fax: 01752 350453
Email: info@zampub.com
Web Site: www.zampub.com

Business:
PO Box 221, Plymouth, Devon PL2 2YJ
Telephone: 01752 367300
Fax: 01752 350453
Email: (as above)
Web Site: (as above)

Directors: Sasha Fenton *(Chief Executive Officer)*
Jan Budkowski *(Managing)*

Industry, Business & Management; Magic & the Occult; Medical (incl. Self Help & Alternative Medicine); Mind, Body, Spirit

New Titles: 5 (2008) , 8 (2009)
No of Employees: 2
Annual Turnover: £35,000

ISBNs, Imprints & Series:
978 0 9533478, 978 1 90306501

Overseas Representation:
Europe: Gardners Books Ltd, Eastbourne, UK
USA & Rest of the World: Sterling Publishing Co Inc, New York, NY, USA

Book Trade Association Membership:
PMA (USA)

2832

ZED BOOKS LTD
7 Cynthia Street, London N1 9JF
Telephone: (020) 7837 4014 & 8466
Fax: (020) 7833 3960
Email: zed@zedbooks.net
Web Site: www.zedbooks.co.uk

Distribution:
NBN International Ltd, Estover, Plymouth PL6 7PZ
Telephone: 01752 202301
Fax: 01752 202331

Trade Representation - UK & Republic of Ireland:
Compass Academic
Telephone: (020) 8994 6477
Email: ca@compass-academic.co.uk
Web Site: www.academic.compass-booksales.co.uk/academic

Directors: Julian Hosie *(Marketing)*
Margaret Ling *(Finance & Company Secretary)*
Commissioning Editors: Tamsine O'Riordan
Ken Barlow
Publicity Officer: Ruvani de Silva
Sales Executive: Ruben Mootoosamy
Production Editor: Jakob Horstmann
Managers: Anneberth Lux *(Sales)*
Dan Och *(Production)*
Rights Executive: Federico Campagna

Academic & Scholarly; Economics; Environment & Development Studies; Gender Studies; Politics & World Affairs; Sociology & Anthropology

New Titles: 46 (2008) , 52 (2009)
No of Employees: 10
Annual Turnover: £1.1M

ISBNs, Imprints & Series:
978 0 86232, 978 0 905762, 978 1 84277, 978 1 84813, 978 1 85649

Overseas Representation:
Australia & New Zealand: Palgrave Macmillan, South Yarra, Vic, Australia
Bangladesh: The University Press Ltd, Dhaka
Canada: Fernwood Books Ltd, Halifax, NS
Egypt: MERIC, Cairo
Fiji: University Book Centre, Suva
Germany: Missing Link International Booksellers, Bremen
Ghana: EPP Books Services Ltd, Accra
Hong Kong: Hong Kong University Press
India: Madhyam International, New Delhi
Iran: Book City, Tehran
Japan: Far Eastern Booksellers, Tokyo
Lebanon: Levant Distributors, Beirut
Malaysia: Gerakbudaya Enterprise, Selangor
Nepal: Everest Media International, Kathmandu
Pakistan: Vanguard Books Pvt Ltd, Lahore
Singapore: Publishers Marketing Services Pte Ltd
Thailand: White Lotus, Bangkok

Uganda: Aristoc Booklex Ltd, Kampala
USA: Palgrave Macmillan, New York, NY
West Africa: EPP Books Services Ltd, Accra, Ghana

Book Trade Association Membership:
IPG

2833

ZERO TO TEN
Evans Publishing Group, Suite 1.3, Coomb House, 7 St John's Road, Isleworth, Middx TW7 6NH
Telephone: (020) 8758 9777
Fax: (020) 8758 9888
Email: tradesales@zerototen.co.uk
Web Site: www.evansbooks.co.uk

Sales Director: Andrew Macmillan

Children's Books

New Titles: 40 (2008) , 50 (2009)
No of Employees: 5
Annual Turnover: £1M

ISBNs, Imprints & Series:
978 0 237 Evans
978 1 84089 Zero to Ten
978 1 84234 Cherrytree

Associated Companies:
Kenya: Evans Brothers (Kenya) Ltd
Nigeria: Evans Brothers (Nigeria Publishers) Ltd
Sierra Leone: Evans Brothers (Sierra Leone) Ltd

Book Trade Association Membership:
EPC

2834

*ZYMURGY PUBLISHING
Hoults Estate, Walker Road, Newcastle upon Tyne NE6 2HL
Telephone: 0191 276 2425
Fax: 0191 276 2425
Email: martin.ellis@ablibris.com

Publisher: Martin Ellis

Biography & Autobiography; Cookery, Wines & Spirits; Crime; Humour; Illustrated & Fine Editions; Natural History; Photography; Travel & Topography

ISBNs, Imprints & Series: 978 1 903506

Book Trade Association Membership:
IPG; Publishers Publicity Circle

3 Packagers

3001

*ALADDIN BOOKS LTD
2–3 Fitzroy Mews, London W1T 6DF
Telephone: (020) 7383 2084
Fax: (020) 7388 6391
Email: sales@aladdinbooks.co.uk
Web Site: www.aladdinbooks.co.uk

Directors: Charles V. Nicholas
   Mrs E. Whittaker
Production: Alexandra Mew
Finance: Emma Rowley
Foreign Rights: Maria Laverty
Editorial: Katie Harker

Children's Books; Educational & Textbooks

ISBNs, Imprints & Series:
978 0 7496 Aladdin/Watts
978 1 59604, 978 1 932799 Creative
   Company/Stargazer

Associated Companies:
Archon Press Ltd; Learning Factory;
   Nicholas Enterprises Ltd
Denmark: Margit Schaleck Agency

Overseas Representation:
China & Taiwan: Andrew Nurnberg
   Associates Ltd, Beijing, P. R. of China
Denmark: Margit Schaleck Agency
Germany: Harry Olechnowitz
Korea: Imprima Agency, Republic of Korea

3002

ALBION PRESS LTD
Spring Hill, Idbury, Oxon OX7 6RU
Telephone: 01993 831094

Directors: Emma Bradford *(Managing)*
   Neil Philip *(Editorial)*

Children's Books

3003

AMBER BOOKS LTD
Bradley's Close, 74–77 White Lion Street,
London N1 9PF
Telephone: (020) 7520 7600
Fax: (020) 7520 7606 & 7607
Email: enquiries@amberbooks.co.uk
Web Site: www.amberbooks.co.uk

Directors: Stasz Gnych *(Managing)*
   Sara Ballard *(Rights)*
   Peter Thompson *(Head of Production)*
Publishing Manager: Charles Catton

*Animal Care & Breeding; Atlases & Maps;
Aviation; Crafts & Hobbies; Crime; Fashion
& Costume; History & Antiquarian; Military
& War; Nautical; Reference Books,*

*Directories & Dictionaries; Sports & Games;
Transport*

New Titles: 14 (2008) , 15 (2009)
No of Employees: 14
Annual Turnover: £4M

ISBNs, Imprints & Series: 978 1 906626

Book Trade Association Membership:
Book Packagers Association

3004

AMOLIBROS
Loundshay Manor Cottage,
Preston Bowyer, Milverton, Taunton,
Somerset TA4 1QF
Telephone: 01823 401527
Fax: 01823 401527
Email: amolibros@aol.com
Web Site: www.amolibros.co.uk

Trade Enquiries & Orders:
Gardners Books, 1 Whittle Drive,
Eastbourne BN23 6QH
Telephone: 01323 521555
Fax: 01323 521666

Managing Consultant: Jane Tatam

*Academic & Scholarly; Animal Care &
Breeding; Biography & Autobiography;
Children's Books; Fiction; Gardening;
Geography & Geology; History &
Antiquarian; Literature & Criticism; Magic &
the Occult; Medical (incl. Self Help &
Alternative Medicine); Music; Nautical;
Philosophy; Poetry; Politics & World Affairs;
Sports & Games; Theatre, Drama & Dance;
Travel & Topography*

New Titles: 30 (2008) , 30 (2009)

3005

ANNO DOMINI PUBLISHING (ADPS)
Book House, Orchard Mews,
18 High Street, Tring, Herts HP23 5AH
Telephone: 0845 868 1333
Email: info@ad-publishing.com
Web Site: www.ad-publishing.com

Children's Books; Religion & Theology

New Titles: 10 (2008) , 10 (2009)
No of Employees: 6

3006

NICOLA BAXTER LTD
PO Box 215, The Brew House,
Framingham Earl Road, Yelverton, Norwich
NR14 7UR
Telephone: 01508 491111
Email: nb@nicolabaxter.co.uk

Web Site: www.nicolabaxter.co.uk

Proprietor: Nicola Baxter

Children's Books; Educational & Textbooks

New Titles: 30 (2008) , 20 (2009)
No of Employees: 3

Book Trade Association Membership:
Association of Book Packagers

3007

BENDER RICHARDSON WHITE
PO Box 266, Uxbridge UB9 5NX
Telephone: 01895 832444
Fax: 01895 835213
Email: brw@brw.co.uk
Web Site: www.brw.co.uk

Directors: Lionel Bender *(Editorial)*
   Kim Richardson *(Sales & Production)*
   Ben White *(Art & Design)*

*Biology & Zoology; Children's Books;
Educational & Textbooks; Natural History;
Reference Books, Directories &
Dictionaries; Religion & Theology*

3008

BLA PUBLISHING LTD
1 Christopher Road, East Grinstead,
West Sussex RH19 3BT
Telephone: 01342 318980
Fax: 01342 410980
Email: eileen@wleducat.freeserve.co.uk

Chairman: Au Bak Ling
Contact: Eileen Parsons *(Company
   Secretary, Sales, Rights & Permissions)*

*Antiques & Collecting; Aviation; Biology &
Zoology; Chemistry; Children's Books;
Computer Science; Medical (incl. Self Help
& Alternative Medicine); Military & War;
Music; Natural History; Nautical; Physics;
Reference Books, Directories &
Dictionaries; Religion & Theology*

ISBNs, Imprints & Series:
Thames Head

Parent Company:
Ling Kee (UK) Ltd

Associated Companies:
Ward Lock Educational Co Ltd

3009

BLUE BEYOND BOOKS
1 Paget Road, Ipswich IP1 3RP
Telephone: 01473 423247
Fax: 01473 214096

Email: martin.spettigue@virgin.net

Manager: Martin Spettigue
Sales Representatives: Mark Thomas
   Nelly Coudoa
   Hita Hirons

*Magic & the Occult; Music; Philosophy;
Poetry; Religion & Theology; Mind Body
Spirit/New Age*

Associated Companies:
USA: Aum Publications; McKeever
   Publishing

Distributor for:
USA: Aum Publications; McKeever
   Publishing

Overseas Representation:
Australia: Wisdom's Delight, Brisbane, Qld
Canada: Peace Publishing, Ottawa, Ont
France: Editions Sri Chinmey, Paris
Germany: The Golden Shore, Nurnberg
USA: Heart-Light Distributors, Seattle, WA

3010

BOOK STREET LTD
Foresters Hall, 25–27 Westow Street,
London SE19 3RY
Telephone: (020) 8771 5115
Fax: (020) 8771 9994
Email: graham@bwj-ltd.com

Directors: Graham Brown *(Managing)*
   Michael Morris

Children's Books; Crafts & Hobbies

3011

BOOKPOWER
[formerly ELST]
120 Pentonville Road, London N1 9JN
Telephone: (020) 7843 1938
Fax: (020) 7837 6348
Email: BookPower@mistral.co.uk
Web Site: www.BookPower.org

Chief Executive: Valerie Teague
Trustee, Treasurer: Jamie Sehmer

*Academic & Scholarly; Accountancy &
Taxation; Animal Care & Breeding; Biology
& Zoology; Computer Science; Economics;
Educational & Textbooks; Engineering;
Industry, Business & Management; Medical
(incl. Self Help & Alternative Medicine);
Scientific & Technical; Veterinary Science;
Vocational Training & Careers*

New Titles: 3 (2009)

ISBNs, Imprints & Series:
BookPower (formerly ELST); ELST

Associated Companies:
ELST (Educational Low-Priced Sponsored Textbooks)

Overseas Representation:
Ghana: Gibrine Adam, EPP Book Services Ltd, Accra
India: Vinod Vasishtha, Viva Group, New Delhi
Kenya: Jimmi Makotsi, Acacia Publishers, Nairobi
Nigeria: L. Adesuyi, Harilah Books, Ikeja; Kolade Mosuro, Mosuro The Booksellers Ltd, Ibadan
Pakistan: British Council, Karachi
Sri Lanka: Pitraban Books, Colombo
Zimbabwe: Maureen Stewart, British Council, Bulawayo

3012

BROWN WELLS & JACOBS LTD
Foresters Hall, 25–27 Westow Street, London SE19 3RY
Telephone: (020) 8771 5115
Fax: (020) 8771 9994
Email: graham@bwj-ltd.com
Web Site: www.bwj.org

Director: Graham Brown *(Managing, Design, Sales & Production)*
Production Manager: Jenny Broom

Children's Books; Crafts & Hobbies

ISBNs, Imprints & Series: 978 1 873829

Distributor for:
Brown Wells & Jacobs Ltd (Packaging)

3013

CAMBRIDGE PUBLISHING MANAGEMENT LTD
Burr Elm Court, Main Street, Caldecote, Cambs CB23 7NU
Telephone: 01954 214006
Fax: 01954 214001
Email: j.dobbyne@cambridgepm.co.uk
Web Site: www.cambridgepm.co.uk

Directors: Jackie Dobbyne *(Managing)*
Tim Newton *(Production)*
Managing Editors: Karen Beaulah
Catherine Buch
Diane Teiltol

Academic & Scholarly; Archaeology; Architecture & Design; Biography & Autobiography; Children's Books; Cookery, Wines & Spirits; Crafts & Hobbies; Educational & Textbooks; English as a Foreign Language; Fine Art & Art History; Gardening; Industry, Business & Management; Medical (incl. Self Help & Alternative Medicine); Military & War; Natural History; Reference Books, Directories & Dictionaries; Religion & Theology; Sports & Games; Travel & Topography; Vocational Training & Careers

No of Employees: 18
Annual Turnover: £1M

Book Trade Association Membership: IPG

3014

CAMERON BOOKS
PO Box 1, Moffat, Dumfriesshire DG10 9SU
Telephone: 01683 220808
Fax: 01683 220012
Email: mail@cameronbooks.co.uk
Web Site: www.cameronbooks.co.uk

Directors: Ian A. Cameron
Jill Hollis

Antiques & Collecting; Architecture & Design; Fine Art & Art History; Natural

History; Film Criticism

ISBNs, Imprints & Series:
978 0 906506 Cameron & Hollis

3015

CORPUS PUBLISHING LTD
PO Box 8, Lydney, Glos GL15 6YD
Telephone: 01594 560600
Fax: 01594 560550
Email: info@firststonepub.co.uk

Publisher: John Sellers

Accountancy & Taxation; Animal Care & Breeding; Children's Books; Medical (incl. Self Help & Alternative Medicine); Sports & Games

ISBNs, Imprints & Series:
978 1 903333 Corpus Publishing
978 1 904439 First Stone Publishing

3016

*COWLEY ROBINSON PUBLISHING LTD
8 Belmont, Bath BA1 5DZ
Telephone: 01225 339999
Fax: 01225 339995
Email:
stewart.cowley@cowleyrobinson.com

Directors: Stewart Cowley
D. Hawcock
P. Fleming
Managers: Leanne Down *(Production)*
Anna Sainaghi *(Senior Sales)*

Children's Books

Parent Company:
Allcloud Ltd

3017

D & N PUBLISHING
8 Fiveways, Baydon, Wilts SN8 2LH
Telephone: 01672 540556
Email: d@dnpublishing.co.uk

Manager/Owner: David Price-Goodfellow
Designer/Owner: Namrita Price-Goodfellow

Animal Care & Breeding; Antiques & Collecting; Aviation; Biology & Zoology; Crafts & Hobbies; Do-It-Yourself; Fine Art & Art History; Gardening; Geography & Geology; Guide Books; History & Antiquarian; Medical (incl. Self Help & Alternative Medicine); Military & War; Natural History; Photography; Reference Books, Directories & Dictionaries; Sports & Games; Theatre, Drama & Dance; Transport; Travel & Topography

No of Employees: 2

3018

DIAGRAM VISUAL INFORMATION LTD
34 Elaine Grove, London NW5 4QH
Telephone: (020) 7485 5941
Fax: (020) 7485 5941
Email: info@diagramgroup.com
Web Site: www.diagramgroup.com

Managing Director: Bruce Robertson

Educational & Textbooks; Geography & Geology; Health & Beauty; Reference Books, Directories & Dictionaries; Sports & Games

Overseas Representation:
Bulgaria: Nika Literary Agency, Sofia
Eastern Europe: DS Druck- und Verlags service, Stuttgart, Germany

Hungary: DS Budapest Kft, Budapest
Japan: Tuttle-Mori Agency Inc, Tokyo
Korea: KCC, Seoul, Republic of Korea
Lithuania: Musa Knyga, Vilnius
Netherlands & Scandinavia: Jan Michael, Amsterdam, Netherlands
Poland: DS Druck Warszawa, Warsaw
Romania: Mast Publishing, Bucharest
Russia: ICSTI, Moscow
Thailand: Big Apple Tuttle-Mori Agency (Thailand) Co Ltd, Bangkok

3019

*EDDISON SADD EDITIONS LTD
St Chad's House, 148 King's Cross Road, London WC1X 9DH
Telephone: (020) 7837 1968
Fax: (020) 7837 2025
Email: info@eddisonsadd.co.uk
Web Site: www.eddisonsadd.com

Accounts:
Facts & Figures
Telephone: 01280 813111
Fax: 01280 817229

Directors: Nick Eddison *(Managing)*
Ian Jackson *(Editorial)*
Susan Cole *(Rights)*
David Owen *(Financial)*
Elaine Partington *(Art)*
Sarah Rooney *(Production)*

Children's Books; Cookery, Wines & Spirits; Health & Beauty; Magic & the Occult; Medical (incl. Self Help & Alternative Medicine); Mind, Body, Spirit; Puzzles

ISBNs, Imprints & Series:
Bookinabox

Associated Companies:
Connections Book Publishing

Overseas Representation:
Worldwide: Melia Publishing Services, UK

3020

EMMA TREEHOUSE LTD
The Studio, Church Street, Nunney, Frome, Somerset BA11 4LW
Telephone: 01373 836233
Fax: 01373 836299
Email: sales@emmatreehouse.com

Directors: David Bailey
Richard Powell
Hilary Allom
Managers: Christine Barham
Margret Heilegenstadt

Children's Books

New Titles: 36 (2008) , 24 (2009)
No of Employees: 5
Annual Turnover: £1.5M

ISBNs, Imprints & Series:
Treehouse Children's Books
978 1 85576

Distributor for:
Macmillan Distribution

Book Trade Association Membership:
Book Packagers Association

3021

ESSENTIAL WORKS LTD
The Green, 29 Clerkenwell Green, London EC1R 0DU
Telephone: (020) 7017 0890
Email: info@essentialworks.co.uk

Directors: John Conway *(Managing)*
Mal Peachey *(Publishing)*
Rights & Co-Editions: Jackie Strachan
Jane Moseley

Biography & Autobiography; Cinema, Video, TV & Radio; Fashion & Costume; Health & Beauty; Humour; Illustrated & Fine Editions; Military & War; Music; Photography; Sports & Games; Transport

3022

FOCUS PUBLISHING (SEVENOAKS) LTD
11A St Botolph's Road, Sevenoaks, Kent TN13 3AJ
Telephone: 01732 742456
Fax: 01732 743381
Email: info@focus-publishing.co.uk
Web Site: www.focus-publishing.co.uk

Directors: Guy Croton *(Managing)*
Caroline Watson *(Publishing)*
Designer: Heather McMillan
Editor: Vicky Hales-Dutton

Animal Care & Breeding; Aviation; Biology & Zoology; Cookery, Wines & Spirits; Crafts & Hobbies; Do-It-Yourself; Gardening; Medical (incl. Self Help & Alternative Medicine); Military & War; Music; Natural History; Nautical; Photography; Sports & Games; Theatre, Drama & Dance; Transport

3023

FREELANCE MARKET NEWS
Sevendale House, 7 Dale Street, Manchester M1 1JB
Telephone: 0161 228 2362
Fax: 0161 228 3533
Email: fmn@writersbureau.com
Web Site: www.freelancemarketnews.com

Editorial & Circulation: Miss Angela Cox

Educational & Textbooks; Fiction; Literature & Criticism; Photography; Poetry

Parent Company:
The Writers Bureau Ltd

3024

GRAHAM-CAMERON PUBLISHING & ILLUSTRATION
The Studio, 23 Holt Road, Sheringham, Norfolk NR26 8NB
Telephone: 01263 821333
Fax: 01263 821334
Email: mike@graham-cameron-illustration.com

Marketing & Sales:
Duncan Graham-Cameron,
59 Hertford Road, Brighton BN1 7GG
Telephone: 01273 385890
Email: duncan@graham-cameron-illustration.com
Web Site: www.graham-cameron-illustration.com

Partners: Mike Graham-Cameron *(Managing & Editorial)*
Helen Graham-Cameron *(Executive, Art & Editorial)*
Duncan Graham-Cameron *(Executive, Marketing & Sales)*

Architecture & Design; Children's Books; Educational & Textbooks; English as a Foreign Language; Military & War; Natural History; Religion & Theology

No of Employees: 3

ISBNs, Imprints & Series: 978 0 947672

Associated Companies:
Graham-Cameron Illustration

Book Trade Association Membership:
IPG; Cambridge Book Association; Pica Club; The Paternosters

3025

HART MCLEOD LTD
14A Greenside, Waterbeach, Cambridge
CB25 9HP
Telephone: 01223 861495
Fax: 01223 862902
Email: inhouse@hartmcleod.co.uk
Web Site: www.hartmcleod.co.uk

Directors: Graham Hart (Editorial)
Chris McLeod (Design)
Joanne Barker (Design)

Academic & Scholarly; Educational &
Textbooks; Sports & Games

3026

THE IVY PRESS LTD
210 High Street, Lewes, East Sussex
BN7 2NS
Telephone: 01273 487440
Fax: 01273 487441
Web Site: www.ivy-group.co.uk

Directors: Stephen Paul (Managing)
Nikki Tilbury (Rights)
Peter Bridgewater (Creative)

Crafts & Hobbies; Fashion & Costume;
Health & Beauty; Illustrated & Fine Editions

New Titles: 40 (2008)
No of Employees: 26

3027

LITTLE PEOPLE BOOKS
The Home of BookBod, Knighton,
Radnorshire LD7 1UP
Telephone: 01547 520925
Email: littlepeoplebooks@thehobb.tv
Web Site: www.thehobb.tv/lpb

Directors: Grant Jessé (Production,
Managing Editor)
Helen Wallis (Rights, Finance)

Audio Books; Children's Books; Educational
& Textbooks; Digital Publications; Water
Environment

ISBNs, Imprints & Series: 978 1 899573

Parent Company:
Grant Jessé

Associated Companies:
Karavadra: Multimedia

Book Trade Association Membership:
IPG; Book Packagers Association

3028

MARKET HOUSE BOOKS LTD
Suite B, Elsinore House,
43 Buckingham Street, Aylesbury, Bucks
HP20 2NQ
Telephone: 01296 484911
Fax: 01296 338934
Email: dainthth@mhbref.com

Directors: Dr John Daintith
Peter Sapsed
Chief Editor: Elizabeth Martin
Production Editor: Anne Stibbs

Computer Science; Industry, Business &
Management; Law; Medical (incl. Self Help
& Alternative Medicine); Music; Psychology
& Psychiatry; Reference Books, Directories &
Dictionaries; Scientific & Technical; Theatre,
Drama & Dance

3029

*MONKEY PUZZLE MEDIA LTD
The Rectory, Eyke, Woodbridge, Suffolk
IP12 2QW
Telephone: 01394 460100

Directors: Roger Goddard-Coote
(Managing)
Paul Mason (Editorial)
Picture Manager: Lynda Lines

Atlases & Maps; Children's Books;
Educational & Textbooks; Fine Art & Art
History; Geography & Geology; Health &
Beauty; History & Antiquarian; Natural
History; Politics & World Affairs; Scientific &
Technical; Sports & Games; Travel &
Topography

3030

ORPHEUS BOOKS LTD
6 Church Green, Witney, Oxon OX28 4AW
Telephone: 01993 774949
Fax: 01993 700330
Email: nicholas@orpheusbooks.com
Web Site: www.orpheusbooks.com

Directors: Nicholas Harris
Sarah Hartley

Children's Books

ISBNs, Imprints & Series:
978 1 901323, 978 1 905473

3031

PARAGON PUBLISHING
4 North Street, Rothersthorpe, Northants
NN7 3JB
Telephone: 01604 832149
Email: mark.webb@tesco.net
Web Site: www.intoprint.net

Proprietor: Mark Webb

Academic & Scholarly; Architecture &
Design; Computer Science; Cookery, Wines
& Spirits; Educational & Textbooks;
Electronic (Educational); Electronic
(Professional & Academic); English as a
Foreign Language; Environment &
Development Studies; Fiction; Languages &
Linguistics; Poetry; Religion & Theology;
Science Fiction; Scientific & Technical;
Sports & Games; Theatre, Drama & Dance

New Titles: 11 (2008) , 25 (2009)

ISBNs, Imprints & Series:
KinderKlub; Primary Modern Language;
Stadium & Arena
978 1 899820 Into Print

3032

PLAYNE BOOKS LTD
Park Court Barn, Trefin, Haverfordwest,
Pembrokeshire SA62 5AU
Telephone: 01348 837073
Fax: 01348 837063
Email: playne.books@virgin.net

Editorial Director: Gill Davies
Production: David Playne

Children's Books; History & Antiquarian;
Theatre, Drama & Dance; Travel &
Topography

New Titles: 10 (2008)
No of Employees: 2

Associated Companies:
Playne Design; Playne Plays; Spinfolds

Book Trade Association Membership:
IPG

3033

TONY POTTER PUBLISHING
1 Stairbridge Court,
Bolney Grange Business Park,
Stairbridge Lane, Bolney, Haywards Heath,
West Sussex RH17 5PA
Telephone: 01444 232889

Fax: 01444 232142
Email: pat@tonypotter.com
Web Site: www.tonypotter.com

Managing Director: Dr Tony Potter
Managing Editor: Pat Hegarty
Rights Consultant: Susannah Moore
Head of Production: Zöe Fawcett

Children's Books; Humour

New Titles: 50 (2008) , 55 (2009)
No of Employees: 13
Annual Turnover: £2M

ISBNs, Imprints & Series:
978 1 905288 Over the Moon
978 1 906013 Teapot Press
978 1 906824 Potter Books

Book Trade Association Membership:
IPG

3034

QUANTUM PUBLISHING
6 Blundell Street, London N7 9BH
Telephone: (020) 7700 6700
Fax: (020) 7700 4191
Email: quantum@quarto.com
Web Site: www.quarto.com

Publisher: Anastasia Cavouras

Antiques & Collecting; Archaeology;
Architecture & Design; Atlases & Maps;
Aviation; Children's Books; Cookery, Wines
& Spirits; Crafts & Hobbies; Do-It-Yourself;
Fashion & Costume; Fine Art & Art History;
Gardening; Health & Beauty; History &
Antiquarian; Magic & the Occult; Medical
(incl. Self Help & Alternative Medicine);
Military & War; Music; Natural History;
Nautical; Photography; Sports & Games;
Transport

ISBNs, Imprints & Series:
Cartographica Press; Oceana; Quantum

Parent Company:
Quarto Publishing Plc

3035

**READER'S DIGEST CHILDREN'S
PUBLISHING LTD**
The Ice House, 124–126 Walcot Street,
Bath BA1 5BG
Telephone: 01225 473200
Fax: 01225 460942
Email: customercare@readersdigest.co.uk

Directors: Paul E. Stuart (Commercial)
Jennifer Fifield (International Sales)

Children's Books; Novelty Books

ISBNs, Imprints & Series:
978 1 84880, 978 1 85724

Parent Company:
USA: The Reader's Digest Association Inc

Associated Companies:
USA: Reader's Digest Children's Publishing
Inc

3036

REGENCY HOUSE PUBLISHING LTD
The Red House, 84 High Street,
Buntingford, Herts SG9 9AJ
Telephone: 01763 274666
Fax: 01763 273501
Email: regency-house@btconnect.com

Managing Director: Miss N. Trodd
Managers: B. H. Trodd
Annabel Trodd

Animal Care & Breeding; Architecture &
Design; Aviation; Children's Books; Crafts &

Hobbies; Magic & the Occult; Military &
War

ISBNs, Imprints & Series: 978 1 85361

3037

Tangerine Designs Ltd

1 Limpley Mill, Lower Stoke, Bath BA2 7JF
Telephone: 01225 720001
Email: enquiries@tangerinedesigns.co.uk
Web Site: www.tangerinedesigns.co.uk

Managing Director: Christine Swift
Co-edition Sales Agents: Trish Pugsley
Rachel Pidcock

Children's Books

Distributor for:
Alligator Books Ltd [Foreign Rights Agents];
Pinwheel [Foreign Rights Agents]

Book Trade Association Membership:
Publishers Association

3038

TOUCAN BOOKS LTD
Third Floor, 89 Charterhouse Street,
London EC1M 6PE
Telephone: (020) 7250 3388
Fax: (020) 7250 3123
Email: ellen@toucanbooks.co.uk

Directors: Ellen Dupont (Managing)
Robert Sackville-West

Animal Care & Breeding; Architecture &
Design; Atlases & Maps; Children's Books;
Crafts & Hobbies; Fine Art & Art History;
Gardening; History & Antiquarian; Natural
History; Reference Books, Directories &
Dictionaries; Travel & Topography

New Titles: 20 (2008) , 15 (2009)

Book Trade Association Membership:
Book Packagers Association

3039

TUCKER SLINGSBY LTD
Fifth Floor, Regal House, 70 London Road,
Twickenham TW1 3QS
Telephone: (020) 8744 1007
Fax: (020) 8744 0041
Email: info@tuckerslingsby.co.uk
Web Site: www.tuckerslingsby.co.uk

Directors: Del Tucker
Janet Slingsby

Children's Books; Cookery, Wines & Spirits;
Crafts & Hobbies; Gardening; Health &
Beauty

ISBNs, Imprints & Series: 978 1 902272

3040

WATERSIDE PRESS
Sherfield Gables, Sherfield-on-Loddon,
Hook RG27 0JG
Telephone: 01256 882250
Fax: 01256 882250
Email: enquiries@watersidepress.co.uk
Web Site: www.watersidepress.co.uk

Managing Editor: Bryan Gibson

Academic & Scholarly; Biography &
Autobiography; Crime; Educational &
Textbooks; Fiction; History & Antiquarian;
Languages & Linguistics; Law; Literature &
Criticism; Reference Books, Directories &
Dictionaries; Sociology & Anthropology;
Theatre, Drama & Dance

New Titles: 9 (2008) , 9 (2009)

ISBNs, Imprints & Series:
978 1 872870, 978 1 904380, 978 1
906534

Associated Companies:
Bryan Gibson Publications

Overseas Representation:
North America: International Specialized
Book Services Inc, Portland, OR, USA

3041 ▄▄▄▄▄▄▄

DAVID WEST CHILDREN'S BOOKS
7 Princeton Court, 55 Felsham Road,
London SW15 1AZ
Telephone: (020) 8780 3836
Fax: (020) 8780 9313
Email: dww@btinternet.com
Web Site:
www.davidwestchildrensbooks.com

Proprietor/Publisher: David West
Publisher: Lynn Lockett

*Architecture & Design; Children's Books;
Cinema, Video, TV & Radio; Crafts &
Hobbies; Fashion & Costume; Geography &
Geology; History & Antiquarian; Military &
War; Music; Natural History; Scientific &
Technical; Sports & Games; Transport*

3042 ▄▄▄▄▄▄▄

YOUNG PEOPLE IN FOCUS
23 New Road, Brighton, East Sussex
BN1 1WZ
Telephone: 01273 693311
Fax: 01273 647322

Email:
publications@youngpeopleinfocus.org.uk
Web Site:
www.youngpeopleinfocus.org.uk

*Educational & Textbooks; Professionals
Working with Parents; Professionals
Working with Teenagers; Research in
Adolescence; Teenagers in Foster Care*

New Titles: 2 (2008)
No of Employees: 15

ISBNs, Imprints & Series: 978 1 871504

4 Authors' Agents

4001

AITKEN ALEXANDER ASSOCIATES
18–21 Cavaye Place, London SW10 9PT
Telephone: (020) 7373 8672
Fax: (020) 7373 6002
Email: reception@gillonaitken.co.uk
Web Site: www.aitkenalexander.co.uk

Directors: Gillon Aitken (Chairman)
Clare Alexander (Joint Managing)
Sally Riley (Joint Managing)
Andrew Kidd
Joaquim Fernandes (Company Secretary)
Foreign Rights: Sally Riley
Film/TV: Lesley Shaw

All MSS except plays, film & TV scripts, short stories & articles if not by existing clients.

Specialization: quality full-length fiction & non-fiction.

Associated Companies:
Hughes Massie Ltd

4002

THE AMPERSAND AGENCY LTD
Ryman's Cottages, Little Tew, Oxon OX7 4JJ
Telephone: 01608 683677 & 683898
Fax: 01608 683449
Email: peter@theampersandagency.co.uk
Web Site:
www.theampersandagency.co.uk

Directors: Peter Buckman (Managing)
Anne-Marie Doulton (Editor)
Consultants: Peter Janson-Smith
Patrick Neale

All MSS except poetry, science fiction, horror, fantasy or illustrated children's books.

Specialization: literary and commercial fiction and non-fiction for all markets. A full range of services including foreign and media rights is offered. Member of the Association of Authors' Agents.

Overseas Representation:
Worldwide: The Buckman Agency, Oxford

4003

DARLEY ANDERSON LITERARY, TV & FILM AGENCY
Estelle House, 11 Eustace Road, London SW6 1JB
Telephone: (020) 7385 6652
Fax: (020) 7386 5571
Email: enquiries@darleyanderson.com
Web Site: www.darleyanderson.com

Sole Proprietor: Darley Anderson (Fiction Agent)
Associate Agents: Zoë King (Non-Fiction)
Camilla Bolton (Crime/Thriller)
Becky Stradwick (Children's)
Film & TV: Steve Fisher
Manager: Madeleine Buston (Head of Rights)

All MSS except short stories, academic or poetry.

Specialization: fiction: all types of thrillers & all types of fiction including contemporary, 20th century romantic sagas, chick lit, bonkbusters, women in jeopardy; also crime (cosy/hard-boiled/historical), horror, comedy & Irish novels; popular culture; non-fiction: celebrity autobiographies, biographies, 'true life' women in jeopardy, popular psychology, self-improvement, diet, health, beauty & fashion, gardening, cookery, inspirational & religious, and children's fiction.

Overseas Representation:
Bulgaria: Anthea Literary Agency, Sofia
China & Taiwan: The Grayhawk Agency, Taipei
Czech & Slovak Republics: Andrew Nurnberg Associates, Prague
Germany: Thomas Schlück Literary Agency, Garbsen
Greece: O A Literary Agency, Markopoulo, Athens
Hungary: Kàtai & Bolza Literary Agents, Budapest
Israel: I. Pikarski Literary Agency, Tel Aviv
Italy: Natoli, Stefan & Oliva Agenzia Letteraria, Milan
Japan: The English Agency Japan Ltd, Tokyo; Japan Uni Agency, Tokyo; Tuttle-Mori Agency Inc, Tokyo
Korea: EYA, Seoul
Netherlands: Jan Michael, Amsterdam
Poland: Graal Ltd, Warsaw
Romania: International Copyright Agency, Bucharest
Russia: Synopsis Literary Agency, Moscow
Scandinavia: Jan Michael, Amsterdam
Serbia: PLIMA Literary Agency, Belgrade
Turkey: Akcali Copyright Agency, Istanbul
USA: Darley Anderson Books, London; Helen Breitwieser, Cornerstone Literary Agency, Los Angeles, CA; Liza Dawson Associates, New York, NY
USA (for film): Steve Fisher APA Talent & Literary Agency, Los Angeles, CA

4004

*ANNETTE GREEN AUTHORS' AGENCY
1 East Cliff Road, Tunbridge Wells, Kent TN4 9AD
Telephone: 01892 514275

Fax: 01892 558262
Email: david@annettegreenagency.co.uk
Web Site: www.annettegreenagency.co.uk

Partners: Annette Green
David Smith

All MSS except sci-fi or fantasy, young children's, poetry or dramatic scripts.

Specialization: literary and commercial fiction, general non-fiction & young adult.

Rights Representative in UK for:
USA: Laura Langlie Literary Agent, Brooklyn, New York, NY

Overseas Representation:
USA: Laura Langlie Literary Agent, Brooklyn, New York, NY

4005

AQUARIUS LIBRARY
[a division of SPM London Ltd]
PO Box 5, 136 Emmanuel Road, Hastings TN34 3ZY
Telephone: 01424 721196
Fax: 01424 717704
Email: aquarius.lib@clara.net
Web Site: www.aquariuscollection.com

Postal Address:
PO Box 5, Hastings, East Sussex TN34 1HR
Telephone: 01424 721196
Fax: 01424 717704
Email: aquarius.lib@clara.net
Web Site: www.aquariuscollection.com

Directors: Gilbert Gibson (Managing)
David Corkill (Picture Library)

Specialization: Hollywood candid photography, film stills (old & new, colour & b/w), showbusiness personalities and all other aspects of international showbusiness and mass entertainment.

Parent Company:
Sun-Pacific Music (London) Ltd

Associated Companies:
UK: Aquarius Collection Ltd

4006

*ARTELLUS LTD
30 Dorset House, Gloucester Place, London NW1 5AD
Telephone: (020) 7935 6972
Fax: (020) 7487 5957
Web Site: www.artellusltd.co.uk

Director: Leslie Gardner

Associate: Darryl Samaraweera (Company Secretary)
Chair: Gabriele Pantucci

All MSS except film scripts.

Specialization: speculative fiction, thrillers, non-fiction – commercial and literary, self-help, history, science. Selective readers service on request.

Rights Representative in UK for:
Eastern Europe: Prava i Prevodi, Belgrade
Far East: Big Apple Tuttle-Mori Agency Inc, Shanghai
Spain & Portugal: Carmen Balcells Agencia Literaria SA, Barcelona

4007

TASSY BARHAM ASSOCIATES
23 Elgin Crescent, London W11 2JD
Telephone: (020) 7229 8667
Fax: (020) 7229 8667
Email: tassy@tassybarham.com

Agent: Tassy Barham

Specialization: Brazil. Representing European and American agencies and publishers in Brazil, and Portuguese-language writers into the UK.

4008

LORELLA BELLI LITERARY AGENCY (LBLA)
54 Hartford House, 35 Tavistock Crescent, Notting Hill, London W11 1AY
Telephone: (020) 7727 8547
Fax: 0870 787 4194
Email: info@lorellabelliagency.com
Web Site: www.lorellabelliagency.com

Proprietor: Lorella Belli

All MSS except children's books, science fiction, fantasy, academic, poetry, original scripts. No reading fee. May suggest revision.

Specialization: general fiction and non-fiction (particularly interested in first-time writers, commercial women's fiction, crime/thrillers, international and multicultural writing, journalists, books on/about Italy). Clients range from commercial fiction to literary fiction to a number of non-fiction writers and journalists. The agency represents a number of bestselling and award-winning authors. Also represents European, Canadian, Australian and American agencies in the UK and abroad. Commission: 15% home; 20% overseas and dramatic rights. Works with co-agents *abroad; film & TV rights handled by an associate agency.*

Rights Representative in UK for:
Australia: Calidris Literary Agency, Goulburn, NSW
USA: Paula Balzer Literary Agency, New York, NY; Creative Culture Agency, New York, NY; Fine Print Agency, New York, NY; Sarah Lazin Books, New York, NY; Mildred Marmur Associates, Larchmont, NY; Susan Schuman Agency, New York, NY

4009 ▬

BLAKE FRIEDMANN LITERARY AGENCY LTD
122 Arlington Road, London NW1 7HP
Telephone: (020) 7284 0408
Fax: (020) 7284 0442
Email: "firstname"@blakefriedmann.co.uk
Web Site: www.blakefriedmann.co.uk

Directors & Agents: Carole Blake *(Book Sales)*
Julian Friedmann *(Film & TV)*
Isobel Dixon *(Book Sales)*
Film, TV & Radio Sales: Conrad Williams
Accounts Manager: Adrian Clark
Agents: Oli Munson *(Book Sales)*
Katie Williams *(Film & TV)*

All MSS except science fiction, plays, poetry & short stories (excluding existing clients).

Specialization: placing book rights internationally; film, television & radio rights.

Overseas Representation:
Bulgaria: Anthea Literary Agency, Sofia
China, Taiwan & Hong Kong: Andrew Nurnberg Literary Agency, Taipei; Andrew Nurnberg Associates, Beijing
Czech Republic: Dilia (Czechoslovak Theatrical & Literary Agency), Prague
France: La Nouvelle Agence, Paris
Germany: Liepman AG, Zurich
Hungary: Kàtai & Bolza, Literary Agents, Budapest
Italy: Natoli, Stefan & Oliva Agenzia Letteraria, Milan
Japan: The English Agency Japan Ltd, Tokyo
Korea: KCC International Ltd, Seoul
Poland: Graal Ltd, Warsaw
Romania: S. Kessler International Copyright Agency, Bucharest
Russia: Andrew Nurnberg Associates, Moscow
Scandinavia: Leonhardt & Hoier Literary Agency, Copenhagen
Spain, Brazil & Portugal: The Foreign Office
Turkey: Anatolialit Agency
USA, Canada & Greece: Blake Friedmann Literary Agency, London

4010 ▬

LUIGI BONOMI ASSOCIATES LTD
91 Great Russell Street, London WC1B 3PS
Telephone: (020) 7637 1234
Fax: (020) 7637 2111
Email: info@bonomiassociates.co.uk
Web Site: www.bonomiassociates.co.uk

Directors: Luigi Bonomi
Amanda Preston
Literary Agent: Molly Stirling
Administration Assistant: Ajda Vucicevic

All MSS except poetry, children's stories or adult science fiction/fantasy.

Specialization: fiction: commercial and literary fiction, thrillers, crime, women's fiction. Non-fiction: history, science, parenting, lifestyle, diet, health, TV tie-ins. Keen to find new authors and help them develop their careers. Send preliminary letter, synopsis and first three chapters. No reading fee. Will suggest revision. Works with foreign agencies and has links with TV presenters' agencies and production companies. Authors include Will Adams, James Barrington, Chris Beardshaw, Sean Black, Gennaro Contaldo, Nick Foulkes, David Gibbins, Richard Hammond, Jane Hill, Matt Hilton, John Humphrys, Graham Joyce, Simon Kernick, Colin McDowell, Dr Gillian McKeith, Richard Madeley and Judy Finnigan, James May, Nicola Monaghan, Mike Morley, Sue Palmer, Andrew Pepper, Melanie Phillips, Jem Poster, Esther Rantzen, John Rickards, Mike Rossiter, Catherine Sampson, Prof Bryan Sykes, Mitch Symons, Alan Titchmarsh, Martin Townsend, Sir Terry Wogan, Sally Worboyes. Founded 2005. Fiction and non-fiction (home 15%, overseas 20%).

Overseas Representation:
Worldwide: Intercontinental Literary Agency, London

4011 ▬

JENNY BROWN ASSOCIATES
33 Argyle Place, Edinburgh EH9 1JT
Telephone: 0131 229 5334
Email: jenny@jennybrownassociates.com
Web Site: www.jennybrownassociates.com

Agents: Jenny Brown
Mark Stanton
Lucy Juckes *(Children's)*
Allan Guthrie
Kevin Pocklington *(Foreign Rights)*

All MSS except academic, poetry, science fiction, horror & fantasy. Submissions: see website for submission information.

Specialization: non-fiction (including sport & music) and literary fiction (including crime & thrillers). Most of the agency's clients are based in Scotland, but the company represents writers from all over the UK, and sells their work worldwide.

4012 ▬

FELICITY BRYAN
2a North Parade, Banbury Road, Oxford OX2 6LX
Telephone: 01865 513816
Fax: 01865 310055
Email: agency@felicitybryan.com
Web Site: www.felicitybryan.com

Directors: Felicity Bryan
Catherine Clarke

All MSS except science fiction, fantasy, romance, gardening, memoirs, self-help, picture/illustrated books, film, TV and play scripts or poetry.

Specialization: adult fiction & general non-fiction, history & popular science, children 8–12 upwards.

Overseas Representation:
China: Big Apple Tuttle-Mori Agency Inc, Shanghai; Andrew Nurnberg Associates, Beijing
Europe, Russia & China: Andrew Nurnberg Associates, London
Japan: Japan Uni Agency, Tokyo; Tuttle-Mori Agency Inc, Tokyo
Korea: EYA, Seoul

4013 ▬

THE BUCKMAN AGENCY
Ryman's Cottage, Little Tew, Oxford OX7 4JJ
Telephone: 01608 683677
Fax: 01608 683449
Email: r.buckman@talk21.com & j.buckman@talk21.com

Also at:
Jessica Buckman, 118 Effra Road, Wimbledon, London SW19 8PR
Telephone: (020) 8544 2674
Fax: (020) 8543 9653

Partners: Rosemarie Buckman *(Literary Agent)*
Jessica Buckman *(Literary Agent)*

Specialization: handling of translation rights in all foreign rights markets for fiction and non-fiction, working on behalf of UK and US agencies.

4014 ▬

BRIE BURKEMAN & SERAFINA CLARKE LTD
14 Neville Court, Abbey Road, London NW8 9DD
Telephone: 0870 199 5002
Fax: 0870 199 1029
Email: brie.burkeman@mail.com

Proprietor: Brie Burkeman

All MSS except academic, text, poetry, short stories, musicals or short films. No reading fee but return postage essential. Unsolicited e-mail attachments will be deleted without opening.

Specialization: commercial and literary full-length fiction and non-fiction books, as well as full length scripts for film and theatre. Worldwide representation, works with sub-agents where necessary. Also independent film and TV consultant to literary agents and publishers. Commission: 15% home, 20% overseas. Member of AAA and PMA.

Overseas Representation:
Worldwide – contact: Brie Burkeman & Serafina Clarke Ltd, London

4015 ▬

CAMPBELL THOMSON & MCLAUGHLIN LTD
50 Albemarle Street, London W1S 4BD
Telephone: (020) 7493 4361
Fax: (020) 7495 8961
Email: cbruton@ctmcl.co.uk
Web Site: www.ctmcl.co.uk

Director: Paul Marsh *(Managing)*
Agent: Charlotte Bruton
Consultant: John McLaughlin

All MSS except children's, poetry, SF; book length MSS only.

Associated Companies:
Peter Janson-Smith Ltd

Rights Representative in UK for:
USA: The Fox Chase Agency Inc, Chesterbrook, PA; Raines & Raines Agency, Medusa, NY

Overseas Representation:
Worldwide (all translation rights): The Marsh Agency, London

4016 ▬

CASAROTTO RAMSAY & ASSOCIATES LTD
Waverley House, 7–12 Noel Street, London W1F 8GQ
Telephone: (020) 7287 4450
Fax: (020) 7287 9128
Email: agents@casarotto.co.uk
Web Site: www.casarotto.uk.com

Directors: Giorgio Casarotto
Tom Erhardt
Jenne Casarotto
Mel Kenyon
Jodi Shields
Rachel Holroyd

Specialization: film scripts, TV scripts, play scripts, radio scripts only after preliminary letter. No books.

4017 ▬

CHAPMAN & VINCENT
7 Dilke Street, London SW3 4JE
Telephone: (020) 7352 5582
Email: chapmanvincent@hotmail.co.uk

Directors: Jennifer Chapman
Gilly Vincent

All MSS except domestic tragedies and academic work.

Specialization: non-fiction only. Write with two sample chapters and SAE. E-mail submissions without attachments can be considered. A small agency whose clients come mainly from personal recommendation. The agency is not actively seeking clients but is happy to consider really original work. Clients include George Carter, Leslie Geddes-Brown, Lucinda Lambton, Rowley Leigh and Eve Pollard. Commission: Home 15%; US & Europe 20%. Member of the Association of Authors' Agents.

Overseas Representation:
USA: Elaine Markson Literary Agency, New York, NY

4018 ▬

***MARY CLEMMEY LITERARY AGENCY**
6 Dunollie Road, London NW5 2XP
Telephone: (020) 7267 1290
Fax: (020) 7813 9757
Email: mcwords@googlemail.com

Literary Agent: Mary Clemmey

All MSS except science fiction, horror, fantasy, poetry or children's books. No unsolicited e-mail submissions.

Specialization: fiction and non-fiction, high quality work with an international market. TV, film, radio and theatre scripts from existing clients only. Please approach only by preliminary letter and synopsis (SAE essential for response).

Rights Representative in UK for:
USA: Betsy Amster Literary Enterprises, Los Angeles, CA; Lynn C. Franklin Associates Ltd, New York, NY; Frederick Hill Bonnie Nadell Associates Literary Agency, San Francisco, CA; The Miller Agency, New York, NY; Roslyn Targ Literary Agency Inc, New York, NY; The Weingel Fidel Agency, New York, NY

Overseas Representation:
USA: Elaine Markson Literary Agency, New York, NY

4019 ▬

ELSPETH COCHRANE PERSONAL MANAGEMENT
16 Trinity Close, The Pavement, London SW4 0JD
Telephone: (020) 7622 3566
Email: elspethcochrane@talktalk.net

Directors: Elspeth Cochrane *(Managing)*
Tony Barlow

Specialization: fiction, non-fiction, biographies, screenplays. Subjects have included Richard Burton, Marlon Brando, Sean Connery, Clint Eastwood, Lord Olivier. Also scripts for all media, with special interest in drama. No unsolicited MSS. Preliminary letter, synopsis and SAE are essential in the first instance. Clients include

Royce Ryton, Robert Tanitch. Commission: 12.5%.

4020

*ROSICA COLIN LTD
1 Clareville Grove Mews, London SW7 5AH
Telephone: (020) 7370 1080
Fax: (020) 7244 6441

All MSS except poetry. No unsolicited submissions please.

Specialization: theatre, film, television, radio & foreign rights.

4021

JANE CONWAY-GORDON LTD
1 Old Compton Street, London W1D 5JA
Telephone: (020) 7494 0148
Fax: (020) 7287 9264
Email: jconway_gordon@dsl.pipex.com

Company Director: Jane Conway-Gordon

All MSS except science fiction, poetry, children's, short pieces; return postage essential.

Overseas Representation:
Europe (excluding Germany & France): Intercontinental Literary Agency, London
France: La Nouvelle Agence, Paris
Germany: Liepman AG, Zurich
USA: Lyons Literary LLC, New York, NY

4022

COOMBS MOYLETT LITERARY AGENCY
120 New Kings Road, London SW6 4LZ
Telephone: (020) 8740 0454
Email: lisa.moylett@btopenworld.com

Proprietor: Lisa Moylett
Editor: Juliet van Oss
Submissions: Sara Stanford

All MSS except science fiction, poetry or children's.

Specialization: commercial and literary fiction and non-fiction. Special interests in fiction are thrillers, crime/mystery; women's literary and contemporary and in non-fiction: biography; history and current affairs. The agency is particularly interested in finding and developing new talent. Services include the selling of subsidiary rights such as film & TV and translation. The agency has good relations with US publishers and is represented in both Japan by Tuttle Mori and in Germany by the Michael Meller Literary Agency. Guidelines for submission: first three chapters, a short synopsis and SAE (essential for the return of material). No e-mail or disc submissions.

Overseas Representation:
Germany: Michael Meller Literary Agency, Munich
Japan: Tuttle-Mori Agency Inc, Tokyo

4023

RUPERT CREW LTD
[International Literary Representation]
1a King's Mews, London WC1N 2JA
Telephone: (020) 7242 8586
Fax: (020) 7831 7914
Email: info@rupertcrew.co.uk
Web Site: www.rupertcrew.co.uk

Founder: F. Rupert Crew
Joint Managing Directors: Doreen Montgomery (*Chairman*)
Caroline Montgomery (*Company Secretary*)

All MSS except science fiction, fantasy, short stories, poetry, film & TV scripts.

Specialization: international business management for authors desiring world representation. Preliminary letter with SAE required. Also acts as publishers' consultants.

Overseas Representation:
China: Big Apple Tuttle-Mori Agency Inc, Shanghai
Eastern Europe: Andrew Nurnberg Associates, London
France: Eliane Benisti, Paris
Germany: Paul & Peter Fritz AG Literary Agency, Zurich
Hungary: Kàtai & Bolza Literary Agents, Budapest
Italy: Agenzia Letteraria Internazionale srl, Milan
Japan: The English Agency Japan Ltd, Tokyo; Tuttle-Mori Agency Inc, Tokyo
Scandinavia & Spain: Sane Töregård Agency, Karlshamn
Taiwan: Big Apple Tuttle-Mori Associates, Shin-Juang
USA: The Martell Agency, New York, NY
Worldwide (Film/TV): MBA Literary Agents, London

4024

CURTIS BROWN
Haymarket House, 28–29 Haymarket, London SW1Y 4SP
Telephone: (020) 7393 4400
Fax: (020) 7393 4401/2
Email: cb@curtisbrown.co.uk
Web Site: www.curtisbrown.co.uk

Directors: Jonathan Lloyd (*Chief Executive Officer*)
Ben Hall (*Chief Operating Officer*)
Jonny Geller (*Managing – Book Department*)
Nick Marston (*Managing – Theatre, Film & TV Department*)
Jacquie Drewe
Sarah Spear
Head of Legal and Business Affairs: Craig Dickson
Operations Manager: Emma Bailey
Literary Agents: Felicity Blunt
Sheila Crowley
Camilla Hornby
Vivienne Schuster
Elizabeth Scheinkman
Karolina Sutton
Steohanie Thwaites
Rights Agents: Kate Cooper (*Joint Head of Foreign Rights*)
Betsy Robbins (*Joint Head of Foreign Rights*)
Carol Jackson
Daisy Meyrick
Katie McGowan
Helen Manders
Elizabeth Iveson

All MSS except short stories & poetry.

Specialization: negotiation in all publishing markets; and television, film & dramatic writing, directing, presenting & acting.

Associated Companies:
Australia: Curtis Brown (Australia) Pty Ltd

Rights Representative in UK for:
USA: Gelfman Schneider Literary Agents Inc, New York, NY

4025

FELIX DE WOLFE LTD
Kingsway House, 103 Kingsway, London WC2B 6QX
Telephone: (020) 7242 5066
Fax: (020) 7242 8119
Email: info@felixdewolfe.com

Director: Caroline de Wolfe

All MSS except non-fiction, children's.

Overseas Representation:
France: Michelle Lapautre, Paris
Italy: Liepman AG, Zurich

4026

ROBERT DUDLEY AGENCY
50 Rannoch Road, London W6 9SR
Telephone: 07879 426574
Email: info@robertdudleyagency.co.uk
Web Site: www.robertdudleyagency.co.uk

Agent: Robert Dudley

All MSS except film scripts.

Specialization: Robert Dudley Agency looks after a variety of authors of both fiction and non-fiction. Non-fiction subjects include sport, management, history, militaria, politics, health and well-being, travel, biography, film and archaeology.

Parent Company:
Bowerdean Publishing Co Ltd

4027

EDWARDS FUGLEWICZ
49 Great Ormond Street, London WC1N 3HZ
Telephone: (020) 7405 6725
Fax: (020) 7405 6726
Email: info@efla.co.uk

Partners: Ros Edwards
Helenka Fuglewicz

All MSS except children's books, science fiction, fantasy or horror. No unsolicited MSS.

Specialization: fiction and non-fiction: biography, history, and popular culture. Founded in 1996.

Rights Representative in UK for:
Republic of Ireland: Poolbeg Press, Dublin
UK: The Bodleian Library, Oxford

4028

FAITH EVANS ASSOCIATES
27 Park Avenue North, London N8 7RU
Telephone: (020) 8340 9920
Fax: (020) 8340 9410
Email: faith@faith-evans.co.uk

Specialization: Small agency. No phone calls or unsolicited MSS.

4029

FOX & HOWARD LITERARY AGENCY
4 Bramerton Street, Chelsea, London SW3 5JX
Telephone: (020) 7352 8691
Fax: (020) 7352 8691

Agents: Chelsey Fox
Charlotte Howard

Specialization: general non-fiction: biography, history and popular culture, reference, business, mind, body and spirit, health (home 15%, overseas 20%). No reading fee, but preliminary letter and synopsis with SAE essential. Founded 1992.

4030

FRASER ROSS ASSOCIATES
6 Wellington Place, Edinburgh EH6 7EQ
Telephone: 0131 553 2759
Email: lindsey.fraser@tiscali.co.uk
Web Site: www.fraserross.co.uk

Also at:
Telephone: 0131 657 4412
Email: kjross@tiscali.co.uk
Web Site: www.fraserross.co.uk

Partners: Lindsey Fraser
Kathryn Ross

All MSS except poetry, short stories & science fiction.

Specialization: representing writers and illustrators for children's books, and writers for adults (home 10–15%, overseas 20%). Send the first three chapters (or equivalent), a synopsis, CV and covering letter. Return postage is essential. Current clients include Thomas Bloor, Joan Lingard, Tanya Landman, Vivian French, Dugald Steer and Jamie Rix.

4031

JÜRI GABRIEL
35 Camberwell Grove, London SE5 8JA
Telephone: (020) 7703 6186
Email: Juri@JuriGabriel.com

Proprietor: Jüri Gabriel

All MSS except screenplays, tele or radio scripts (only handles performance rights in existing works for existing clients); science fantasy; children's books, poetry, short stories or articles.

Specialization: literary fiction, popular academic and anything that combines intellect, originality and wit. In first instance please send a two page synopsis, three sample chapters, a brief c.v. and return postage if you want the material back. No submissions by fax or e-mail. Clients include Maurice Caldera, Diana Constance, Miriam Dunne, Matt Fox, Paul Genney, Pat Gray, Mikka Haugaard, Robert Irwin, Andrew Killeen, John Lucas, David Madsen, Richard Mankiewicz, David Miller, Andy Oakes, John Outram, Phil Roberts, Roger Storey, Dr Stefan Szymanski, Dr Terence White. Commission: home 10%, US & translation 20%.

4032

DAVID GODWIN ASSOCIATES
55 Monmouth Street, London WC2H 9DG
Telephone: (020) 7240 9992
Fax: (020) 7395 6110
Web Site: www.davidgodwinassociates.co.uk

Literary Agent: David Godwin
Company Secretary: Heather Godwin
Managers: Kirsty McLachlan (*Film & TV Rights*)
Kerry Glencourse (*Foreign & US Rights*)

All MSS except science fiction & children's.

Specialization: UK, US and translation rights, TV & film.

4033

GRAHAM MAW CHRISTIE
19 Thornhill Crescent, London N1 1BJ
Telephone: (020) 7737 4766
Email: enquiries@grahammawchristie.com
Web Site: www.grahammawchristie.com

Directors: Jane Graham Maw
Jennifer Christie

All MSS except fiction, children's or poetry.

Specialization: literary agents for general non-fiction: autobiography/memoir, humour and gift, business, web-to-book, food and drink, health, lifestyle, parenting, personal development, popular culture, popular science and popular philosophy, reference, TV tie-in. No reading fee. Will suggest revision. See website for guidance on submissions.

4034

*LOUISE GREENBERG BOOKS LTD
The End House, Church Crescent, London
N3 1BG
Telephone: (020) 8349 1179
Fax: (020) 8343 4559
Email: louisegreenberg@msn.com

All MSS except sport, leisure, poetry,
children's. No telephone approaches from
authors.

Specialization: full length literary fiction and
serious non-fiction. Screen work for book
clients only.

Associated Companies:
UK: Sarah Manson Literary Agents
[Children's Books]

Rights Representative in UK for:
USA: Rosalie Siegel International Literary
Agent, Penington, NJ

4035

*GREENE & HEATON LTD
37 Goldhawk Road, London W12 8QQ
Telephone: (020) 8749 0315
Fax: (020) 8749 0318
Email: info@greeneheaton.co.uk
Web Site: www.greeneheaton.co.uk

Directors: Carol Heaton
Charles Elliott (Company Secretary)
Judith Murray
Antony Topping

All MSS except plays, TV & film-scripts,
articles & poetry, stories (other than from
existing clients), science fiction or fantasy.
Preliminary letter and return postage
required.

Rights Representative in UK for:
Canada: The Cooke Agency, Toronto, Ont
USA: Jean V. Naggar Literary Agency, New
York, NY; The Sagalyn Literary Agency,
Bethesda, MD; Denise Shannon Literary
Agency, New York, NY

Overseas Representation:
Canada: The Cooke Agency, Toronto, Ont
France: VVV Agency, Paris
German-speaking countries: Paul & Peter
Fritz AG Literary Agency, Zurich;
Liepman AG, Zurich
Italy: Antonella Antonelli Agenzia
Letteraria, Milan
Japan: Tuttle-Mori Agency Inc, Tokyo
Netherlands, Eastern Europe & Russia:
Andrew Nurnberg Associates, London
Scandinavia: The Buckman Agency, Oxford
Spain: Carmen Balcells Agencia Literaria SA,
Barcelona
USA: Jean V. Naggar Literary Agency, New
York, NY; Denise Shannon Literary
Agency, New York, NY

4036

GREGORY & COMPANY AUTHORS' AGENTS
3 Barb Mews, London W6 7PA
Telephone: (020) 7610 4676
Fax: (020) 7610 4686
Email: info@gregoryandcompany.co.uk
Web Site: www.gregoryandcompany.co.uk

Proprietor: Jane Gregory
Editorial: Stephanie Glencross
Rights: Claire Morris
Jemma McDonagh
Accounts: Terry Bland

All MSS except children's, juvenile,
academic & technical books, poetry & plays,
TV & film scripts, science fiction, short
stories. Preliminary letter with synopsis, first
three chapters and SAE essential.

Specialization: fiction: commercial, crime,
literary, suspense and thrillers. Editorial
advice given to own authors. Film & TV
rights for own published authors only, no
original scripts.

Associated Companies:
The Jane Gregory Agency

Overseas Representation:
Brazil: Tassy Barham Associates, London
Bulgaria: Interrights Literary & Translation
Agency, Sofia
China: Big Apple Tuttle-Mori Associates,
Shin-Juang
Croatia: Zvonimir Majdak, Zagreb
Czech Republic & Slovakia: Andrew
Nurnberg Associates, Prague
France: La Nouvelle Agence, Paris
Hungary: Lex Copyright, Budapest
Israel: Ilana Pikarski, Tel Aviv
Japan: Japan Uni Agency Inc, Tokyo; Tuttle-
Mori Agency Inc, Tokyo
Korea: EYA, Seoul
Poland: Andrew Nurnberg Associates,
Warsaw
Romania: Simona Kessler International
Copyright Agency Ltd, Bucharest
Russia: Andrew Nurnberg Associates,
Moscow
Scandinavia: Leonhardt & Hoier Literary
Agency, Copenhagen
Spain: Carmen Balcells Agencia Literaria SA,
Barcelona
Turkey: Akcali Copyright Trade & Tourism
Co Ltd, Istanbul

4037

THE HANBURY AGENCY
28 Moreton Street, London SW1V 2PE
Telephone: (020) 7630 6768
Email: enquiries@hanburyagency.com
Web Site: www.hanburyagency.com

Proprietor: Margaret Hanbury
Assistant: Stuart Rushworth

Specialization: quality fiction and non-
fiction (home 15%, overseas 20%). See
website for submission details. Authors
include George Alagiah, J. G. Ballard, Simon
Callow, Judith Lennox, Katie Price. Founded
in 1983.

Overseas Representation:
Brazil: Tassy Barham, London
Eastern Europe, Russia & Baltic States:
Prava i Prevodi, Belgrade
France: Michelle Lapautre, Paris
Germany: Mohrbooks Literary Agency,
Zurich
Greece: JLM Literary Agency, Athens
Hungary: Lex Copyright, Budapest
Israel: Ilana Pikarski Literary Agency, Tel Aviv
Italy: Luigi Bernabó Associates Srl, Milan
Japan: The English Agency Japan Ltd, Tokyo
Korea: The Eric Yang Agency, Seoul
Netherlands: Jan Michael, Amsterdam
Scandinavia: Licht & Burr Literary Agency,
Copenhagen
Spain & Portugal: International Editors Co,
Barcelona
Turkey: Akcali Copyright Agency, Istanbul
USA: Robin Straus Inc, New York, NY

4038

ANTONY HARWOOD LTD
103 Walton Street, Oxford OX2 6EB
Telephone: 01865 559615
Fax: 01865 310660
Email: mail@antonyharwood.com
Web Site: www.antonyharwood.com

Agents: Antony Harwood
James MacDonald Lockhart

All MSS except screenwriting, poetry.

Specialization: handles fiction and non-
fiction. Founded 2000.

4039

A. M. HEATH & CO LTD
6 Warwick Court, London WC1R 5DJ
Telephone: (020) 7242 2811
Fax: (020) 7242 2711
Web Site: www.amheath.com

Directors: William Hamilton (Managing)
Euan Thorneycroft (Company Secretary)
Victoria Hobbs
Jennifer Custer (Foreign Rights)
Agent: Sarah Molloy (Children's)

All MSS except plays, scripts, poetry,
scientific, technical for the layman only.

Rights Representative in UK for:
USA: Miriam Altshuler Literary Agency, Red
Hook, NY; Brandt & Hochman Inc, New
York, NY; Jane Chelius Literary Agency,
Brooklyn, NY; Anne Edelstein Literary
Agency, New York, NY; Lescher &
Lescher Ltd, New York, NY; Gina
Maccoby Literary Agency, New York, NY

Overseas Representation:
Brazil: Tassy Barham, London
Bulgaria & Serbia: Andrew Nurnberg
Literary Agency, Sofia
China & Taiwan: Andrew Nurnberg Literary
Agency, Shanghai; Andrew Nurnberg
Literary Agency, Taipei
Czech & Slovak Republics & Slovenia:
Andrew Nurnberg Associates, Prague
France: La Nouvelle Agence, Paris
Germany, Switzerland & Austria:
Mohrbooks Literary Agency, Zurich
Hungary & Croatia: Andrew Nurnberg Ltd,
Budapest
Israel: Deborah Harris Agency, Jerusalem
Italy: Luigi Bernabó Associates Srl, Milan
Japan (fiction): The English Agency Japan
Ltd, Tokyo
Japan (non-fiction): Tuttle-Mori Agency Inc,
Tokyo
Korea: EYA, Seoul
Poland: ANAW Literary Agency, Warsaw
Romania: Simona Kessler International
Copyright Agency Ltd, Bucharest
Russia: Andrew Nurnberg Associates,
Moscow
Scandinavia: Licht & Burr Literary Agency,
Copenhagen
Thailand: Big Apple Tuttle Mori Agency
(Thailand) Co Ltd, Bangkok
Turkey, Greece, Indonesia, Portugal, Latvia,
Lithuania, Estonia, Spain & Netherlands:
A. M. Heath & Co Ltd, London

4040

DAVID HIGHAM ASSOCIATES
5–8 Lower John Street, Golden Square,
London W1F 9HA
Telephone: (020) 7434 5900
Fax: (020) 7437 1072
Email: dha@davidhigham.co.uk
Web Site: www.davidhigham.co.uk

Specialization: agents for the negotiation of
all rights in fiction, general non-fiction,
children's fiction and picture books, plays,
film and TV scripts. Represented in all
foreign markets. Preliminary letter and
return postage essential. No reading fee.
Founded 1935.

4041

KATE HORDERN LITERARY AGENCY
18 Mortimer Road, Clifton, Bristol BS8 4EY
Telephone: 0117 923 9368
Email: katehordern@blueyonder.co.uk &
annewilliamskhla@googlemail.com

Proprietor: Kate Hordern
Associate Agent: Anne Williams

Specialization: quality literary and
commercial fiction, including women's
fiction, crime and thrillers, and general non-

fiction. Clients include Jeff Dawson, Richard
Bassett, J. T. Lees, Will Randall, Leigh
Eduardo, Duncan Hewitt, Kylie Fitzpatrick.

4042

*VALERIE HOSKINS ASSOCIATES
20 Charlotte Street, London W1T 2NA
Telephone: (020) 7637 4490
Fax: (020) 7637 4493
Email: vha@vhassociates.co.uk

Managing Director: Valerie Hoskins
Agent: Rebecca Watson
Assistant: Georgina Paget

Specialization: film & television rights for
published work. The company is not a
publishing agency.

4043

IMG UK LTD
McCormack House, Burlington Lane,
London W4 2TH
Telephone: (020) 8233 5300
Fax: (020) 8233 5268
Email: sarah.wooldridge@imgworld.com
Web Site: www.imgworld.com

Consultant: Sarah Wooldridge
Accountant: Sally Matthews

All MSS except science fiction, fiction,
children's, short stories and poetry.

Specialization: non-fiction. No reading fee.
Please send synopsis with sample chapter
and SAE. Also handle IMG speakers. 20%
commission.

Associated Companies:
Worldwide: IMG

4044

THE INSPIRA GROUP
5 Bradley Road, Enfield, Middx EN3 6ES
Telephone: (020) 8292 5163
Fax: 0870 139 3057
Email: darin@theinspiragroup.com
Web Site: www.theinspiragroup.com

Managing Director: Darin Jewell
Rights: Shaun Ebelthite
Administration: Charlene Webber

Specialization: children's books, fantasy/sci-
fi, and general fiction. Manuscripts in all
genres are considered. Clients include
Michael Tolkien, Simon Hall, John Wilson
and Simon Brown. Authors should e-mail
their full MSS, synopsis and short literary CV
(with their postal address and landline tel.
no.) to darin@theinspiragroup.com

4045

INTERCONTINENTAL LITERARY AGENCY
Centric House, 390 Strand, London
WC2R 0LT
Telephone: (020) 7379 6611
Fax: (020) 7240 4724
Email: ila@ila-agency.co.uk
Web Site: www.ila-agency.co.uk

Agents: Nicki Kennedy
Sam Edenborough
Mary Esdaile
Tessa Girvan
Katherine West
Jenny Robson

Specialization: translation rights exclusively.

Rights Representative in UK for:
see website at:: Intercontinental Literary
Agency, London

4046

JANKLOW & NESBIT (UK) LTD
33 Drayson Mews, London W8 4LY
Telephone: (020) 7376 2733
Fax: (020) 7376 2915
Email: queries@janklow.co.uk

Literary Agents: Tif Loehnis
Claire Paterson
Will Francis
Foreign Rights: Rebecca Folland

All MSS except poetry, plays, film & TV scripts.

Specialization: fiction and non-fiction; commercial and literary. Send full outline (non-fiction), synopsis and first three sample chapters (fiction) plus informative covering letter and return postage.

Overseas Representation:
USA: Janklow & Nesbit Associates, New York, NY

4047

JOHNSON & ALCOCK LTD
Clerkenwell House,
45–47 Clerkenwell Green, London
EC1R 0HT
Telephone: (020) 7251 0125
Fax: (020) 7251 2172
Email: info@johnsonandalcock.co.uk
Web Site: www.johnsonandalcock.co.uk

Directors: Andrew Hewson
Michael Alcock
Agents: Anna Power
Ed Wilson

All MSS except technical or academic material, poetry, plays, fantasy, horror. No unsolicited manuscripts; please send synopsis, full CV, sample opening chapters and SAE in the first instance. No reading fee.

Specialization: fiction and non-fiction. General non-fiction, mainly biography, history, current affairs, health and lifestyle; literary and commercial fiction; graphic novels.

Rights Representative in UK for:
USA: Soho Press, New York, NY

Overseas Representation:
Worldwide - contact: Johnson & Alcock Ltd, London

4048

JANE JUDD LITERARY AGENCY
18 Belitha Villas, London N1 1PD
Telephone: (020) 7607 0273
Fax: (020) 7607 0623
Web Site: www.janejudd.com

Proprietor: Jane C. Judd

All MSS except plays, poetry and short stories.

Specialization: general non-fiction & fiction.

Rights Representative in UK for:
USA: Mercury House, San Francisco, CA; Permanent Press, Sag Harbor, NY; RLR Associates, New York, NY; Chris Tomasino, New York, NY; Marian Young, New York, NY

Overseas Representation:
France: La Nouvelle Agence, Paris
Germany: Thomas Schlück Literary Agency, Garbsen
Italy: Stefania Fietta ALI, Milan
Netherlands & Scandinavia: Jan Michael, Amsterdam

Spain & Portugal: Julio F Yañez Literary Agency, Barcelona
USA: The Unter Agency, New York, NY

4049

MICHELLE KASS ASSOCIATES
85 Charing Cross Road, London
WC2H 0AA
Telephone: (020) 7439 1624
Fax: (020) 7734 3394
Email: office@michellekass.co.uk

Agents: Michelle Kass
Andrew Mills

Specialization: an agency representing novelists, writers and directors for film, TV and theatre.

4050

*THE FRANCES KELLY AGENCY
111 Clifton Road, Kingston-upon-Thames, Surrey KT2 6PL
Telephone: (020) 8549 7830
Fax: (020) 8547 0051

Proprietor: Frances Kelly

Specialization: general non-fiction, all academic & professional disciplines; return postage & preliminary letter requested.

4051

KNIGHT FEATURES
20 Crescent Grove, London SW4 7AH
Telephone: (020) 7622 1467
Fax: (020) 7622 1522
Email: peter@knightfeatures.co.uk

Proprietor: Peter Knight
Associates: Gaby Martin
Andrew Knight
Samantha Ferris

All MSS except short stories, poetry & unsolicited MSS (reading fee). No e-mail submissions.

Specialization: worldwide selling of strip cartoons, major features and serializations. Exclusive syndication agent in UK & Irish Republic for United Feature Syndicate (Peanuts, Dilbert, etc.) & Newspaper Enterprise Association (Frank & Ernest, Born Loser, King Baloo, etc.), also Paws Inc (Garfield), Creators Syndicate (The Far Side).

Rights Representative in UK for:
New Zealand: The Puzzle Co
USA: Paws Inc; United Media Inc, New York, NY

4052

LENZ-MULLIGAN RIGHTS & CO-EDITIONS
15 Sandbourne Avenue, London
SW19 3EW
Telephone: (020) 8543 7846
Email: lenzmulligan@btinternet.com

Rights Manager: Gundhild Lenz-Mulligan

All MSS except poetry and film scripts.

Specialization: sale of co-editions and rights in the Nordic countries and Dutch, English and German-speaking markets. Particularly interested in children's books. Also offers proofreading and translation services of German language material. Represents European, American and Australian publishers, packagers and authors.

Rights Representative in UK for:
Australia: Tracy Marsh Publications, West Beach, SA
Germany: Ars Edition

Netherlands: Image Books Factory, Eindhoven

4053

BARBARA LEVY LITERARY AGENCY
64 Greenhill, Hampstead High Street, London NW3 5TZ
Telephone: (020) 7435 9046
Fax: (020) 7431 2063

Associate: John F. Selby *(Solicitor)*

Specialization: general fiction & non-fiction, and TV presenters.

Rights Representative in UK for:
USA: Arcadia, Danbury, CT; Richard Parks, New York, NY

Overseas Representation:
Foreign Language Markets: The Buckman Agency, London
USA: Marshall Rights, London

4054

LIMELIGHT MANAGEMENT
33 Newman Street, London W1T 1PY
Telephone: (020) 7637 2529
Fax: (020) 7637 2538
Email: limelight.management@virgin.net
Web Site:
www.limelightmanagement.com

Owner/Founder: Fiona Lindsay *(Managing Director)*
Agent: Mary Bekhait

Specialization: full-length book MSS. Commercial fiction and non-fiction. Food, wine, health, crafts, gardening, biography/ memoirs, popular culture, travel, women's interest (home 15%, overseas 20%), TV and radio rights (15–20%); will suggest revision where appropriate. No reading fee.

4055

*CHRISTOPHER LITTLE LITERARY AGENCY
10 Eel Brook Studios,
125 Moore Park Road, London SW6 4PS
Telephone: (020) 7736 4455
Fax: (020) 7736 4490
Email: info@christopherlittle.net
Web Site: www.christopherlittle.net

Proprietor: Christopher Little *(Agent)*
Agent: Patrick Janson-Smith

All MSS except poetry, plays, science fiction, fantasy, textbooks, illustrated children's or short stories. Film scripts for established clients only.

Specialization: full length commercial fiction and non-fiction. No reading fee. Send detailed letter plus synopsis and three sample chapters, and SAE in first instance.

4056

LONDON INDEPENDENT BOOKS
26 Chalcot Crescent, London NW1 8YD
Telephone: (020) 7706 0486
Fax: (020) 7724 3122

Literary Agent: Carolyn Whitaker

All MSS except computers & young children's.

Specialization: fiction & non-fiction, particularly travel & fantasy.

4057

ANDREW LOWNIE LITERARY AGENCY LTD
36 Great Smith Street, London SW1P 3BU
Telephone: (020) 7222 7574

Fax: (020) 7222 7576
Email: lownie@globalnet.co.uk
Web Site: www.andrew.lownie.co.uk

Proprietor: Andrew Lownie

Specialization: non-fiction only. History, biography, packaging celebrities for book market and representing book projects for journalists. Titles agented include the Oxford Classical Dictionary, Cambridge Guide to Literature in English, Norma Major's books on Joan Sutherland and Chequers, Juliet Barker, Duncan Falconer, Laurence Gardner, Lawrence James, Damien Lewis, David Stafford, Alan Whicker, Sir John Mills, authorized lives of Sir Henry Cooper and Dick Emery, Desmond Seward, Daniel Tammet, Cathy Glass, Joyce Cary and Julian Maclaren - Ross Estates, numerous books about the SAS. Return postage essential. No reading fee. Commission 15% worldwide.

Overseas Representation:
Worldwide (excluding USA & Japan): The Marsh Agency, London

4058

LUTYENS & RUBINSTEIN
231 Westbourne Park Road, London
W11 1EB
Telephone: (020) 7792 4855
Fax: (020) 7792 4833
Email:
submissions@lutyensrubinstein.co.uk

Partners: Felicity Rubinstein
Sarah Lutyens

All MSS except poetry, screenplays, scripts for theatre and/or TV and radio.

Specialization: general adult non-fiction and fiction.

Overseas Representation:
France: La Nouvelle Agence, Paris
Germany: Eggers & Landwehr, Berlin
Italy: Grandi & Associates, Milan
USA: Inkwell Management, New York, NY

4059

DUNCAN MCARA
28 Beresford Gardens, Edinburgh EH5 3ES
Telephone: 0131 552 1558
Email: duncanmcara@mac.com

All MSS except 'genre' fiction, educational & children's.

Specialization: literary fiction; non-fiction: art, architecture, archaeology, biography, history, military, Scottish. Home: 10%; Overseas: 20%. Preliminary letter with SAE essential. No reading fee. Also acts as editorial consultant on all aspects of general trade publishing. Editing, re-writing, copy-editing, proof correction for wide range of UK publishers.

4060

*THE MCKERNAN LITERARY AGENCY & CONSULTANCY
5 Gayfield Square, Edinburgh EH1 3NW
Telephone: 0131 557 1771
Email: maggie@mckernanagency.co.uk
Web Site: www.mckernanagency.co.uk

Agent: Maggie McKernan

All MSS except film scripts, screenplays, picture books for children.

Specialization: assisting and developing writers, as well as representing their interests in their dealings with publishers, selling rights and handling negotiations of contracts. Handle fiction and non-fiction (commercial and literary novels of all kinds, including crime, historical, contemporary). Consideration will be given to novels for children over the age of 10, but not picture books.

Overseas Representation:
USA & Worldwide (translation rights):
Capel & Land Ltd, London

4061

EUNICE MCMULLEN LTD
Low Ibbotsholme Cottage, off Bridge Lane, Troutbeck Bridge, Windermere, Cumbria LA23 1HU
Telephone: 01539 448551
Email: eunicemcmullen@totalise.co.uk
Web Site: www.eunicmcmullen.co.uk

Specialization: children's books (fiction only) for all ages including picture books for co-edition market and early teen fiction. No unsolicited MSS.

4062

ANDREW MANN LTD
1 Old Compton Street, London W1D 5JA
Telephone: (020) 7734 4751
Fax: (020) 7287 9264
Email: info@andrewmann.co.uk
Web Site: www.andrewmann.co.uk

Directors: Anne Dewe
Tina Betts

All MSS except poetry.

Specialization: fiction, general non-fiction & film/TV/radio scripts. No unsolicited MSS. Preliminary letter, synopsis - first 30 pages and SAE essential. No reading fee. No e-mail submissions, synopses only.

Rights Representative in UK for:
USA: Richard McDonough, Irvine, CA

Overseas Representation:
China (Mainland): Big Apple Tuttle-Mori Agency Inc, Shanghai
France: VVV Agency, Paris
Germany: Thomas Schlück Literary Agency, Garbsen
Hungary: Kàtai & Bolza Literary Agents, Budapest
Israel: Deborah Harris Agency, Jerusalem
Italy: Living Literary Agency, Milan
Japan: Tuttle-Mori Agency Inc, Tokyo
Poland, Bulgaria, Czech Republic & Slovakia: Andrew Nurnberg Associates, London
Romania: Simona Kessler International Copyright Agency Ltd, Bucharest
Russia: Author Rights Agency
Taiwan: Big Apple Tuttle-Mori Associates, Shin-Juang
Thailand: Silk Road Agency, Bangkok
Turkey: Asli Karasuil Agency, Istanbul
USA: Jonathan Lyons, New York, NY

4063

SARAH MANSON LITERARY AGENT
6 Totnes Walk, London N2 0AD
Telephone: (020) 8442 0396
Email: info@sarahmanson.com
Web Site: www.sarahmanson.com

Proprietor: Sarah Manson

All MSS except poetry and picture books.

Specialization: fiction for children and young adults. List of clients includes both well-established writers and promising new talent.

4064

MARJACQ SCRIPTS
34 Devonshire Place, London W1G 6JW
Telephone: (020) 7935 9499

Fax: (020) 7935 9115
Email: enquiries@marjacq.com
Web Site: www.marjacq.com

Agents: Philip Patterson *(Literary)*
Luke Speed *(Film)*
Isabella Floris *(Literary)*

All MSS except poetry or stage plays.

Specialization: literary and commercial fiction, crime, thrillers, science fiction and women's fiction, and general non-fiction. Please submit three sample chapters and synopsis in first instance. SAE essential for return of MS.

Overseas Representation:
Austria, Germany, Switzerland & parts of Eastern Europe: Transnet Contracts Ltd, Vienna
France: VVV Agency, Paris
Hungary: Kàtai & Bolza Literary Agents, Budapest
Israel: Ilana Pikarski Literary Agency, Tel Aviv
Italy: Agenzia Piergiorgio Nicolazzini, Milan
Japan: The English Agency Japan Ltd, Tokyo
Poland: Graal Ltd, Warsaw
Russia: Prava i Prevodi RAO, Moscow
Scandinavia, Netherlands, Spain & Portugal: Lennart Sane Agency, Karlshamn
Turkey: Kayi Literary & Merchandising Agency, Istanbul

4065

THE MARSH AGENCY LTD
50 Albemarle Street, London W1S 4BD
Telephone: (020) 7493 4361
Fax: (020) 7495 8961
Email: enquiries@marsh-agency.co.uk
Web Site: www.marsh-agency.co.uk

Managing Director: Paul Marsh
Manager: Camilla Ferrier *(Foreign Rights)*
Agents: Geraldine Cooke
Jessica Woollard
Caroline Hardman

All MSS except children's, poetry, drama, TV, film & radio.

Specialization: selling of rights in the work of English-language writers throughout the world, representing a number of British and American agencies and publishers.

Parent Company:
UK: Campbell Thomson & McLaughlin Ltd

Associated Companies:
UK: Paterson Marsh Ltd

Rights Representative in UK for:
Worldwide: see Website for full list

4066

BLANCHE MARVIN
21a St Johns Wood High Street, London NW8 7NG
Telephone: (020) 7722 2313
Fax: (020) 7722 2313

Director: Blanche Marvin

Specialization: theatre, film, TV, radio & publishing for UK & USA. MSS from published authors only.

4067

MBA LITERARY AGENTS
62 Grafton Way, London W1T 5DW
Telephone: (020) 7387 2076
Fax: (020) 7387 2042
Email: firstname@mbalit.co.uk
Web Site: www.mbalit.co.uk

Directors: Diana Tyler *(Managing)*
Meg Davis

Timothy Webb *(Financial)*
Laura Longrigg

All MSS except poetry, short stories.

Specialization: fiction and non-fiction. Also scripts for film, TV, radio & theatre.

Rights Representative in UK for:
USA: Beacon Artists, New York, NY; Frances Collin Agency, New York, NY; Donald Maass Agency, New York, NY; Martha Millard Literary Agency, New York, NY

Overseas Representation:
Brazil: Tassy Barham, London
Eastern Europe & Greece: Prava i Prevodi, Belgrade
France: Lora Fountain Associates, Paris
Germany: Mohrbooks Literary Agency, Zurich; Thomas Schlück Literary Agency, Garbsen
Israel: I. Pikarski Literary Agency, Tel Aviv
Italy: Vicki Satlow Literary Agency, Milan
Japan: Tuttle-Mori Agency Inc, Tokyo
Netherlands: Caroline Van Gelderen Literary Agency, Hilversum
Russia: Prava i Prevodi RAO, Moscow
Scandinavia: Licht & Burr Literary Agency, Copenhagen
Spain: Carmen Balcells Agencia Literaria SA, Barcelona

4068

THE CATHY MILLER FOREIGN RIGHTS AGENCY
29A The Quadrangle, 49 Atalanta Street, London SW6 6TU
Telephone: (020) 7386 5473
Fax: (020) 7385 1774
Email: cathy@millerrightsagency.com

Principal/Managing Director: Mrs Cathy Miller

All MSS except poetry & educational.

Specialization: foreign rights; acting as consultants to publishers on sales of foreign rights of non-fiction titles (psychoanalysis, medical, business & management, esoteric, health & general trade books); handling market research for lists or one-off projects; helping to set up rights departments; advising on all matters concerning translation rights and negotiations with foreign publishers.

Rights Representative in UK for:
Canada: Mark Fisher; Golden Globe Publishing, Notre Dame-de-l'Ile Perrot, PQ; Fletcher Peacock
UK: Artemis Music Publishing; Foulsham Publishers; Free Association Books; Ann Henning-Jocelyn, Countess of Roden; Karnac Books; Phantom Genius Ltd; Shepheard-Walwyn; Thorogood Publishing Ltd

Overseas Representation:
China: Mei Yao, New York, NY
Greece: Read n Right Agency, Cahlkida
Japan: The English Agency Japan Ltd, Tokyo
Korea: EYA, Seoul
Poland: Graal Ltd, Warsaw
Russia: Alexander Korzhenevski Literary Agency, Moscow
Spain: Julio F Yañez Literary Agency, Barcelona

4069

*NEW AUTHORS SHOWCASE
Rivendell, Kingsgate Close, Torquay TQ2 8QA
Telephone: 01803 326617
Email: mail@newauthors.org.uk
Web Site: www.newauthors.org.uk

Proprietor: Barrie James

Specialization: the UK's first Internet site for displaying new authors and poets to publishers. Most genres included. Established in August 1997 it now has in excess of 500 writers.

4070

NEW WRITING NORTH
Holy Jesus Hospital, City Road, Newcastle-upon-Tyne NE1 2AS
Telephone: 0191 233 3850
Email: claire@newwritingnorth.com
Web Site: www.newwritingnorth.com

Directors: Claire Malcolm
Anna Disley *(Deputy)*
Finance & Administration: Cath Robson
Marketing: Olivia Mantle

4071

NEW WRITING SOUTH
9 Jew Street, Brighton BN1 1UT
Telephone: 01273 735353
Email: admin@newwritingsouth.com
Web Site: www.newwritingsouth.com

Director: Chris Taylor
Manager: Mark Bryant
Education: Beth Miller

Specialization: nurturing and developing writers and encouraging a thriving new writing economy in the south.

4072

THE MAGGIE NOACH LITERARY AGENCY
7 Peacock Yard, Iliffe Street, London SE17 3LH
Telephone: (020) 7708 3073
Email: info@mnla.co.uk

All MSS except short stories, poetry, plays, screenplays, cookery, gardening, mind/ body/spirit, illustrated children's, scientific/ academic/specialist non-fiction. Absolutely no illustrated books.

Specialization: fiction, general non-fiction and children's books. No unsolicited manuscripts – submissions by arrangements only. Home 15%, USA & translation 20%.

Overseas Representation:
Worldwide: Jill Hughes, Aubourn, Lincs

4073

*ANDREW NURNBERG ASSOCIATES LTD
45-47 Clerkenwell Green, London EC1R 0QX
Telephone: (020) 7417 8800
Fax: (020) 7417 8812
Email: contact@nurnberg.co.uk
Web Site: www.andrewnurnberg.com

Directors: Andrew Nurnberg *(Managing)*
Sarah Nundy
Vicky Mark

Specialization: representing leading British & American agents & authors, as well as sale of translation rights throughout the world.

Associated Companies:
Bulgaria: Andrew Nurnberg Associates, Sofia
Czech Republic: Andrew Nurnberg Associates, Prague
Hungary: Andrew Nurnberg Associates, Budapest
Latvia: Andrew Nurnberg Associates, Baltic
P. R. of China: Andrew Nurnberg Literary Agency, Beijing
Poland: Andrew Nurnberg Associates, Warsaw
Russia: Andrew Nurnberg Literary Agency, Moscow

Taiwan: Andrew Nurnberg Literary Agency, Taipei

4074

DEBORAH OWEN LTD
78 Narrow Street, Limehouse, London E14 8BP
Telephone: (020) 7987 5119 & 5441
Fax: (020) 7538 4004
Email: do@deborahowen.co.uk

Literary Agent: Deborah Owen

Specialization: small agency representing Amos Oz and Delia Smith. No new authors.

4075

PATERSON MARSH LTD
50 Albemarle Street, London W1S 4BD
Telephone: (020) 7493 4361
Fax: (020) 7495 8961
Email: paterson@patersonmarsh.co.uk
Web Site: www.patersonmarsh.co.uk

Managing Director: Paul Marsh
Consultant: Mark Paterson
Agent: Stephanie Ebdon

All MSS except fiction, children's, poetry, drama, TV, film & radio.

Specialization: professional psychology, psychoanalysis, psychotherapy, general non-fiction. Preliminary letter and return postage required.

Associated Companies:
UK: Sigmund Freud Copyrights

Rights Representative in UK for:
UK: Sigmund Freud Copyrights, London; Hammersmith Press, London; New Library of Psychoanalysis, London
USA: The Analytic Press, New York, NY; International Universities Press, Madison, CT; Other Press LLC, New York, NY; Pitchstone Publishing, Los Angeles, CA; Routledge US, New York, NY; Zeig, Tucker & Theisen Inc, Redding, CT

4076

JOHN PAWSEY
8 Snowshill Court, Giffard Park, Milton Keynes, Bucks MK14 5QG
Telephone: 01908 217179

Sole Proprietor: John Pawsey

All MSS except fiction, poetry, short stories, journalism, children's, original film & stage scripts.

Specialization: sport, popular culture.

Rights Representative in UK for:
USA: Alison J. Picard, Cotuit, MA; Bobbe Siegel, New York, NY

Overseas Representation:
France: Lora Fountain Associates, Paris
Germany: Thomas Schlück Literary Agency, Garbsen
Hungary: Lex Copyright, Budapest
Italy: Living Literary Agency, Milan
Japan: The English Agency Japan Ltd, Tokyo
Korea: Korea Copyright Center, Seoul
Netherlands: International Literatur Bureau BV, Hilversum
Russia: Prava i Prevodi RAO, Moscow
Scandinavia: Sane Töregård Agency, Karlshamn
Spain & South America: International Editors Co, Barcelona
USA: Alison J. Picard, Cotuit, MA
Yugoslav States: Prava i Prevodi, Belgrade

4077

POLLINGER LTD AUTHORS' AGENTS
9 Staple Inn, Holborn, London WC1V 7QH
Telephone: (020) 7404 0342
Fax: (020) 7242 5737
Email: info@pollingerltd
Web Site: www.pollingerltd.com

Directors: Lesley Pollinger *(Managing)*
Leigh Pollinger
Literary Agents: Joanna Devereux
Tim Bates
Hayley Yeeles *(Rights)*
Film & TV Agent: Ruth Needham
Company Secretary: John Furzer

All MSS except poetry & articles – see website for submission details.

Specialization: adult fiction and non-fiction, children's and literary estates.

Associated Companies:
Laurence Pollinger Ltd

Rights Representative in UK for:
UK: Accent Press; Wallflower Press, London
UK (dramatic rights): Summersdale
USA: New Directions Publishing Corporation, New York, NY

Overseas Representation:
China: Big Apple Tuttle-Mori Agency, Taipei
Denmark, Finland, Norway & Sweden: Licht & Burr Literary Agency, Copenhagen
France: Michelle Lapautre Agency, Paris
Germany & Switzerland: Mohrbooks Literary Agency, Zurich
Greece: Read n Right Agency, Cahlkida
Hungary: Lex Copyright, Budapest
Israel: The Book Publishers Association of Israel, Tel Aviv
Japan: Tuttle-Mori Agency Inc, Tokyo
Korea: The Eric Yang Agency, Seoul
Portugal & Brazil: Ilidio da Fonseca Matos, Lisbon
Spain & South America: Carmen Balcells Agencia Literaria SA, Barcelona
Turkey: ONK Agency Ltd, Istanbul
Yugoslav States, Bulgaria, Poland, Czech/ Slovak Rep., Russia & Romania: Prava i Prevodi, Belgrade

4078

SHELLEY POWER LITERARY AGENCY LTD
13 rue du Pré Saint Gervais, 75019 Paris, France
Telephone: +33 1 42 38 36 49
Fax: +33 1 40 40 70 08
Email: shelley.power@wanadoo.fr

Director, Literary Agent: Shelley Power

All MSS except children's books, poetry, plays or film scripts. No horror, science fiction or fantasy.

Specialization: literary agency.

Rights Representative in UK for:
USA: The Feminist Press, New York, NY

Overseas Representation:
China: Big Apple Tuttle-Mori Agency Inc, Shanghai; Big Apple Tuttle-Mori Agency, Taipei
Czech Republic: Transnet Contracts
France: Lora Fountain Associates, Paris
Germany: Liepman AG
Greece: JLM Literary Agency, Athens
Hungary: Kàtai & Bolza Literary Agents, Budapest
Israel: Ilana Pikarski Literary Agency, Tel Aviv
Italy: Natoli, Stefan & Oliva Agenzia Letteraria, Milan
Japan: The English Agency Japan Ltd, Tokyo
Korea: The Eric Yang Agency, Seoul
Poland: Graal Ltd, Warsaw

Romania: Simona Kessler International Copyright Agency Ltd, Bucharest
Scandinavia: Licht & Burr Literary Agency, Copenhagen
Spain: Julio F Yañez Literary Agency, Barcelona

4079

REAL CREATIVES WORLDWIDE (RCW)
14 Dean Street, London W1D 3RS
Telephone: (020) 7437 4188
Email: malcolm.rasala@realcreatives.com
Web Site: www.realcreatives.com

Chief Executive Officer: M. Rasala
COO: M. Maco
Sales: Natasha Ganea

Specialization: literary agency for books; film agent for motion pictures (recognized agent in Hollywood); TV agent for TV programmes worldwide; advertiser - supply TV programme agents; agent representing 200 professionals (directors, producers, creatives, etc.) in the motion picture, TV and advertising industries, 120 professors (Harvard, Yale, MIT, Stanford, Oxford, etc.).

Associated Companies:
USA: www.tvmyworld.com

Overseas Representation:
Italy: Marco Fichera, Rome

4080

REDHAMMER MANAGEMENT LTD
186 Bickenhall Mansions, London W1U 6BX
Telephone: (020) 7486 3465
Fax: (020) 7000 1249
Web Site: www.redhammer.info

Chief Executive Officer: Peter Cox

Specialization: rights representation, including literary and publishing, film and TV; merchandising. The company has a small number of successful clients who wish to accelerate the momentum of their success. Currently published writers can visit our website if they would like more information; if you have not yet been published, your submission will be considered if you follow the Submissions Procedure.

4081

*ROBINSON LITERARY AGENCY LTD
Block A511, The Jam Factory, 27 Green Walk, London SE1 4TT
Telephone: (020) 7096 1460
Email: info@rlabooks.co.uk
Web Site: www.rlabooks.co.uk

Managing Director: Peter Robinson
Agent: Sam Copeland

All MSS except lifestyle, cookery or gardening titles.

Specialization: all areas of fiction (general, crime, literary and children's), general non-fiction (history, biography, travel, current affairs, popular culture and humour). Aims to offer a bespoke service to clients across all media. In addition to handling book rights in all languages and territories, the agency also handles TV documentary rights and presenters, film rights and merchandising. It believes in establishing long-term relations with clients and nurturing writers' careers over many years. It will offer editorial advice where appropriate and is active in seeking out new talent. Represents a broad range of authors and clients from internationally bestselling novelists to academic historians and award-

winning children's writers. Works in association with specialist film agents, Sayle Screen Ltd, for the handling of film and theatre rights. Commission: 15% home, 20% overseas. Established in 2005.

Overseas Representation:
All translation markets: Rogers, Coleridge & White Ltd, London
USA: Fletcher & Parry, New York, NY; Inkwell Management, New York, NY

4082

ROGERS, COLERIDGE & WHITE LTD
20 Powis Mews, London W11 1JN
Telephone: (020) 7221 3717
Fax: (020) 7229 9084
Web Site: www.rcwlitagency.com

Chairman: Deborah Rogers
Directors: Peter Straus *(Managing)*
Gill Coleridge
Patricia White
David Miller
Laurence Laluyaux *(Foreign Rights)*
Stephen Edwards *(Foreign Rights)*
Zoe Waldie
Peter Robinson
Agents: Hannah Westland
Catherine Pellegrino *(Children's)*
Sam Copeland

All MSS except screenplays, plays or technical books. No unsolicited MSS, please and no submissions by e-mail.

Specialization: handles fiction, non-fiction and children's books. Literary agency. Founded 1967. Rights representative in UK and translation for several New York agents. Commission: Home 15%; US & translation 20%.

Associated Companies:
UK: Robinson Literary Agency

4083

THE SAYLE LITERARY AGENCY
1 Petersfield, Cambridge CB1 1BB
Telephone: 01223 303035
Fax: 01223 301638
Web Site: www.sayleliteraryagency.com

Proprietor: Rachel Calder

All MSS except children's, poetry, technical.

Specialization: fiction (literary & crime), biography, history, current affairs, travel, social issues.

Rights Representative in UK for:
USA: Darhansoff Verrill Feldman Literary Agency, New York, NY; New England Publishing Associates, CT

Overseas Representation:
Europe & Rest of the World: The Marsh Agency, London
USA: Dunow, Carlson & Lerner Agency, New York, NY

4084

CAROLINE SHELDON LITERARY AGENCY
71 Hillgate Place, London W8 7SS
Telephone: (020) 7727 9102
Email: carolinesheldon@carolinesheldon.co.uk & pennyholroyde@carolinesheldon.co.uk
Web Site: www.carolinesheldon.co.uk & www.carolinesheldonillustrators.co.uk

Literary Agents: Caroline Sheldon
Penny Holroyde

All MSS except short stories.

Specialization: fiction, women's fiction & children's books, human interest non-fiction.

4085

DORIE SIMMONDS LITERARY AGENCY
Riverbank House,
1 Putney Bridge Approach, London
SW6 3JD
Telephone: (020) 7736 0002
Fax: (020) 7736 0010
Email: dorie@doriesimmonds.com

Proprietor: Dorie Simmonds
Rights Executive: Frances Lubbe

All MSS except plays, poetry or short stories.

Specialization: commercial fiction and non-fiction in both the adult and children's markets.

4086

JEFFREY SIMMONS
15 Penn House, Mallory Street, London
NW8 8SX
Telephone: (020) 7224 8917
Email: jasimmons@unicombox.co.uk

All MSS except children's books, cookery, science-fiction, romances & some specialist subjects.

Specialization: biography & memoirs; cinema, drama & the arts; general fiction; history; law & crime; literature; politics & world affairs.

Overseas Representation:
Japan: The English Agency Japan Ltd, Tokyo
Spain: Julio F Yañez Literary Agency, Barcelona

4087

SINCLAIR-STEVENSON
3 South Terrace, London SW7 2TB
Telephone: (020) 7581 2550
Fax: (020) 7581 2550

Translation Rights:
c/o David Higham Associates Ltd,
5–8 Lower John Street, Golden Square,
London W1F 9HA

All MSS except children's books, science fiction, science, fantasy, film or play scripts.

Specialization: non-fiction – biography and autobiography, the arts, politics and current affairs, travel, history; and fiction.

Rights Representative in UK for:
USA: T. C. Wallace Ltd, New York, NY

Overseas Representation:
USA: T. C. Wallace Ltd, New York, NY

4088

ROBERT SMITH LITERARY AGENCY LTD
12 Bridge Wharf, 156 Caledonian Road,
London N1 9UU
Telephone: (020) 7278 2444
Fax: (020) 7833 5680
Email:
robertsmith.literaryagency@virgin.net

Directors: Robert Smith *(Managing)*
Anne Smith

All MSS except fiction, poetry, children's books or reference. Writers may submit synopses but no unsolicited manuscripts.

Specialization: the agency sells books, series and articles to book publishers, newspapers and magazines across the world. It operates

only in non-fiction. Main areas are autobiography and biography, show business, hot topics, history, health, lifestyle and true crime.

Overseas Representation:
Germany: Thomas Schlück Literary Agency, Garbsen
Italy: Natoli, Stefan & Oliva Agenzia Letteraria, Milan
Spain: RDC Agencia Literaria, Madrid

4089

SHIRLEY STEWART LITERARY AGENCY
3rd Floor, 4a Nelson Road, London
SE10 9JB
Telephone: (020) 8293 3000

Director: Shirley Stewart

All MSS except children's books, poetry, plays, science fiction and fantasy.

Specialization: full-length MSS only. Fiction and non-fiction (home 10–15%, overseas 20%). No reading fee but preliminary letter and return postage essential.

Rights Representative in UK for:
USA: Curtis Brown Ltd, New York, NY

4090

THE SUSIJN AGENCY LTD
3rd Floor, 64 Great Titchfield Street,
London W1W 7QH
Telephone: (020) 7580 6341
Fax: (020) 7580 8626
Email: info@thesusijnagency.com
Web Site: www.thesusijnagency.com

Literary Agents: Laura Susijn
Nicola Barr

All MSS except children's books, sci-fi, romantic fiction, fantasy, sagas, self-help, business, military and computer books.

Specialization: selling rights world-wide in literary fiction and non-fiction. Also represents non-English language publishers and authors for UK, US and translation rights world-wide. Particularly interested in literature from mixed cultural background. Deals direct, using sub-agent in Eastern Europe, Israel and the Far East. Preliminary letter, synopsis and first two chapters preferred. No reading fee.

4091

THE TENNYSON AGENCY
10 Cleveland Avenue, London SW20 9EW
Telephone: (020) 8543 5939
Email: submissions@tenagy.co.uk
Web Site: www.tenagy.co.uk

Partner: Adam Sheldon

All MSS except poetry, short stories, science fiction, popular romantic and historical fiction, children's books and non-fiction unrelated to the arts.

Specialization: writing for the theatre, TV, radio and film. Related subjects and literary fiction are considered on an ad hoc basis. Commission rates: literature: 12.5%, drama: 15%, overseas: 20%. Submissions by post, on invitation, following introductory letter. Full details on the agency's website.

4092

J. M. THURLEY MANAGEMENT
Archery House, 33 Archery Square, Walmer,
Deal CT14 7AY
Telephone: 01304 371721
Fax: 01304 371416

Email: jmthurley@aol.com
Web Site: www.thecuttingedge.biz

Contacts: Jon Thurley
Patricia Preece

All MSS except short stories & poetry.

Specialization: will give editorial help by arrangement on all types of projects.

4093

LAVINIA TREVOR
29 Addison Place, London W11 4RJ
Telephone: (020) 7603 5254
Fax: 0870 129 0838
Web Site: www.laviniatrevor.co.uk

Agent: Lavinia Trevor

Specialization: fiction and non-fiction for the general trade market (see website). No unsolicited material.

4094

JANE TURNBULL AGENCY
58 Elgin Crescent, London W11 2JJ
Telephone: (020) 7727 9409
Web Site: www.janeturnbull.co.uk

Mailing Address:
Barn Cottage, Veryan, Truro, Cornwall
TR2 5QA
Telephone: 01872 501317

Proprietor: Jane Turnbull

All MSS except science or romantic fiction, children's fiction, poetry or plays.

Specialization: literary fiction, current affairs, biography, design, lifestyle, health, TV tie-ins, humour, natural history. Initial letter essential; no unsolicited MSS. Commission 15% home sales, 20% US, 20% translation, 15% radio/TV/film. Founded 1986, member of the Association of Authors' Agents.

Overseas Representation:
Worldwide: Aitken Alexander Associates, London

4095

UNITED AGENTS LTD
12–26 Lexington Street, London W1F 0LE
Telephone: (020) 3214 0800
Fax: (020) 3214 0801
Web Site: www.unitedagents.co.uk

Joint Heads, Books Department: Simon Trewin
Caroline Dawnay
Agents: Sarah Ballard
Rosemary Canter
James Gill
Robert Kirby
Rosemary Scoular
Charles Walker
Anna Webber
Jessica Craig *(Foreign Rights)*
Jane Willis *(Foreign Rights)*
Sara Starbuck *(Audio & Straight Reading Rights)*

Specialization: literary and talent agency, operating across books, theatre, film, TV and commercials. Offers a full service to its client base and is always interested in new clients. Please consult wrbsite at www.unitedagents.co.uk for full submission guidelines.

4096

ED VICTOR LTD
6 Bayley Street, Bedford Square, London
WC1B 3HE
Telephone: (020) 7304 4100

Fax: (020) 7304 4111
Email: mary@edvictor.com

Directors: Ed Victor *(Executive Chairman)*
Margaret Phillips *(Joint Managing)*
Sophie Hicks *(Foreign Rights & Joint Managing)*
Leon Morgan
Carol Ryan
Graham Greene CBE
Hitesh Shah

All MSS except short stories; poetry; technical.

Specialization: fiction, non-fiction, biography, children's books.

4097

*WADE & DOHERTY LITERARY AGENCY LTD
33 Cormorant Lodge, Thomas More Street,
London E1W 1AU
Telephone: (020) 7488 4171
Fax: (020) 7488 4172
Email: rw@rwla.com
Web Site: www.rwla.com

Partner: Broo Doherty

All MSS except scripts, poetry, plays or short stories.

Specialization: handles general fiction and non-fiction including children's books. Send detailed synopsis and first 10,000 words by e-mail. No reading fee. Commission: home 10%, overseas and translation 20% (fees negotiable if a contract has already been offered). Founded 2001.

4098

WATSON, LITTLE LTD
48–56 Bayham Place, London NW1 0EU
Telephone: (020) 7388 7529
Fax: (020) 7388 8501
Email: office@watsonlittle.com
Web Site: www.watsonlittle.com

Directors: Mandy Little *(Managing)*
James Wills *(Senior Agent)*
Literary Agent: Sally Anne Sweeney

All MSS except short stories, plays, poetry, works for very small children & articles (except by established columnists).

Specialization: literary and commercial fiction, serious non-fiction, psychology, self-help, popular culture, celebrity, health, sport, humour, children's.

Rights Representative in UK for:
USA (children's): The Chudney Agency, New York, NY

Overseas Representation:
USA (adult): Howard Morhaim Literary Agency, New York, NY
USA (children's): The Chudney Agency, New York, NY
Worldwide: The Marsh Agency, London
Worldwide (film & TV associates): MBA Literary Agents, London; The Sharland Organisation, Raunds, Northants

4099

A. P. WATT LTD
20 John Street, London WC1N 2DR
Telephone: (020) 7405 6774
Fax: (020) 7831 2154
Email: apw@apwatt.co.uk
Web Site: www.apwatt.co.uk

Directors: Caradoc King
Linda Shaughnessy
Derek Johns
Georgia Garrett

Natasha Fairweather
Rob Kraitt *(Associate)*

All MSS except poetry.

Specialization: general fiction and non-fiction. No unsolicited manuscripts.

4100

JOSEF WEINBERGER PLAYS LTD

[formerly Warner/Chappell Plays Ltd]
12–14 Mortimer Street, London W1T 3JJ
Telephone: (020) 7580 2827
Fax: (020) 7436 9616
Email: general.info@jwmail.co.uk
Web Site: www.josef-weinberger.com

Manager: Michael Callahan

Specialization: stage plays. Works in conjunction with overseas agents. No unsolicited manuscripts, preliminary letter essential.

Parent Company:
UK: Josef Weinberger Ltd

Rights Representative in UK for:
USA: Dramatists Play Service Inc, New York, NY

Overseas Representation:
Australia: Hal Leonard (Australia) Ltd, Melbourne, Vic
Canada & USA: Dramatists Play Service Inc, New York, NY
New Zealand: Play Bureau (NZ) Ltd, New Plymouth
South Africa: Dalro (Pty) Ltd, Johannesburg
Zimbabwe: National Theatre Organization, Harare

4101

EVE WHITE LITERARY AGENT

1a High Street, Kintbury, Berks RG17 9TJ
Telephone: 01488 657656
Fax: 01488 657656
Email: eve@evewhite.co.uk
Web Site: www.evewhite.co.uk

Director: Eve White

Specialization: UK agency representing internationally published authors of commercial and literary fiction and non-fiction, children's fiction and picture books. The company does not represent poets and screen writers. Foreign rights handled in conjunction with Diana Mackay at Melcombe International Ltd. Authors should refer to our website for submission

requirements. Clients include: Rae Earl, Tim Clark, Chris Pascoe, Alexander Stobbs, Ruth Saberton, Vijay Medtia & Shanta Everington. Children's authors: Andy Stanton, Jimmy Docherty, Susannah Corbett, Gillian Rogerson, David Flavell, Kate Maryon, Carolyn Ching, Rachael Mortimer, Tracey Corderoy & Abie Longstaff.

Overseas Representation:
Commonwealth countries & USA: Eve White, Kintbury
Worldwide (excluding Commonwealth countries & USA): Melcombe International, Somerset

4102

DINAH WIENER LTD

12 Cornwall Grove, London W4 2LB
Telephone: (020) 8994 6011
Fax: (020) 8994 6044

Directors: Dinah Wiener
   D. P. Wiener
   B. M. Wiener

All MSS except juvenile, plays, film scripts, poetry & short stories.

Specialization: general fiction and non-fiction.

4103

JONATHAN WILLIAMS LITERARY AGENCY

Rosney Mews, Upper Glenageary Road, Glenageary, Co Dublin, Republic of Ireland
Telephone: +353 (01) 280 3482
Fax: +353 (01) 280 3482

Director: Jonathan Williams

All MSS except plays or film scripts. Return postage and packing is appreciated. Irish postage stamps or international postal coupons, please.

Specialization: typescripts of Irish interest.

Overseas Representation:
Italy: Agenzia Piergiorgio Nicolazzini, Milan
Japan: Tuttle-Mori Agency Inc, Tokyo
Netherlands & Germany: International Literatuur Bureau, Amsterdam
Spain & Spanish-speaking Latin America: Antonia Kerrigan Literary Agency, Barcelona

5 Trade & Allied Associations

5.1 INTERNATIONAL

5001

ENGLISH-SPEAKING UNION OF THE COMMONWEALTH
37 Charles Street, London W1J 5ED
Telephone: (020) 7529 1550
Fax: (020) 7495 6108
Email: esu@esu.org
Web Site: www.esu.org

President: HRH The Duke of Edinburgh KG, KT, OM
Chairman: The Lord Hunt of the Wirral MBE, PC
Director General: Mrs Valerie Mitchell OBE

The English-Speaking Union is an international organization represented in 59 countries and with headquarters in London and New York. It is a registered charity with the aim of promoting international friendship and understanding through the English language.

The ESU runs several awards: the Duke of Edinburgh English Language Book Award, the President's Award for the best non-book language materials, the Marsh Biography Award and the Marsh Children's Literature in Translation Award.

5002

*FEDERATION OF EUROPEAN PUBLISHERS
31 rue Montoyer, Box 8, 1000 Brussels, Belgium
Telephone: +32 (02) 770 11 10
Fax: +32 (02) 771 20 71
Email: info@fep-fee.eu
Web Site: www.fep-fee.eu

Director: Ms Anne Bergman-Tahon
Legal Advisor: Ms Olga Martin Sancho

Lobbying European institutions on behalf of the European publishing community.

5003

IBBY – INTERNATIONAL BOARD ON BOOKS FOR YOUNG PEOPLE
Nonnenweg 12, Postfach, 4003 Basel, Switzerland
Telephone: +41 ((0)61) 272 29 17
Fax: +41 ((0)61) 272 27 57
Email: forest.zhang@ibby.org
Web Site: www.ibby.org

Executive Director: Elizabeth Page
President of the Executive Committee: Patricia Aldama
Deputy Director of Administration: Forest Zhang

Promotion of children's books and reading worldwide.

5004

PRIVATE LIBRARIES ASSOCIATION
Ravelston, South View Road, Pinner, Middx HA5 3YD
Email: dchambrs@aol.com
Web Site: www.plabooks.org

Hon President: Keith Fletcher
Hon Secretary: Stan Brett
Hon Editor & Hon Publications Secretary: David Chambers
Hon Treasurer: Dean A. Sewell

An international society of book collectors, run on a voluntary basis. Publications include a quarterly journal and *The Exchange List*, which circulate among member collectors throughout the world, *Private Press Books*, an annual bibliography, and other books concerned with book collecting.
5.2 United Kingdom & Republic of Ireland

5.2 UNITED KINGDOM & REPUBLIC OF IRELAND

5005

YR ACADEMI GYMREIG
Mount Stuart House, Mount Stuart Square, Cardiff CF10 5FQ
Telephone: (029) 2047 2266
Fax: (029) 2049 2930
Email: post@academi.org
Web Site: www.academi.org

Glyn Jones Centre for Writers:
Wales Millennium Centre, Bute Place, Cardiff CF10 5AL
Telephone: (as above)
Fax: (029) 2047 0691
Email: (as above)
Web Site: (as above)

Chief Executive: Peter Finch
Deputy: Lleucu Siencyn

Founded in 1959, Yr Academi Gymreig / The Welsh Academy is the national society which promotes the writers and literatures of Wales. The Academi runs courses, competitions (including the Cardiff International Poetry Competition), conferences, tours by authors, international exchanges, events for schools, readings, literary performances and festivals. The Academi also offers advice to authors, a writers' critical and mentoring service and financial bursaries, and runs the annual Book of the Year Award. It works in partnership with Tŷ Newydd, the Criccieth-based residential writers' centre.

Publications include *A470*; *Taliesin*, a quarterly literary journal in the Welsh language; *The Oxford Companion to the Literature of Wales*; *The Welsh Academy English-Welsh Dictionary*; *The Welsh Academy Encyclopaedia of Wales* published with the support of the Lottery, and a variety of translated works.

In 2004 Academi became a resident at the Wales Millennium Centre. The Glyn Jones Centre for Writers opened in 2005.

5006

ACADEMIC AND PROFESSIONAL DIVISION OF THE PUBLISHERS ASSOCIATION
29B Montague Street, London WC1B 5BW
Telephone: (020) 7691 9191

Fax: (020) 7691 9199
Email: gtaylor@publishers.org.uk
Web Site: www.publishers.org.uk

Director: Graham Taylor

Parent Company:
UK: The Publishers Association

The Academic and Professional Division of The Publishers Association represents the interests of publishers serving higher education, scholarly communication and the professional and commercial market. Collective activities are organized on their behalf. Membership is open to any publisher in membership of the Publishers Association who produces books, journals or similar published material for these markets.

5007

ALLIANCE OF LITERARY SOCIETIES (ALS)
59 Bryony Road, Selly Oak, Birmingham B29 4BY
Telephone: 0121 475 1805
Email: l.j.curry@bham.ac.uk
Web Site: www.allianceofliterarysocieties.org.uk

Chair: Linda J. Curry
Hon Treasurer / Membership Secretary: Julie Shorland
Secretary: Anita Fernandez-Young

The ALS is an umbrella organization for literary societies/groups within the UK. The AGM is hosted by different member societies each year, with accompanying talks etc covering a weekend (usually in April or May). Members of affiliated societies are welcome to attend but only the delegate of the affiliated society may have a vote. Details are on the website – including subscription rates. An annual journal (*ALSo...*) is also produced. This is freely available to member societies but can be purchased by non-members.

5008

ARTS COUNCIL ENGLAND
14 Great Peter Street, London SW1P 3NQ
Telephone: 0845 300 6200
Fax: (020) 7973 6590
Email: enquiries@artscouncil.org.uk
Web Site: www.artscouncil.org.uk

Chair: Dame Liz Forgan
Chief Executive: Alan Davey

Arts Council England is the national development agency for the arts in England, distributing public money from government and the national lottery.

Arts Council England's main funding programme is Grants for the arts. It is open to individuals, art organizations, national touring and other people who use the arts in their work. The grants are for activities that benefit people in England or that help artists and arts organizations from England to carry out their work.

Arts Council England has one national and nine regional offices. Founded in 1946.

5009

ASSOCIATION OF AUTHORS' AGENTS
c/o Watson, Little, 48–56 Bayham Place, London NW1 0EU
Email: jw@watsonlittle.com
Web Site: www.agentsassoc.co.uk

President: Philippa Milnes-Smith
Vice-President: Anthony Goff
Treasurer: Anna Davis
Secretary: James Wills

Founded in 1974 to institute and maintain a code of professional behaviour, to discuss matters of common professional interest and to provide a vehicle for representing the view of authors' agents in discussions on matters of common interest with other professional bodies.

5010

ASSOCIATION OF FREELANCE EDITORS, PROOFREADERS & INDEXERS (IRELAND)
11 Clonard Road, Sandyford, Dublin 16, Republic of Ireland
Telephone: +353 (0)1 295 2194 & (0)58 48458
Email: poweredting@eircom.net &
Brenda@ohanlonmedia.com
Web Site: www.afepi.ie

Co-Chair: Winifred Power
Brenda O'Hanlon

The AFEPI was established to provide information to publishers on Irish freelancers working in this field, and to protect the interests of those freelancers. Membership is restricted to freelancers with experience and/or references, but skills of members are not tested or evaluated.

5011

ASSOCIATION OF ILLUSTRATORS
2nd Floor Back Building, 150 Curtain Road, London
EC2A 3AT
Telephone: (020) 7613 4328
Fax: (020) 7613 4417
Email: info@theaoi.com
Web Site: www.theaoi.com

Managing Director: Ramon Blomfield
Managers: Derek Brazell (Special Projects)
Ian Veacock (Finance Officer)
Jareh Das (Events & Marketing Co-ordinator)
Nicolette Hamilton (Membership Co-ordinator)
Becky Brown (Membership Co-ordinator)

Established in 1973 to advance and protect illustrators' rights, the AOI is a non-profit making trade association dedicated to its members' professional interest and the promotion of illustration.
    Corporate members (agents and clients) receive free copy of the *Images Annual*, discounts on events, publications and our Images competition entry, plus *Varoom* – the journal of illustration and made images, published three times per year.

5012

ASSOCIATION OF LEARNED & PROFESSIONAL SOCIETY PUBLISHERS
1 Abbey Cottages, The Green, Sutton Courtenay, Oxon
OX14 4AF
Telephone: 01235 847776 & 0796 850 4763 (mobile)
Fax: 0870 706 0332
Email: ian.russell@alpsp.org
Web Site: www.alpsp.org

Chief Operating Officer:
Nick Evans, 9 Stanbridge Road, Putney, London SW15 1DX
Telephone: (020) 8789 2394
Fax: (020) 8789 2394
Email: nick.evans@alpsp.org
Web Site: www.alpsp.org

Chief Executive: Ian Russell
Managers: Nick Evans (Chief Operating Officer)
Ian Hunter (Finance & Administration)
Co-ordinators: Lesley Ogg (Events)
Amanda Whiting (Training)
Suzy Fotheringham (Marketing & Membership)
Dee French (Administration)
Editor: Alan Singleton (Editor-in-Chief, Learned Publishing)
North American Executive Director: Isabel Czech
Training Administrator: Barbara Holmes

ALPSP is an international trade association for the community of not-for-profit publishers and those who work with them to disseminate academic and professional information; it was founded in 1972, and currently has over 350 members in more than 40 countries. ALPSP carries out research and other projects, monitors national and international issues and represents members' interests to the wider world. The Association provides co-operative services such as the ALPSP Learned Journals Collection. It also offers an extensive programme of courses and seminars, an informative website (www.alpsp.org), a quarterly journal, *Learned Publishing*, and a monthly electronic newsletter, *ALPSP Alert*.

5013

ASSOCIATION OF ONLINE PUBLISHERS (AOP)
Queens House, 28 Kingsway, London WC2B 6JR
Telephone: (020) 7400 7510
Fax: (020) 7404 4167
Email: info@ukaop.org.uk
Web Site: www.ukaop.org.uk

Directors: Ruth Brownlee
Rebecca Winfied (Finance – Periodical Publishers
    Association)
Website & Database Manager: Ron Nussey
Events & Marketing Executive: Tilly Martin
Head of Research & Insights: Tim Cain

Parent Company:
UK: Periodical Publishers Association

The UK Association of Online Publishers (AOP) is an industry body representing online publishing companies that create original, branded, quality content. AOP champions the interests of approximately 160 publishing companies from diverse backgrounds including newspaper and magazine publishing, TV and radio broadcasting, and pure online media.
    AOP presents a unified voice to industry and Government, specifically to address issues and concerns relating to all areas of online publishing. AOP publishes original research and hosts forums, awards and conferences, covering a range of topics from paid-for-content, subscription models and data protection, through to copyright, content management, new technologies and audience measurement.
    The primary mission of UK AOP is to drive standards and revenue across all areas of online publishing to raise the credibility and profile of the industry.

5014

*ASSOCIATION OF SUBSCRIPTION AGENTS AND INTERMEDIARIES
10 Lime Avenue, High Wycombe HP11 1DP
Telephone: 01494 534778
Email: rollo.turner@dsl.pipex.com
Web Site: www.subscription-agents.org

Chief Executive Officer: Rollo Turner (Secretary General)

Represents the interests of subscription agents and intermediaries who supply periodicals and related material in both paper and electronic form to libraries, companies and individuals worldwide.

5015

AUDIOBOOK PUBLISHING ASSOCIATION
[formerly SWPA]
Telephone: 07531 902975
Email: info@theapa.net
Web Site: www.theapa.net

Administrator: Laura Briscall
Chair: Alison Muirden
Vice-Chair: Zoe Howes

The UK association for the audiobook industry, formerly the Spoken Word Publishing Association. Its broad membership covers all those involved in spoken word audio, one of the fastest-growing areas in publishing.

5016

AUTHORS' FOUNDATION
84 Drayton Gardens, London SW10 9SB
Telephone: (020) 7373 6642
Fax: (020) 7373 5768
Email: info@societyofauthors.org
Web Site: www.societyofauthors.org

Trustees: Lady Antonia Fraser
Michael Holroyd
Simon Brett
Secretary: Mark Le Fanu

Founded in 1984 to mark the centenary of the Society of Authors, the Foundation offers grants to published writers who need additional funding for research, travel, etc. Open to fiction, poetry and non-fiction. The Foundation incorporates the Phoenix Trust. Closing dates for applications: 30 April and 30 September.

5017

AUTHORS' LICENSING & COLLECTING SOCIETY (ALCS)
The Writers' House, 13 Haydon Street, London EC3N 1DB
Telephone: (020) 7264 5700
Email: alcs@alcs.co.uk
Web Site: www.alcs.co.uk

Chief Executive: Owen Atkinson
Deputy Chief Executive: Barbara Hayes
Communications Officer: Alison Baxter

The Authors' Licensing & Collecting Society is the UK collective rights management society for writers of all genres. Members grant to the Society the right to administer on their behalf those rights which an author is unable to exercise as an individual or which are best handled on a collective basis. These include photocopying, rental and lending right, off-air and private recording, electronic rights, broadcast rights for BBC Prime and BBC World Service TV, cable retransmission and rights for the public reception of broadcasts. Membership costs a one-off lifetime fee of £25. Please contact the Society for further information. The ALCS administers these rights in the UK and Northern Ireland. Under reciprocal arrangements with foreign collecting societies other territories are also covered. Distributions to members are made bi-annually. For advice and further information please contact the ALCS office or click www.alcs.co.uk.

5018

BAPLA (BRITISH ASSOCIATION OF PICTURE LIBRARIES AND AGENCIES)
18 Vine Hill, London EC1R 5DZ
Telephone: (020) 7713 1780
Fax: (020) 7713 1211
Email: enquiries@bapla.org.uk
Web Site: www.bapla.org.uk

Picture Buyers' Fair:
18 Vine Hill, London EC1R 5DZ
Telephone: (020) 7713 1780
Fax: (020) 7713 1211
Email: pbf@bapla.org.uk
Web Site: www.pbf.org.uk

Executive Director: Simon Cliffe
Association Administrator: Damalie Nakalema
Membership & Communications Manager: Susanne
Kittlinger

The British Association of Picture Libraries and Agencies, or BAPLA, is the trade association for picture libraries in the UK and one of the largest organizations of its kind in the world. With over 380 member companies, it represents the vast majority of commercial picture libraries and agencies in the UK. Please see the website for details: www.bapla.org.uk

5019

THE BIBLIOGRAPHICAL SOCIETY
c/o Institute of English Studies, Senate House, Malet Street, London WC1E 7HU
Telephone: (020) 7862 8679
Fax: (020) 7862 8720
Email: admin@bibsoc.org.uk
Web Site: www.bibsoc.org.uk

Hon Secretary: Margaret Ford

The Bibliographical Society promotes the study of historical, analytical, descriptive and textual bibliography. It publishes its own journal, *The Library*, and supports a publishing programme of books and monographs on bibliographical subjects.

5020

BOOK AID INTERNATIONAL
39–41 Coldharbour Lane, Camberwell, London SE5 9NR
Telephone: (020) 7733 3577
Fax: (020) 7978 8006
Email: info@bookaid.org
Web Site: www.bookaid.org

Patron: HRH The Duke of Edinburgh KG, KT, OM
Chair: James Arnold Baker
Director: Clive Nettleton

Book Aid International is the major UK support for libraries in sub-Saharan Africa. It is a cost-effective agency that believes in people's potential for self-development and transformation through learning – and that the development of human capacity is essential for escaping poverty. Support for the long-term development of the local book trade is a high priority. The aim is that locally produced and culturally relevant books should be made available for readers in Africa and elsewhere.

Book Aid International works with partners that give the widest possible access to books and information, including public library services, community resource centres, universities, colleges, schools and non-governmental organizations. Carefully selected materials are made available to these organizations in 18 developing countries – most resources are targeted in 17 countries in sub-Saharan Africa; other programmes focus on Palestine.

Currently two-thirds of all donations come from UK publishers, taking advantage of the wealth of surplus runs, superseded editions and returns that exist in the publishing industry. The rest are given by schools, colleges, libraries and individuals.

For more information about how you can help Book Aid International please contact the Book Acquisitions Officer.

5021

BOOK INDUSTRY COMMUNICATION
39–41 North Road, London N7 9DP
Telephone: (020) 7607 9021
Fax: (020) 7607 0415
Email: info@bic.org.uk
Web Site: www.bic.org.uk

Chairman: Michael Holdsworth
Executive Director: Peter Kilborn

Book Industry Communication (BIC) is an independent organization set up and sponsored by the Publishers Association, Booksellers Association, the Chartered Institute of Library and Information Professionals and the British Library to promote supply chain efficiency in all sectors of the book world through e-commerce and the application of standard processes and procedures. Its subscribers include most of the UK's major publishers, booksellers and service providers.

5022

BOOKSELLERS ASSOCIATION OF THE UNITED KINGDOM & IRELAND LTD
Minster House, 272 Vauxhall Bridge Road, London SW1V 1BA
Telephone: (020) 7802 0802
Fax: (020) 7802 0803
Email: mail@booksellers.org.uk
Web Site: www.booksellers.org.uk

President: Sharon Murray
Chief Executive: Tim Godfray

Associated Companies:
UK: Batch.co.uk Ltd; Book Industry Communication Ltd; Book Tokens Ltd; Word Book Day Ltd

Founded in 1895. Represents over 4400 outlets. Promotes and looks after the interests of booksellers, helps booksellers become more efficient, fights for better distribution in the trade, helps booksellers increase sales and reduce costs and gives advice on opening and running a bookshop. Among other services, the Association produces catalogues for distribution throughout the retail trade at Christmas and directories of members, publishers and services.

5023

BOOKTRUST
Book House, 45 East Hill, London SW18 2QZ
Telephone: (020) 8516 2977
Fax: (020) 8516 2978

Email: query@booktrust.org.uk
Web Site: www.booktrust.org.uk

Patron: HRH the Prince Philip, Duke of Edinburgh
Chief Executive: Viv Bird

Booktrust is an independent national charity that encourages people of all ages and cultures to discover and enjoy reading.

5024

BRITISH ASSOCIATION OF COMMUNICATORS IN BUSINESS
Suite GA2, Oak House, Woodlands Business Park, Linford Wood, Milton Keynes MK14 6EY
Telephone: 01908 313755
Fax: 01908 313661
Email: enquiries@cib.uk.com
Web Site: www.cib.uk.com

Chief Executive: Kathie Jones

The Association aims to be the market leader for those involved in internal and corporate communications by providing professional, authoritative, dynamic, supportive and innovative services.

Membership is open to all individuals engaged in corporate communications. Major activities include the annual Communicators in Business Awards competition, an annual conference and a regular programme of educational and training events. Publications include *Communicators* magazine and *CiBNews*.

5025

BRITISH CENTRE FOR LITERARY TRANSLATION (BCLT)
University of East Anglia, Norwich NR4 7TJ
Telephone: 01603 592785
Fax: 01603 592737
Email: bclt@uea.ac.uk
Web Site: www.uea.ac.uk/bclt

Directors: Amanda Hopkinson
  Valerie Henitiuk *(Associate)*
Co-ordinator: Catherine Fuller

Parent Company:
UK: University of East Anglia

Raises the profile of literary translation and the professional development of literary translators. Organizes events, readings, workshops aimed at translators, professionals in arts and publishing and the general public.

5026

*BRITISH FANTASY SOCIETY
56 Leyton Road, Birmingham B21 9EE
Telephone: 07845 897760
Email: secretary@britishfantasysociety.org
Web Site: www.britishfantasysociety.org

President: Ramsey Campbell
Chairman: Marie O'Regan
Secretary & Treasurer: Vicky Cook
Editors: Stephen Theaker *(Dark Horizons)*
  Lee Harris *(Newsletter)*
  Andrew Hook *(New Horizons)*

Formed for devotees of fantasy, horror and related fields in literature, art and the cinema. Publications include *Prism* (quarterly), featuring news and reviews, and *Dark Horizons* and *New Horizons* (every six months alternating), featuring fiction and articles from new and established authors, plus other more occasional publications listing fiction and nonfiction of interest. There is a small press library and an annual convention, 'FantasyCon', which features the British Fantasy Awards sponsored by the Society. Please visit our website for full information. Membership fees: UK £30 (£45 joint); Europe £40 (£60 joint); Rest of World £55 (£80 joint).

5027

THE BRITISH GUILD OF TRAVEL WRITERS
26 Needham House, Woodberry Down, London N4 2TN
Telephone: (020) 8144 8713
Web Site: www.bgtw.org

Chair: Melissa Shales

The Guild has a membership of around 230, all professional journalists, broadcasters and photographers who derive the majority of their earnings from travel writing or broadcasting. Monthly meetings are devoted to discussion of travel topics, usually with outside speakers, and take place at a variety of venues. There is a monthly *Newsletter* for members. An annual year book giving full details of all members together with comprehensive lists of PRs and other contacts in the travel trade is available for purchase.

5028

BSI
389 Chiswick High Road, London W4 4AL
Telephone: (020) 8996 9000
Fax: (020) 8996 7553
Email: info@bsigroup.com
Web Site: www.bsigroup.com

Chairman: Sir David John
Directors: Clive Mosey *(Financial)*
  Vincent Cassidy *(Commercial)*
  Peter McKay *(Publishing)*
  Shirley Bailey-Wood *(Operations)*

Parent Company:
UK: BSI Group

BSI British Standards is a division of the BSI Group. BSI British Standards has a range of products and services (from guide books to online products) centred on standards (45,000 international standards), standardization and codes of practice for all industries, systems and technologies. BSI also offers customers a full range of training products, international technical assistance and private standardization services.

5029

BTBS THE BOOK TRADE CHARITY
The Foyle Centre, The Retreat, Kings Langley, Herts WD4 8LT
Telephone: 01923 263128
Fax: 01923 270732
Email: btbs@booktradecharity.demon.co.uk & david@btbs.org
Web Site: www.btbs.org.uk

Chairman: Jo Henry
Housing Manager, The Retreat: Jackie Bright
Chief Executive: David Hicks
Treasurer: Nigel Batt

The welfare charity of the book trade, offering support to colleagues in difficult personal circumstances.

BTBS gives direct financial support, regular and one-off, to individuals, to help with a wide range of problems.

Accommodation at The Retreat, Kings Langley, offers pre-retirement and retirement housing.

The book trade helpline (freephone 0808 100 2304) provides sympathetic, confidential help.

Anyone who has worked in the book trade (publishing, distribution, bookselling, etc. for more than one year, employed, self-employed or freelance) is eligible to apply for assistance.

5030

CHARTERED INSTITUTE OF JOURNALISTS
2 Dock Offices, Surrey Quays Road, London SE16 2XU
Telephone: (020) 7252 1187
Fax: (020) 7232 2302
Email: memberservices@cioj.co.uk
Web Site: www.cioj.co.uk

President: Liz Justice
Treasurer: Norman Bartlett
General Secretary: Dominic Cooper

The senior professional society of journalists worldwide. Incorporated by Royal Charter in 1890, it had its origin in the National Association of Journalists, which was founded in 1884 and converted into the Institute in 1889. Its primary object is 'the promotion by all reasonable means of the interests of journalists and journalism'. Representing the profession as a whole, it is a completely independent body free of political partiality. It gives equal rights of membership to all members of the profession, including radio and television journalists, press photographers and public relations officers with journalistic qualifications. Trade union representation is provided by the IOJ (TU), an independent certificated trade union.

5031

*THE CHARTERED INSTITUTE OF LINGUISTS
Saxon House, 48 Southwark Street, London SE1 1UN
Telephone: (020) 7940 3100
Fax: (020) 7940 3125
Email: info@iol.org.uk
Web Site: www.iol.org.uk

Chief Executive: John Hammond
Director of Communications: Cetty Zambrano

The Chartered Institute of Linguists (IoL) is an international professional membership organization. It promotes proficiency in modern languages worldwide amongst professional linguists, including translators, interpreters and educationalists, as well as those in the public and private sectors for whom languages are an important skill.

Through its wholly-owned subsidiary IoL Language Services Ltd (LSL) it offers translation, production and recruitment services, validation of language qualifications and assessments as well as training courses. The IoL Educational Trust, an associated charity, is an accredited awarding body offering high-level exams. The Institute helps to ensure equal access for all to the public services (law, health, local government) by providing interpreting qualifications in most of the languages spoken in the UK, and running the National Register of Public Service Interpreters (NRPSI Ltd).

The Linguist is the bi-monthly publication of the Chartered Institute of Linguists (published six times per year). It is free to all members, non-members can receive it on subscription.

5032

CHILDREN'S BOOKS IRELAND
17 North Great George's Street, Dublin 1,
Republic of Ireland
Telephone: +353 (0)1 872 7475
Fax: +353 (0)1 872 7476
Email: info@childrensbooksireland.com
Web Site: www.childrensbooksireland.com

Director: Mags Walsh
Programme Officer: Tom Donegan
Administrator: Jenny Murray
Editors – Inis Magazine: Patricia Kennon
    Marion Keyes

Children's Books Ireland is the national children's book organization of Ireland. The aim of Children's Books Ireland is to promote quality children's books and reading. CBI runs an annual nationwide Children's Book Festival, the Bisto/CBI Book of the Year awards, publishes *Inis*, a quarterly magazine, which carries a wide range of articles about children's books in Ireland and abroad as well as an extensive review section, and hosts an annual Children's Books conference.

CBI is a resource and support organization for teachers, pupils, writers, publishers, booksellers, librarians as well as an imaginative programmer of events for young readers.

5033

CHILDREN'S WRITERS & ILLUSTRATORS GROUP
The Society of Authors, 84 Drayton Gardens, London
SW10 9SB
Telephone: (020) 7373 6642
Fax: (020) 7373 5768
Email: jmccrum@societyofauthors.org
Web Site: www.societyofauthors.org

Secretary: Jo McCrum

Parent Company:
UK: The Society of Authors

The Children's Writers and Illustrators Group is an organization, founded in 1963, for writers and illustrators of children's books, who are members of the Society of Authors. Meetings are held regularly, with opportunities for members to meet each other, as well as to hear talks or discussions on various aspects of their work.

5034

CILIP (CHARTERED INSTITUTE OF LIBRARY AND INFORMATION PROFESSIONALS)
7 Ridgmount Street, London WC1E 7AE
Telephone: (020) 7255 0500 & (020) 7255 0505 (textphone)
Fax: (020) 7255 0501

Email: info@cilip.org.uk
Web Site: www.cilip.org.uk

Chief Executive: Bob McKee
Managing Director, CILIP Enterprises: John Woolley
Publishing Director, Facet Publishing: Helen Carley

CILIP: the Chartered Institute of Library and Information Professionals is a leading professional body for librarians, information specialists and knowledge managers.

CILIP forms a community of around 36,000 people engaged in library and information work, of whom approximately 21,000 are CILIP members and about 15,000 are regular customers of CILIP Enterprises.

5035

COMHAIRLE NAN LEABHRAICHEAN / THE GAELIC BOOKS COUNCIL
22 Mansfield Street, Glasgow G11 5QP
Telephone: 0141 337 6211
Fax: 0141 341 0515
Email: brath@gaelicbooks.net
Web Site: www.gaelicbooks.org

Chair: Prof Roibeard Ó Maolalaigh
Director: Ian MacDonald

The Council was set up in 1968 to administer the Gaelic Books Grant awarded by the Scottish Education Department, and its purpose is to stimulate Gaelic publishing. It normally has about ten members as its board, and a paid staff of four. In April 1983 the Scottish Arts Council became its main funding body, and its Assessor attends meetings. The Council became a charitable company in July 1996.

It provides financial assistance in the form of publication grants (paid to the publisher) for individual Gaelic books, and also commission grants for authors. Editorial advice is available, and a word-processing and proof-reading service.

In 2003 it launched the highly successful Ùr-Sgeul imprint for prose work in Gaelic, with the associated books, CDs and DVDs being issued by the publisher Clàr.

As a retailer, the Council stocks all Gaelic and Gaelic-related works in print, regular lists of these being published in its catalogue, *Leabhraichean Gàidhlig*, and on its website. It has its own shop at the address above, and also does mail order and mobile selling at selected events, as well as running a book club (A' Chiste Leabhraichean).

5036

COPYRIGHT TRIBUNAL
2nd Floor, 21 Bloomsbury Street, London WC1B 3HB
Telephone: (020) 7034 2836
Fax: (020) 7034 2826
Email: catherine.worley@ipo.gov.uk
Web Site: www.ipo.gov.uk/ctribunal.htm

Chairman: Judge Fysh QC
Secretary/Head: Catherine Worley

The main function of the Tribunal is to decide, where the parties cannot agree between themselves, the terms and conditions of licences offered by, or licensing schemes operated by, collective licensing bodies in the copyright and related rights area. It has the statutory task of conclusively establishing the facts of a case and of coming to a decision which is reasonable in the light of those facts. Its decisions are appealable to the High Court only on points of law. (Appeals on a point of law against decisions of the Tribunal in Scotland are to the Court of Session.)

Broadly, the Tribunal's jurisdiction is such that anyone who has unreasonably been refused a licence by a collecting society or considers the terms of an offered licence to be unreasonable may refer the matter to the Tribunal. The Tribunal also has the power to decide some matters even though collecting societies are not involved. For example, it can settle disputes over the royalties payable by publishers of TV programme listings to broadcasting organizations.

5037

THE CRITICS' CIRCLE
c/o 69 Marylebone Lane, London W1U 2PH
Telephone: (020) 7224 1410
Web Site: www.criticscircle.org.uk

President: Charles Spencer
Honorary General Secretary: William Russell

Founded in 1913 by J. T. Grein, S. R. Littlewood and John Parker. Aims to promote the art of criticism and to uphold its

integrity in practice; to foster and safeguard the professional interests of its members and to provide opportunities for social intercourse among them and to support the advancement of the arts. Membership is only by invitation of the Council and is confined to persons engaged professionally, regularly and substantially in the writing or broadcasting of criticism of theatre, music, film, dance and art and architecture. There is no literary section *per se*.

5038

DATA PUBLISHERS ASSOCIATION (DPA)
Queen's House, 28 Kingsway, London WC2B 6JR
Telephone: (020) 7405 0836
Fax: (020) 7404 4167
Email: sarah.gooch@dpa.org.uk
Web Site: www.dpa.org.uk

Executive Director: Jerry Gosney
Marketing Co-ordinator: Sarah Gooch

The Data Publishers Association (DPA) is the industry body representing data and directory publishers in the UK. Its role is to protect and promote the interests of the industry, both in print and online.

5039

DESIGN AND ARTISTS COPYRIGHT SOCIETY
33 Great Sutton Street, London EC1V 0DX
Telephone: (020) 7336 8811
Fax: (020) 7336 8822
Email: info@dacs.org.uk
Web Site: www.dacs.org.uk

Chief Executive: Gilane Tawadros
Directors: John Robinson (*Legal & International*)
    Tania Spriggens (*Communications*)
    Jane Sandeman (*Finance*)
    Jeremy Stein (*Services*)

Founded in 1984 by artists for artists. DACS is a not-for-profit organization established to administer and protect the rights of artists in the UK, including copyright and Artist's Resale Right.

Membership is open to any artist of any discipline and to the estate of an artist still in copyright.

DACS represents over 52,000 artists, including Picasso, Dali, Matisse, Wadsworth, Hamilton, Spencer and Lichtenstein.

Any publisher wishing to reproduce works of art in copyright should contact DACS in the first instance to obtain clearance prior to publication.

5040

EDUCATIONAL PUBLISHERS COUNCIL
[Schools Division of The Publishers Association]
The Publishers Association, 29B Montague Street, London
WC1B 5BW
Telephone: (020) 7691 9191
Fax: (020) 7691 9199
Email: gtaylor@publishers.org.uk
Web Site: www.publishers.org.uk

Director: Graham Taylor

Parent Company:
UK: The Publishers Association

The Educational Publishers Council is particularly concerned with making known, both to the educational system and to the general public, the nature and importance of educational publishers' work. It is charged with assessing and putting forward the co-ordinated views of educational publishers. Membership is open to any firm which is in membership of The Publishers Association and gives proof of a *bona fide* interest in publishing or producing books or other permanent forms of instruction intended for classroom use.

5041

EDUCATIONAL WRITERS GROUP
The Society of Authors, 84 Drayton Gardens, London
SW10 9SB
Telephone: (020) 7373 6642
Fax: (020) 7244 0743
Email: info@societyofauthors.org
Web Site: www.societyofauthors.org

Secretary: Elizabeth Haylett Clark

Parent Company:
UK: The Society of Authors

The Educational Writers Group is a subsidiary group of the Society of Authors. Its purpose is to advise members on their publishing problems etc, to study the conditions peculiar to the market at home and overseas, to watch developments in teaching as they affect the educational writer, and to hold meetings at which experience can be pooled, and matters of mutual interest discussed.

5042

ENGLISH ASSOCIATION
University of Leicester, University Road, Leicester LE1 7RH
Telephone: 0116 252 3982
Fax: 0116 252 2301
Email: engassoc@le.ac.uk
Web Site: www.le.ac.uk/engassoc

Chief Executive: Helen Lucas
Assistant: Julia Hughes

Founded in 1906 to promote the knowledge, enjoyment and study of the English language and its literatures.

The Year's Work in English Studies – the annual qualitative narrative bibliographical overview of scholarly work on English language and literature written in English. Published annually in December.

The Year's Work in Critical and Cultural Theory – companion volume to YWES, providing a narrative bibliography of work in the field of critical and cultural theory.

Order from: Julia Hughes.

5043

THE FEDERATION OF CHILDREN'S BOOK GROUPS
2 Bridge Wood View, Horsforth, Leeds LS18 5PE
Telephone: 0113 258 8910
Email: info@fcbg.org.uk
Web Site: www.fcbg.org.uk

A national, voluntary organization concerned with children and their books. The Federation's aim is to promote enjoyment and interest in children's books and reading, and to encourage the availability of a range of literature for all ages, from pre-school to teenage. The Federation liaises with schools, playgroups, publishers, libraries and other official bodies.
   National activities include:
   – organizes, annually, The Red House Children's Book Award
   – promotes National Share-a-Story Month in May
   – organizes an annual conference each spring.
   Members are able to receive Federation publications, including the *Federation Newsletter*, the annual *Red House Children's Book Award 'Pick of the Year' Top Fifty Booklist*, and information about National Share-a-Story Month.

5044

GAY AUTHORS WORKSHOP
BM Box 5700, London WC1N 3XX
Email: eandk2@btinternet.com

Secretary: Kathryn Byrd

Associated Companies:
UK: Gay Authors Self-Publishing Society

Gay Authors Workshop is an association of lesbians, gay men and bisexuals who are creative writers – poets, dramatists, fiction writers. Its aim is to raise the standard of gay literature by providing opportunities for gay writers to meet, read, discuss and criticize their work in a constructive way. Monthly meetings are held at different places in the London area for that purpose, and to share information about publishing outlets and competitions. Although London-based, it is a national organization. The quarterly newsletter (print and tape) keeps members in touch with activities. Membership is open to all gay writers, beginners as well as published authors. The subscription is £7 a year, £3 unwaged.

5045

GIBB MEMORIAL TRUST
2 Penarth Place, Cambridge CB3 9LU
Telephone: 01223 566630

Email: PRBligh@ntlworld.com
Web Site: www.gibbtrust.org

Book Distribution:
Oxbow Books Ltd, 10 Hythe Bridge Street, Oxford OX1 2BW
Telephone: 01865 241249
Fax: 01865 794449
Email: oxbow@oxbowbooks.com
Web Site: www.oxbowbooks.com

Secretary to the Trustees: P. R. Bligh *(Finance & Administration)*

The Trust is a registered charity whose aim is to support the publication of works of scholarly research within the areas of the history, literature, philosophy and religion of the Persians, Turks and Arabs. Its activities are in financing and organizing the production and publication of books, and in marketing the published works. The books are distributed by Oxbow Books in Oxford, UK, and Oakville, USA.

5046

GUILD OF FOOD WRITERS
255 Kent House Road, Beckenham, Kent BR3 1JQ
Telephone: (020) 8659 0422
Email: gfw@gfw.co.uk
Web Site: www.gfw.co.uk

The Guild of Food Writers is the professional association of food writers and broadcasters in the UK. Established in 1984, it now has 350 authors, columnists, freelance journalists and broadcasters amongst its members.
   The objectives of the Guild as set out in its constitution are as follows:
   To bring together professional food writers..., to print and issue an annual list of members, to extend the range of members' knowledge and experience..., and to encourage the development of new writers by every means including competitions and awards. To contribute to the growth of public interest in, and knowledge of, the subject of food and to campaign for improvements in the quality of food.
   The Guild is a self-supporting body that offers its members a busy calendar that includes an annual lecture dinner and AGM, annual awards, monthly workshops and occasional professional and social events. It also publishes a monthly newsletter and comprehensive and detailed annual directory of members.
   The Guild offers professional support and guidance to its members. In the public forum it campaigns with authority for improvements in the awareness and quality of food in every sector of society.

5047

INDEPENDENT PUBLISHERS GUILD (IPG)
PO Box 12, Llain, Whitland SA34 0WU
Telephone: 01437 563335
Fax: 01437 562071
Email: info@ipg.uk.com
Web Site: www.ipg.uk.com

Chief Executive: Bridget Shine

The Independent Publishers Guild (IPG) actively represents the interests of independent publishers in the UK and is represented on many committees and forums, which form the strategy for the UK book trade. The IPG helps publishers to do better business, somewhere they can find advice, ideas and information.
   With over 450 members and steadily growing with combined revenues of over £500M, the IPG provides a vibrant networking base. Members receive regular e-newsletters, training courses and seminars covering important areas. It also organizes an annual conference.
   The IPG runs a collective stand for members at leading international book fairs including Frankfurt and London.

5048

INFORMATION COMMISSIONER'S OFFICE
Wycliffe House, Water Lane, Wilmslow, Cheshire SK9 5AF
Telephone: 0845 630 6060 or 01625 545745
Fax: 01625 524510
Email: mail@ico.gsi.gov.uk
Web Site: www.ico.gov.uk

Information Commissioner: Richard Thomas

The Information Commissioner's Office is the UK's independent public body set up to promote access to official information and to protect personal information.
   It regulates and enforces the Data Protection Act, the Freedom of Information Act, the Privacy and Electronic Communications Regulations and the Environmental Information Regulations.
   The ICO provides guidance to organizations and individuals. It rules on eligible complaints and can take action when the law is broken.
   Reporting directly to Parliament, the Commissioner's powers include the ability to order compliance, using enforcement and decision notices, and prosecution.

5049

INSTITUTE OF SCIENTIFIC AND TECHNICAL COMMUNICATORS (ISTC)
Airport House, Purley Way, Croydon CR0 0XZ
Telephone: 020 8253 4506
Fax: 020 8253 4510
Email: istc@istc.org.uk
Web Site: www.istc.org.uk

President: Simon Butler
Treasurer: Peter Fountain
Editor: Marian Newell *(Communicator – ISTC Journal)*
Administration: Elaine Cole
Marketing Director: Paul Ballard

Formed in 1972 as a result of the amalgamation of the Presentation of Technical Information Group (1948), the Institution of Technical Authors and Illustrators (originally the Technical Publications Association), formed in 1953, and the Institute of Technical Publicity and Publications (1963).
   The Institute aims to establish and maintain professional codes of practice for those employed in all branches of scientific and technical communication. It provides a forum for the exchange of views between its members, and aims to further their expectations and interests. The membership embodies a wide range of specialist knowledge of the principles and modern practices of effective communication of scientific and technical information. Through its publications and meetings, the Institute disseminates this experience to a growing profession and to those who employ the services of its members.
   The Institute represents Great Britain on the International Council for Technical Communication (INTECOM).
   Publications: *The Communicator* (UK subscription: £37 per year).

5050

INSTITUTE OF TRANSLATION & INTERPRETING
Fortuna House, South Fifth Street, Milton Keynes MK9 2EU
Telephone: 01908 325250
Fax: 01908 325259
Email: info@iti.org.uk
Web Site: www.iti.org.uk

Chairman: Catherine Greensmith
General Secretary: Alan Wheatley

The Institute of Translation and Interpreting (ITI) is the UK's main professional association for translators and interpreters and aims to promote the highest standards in translating and interpreting. It has a strong corporate membership and runs professional development courses and conferences, sometimes in conjunction with its language, regional and subject networks. Membership is open to those with a genuine and proven involvement in translation and interpreting. As a full and active member of the International Federation of Translators, it maintains good contacts with translators and interpreters worldwide. ITI's bi-monthly bulletin is available on subscription through the ITI office in Milton Keynes.
   ITI's directory of translators and interpreters may be accessed from the website at www.iti.org.uk.

5051

IP3 (INSTITUTE OF PAPER, PRINTING & PUBLISHING)
Runnymede House, off Hummer Road, Egham, Surrey TW20 9BD
Telephone: 0870 330 8625
Fax: 0870 330 8615
Email: info@ip3.org.uk
Web Site: www.ip3.org.uk

Also at:
Colin Walsh, Director, IP3, 25–27 High Street, Chesterton, Cambridge CB4 1ND

Telephone: 01223 352790
Fax: 01223 460718
Email: csw@bpccam.co.uk

Directors: Tim Feest
Colin Walsh
David Pryke

Fostering excellence in publishing through:
– the promotion, support and endorsement of a programme of educational training, research and development
– the introduction of a code of practice
– the development of standards of occupational compe-
tence
– the publication of bulletins, handbooks, reports and
research designed to assist in the improvement of individual
performance
– the development of professional publishing qualifications
– meetings, seminars and conferences.
The Institute will offer individuals:
– membership of an active community of people working
in publishing
– the opportunity to participate in and influence the direction of a body that has their best interests at heart
– a community that can raise professional standards and,
as a consequence, individual and collective status
– opportunities to network, seek advice, guidance and
career counselling
– access to career, education and training information
– a range of cost-saving services and activities.
The Institute of Publishing will be a forum providing
opportunities for individuals in publishing to develop themselves and progress in their careers and to meet the chal-
lenges of an increasingly competitive business.

5052

IRISH BOOK PUBLISHERS ASSOCIATION (CLÉ)
Guinness Enterprise Centre, Taylor's Lane, Dublin 8,
Republic of Ireland
Telephone: +353 (01) 415 1210
Email: info@publishingireland.com
Web Site: www.publishingireland.com

President: Seán Ó Cearnaigh *(Publisher, CoisLife)*
Project Manager: Jolly Ronan
Administrator: Karen Kenny

The Irish Book Publishers Association (CLÉ) promotes the
publication, distribution, sale and publicity of books at home
and abroad. There are over 90 members of the association.
CLÉ is a member of the Federation of European Publishers
and of the International Publishers Association.

5053

ISBN AGENCY - UK AND IRISH REPUBLIC
3rd Floor, Midas House, 62 Goldsworth Road, Woking
GU21 6LQ
Telephone: 0870 777 8712
Fax: 0870 777 8714
Email: isbn.agency@nielsen.com
Web Site: www.isbn.nielsenbook.co.uk

Senior Manager: Julian Sowa
Manager: Diana Williams

Associated Companies:
UK: ISTC Agency; Nielsen Book; SAN Agency
USA: The Nielsen Company

The UK International Standard Book Numbering Agency is
responsible for assigning ISBN prefixes to publishers based in
the UK or the Irish Republic.
The UK ISBN Agency cannot assign ISBNs to publishers
based in other countries.
The Agency:
– allocates ISBN publisher prefixes to eligible publishers
based on the information provided by the publisher;
– advises publishers on the correct and proper implementation of the ISBN system;
– maintains a database of publishers and their prefixes
for inclusion in the *Publishers' International ISBN Directory;*
– encourages and promotes the use of the Bookland
EAN bar code format;
– encourages and promotes the importance of the ISBN
for a proper listing of titles with bibliographical agencies;
– provides technical advice and assistance to publishers
and the booktrade on all aspects of ISBN usage.

Any new publishers wishing to apply for an allocation of
ISBNs should contact the ISBN Agency for an application
pack. A registration fee is payable.

5054

ISSN UK CENTRE
The British Library, Boston Spa, Wetherby, West Yorkshire
LS23 7BQ
Telephone: 01937 546959
Fax: 01937 546562
Email: issn-uk@bl.uk
Web Site: www.bl.uk/issn

Assigns ISSN (International Standard Serial Numbers) to
serial titles published in the UK.

5055

ISTC AGENCY
3rd Floor, Midas House, 62 Goldsworth Road, Woking,
Surrey GU21 6LQ
Telephone: 0870 777 8712
Fax: 0870 777 8714
Email: istc.agency@nielsen.com
Web Site: www.istc.nielsenbook.co.uk

Managers: Julian Sowa *(Senior)*
Diana Williams

Parent Company:
UK: Nielsen Book
USA: The Nielsen Company

Associated Companies:
UK: ISBN Agency; SAN Agency

The International Standard Text Code (ISTC) is a global iden-
tification system for textual works, i.e. the content in text-
based publications. Nielsen Book operates one of the first
ISTC registration agencies, enabling authors, publishers and
other authorized representatives to register textual works
with an ISTC. It also provides advice and guidance on how to
make the most of this important new system. Nielsen Book
also runs the ISBN and SAN agencies.

5056

MEDICAL WRITERS GROUP
The Society of Authors, 84 Drayton Gardens, London
SW10 9SB
Telephone: (020) 7373 6642
Fax: (020) 7373 5768
Email: info@societyofauthors.org &
sbaxter@societyofauthors.org
Web Site: www.societyofauthors.org

Secretary: Sarah Baxter

The Medical Writers Group, established in 1979, is a group
within the Society of Authors. Its principal objects are to represent its members in all matters affecting their interests as
medical writers; to hold meetings from time to time for the
discussion of matters of common interest; and to provide,
through the Society, advice to members on the special problems of medical authorship. Authors who have had a book
accepted for publication, but not yet published, can join the
Society and obtain advice. Also administers the Medical
Book Awards.

5057

MUSIC PUBLISHERS ASSOCIATION
6th Floor, British Music House, 26 Berners Street, London
W1T 3LR
Telephone: (020) 7580 0126
Fax: (020) 7637 3929
Email: info@mpaonline.org.uk
Web Site: www.mpaonline.org.uk

Chief Executive: Stephen Navin
Editor, MPA Catalogue: Jake Kirner

Associated Companies:
UK: MCPS Ltd

The Music Publishers Association (MPA) was established in
1881 and is governed by an elected Board. The MPA exists
to safeguard the interests of music publishers and the writers signed to them. It provides them with a forum and a collective voice, and aims to inform and to educate the wider
public in the importance and value of copyright.

The MPA offers a range of services and publications to
those interested in music publishing and participates in education and information initiatives across the music industry.

5058

NATIONAL ACQUISITIONS GROUP
12–14 King Street, Wakefield WF1 2SQ
Telephone: 01924 383010
Fax: 01924 383010
Email: nag@btconnect.com
Web Site: www.nag.org.uk

Chair: Paul Dalton
Hon. Secretary: Sarah Armitage
Hon. Treasurer: Mark Merrill *(Publications Officer)*
Administrator: Jane Butler

Established in 1986, NAG is a broadly based organization
which stimulates, co-ordinates and publicizes developments
in library acquisitions and the book trade. The membership
includes individuals and organizations within publishing,
bookselling and systems supply, as well as librarians responsible for choosing and buying books for academic, public,
national, government and special institutions.
NAG has two main aims:
– to bring together all those in any way concerned with
library acquisitions, to assist them in exchanging information
and comment and to promote understanding and good
practice between them;
– to seek to influence other organizations and individuals
to adopt its opinions and standards.
NAG's objectives are to:
– provide a forum for discussion and the exchange of
information;
– extend knowledge and understanding of technological
developments;
– promote the dissemination of information about library
acquisitions;
– develop the awareness of producers, suppliers and
librarians;
– act as a channel of communication with Government
and other bodies.

5059

NATIONAL ASSOCIATION FOR THE TEACHING OF
ENGLISH
50 Broadfield Road, Sheffield S8 0XJ
Telephone: 0114 555 419
Fax: 0114 555 296
Email: info@nate.org.uk
Web Site: www.nate.org.uk

Development & Communications Director: Ian McNeilly
Publications Manager: Anne Fairhall
Company Secretary: Lyn Fairfax

NATE is the UK subject association for all aspects of English
teaching from pre-school to university. NATE publishes its
own and distributes other titles covering:
– *classroom resources:* primary, secondary, post 16
– *teaching English:* theoretical titles including: language,
literacy, literature, speaking and listening, media, drama,
information and communications technologies, assessment,
theory, equal opportunities
– *management & staff development:* curriculum, planning, managing the English department, whole school
issues relating to English teaching.
The Association publishes four periodicals: *English in
Education, NATE News, English Drama Media* and *Classroom.*

5060

NATIONAL LITERACY TRUST
68 South Lambeth Road, London SW8 1RL
Telephone: (020) 7587 1842
Fax: (020) 7587 1411
Email: contact@literacytrust.org.uk
Web Site: www.literacytrust.org.uk

National Literacy Trust:
National Reading Campaign; Reading Champions; Reading
Connects; Reading Is Fundamental, UK; Reading The
Game; Talk To Your Baby

The National Literacy Trust is an independent charity (no
1116260) that changes lives through literacy. It has a vision
of a society in which everyone has the reading, writing,
speaking and listening skills that they need to fulfil their own
and, ultimately, the nation's potential. It aims to empower

learners, support professionals and influence policy and practice.

To make a real difference, whole communities need to work together. It helps to make this happen. It supports those who work with learners through its innovative programmes, information and research and it brings together key organizations to lead literacy promotion in the UK.

Programmes include Reading Is Fundamental, UK – providing free books for children to choose and keep; Reading The Game – involving the professional football community; Reading Connects – developing a whole-school approach to reading for pleasure; Reading Champions – putting the boys in charge of their reading; and the Talk To Your Baby campaign, which supports parents and professionals. For more information visit www.literacytrust.org.uk

5061

NEW WRITING NORTH
Holy Jesus Hospital, City Road, Newcastle upon Tyne NE1 2AS
Email: claire@newwritingnorth.com
Web Site: www.newwritingnorth.com

Directors: Cath Robson *(Finance)*
   Anna Disley *(Deputy, Theatre & Education)*
Projects & Marketing Officer: Olivia Mantle

New Writing North is the literature development agency for the north-east of England.

5062

NIELSEN BOOKDATA
3rd Floor, Midas House, 62 Goldsworth Road, Woking, Surrey GU21 6LQ
Telephone: 01483 712200
Fax: 01483 712201
Email: info.bookdata@nielsen.com
Web Site: www.nielsenbookdata.co.uk

Directors: Ann Betts *(Commercial)*
   Simon Skinner *(Sales)*
Head of Marketing: Mo Siewcharran
Head of Data Sales: Paul Dibble
Managers: Vesna Nall *(Publisher Subscriptions)*
   Lucy Huddlestone *(UK Sales)*

Parent Company:
UK: Nielsen Book
USA: The Nielsen Company

Associated Companies:
UK: Nielsen BookNet; Nielsen BookScan

Nielsen BookData is a book information provider worldwide. The company has a range of products and services which provide content-rich, accurate and timely book information for English-language titles published internationally. These services are sold to booksellers, libraries and publishers in over 100 countries, including the UK, Ireland, Europe, Australia, New Zealand, South Africa and the USA.

5063

PERIODICAL PUBLISHERS ASSOCIATION
Queens House, 28 Kingsway, London WC2B 6JR
Telephone: (020) 7404 4166
Fax: (020) 7404 4167
Email: info1@ppa.co.uk
Web Site: www.ppa.co.uk

Chief Executive: Jonathan Shephard
Chief Operating Officer: Sarah Tunstall

Associated Companies:
Republic of Ireland: Periodical Publishers Association Ireland
UK: Association of Publishing Agencies; Periodical
   Publishers Association Scotland; Periodicals Training
   Council; PPA Interactive; Teenage Magazine Arbitration
   Panel (TMAP)

Trade association representing publishers of consumer, business-to-business and customer magazines.

5064

THE POETRY SOCIETY
22 Betterton Street, London WC2H 9BX
Telephone: (020) 7420 9880
Fax: (020) 7240 4818

Email: info@poetrysociety.org.uk
Web Site: www.poetrysociety.org.uk

Director: Judith Palmer
Editor, Poetry Review: Fiona Sampson
Press & Marketing Manager: Lisa Roberts

The Society's principal activities include: the quarterly publication of the UK's world-class poetry magazine, *Poetry Review*; an Advice and Information Service; the Society's newsletter, *Poetry News*; the National Poetry Competition which awards over £7000 in prizes each year and has brought many poets to national attention; the annual Foyle Young Poets of the Year Award (11–17 year olds). The Poetry Society also produces a range of publications including *The Poetry Book for Primary Schools* and *Jumpstart: Poetry in the Secondary School* as well as books exploring the links between poetry and pop, poetry and gardens, and poetry and personal development. Other resources include *poetryclass*, an invaluable teacher-training resource for both primary and secondary school teachers, free National Poetry Day materials, display materials (including Poems on the Underground posters) and The Library Poetry Pack, an information pack available with membership.

5065

PUBLIC LENDING RIGHT
Richard House, Sorbonne Close, Stockton-on-Tees TS17 6DA
Telephone: 01642 604699
Fax: 01642 615641
Email: authorservices@plr.uk.com
Web Site: www.plr.uk.com

Registrar: Jim Parker

Public Lending Right (PLR) exists to make payments to authors for the borrowing of their books from public libraries. PLR is funded by the Department for Culture, Media and Sport, and is headed by a Registrar. To qualify, authors must register their books with the PLR office. Payment calculations are based on book loans from a representative sample of public libraries. Payments are made annually. No author may receive more than £6600.

5066

THE PUBLISHERS ASSOCIATION
29B Montague Street, London WC1B 5BW
Telephone: (020) 7691 9191
Fax: (020) 7691 9199
Email: mail@publishers.org.uk
Web Site: www.publishers.org.uk

Chief Executive: Simon Juden
Directors: Graham Taylor *(Educational, Academic &
   Professional Publishing)*
   Emma House *(International)*

The Publishers Association is a trade organization serving book, journal and electronic publishers in the UK. It brings publishers together to discuss the main issues facing the industry and to define the practical policies that will take the industry forward. The aim of The Publishers Association is to serve and promote by all lawful means the interest of book, journal and electronic publishers and to protect their interests.

5067

PUBLISHERS LICENSING SOCIETY LTD
37–41 Gower Street, London WC1E 6HH
Telephone: (020) 7299 7730
Fax: (020) 7299 7780
Email: pls@pls.org.uk
Web Site: www.pls.org.uk

Chairman: Graham Taylor
Managers: Tom West *(Operations)*
   Lydia Murray *(Finance)*
   David Bishop *(Licensing & Communications)*
Consultant: Mark Bide
Chief Executive: Alicia Wise

The Publishers Licensing Society (PLS) obtains mandates from publishers which grant PLS the authority to license photocopying and digitization of pages from published works. PLS also consults with publishers on the development of licences.

PLS aims to maximize revenue from licences for mandating publishers and to expand the range and repertoire of

mandated publishers available to licence holders. It supports the Copyright Licensing Agency (CLA) in its efforts to increase the number of legitimate users through the issuing of licences and pursues any infringements of copyright works belonging to rights holders.

5068

PUBLISHERS PUBLICITY CIRCLE
65 Airedale Avenue, London W4 2NN
Telephone: (020) 8994 1881
Email: ppc-@lineone.net
Web Site: www.publisherspublicitycircle.co.uk

Secretary/Treasurer: Heather White

For over 50 years, the Publishers Publicity Circle has enabled book publicists - both from publishing houses and freelance PR agencies - to meet and share information regularly. Representatives of the media are invited to speak about the ways in which they can feature authors and their books, and how book publicists can provide most effectively the information and material needed.

Annual prizes are awarded for the best publicity campaigns of the year.

A directory of the PPC membership is published each year and distributed to over 2500 media contacts, providing the names of publicity staff, their fax and telephone numbers, and email addresses.

5069

PUBLISHING SCOTLAND
Scottish Book Centre, 137 Dundee Street, Edinburgh EH11 1BG
Telephone: 0131 228 6866
Fax: 0131 228 3220
Email: enquiries@publishingscotland.org
Web Site: www.publishingscotland.org

Chief Executive: Marion Sinclair
Member Services & Marketing Manager: Jane Walker
Administrators: Carol Lothian *(Finance & Office)*
   Joan Lyle *(Information & Training)*

Associated Companies:
UK: BookSource Ltd

Publishing Scotland has grown from the work of the Scottish Publishers Association (SPA), a trade association in existence for over 30 years, representing over 75 book and journal publishers. It now offers a network membership of the organization.

Publishing Scotland is an organization with responsibility for support and development of the publishing sector in Scotland. The remit is to work with companies, organizations and individuals in the industry, and to co-ordinate joint initiatives and partnerships. Publishing Scotland provides a forum for discussions, events and for linking services and skills to needs and opportunities. Publishing Scotland provides all the services for publishers that were previously the work of the SPA.

Publishing Scotland represents its members' interests in a number of capacities, in co-operative promotion and marketing of their books, attendance at international book fairs, joint catalogue mailings, export services and training.

5070

ROMANTIC NOVELISTS ASSOCIATION
Nevermore, Little Birch, Hereford HR2 8BB
Telephone: 01981 541235
Email: RNAhonsec@emryle.waitrose.com
Web Site: www.rna-uk.org

Secretary: E. M. Ryle

The Association aims to raise the prestige of good quality romantic fiction and makes annual awards for the best romantic (including historical) novel, and for the best first novel by a hitherto unpublished writer accepted for publication. A new annual award for Category Romance was made in 2003.

5071

ROYAL SOCIETY OF LITERATURE
Somerset House, Strand, London WC2R 1LA
Telephone: (020) 7845 4676
Fax: (020) 7845 4679
Email: info@rslit.org
Web Site: www.rslit.org

President: Sir Michael Holroyd CBE, FRHistS, FRSL
Chair: Anne Chisholm FRSL
Secretary: Maggie Fergusson FRSL

The Society's purpose is to sustain all that is best, whether traditional or experimental, in English Letters, and to encourage a catholic appreciation of literature. Lectures and poetry readings take place monthly at Somerset House. The Society administers a number of trusts for the advancement of Letters. The Royal Society of Literature Award under the Heinemann bequest is presented annually to one or more writers on the strength of a published work of high literary merit. The V. S. Pritchett Memorial Prize is a new prize for a previously unpublished short story. The Royal Society of Literature Ondaatje Prize was launched in 2003. The £10,000 prize will be awarded annually to the book of the highest literary merit, fiction or non-fiction, which evokes the spirit of a place.

5073

RSA (THE ROYAL SOCIETY FOR THE ENCOURAGEMENT OF ARTS, MANUFACTURES AND COMMERCE)

8 John Adam Street, London WC2N 6EZ
Telephone: (020) 7451 6902
Fax: (020) 7839 5805
Email: editor@rsa.org.uk
Web Site: www.theRSA.org

Publisher:
Wardour Publishing & Design, Elsley Court,
20–22 Great Titchfield Street, London W1W 8BE
Telephone: (020) 7016 2555
Web Site: www.wardour.co.uk

Chairman: Luke Johnson
Chief Executive: Matthew Taylor
Directors: Stephen King (Chief Operating Officer)
Nina Bolognesi (External Affairs)
Belinda Lester (Fellowship)
Rachel O'Brien (Interim, Projects)
Carrie Walsh (Commercial)
Editor: Frances Hedges

Publishes quarterly RSA Journal and reports, conference papers and occasional books.

5073

SAN AGENCY – UK & IRISH REPUBLIC

3rd Floor, Midas House, 62 Goldsworth Road, Woking, Surrey GU21 6LQ
Telephone: 0870 777 8712
Fax: 0870 777 8714
Email: san.agency@nielsen.com
Web Site: www.san.nielsenbook.co.uk

Managers: Julian Sowa (Senior)
Diana Williams

Parent Company:
UK: Nielsen Book
USA: The Nielsen Company

Associated Companies:
UK: ISBN Agency; ISTC Agency

SANs, Standard Address Numbers, are unique for geographical locations and can be assigned to the addresses of organizations involved in the bookselling or publishing industries. The SAN Agency is responsible for managing the scheme on behalf of Book Industry Communication in the UK and Republic of Ireland. Nielsen Book also runs the ISBN and ISTC agencies.

5074

SCBWI (SOCIETY OF CHILDREN'S BOOK WRITERS & ILLUSTRATORS (BRITISH ISLES REGION))

36 Mackenzie Road, Beckenham, Kent BR3 4RU
Telephone: (020) 8249 9716
Email: ra@britishscbwi.org
Web Site: www.britishscbwi.org

Regional Advisor (Chair): Natascha Biebow
Newsletter Editor: Eileen Ramchandran
Co-ordinators: Anne-Marie Perks (Illustrator)
Candy Gourlay (Website)
Sue Hyams (Membership)

Parent Company:
USA: SCBWI

The SCBWI is an international professional organization for writers and illustrators of children's books. It is a network for the exchange of knowledge between writers, illustrators, editors, publishers, agents, librarians, educators, booksellers and others involved with literature for young people. There are currently more than 18,000 members worldwide, in over 70 regions.

The SCBWI International sponsors three annual conferences on writing and illustrating books and multimedia, one in New York in February, one in Bologna, Italy, and one in Los Angeles in August, as well as dozens of regional conferences and events throughout the world. It also publishes a bi-monthly newsletter, The Bulletin, awards grants for works in progress, and provides many informational publications on the art and business of writing and selling written, illustrated and electronic material. The SCBWI also presents numerous grants and awards, including the Golden Kite Award for the best fiction and non-fiction books.

The SCBWI British Isles (SCBWI-BI) region meets bi-monthly, usually in London, for a speaker or workshop event. It also sponsors local critique groups, master classes and regional networks events, and publishes a quarterly newsletter, Words and Pictures, which includes up-to-date events and marketing information, and articles on the craft of children's writing and illustrating. It also runs a yearly Writer's and Illustrator's Conference with hands-on workshops on improving your craft and the opportunity to meet publishing professionals and find out what they are looking for. SCBWI-BI runs a listserve and social networking site where writers and illustrators can set up their own promotional website.

SCBWI is open to both published and unpublished writers and illustrators.

Full membership is open to those whose work for children's books, illustrations or photographs, films, electronic media, articles, poems or stories has been published or produced.

Associate membership is open to all those with an interest in children's literature or media, whether or not they have published.

To join, see our web site www.britishscbwi.org

5075

SCHOOL LIBRARY ASSOCIATION

Unit 2, Lotmead Business Village, Lotmead Farm, Wanborough, Swindon SN4 0UY
Telephone: 01793 791787
Fax: 01793 791786
Email: info@SLA.org.uk
Web Site: www.SLA.org.uk

Editor: Steve Hird
Review Editor: Chris Brown
Production Editor: Richard Leveridge

The School Library Association is an independent organization working to promote the development of school libraries, primary and secondary. Services to members include advice and information, publications at reduced prices, The School Librarian, a quarterly journal of articles and reviews, training courses and a network of area branches. Membership includes schools, colleges, local education authorities, public libraries, publishers and individuals in the United Kingdom and overseas. Membership costs £69.50 p.a.

5076

SCOTTISH BOOK TRUST

Sandeman House, Trunks Close, 55 High Street, Edinburgh EH1 1SR
Telephone: 0131 524 0160
Fax: 0131 524 0161
Email: info@scottishbooktrust.com
Web Site: www.scottishbooktrust.com

Chief Executive Officer: Marc Lambert
Managers: Jeanette Harris (General)
Sophie Moxon (Head of Programme)
Marion Bourbouze (Marketing & Audience Development)

Scottish Book Trust is a leading agency for the promotion of literature in Scotland, developing innovative projects to encourage adults and children to read, write and be inspired by books.

It promotes children's literature and the joys of reading and writing by organizing book awards, author tours and talks, and writing competitions, and by developing interactive online projects. It supports writers with a range of

projects including skills development and bursaries, the funding of literature events, book awards and the promotion of Scottish writing to over 10 million people worldwide. It fosters readers and writers by offering a variety of events, advice and online information on books and authors. It works with learning professionals all over Scotland to create innovative and effective resources and events which inspire people through literature.

5077

SOCIETY FOR EDITORS & PROOFREADERS

Erico House, 93–99 Upper Richmond Road, London SW15 2TG
Telephone: (020) 8785 5617
Fax: (020) 8785 5618
Email: admin@sfep.org.uk
Web Site: www.sfep.org.uk

Chair: Sarah Price
Executive Secretary: Justina Amenu

Founded in 1988 with the twin aims of promoting high editorial standards and achieving recognition of its members' professional status, the Society works to disseminate information and training, foster good relations between members and their clients, and combat the isolation often experienced by freelances. It supports recognized standards of training and accreditation for editors and proofreaders, and is establishing recognized standards for its own members. Membership in 2008 was approximately 1400.

Benefits of membership include: annual directory of members seeking work; free regular newsletter; local groups throughout the country; online discussion group; annual conference; meetings and training sessions in several centres, covering aspects of current professional practice and business matters; legal helpline; discounts on selected products and services.

5078

SOCIETY OF ARCHIVISTS

Prioryfield House, 20 Canon Street, Taunton, Somerset TA1 1SW
Telephone: 01823 327030 & 327077
Fax: 01823 271719
Email: societyofarchivists@archives.org.uk
Web Site: www.archives.org.uk

Executive Director: John Chambers
Membership Administrator: Lorraine Logan

Publication of texts/periodicals on archives and records management. Conferences and training courses.

5079

SOCIETY OF AUTHORS

84 Drayton Gardens, London SW10 9SB
Telephone: (020) 7373 6642
Fax: (020) 7373 5768
Email: info@societyofauthors.org
Web Site: www.societyofauthors.org

Chairman: Margaret Drabble
General Secretary: Mark Le Fanu

An independent trade union for authors. Its purpose is to further the interests of its 8500 members through individual advice and general campaigning. It is controlled by an elected Committee of Management and administered by a staff with long experience in the business and legal aspects of authorship. Members have access to a comprehensive advisory service and may seek advice on all forms of contracts. The Society also serves the interests of specialist writers through a number of subsidiary groups – viz the Broadcasting Group, the Translators Association, Children's Writers and Illustrators, Educational Writers, Academic Writers and Medical Writers Groups. It makes representations to government departments and promotes campaigns on behalf of the profession as a whole (eg public lending right, tax concessions for authors, etc). It also administers literary estates, publishes a quarterly journal, The Author, issues numerous Quick Guides to its members and manages a variety of awards and trust funds for authors.

5080

SOCIETY OF AUTHORS PENSION FUND

84 Drayton Gardens, London SW10 9SB
Telephone: (020) 7373 6642
Fax: (020) 7373 5768

Email: info@societyofauthors.org
Web Site: www.societyofauthors.org

Secretary: Mark Le Fanu

A small number of pensions is granted by the Pension Fund Committee to authors over the age of 60 who have been members of the Society for 10 years. Pensions are normally £1700 per annum.

5081

SOCIETY OF EDITORS
University Centre, Granta Place, Cambridge CB2 1RU
Telephone: 01223 304080
Fax: 01223 304090
Email: info@societyofeditors.org
Web Site: www.societyofeditors.org

Executive Director: Bob Satchwell

The Society of Editors has more than 400 members in national, regional and local newspapers, magazines, broadcasting and new media, journalism, education and media law.

It campaigns for media freedom, self-regulation, the public's right to know and the maintenance of standards in journalism.

5082

SOCIETY OF INDEXERS
Woodbourn Business Centre, 10 Jessell Street, Sheffield S9 3HY
Telephone: 0114 244 9561 or 07757 813134
Email: admin@indexers.org.uk
Web Site: www.indexers.org.uk

Secretary: Judith Menes

Founded 1957 to raise the standards of indexing of books, periodicals and documents by holding meetings, courses and conferences and to issue a journal, *The Indexer*, and regular newsletters. Publishes and runs an open-learning course 'Training in Indexing'. The Society publishes a directory of members (*Indexers Available*) competent to do indexing in a wide range of both simple and specialized subject fields. Copies may be obtained from the Society's office, or be viewed on its website. Minimum scales of payment are recommended by the Society for use by members as a basis for negotiation with publishers. The Society wishes to impress on both publishers and authors the need for adequate and competent indexes in non-fiction works.

5083

SOCIETY OF MEDICAL WRITERS
Ashlett House, 24 Rochester Way, Sudbury, Essex CO10 1LP
Telephone: 01787 374879
Email: raymond.hume@btinternet.com
Web Site: www.somw.org.uk

Chairman: Dr Raymond Hume
Finance Officer: Dr Richard Cutler
Editor: Dr Michael Lasserson

Membership of the Society of Medical Writers is open to anyone who publishes or aspires to publish their work of whatever nature – medical or non-medical, fact or fiction, prose or poetry. It is intended that the association should be enjoyable, stimulating and educational so that writing from medical practice, including general practice, is improved and encouraged.

The aims of the Society are therefore to:
- improve standards of writing by medical practitioners;
- encourage literacy whether in scientific papers, review articles, historical or anecdotal essays;
- provide meetings for practitioners interested in writing, for the exchange of views, skills and ideas;
- provide education on the preparation, presentation and submission of written material for publication;

- act as a means of introduction between practitioners and suitable publishers and editors;
- maintain a register of members of the SOMW, available to commissioning editors and others;
- advise on sources of assistance with regard to technical, legal and financial aspects of writing;
- consider questions of ethics relating to writing and publication;
- further developments in the art of writing and to facilitate access to educational opportunities for those motivated to become better writers.

5084

SOCIETY OF YOUNG PUBLISHERS
The Publishers Association, 29B Montague Street, London WC1B 5BW
Email: sypchair@thesyp.org.uk
Web Site: www.thesyp.org.uk

Chair: Angela Solomon
Treasurer: Laura Palosuo
Marketing Officer: Simon Hagan

Established in 1949, the Society of Young Publishers is open to anyone in publishing or a related trade (in any capacity) – or who is hoping to be soon. Its aim is to assist, inform and enthuse anyone trying to break into the publishing industry or progress within it.

It organizes monthly speaker meetings which discuss different topics of relevance to the publishing industry. Guest speakers are drawn from a variety of backgrounds.

Members receive approximately five issues per year of its magazine, *InPrint*, to keep them up-to-date with the society and events and issues within the industry. The SYP receives regular notice of situations vacant which members receive through its Jobs Bulletin.

5085

TRANSLATORS ASSOCIATION
84 Drayton Gardens, London SW10 9SB
Telephone: (020) 7373 6642
Fax: (020) 7373 5768
Email: info@societyofauthors.org
Web Site: www.societyofauthors.org

Secretary: Jo McCrum

The Translators Association is a subsidiary of the Society of Authors and advises literary translators on such matters as contracts and fees. Publishers seeking book translators can search the online database.

5086

TRAVELLING SCHOLARSHIP FUND
Society of Authors, 84 Drayton Gardens, London SW10 9SB
Telephone: (020) 7373 6642
Fax: (020) 7373 5768
Email: info@societyofauthors.org
Web Site: www.societyofauthors.org

Secretary: Mark Le Fanu

Founded in 1944 by an anonymous donor, to enable British creative writers to travel and to keep in touch with their colleagues abroad. A special committee annually reviews the field of contemporary literature before making its awards, which are not for open candidature, and are normally made to established writers of over 30 years of age. The Fund is administered by the Society of Authors.

5087

WATCH (WRITERS ARTISTS & THEIR COPYRIGHT HOLDERS)
The Library, University of Reading, PO Box 223, Whiteknights, Reading RG6 6AE
Telephone: 0118 378 8783
Fax: 0118 378 6636

Email: d.c.sutton@reading.ac.uk
Web Site: www.watch-file.com

Director: Dr D. Sutton

WATCH provides a free online database of information about the copyright holders of literary authors, artists and prominent persons. The database is in the form of an open-access public website, jointly maintained by the Universities of Texas and Reading.

5088

WELSH BOOKS COUNCIL / CYNGOR LLYFRAU CYMRU
Castell Brychan, Aberystwyth, Ceredigion SY23 2JB
Telephone: 01970 624151
Fax: 01970 625385
Email: castellbrychan@cllc.org.uk
Web Site: www.cllc.org.uk & www.gwales.com

Director: Gwerfyl Pierce Jones
Head of Department: Sion Ilar *(Design)*
Marian Beech Hughes *(Editorial)*
D. Philip Davies *(Information Services)*
Menna Lloyd Williams *(Children's Books)*
Dafydd Charles Jones *(Distribution)*
Arwyn Roderick *(Finance)*
Elwyn Jones *(Administration & Public Relations)*
Helgard Krause *(Sales & Marketing)*

The Welsh Books Council is a national organization with charitable status funded by the Welsh Assembly Government. Established in 1961, it is responsible for promoting all sectors of the publishing industry in Wales, in both languages, in conjunction with publishers, booksellers, libraries and schools. The Council is also responsible for distributing publishing grants for Welsh-language publishing and Welsh writing in English. Its Wholesale Distribution Centre stocks the vast majority of Welsh-interest titles currently available. www.gwales.com, the Council's on-line information and ordering service, is a one-stop shop for titles of relevance to Wales.

5089

WORSHIPFUL COMPANY OF STATIONERS AND NEWSPAPER MAKERS
Stationers' Hall, Ave Maria Lane, London EC4M 7DD
Telephone: (020) 7248 2934
Fax: (020) 7489 1975
Email: admin@stationers.org
Web Site: www.stationers.org

Master: R. D. Brewster
Clerk: Brigadier D. G. Sharp AFC

The Worshipful Company of Stationers had its beginnings in a Guild dating back at least to 1403; the original Charter was granted in 1557. The Company was expanded in modern times (1933) to include the Newspaper Makers. For nearly four centuries it was essential for the protection of copyright to register books at Stationers' Hall; since 1924 an extensively used system of voluntary registration has been in force. This was discontinued in February 2000.

The Company's object has always been to promote the interests of the printing and allied trades, among them publishing and bookbinding. Its activities at the present day include the binding of apprentices and the award of scholarships to young men and women in these trades and the provision of pensions and financial help for tradesmen and their widows. The Company also plays a full part in the life of the City of London.

The Stationers' Hall may be hired for functions.

6 Trade & Allied Services

6.1 EDITORIAL SERVICES

6001

ACUPUNCTUATION LTD
4 Harbidges Lane, Long Buckby, Northampton NN6 7QL
Telephone: 01327 844119
Email: acuedit@fireflyuk.net
Web Site: www.acuedit.co.uk

Contact: David Price

Writing, rewriting, editing, proofreading.
Special interests:
– Fine Art (particularly Modern Art);
– Music (particularly operettas and musicals, pop and rock music);
– Travel Guides;
– Modern European History and Politics (particularly Eastern Europe and the former Soviet Union);
– Social and Cultural History.

6002

AESOP (ALL EDITORIAL SERVICES ONLINE FOR PUBLISHERS & AUTHORS)
28 Abberbury Road, Iffley, Oxford OX4 4ES
Telephone: 01865 429563
Fax: 08700 635449
Email: mart@copyedit.co.uk
Web Site: www.copyedit.co.uk

Owner/Editor: Martin Noble

AESOP provides the following editorial services to publishers, authors, academics and businesses: copy-editing; proof-reading; structural editing; rewriting; co-writing; ghost-writing; thesis and dissertation editing and printing; improving use of English of non-native English writers of academic reports and books; indexing; editorial reports and reviews; advice to publishers, authors and literary agents; novelization; research; fact-checking; bibliographical research; CRC (camera ready copy) in Word format; text capture; scanning/OCR; e-book production on CD-ROM or online; keying in MSS; audio transcription; tagging. Specializes in fiction, literature, poetry, media, music, performing arts, humour, biography, memoirs, travel, education, economics, psychology, history, alternative health, new age, esoteric and spiritual subjects, special needs.

6003

ASGARD PUBLISHING SERVICES
75 Woodside View, Leeds LS4 2QS
Telephone: 0113 274 1037
Fax: 0113 274 1037
Email: andrew.shackleton@asgardpublishing.co.uk
Web Site: www.asgardpublishing.co.uk

Also at:
Allan Scott
Telephone: 01449 741747
Fax: 01449 740118
Email: allanscott@compuserve.com

Personnel: Philip Gardner
Michael Scott Rohan
Allan Scott
Andrew Shackleton

Established in 1984. Full editorial service, including writing and re-writing, translating, copy-editing, proof-reading, indexing, design and layout. Projects can be taken from manuscript to film, or to Quark XPress files. Extensive experience with DTP, computer-based multimedia projects (including video production) and electronic publishing. Reference material is a speciality.

6004

*BBR SOLUTIONS LTD
12 Cutthorpe Road, Chesterfield S42 7AE
Telephone: 01246 271662
Fax: 01246 271662
Email: solutions@bbr-online.com
Web Site: www.bbr-online.com/solutions

Directors: Chris Reed
Amanda Thompson

Associated Companies:
UK: BBR Distribution

BBR Solutions is an editorial and design consultancy with over 20 years' experience in publishing. It proofs and edits manuscripts for publication, and creates clean typography-led designs for books and journals. Please take a look at the company's website for some examples.

6005

BLACK ACE BOOK PRODUCTION
PO Box 7547, Perth PH2 1AU
Telephone: 01821 642822
Fax: 01821 642101
Web Site: www.blackacebooks.com

Directors: Hunter Steele
Boo Wood

Book production and text processing, including text capture (or scanning), editing, proofing to camera-ready/film, printing and binding, jacket artwork and design. Delivery of finished books; can sometimes help with distribution.

6006

BOOK CREATION LTD
20 Lochaline Street, London W6 9SH
Telephone: (020) 8563 9982
Fax: (020) 8626 1851
Email: hal@bookcreation.com
Web Site: www.bookcreation.com

Managing Director: Hal Robinson

Associated Companies:
UK: Librios Ltd

Book Creation provides editorial, translation, design and packaging/repackaging services, using Mac and PC technol-ogy, to text and layouts or final film, primarily in illustrated non-fiction, partworks, dictionaries and general reference, often involving re-use of existing illustrative or text resources.
Its sister company, Librios, provides comprehensive, XML-based electronic publishing and content management services.

6007

*CHAMELEON HH PUBLISHING LTD
The Quarry House, East End, Witney, Oxon OX29 6QA
Telephone: 01993 880223
Email: chameleon@chameleonhh.co.uk
Web Site: www.chameleonhh.co.uk

Directors: Marion Hebblethwaite *(Managing)*
Robert White *(Editorial)*
Company Secretary: Helen Hazzledine

Editorial services for self-publishers, electronic publishing services, training in MS Word / Adobe for press quality files.

6008

COPYTRAIN
Pitts, Great Milton, Oxford OX44 7NF
Telephone: 01844 279345
Fax: 01844 279345
Email: rbalkwill@aol.com

Proprietor: Richard Balkwill

Copytrain provides a consultancy and advisory service to publishers in the training and copyright fields.
Training: Publishing Training Centre lecturer in editorial management, financial planning and copyright. Seminars in contracts, copyright and rights. Courses in all aspects of publishing and management.
Copyright: Advice to publishers on rights and copyright matters. Review of authors' and suppliers' contracts and agreements. Associate of Rightscom.
Clients include CAB International, the British Council and the Publishers Licensing Society.
Copytrain provides 'work-for-hire' writing commissions, especially in the children's reference area (non-fiction, history, railways).

6009

FIRST EDITION TRANSLATIONS LTD
6 Wellington Court, Wellington Street, Cambridge CB1 1HZ
Telephone: 01223 356733
Fax: 01223 316232
Email: info@firstedit.co.uk
Web Site: www.firstedit.co.uk

Contact: Sheila Waller

First Edition offers complete and specialized editorial and translation services, including all necessary liaison: translation, research, editing, Americanization, proofreading, indexing, desktop publishing, print ready PDF or CD output. Assessment of foreign language books for the market.

6010

GEO GROUP & ASSOCIATES
4 Christian Fields, London SW16 3JZ
Telephone: (020) 8764 6292
Fax: 0115 981 9418
Email: Nyala.publishing@geo-group.co.uk
Web Site: www.geo-group.co.uk

Also at:
Nyala Publishing, 97 Rivermead, West Bridgford,
Nottingham NG2 7RF
Telephone: 0115 981 9418
Email: (as above)
Web Site: (as above)

Director: John Douglas

Associated Companies:
UK: Nyala Publishing

Publishing services: pre-press, editing, design, proofreading,
reading.

6011

ALEXANDRA NYE, LITERARY CONSULTANT
6 Kinnoull Avenue, Dunblane, Perthshire FK15 9JG
Telephone: 01786 825114

Literary Consultant: Alexandra Nye *(Editorial Director)*

Provides a consultancy service for all types of fiction, with
special interest in literary fiction, Scottish history, upmarket
thrillers. Children's fiction age range 9–12, teens and young
adult. Will supply detailed 5-page report on MSS. Does not
accept poetry, plays, TV scripts or biographies.

6012

CHRISTOPHER PICK
41 Chestnut Road, London SE27 9EZ
Telephone: (020) 8761 2585
Fax: (020) 8761 6388
Email: christopher@the-picks.co.uk

Publications Consultant: Christopher Pick

I research, write, edit and produce information materials for
public- and voluntary-sector agencies and for the corporate
sector. I specialize in producing documents (e.g. policy and
research reports, annual reports, handbooks) that are acces-
sible and clearly written and that meet the needs of the target audience/readership. I also write and produce family
memoirs and 'popular' histories of organizations, companies, etc.

6013

THE PUZZLE HOUSE
Ivy Cottage, Battlesea Green, Stradbroke, Suffolk IP21 5NE
Telephone: 01379 384656
Fax: 01379 384656
Email: puzzlehouse@btinternet.com
Web Site: www.thepuzzlehouse.co.uk

Partners: Roy Preston
Sue Preston

The Puzzle House supplies crossword, quiz and puzzle material for books and magazines. Full editorial service is offered
on projects ranging from a one-off puzzle to full CRC book.
All subject areas and age ranges catered for. Specialist interest and experience in the children's activity market. Established 1988. Puzzles available for syndication.

6014

RONNE RANDALL
26 Oak Tree Avenue, Radcliffe-on-Trent, Nottingham
NG12 1AD
Telephone: 0115 933 5804
Email: ronnerandall@aol.com
Web Site: www.freelancersintheuk.co.uk/ronne-randall-
i430.html

Proprietor: Ronne Randall

Accurate Americanization by a native of the USA, as well as
editorial services including editing, copy editing, writing,
rewriting/adaptation, and proofreading. Special interest and
experience in children's books (including licensed charac-

ters). Clients include Ladybird, Macmillan, Hodder Children's
Books, Templar and Parragon.

6015

READING AND RIGHTING
[Robert Lambolle Services]
618b Finchley Road, London NW11 7RR
Telephone: (020) 8455 4564
Email: lambhorn@gmail.com
Web Site: readingandrighting.netfirms.com

Managing Director: Robert Lambolle *(Literary/Script
Consultant)*

Established in 1987, Reading & Righting is an independent
script consultancy providing evaluation and editing services,
based on wide-ranging agency and publishing experience.
Detailed assessment, analysis of prospects and next-step
guidelines for fiction, non-fiction, screenplays, plays and
poetry, plus full editing service, one-to-one tutorials, mentoring, lectures, creative writing courses, and research. Prospective clients should consult website or request leaflet
outlining procedure and terms.
Specialist interests include cinema, the performing arts,
popular culture, psychotherapy and current affairs.

6016

SANDHURST EDITORIAL
36 Albion Road, Sandhurst, Berks GU47 9BP
Telephone: 01252 877645
Email: lionel.browne@sfep.net
Web Site: www.sandhurst-editorial.co.uk

Proprietor: Lionel Browne

Current clients include:
UK: CAPDM Ltd; Folens; IHS BRE Press; ILM Publications;
London Business School; McGraw-Hill; Palgrave
Publishers; Pearson Education; Publishing Training
Centre; Soundbite Learning; Thomas Telford; Whittles
Publishing; Wiley Blackwell

Sandhurst Editorial provides a complete editorial service for
clients inside and outside the UK, both private sector and
public sector: academic and educational publishers, research
associations, commercial clients, and government departments. The skills on offer include editorial development and
consultancy, project management, writing, rewriting, copy-
editing and proofreading.
The company specializes in science and technology, but
has handled projects as diverse as bibles, biography, travel
guides and corporate reports.

6017

*SUNRISE SETTING LTD
12a Fore Street, St Marychurch, Torquay, Devon TQ1 4NE
Telephone: 01803 322635
Fax: 01803 323565
Email: enquiries@sunrise-setting.co.uk
Web Site: www.sunrise-setting.co.uk

Directors: Jessica Stock *(Finance & Marketing)*
Alistair Smith *(Technical)*

Sunrise Setting Ltd has over 20 years' experience of providing a high-quality typesetting, editorial and project management service to STM publishers, including copyediting, a full
XML workflow, graphics manipulation, project management
of conference proceedings, books and journals, and the
writing of LaTex class files and author support.

6018

HANS ZELL PUBLISHING CONSULTANTS
Glais Bheinn, Lochcarron, Ross-shire IV54 8YB
Telephone: 01520 722951
Fax: 01520 722953
Email: hanszell@hanszell.co.uk
Web Site: www.hanszell.co.uk/

Proprietor: Hans M. Zell

Associated Companies:
UK: Hans Zell Publishing

Consultancy service to publishers and academic institutions,
in particular providing advisory services and individual
project management for publishers, research institutes, and

the book community in Africa and in other developing countries.
Specialization:
– scholarly publishing, especially university press publishing, and publishing by research institutions and NGOs,
including editorial and financial management, administration, marketing and promotion, pricing and distribution,
general publishing management, and dealing with author
and publisher contracts
– journals publishing management, including subscription
management and fulfilment, financial control, journals promotion, and market assessments
– reference book publishing, particularly for reference
resources focusing on Africa and the developing world,
including research, project evaluations, editorial services,
and market assessments
– training – in-house or through workshops and seminars
– in editorial and production management, financial planning, and all areas of marketing
– marketing and distribution of books on African and
development studies, and African literature and culture –
providing a range of specialist mailing list services in this
area, full details available on request.
– Internet training for the book professions in developing
countries.
Also publisher of information resources (print and online)
on Africa, African studies and African publishing.
6.2 Design & Production Services

6.2 DESIGN & PRODUCTION SERVICES

6019

BOOK PRODUCTION CONSULTANTS LTD
25–27 High Street, Chesterton, Cambridge CB4 1ND
Telephone: 01223 352790
Fax: 01223 460718
Email: bpc@bpccam.co.uk
Web Site: www.bpccam.co.uk

Also at:
The Baltic Exchange, St Mary Axe, London EC3A 8EX
Telephone: (020) 7623 2308
Fax: (020) 7623 2309
Email: bpc@bpccam.co.uk
Web Site: www.bpccam.co.uk

Managing Director: Colin Walsh
Managers: Jo Littlechild *(Marketing)*
Susan Buck *(Accounts)*
Jo'e Coleby *(Editorial Project)*

Associated Companies:
UK: Book Connections; Granta Editions

A totally comprehensive publishing service including editing,
sub-editing, designing, technical mark-up, illustrating, technical drawing, estimating, paper buying, typesetting and
origination. BPC arranges the printing and binding of black-
and-white or colour publications in the UK or overseas and
supervises quality control and delivery schedules; also computer software packs including design of packaging and
manufacture of boxes, tapes and discs. Other specialities
include the design and production of illustrated books,
music and foreign language setting projects, academic journals and institutional publications, producing company
sponsored books and company histories. Electronic publishing and CD-ROM origination, particularly as joint ventures,
form part of current expansion. Specialist divisions include
business histories (providing authors, archivists and picture
researchers), contract magazine production and company
literature.

6020

BOOKCRAFT LTD
18 Kendrick Street, Stroud, Glos GL5 1AA
Telephone: 0870 1601900
Fax: 0870 1601901
Email: information@bookcraft.co.uk
Web Site: www.bookcraft.co.uk

Director: John Button *(Publishing)*

Clients include:
UK: Collector's Library; Pearson; Taylor & Francis

Bookcraft provides publishers with a wide range of editorial, design, technical and training services.

Main areas of activity are:

- publishing consultancy
- publishing software training
- design services
- editorial and proofreading services
- project management.

6021

CHASE PUBLISHING SERVICES LTD
33 Livonia Road, Sidmouth, Devon EX10 9JB
Telephone: 01395 514709
Fax: 01395 514709
Email: r.addicott@chase-publishing.co.uk

Director: Ray Addicott

Chase offers a complete editorial and production service to authors and publishers – from copy-editing of the author's typescript to finished books at the delivery point. It specializes in academic books. Founded in 1989.

6022

DISCRIPT LTD
24 Bedfordbury, Covent Garden, London WC2N 4BN
Telephone: (020) 7240 3196
Fax: (020) 7379 8559
Email: info@discript.com
Web Site: www.discript.com

Directors: Richard Bates (Managing)
F. R. Bates (Finance)

Discript can provide editorial, proofreading, production, book design and typography, including text keyboarding, OCR capture and indexing. Whether a large technical document, illustrated book or colour leaflet is required, Discript can provide a fast efficient service. It also helps authors to self-publish.

6023

*FOTOLIBRA
22 Mount View Road, London N4 4HX
Telephone: (020) 8348 1234
Email: professionals@fotoLibra.com
Web Site: www.fotoLibra.com

Directors: Gwyn Headley
Yvonne Seeley

Associated Companies:
USA: Idea Logical Company Inc

Organizations who have used fotoLibra's services include:
UK: Bemrose; Carlton Books; Compendium; Hodder Headline; Macmillan; Pearson; Penguin; Quarto; Random House

fotoLibra is a picture library set up by publishers for publishers. The company has 18,000+ photographers in over 150 countries to take the required image if it is not already in the library – and there's no obligation to buy. Over 250,000 images on line.

6024

GRAHAM-CAMERON ILLUSTRATION
The Studio, 23 Holt Road, Sheringham, Norfolk NR26 8NB
Telephone: 01263 821333
Fax: 01263 821334
Email: enquiry@graham-cameron-illustration.com
Web Site: www.graham-cameron-illustration.com

Sales & Marketing:
Duncan Graham-Cameron, 59 Hertford Road, Brighton BN1 7GG
Telephone: 01273 385890
Email: duncan@graham-cameron-illustration.com
Web Site: (as above)

Partners: Mike Graham-Cameron (Finance)
Helen Graham-Cameron (Art)
Duncan Graham-Cameron (Sales & Marketing)

Parent Company:
UK: Graham-Cameron Publishing

Associated Companies:
UK: Helen Herbert, Fine Art

This agency has some 37 qualified professional illustrators who have a wide range of techniques, media and artistic skills. GCI specializes in pictures for educational and children's books, ELT and for general information publications.

6025

HOLBROOK DESIGN OXFORD LTD
Holbrook House, 105 Rose Hill, Oxford OX4 4HT
Telephone: 01865 459000
Email: info@holbrook-design.co.uk
Web Site: www.holbrook-design.co.uk

Directors: Peter Tucker (Design)
Alex Tucker (Production)

Holbrook Design Oxford Ltd was founded as PGT Design in 1974. It offers the following services: typography, editorial design and art direction, photography; from concept through dummies, mark-up and typesetting, page layouts to artwork, in consultation with photographers, illustrators and printers. Clients include many national and international publishers. Holbrook Design has particular experience in educational and general publishing; subject areas covered range from science to religion, cookery to history and first readers to A-level.

6026

HOLBROOK HOSTING
Holbrook House, 105 Rose Hill, Oxford OX4 4HT
Telephone: 01865 459000
Email: info@holbrookhosting.com
Web Site: www.holbrookhosting.com

Partner: Peter Tucker (Consultant)

Design Systems is a consultancy providing both technical and design expertise in the implementation and use of both Macs and PCs in graphics and publishing industries. Agents include Adobe, Quark, Ventura Software, Monotype, Linotype and other associated companies. Affiliated to Holbrook Design Oxford Ltd, for many years designers in publishing and print.

6027

HYBERT DESIGN LTD
Suite 3, Maple Court, Grove Park, White Waltham, Berks SL6 3LW
Telephone: 01628 822700
Fax: 01628 822288
Email: info@hybertdesign.com
Web Site: www.hybertdesign.com

Also at:
Buterud P1 8722, 464 91 Dals Rostock, Sweden
Telephone: +46 (0)530 30084

Director: Tom Hybert
Company Secretary: Kate Hybert
Senior Designer: Linda Elliott

Established in 1975, Hybert Design specializes in marketing, promotion and cover design for publishers in all areas, including education, science and technology, journal and business publishing.

6028

IMAGO PUBLISHING LTD
Albury Court, Albury, Thame, Oxon OX9 2LP
Telephone: 01844 337000
Fax: 01844 339935
Email: reception@imago.co.uk
Web Site: www.imago.co.uk

Directors: Colin Risk (Managing)
Jim Allpass (Finance)
Angela Young
Debbie Knight
Cherry Jaquet (Production)
Martina Scheible
Paolo Scaramuzza

Offers production consultancy, print broking and training to the publishing industry. With offices in the UK, Paris, Hong Kong, China, Singapore, Malaysia, India, Sydney, New York and California, the group is able to locate and control sources of manufacture on a world-wide basis. The group works with a wide range of customers, and can offer its extensive expertise in many ways, from running all the production needs for small publishers/packagers, to sourcing and arranging for the manufacture of individual projects on a competitive brokerage basis. All types of work are handled, including colour separation, children's books, novelty products, short- and long-run general books and magazines. Training courses in colour, toy safety, paper, assessing digital images, CTP, InDesign, Quark and Photoshop run regularly.

6029

MY WORD!
PO Box 4575, Rugby, Warwickshire CV21 9EH
Telephone: 01788 571294
Fax: 01788 550957
Email: enquiries@myword.co.uk
Web Site: www.myword.co.uk

Partners: Roderick Grant
Janet Grant
DTP Operator: Sally Stow

My Word! is a family business which specializes in typesetting of materials for both printing and the Internet.

Its range includes magazines, books, newsletters, newspapers, brochures, conference and sales materials, leaflets, posters and stationery.

Clients come from both the charity and commercial sectors.

6030

SMALL PRINT
The Old School House, 74 High Street, Swavesey, Cambridge CB24 4QU
Telephone: 01954 231713 (mobile: 07760 430206)
Fax: 01954 205061
Email: info@smallprint.co.uk
Web Site: www.smallprint.co.uk

French Fotos:
(as above)
Telephone: (as above)
Fax: (as above)
Email: frenchfotos@aol.com
Web Site: www.frenchfotos.co.uk

Proprietor: Naomi Laredo
Photographer: Louise John

A flexible publishing and translation resource for publishers and businesses producing educational, training and information material.

Project management and production service includes research, copywriting, editing and proofreading, design and layout for web or print, audio and video production.

Translation and language-checking service covers most European and Asian languages.

French Fotos offers up-to-date images of France and the French, from stock or taken to order.

Clients to date include ACCA, Berlitz, Cambridge University Press, Channel 4 Learning, Dorling Kindersley, Henley Management College, Nelson Thornes.
6.3 Electronic Publishing Services

6.3 ELECTRONIC PUBLISHING SERVICES

6031

ATTWOOLL ASSOCIATES LTD
90 Divinity Road, Oxford OX4 1LN
Telephone: 01865 422230
Fax: 01865 791192
Email: david@attwoollassociates.com
Web Site: www.attwoollassociates.com

Director: David Attwooll
Associate: Clare Painter

Attwooll Associates Ltd is a publishing consultancy and licensing agency specializing in electronic and print media, in North American and UK markets. It was founded in April 2002.

Activities include:

- publishing and media strategy
- intellectual property exploitation and licensing
- project management and innovation
- market-driven content creation and acquisition
- information mapping and knowledge management
- mergers and acquisitions advice
- training seminars and lectures.

Please see www.attwoollassociates.com

6032

GLOBAL MAPPING

Manor Road, Brackley, Northants NN13 6EE
Telephone: 01280 840770
Fax: 01280 840816
Email: sales@globalmapping.uk.com
Web Site: www.globalmapping.uk.com

Managing Director: Alan Smith

Publishes its own range of maps. Also creates bespoke map products for other publishers including interactive map-based websites. Online retailer of map-based products such as wall maps, postcode maps, ordnance survey data, atlases, globes and guides. Global Mapping aims to be a one-stop shop for all map-based requirements.

6033

KOALA PUBLISHING LTD

Downend House, 112 North Street, Downend, Bristol BS16 5SE
Telephone: 0117 910 9111
Fax: 0117 910 9222
Email: sales@koalapub.co.uk
Web Site: www.koalapub.co.uk

Directors: Gordon Dennis *(Commercial)*
  Vivienne Willoughby-Ellis *(Managing)*
Marketing Manager: Robin Shobbrook

Koala helps suppliers of complex products and services who need to:
–   create straightforward, easy to use documentation and get it to their customers in the most effective way possible – from PDAs to printer manuals;
–   efficiently organize, write and deliver their technical manuals, policies and procedures;
–   reduce the cost and time constraints on professional staff of providing information to their customers, and reduce the long-term risks of litigation caused by faulty documentation.
  Koala provides software products for publishing technical documentation including manuals, training materials, catalogues, directories and listings. Services include project management and control; analysis and design; bespoke programming; data format conversion; and full training and support.

6034

LIGHTNING SOURCE UK LTD

Chapter House, Pitfield, Kiln Farm, Milton Keynes MK11 3LW
Telephone: 0845 121 4567
Fax: 0845 121 4594
Email: enquiries@lightningsource.co.uk
Web Site: www.lightningsource.com

President: David Taylor
Directors: Dave Piper *(Managing)*
  Suzanne Wilson-Higgins *(Commercial)*
  Terry Gridley *(Operations)*
  Frank Devine *(Finance)*
Marketing Manager: Lawrence Felice

Parent Company:
USA: Ingram

Associated Companies:
USA: Lightning Source

Lightning Source offers quality, e-book, one-off book manufacturing and access to comprehensive distribution solutions in the publishing industry.

6035

MMT

[trading as MMT Digital]
1A Uppingham Gate, Ayston Road, Uppingham, Rutland LE15 9NY

Telephone: 01572 822278
Fax: 01572 820213
Email: info@mmtdigital.co.uk
Web Site: www.mmtdigital.co.uk

London Office:
Suite 54–55, 88–90 Hatton Gardens, London EC1N 8PN
Telephone: (020) 7242 5698
Fax: (as above)
Email: (as above)
Web Site: (as above)

Directors: Peter Cannings *(Managing & Finance)*
  Ben Rudman *(Marketing)*
  James Cannings *(Production)*
  Will Hawkins *(New Business)*

Currently working with Hodder on their e-titles.

6036

NIELSEN BOOKNET

3rd Floor, Midas House, 62 Goldsworth Road, Woking, Surrey GU21 6LQ
Telephone: 01483 712200
Fax: 01483 712201
Email: sales.booknet@nielsen.com
Web Site: www.nielsenbooknet.co.uk

Director: Ann Betts *(Commercial, President)*
Head of BookNet Sales: Stephen Long
Head of Marketing: Mo Siewcharran
Business Development Manager: Joanna De Courville
Head of Data Sales (Libraries): Paul Dibble

Parent Company:
UK: Nielsen Book
USA: The Nielsen Company

Associated Companies:
UK: Nielsen BookData; Nielsen BookScan

Nielsen BookNet provides a range of e-commerce services that allow electronic trading between booksellers, distributors, publishers, libraries and other suppliers, regardless of their size and location. Services include BookNet Transaction Services for booksellers and publishers/distributors, TeleOrdering and EDI. Nielsen BookNet is uniquely placed in the book trade to be the trading hub for orders, invoices, delivery notes and other EDI messaging.

6037

TRILOGY GROUP

Aries House, 43 Selkirk Street, Cheltenham, Glos GL52 2HJ
Telephone: 01242 222132
Fax: 01242 235103
Email: alex–dare@trilogygroup.com
Web Site: www.trilogygroup.com

Directors: Alex Dare *(Managing)*
  Simon Gough *(IT)*
  Mike Ribbins *(Group Chairman)*

The Trilogy Group specializes in software for the specialist publisher, especially those requiring a totally integrated business solution to handle publishing management, administration, direct and distribution sales together with active marketing. Our software, which uses Microsoft SQL Server technology, offers:
–   title management
–   customer management with profiles and buying history
–   active marketing facilities
–   direct mail management with optional integration to MailSort
–   subscriptions management
–   royalties
–   integration to accounting systems
–   vast range of 'real time' management reports
–   real-time stock management
–   warehouse and despatch management
–   integrated on-line shopping facilities with web hosting
–   multi-site management
–   EPOS
–   production control, scheduling and job costing.

6038

*VISTA

[a division of Publishing Technology]
Link House, 19 Colonial Way, Watford, Herts WD24 4JL
Telephone: 01923 830200

Fax: 01923 238789
Email: solutions@vistacomp.com
Web Site: www.vistacomp.com

Director: Colin Bottle *(Managing)*
Managers: Morayea Pindziak *(International Marketing)*
  John Lawson *(UK Business Development)*

Parent Company:
UK: Publishing Technology Plc

Associated Companies:
Australia: Vista
USA: Vista Inc

A worldwide provider of print and online software solutions and services for the publishing industry. Vista's author2reader™ enterprise-wide applications framework is designed to meet the unique demands of the publishing industry at all stages of the publishing process. The framework provides a modular approach that allows Vista to assemble software components that meet the needs of individual publishers from a standard set of applications. The applications are supported by an array of specialized services, from data conversion and system integration to implementation to consulting to applications hosting.
  Solutions include:
– fulfilment and distribution for books and journals
– warehouse management
– web-based customer service
– title and bibliographic data management
– production management
– business intelligence
– rights and royalties
– digital asset management
– online digital solutions
– off-shore development and support services
– content delivery and web sites.
6.4 Translation Services

6.4 TRANSLATION SERVICES

6039

*AMERICAN PIE

179 Kings Cross Road, London WC1X 9BZ
Telephone: (020) 7278 9490
Fax: (020) 7278 2447
Email: bacon@americanization.com
Web Site: www.langservice.com

Also at:
215 West Red Oak #1, Sunnyvale, CA 94086-6632, USA
Email: DHenderson@aol.com
Web Site: www.americanization.com

Directors: Josephine Bacon *(Managing)*
  Dan Henderson
Secretary: Azmi Jbeily

Parent Company:
USA: American Eyes Ltd

Associated Companies:
UK: Tamr Translations Ltd

American Pie is a company of translators, book packagers and designers, specializing in publishing work and foreign language typesetting. American Pie, with offices in London and Sunnyvale, California, translates between British and American English.

6040

*BRITISH CENTRE FOR LITERARY TRANSLATION (BCLT)

University of East Anglia, Norwich NR4 7TJ
Telephone: 01603 592785
Fax: 01603 592737
Email: bclt@uea.ac.uk
Web Site: www.uea.ac.uk

Director: Amanda Hopkinson
Co-ordinator: Catherine Fuller

Parent Company:
UK: University of East Anglia

Raises the profile of literary translation and the professional development of literary translators. Organizes events, readings, workshops aimed at translators, professionals in arts and publishing and the general public.

6041

FIRST EDITION TRANSLATIONS LTD
6 Wellington Court, Wellington Street, Cambridge CB1 1HZ
Telephone: 01223 356733
Fax: 01223 316232
Email: info@firstedit.co.uk
Web Site: www.firstedit.co.uk

Contact: Sheila Waller

Translations – commercial, technical, academic and of any length – undertaken in any language according to publisher's requirements. Editing, proofreading, Americanization, indexing, typesetting/desktop publishing. Output to print ready PDF or CD. Quotations given without obligation.

6042

SATRAP PUBLISHING & TRANSLATION
Suite 21, London House, 271 King Street, Hammersmith, London W6 9LZ
Telephone: (020) 8748 9397
Fax: (020) 8748 9394
Email: satrap@btconnect.com
Web Site: www.satrap.co.uk

Managing Director: Alex Vahdat
Manager: Mrs Homa Lohrasb (Technical)

Satrap Publishing is a UK-based international company, specializing in the fields of translation, typesetting and print services in Oriental and East European languages.

The company produces promotional literature, exhibition catalogues, information pamphlets, books, reports, manuals, business stationery, product labels, diaries etc for Western European companies, trade centres and various organizations which have foreign language requirements for their overseas trade links.

The human resources and advanced technical facilities available are ideal for those clients who wish to target ethnic minorities for their social, cultural and educational programmes. Satrap Publishing offers a complete package of expert translation, typesetting, professional graphic design as well as printing. Production of exclusive greeting cards and wedding stationery in non-European languages are among other services from Satrap Publishing.

6043

SWEDISH-ENGLISH LITERARY TRANSLATORS ASSOCIATION (SELTA)
3 Roseacre Close, London W13 8DG
Telephone: (020) 8997 1218
Web Site: www.selta.org.uk & www.swedishbookreview.com

Hon Secretary: Peter Linton
Editor, Swedish Book Review: Sarah Death

SELTA aims to promote the publication of Swedish literature in English and to represent the interests of those involved in its translation. Publishes *Swedish Book Review* (**ISSN:** 0265 8119): biannual, £15 p.a.

6044

UPS TRANSLATIONS
111 Baker Street, London W1U 6RR
Telephone: (020) 7224 1220
Fax: (020) 7486 3272
Email: info@upstranslations.com
Web Site: www.upstranslations.com

Chairman & Managing Director: Bernard Silver
Company Secretary: Denise McKenzie
Sales Director: Justin Silver

Parent Company:
UK: United Publicity Services Plc

Translation of books from manuscript to final film, into and from all the languages of the world, and Americanization.

6045

SALLY WALKER LANGUAGE SERVICES
43 St Nicholas Street, Bristol BS1 1TP
Telephone: 0117 929 1594
Fax: 0117 929 0633
Email: translations@sallywalker.co.uk
Web Site: www.sallywalker.co.uk

Also at:
Perch Buildings, 9 Mount Stuart Square, Cardiff CF10 5EE
Telephone: (029) 2048 0747
Fax: (029) 2048 8736
Email: languages@sallywalker.co.uk
Web Site: www.sallywalker.co.uk

Directors: Sally Walker
David Poole (Sales & Marketing)

Established in 1969 Sally Walker Language Services provides a 70 language capability. Languages include all European and major Middle Eastern and Far Eastern. Additionally most Indian and African languages are offered.

6046

WESSEX TRANSLATIONS LTD
Barn 500, The Grange, Romsey Road, Michelmersh, Romsey, Hants SO51 0AE
Telephone: 0870 1669 300
Fax: 0870 1669 299
Email: sales@wt-lm.com
Web Site: www.wt-lm.com

Directors: Jonathan Nater
Robin Weber
Paul Stewart

Associated Companies:
France: Wessex Traductions

In addition to translation our services include interpreting, typesetting, DTP and artwork, editing and proofreading, copywriting, software localization, language training, audio and video transcription, voice-overs and website translations.

Translators always work into their mother tongue, and all translations are double-checked, and then re-worked, DTPed if required and checked again before despatch. The final text is sent by email with hard copy if required to meet clients' individual software requirements, ready to print wherever possible.

A special urgent Tender Translation Service is also offered. 6.5 Sales & Marketing Services

6.5 SALES & MARKETING SERVICES

6047

AMALGAMATED BOOK SERVICES LTD
The Old Mill House, Mill Lane, Uckfield, East Sussex TN22 5AA
Telephone: 01825 746050
Fax: 01825 764925
Email: richard@vinehouseuk.co.uk
Web Site: www.amalg.co.uk

Managing Director: Richard Squibb
Senior Sales Executives: Paul Cook
Glenn Wilson

Associated Companies:
UK: Vine House Distribution Ltd

Sales representation for publishers covering the UK, Ireland and elsewhere.

6048

BERTOLI MITCHELL LLP
53 Chandos Place, Covent Garden, London WC2N 4HS
Telephone: (020) 7812 6416
Fax: (020) 7812 6677
Email: nb@bertolimitchell.co.uk
Web Site: www.bertolimitchell.co.uk

Partners: William Mitchell (Managing)

Natalina Bertoli
Senior Associate: Paul Mitton

Bertoli Mitchell LLP is a specialist mergers and acquisitions advisory firm in the publishing and information industries.

The partnership offers corporate finance services for mergers, acquisitions and divestitures including:
- sell-side advisory representation to sellers of privately held businesses and corporate clients seeking to divest business units or assets
- buy-side advisory services and representation
- commercial and contracts due diligence
- valuations

Since Bertoli Mitchell was founded in 1994 it has advised successfully on over 80 transactions.

Bertoli Mitchell also undertakes strategic research and consultancy. Activities include:
- profiling, analysis, forecasting and recommendations for clients considering entry into specific markets or sectors
- benchmarking, cost audits and development of financial targets
- development of business plans

Clients range from large fully listed international companies to shareholders of small and medium-sized private businesses.

6049

BEST MAILING SERVICES LTD
Merlin Way, North Weald, Epping, Essex CM16 6HR
Telephone: 01992 524343
Fax: 01992 524552
Email: sales@bestmailing.co.uk
Web Site: www.bestmailing.co.uk

Directors: Mrs Lyn Reed (Managing)
Peter Cook (Client Services)

BMS offers a complete direct mail production facility.

Comprehensive services include database management, data capture, laser printing, mail order fulfilment, subscription management, machine and hand enclosing, bulk despatch, overseas and UK postal discounts.

BMS also provides high volume digital printing and on demand publishing, backed up with a professional finishing service which includes booklet making and collating.

6050

*THE BOOK DEPOT
111 Woodcote Avenue, London NW7 2PD
Telephone: (020) 8906 3708
Email: conrad@adword.fsnet.co.uk

Proprietor: Conrad Wiberg

Sales, marketing, promotion campaigns, special sales service, out of print and antiquarian bookfinding service.

6051

BOOKLINK
43 Maycock Grove, Northwood, Middx HA6 3PU
Telephone: 01923 828612
Fax: 01923 828455
Email: info@booklink.co.uk
Web Site: www.booklink.co.uk

Managing Director: Evelyne Duval (Agent)

Associated Companies:
UK: Musketeer Books Ltd

An international connection for foreign rights sales and consultancy. Representing French, English and American publishers/packagers.

6052

BOOKPLATE
12 Hids Copse Road, Oxford OX2 9JJ
Telephone: 01865 861669
Email: sue.miller@oxfordcreative.com
Web Site: www.bookplate.org.uk

Yale Representation:
47 Bedford Square, London WC1B 3DP
Telephone: (020) 7079 4900

Marketing: Sue Miller
Sales: Kate Pocock

Andrew Jarmain
Distribution: John Holloran

Bookplate brings together Yale Representation, Oxford Creative Marketing and Marston – to provide a one-stop sales, marketing and distribution package for publishers.
    Working with Bookplate, publishers benefit from:
    – individual marketing for each publisher ensuring maximum visibility and profile raising
    – wide-ranging, flexible services customized for each publisher
    – direct access to the individual sales, marketing and distribution companies
    – total transparency in reporting on customers and sales
    – 24/7 access to all sales and customer information – fully downloadable
    – a pre-agreed fee encompassing the services of all three companies payable as a percentage of net sales.
    Contact Sue Miller at Oxford Creative Marketing for more information or meet us at the London and Frankfurt Book Fairs, and at BEA.

6053

BOOKS ON MUSIC
3 Kendal Green, Kendal, Cumbria LA9 5PN
Telephone: 01539 740049
Fax: 01539 737744
Email: (via website)
Web Site: www.booksonmusic.co.uk

Manager: Rosemary Dooley

European distributor for:
USA: Pendragon *(books on music)*

World distributor for:
UK: The British Journal for Ethnomusicology; Royal Musical Association Research Chronicle *(journal)*

Books on Music runs collaborative publishers' exhibitions at academic music conferences. Specialization in music.

6054

BROOKSIDE PUBLISHING SERVICES LTD
2 Brookside, Dundrum Road, Dublin 14, Republic of Ireland
Telephone: +353 (01) 298 9937
Fax: +353 (01) 298 2783
Email: sales@brookside.ie

Managing Director: Edwin Higel
Sales & Marketing Manager: Conor Graham
Senior Academic Sales Rep: Michael Darcy
Sales & Marketing Co-ordinator: Mariel Deegan

Agents for various imprints in Ireland including:
Cambridge University Press; Clarus Press; Continuum; A & A Farmar; First Law; Gazelle Academic; Nick Hern; Houghton Mifflin; Institute of Chartered Accountants in Ireland; Irish Academic Press; Irish Theatre Handbook; Jones & Bartlett; Jessica Kingsley; Learning Matters; Pharmaceutical Press; Pluto; Radcliffe Medical; Routledge / Taylor & Francis; Special Stories Publishing; Taxation Advice Bureau Guide; Tottel Publishing

Represents both trade and academic publishers.

6055

BROOMFIELD BOOKS
36 De La Warr Road, East Grinstead, West Sussex RH19 3BP
Telephone: 01342 313237
Fax: 01342 322525
Email: nic@broomfieldbooks.co.uk

Directors: Nic Webb
    Andrea Grant-Webb

Broomfield Books is a publishing consultancy for small and medium publishers of non-fiction and fiction. The sales agency covers London and the south-east of England, together with UK key accounts and the export market.

6056

THE CENTRE FOR INTERFIRM COMPARISON
32 St Thomas Street, Winchester, Hants SO23 9HJ
Telephone: 01962 844144
Fax: 01962 843180
Email: mikebayliss@cifc.co.uk
Web Site: www.cifc.co.uk

Director: M. J. Bayliss

An independent organization established in 1959 by the British Institute of Management and the British Productivity Council specifically to meet the demand for a neutral specialist body to conduct interfirm comparisons (IFCs) and benchmarking projects on a confidential basis as a service to management.
    The Centre has run a series of confidential IFCs specifically designed for book publishers in conjunction with the Publishers Association. These provided participants with measures for assessing how their overall performance compared, where and why it differed, and lines of action for improvement. More recently the Centre carried out projects for learned journal and magazine publishers. It has become a specialist in conducting in-depth and carefully defined benchmarking projects for firms and organizations of all kinds, based on information supplied confidentially by participants.

6057

COLMAN GETTY LTD
28 Windmill Street, London W1T 2JJ
Telephone: (020) 7631 2666
Fax: (020) 7631 2699
Email: info@colmangetty.co.uk
Web Site: www.colmangetty.co.uk

Also at:
5 Gayfield Square, Edinburgh EH1 3NW

Chief Executive: Dotti Irving
Directors: Liz Sich *(Managing)*
    Mark Hutchinson

Colman Getty is a London- and Edinburgh-based consumer PR consultancy, founded in 1987 and headed by Dotti Irving, formerly Publicity Director of Penguin Books. The agency specializes in book publishing, arts' campaigns and issues-related PR and has an established reputation for handling complex, high-profile campaigns, individual promotions, literary awards and longer term consultancies. As well as offering a wide-based expertise in PR and publicity, Colman Getty can also handle every aspect of marketing projects – from copywriting and print production to sales promotion and advertising. Client list includes The Man Booker Prize for Fiction, the Art Fund Prize for museums and galleries, National Poetry Day, *The Times* Cheltenham Literature Festival, World Book Day and a number of individual writers such as J. K. Rowling, Nigella Lawson and Patricia Cornwell. Other clients include the Association of Graduate Recruiters and *Management Today*.

6058

THE COLUMBA BOOKSERVICE
55A Spruce Avenue, Stillorgan Industrial Park, Blackrock, Co Dublin, Republic of Ireland
Telephone: +353 (01) 294 2556
Fax: +353 (01) 294 2564
Email: info@columba.ie
Web Site: www.columba.ie

Directors: Séan O Boyle *(Managing)*
    Cecilia West *(Sales)*

UK distributor/representative for:
Canada: Novalis
Republic of Ireland: The Columba Press
USA: Church Publishing; Michael Glazier Books; The Liturgical Press; Loyola Press; Morehouse Publishing; Paraclete Press; Paulist Press; Pueblo Books; Resource Publications; Twenty-third Publications

The Columba Bookservice provides trade representation, sales and marketing services for a number of religious publishers.

6059

COMPASS DSA LTD
13 Progress Business Park, Whittle Parkway, Slough SL1 6DQ
Telephone: 01628 559500
Fax: 01628 663876
Email: alan@compass-dsa.co.uk
Web Site: www.compass-dsa.co.uk

Directors: Alan Jessop *(Joint Managing)*
    Derek Searle *(Joint Managing)*

Bob Cripps
June Searle

Associated Companies:
Republic of Ireland: Compass Ireland Ltd
UK: Compass Academic Ltd

Client publishers:
Republic of Ireland: The Collins Press; New Island Books Ltd; The O'Brien Press Ltd
UK: Absolute Press; Accent Press; ALMA Books; Assouline; Benefactum; Birlinn Ltd; Black & White Publishing; Capuchin Classics; Carcanet Press; Chronosport; Comma Press; Compendium Publishing; Diffords Guides; Enitharmon Press; Gallic Books; Gibson Square; Good Hotel Guide; Greatest in the World; Hay House Publishers; Nick Hern Books; Hesperus Press; Highdown Books; How to Books / Springhill; Interact; Know the Score; Little Books; Malavan Media; Myrmidon Books; Oldie Publications; Peter Owen; Oxygen Books; Pennant Books; Plexus; Polygon Ltd; Pomona Books; Pushkin Press; Radio Times; Ryland, Peter & Small / Cico; Saqi / Telegram; Sport Media; Summersdale; Thorogood; TMI; Visit Britain; Which?

Compass DSA is one of the leading independent sales companies, providing sales and marketing services for publishers to both the traditional and non-traditional markets across the UK and Ireland.

6060

DAVENPORT PUBLISHING SERVICES – SALES & MARKETING
11 Silbury Rise, Keynsham, Bristol BS31 1JP
Telephone: 0117 986 2914
Fax: 0117 986 2074
Email: anne@annedavenport.demon.co.uk

Proprietor & Consultant: Anne Davenport

Davenport Publishing Services offers consultancy in marketing, promotion, sales and distribution for academic, STM and society publishers.
    Projects successfully completed include marketing planning and market research, promotion planning, sales advice, sourcing of overseas agents, representatives and distributors, and lapsed subscriber chasing. Davenport Publishing Services offers a full service from consultancy to implementation of marketing campaigns. Long-term or short-term projects are welcome. Clients include society publishers, university presses and independent institutions with publishing interests.

6061

DURNELL MARKETING LTD – PUBLISHERS EUROPEAN MARKETING AGENCY
2 Linden Close, Tunbridge Wells TN4 8HH
Telephone: 01892 544272
Fax: 01892 511152
Email: admin@durnell.co.uk & orders@durnell.co.uk
Web Site: www.durnell.co.uk

Proprietors/Directors: Andrew Durnell *(Managing)*
    Julia Lippiatt *(Finance)*

Durnell Marketing provides a solution for publishers wishing to maximize their sales – via a single sales force – to all of Eastern and Western Europe's diverse markets, including Ireland (but excluding the UK). A team of multilingual sales representatives ensures maximum, effective and personal coverage of publishers' potential customers, be they library suppliers, wholesalers, bookshop chains, specialist independents, campus bookshops, non-trade, museum or institutional accounts. Travelling representatives are supported and enhanced by office-based specialists who provide extra sales backup by promoting potential textbooks and major reference works to individual academics and institutions. In addition, Durnell Marketing organizes specific promotions, exhibitions, mailings, author signings and much more.

6062

EDUCATION DIRECT
Riverside House, Sir Thomas Longley Road, Rochester, Kent ME2 4FN
Telephone: 01634 291122
Fax: 01634 720269
Email: info@education.co.uk
Web Site: www.education.co.uk

Directors: Jason Gould *(Managing)*
David Edwards *(Operations)*
Tim Roger *(Finance)*
Company Secretary: Martin Thorpe

Education Direct provides a complete range of services for companies promoting their products and services to schools, colleges and universities, including:
– a list of educational establishments and contact names;
– award-winning marketing software;
– direct mail services to the education sector;
– project management;
– dedicated telesales and customer services department.

6063

*GAZELLE ACADEMIC
White Cross Mills, Hightown, Lancaster LA1 4XS
Telephone: 01524 68765
Fax: 01524 63232
Email: sales@gazellebooks.co.uk
Web Site: www.gazellebookservices.co.uk

Directors: Trevor Witcher *(Managing)*
Brian Haywood *(Finance)*
Mark Trotter *(Sales & Distribution)*

Parent Company:
UK: Gazelle Book Services Ltd

Clients:
Australia: FHA Publishing & Communication
Belgium: EuroComment
Canada: Calgary University Press; Canadian Humanist Publications; Wilfrid Laurier University Press; Museum of New Mexico Press; New Society Publishers
Denmark: Aarhus University Press; Museum Tusculanum Press
Finland: Finnish Literature Society; PG-Team Oy; Sophi Academic Press
Germany: Ontos-verlag.de
Israel: Yad Ben Zvi
Netherlands: Aspekt Uitgeverij BV; Nova Vista Publishing; VU University Press
Norway: Tapir Academic Press
Sweden: International Idea; Nordic Academic Press; Student Litteratur
Switzerland: INU Press
UK: Arabian Publishing; Boulevard Books; Clinical Press – Europe; Elector Electronics; William Harvey Press Ltd; Institute of Economic Affairs; Merit Publishing (Medical); Sponsorship Unit; Sussex Academic Press; TFM Publishing Ltd (Medical); World Council of Churches
USA: Ariadne Press; Colorado University Press; Current Clinical Strategies Publishing; Darwin Press; Duquesne University Press; Encounter Books; Feminist Press; Hackett Publishing Co; Harlan Davidson Inc; Ibex Publishers; J & S Publishing Co Inc; Liberty Fund; Mage Publishers; MediPress; Nova Science Publishers Inc; Scientific Publishing Co; Truman State University Press; University of Alberta Press; University of New Mexico Press; Woodbine House Inc

Gazelle Academic is now a division of Gazelle Book Services.

6064

GLOBAL BOOK MARKETING LTD
99B Wallis Road, London E9 5LN
Telephone: (020) 8533 5800
Fax: (020) 8533 5800
Email: info@globalbookmarketing.co.uk

Managing Director: A. Zurbrugg
Managers: A. Howe *(Sales)*
A. Hanson *(IT)*

European agents for:
Canada: Between the Lines; Fernwood Publishing
France: Cacimbo Editions
Germany: Bayreuth African Studies; Barbara Budrich; LIT Verlag
Jamaica: Ian Randle Publishers; Universities of the Caribbean Press
Kenya: Camerapix
Netherlands: International Books (Utrecht); Techne
Nigeria: Kachifo
South Africa: Blue Weaver Marketing; Fernwood Press; Human & Rousseau; Jacana Education; Kwela Books; Pharos; David Philip / Spearhead / New Africa Books Consortium; Tafelberg
Sweden: Nordic Africa Institute

Switzerland: Basler Afrika Bibliografien
Tanzania: Blue Mango Publishing
UK: African Rights; Battlebridge; Eastern Arts / Saffron; Horniman Museum Publications
USA: Human Rights Watch; International Publishers (New York)
Zimbabwe: African Publishing Group

Agents and representatives. Many publishers are distributed by Central Books Ltd.

6065

HAWKINS PUBLISHING SERVICES
12 Parkview Cottages, Crowhurst Lane End, Oxted, Surrey RH8 9NT
Telephone: 01342 893029
Fax: 01342 893316
Email: gill.hawkins@virgin.net

Director: Gillian Hawkins

Distributor for:
UK: James Clarke; Green Umbrella Publishing; Lutterworth Press; The National Archive; Shepheard Walwyn

Sales, marketing, publicity, rights and distribution.

6066

HUMPHRYS ROBERTS ASSOCIATES
5 Voluntary Place, Wanstead, London E11 2RP
Telephone: (020) 8530 5028
Fax: (020) 8530 7870
Email: humph4hra@aol.com

Also at:
Terry Roberts, Humphrys Roberts Associates, Caixa Postal 801, Agencia Jardim da Gloria, 06700-990 Cotia SP, Brazil
Telephone: +55 (11) 4702 4496 & 4702 6997
Fax: +55 (11) 4702 6896
Email: hrabrasil@intercall.com.br

Also at:
Christopher Humphrys, Humphrys Roberts Associates, Apartado 83, Calle Teodoro de Molina 9, 29480 Gaucin, Malaga, Spain
Telephone: +34 (952) 151462
Fax: +34 (952) 151463
Email: humph4hra@gmail.com

Joint Managing Directors: Christopher Humphrys
Terry Roberts

Publishers' agents and representatives, representing UK and US publishers in South America, Central America, Mexico, the Caribbean, Spain, Portugal and Gibraltar.

6067

BRIAN INNS BOOKSALES & SERVICES
9 Ashley Crescent, Warwick CV34 6QH
Telephone: 01926 498428
Fax: 01926 498428
Email: brian.inns@btinternet.com

Managing Director: Brian Inns

Specialization: general non-fiction and technical books.
Services: consultancy and solutions for publishers. Development of business with multiple bookselling groups and key accounts handled personally by Brian Inns. Specialist at improving market penetration. Representation in UK. Distribution arranged.

6068

CHRIS LLOYD SALES & MARKETING SERVICES
50a Willis Way, Poole, Dorset BH15 3SY
Telephone: 01202 649930
Fax: 01202 649950
Email: chrlloyd@globalnet.co.uk
Web Site: www.chrislloydsales.co.uk

Distribution:
Orca Book Services
Telephone: 01202 665432

Proprietor: Christopher Lloyd

Publishers & Imprints represented include:
Belgium: Tectum
Canada: Annick Press; Boston Mills Press; Firefly Books; Master Point Press; Robert Rose
France: Heimdal Editions; Herrisey Editions; Histoire & Collections
Netherlands: Miller Books
New Zealand: Ventura Publications
Spain: Andrea Press; Udyat Books
UK: Amateur Winemaker Books; Argus Books; Bromley Books; D & B Publishing; Finesse Bridge Books; Galago Books; Herridge & Sons; Jaguar Daimler Heritage Trust; Key Books; LDA (Learning Development Aids); Mindsports; Mushroom Model Publications; Plane Essentials; Special Interest Model Books *(formerly Nexus Special Interests)*; Veloce Publishing
USA: Black Dog & Leventhal; Cycle Publishing / van der Plas Publications; Meadowbrook Press; Mikaya; Potomac Books *(formerly Brasseys Inc)*; Marianne Richmond Studios

An independent sales and marketing agency for small and medium sized publishers.

6069

THE MANNING PARTNERSHIP LTD
6 The Old Dairy, Melcombe Road, Oldfield Park, Bath BA2 3LR
Telephone: 01225 478444
Fax: 01225 478440
Email: karen@manning-partnership.co.uk
Web Site: www.manning-partnership.co.uk

Joint Managing Directors: Garry Manning
Roger Hibbert
Managers: James Wheeler *(Sales)*
Karen Twissell *(Office)*
Office Assistant: Jo Hughes

Associated Companies:
UK: Brown Dog Books; Nightingale Press

UK Distributor for:
UK: Anness; Brimax; Carroll & Brown; Five Mile Press; Flair; Globe Pequot Press; Interpet Publishing; Oval Books; Tony Potter; Mathew Price; RICS Books; Search Press; Selectabook; Source Books

The Manning Partnership Ltd offers a total sales, marketing and distribution solution for publishers both in the UK and in English-language export markets. Formed in March 1997. Traditional and non-traditional markets are serviced.

6070

MARKETABILITY (UK) LTD
12 Sandy Lane, Teddington, Middx TW11 0DR
Telephone: (020) 8977 2741
Fax: (020) 8977 2741
Email: rachel@marketability.info
Web Site: www.marketability.info

Director: Rachel Maund

Current and recent clients include:
Canada: B. C. Decker
China: Higher Education Press
Republic of Ireland: New Island
Singapore: National Book Development Council; Singapore Book Publishers' Association; Taylor & Francis; World Scientific
UK: BBC Active; Bradt Travel Guides; Brilliant Publications; Cambridge University Press; Centre for Alternative Technology; Church House Publishing; Compass Maps and Guides; Continuum; Dundee University Press; Elsevier; European Database of Libraries; HarperCollins Publishers; Hodder Education; Hymns Ancient and Modern; Lonely Planet; Macmillan; McGraw Hill; Natural History Museum Publications; NBN International; NCVO (National Council for Voluntary Organisations); Oxford University Press; Palgrave Macmillan; Paperless Proofs; Pearson Education; Pen and Sword Books; Pluto Press; ProQuest; Royal Society; Sage Publications; Taylor & Francis Group; University of Wales Press; Wiley-Blackwell Publishing; World Scientific

Marketability is a group of experienced publishing consultants, all ex-publishers, providing complete support to publishers' marketing departments, from campaigns to consultancy. It supplies resources when needed: to manage catalogue or direct marketing campaigns, devise and conduct market research, or provide consultancy and advice on strategic and practical issues. Its experience is across all publishing sectors, and with both small and large organizations.

Also provides in-company and external training courses – see our separate entry under Training.

6071

MIDAS PUBLIC RELATIONS LTD
10–14 Old Court Place, Kensington, London W8 4PL
Telephone: (020) 7361 7860
Fax: (020) 7938 1268
Email: info@midaspr.co.uk
Web Site: www.midaspr.co.uk

Chairman: Tony Mulliken
Directors: Steven Williams *(Managing)*
Jacks Thomas *(Managing)*
Emma Draude *(Deputy Managing)*

Midas has established a reputation as one of the leading PR agencies for the book, magazine and publishing industry, through its work with major publishing houses, high profile authors, corporate communications, trade and consumer events and awards, and the Direct Marketing Industry. Originally formed in 1990 to service the publishing industry, its areas of expertise now span related sectors including the arts, awards, media, home entertainment, music, children's and the direct marketing industry. A fully accredited member of the PRCA.

6072

MOMENTA PUBLISHING LTD
2 Moorlands Close, Hindhead, Surrey GU26 6SY
Telephone: 01428 606339
Fax: 01428 606339
Email: roblmomenta@compuserve.com

Director: Robert Leech
Company Secretary: Mahara Collier

Founded 1972. Momenta represents various publishing houses, mainly specializing in academic, scholastic, technical, architectural, scientific and medical books, located in continental Europe and the USA as well as the UK.

Momenta offers the following services:

full sales representation in the UK and Western Europe; visits to bookshops, sci-tech, academic and medical centres, universities, libraries;

medical and sci-tech lecturers and personnel; participation in book fairs, congresses and exhibitions; detailed visit reports containing comments, impressions and recommendations;

market research;

contact with overdue debtors;

book distribution if required.

Momenta is a dynamic company with a wide experience in book sale and promotion.

6073

NIELSEN BOOKSCAN
3rd Floor, Midas House, 62 Goldsworth Road, Woking GU21 6LQ
Telephone: 01483 712222
Fax: 01483 712220
Email: info.bookscan@nielsen.com
Web Site: www.nielsenbookscan.co.uk

Head of Marketing: Mo Siewcharran
Commercial Director: Ann Betts
UK Business Director: Julie Meynink
Managers: Reeta Windsor *(Publisher Account)*
Carol Brownlee *(Retail Account)*
Head of Data Services (Libraries): Paul Dibble

Parent Company:
UK: Nielsen Book
USA: The Nielsen Company

Associated Companies:
UK: Nielsen BookData; Nielsen BookNet

Nielsen BookScan is a continuous book sales tracking service operating in the UK, Ireland, Australia, the USA, South Africa, Italy, New Zealand, Denmark and Spain. BookScan collects total transaction data at the point of sale directly from tills and dispatch systems of all major book retailers. This ensures that detailed and highly accurate sales information on what books are selling, and at what price, is available

to the book trade. LibScan measures book borrowings in public libraries.

6074

OXFORD CREATIVE MARKETING
12 Hids Copse Road, Oxford OX2 9JJ
Telephone: 01865 861669
Email: info@oxfordcreative.com
Web Site: www.oxfordcreative.com

Managing Director: Sue Miller

Oxford Creative Marketing provides wide-ranging marketing, publicity and consultancy serevices for academic, educational, professional and trade publishers.

Services include: marketing planning and new strategy advice; copywriting for corporate material, catalogues, fliers, newsletters, etc.; direct mail campaigns; and publicity campaigns for trade and academic books, and any work usually handled by an in-house marketing department.

As well as handling one-off projects, OCM can provide on-going marketing support.

In conjunction with Yale Representation and Marston, OCM is a partner in a venture called Bookplate, providing a one-stop, combined sales, marketing and distribution service for publishers.

6075

OXFORD PUBLICITY PARTNERSHIP LTD
5 Victoria House, 138 Watling Street East, Towcester NN12 6BT
Telephone: 01327 357770
Fax: 01327 359572
Email: info@oppuk.co.uk
Web Site: www.oppuk.co.uk

Director: Gary Hall

Launched in 1989, the Oxford Publicity Partnership provides a comprehensive range of sales and marketing services for general non-fiction, academic and professional publishers on an on-going or freelance basis.

OPP acts as the UK and European sales and marketing office for a number of British and North American publishers and its focus is on the development of their presence in these markets to achieve wider recognition and enhanced sales.

OPP's team of experienced marketing staff work with clients to achieve the best combination of publicity and PR, direct mail, electronic marketing, advertising, and exhibition participation. It also has close links with reps, distributors, and the book trade.

6076

*PARKER ASSOCIATES
Cedar House, 35 Chichele Road, Oxted, Surrey RH8 0AE
Telephone: 01883 730207
Fax: 01883 730188
Email: 101341.1235@compuserve.com

Managing Director: Adrian Parker

Representing:
UK: Saraband; Sheldrake Press

Sales and marketing group for publishers. Selling to the UK and Ireland book trade and also to the European book trade. Eight representatives sell to the UK book trade and two to the Irish book trade. Four representatives sell to the European book trade.

6077

*PUBLISHING SERVICES
9 Curwen Road, London W12 9AF
Telephone: (020) 8222 6800
Fax: (020) 8222 6799
Email: susanne@publishing-services.co.uk
Web Site: www.publishing-services.co.uk

Sales Force:
Signature Book Services, 20 Castlegate, York YO1 9RP
Telephone: 01904 633633
Fax: 01904 675445
Email: sales@signaturebooks.co.uk
Web Site: www.signaturebooks.co.uk

Clients include:
UK: Peter Lang Ltd; Lucas Publications; The Tagman Press

Publishing Services offers smaller publishers and media-friendly authors everything from third-party sales and distribution to editing, production and marketing. Our main areas are general fiction/non-fiction and trade niche areas.

It works in association with Signature Books Services and Central Books for UK sales and distribution respectively.

Core marketing services include:

– preparing sales & marketing material in association with the author and publisher

– preparing marketing plans

– implementing publicity campaigns

– liaising with the repforce about dues, sales and publicity

Publishing Services is currently running a series of seminars on grassroots marketing for the Society of Authors.

Other services vary according to the needs of the publisher and include:

– rights submissions

– website advice

– feedback on cover and inside-page design, editing, format, price and timing

– setting up systems – e.g. costings, production schedules, contracts

– special sales

Publishing Services maintains a 'virtual' office of assistants and third-party suppliers, whose services are available to clients at cost, as well as a database of independent bookshops.

6078

JOHN RULE, PUBLISHERS SALES AGENT
40 Voltaire Road, London SW4 6DH
Telephone: (020) 7498 0115
Email: johnrule@johnrule.co.uk

Manager: John Rule

Sales and distribution services for small publishers into UK and export markets.

6079

SEOL LTD
West Newington House, 10 Newington Road, Edinburgh EH9 1QS
Telephone: 0131 668 1456
Fax: 0131 668 4466
Email: info@seol.co.uk

Joint Managing Directors: Hugh Andrew
Carol Crawford
Harry Ward
Carole Hamilton
Financial Manager: Rona Stewart

Clients include:
UK: Appletree Press Ltd; Argyll Publishing; Atelier; Colin Baxter; Birlinn Ltd; Clan Books; John Donald; Fort Publishing; Goblinshead; Hallewell Publications; House of Lochar; Glen Murray Publishing; Polygon; RCAHMS (Royal Commission on the Ancient & Historical Monuments of Scotland); Rucksack Readers; Saltire Society; Usborne

A sales representation agency to the trade and non-traditional outlets in Scotland.

6080

*WILLIAM SNYDER PUBLISHING ASSOCIATES
5 Five Mile Drive, Oxford OX2 8HT
Telephone: 01865 513186
Fax: 01865 513186
Email: snyderpub@aol.com
Web Site: www.hoovers-europe.com

Managing Director: W. A. Snyder

Publishers represented include:
Belgium: Euroconfidentiel
Canada: Canadian Almanac & Directory
Germany: Germany's Top 500
UK: ELC International
USA: Bernan Press; Grey House Publishing; Hoover's Business Press; Omnigraphics; Peachtree Publishers

A specialist provider of business information on companies, people and regions. The company has formed links with several US and Canadian producers of information in reference book form, journals and in electronic formats.

In addition, a consultancy service for organizations interested in international publishing and marketing is provided.

6081

STAR BOOK SALES
PO Box 20, Whimple, Exeter EX5 2WY
Telephone: 0845 156 7082
Fax: 01404 823820
Email: enquiries@starbooksales.com
Web Site: www.starbooksales.com

Sales Director: Dennis Buckingham

UK distributor for:
UK: Cadmos Books; Edit Vallard; Evans Mitchell Books; JB
Publishing; Parker House Publishing; Redcliffe Press

Providing sales, marketing and distribution services for UK
and international publishers. Territories covered in primary
market: UK and Europe.
Through associated organizations it can provide global
coverage for English language titles.

6082

UNIVERSITY PRESSES MARKETING
The Tobacco Factory, Raleigh Road, Southville, Bristol
BS3 1TF
Telephone: 0117 902 0275
Fax: 0117 902 0294
Email: sales@universitypressesmarketing.co.uk
Web Site: www.universitypressesmarketing.co.uk

Chief Executive Officer: Andrew Gilman
Managers: Paul Skinner (Office)
Helena Svojsikova (Area)

Sales agent for (mainly) American university presses in the
UK and Europe.

6083

*THE UNIVERSITY PRESSES OF CALIFORNIA, COLUMBIA & PRINCETON LTD
John Wiley & Sons Ltd, Distribution Centre,
1 Oldlands Way, Bognor Regis, West Sussex PO22 9SA
Telephone: 01243 842165
Fax: 01243 842167
Email: lois@upccp.demon.co.uk

Managing Director: Andrew Brewer
Business Manager: Lois Edwards

6084

PETER WARD BOOK EXPORTS
Unit 3, Taylors Yard, 67 Alderbrook Road, London
SW12 8AD
Telephone: (020) 8772 3300
Fax: (020) 8772 3309
Email: richard@pwbookex.com

Senior Partner: Richard Ward

Publishers' sales representatives in Middle East, North Africa,
Cyprus, Turkey, Malta, Greece and Israel.
6.6 Distributors

6.6 DISTRIBUTORS

6085

ACTIVAIR LTD
Action Court, Ashford Road, Ashford, Middx TW15 1XS
Telephone: 01784 890005
Fax: 01784 890013
Email: paul.barrett@activair.com
Web Site: www.activair.com

Oceanfreight Division:
Activsea Ltd, Unit B2 Zenith, Payecocke Road, Basildon,
Essex SS14 3DW
Telephone: 01268 595320
Fax: 01268 287597
Email: martin.caines@activsea.com

Directors: Paul Barrett (Sales)
Steve Lai (Financial)
Martin Caines (Oceanfreight Sales)

Parent Company:
USA: OHL Inc

Freight forwarder to the publishing industry, providing efficient cost-effective services specifically designed for the
worldwide movement of trade and academic books. Services offered are by air, sea and road between publisher's
warehouse and bookshop door. Sponsor of the British Book
Awards.

6086

AFRICAN BOOKS COLLECTIVE
PO Box 721, Oxford OX1 9EN
Telephone: 01869 349110
Fax: 01869 349110
Email: orders@africanbookscollective.com
Web Site: www.africanbookscollective.com

Head: Mary Jay
Sales & Marketing: Justin Cox

Participating publishers include:
Benin: Centre Panafricain de Prospective Sociale / Pan-
African Social Prospects Centre
Botswana: Lightbooks Publishers; Pyramid Publishing
Cameroon: University of Buea
Eritrea: Hdri Publishers
Ethiopia: Development Policy Management Forum (DPMF);
Forum for Social Studies; Organisation for Social Science
Research in Eastern and Southern Africa (OSSREA)
Ghana: Afram Publications (Ghana) Ltd; Africa Christian
Press; Association of African Universities Press;
Blackmask; Freedom Publishers; Ghana Universities Press;
Sedco Publishing; SEM Financial Training Centre Ltd;
Sub-Saharan Publishers; Third World Network Africa;
Woeli Publishing Services; Women's Health Action
Research Centre
Kenya: Academy Science Publishers; East African
Educational Publishers; Focus Books; Kwani Trust;
LawAfrica; Nairobi University Press
Lesotho: Institute of Southern African Studies, National
University of Lesotho; Law Society of Lesotho
Malawi: Central Africana; Chancellor College Publishers;
Kachere Series
Namibia: Reader in Namibian Sociology; University of
Namibia Press
Nigeria: African Heritage Press; College Press Publishers;
CSS Ltd; Enicrownfit Publishers; Fourth Dimension
Publishing Co Ltd; Heinemann Educational Books
(Nigeria); Ibadan Cultural Studies Group; Ibadan
University Press; Kraft Books; Maiyati Chambers;
Malthouse Press Ltd; New Horn Press Ltd; Obafemi
Awolowo University Press; Onyoma Research
Publications; Saros International Publishers; Spectrum
Books Ltd; University of Lagos Press; University Press Ltd
Senegal: African Renaissance; Council for the Development
of Social Science Research in Africa (CODESRIA)
Sierra Leone: PenPoint Publishers
South Africa: Africa Institute of South Africa; Brenthurst
Collection / Frank Horley Books; Ikhwezi Afrika
Publishers; Mail and Guardian Books; UNISA Press
Swaziland: JAN Publishing Centre
Tanzania: Centre for Energy, Environment, Science &
Technology (CEEST); Dar es Salaam University Press; E &
D Ltd; Mkuki na Nyota Publishers; Tanzania Publishing
House
Uganda: Femrite (Uganda Women Writers' Association);
Fountain Publishers
Zambia: Bookworld Publishers; Multimedia Zambia;
University of Zambia; Zambia Women Writers'
Association
Zimbabwe: Africa Community Publishing & Development
Trust; Baobab Books; Kimaathi Publishing House;
Mambo Press; Southern African Printing and Publishing
House / SAPES Trust; University of Zimbabwe
Publications; Weaver Press Ltd; Women and Law in South
Africa Research Trust; Zimbabwe International Book Fair
Trust; Zimbabwe Publishing House Ltd

African Books Collective is a major initiative to promote Afri-
can-published books in Europe, North America, and in Commonwealth countries outside Africa. It is owned by the
founding publishers, and is non-profit making on its own
behalf. Centralized billing and shipping is provided from
Oxford; and for North America by Michigan State University
Press. The greater part of the list is available print-on-
demand. A range of joint catalogues and other promotional
material is mailed to libraries and other book buyers. English-language material is stocked, with an emphasis on
scholarly, literature and children's titles. A small number of
titles in French and children's titles in Swahili are also
stocked. Standing order / blanket order plans are available
and can be geared to meet libraries' specific requirements or
acquisitions profiles. Trading started in May 1990.

6087

THE ANGLO-AMERICAN BOOK CO LTD
Crown Buildings, Bancyfelin, Carmarthen SA33 5ND
Telephone: 01267 211880
Fax: 01267 211882
Email: books@anglo-american.co.uk
Web Site: www.anglo-american.co.uk

Directors: Mr D. Bowman (Managing)
Mrs C. Lenton (Marketing)

UK Distributor/Representative for:
USA: Center Press; Milton H. Erickson Foundation Press;
Free Spirit Publishing; Genesis II; International Society of
Neuro-Semantics; Kagan & Kagan; Kendall/Hunt;
Leading Edge Communications; Meta Publications;
Network 3000 Publishing; NLP Comprehensive; Science
and Behavior Books; Success Strategies; Teacher Created
Materials; Transforming Press; Westwood Publishing

The Anglo-American Book Co is a stockholding distributor
of British and American books with particular expertise in
the NLP, personal growth, hypnotherapy, accelerated learning and psychotherapy fields. Stock book orders received by
2.30 pm are dispatched the same day.
Order Department opening times: 9–5 Monday to Friday.

6088

ATLANTIC BOOKS
The Bookhouse, 18 Great Footway, Tunbridge Wells, Kent
TN3 0DT
Telephone: 01892 864951
Fax: 01892 864950
Email: esther@atlanticbooks.co.uk
Web Site: www.atlanticbooks.co.uk

Managers: Esther Matthews (Proprietor)
Andy Ackerley (Sales & Marketing)
Jayne Robinson (Customer Service)
Joe Ackerley (Warehouse)

Supplier of all US published material; any American title.

6089

AVANTIBOOKS LTD
Unit 9, The io Centre, Whittle Way, Arlington Business Park,
Stevenage SG1 2BD
Telephone: 01438 747000
Fax: 01438 741131
Email: orders@avantibooks.com
Web Site: www.avantibooks.com

Directors: Hilary Rosenberg
Sue Ravitz

UK distributor/representative for:
Australia: ARIS
South Africa: University of Kwa-Zulu-Natal; Viva Books
UK: Brown & Brown Publishing; Gatehouse Media; LLU+;
Newleaf Books; Suffolk Community Learning & Skills
Dept; Suffolk Family Learning
USA: New Readers Press; Peppercorn Books & Press

Mail order bookshop, specializing in educational titles for
basic skills teaching and ESOL/ELT.

6090

BBR DISTRIBUTION
12 Cutthorpe Road, Chesterfield S42 7AE
Telephone: 01246 271662
Fax: 01246 271662
Email: distribution@bbr-online.com
Web Site: www.bbr-online.com/catalogue

Director: Chris Reed

Parent Company:
UK: BBR Solutions Ltd

UK distributor for:
Australia: Aurealis; Chimaera Publications
Canada: Tesseract Books
Republic of Ireland: Aeon Press; Albedo One
UK: Bowland Press; British Association for Korean Studies
(BAKS); EAHMH Publications; Endcliffe Press; European
Association for the History of Medicine and Health
Publications; Hilltop Press
USA: Automatism Press; Cambrian Publications; Cyber-

Psycho's A.O.D.; Dreams and Nightmares; Fairwood Press; Jazz Police Books; New York Review of S.F.; Not One of Us; Nova Express; Ocean View Books; Permeable Press; Space & Time; Talebones; Wordcraft of Oregon

BBR is an editorial and design consultancy with 25 years' experience in publishing. It proofs and edits manuscripts for publication, and creates typography-led designs for books and journals. Please take a look at the company's website for examples of recent work.

6091

BEBC DISTRIBUTION
Albion Close, Parkstone, Poole, Dorset BH12 3LL
Telephone: 01202 715555
Fax: 01202 715556
Email: karen@bebc.co.uk
Web Site: www.bebcdistribution.co.uk

Managing Director: John Walsh
Managers: Charles Kipping *(Marketing)*
Rosy Jones *(Operations)*
Karen Bickers *(Client)*

Parent Company:
UK: The Bournemouth English Book Centre Ltd

UK Distributor/Representative for:
UK: Academic Book Collection; Actual Enterprises; Adams & Austen Press; John Benjamins; Boyer Education; Brilliant Publications; Brookemead ELT; Catt Publishing; Chancerel; Coat Mear Press; College of Law Publishing; Commonwealth Secretariat; Gem Publishing; Global Legal English; Insearch Publications; The Language Factory; Learning Matters; Listen & Speak Publications; NCELTR; Oxfam; Practical Pre-School Books; Redhead Music; Reflect Press; Smile Mathematics; TP Publications; White Adder; York Associates

Distribution of publishers involved with business books, law books, English language teaching, ICT books, human rights and conservation.

6092

BETTER BOOKS
3 Paganel Drive, Dudley DY1 4AZ
Telephone: 01384 253276
Fax: 0871 715 0236
Email: sales@betterbooks.com
Web Site: www.betterbooks.com

Proprietor: P. J. Wilkes

UK distributor/representative for:
USA: Educators Publishing Service

Mail order distributor of books relating to dyslexia and other special educational needs.

6093

THE BOOK SERVICE LTD
Colchester Road, Frating Green, Colchester, Essex CO7 7DW
Telephone: 01206 256000 (orders: 255678)
Fax: 01206 255929 (orders: 255930)
Email: sales@tbs-ltd.co.uk
Web Site: www.TheBookService.co.uk

Transworld Distribution Centre:
Sanders Road, Finedon Road Industrial Estate, Wellingborough NN8 4NL
Telephone: 01933 225761

Directors: M. Williams *(Managing)*
Colin James *(Deputy Managing)*
Justin Smith *(Finance & Commercial)*

Parent Company:
UK: The Random House Group Ltd

Associated Companies:
UK: Grantham Book Services

Distribution services offered to:
Andersen Press; Atlantic Books; BBC Audio Books; Nicholas Brealey; Canongate Books; Constable & Robinson; Faber & Faber; Granta Books; Know the Score; Little Brown Book Group; Mainstream Publishing; Methuen

Publishing; Parragon Disney; Profile Books; Quercus; Random House Group; Sort of Books; Transworld International; Virgin Books

Distribution covers order receipt, by telephone, post, EDI and teleordering, telesales, year-round hotline service, cyclical invoicing, despatch via Parceline, Countrywide, post and own vehicles. Also included is a full sales ledger and cash collection service. Sales and stock information and royalties are offered. Debt and stock insurance available. Ancillary work such as mailing, shrink-wrapping, repricing, dump-bin and counterpack make up is also available.

6094

BOOK SYSTEMS PLUS LTD
BSP House, Station Road, Linton, Cambs CB21 4NW
Telephone: 01223 894870
Fax: 01223 894871
Email: bsp2b@aol.com
Web Site: www.booksystemsplus.com

Managing Director: George J. Papa
Marketing & New Business: Shirley Greenall

Parent Company:
UK: Whittet Books Ltd

Publishers represented:
Australia: A & B Publishers Pty Ltd; Bookbiz International
Canada: The Althouse Press; The Charlton Press; Detselig Enterprises Ltd; Greatest Escapes.com
Germany: Chateaux & Manoirs
Netherlands: Mo' Media
South Africa: Dreams 4 Africa
UK: Aardvark Publishing; Alice & Fred Books; Caister Academic Press; Chakula Press Ltd; Classic Locations; Cobwebs Brentwood; Cracking It; Delfryn Publications; EFL Ltd; Fitzwarren Publishing; Focus Publications Ltd; Gudrun Publishing / Edda UK; Hiller Airguns; Hoopoe Books; Idlewild Publishers; Institute for Psychophysical Research; Oxford Forum; Pathfinder Audio; Porpoise Books; Raleo Publishing Ltd; Revenge Ink Ltd; UK International Ceramics; Vista Consulting Team Ltd; Whittet Books Ltd; Wild Boar Trading
USA: John F. Blair, Publisher

Book Systems Plus provides full distribution, invoicing and customer services to publishers from the UK and overseas. It also offers bookshop representation and marketing support. It has particular marketing expertise with travel guides and books on antiques and collectables. It acts as the UK sole agent for publishers in North America, Australia, South Africa and Europe.

6095

*BOOKMART LTD
Blaby Road, Wigston, Leicester LE18 4SE
Telephone: 0116 275 9060
Fax: 0116 275 9090
Email: books@bookmart.co.uk
Web Site: www.bookmart.co.uk

Directors: P. E. Parkin *(Managing)*
A. J. Painter *(Finance)*
D. I. Button *(Purchasing)*
L. Williams *(Rights)*
R. J. Parkin *(Sales (Books/ Distribution/ Stationery))*

Promotional books, publisher and distributor.

6096

BOOKPOINT LTD
130 Milton Park, Abingdon, Oxon OX14 4SB
Telephone: 01235 400560
Fax: 01235 832068
Web Site: www.bookpoint.co.uk

Directors: Chris Emerson *(Chief Operating Officer)*
Martyn Burchall *(Operations)*
Alison Rennie *(Customer Service)*
Graham Money *(General Manager)*
Micheline Jebb *(Commercial)*
Lesley Morgan *(Group IT)*

Parent Company:
UK: Hachette UK

Distributor for:
UK: Ashgate/Gower Publishing; Debretts; Facet Publishing *(formerly Library Association)*; Hachette Children's; Headline Book Publishing; Hodder & Stoughton; Hodder Education; Hodder Gibson; Hodder Religious; In Easy Steps; Frances Lincoln; John Murray; Pedigree Books; Plexus Publishing; Souvenir Press; Taylor & Francis

Bookpoint services encompass a number of industry leading initiatives, plus a full suite of EDI applications, order processing, accounting, royalty maintenance, management reporting, warehousing, despatch and ancillary functions. Bookpoint also operate a Premier Next Day Service, and offer PUBEASY to booksellers.

6097

BOOKSOURCE
50 Cambuslang Road, Cambuslang, Glasgow G32 8NB
Telephone: 0845 370 0063
Fax: 0845 370 0064
Email: info@booksource.net
Web Site: www.booksource.net

Directors: Davinder Bedi *(Managing)*
Lorraine Fannin
Mike Miller
Christian Mclean
Dr Keith Whittles
Marion Sinclair
Managers: Louise Wilson *(Client Services)*
David Warnock *(Systems & Facilities)*
Lavinia Drew *(Credit Controller)*
Derek Withers *(Customer Service)*
Jim O'Donnell *(Distribution)*

Distribution on behalf of:
UK: Acair Ltd; Appletree Press; Argyll Publishing; Association for Scottish Literary Studies; Atelier Books; B & W Publishing; Balnakeil Press; Benchmark Books; BILD Publications; Birlinn Ltd; Black & White Publishing; Blue Cow Books; Books Noir; Carnegie Publishing; Cicerone Press; Clairview Books; Clan Publishers; John Donald; R. R. Donnelley *(for the Scottish Executive)*; Richard Drew Ltd; Dundee University Press; Floris Books; Fort Publishing; Geddes & Grosset Ltd; Gullane Children's Books; Hallewell Publications; Hawthorn Press; House of Lochar; IPC Media; Islands Book Trust; Librario Publishing; Meadowside Children's Books; Mercat Press; Moonlight Publishing; Glen Murray Publishing; NMS Enterprises Ltd Publishing; Polygon; Publishing Scotland; Real Reads; Rider French Publications; Roving Press; Royal Commission on the Ancient and Historical Monuments of Scotland; Rucksack Readers; Saltire Society; Sandstone Press; Saraband; Steve Savage Publishing; Scottish Society for Northern Studies; Scottish Text Society; Starlet; Rudolf Steiner Press; Strident Publishing; Sunday Herald Books; Temple Lodge Publishing; Tuckwell Press; Two Ravens Press; Waverley Press; Whittles Publishing; Wild Goose Publications; Neil Wilson Publishing; Windhorse Publications

Established in 1995, BookSource offers warehousing and worldwide distribution services to book trade publishers, charities and funded institutions, and other commercial enterprises.

6098

BUSHWOOD BOOKS LTD
6 Marksbury Avenue, Kew Gardens, Surrey TW9 4JF
Telephone: (020) 8392 8585
Fax: (020) 8392 9876
Email: info@bushwoodbooks.co.uk
Web Site: www.bushwoodbooks.co.uk

Director: Richard Hansen
PA: Victoria Hansen
Sales: Ian McLellan

Exclusive distributor for:
USA: Schiffer *(Mind, Body, Spirit titles)*; Schiffer Collectibles Arts & Crafts; Schiffer Publishing Ltd *(Military Aviation)*

The company also carries in stock hundreds of titles on antiques and collectibles, predominantly horology, jewellery, ceramics and glass. It specializes in providing a service for UK customers to purchase from North American publishers.
Bushwood Books is one of the leading UK distributors of German World War II titles in English, and also carries the Schiffer Mind, Body, Spirit list.

6099

CENGAGE LEARNING SERVICES
[a division of Cengage Learning]
Cheriton House, North Way, Andover, Hants SP10 5BE
Telephone: 01264 332424
Fax: 01264 342732
Web Site: www.cengage.co.uk

Directors: Jill Jones (Chief Executive Officer)
Chad Bonney (Chief Financial Officer)
Carrie Willicome (Operations)

Distributors for:
UK: Cengage Learning (selected imprints); Evans Publishing Group; Janes; Sweet & Maxwell [S&M Ltd, W. Green & Sons, Gee Publishing]

6100

CENTRAL BOOKS
99 Wallis Road, London E9 5LN
Telephone: 0845 458 9911
Fax: 0845 458 9912
Email: orders@centralbooks.com
Web Site: www.centralbooks.com

Directors: William Norris (Managing)
Mark Chilver (Sales)
Managers: Bob Moheebob (Accountant)
Eric McCorkle (Warehouse)
Indy Kaur Naura (Customer Services)
Karen Short (Human Resources)
Mike Drabble (Mail Order)
Sasha Simic (Magazine Sales Rep)
Regina Henrich (Publisher Liaison)

Distribution for:
Australia: Fremantle Arts Centre Press
Canada: Black Rose Books; Fernwood Press
France: Zulma
Germany: European Photography
Greece: Intrac
Italy: Giancarlo Politi Editore
Jamaica: Ian Randle
Kenya: Camerapix
Netherlands: CEDLA; Get Lost Publishing; International Books; Thesis
Republic of Ireland: Dedalus Press; A & A Farmer; Galway University Press; The Lilliput Press Ltd; Oishin Publishing; Salmon Publishing Ltd; University College Dublin Press
Scandinavia: Nordic Institute of Asian Studies; Nordiska Afrikainstitutet (Scandinavian Institute of Africa)
South Africa: Cape Town University Press; Fernwood Press; Kwela; Londolozi Publishers; David Philip; Ravan Press; University of Capetown Press; University of Natal Press; Witwatersrand University Press
Switzerland: Parkett Verlag
UK: 21; Absolute Press; Accent Press; Agraphia Press; Ambit Books; Amnesty Publications; Anthem Press; Archetype; Argyll Publishing; Aurora Books; Aurora Metro; Auteur; Battlebridge; Birmingham University Press; Blue Island Publishing; Bowerdean Publishing Co Ltd; Marion Boyars Publishers; British Council for Archaeology; British Film Institute; Broadcast Books; Cadmos; CAF (Charities Aid Foundation); Calouste Gulbenkian Foundation; Jon Carpenter Publishing; Catalyst Press; Centre for Policy on Ageing; The Children's Society; CILT; Comerford & Miller; Corvo Books; CPAG (Child Poverty Action Group); Dedalus; Demos; Directory of Social Change; Disability Alliance; English Heritage; Enitharmon Press; Five Leaves Publications; Flambard; Flowers East; Foreign Policy Centre; Format Publishing; Friction Press; Gambit; Gibson Square Press; Golgonooza; Green Books; Green Guide Publishing; Greenprint; Greenwich Exchange; Harbord Publishing; Heretic Books Ltd (formerly GMP Publishers Ltd); Holo Books; Hood Hood Books; Human Givens; Human Rights Watch; Hyphen Press; Imprint Academic; Institute for Public Policy Research; Latin America Bureau; Lawrence & Wishart; Libris Ltd; Loki Books; London Art & Artists; Lucas Publications Ltd; Mares Nest; Menard Press; Merlin Press; Middlesex University Press; Minority Rights Group; Muslim Academic Trust; National Autistic Society (NAS); New Clarion Press; New Economics Foundation; New European Publications Ltd; NIACE (National Institute for Adult Continuing Education); Northway; Open Gate Press; Peter Owen Ltd; Peepal Tree Books; Pomona Books; Prospect Books; Quill; Quilliam; Redstone Press; Refugee Council; Resource Publications; Right Angle Publishing; Route; Runnymede Trust; Seafarer; Seren; Serif; Smith / Doorstep; Smith Institute; Social Market

Foundation; Stacey International; Totterdown Books; University of Hertfordshire Press; Vegan Society; Wallflower Press; Josef Weinberger Ltd; Weston Publishing; Westworld International; Wooden Books; WorldView
USA: International Publishers NY; McPherson & Co; Monthly Review; Pamphleteer's Press

The main activity and purpose of Central Books is to assist independent publishers to reach the widest possible audience for their books. Central Books offer warehousing, distribution, representation and some help with marketing and promotion. It supplies booksellers and library suppliers throughout the world. The company is one of Europe's leading distributors of magazines and journals to the book trade.

6101

COMBINED ACADEMIC PUBLISHERS LTD
15a Lewins Yard, East Street, Chesham, Bucks HP5 1HQ
Telephone: 01494 581601
Fax: 01494 581602
Email: nickesson@combinedacademic.co.uk
Web Site: www.combinedacademic.co.uk

Managing Director: Nicholas Esson
Managers: Ms Julia Monk (Marketing)
Ms Denise Martin (Accounts)
Representative: Keith Woods

UK & European distributor for:
Canada: McGill-Queen's University Press
USA: Duke University Press; Indiana University Press; New York University Press; Temple University Press; University of Illinois Press; University of Nebraska Press; University of Texas Press; University of Washington Press

Combined Academic Publishers, in association with Marston Book Services, is a professional representation and distribution agency for academic and university presses.

UK and Republic of Ireland field sales are handled by our own representative and a team of experienced commisson agents, while agents are active in five continental European territories – Scandinavia; the Netherlands and Belgium; Southern Europe; Germany, Austria and Switzerland; Central and Eastern Europe – as well as the Middle East and Africa.

CAP has a pro-active marketing department offering direct mail campaigns, space advertising and review copy distribution.

6102

COMBINED BOOK SERVICES LTD
Unit Y, Paddock Wood Distribution Centre, Paddock Wood, Tonbridge, Kent TN12 6UU
Telephone: 01892 837171
Fax: 01892 837272
Email: info@combook.co.uk
Web Site: www.combook.co.uk

Directors: Keith Neale (Distribution)
Allan Smith (Customer Services)

Distributors for:
Italy: LEM Art Group
UK: A Jot Publishing; J. A. Allen (Equestrian); Anshan Publishers; John Calder; Claerhout Publishing; Discovery Books; Eddington Hook; Encyclopaedia Britannica; Freehand Publishing; Robert Hale; Hammersmith Press; Hoberman Collection; Korero Books; Lotus Publishing; Management Books 2000; Momenta Publishing; NAG Publishers; New Age Science; Northcote House Publishers; Oneworld Classics; Phoenix Publishers; Pocket Issue; Pucci Books [formerly Oblique]; Pushkin Press; Splendid Books; Thomas Telford Ltd (Institute of Civil Engineers); teneues Publishing UK; Woodhead Publishing

Combined Book Services provides full distribution services for publishers of trade, academic and professional books. The service includes invoicing and cash collection together with a comprehensive range of management reports. CBS also distributes calendars and stationery products.

6103

CONTOUR MANAGEMENT SERVICES (CMS)
PO Box 3042, New Milton, Hants BH25 7XG
Telephone: 01425 620532
Fax: 01425 620532
Email: sales@contourmanagementservices.com
Web Site: www.contourmanagementservices.com

Partners: Mike Cranidge (Managing)
Sue Cranidge

Agent and distributor for:
Australia: Meridian Maps
Baltic States: Jāna Sēta Map Publishers
Portugal: Turinta
USA: Hedberg Maps Inc; Map Link

Importers and distributors of maps with a difference.

6104

CORNERHOUSE PUBLICATIONS
70 Oxford Street, Manchester M1 5NH
Telephone: 0161 200 1503
Fax: 0161 200 1504
Email: Publications@Cornerhouse.org
Web Site: www.Cornerhouse.org/books

Publications Director: Paul Daniels
Administrator: Debbie Fielding
Publications Officer: Suzanne Davies

Clients include:
Germany: Walther König
Switzerland: JRP / Ringier
UK: British Council Visual Arts; Hayward Gallery; ICA; Ikon; Modern Art Oxford; Saatchi Gallery

Distributor of visual arts and photography books for publishers, museums amd galleries world-wide. A full list of publishers we distribute is available in our catalogue or at our web site: www.Cornerhouse.org/books.

6105

*COUNTER CULTURE
The Long Barn, Sutton Mallet, Somerset TA7 9AR
Telephone: 01278 722888
Fax: 01278 722565
Email: info@counterculture-books.co.uk
Web Site: www.counterculture-books.co.uk

Owner: Peter Gotto

Associated Companies:
UK: Green Magic

Distributors for:
UK: Aeon Press; Ariadne Publications; Avalon; Avalonia; Blackstone; Bluestone Press; Bossiney Books; Caine Books; Capall Bann; Chalice Well; Compassbooks; Connections; Jonathon Cope; Crescent Books; Cygnus Books; Dilston Press; Sheridan Douglas; Druid Ways; Edfu; Eric; Glennie Kindred; Godsfield Press; Gothic Image; Green Books; Green Magic; Robert Hale; Hay House; Heart of Albion Press; Hermitage Publishing; Ignotus Press; Kindred Books; Kindred Press; Knockabout Comics; Lear Books; Living Wood; Mandrake; Meym Mamvro; Mythos; Neptune; Pan Dimensional; Pendragon Press; Penwith Press; Permanent Publications; Points Press; Poppy Palin; Scandinavian Yoga & Meditation School; Speaking Tree; Tagman Press; Thoth Publications; Wessex Books; Whitaker Publishing; Wild Spirit; Wooden Books
USA: Abramelin Press; Adventures Unlimited; Ash Tree Publishing; Blue Water Publishing; Book Publishing Company; Citadel Press; Crossing Press; Eaglewing; Earth Love; Mara Freeman; Granite Publishing; Hanford Mead; Heart of the Sun; Heaven and Earth Publishing; Hulogosi Press; Llewellyn; Moosewood; New Page Books; New Trends; Perelandra; Raw Family; Red Wheel/Weiser Books; Shelter; Swan Raven & Co; Ultra; US Games; Vision; Wild Flower; Witches Almanac

Book distribution and worldwide sales.

6106

DEEP BOOKS LTD
Unit 3, Goose Green Trading Estate, 47 East Dulwich Road, London SE22 9BN
Telephone: (020) 8693 0234
Fax: (020) 8693 1400
Email: sales@deep-books.co.uk
Web Site: www.deep-books.co.uk

Managing Director: Chris Custance
Managers: Linda Doolin (Sales)
Alan Ritchie (Marketing)
Paul Woodfield

Client Publishers include:

Australia: Michelle Anderson Publishing [formerly Hill of Content Publishing]; Finch Publishing; Barry Long Books (Australia); Milne Books
Austria: Ennsthaler Publishing House
Israel: Astrolog Publishing House
Italy: Lo Scarabeo
Netherlands: Altamira-Becht; Binkey Kok Publications; Gottmer Publishing Group
Singapore: Lotus Bloom Publishing
UK: Camino Guides; Earthdancer; Findhorn Press; From Within; Khaniqahi Nimatullahi Publications (KNP); KNP London; Barry Long Books (Britain); Polair Publishing
USA: Acropolis Books; Alliance Book Company; Alpha Books / Penguin USA; Amber Lotus; ARE Press; Ariel Press; Avery/Penguin USA; Basic Health Publications; Bear & Co; Bear Cub Books; Berkley Publishing Group; Bindu Books; Blue Dolphin Publishing Inc; Bluestar Communications; Boys Town Press; Career Press; Chamberlain Bros / Penguin USA; Chiron Publications; Alan Cohen Publishing; Crystal Clarity Publishers; Crystal Quartz Depot; Dawn Publications; Dawnhorse Publications; De Vorss & Co; Destiny Audio Books; Destiny Books; Dragonhawk Publishing; Dutton / Penguin USA; Earth Magic Productions Inc; Enthea Press; Golden Sufi Center; Gotham Books / Penguin USA; Hampton Roads Publishing; Nicolas Hays; Healing Arts Press; Himalayan Institute Press; Hudson Street / Penguin USA; Hunter House Inc; Ibis Press; Inner Traditions International; Inner Travel Books; Integral Yoga Publications; Jewish Light Publishing; JZK Publishing; Kali Press; Veronica Lane Books; Lantern Books; Music Design; Namaste Publishing; New Page Books; Oral Traditions; Original Publications; Park St Press; Perigee/ Penguin; Portfolio / Penguin USA; Power Press; Putnam / Penguin USA; Riverhead Books / Penguin USA; Self Realization Fellowship; Skylight Paths; Squareone Publishers; Synergetic Press; Jeremy P. Tarcher / Penguin USA; Threshold Books; Timeless Books; Vital Health Publishing; Witches' Almanac; Words of Wizdom; World Wisdom Books

Specialist mind body spirit distributors. Deep Books handles publishers lists from the UK, the USA and Australia. It provides sales and distribution for these publishers throughout the UK, Republic of Ireland, mainland Europe and Scandinavia and acts as their exclusive agents in that territory.

6107 ■

EUROPEAN SCHOOLBOOKS LTD
Ashville Trading Estate, The Runnings, Cheltenham GL51 9PQ
Telephone: 01242 245252
Fax: 01242 224137
Email: direct@esb.co.uk
Web Site: www.eurobooks.co.uk

Managing Director: Frank Preiss
Marketing: Ruth Trippett

Distributor for:
Brazil: Pontes Editores
Denmark: Grafisk Forlag
France: 10/18; Assimil; Bordas; Casterman; CLE International; Armand Colin; Didier; Ecole des loisirs; Editions du Fallois; Editions du Seuil; Flammarion; Folio; Foucher; Gallimard; Garnier Flammarion; Gault Millau; Hachette; Hatier; J'ai lu; Larousse; Livres de poche; Minuit; Nathan; Presses de la cité; Presses Pocket; Presses Universitaires de France; Presses Universitaires de Grenoble; Le Robert
Germany: Arena; Bibliographisches Institut Mannheim; Brockhaus; Carlsen; Cornelsen; Deutscher Taschenbuch Verlag; Diogenes; Duden; Fischer; Gilde Buchhandlung; Goldmann; Heyne; Max Hueber Verlag; Insel; Kiepenheuer & Witsch; Knaur; Langenscheidt; Luchterhand; Reclam; Rowohlt; Suhrkamp; Ullstein; Verlag Dürr & Kessler; Verlag für Deutsch; Verlag Moritz Diesterweg
Italy: Alma Edizioni; Bonacci Editore; Edilingua; Einaudi; European Language Institute; Fabbri-Bompiani; Feltrinelli; Garzanti; Giunti; Guerra; Mondadori; Le Monnier; Oscar; Piemme; Rizzoli; Rux; La Spiga; Zanichelli
Netherlands: Intertaal
Portugal: Dinapress; Lidel Edições Técnicas; Porto Editora Lda; Public. Europa-America

Spain: Alfaguara; Alianza; Anaya; Anaya ELE; Austral; Catedra; Colegio de España; Destino; Difusión; EDELSA; Ediciones Edhasa; Ediciones Edinumen; Ediciones Molino; Ediciones SM; Espasa-Calpe; Everest; Grijalbo; Juventud; Mondadori España; Planeta; Plaza & Janes; Santillana; Seix Barral; SGEL; Sopena; Javier Vergara
UK: European Schoolbooks Publishing Ltd; Understanding Global Issues

Distributors of some 80,000 titles in the main European languages on behalf of over 100 publishers. Large-scale promotion in all sectors of the foreign languages educational market. Suppliers of foreign-published stock to academic and general bookshops. General wholesale service for non-stock titles.

6108 ■

THE EUROSPAN GROUP
3 Henrietta Street, Covent Garden, London WC2E 8LU
Telephone: (020) 7240 0856
Fax: (020) 7379 0609
Email: info@eurospangroup.com
Web Site: www.eurospanbookstore.com

Directors: Michael Geelan *(Managing & Chairman)*
Kate Fraser *(Operations)*
Stephen Lustig *(Marketing)*

A complete list of publishers and subsidiary imprints distributed by Eurospan is available on request.

6109 ■

FREELANCE MARKET NEWS
Sevendale House, 7 Dale Street, Manchester M1 1JB
Telephone: 0161 228 2362
Fax: 0161 228 3533
Email: fmn@writersbureau.com
Web Site: www.freelancemarketnews.com

Managing Editor: Miss Angela Cox

Parent Company:
UK: The Writers Bureau Ltd

Distributor for:
USA: Writer's Digest Books *(books on writing)*

6110 ■

GAZELLE BOOK SERVICES LTD
White Cross Mills, Hightown, Lancaster LA1 4XS
Telephone: 01524 68765
Fax: 01524 63232
Email: sales@gazellebooks.co.uk
Web Site: www.gazellebooks.co.uk

Directors: Trevor Witcher *(Managing)*
Brian Haywood *(Company Secretary & Finance)*
Mark Trotter *(Distribution & Sales)*
Managers: Kevin Dixon *(Warehouse)*
Lee Hodgkiss *(Marketing & Exhibitions)*
Gareth Hindson *(Customer Service)*
Melanie Warren *(Sales & Marketing)*
Bookkeeper: Analyn Dixon

Gazelle Book Services handles both trade and academic lists and covers the whole of the UK and Europe. It provides:
fast order turn-round;
comprehensive stock and regular stock replenishment;
efficient reporting and information service to customers;
regular sales calling and regular liaison with booksellers in connection with promotion, exhibitions, special events, etc;
following through;
friendly, helpful service;
regular and adaptable reporting to publishers;
flexibility and co-operation.
Complete list of client publishers is available on request.

6111 ■

GRANTHAM BOOK SERVICES
Trent Road, Grantham, Lincs NG31 7XQ
Telephone: 01476 541000 (orders: 541080)
Fax: 01476 541060 (orders: 541061)
Email: orders@gbs.tbs-ltd.co.uk
Web Site: www.granthambookservices.co.uk

Directors: Mark Williams *(Managing)*
Andy Willis *(Client Services)*
Justin Smith *(Finance & Commercial)*

Managers: David Goodere *(Customer Services)*
Colleen McMorran *(Client Services)*
Simon Goldstein *(Head of Operations, Grantham)*
Duty Managers: Steve Bower *(Operations)*
Sam Beveridge *(Logistics)*
Martin Wells *(Operations)*

Parent Company:
UK: Random House UK

Clients include:
France: La Martiniere
UK: AA Special Sales; Alma Books; Bounce Sales & Marketing; Chronicle; Compass Maps; Thomas Cook; Crown House; The Crowood Press; David & Charles; Duckworth; Footprint Handbooks; Geocentre International UK Ltd; Harbour Books; Hay House; Nick Hern Books; Hesperus; How To Books; Kraken; Landmark Publishing; Lerner; Lonely Planet; Manning Partnership; Melia Publishing Services; National Archives; National Portrait Gallery; New Holland; One World; Osprey Publishing; Oval Books; Perseus Books; PGUK; Piccadilly Press; QED; Quiller; Reaktion Books; Rotovision; Severn House Publishers; Sound Entertainment; Templar Publishing; Timber Press; Titan Books
USA: Everyman; MBI; Rockport; Workman Publishing

Grantham Book Services provides a very fast and efficient distribution service for publishers. Service includes order receipt by post, fax, telephone and teleordering; invoicing and despatch. A next day delivery service, from receipt of order to delivery of books, is provided to the UK trade. Also sales ledger and cash collection service. Comprehensive range of computer reports; plus all the usual ancillary work such as shrinkwrapping, repricing, dumpbin and counter-pack make up.

6112 ■

KUPERARD PUBLISHERS
59 Hutton Grove, London N12 8DS
Telephone: (020) 8446 2440
Fax: (020) 8446 2441
Email: enquiries@kuperard.co.uk
Web Site: www.kuperard.co.uk

Chief Executive: Joshua Kuperard
Managers: Martin Kaye *(Sales & Marketing)*
Linda Tenenbaum *(Special Sales)*

Publishers of:
Chic Guides; Culture Smart! Guides; Customs & Etiquette; FHG Guides; Kuperard Books; NFT Guides; Simple Guides

Distributor for Religious books:
USA: HarperCollins; Lerner Books; Penguin; Random House; Schocken Books / Random House; Simon & Schuster

Distributor for classic literature:
USA: The Modern Library (Random House)

Distributor for Montessori books:
USA: Penguin; Schocken Books

Distributor for Self-Study Language Courses:
USA: Living Language (Random House)

Kuperard, a division and imprint of Bravo Ltd, acts as publishers, co-publishers and distributors, handling marketing and representation. Kuperard handle over 30 UK and overseas publishers. Stocklists, catalogues and brochures are available upon request.
Travel subjects include leisure guides covering a wide variety of destinations and markets. Kuperard publishes cross-cultural guides for business people and travellers. Religion subjects covered include art, cookery, the Holy Land, history, language, mysticism, holocaust, faith and spirituality.

6113 ■

LITTLEHAMPTON BOOK SERVICES LTD
Faraday Close, Durrington, Worthing, West Sussex BN13 3RB
Telephone: 01903 828500
Fax: 01903 828625
Email: ...@lbsltd.co.uk
Web Site: www.lbsltd.co.uk

Directors: Chris Emerson *(Chief Executive Officer)*
Simon Davidson *(Managing)*
Basil May *(Finance)*
Lesley Morgan *(Group IT)*

Bridget Radnedge *(Publishing Services)*
Alan Rakes *(Inventory)*

Parent Company:
UK: Hachette UK Publishing Group

Clients include:
3C Publishing (Columbia Marketing Ltd); Ian Allan; Anvil Poetry Press; Aurum Press, Apple & JR Books; Automobile Association; Barefoot Books; John Blake Publishing; Bloodaxe; Carcanet; Crombie Jardine Publishing; Cyan; DAAB; Express Newspapers; Eye Books Ltd; Gallic Books; Gibson Square Publishing; Gloucester Publishers [formerly Everyman]; The Good Hotel Guide Ltd; The Greatest in the World; Grub Street; Haus Publishing; Infinite Ideas Co; Interact Publishing Ltd; Kogan Page; Kyle Cathie; Little Books; Make Believe Ideas Ltd; Marshall Cavendish; Myrmidon Books; Northumbria University Publishing; Michael O'Mara Books; Octopus Publishing Group; Old St Publishing; Oldie Publications; Orion Group; PC Publishing; Pitch Publishing Ltd; Private Eye; Raceform / Highdown Publishing; Radio Times; Alan Rogers' Guides Ltd; Serpent's Tail; Snowbooks Ltd; Sport Media; Summersdale; Tantor Media Inc; Taschen; Thames & Hudson; Vertigo Communications LLB; Vision; Visit Britain; Which? The Consumer Association

Littlehampton Book Services provides publishers with full warehouse management and distribution services that include credit control and trust accounting, sophisticated management reporting, telesales, customer service and royalty accounting.

6114

B. McCALL BARBOUR
28 George IV Bridge, Edinburgh EH1 1ES
Telephone: 0131 225 4816
Fax: 0131 225 4816
Web Site: www.mccallbarbour.co.uk

Managing Partner: Rev Dr T. C. Danson-Smith
Despatch Manager: Miss G. A. Danson-Smith

USA companies represented:
USA: AMG Publishers; Chick Publications; Dake Bible Sales; Discovery House; Kirkbride Bible Co; Living Stories Inc; Thomas Nelson & Sons; Oxford University Press [Bibles]; John Peterson Music; Rainbow Study Bibles; Schoettle Publishing House; Singspiration Inc; Sword of the Lord Publishers; Zondervan Corporation

Distributor of Bibles, Christian books and greeting cards, also videos, DVDs, gifts.

6115

MACMILLAN DISTRIBUTION (MDL)
Brunel Road, Houndmills, Basingstoke, Hants RG21 6XS
Telephone: 01256 302840
Fax: 01256 841426
Email: www-mdl@macmillan.co.uk
Web Site: www.macmillandistribution.co.uk

Directors: Lawrence Jennings *(Chairman)*
David Smith *(Managing)*
Andrew May-Miller *(Information Services)*
Guy Browning *(Distribution)*

Parent Company:
UK: Macmillan Ltd

Macmillan Publishers:
Boxtree; W. H. Freeman & Worth Publishers; Macmillan Children's Books; Macmillan Digital Audio; Macmillan Education; Nature Publishing Group; Office for National Statistics (ONS); Palgrave; Pan Macmillan; Picador; Priddy Books; Sinauer Associates; University Science Books

Client Publishers:
Accent Press Ltd; Alligator Books; Arcturus Publishing Ltd; Arden Shakespeare; Barrington Stoke; Berg Publishers; A. & C. Black; Bloomsbury Publishing Plc; Camra; Cico Books; Class Publishing (London) Ltd; CRW Publishing Ltd; Earthscan / James & James; Elliott & Thompson Ltd; Fairchild; Featherstone; First Second Editions; W. Foulsham & Co Ltd; Guinness World Records Ltd; Jones & Bartlett; Jessica Kingsley Publishers; Little Tiger Press (Magi); Methuen Drama; Murdoch Books (UK) Ltd; Panini Books; Persephone Book Ltd; Prestel Publishing Ltd; Quadrille Publishing Ltd; Revolver Books; Ryland Peters &

Small; Spy Publishing Ltd; I. B. Tauris; Tokyopop; V & A Publications; Walker Books Ltd; John Wisden & Co Ltd

Macmillan Distribution (MDL) offers a full book distribution service to the Macmillan publishers as well as a wide range of third-party clients. It provides order fulfilment in a variety of electronic formats as well as more traditional forms, cash collection and information provision through its sophisticated sales analysis system. MDL was one of the first publisher's distribution companies to obtain ISO9000 certification, the internationally recognized standard for quality systems, and is fully e4 books commended. It consciously looks for ways to expand and improve the services it offers, which include printing, catalogue despatch A.I. provision and links with reps using PDAs for order transfer and title and price availability. It recently invested in 120,000 sq feet of new state-of-the-art warehousing, and refinements of its warehousing and stock systems are ongoing.

6116

MARSTON BOOK SERVICES LTD
160 Milton Park, Abingdon, Oxon OX14 4SD
Telephone: 01235 465604
Fax: 01235 465655
Email: monica.harding@marston.co.uk
Web Site: www.marston.co.uk

Chairman: John Holloran
Directors: Ross Clayton *(Managing)*
Graham Cooper *(Financial)*
Managers: Melanie Khosa *(Customer Service)*
Donna Green *(Trade)*
Monica Harding *(Client Development & Service)*

Associated Companies:
UK: Orca Book Services

Clients represented:
Belgium: Brepols Publishing; Harvey Miller Publishers
Denmark: Copenhagen Business School Press
Germany: Berghahn; Boerm Bruckmeier Verlag GmbH
Italy: Damiani Editore
Netherlands: Asian Studies Book Services
Republic of Ireland: Cork University Press / Attic Press
Singapore: World Scientific Publishing
UK: Actar D; Acumen Publishing; Adamson Publishing; Alban Books; Alpha Science International Ltd; Anthem Press; Arts Council of England; Assouline Publishing Inc; Atrium Group; The Barbirolli Society; Bennett & Bloom; Bibles for Children; Black Dog Publishing Ltd; Bonnier Books; Burke Publishing; CIPAC; Clinical Publishing; Combined Academic Publishers Ltd; James Currey Publishers; Edinburgh University Press; Edward Elgar Publishing Ltd; Equinox; Flame Tree Publishing; Die Gestalten Verlag UK; Gibraltar Research; Greenwood Publishing Group; Harriman House Ltd; The History Press; Hurst & Co (Publishers) Ltd; ICSA; Institute of Physics *(education only)*; Island Press; Peter Lang Ltd; Library Reference; Lion Hudson Plc; Liverpool University Press; Manchester University Press; Manticore Books Ltd; Mapin; Merrell Publishers Ltd; Multilingual Matters Ltd / Channel View Publications; NIAS; Now Publishing; Oberon; Orthodox Christian Books Ltd; Permillion; Pluto Press; The Policy Press; Princeton Architectural Press; Public Catalogue Foundation; Research Studies Press; The Royal Society of Medicine Press Ltd; John Rule Sales & Marketing; Saint Andrew Press; Saqi; Scottish Council for Law Reporting; Society for Promoting Christian Knowledge; Terra Publishing; Third Millennium Publishing Ltd; Thorogood Publishing; Tottel Publishing; Turning Point; Unicorn Press; University of Buckingham; Verso; The Voltaire Foundation; John Wilson Booksales
USA: CQ Press; Enisen Publishing; National Academies Press; Rizzoli International Publications; University of Pennsylvania Press

Provides fulfilment services to the publishing world.
Services available include: order processing; customer service; credit control; management reporting; production of royalty statements; pick, pack and despatch (automated warehouse management system); digital print facility; journal fulfilment; ancillary work; exhibition services; EDI; IT support and development.

6117

MDS BOOK SALES
128 Pikes Lane, Glossop, Derbys SK13 8EH
Telephone: 01457 861508
Fax: 01457 868332

Email: mdsbooksales@aol.com
Web Site: www.mdsbooks.co.uk

Proprietor: Mark Senior

Associated Companies:
UK: Venture Publications Ltd

Distributor for:
UK: Birmingham Transport Historical Group; DTS Sales; John Hambley Books; Senior Publications; Venture Publications Ltd; Peter Watts Publishing

Book wholesalers and distributors specializing in transport related lists.

6118

MELIA PUBLISHING SERVICES LTD
The White House, 2A Meadrow, Godalming, Surrey GU7 3HN
Telephone: 01483 869839
Fax: 01483 869845
Email: melia@melia.co.uk
Web Site: www.melia.co.uk

Directors: Terry Melia *(Managing)*
Billy Adair *(Sales)*
Cleve Vine *(Finance)*
Managers: Joanna Melia *(Sales)*
Linda West *(Accounts)*

Distributor for:
UK: Connections; Ivy Press; Psychology News; Snake River Press; Worth Press Ltd
USA: Algonquin; Artisan; Tom Doherty Association; Farrar, Straus & Giroux; Filipacchi; Forgie; Griffin; Harcourt Trade Books; Henry Holt; Houghton Mifflin Harcourt; Kensington Publishing Corporation; Minotaur; Newmarket Press; Owl; Papercutz; Picador; Rodale; Seven Seas; St Martins Press; Storey Books; Time Inc Home Entertainment; Toby Press LLC; Tor; Workman Publishing

Sales and distribution for English language publishers.

6119

MK BOOK SERVICE
7 East Street, Hartford Road, Huntingdon PE29 1WZ
Telephone: 01480 353710
Fax: 01480 431703
Email: mkbooks@tiscali.co.uk

Owner: M. R. King

UK distributor/representative for clients including:
Argentina: Del Nuevo Extremo; Lola
Australia: Academic English Press; Gary Allen Pty Ltd NSW; Art Media; Ausmed; Australian Medical Publications; Blue Cat Books; E. J. Bowles; Coffee School Melbourne; Corkwood Press; Crossing Press; Ken Duncan Panographs; Eagles Nest Golf Guides; East Street Publications; Golden Point Press; Haese & Harris; Hobby Investment; IBID Press; Indo Lingo Surf; JB Books; Linford; Melting Pot Press; Mitchell Wordsmith; Parrot Books; Perfect Potion; Piscean Books; Slouch Hat Publications; Wizard Study Guides; Woodmore
Bangladesh: University Press Dhaka
Canada: Creative Newfoundland; Empty Mirror Press; Fitzhenry & Whiteside; St James Publishing BC
Estonia: Periodika
France: Editions Pelisser
Germany: ADAC
Iceland: Forglaid; Iceland Review; Mimir
India: Aditya Prakashan; Allied Publications; Anmol; Asa; Ashish/APH; Asia Bookclub; Atlantic Publishing; Authors Press; Best Books Kolkata; Biotech; Book Enclave; Concord Press; Daya; Deep & Deep; Diamond Pocket Books; DK Printworld Pty Ltd; Galaxy; Gene-Tech Books; India Research Press; Indus; Intellectual Book Corner; ISPCK; Kaushal; Low Price Publications; Mahaveer & Sons; Minerva Associates; Modern Publishers; National Book Trust; Papyrus; Prestige; Rajesh; Regency; South Asian Publications; Vine Press
Israel: Beit Yochmann; Ben Zvi Press; Bible Lands Museum; Carta; Francisian Printing Press; Gefen; Israel Academy of Sciences; Israel Exploration Society; Magnes Press; Rubin Mass Publishing Jerusalem; Yad Vaschem
Italy: Biblico Pontificio; Palombi *(English language titles only)*
Latvia: Avots
Mexico: Funentes

Nepal: Nirala
New Zealand: Catt Publishing; Craig Printing; Jenn Falconer Books; Holst Ltd; Hyndmans; Kingsley Wood; Look Around Design; Manaaki Whenuka Press; Marlborough Wine; Nationwide; Photo Image; SPSS Ashburton; Wises Publications
Pakistan: Iqbal Institute; Sang-e-meel; Vanguard
Philippines: Asia Type
Portugal: Quinta do Pinhal; Vista Iberica
Russia: Raduga
Russian Federation: Literatura
South Africa: Galago Books; Tortoise Press
Taiwan: Far East Book Co; SMC Publishing
Thailand: Dragondance; White Lotus
UK: John Bell Training; Hakedes; Pelican Publishing; Popular Publications; Soul to Sole; George Thompson Brake; Willingham Press
Uruguay: Editions Trilice
USA: American Historical Press; Eisenbrauns; Floating Gallery Press; Global Health Solutions; Learning Unlimited; Nova Books; Tarrak; Tusitlal Publishing
Zimbabwe: Argosy Press; Modus Publications

Distributor for overseas publishers; importer from overseas, for whom we are not agents; distributor for selected UK publishers; library supply; booksearch for out of print UK books.

6120

MOTILAL (UK) – BOOKS OF INDIA
367 High Street, London Colney, St Albans, Herts AL2 1EA
Telephone: 01727 761677
Fax: 01727 761357
Email: info@mlbduk.com

Managing Director: R. J. McLennan
Finance: Ms Ann Moister
Customer Services: Richard Neil
Barbara Doffman

Parent Company:
UK: Moneysavers (Ldn) Ltd

Associated Companies:
UK: Ahimsa Books

Distributor for:
Australia: Chakra Press
India: Bhaktivedanta Book Trust; Motilal Banarsidass
UK: Ahimsa Books
USA: Bala Books; Bhaktivedanta Book Trust; Govardhan Hill; Hari-Nama Press; World Relief Network

Indian publishers represented include:
India: Abhinav Publications; Amexfel Publishers; Anmol Publications; Aravali Books International; Aryan Books International; Asian Educational Services; Asiatic Publishing House; Banjara Academy; Bihar School of Yoga; Bookwell Publications; BPB Publications; BPI (India) Pvt Ltd; Brijbasi Art Press; Centre for Studies in Civilizations; Chand (S.) & Co Ltd; Commonwealth Youth Programme; Cosmo Publications; Crest Publishing House; Deep & Deep; DK Printworld; Excel Books; Foundation Books; Full Circle; Gemini Books; Gulshan Publishers; Gyan Publishing House; HarperCollins India; Hind Pocket Books; Indian Book Centre; Indiana Publishing House; Indica; Indus Publishing; Institute for Human Development; Jaico Publishing House; Jaya Books; Jaypee Brothers Medical Publishers; Ben Johnston Publishing; Kalpaz Publications; Katha; Kitab Bhavan; Laxmi Publications; Low Price Publications; Malhotra Publishing; Manas; Manohar Publishers; Motilal Banarsidass; New Age Books; Orient Paperbacks; Paljor Publications; Pentagon Press; Pragati; Sandeep Prakashan; Prentice-Hall of India Pvt Ltd; Pustak Mahal; Rawat; Readworthy; Sahasrara Publications; Sanskrit Religious Institute; Sanskriti; Shubhi Publications; Spectrum Publications; Sura Books; Torchlight Publishing; Unisun Publications; Universal Law Publishing; Vanity Books International; Wordspeak; Worldview; Zubaan

Distributor of books and other materials dealing with the philosophies, religions and cultures of India.
In November 1998 the company took over Motilal Books, who are the European distributors for Motilal Banarsidass Ltd (MLBD) of New Delhi. MLBD are the foremost publishers for the academic market on the topics of Hinduism, Buddhism, Jainism and all titles from India. We supply all markets with titles in all fields, books from India in general, representing all major Indian publishers.

The company now represents 300 Indian publishers as their UK distributor, with over 35,000 English titles listed on Nielsen BookData.

6121

NMD TRADING CO
[trading as Mayfield Books & Gifts]
9 Orgreave Close, Sheffield S13 9NP
Telephone: 0114 288 9522
Fax: 0114 269 1499
Email: sales@mayfield-books.co.uk

Directors: David N. Smith *(Managing)*
Andrew Smith *(Sales)*

Supply bookshops and other trade outlets through the Midlands and Northern England with maps and guides and local book product. Specialize in walking and outdoor activity books. Four representatives call regularly throughout the year. Main suppliers are Ordnance Survey, George Philips, Collins and Geographers A-Z Map Co. Provide a service for small publishers into the multiple chains, e.g. W. H. Smith, Waterstone's. Distributor for Myriad Books.
Sole supplier of LAM-fold maps. Also supply laminated flat maps and other special product, such as library supply.

6122

ORCA BOOK SERVICES LTD
Unit A3, Fleets Corner, Poole, Dorset BH17 0HL
Telephone: 01202 665432
Fax: 01202 666219
Email: orders@orcabookservices.co.uk
Web Site: www.orcabookservices.co.uk

Directors: Martyn Chapman *(Commercial)*
Colin Smith *(IT)*
Ian Whyte *(Logistics)*
Manager: Denise Shonfeld *(Finance)*
Customer Services: Trisha Clapp
Credit Control: Maggie Johnson

Parent Company:
UK: Marston Book Services Ltd

UK distributor for:
Age Concern; Amberley Publishing; Ammo Books; Arris Publishing; Black Dog & Leventhal; The Book Foundation; Burns & Oates; Compendium; Continuum International Publishing Group; CSA Word; Dynasty Press; Evans Mitchell Books; Family Doctor Publications; Firefly Books; Francis Frith Book Co; Global Oriental; GMB Publishing; Guild of Master Craftsman Publications; Histoires et Collections; John Hunt Publishing; Industrial Press; Islamic Texts; JB Publishing; Kuperard Publishers; Lark Books; Learning Development Aids; Lifetime Careers Publishing; Maverick Arts; Mi-Vox; O Books; Palazzo Editions; Parkstone Press; Peerless Editions; Pepin Press; A. K. Peters; Potomac Books; Ravette Publishing; Redcliffe Press; Reynolds & Hearn; Romain Pages; Roundhouse Publishing; Special Interest Model Books; Sterling Publishing; Taunton Press; Thalamus Publishing; Ticktock Media; Van der Plas Publications; Veloce Publishing; Vine House; White Star Publishers

Orca Book Services provides a full distribution service to general, academic and specialist publishers. A comprehensive package of management reports comes as standard, and this can be tailored to the individual publisher's requirements if necessary. Royalty accounting is also available as well as representation through the various sales agencies with which we have arrangements.

6123

ORTHODOX CHRISTIAN BOOKS LTD
Studio 3, Unit 5, Silverdale Enterprise Park, Kents Lane, Newcastle-under-Lyme, Staffs ST5 6SR
Telephone: 01782 444561
Fax: 01782 624106
Email: orthbook@aol.com
Web Site: www.orthodoxbooks.co.uk

Managing Director: Nicholas Chapman

UK distributor for:
Greece: EN PLO Editions; Denise Harvey; Uncut Mountain Publishers
USA: Antiochian Archdiocese Publications Department; Conciliar Press; Holy Cross Press; Holy Trinity Monastery; St Herman of Alaska Press; St Nectarios Press; St

Nikodemos Orthodox Publication Society; St Tikhon's Seminary Press; St Vladimir's Seminary Press

Specialist distributor, wholesaler and retailer of books and other items pertaining to the faith, life and worship of the Orthodox Christian Churches. For some publishers it has exclusive distribution rights for the UK, European Union and British Commonwealth.

6124

POMEGRANATE EUROPE LTD
Unit 1, Hurlbutt Road, Heathcote Business Centre, Warwick CV34 6TD
Telephone: 01926 430111
Fax: 01926 430888
Email: sales@pomeurope.co.uk
Web Site: www.pomegranate.com

Directors: Thomas Burke *(Managing)*
Ley S. Bricknell *(Sales)*
Katie Burke *(Publisher)*

Associated Companies:
USA: Pomegranate Communications Inc

UK Distributor for:
USA: Pomegranate

Pomegranate (Europe) Ltd represent, distribute and publish a high-quality range of fine art and photographic calendars, posters, cards, diaries, books of days, postcards, books and much more.

6125

REARDON PUBLISHING
PO Box 919, Cheltenham, Glos GL50 9AN
Telephone: 01242 231800
Email: reardon@bigfoot.com
Web Site: www.reardon.co.uk &
www.cotswoldbookshop.com

Director: Nicholas Reardon

UK distributor for:
UK: Cassell *(selected publications)*; Cicerone *(selected publications)*; Cordee *(selected publications)*; Corinium Publications; Estate Publications; Flukes UK *(illustrated maps)*; The Gloucestershire Ramblers Association; Harvey Maps *(all maps)*; Ordnance Survey *(all maps)*; Orion *(selected publications)*; Philips Maps; Video Ex *(selected titles)*

Reardon Publishing offers a wide range of Costwold books, maps, videos, CDs and postcards and prints mostly in the specialized areas of walking, cycling, driving, folklore, leisure and tourism in both the Cotswold and associated counties, plus a new range of books on Antarctica and Antarctic heroes.

6126

*JOHN RITCHIE LTD
40 Beansburn, Kilmarnock, Ayrshire KA3 1RL
Telephone: 01563 536394
Fax: 01563 571191
Email: sales@johnritchie.co.uk
Web Site: www.johnritchie.co.uk

Directors: Kenneth Munro *(Managing)*
Edwin Taylor

UK distributor for:
Canada: Lawson Falle
UK: Cambridge Bibles; John Ritchie Ltd Publications
USA: AMG Publications; Broadman & Holman; Gospel Folio Press; Thomas Nelson (Nashville TN); Standard Publishing

Publishing and distributing Christian, i.e. religious books, magazines, etc. Providing wholesale supply to Christian bookshops for major UK and US publishers.

6127

SCANDINAVIA CONNECTION
26 Woodsford Square, London W14 8DP
Telephone: (020) 7602 0657
Email: books@scandinavia-connection.co.uk
Web Site: www.scandinavia-connection.co.uk

Chairman: Max Morgan-Witts

Parent Company:
UK: Max Morgan-Witts Productions Ltd

UK distributor for:
Denmark: Aschehoug; Borgen; Nyt Nordisk
Finland: Otava
Iceland: EDDA; Forlagid; JPV
Norway: Cappelen; Index; KOM; Normann's; Wennergren-Cappelen
Sweden: Atlantis; ICA; J-P Lahall
USA: Pelican *(for Norway B&B Book)*

Sole UK supplier for various Scandinavian publishers of non-fiction English edition Scandinavian books, maps, videos and CD-ROMs; UK book distributor for non-fiction English editions by Norwegian, Finnish, Icelandic, Danish and Swedish publishers.

6128 ▬▬▬▬▬

*SQUADRON SIGNAL / POCKETBOND LTD
PO Box 80, Welwyn, Herts AL6 0ND
Telephone: 01707 391509
Fax: 01707 327466
Email: sales@pocketbond.co.uk

Director: Phillip Brook
Manager: Neil Fraser

Pocketbond Ltd is the UK importer of Squadron Signal Publications and Detail & Scale Publications, USA. These lists are sold and distributed in the UK and the
Republic of Ireland to bookshops, book wholesalers, etc.

6129 ▬▬▬▬▬

TRADE COUNTER DISTRIBUTION
Mendlesham Industrial Estate, Norwich Road, Mendlesham, Norfolk IP14 5NA
Telephone: 01449 766629
Fax: 01449 767122
Email: patrick.curran@tradecounter.co.uk
Web Site: www.tradecounter.co.uk

Managing Director: Patrick Curran
General Manager: Martin Leigh
Chairman: Brian Barron

Storage, packing and distribution of books for publishers. Order processing and credit centre. Operates both full service and fulfilment.

6130 ▬▬▬▬▬

TRANSATLANTIC PUBLISHERS GROUP LTD
Unit 242, 235 Earls Court Road, London SW5 9FE
Telephone: (020) 7373 2515
Fax: (020) 7244 1018
Email: Richard@TPGLtd.co.uk
Web Site: www.TransatlanticPublishers.com

Directors: Richard Williamson *(Managing)*
Mark Chaloner *(Sales & Marketing)*

UK distributor for:
Australia: Advanced Knowledge International
India: Hindustan Book Co
USA: American Institute of Aeronautics & Astronautics; American Institute of Mathematical Sciences; American Pharmacists Associations; American Society of Health Systems Pharmacists (ASHP); Business Expert Press Inc; Demos Medical Publishers; Destech Publications; ESRI Press; Franklin Beedle & Associates; Industrial Press; Joint Commission Resources; Lexicomp Inc; Momentum Press; A. K. Peters; Potomac Books; Zero to Three Press

Distributors and agents for academic publishers in the UK, Europe and the Middle East.

6131 ▬▬▬▬▬

TURNAROUND PUBLISHER SERVICES LTD
Unit 3, Olympia Trading Estate, Coburg Road, London N22 6TZ
Telephone: (020) 8829 3000
Fax: (020) 8881 5088
Email: sales@turnaround-uk.com
Web Site: www.turnaround-uk.com

Directors: Bill Godber *(Managing & Sales)*
Claire Thompson *(Marketing & Company Secretary)*

Sue Gregg *(Finance)*
Andy Webb *(UK Sales)*

Clients include:
Australia: 4 Ingredients; Etram Publishing; Outre Gallery & Publishing
Canada: Tradewind Books
Czech Republic: Magic Realist Press
Finland: Desura Ltd
France: BIGfib; Editions Intervalles; Heolis; JNF Productions
Germany: Editions Braus; From Here to Fame; Kehrer Verlag; Konkursbuch Verlag; Mannerschwarm; Mix of Pix
Italy: Europa Editions
Jamaica: LMH Publishing Ltd
Japan: Kumon Publishing Group
Republic of Ireland: Maverick House
Sweden: Dokument; Nicotext; Premium Publishing
Thailand: Creation; Creation / Oneiros Books; Creation / Solar Books; Creation / Wet Angel
UK: Abaddon; Adelita Ltd; AK Press; Anvil Books; The Aquarium; Arcadia Books; Arcadia E-Books; Artists' & Photographers' Press Ltd; Ayebia Clarke Publishing Ltd; B A for Adoption & Fostering; Black Spring; Blackamber Books; Bliss; Bloody Books; Bobcat Press; Bookmarks; Borderline Publications; Burning House; Cinebook; Creative Essentials; Creme de la Crime Ltd; Crocus Books; Dalen Books; Dexter Haven Publishing; Education Now Books; Emerald Publishing; Erotic Review Books; Eurocrime; Exact Change; Facts, Figures & Fun; Fanfare; Guerilla Books; Hansib Publications; Helter Skelter; High Stakes Publishing; Honno Welsh Women's Press; Inglis Publications; Kamera; Dewi Lewis Publishing; Lifeguides; Little Roots; London Books; LVSC; Magnum Music Group; Meadow & Black; Monday Books; Myriad Editions; New Internationalist; Noir Publishing; Rankin Photography Ltd; Susan Russell Publishing; SAF Publishing Ltd; Satchel; Selfmadehero; Shubrook Brothers; Sorted; Southbank Publishing; Sportsbooks; Straightforward Publishing; Strange Attractor; Stray Cat Publishing Ltd; Suitcase Press; True Crime Library; Vice UK; Zidane Press; Ziji Publishing
USA: Africa World Press Inc; Angel City Press; Arcata Arts; Atlas & Co; Avalon Press; Bantam *(select stock holdings only)*; Barricade Books; Ben Bella; Berkley Boulvard *(select stock holdings only)*; Blood Moon Productions; Bywater Books; Catbird Press; Checker Publishing; Consafos Books; Counterpoint; Demo; DGN Productions Inc; Disinformation Co Ltd; Disney Editions *(select stock holdings only)*; Dominion Press; Doubleday *(select stock holdings only)*; Fantagraphics; Ferine Books; Fulcrum; Green Candy Press; Green Integer; Hachette Book Group USA *(select stock holdings only)*; HarperCollins US *(select stock holdings only)*; Haymarket Books; Holloway House Publishing; Hyperion *(select stock holdings only)*; IG Publishing; Intrigue Press; Last Gasp; Lee & Low; Lerner Publishing Group; Magic Carpet Books; Majority Press; Manic D Press; Helen Marx Books; Melrose Square; Melville House; Naked Ambition LLC; The Nazca Plains; NBM; Netcomics; The New Press; Palgrave *(select stock holdings only)*; Penguin Book Group USA *(select stock holdings only)*; Process; Quiver; Random House Group USA *(select stock holdings only)*; The Red Sea Press; Santa Monica Press; Sierra Club Books; Simon & Schuster Group USA *(select stock holdings only)*; Speck Press; St Martins Press Group *(select stock holdings only)*; Starbooks; Steerforth Press; Testify Books; Turtle Point Press; Van Patten

Distribution only:
UK: Allison & Busby

Sales only:
Canada: Black Rose Books (Central Books)
UK: Anvil Books; Marion Boyars; Duckworth/Overlook; Five Leaves; Maia Press; Serif

Turnaround provides a sales, marketing and distribution service for a range of UK, US and Irish publishers in the UK and Europe.

6132 ▬▬▬▬▬

TURPIN DISTRIBUTION
Pegasus Drive, Stratton Business Park, Biggleswade, Beds SG18 8TQ
Telephone: 01767 604868
Fax: 01767 604949
Email: neil.castle@turpin-distribution.com

Also at:
Turpin North America, The Bleachery, 143 West Street, New Milford, CT 06778, USA

Telephone: +1 (860) 350 0041
Fax: +1 (860) 350 0039

Managing Director: Lorna Summers
Company Accountant: Richard Stroud
Head Customer Relations & Distribution: Neil Castle

Parent Company:
UK: Eurospan

Clients include:
France: Organisation for Economic Cooperation and Development (OECD); SaS-Lavoisier
Germany: Dechema
Greece: Adcotec
Japan: Japanese Society for Analytical Chemistry
Netherlands: Brill Academic Publishers; Kluwer Law International; New in Chess
Russia: Turpion-Moscow
UK: Abington Publishing; Adcotec; Philip Allan Updates *(magazines)*; Association of Learned and Professional Society Publishers (ALPSP); The Association of Project Managers; Beech Tree Publishing; Berg Publishing; The Bodleian Library; The British Library; The British Psychological Society; Chandos Publishers; Dunedin Academic Press; Equinox Publishing; Euromoney PLC; The Eurospan Group; Fiscal Publications; Global Oriental; John Harper Publishing; Institute of Cast Metal Engineers; Intellect Journals; Internet Archaeology; IP Publishing; Journal of Transport & Economic Policy; Logos Journal; Pharmaceutical Press; Pickering & Chatto; Pion Publishers; Royal College of Obstetricians and Gynaecologists; Royal College of Psychiatrists; Sapiens; Science & Technology Letters; Society of Chemical Industry; Spiramus; The Way; White Horse Press
USA: American Association Cancer Research; American School of Classical Studies; Aspen Publishers Inc; Berghahn Journals; Greenwood *(journals)*; Idea Group Inc. Journals; Nova Science Publishers *(journals)*; United Nations

Turpin specializes in worldwide distribution of learned and academic book and journal publications. It sends out renewals/invoices etc. in the publisher's name with their logo and trading terms. It bills and collects in multiple currencies and provides multilingual customer care. Publishers' sales and financial reports are delivered via secure internet access. Turpin can handle both print and online products. Customer care and warehousing in the UK and the USA.

6133 ▬▬▬▬▬

VINE HOUSE DISTRIBUTION LTD
Waldenbury, North Chailey, East Sussex BN8 4DR
Telephone: 01825 723398
Fax: 01825 724188
Email: richard@vinehouseuk.co.uk
Web Site: www.vinehouseuk.co.uk

Customer Services:
The Old Mill House, Mill Lane, Uckfield, East Sussex TN22 5AA
Telephone: 01825 767396
Fax: 01825 765649
Email: sales@vinehouseuk.co.uk
Web Site: www.vinehouseuk.co.uk

Directors: Richard Squibb
Sarah Squibb
Tara Horwood
Customer Services Manager: Pauline Gosden

Associated Companies:
UK: Vine House Book Promotion

Clients include:
Australia: Clockwork Media; Epic Guides; Inn Australia
Finland: Fine Publishing
Italy: Mediane
Monaco: Christian Philippsen
New Zealand: Travelwise
South Africa: Outstanding 100
Spain: Editorial Moll
Sweden: MagDig Media
Switzerland: Chronosports; Editions J. R. Piccard
UK: Ashgrove Publishing; Association of Illustrators; At Heart Publishing; Bearmondsey Publishing; Berkut International; Boleyn Books; The Book Guild; British Institute of Radiology; Dance Books; Delancey Press *(imprint of The Book Guild)*; Dove Publishing; Fitzjames

Press; Football World; Good Life Press; Haldane Mason;
Hochland Communications; Martin Holmes Rallying;
Honeyglen Publishing; Horse's Mouth Publications;
Immel Publishing; Jaspal Jandu Photography; Sheila
Markham Rare Books; Andrew Martin International;
Masquerade Publications; Motor Racing Publications;
Oxbridge Applications; Park Lane Books; Picnic
Publishing; PMM Books; Puck Books; Julian Richer
Publishing; Royal Academy of Dancing; Safety House;
Saxon Books; R. D. & A. S. Shepherd Partnership; Silent
But Deadly Publications; Superbrands; Sylph Editions;
Tartarus Press; Temple House Books; Tiger Books; Tonto
Books; Touchstone Books; Troubador Publishing; John
van Weenen; Wooden Dragon Press
USA: Dance Horizons; Princeton Book Co; Wine
Appreciation Guild

Vine House Distribution provides a comprehensive range of
services for small and medium sized book publishers, including representation, distribution, marketing, publicity and
promotion, and mail order fulfilment.

6134

VIRTUE BOOKS LTD
Edward House, Tenter Street, Rotherham S60 1LB
Telephone: 01709 365005
Fax: 01709 829982
Email: info@virtue.co.uk
Web Site: www.virtue.co.uk

Directors: Richard Russum *(Commercial)*
Peter Russum *(Managing)*

Parent Company:
UK: E. Russum & Sons Ltd

Specialist distributor, concentrating almost exclusively on
books on cookery, food and drink. Virtue holds stocks of
over 300 titles and supplies mainly to professional and
domestic kitchen shops, cook shops, food shops, delicates-
sens, etc. Some of the titles on its list are exclusive to Virtue,
but the majority are sourced from British, American and
some continental publishers.

6135

WINDSOR BOOKS LTD
5 Castle End Park, Castle End Road, Ruscombe, Berks
RG10 9XQ
Telephone: 0118 934 6367
Fax: 0118 934 6368
Email: geoffcowen@windsorbooks.co.uk
Web Site: www.windsorbooks.co.uk

Managing Director: Geoff Cowen
Managers: Angela Prysor-Jones *(Publicity)*
Eileen Johnson *(Credit Control)*

Associated Companies:
UK: Meyer & Meyer Sport (UK); Star Book Sales

UK Distributor/Representative for:
Germany: Meyer & Meyer Verlag

Windsor Books Ltd, through its subsidiary, Star Book Sales,
provides distribution combined with sales representation
and marketing in the UK and European markets, linked to
Orca Distribution Services Ltd. The Star sales team consists of
six representatives in the UK and Republic of Ireland and six
covering West and Eastern Europe.
6.7 Remainder Merchants

6.7 REMAINDER MERCHANTS

6136

*AB BOOKS
21 Chalice Court, Hedge End, Southampton SO30 4TA
Telephone: 01489 799082
Fax: 01489 799082
Email: abbooks@tiscali.co.uk

Proprietor: A. C. Butler

Remainder and bargain book sales.

6137

BOOKMARK REMAINDERS LTD
Rivendell, Illand, Launceston, Cornwall PL15 7LS
Telephone: 01566 782728
Fax: 01566 782059
Email: andrew.rattray@book-bargains.co.uk
Web Site: www.book-bargains.co.uk

Directors: Andrew Rattray
Carol Rattray

A wide range of genuine remainders and bargain books.
Prompt payment to publishers, authors for surplus stocks.

6138

FANSHAW BOOKS LTD
Unit 7, Lysander Mews, Lysander Grove, London N19 3QP
Telephone: (020) 7281 9387
Fax: (020) 7561 3502
Email: info@roybloom.com
Web Site: www.roybloom.com

Managing Director: Adam Bloom
Chairman: Roy Bloom

Remainder company specializing in real UK publishers'
books, mainly non-fiction, art, military, history, etc. It also
has a number of retail stores, so customers can buy from one
to 50,000 copies of a book.

6139

OCTAGON BOOKS (WHOLESALE) LTD
The Old Exchange, New Pond Road, Holmer Green,
High Wycombe, Bucks HP15 6SU
Telephone: 01494 711717 (mobile: 07718 364857)
Fax: 01494 711176
Email: ronive@lineone.net

Directors: Ron Ive
Bernard McDonnell *(Commercial)*

All types of remainders and promotional reprints.

6140

JIM OLDROYD BOOKS
14–18 London Road, Sevenoaks, Kent TN13 1AJ
Telephone: 01732 463356
Fax: 01732 464486
Email: jim@oldroyd.co.uk & paula@oldroyd.co.uk
Web Site: www.oldroyd.co.uk

Directors: Jim Oldroyd
Paula Ireland
Manager: Niki Oldroyd *(Buyer)*

Remainders, bargain books and overstocks of adult and children's books. All ages and all interests.

6141

PR BOOKS LTD
Unit 2, Mealbank Trading Estate, Mealbank, Kendal,
Cumbria LA8 9DL
Telephone: 01539 733332
Fax: 01539 733375
Email: info@prbooks.co.uk
Web Site: www.prbooks.co.uk

Joint Managing Directors: Paul Farrar
Ruth Farrar
Regional Sales: Thomas Seddon
Sales Director: Mark Farrar

Associated Companies:
UK: Caxton Publishing Ltd; Greenwich Book Time; Henry
Roberts Bookshops

PR Books Ltd is an international book wholesaler. It is located
in the north-west of England and has been in business for 20
years. It currently has close to 6000 remainder titles, covering the following subjects: children's, educational, natural
history, military history, fiction, non-fiction, cookery, travel,
arts & crafts, social, reference, dictionaries, language packs,
fitness, wellbeing, gardening and interior design.

6142

*SANDERSON BOOKS LTD
Front Street, Klondyke, Cramlington, Northumberland
NE23 6RF
Telephone: 01670 735855
Fax: 01670 730974
Email: sales@sandersonbooks.com
Web Site: www.sandersonbooks.com

Director: John Sanderson
Manager: Anne Pearson

6143

SANDPIPER BOOKS LTD
24 Langroyd Road, London SW17 7PL
Telephone: (020) 8767 7421
Fax: (020) 8682 0280
Email: enquiries@sandpiper.co.uk
Web Site: www.sandpiper.co.uk

Managing Director: Robert Collie

Hardback reprints of Oxford University Press monographs in
classical and mediaeval studies, philosophy and history,
retailing at paperback prices and retaining the OUP imprint.
These OUP books are exclusive to Sandpiper. The company
also buys remainders exclusively from university presses and
the scholarly divisions of major publishers as well as from
smaller companies, and supplies an extensive network of
trade and non-trade outlets both in the UK and overseas.
6.8 Main Wholesalers

6.8 MAIN WHOLESALERS

6144

*AQUAPRESS
25 Farriers Way, Temple Farm Industrial Estate,
Southend-on-Sea, Essex SS2 5RY
Telephone: 0870 830 8120
Fax: 0870 830 8280
Email: info@aquapress.co.uk
Web Site: www.aquapress.co.uk

Registered Office:
9 Nelson Street, Southend-on-Sea, Essex SS1 1EH

Proprietor: Chris Davey
Sales Manager: Angela Davey
Marketing: Magdalena Strzyminska

UK distributor for:
USA: Best Publishing; Cornell Maritime Press; Gary Gentile
Productions; Watersport Publishing Inc

AquaPress is a specialist publisher and distributor for diving
and medical books, and also specializes in printing water-
proof manuals and books. AquaPress supplies wholesale to
the diving and medical industry both UK and overseas as
well as the general book trade.

6145

ARGOSY LIBRARIES LTD
Unit 12, North Park, North Road, Finglas, Dublin 11,
Republic of Ireland
Telephone: +353 (01) 823 9500
Fax: +353 (01) 823 9599
Email: info@argosybooks.ie
Web Site: www.argosybooks.ie

Managing Director: Fergal Stanley
Managers: Eddie Walsh *(General)*
Ronan Richmond *(Sales)*
Mary Healy *(Buyer)*

Trade book wholesaler specializing in books of Irish interest
and maps and guides to Ireland. Export service available.

6146

BAKER & TAYLOR UK LTD
Unit B, Charbridge Way, Bicester, Oxon OX26 4ST
Telephone: 01869 363500
Fax: 01869 363555

Directors: Diane White *(Buying)*

Annette Burgess *(Commercial)*
Gareth Powell *(Managing)*

Parent Company:
USA: Baker & Taylor

Baker & Taylor offers book distribution and merchandising service. A full-time sales force covers the entire UK and Northern Ireland, supported by five senior managers.

Operating from its computerized distribution centre at Bicester, Baker & Taylor offers over 10,000 titles from stock totally geared to the specialist markets it services, delivered fast. Baker & Taylor's range extends to gardening, DIY and the home, cookery, natural history, travel and leisure, illustrated stationery, gift books and children's books. It supplies books mainly to garden centres, home and DIY outlets, department stores, the natural history / heritage markets and the gift sector, and offers a specialist service to non-traditional children's book outlets and club warehouses.

6147

BERTRAMS
1 Broadland Business Park, Norwich NR7 0WF
Telephone: 0871 803 6666
Fax: 0871 803 6709 (customer services)
Email: sales@bertrams.com
Web Site: www.bertrams.com

Directors: Michael Neil *(Managing)*
Ian Hendrie *(Finance & Commercial)*
Chris Rushby *(Buying & Marketing)*

Parent Company:
UK: Smiths News Plc

Bertrams is wholly owned by Smiths News Plc, one of the UK's leading wholesalers of newspapers and magazines. It celebrated 40 years of trading in 2008. Bertrams has a stockholding of over 920,000 titles from over 6000 publishers and can source over 5 million English language titles from both the UK and USA. Customers, from independent booksellers to online retailers, multinationals to non-book trade outlets in both the UK and international markets, can access availability of stock, product information, ordering and shipping details in real time through Bertrams.com, Bertmail, Bertrams' ordering system, as well as Bertrams' Customer Services department. A proactive marketing program enables publishers to market their titles effectively and efficiently through all sales channels, both business to business and to the end consumer. The warehouse works at 24/7 at peak capacity and provides an accurate and robust service in a secure site.

Bertram Library Services business in Leeds provides stock and selection advice for public libraries throughout the country. Bertram Publisher Services, the distribution arm of the group, provides distribution facilities for a range of publishers and retailers.

Bertrams is a key industry player with membership of the BA and BIC, working towards improving the supply chain throughout the book industry.

6148

BOOKSPEED
16 Salamander Yards, Edinburgh EH6 7DD
Telephone: 0131 467 8100
Fax: 0131 467 8008
Email: sales@bookspeed.com
Web Site: www.bookspeed.com

Director: Kingsley Dawson
Sales Manager: Fiona Stout
Buyer: Matthew Perren

Parent Company:
UK: Rhodawn Ltd

Consultants and suppliers of books to specialist retailers in the gift, leisure and heritage markets.

6149

BOOKWORLD WHOLESALE LTD
Unit 10, Hodfar Road, Sandy Lane Industrial Estate, Stourport-on-Severn, Worcs DY13 9QB
Telephone: 01299 823330
Fax: 01299 829970
Email: info@bookworldws.co.uk
Web Site: www.bookworldws.co.uk

Director: Justin Gainham *(Sales)*
Manager: Andrea Gainham *(Warehouse)*

Transport, military and modelling book specialist distributor, now selling craft, doll and martial arts books, mainly to the UK; some export sales to Europe and the USA.

Minimum order one book, full trade terms given but postage added to orders under £50 in value. Teleordering mnemonic BK WORLD.

Range of distribution whole of UK. Number of publishers for whom we distribute is in excess of 70.

6150

GARDNERS BOOKS LTD
1 Whittle Drive, Eastbourne, East Sussex BN23 6QH
Telephone: 01323 521555
Fax: 01323 521666
Email: sales@gardners.com
Web Site: www.gardners.com

Chairman: Alan Little
Directors: Jonathan Little *(Managing)*
Jean Little
Andrew Little *(Technical)*
Bob Jackson *(Commercial)*
Simon Morley *(Buying)*
Nicky Little *(Finance)*
David O'Reilly *(Warehouse)*
Managers: Phil Edwards *(Senior Buying)*
Gail Harbour *(Buying)*
David Brewster *(Customer Care)*
Gary Sheppard *(Marketing)*

Gardners Books is a leading independent book and entertainment product wholesaler offering one of the largest stock ranges available from any UK wholesaler, wih in excess of 1 million titles available from over 5000 publishers, 70,000+ eBook files and 35,000 DVDs and Blu-ray discs. Gardners offers a comprehensive range of e-commerce solutions including bespoke data feeds and drop-ship fulfilment to meet retailers' business requirements. Orders can be placed 24 hours a day via its account holders' website, Gardlink electronic ordering system, Gardcall automated telephone enquiry service, fax and EDI. Its experienced customer care team is available from Monday to Saturday between 9am and 6pm to take orders and assist customers.

Gardners Books trade website, www.gardners.com, is free to account holders and features data on over 1.2 million British books in print, as well as real-time stock figures, invoices, backorders and promotional offers. Information on additional services Gardners offers, such as B2B abd B2C home delivery fulfilment to marketing materials, distribution services and print on demand can also be found on the site.

6151

SHOGUN INTERNATIONAL LTD
87 Gayford Road, London W12 9BY
Telephone: (020) 8749 2022
Fax: (020) 8740 1086
Email: info@shoguninternational.com

Manager: G. Blanc

Sole UK agent for:
Hong Kong: Leung Ting Publications
Sweden: Japanska
USA: Dragon Books Publishing Corp; Ohara Publications (Black Belt Communications Inc); Unique Publications

Shogun International deals exclusively with wholesaling of martial arts goods and related sports books.
6.9 Main Library Suppliers

6.9 MAIN LIBRARY SUPPLIERS

6152

THE HOLT JACKSON BOOK CO LTD
Park Mill, Great George Street, Preston PR1 1TJ
Telephone: 01772 798000
Email: info@holtjackson.co.uk
Web Site: www.holtjackson.co.uk

Chairman: Yvette Stafford
Directors: Kathryn Pattinson *(Managing)*
J. Little

A. Little
Senior Manager: Mrs J. Holborn *(Customer Care)*

Parent Company:
UK: The Little Group Ltd

Booksellers.

6153

STEVEN SIMPSON BOOKS
5 Hardingham Road, Hingham, Norwich NR9 4LX
Telephone: 01953 850471
Fax: 01953 850471
Email: info@aquariumatlas.co.uk
Web Site: www.aquariumatlas.co.uk

Proprietor: S. J. Simpson

UK distributor for:
Germany: Hans A. Baenasch / Mergus Verlag GmbH (exclusive); Birgit Schmettkamp Verlag (exclusive); Verlag ACS Aqualog GmbH (exclusive); Verlag Eugen Ulmer KG (exclusive)
Italy: Aquapress Publishers (exclusive); FAO (Food & Agriculture Organization of the United Nations)
Nepal: T. K. Shrestha (exclusive)

Distributor to the trade for overseas publishers in the field of natural history.

6154

STARKMANN LTD
6 Broadley Street, London NW8 8AE
Telephone: (020) 7724 5335
Fax: (020) 7724 9863
Email: orders@starkmann.co.uk
Web Site: www.starkmann.com

Delivery Address:
6 Plympton Place, London NW8 8AD

Managing Director: Dr Bernard Starkmann
Managers: Sheikh Obarey *(Accounts)*
Martin Illmann *(Sales)*
Steven Wright *(Operations)*
Rodney Latham *(IT)*
Kerstin Peter *(Customer Service)*

Suppliers of academic and scientific books and ebooks to university, college, industrial and research libraries in Europe. Customers and potential customers receive frequent and accurate new book information. Distribution of the main line publishers from UK, USA, Netherlands, Germany and Switzerland. Supplies made at publisher's list price. Fast airfreight service of US books. Comprehensive website featuring bibliographic database, online ordering, order tracking, new title alert service and special offers.

6155

ROY YATES BOOKS
Smallfields Cottage, Cox Green, Rudgwick, Horsham, West Sussex RH12 3DE
Telephone: 01403 822299
Fax: 01403 823012
Email: roy@royyatesbooks.fsnet.co.uk

Managing Director: Roy Yates

Specialist supplier of children's books to schools and libraries; distributes multilingual books; distributes foreign-language books.
6.10 Book Clubs

6.10 BOOK CLUBS

6156

ARTISTS' CHOICE LTD
The Old Post Office, Bythorn, Huntingdon, Cambs PE28 0QN
Telephone: 01832 710201
Fax: 01832 710488
Email: henry@artists-choice.co.uk
Web Site: www.artists-choice.co.uk & www.acaward.com

Managing Director: Henry Malt

Book club aimed at the amateur artist.

6157

BIBLIOPHILE BOOKS
Unit 5 Datapoint Business Centre, 6 South Crescent,
London E16 4TL
Telephone: (020) 7474 2474
Fax: (020) 7474 8589
Email: orders@bibliophilebooks.com
Web Site: www.bibliophilebooks.com

General Manager: Jackie McDaid
Distribution: Steven Lee
Director: Anne Quigley

Produces 10 catalogues a year, offering books at bargain
prices to private buyers. Range: general, eg biography, history, travel, handicrafts, humour, literature.

6158

*LETTERBOX LIBRARY
71–73 Allen Road, Stoke Newington, London N16 8RY
Telephone: (020) 7503 4801
Fax: (020) 7503 4800
Email: info@letterboxlibrary.com
Web Site: www.letterboxlibrary.com

Contacts: Kerry Mason
Maikim Stern
Fen Coles

Letterbox Library is a children's bookseller specializing in children's books which celebrate equality and diversity. Quarterly catalogues are produced with up to 50 new titles,
offered at discounts to members. Books are multicultural
and non-sexist, and also show groups of people traditionally
under-represented in children's books, e.g. different faith
groups, disabled children, refugees. All books are approved
by an independent team of reviewers. Subscription is £5 a
year and entitles members to discounts. Non-members can
buy books at the retail price. Letterbox Library also provides
book displays for schools and libraries and attends exhibitions. Letterbox Library is a social enterprise.

6159

POETRY BOOK SOCIETY
4th Floor, 2 Tavistock Place, London WC1H 9RA
Telephone: (020) 7833 9247
Fax: (020) 7833 5990
Email: info@poetrybooks.co.uk
Web Site: www.poetrybooks.co.uk &
www.poetrybookshoponline.com

Director: Chris Holifield

Publicly funded charity, membership organization, mail
order book club promoting contemporary poetry titles to an
international readership. Quarterly publication of *Bulletin*
magazine featuring selected new poetry titles. Also has Children's Poetry Bookshelf, relaunched 2005 with new website
(www.childrenspoetrybookshelf.co.uk) and parent and
library memberships. The Society also acts as sole distributor
for The Poetry Archive CDs, and awards the annual T. S. Eliot
Prize for Poetry.
  Membership from £12 p.a.
  Also runs www.poetrybookshoponline.com, selling a
wide range of poetry and SoundBlast performance poets'
CDs.
6.11 Literary & Trade Events

6.11 LITERARY & TRADE EVENTS

6160

BOOKSELLERS ASSOCIATION ANNUAL CONFERENCE
Minster House, 272 Vauxhall Bridge Road, London
SW1V 1BA
Telephone: (020) 7802 0802
Fax: (020) 7802 0803
Email: naomi.gane@booksellers.org.uk
Web Site: www.booksellers.org.uk

Chief Executive: Tim Godfray

Conference Organizer: Naomi Gane
Head of Marketing & Events: Alan Staton

Major UK book trade event. The Conference provides
opportunity for those supplying or serving the retail book
trade to meet trade customers and for both to learn from
business programme. **Details from:** above address.

6161

THE TIMES CHELTENHAM LITERATURE FESTIVAL
Cheltenham Festivals Ltd, 109 Bath Road, Cheltenham,
Glos GL53 7LS
Telephone: 01242 775861
Fax: 01242 256457
Email: clair.greenaway@cheltenhamfestivals.com
Web Site: www.cheltenhamfestivals.com

Chief Executive: Donna Renney
Artistic Director: Sarah Smyth
Executive Director: Clair Greenaway

Annual in October. Promoted by Cheltenham Festivals Ltd.
Performances, poetry readings, talks and discussions by liter-
ary personalities. Includes Book It! Festival for Children,
Voices Off Fringe Festival and Write Away creative writing
workshops.
  Details from: Artistic Director: Sarah Smyth or Executive
Director: Clair Greenaway.

6162

CHILDREN'S BOOK WEEK
Booktrust, Book House, 45 East Hill, Wandsworth, London
SW18 2QZ
Telephone: (020) 8516 2976
Fax: (020) 8516 2992
Email: education@booktrust.org.uk
Web Site: www.booktrust.org.uk

Patron: HRH The Prince Philip Duke of Edinburgh
Chief Executive: Viv Bird
Chair: Sue Horner

Children's Book Week is an annual event which takes place
every October. It is a national event promoting the idea that
reading and books are fun!
  Promotional resource materials are sent to schools and
libraries in England.

6163

CIANA LTD
24 Langroyd Road, London SW17 7PL
Telephone: (020) 8682 1969
Fax: (020) 8682 1997
Email: enquiries@ciana.co.uk
Web Site: www.ciana.co.uk

Directors: Robert Collie
Sarah Weedon

Organizers of two annual trade fairs for the remainder, over-
stock and promotional book market. Over 100,000 discounted books, stationery items, CDs and DVDs. The
September Fair is held in London Islington. The January Fair
is in the Barbican in the City of London.

6164

EDINBURGH INTERNATIONAL BOOK FESTIVAL
5A Charlotte Square, Edinburgh EH2 4DR
Telephone: 0131 718 5666
Fax: 0131 226 5335
Email: admin@edbookfest.co.uk
Web Site: www.edbookfest.co.uk

Directors: Catherine Lockerbie
Sara Grady (*Children & Education Programme*)
Andrew Coulton (*Administrative*)
Managers: Amanda Barry (*Marketing & PR*)
Lois Wolffe (*Sponsorship & Development*)

The Edinburgh International Book Festival began in 1983
and is now an annual event. It exists to promote books and
reading to all ages and is primarily for the public.
  The festival runs its own, independent book sales operation on the site – a tented village in Edinburgh's Charlotte
Square Gardens.
  More than 700 events take place over 17 days in August,
representing both adult and children's literature.

6165

FRANKFURT BOOK FAIR
Reineckstrasse 3, 60313 Frankfurt am Main, Germany
Telephone: +49 69 2102 0
Fax: +49 69 2102 227 & 277
Email: info@book-fair.com
Web Site: www.book-fair.com

Chief Executive Officer: Juergen Boos
Director, Marketing & Sales: Thomas Minkus

Parent Company:
Germany: Börsenverein des Deutschen Buchhandels

The Frankfurt Book Fair is one of the largest book fairs in the
world with more than 7000 exhibitors from over 100 countries. Open exclusively to the trade for the first three days
and to the public for the last two days it attracts publishers,
booksellers, authors, agents, distributors and the whole
range of multimedia companies.
  The Frankfurt Book Fair also organizes the participation of
German publishers at more than 25 international book fairs
and is associated with the Cape Town Book Fair in South
Africa and the Abu Dhabi International Book Fair. The Frankfurt Book Fair is a subsidiary of the German Publishers &
Booksellers Association.

6166

GENERAL DIRECTORATE OF INTERNATIONAL BOOK EXHIBITIONS & FAIRS
Malaya Dmitrovka Street 16, Moscow 127006, Russia
Telephone: +7 (495) 699 4034, 699 9790 & 699 3466
Fax: +7 (495) 699 2539 & 299 1110
Email: mibf@mibf.ru & vBelov@mibf.ru
Web Site: www.mibf.ru

General Director: Nikolay Ph. Ovsyannikov
Head of Foreign Relations Department: Nina Sudjina
Project Manager: Valery Belov

Organization of annual Moscow International and Russian
National Book Fairs, as well as collective and national book
stands of Russian publishers at the international book fairs.

6167

GÖTEBORG BOOK FAIR
412 94 Göteborg, Sweden
Telephone: +46 (031) 708 8400
Fax: +46 (031) 209103
Email: info@goteborg-bookfair.com
Web Site: www.goteborg-bookfair.com

Public Relations Manager: Birgitta Jacobsson Ekblom
Managing Director: Anna Falck

Göteborg Book Fair is one of the biggest bookfairs in northern Europe; 100,000 visits in four days, 900 exhibitors, 450
seminars and more than 1000 journalists covering the fair.
  Göteborg Book Fair is arranged annually in September,
and takes place at the Swedish Exhibition Centre located in
the centre of the city of Göteborg.

6168

LEIPZIG BOOK FAIR
Leipziger Messe GmbH, Messe-Allee 1, 04356 Leipzig,
Germany
Telephone: +49 (0)341 678 8240
Fax: +49 (0)341 678 8242
Email: info@leipziger-buchmesse.de
Web Site: www.leipziger-buchmesse.de

Exhibition Director: Oliver Zille

The Leipzig Book Fair is an independent, general book fair
concentrating on the German-speaking countries of Europe
(Germany, Austria and Switzerland). It also features international book art and is additionally characterized by general
themes (e.g. audio books, travelling) which change from
year to year and which are highlighted by special events
relating to these themes. The commercial aspect of the Leipzig Book Fair is accompanied by a wide range of fringe
events, including a section for antique books and prints.
  Visitors to the Leipzig Book Fair are mainly made up of
representatives from publishers, the book trade, libraries,
the newer media, the printing industry, and all other areas
connected with the production of books, including book
illustrators and graphic designers.
  2010 dates: 18–21 March.

6169 ∎

THE LONDON BOOK FAIR

Gateway House, 28 The Quadrant, Richmond, Surrey
TW9 1DN
Telephone: (020) 8910 7197
Fax: (020) 8334 0688
Email: emma.lowe@reedexpo.co.uk
Web Site: www.londonbookfair.co.uk

Group Exhibition Director: Alistair Burtenshaw
Managers: Amy Webster (International Key Accounts)
    Emma Lowe (Sales)
    Matt Colgan (Sales)
    Barbara Davis (International Sales)
    Gwen Wilcox (Content)
Executives: Rachel Jones (Sales)
    Rebecca Hearn (Marketing)
Exhibition Administrators: Erin Dowling
    Christine Dolan

The London Book Fair is a global marketplace for rights
negotiation and the sale and distribution of content across
print, audio, TV, film and digital channels, bringing three
days of focused access to customers content and emerging
markets.
2010 Fair: 19–21 April at Earls Court, London. For further
information, please visit our website www.londonbook-
fair.co.uk

6170 ∎

THE LONDON LITERARY MAFIA

618b Finchley Road, London NW11 7RR
Telephone: (020) 8455 4564
Email: lambhorn@gmail.com
Web Site: www.phantomcaptain.netfirms.com

Director: Neil Hornick (Artistic)

Parent Company:
UK: The Phantom Captain

'Are You Reading Me?' – Established in 1997, The London
Literary Mafia (a.k.a. The Phantom Captain Literary Lions) is
a performance company specializing in entertainments,
talks and readings devised to brighten up literature festivals,
conferences, book launches, award ceremonies, promotions, luncheons and dinners, book fairs, writing courses
and related writer/reader-themed events. Activities draw on
the extensive experience of Neil Hornick, artistic director of
the company, as writer-director-actor and (under a pen-
name) as a professional literary consultant. Events can be
commissioned and designed for specific occasions.

6171 ∎

SALON DU LIVRE DE MONTREAL

300 rue St-Sacrement, Bureau 430, Montreal, PQ,
Canada H2Y 1X4
Telephone: +1 (514) 845 2365
Fax: +1 (514) 845 7119
Email: slm.info@videotron.ca
Web Site: www.salondulivredemontreal.com

General Manager: Francine Bois

The Salon du Livre de Montréal is a public book fair which
aims to promote reading.

6172 ∎

*TOKYO INTERNATIONAL BOOK FAIR

Reed Exhibitions Japan Ltd, 18F Shinjuku Nomura Building,
1-26-2 Nishi-Shinjuku, Shinjuku-ku, Tokyo 163-0570, Japan
Telephone: +81 3 3349 8507
Fax: +81 3 3345 7929
Email: tibf-eng@reedexpo.co.jp
Web Site: www.bookfair.jp/english

International Sales Director: Kaoru Iwata
International Sales Manager: Janet Or
Show Director: Keisuke Amano

Parent Company:
UK: Reed Exhibition Companies

Tokyo International Book Fair (TIBF) represents the world's
second largest single publishing market - Japan. TIBF has
built its success upon the full support of its joint organization
committee comprising the seven most influential Japanese
publishing trade associations.

TIBF offers exhibitors opportunities to meet major book
publishers, literary agents, distributors and booksellers from
all over Japan and neighbouring countries such as Korea,
Taiwan, Hong Kong and China, and develop extensive business opportunities including:
    – international rights negotiation
    – joint publishing projects
    – direct book exports.
    2009 Fair: 9–13 July at Tokyo Big Sight.
    For more information, please contact Reed Exhibitions in
Tokyo.

6173 ∎

WORLD BOOK DAY

c/o Booksellers' Association,
272–274 Vauxhall Bridge Road, London SW1V 1BA
Telephone: (020) 7802 0802
Email: cathy.schofield@blueyonder.co.uk
Web Site: www.worldbookday.com

Word Book Day Co-ordinator: Cathy Schofield

One of the UK's biggest celebrations of books and reading,
held on the first Thursday in March. It is a partnership of
publishers, booksellers and interested parties who work
together to promote books and reading for the personal
enrichment and enjoyment of all. One of the main aims of
World Book Day is to encourage children to explore the
pleasures of reading by providing them with the opportunity
to have a book of their own. Thanks to the generosity of
National Book Tokens and participating booksellers, school-
children are entitled to receive a World Book Day £1 book
token, which can be exchanged for one of the specially published £1 books or is redeemable against a book or audiobook of their choice.
6.12 Publishing Reference Books & Periodicals

6.12 PUBLISHING REFERENCE BOOKS & PERIODICALS

6174 ∎

THE AUTHOR

84 Drayton Gardens, London SW10 9SB
Telephone: (020) 7373 6642
Fax: (020) 7373 5768
Email: TheAuthor@societyofauthors.org
Web Site: www.societyofauthors.org

Editor: Andrew Rosenheim
Manager: Kate Pool

Parent Company:
UK: The Society of Authors

Free to members. £12, post free, per copy for others. Annual
subscription: £30, post free.

The quarterly journal of the Society of Authors. Articles on
the legal, commercial and technical side of authorship.

6175 ∎

BOOKS FOR KEEPS

1 Effingham Road, London SE12 8NZ
Telephone: (020) 8852 4953
Fax: (020) 8318 7580
Email: enquiries@booksforkeeps.co.uk
Web Site: www.booksforkeeps.co.uk

Managing Director: Richard Hill
Editor: Rosemary Stones

ISSN: 0143-909X

6 issues pa. Annual subscription: £26.50 (UK), £29.50
(Europe), £32.50 (worldwide: airmail only).

Reviews all children's books and carries articles/features
about authors, publishing, education, etc. Main readership -
teachers, librarians and parents.

6176 ∎

BOOKS IN PRINT 2009–2010

Bowker (UK) Ltd, 1st Floor, Medway House,
Cantelupe Road, East Grinstead, West Sussex RH19 3BJ
Telephone: 01342 310450
Fax: 01342 310486
Email: sales@bowker.co.uk
Web Site: www.bowker.co.uk

Directors: Doug McMillan (Managing)
    Pam Roud (Sales)
Marketing Manager: Jo Grange

Associated Companies:
USA: R. R. Bowker LLC; Cambridge Information Group

ISBN: 978 0 8352 5014 6

Published August 2009, 7 volumes, hbk, £640.

Full bibliographic and ordering information for over two million titles published or distributed in the USA. There are
164,000 titles new to this edition.

6177 ∎

THE BOOKSELLER

5th Floor, Endeavour House, 189 Shaftesbury Avenue,
London WC2H 8TJ
Telephone: (020) 7420 6006
Fax: (020) 7420 6103
Email: letters-to-editor@bookseller.co.uk
Web Site: www.theBookseller.com

Managing Director: Nigel Roby
Managers: Nicola Chin (Deputy Sales)
    Samantha Missingham (Marketing)
Editor-in-Chief: Neill Denny

Parent Company:
USA: Nielsen Entertainment Media

ISSN: 0006-7539

Weekly £4.40. Annual subscription: £177 (UK: public libraries), £186 (UK: all other businesses), £192 (Europe – airmail),
£264 (rest of world – airmail).

The weekly newspaper of the book trade, offering in the
course of a year over 7000 pages of news, analysis, features,
letters, advertising and lists of books published in the UK.
Major national and international events reported, regular
authoritative articles on matters of trade, special features,
book features and rights, stock market, legal and financial
pages. Twice a year a six-month special issue of over 700
pages provides the best reference source for British publishers' publishing plans. Regular supplements in specialist
areas.

6178 ∎

BOOKSELLER + PUBLISHER

Thorpe-Bowker, PO Box 6509, St Kilda Road Central, Vic,
Australia 8008
Telephone: +61 (03) 8517 8333
Fax: +61 (03) 8517 8399
Email: bookseller.publisher@thorpe.com.au
Web Site: www.booksellerandpublisher.com.au

General Manager: Gary Pengelly
Publisher: Tim Coronel
Advertising Manager: Xeverie Swee
Production & Design: Silvana Paolini
Editor: Matthia Dempsey

Parent Company:
Australia: Thorpe-Bowker
USA: R. R. Bowker LLC

Published continuously since 1921, Bookseller + Publisher
magazine (and its offshoots the Weekly Book Newsletter,
WBN Media Extra and Australian Library News) is the trade
publication of the book industry for Australia and the
region.

6179 ∎

CHILDREN'S BOOKS IN PRINT 2009

Bowker (UK) Ltd, 1st Floor, Medway House,
Cantelupe Road, East Grinstead, West Sussex RH19 3BJ
Telephone: 01342 310450

Fax: 01342 310486
Email: marketing@bowker.co.uk
Web Site: www.bowker.co.uk

Directors: Doug McMillan *(Managing)*
  Pam Roud *(Sales)*
Marketing Manager: Jo Grange

Associated Companies:
USA: R. R. Bowker LLC; Cambridge Information Group

ISBN: 978 0 8352 5025 2

Published December 2009, 2 volumes, £190.

Most complete list of currently available children's books published in the USA.

6180

CHILDREN'S WRITERS' & ARTISTS' YEARBOOK
A. & C. Black Publishers Ltd, 36 Soho Square, London
W1D 3QY
Telephone: (020) 7758 0201
Fax: (020) 7758 0222
Email: wayb@acblack.com
Web Site: www.acblack.com &
www.writersandartists.co.uk

Directors: Jill Coleman *(Managing)*
  Jonathan Glasspool *(Deputy Managing)*

Parent Company:
UK: Bloomsbury Publishing Plc

ISBN: 978 1 4081 11277

Annual. 2010 edition, published June 2009, £14.99.

A comprehensive guide to markets in all areas of children's media. Contains articles and information on a wide range of topics written by well-known authors and illustrators, best-selling publishers and editors, leading figures in TV and radio and other children's media experts. Also contains market contacts including book publishers and packagers, literary and art agents, magazines, TV and radio, festivals, courses and bookshops.

6181

THE COMPLETE DIRECTORY OF LARGE PRINT BOOKS AND SERIALS 2009
Bowker (UK) Ltd, 1st Floor, Medway House,
Cantelupe Road, East Grinstead, West Sussex RH19 3BJ
Telephone: 01342 310450
Fax: 01342 310486
Email: marketing@bowker.co.uk
Web Site: www.bowker.co.uk

Directors: Doug McMillan *(Managing)*
  Pam Roud *(Sales)*
Marketing Manager: Jo Grange

Associated Companies:
USA: R. R. Bowker LLC; Cambridge Information Group

ISBN: 978 0 8352 4976 8

Published January 2009, 1 volume, £215.

Bigger than ever, this invaluable guide covers the large print field like no other resource. Inside you'll discover current, accurate bookfinding and ordering information on some 22,500 titles.

6182

DIRECTORY OF UK & IRISH BOOK PUBLISHERS
The Booksellers Association of UK & Ireland,
272 Vauxhall Bridge Road, London SW1V 1BA
Telephone: (020) 7802 0802
Fax: (020) 7802 0803
Email: mail@booksellers.org.uk
Web Site: www.booksellers.org.uk

Chief Executive: Tim Godfray

ISBN: 978 0 9552233 8 9

Annual. 2009 edition, £77.63 (plus P&P overseas), £60.38 (BA members).

Contains addresses and comprehensive information (including personnel, e-mail and www sites) about UK and Irish publishers, sales agents, remainder dealers, distributors and book wholesalers, including distribution arrangements in the UK for overseas publications. Also includes trade terms and returns information, details of product specialization such as audio books, electronic publishing and maps, plus a subject specialization index and ISBN prefixes.

The *Directory of UK & Irish Book Publishers* – jointly published by the Booksellers Association and Nielsen Book – combines and replaces the old BA *Directory of UK & Irish Book Publishers* and BookData's *The Red Book: Directory of Publishers*.

There is a more detailed listing available simultaneously as an online searchable database at www.ukpublishers.net. Purchasers of the book will automatically have access to the online service for the subscription period of one year. The online Directory also includes additional information and 6000+ entries not included in the print version and will be updated with new entries and amendments throughout the year.

6183

DIY: BOOKFINDING AND BOOKSELLING
Magna Graecia's Publishers, PO Box 342, Oxford OX2 7YF
Telephone: 01865 553653
Fax: 01865 553653
Email: info@magnagraeciaspublishers.co.uk
Web Site: www.magnagraeciaspublishers.co.uk

Director: Luigi Gigliotti *(Research Editor)*

Single parts: £29.95 each, except Volume 5: £19.95. Complete set: £229.60 plus p&p.

List of titles reported wanted by our members, clients in the UK and worldwide. The Register is updated daily. It is available on-line or in print format.

Set of eight parts: Volume One (3 parts) by authors; Volume Two (2 parts) by titles; Volume Three (1 part) by categories; Volume Four (1 part) by subjects; Volume Five (1 part) by subjects.

6184

GLOBAL BOOKS IN PRINT ONLINE
Bowker (UK) Ltd, 1st Floor, Medway House,
Cantelupe Road, East Grinstead, West Sussex RH19 3BJ
Telephone: 01342 310450
Fax: 01342 310486
Email: marketing@bowker.co.uk
Web Site: www.bowker.co.uk

Directors: Doug McMillan *(Managing)*
  Pam Roud *(Sales)*
Marketing Manager: Jo Grange

Associated Companies:
USA: R. R. Bowker LLC; Cambridge Information Group

Annual subscription: from £2220.

Over 2.7 million records of English-language titles. Single most complete listing of English language titles. Available on the web – www.globalbooksinprint.com.

This is no longer offered on CD. Online version only.

6185

THE NEW WALFORD: GUIDE TO REFERENCE RESOURCES
Facet Publishing, 7 Ridgmount Street, London WC1E 7AE
Telephone: (020) 7255 0597
Fax: (020) 7255 0591
Email: info@facetpublishing.co.uk
Web Site: www.facetpublishing.co.uk

Managing Director: John Woolley
Managers: Lena Stuart *(Marketing)*
  Rohini Ramachandran *(Sales)*
Publisher: Helen Carley
Production: Kathryn Beecroft
Commissioning Editor: Louise Le Bas
Desk Editor: Lin Franklin

In three volumes. Vol. 1: Science, Technology and Medicine (**ISBN**: 978 1 85604 495 0, June 2005, 848 pp, hbk, £149.95). Vol. 2: The Social Sciences (**ISBN**: 978 1 85604 498 1, 2007, 720 pp, hbk, £159.95). Vol. 3: Arts, Humani-

ties and General Reference (**ISBN**: 978 1 85604 499 8, 2010, 800 pp, hbk, £159.95).

6186

NEW WELSH REVIEW
PO Box 170, Aberystwyth, Ceredigion SY23 1WZ
Telephone: 01970 628410
Email: admin@newwelshreview.com
Web Site: www.newwelshreview.com

Editor: Kathryn Gray
Development Manager: Sue Fisher

New Welsh Review is a quarterly magazine which brings its readers a selection of new writing from Wales and the UK. Each issue includes a range of critical articles, book reviews, fiction and poetry. While the magazine's focus is on Welsh writing in English, its outlook is deliberately eclectic, encompassing broader European and international literary contexts.

6187

PUBLISHING, BOOKS & READING IN SUB-SAHARAN AFRICA: A CRITICAL BIBLIOGRAPHY
Hans Zell Publishing Consultants, Glais Bheinn, Lochcarron,
Ross-shire IV54 8YB
Telephone: 01520 722951
Fax: 01520 722953
Email: hanszell@hanszell.co.uk
Web Site: www.hanszell.co.uk/pbrssa/index.shtml

Editor: Hans Zell

ISBN: 978 0 9541029 5 1

Published October 2008, 762 pp, cased, £130/€195/$260. Print and online (online access bundled with print).

A completely revised and fully updated edition, covering both print and online resources. *Publishing, Books & Reading in Sub-Saharan Africa: A Critical Bibliography* charts the growth of publishing and book development in the countries of Africa south of the Sahara, as well as including a very large number of entries on many other topics as they relate to books and reading in Africa. It is a detailed documentation resource on the current state of the book on the African continent.

6188

PUBLISHING NEWS
Publishing News Ltd, 39 Store Street, London WC1E 7DS
Telephone: (020) 3089 4460
Web Site: www.britishbookindustryawards.co.uk

Managing Director: Jo Henry

Associated Companies:
UK: BML Ltd; British Book Awards; British Book Industry Awards

Weekly. £110 a year (UK only), £125 (Europe), £140 (elsewhere).

Weekly newspaper of the book trade. Hardback and paperback reviews and extensive listings of new paperbacks. Interviews with leading personalities in the trade, authors, agents and features on specialist book areas. Full international coverage.

6189

SHEPPARD'S DIRECTORIES
Richard Joseph Publishers Ltd, PO Box 15, Torrington,
Devon EX38 8ZJ
Telephone: 01805 625750
Email: office@sheppardsworld.co.uk
Web Site: www.sheppardsworld.co.uk

Managing Director: Richard Joseph

Sheppard's Directories are a comprehensive set of reference books available for the secondhand and antiquarian book trades. Information is presented in the same format for each directory; the principal section gives full details of dealerships, arranged geographically; an Alphabetical Business Index, Proprietor's index and a detailed Speciality Index. Valuable information is also given in the introductory pages. Volumes include: British Isles, Europe, North America, Australia and New Zealand, Latin America and Southern Africa,

International Print and Map Sellers and International Ephemera Dealers. Sheppard's Directories are sold to dealers throughout the world. Now available for online searches.

6190

THE TIMES LITERARY SUPPLEMENT
Times House, 1 Pennington Street, London E98 1BS
Telephone: (020) 7782 5000
Fax: (020) 7782 4966
Email: letters@the-tls.co.uk
Web Site: www.the-tls.co.uk

Editors: Sir Peter Stothard
   Alan Jenkins *(Deputy)*
   Robert Potts *(Managing)*

The *TLS* is a weekly literary review, which carries reviews by leading authorities on up to 3000 books a year on literature and language, history, politics, philosophy, the arts and music, social studies, economics, natural history and many other subjects. It also reviews exhibitions and performing arts, carries articles of general interest, publishes poetry and has a letters page which is the principal forum for literary debate. It is essential reading for librarians, booksellers and academics, and also for its broad, worldwide general readership.

6191

WRITERS' & ARTISTS' YEARBOOK
A. & C. Black Publishers Ltd, 36 Soho Square, London W1D 3QY
Telephone: (020) 7758 0201
Fax: (020) 7758 0222
Email: wayb@acblack.com
Web Site: www.acblack.com & www.writersandartists.co.uk

Directors: Jill Coleman *(Managing)*
   Jonathan Glasspool *(Deputy Managing)*

Parent Company:
UK: Bloomsbury Publishing Plc

ISBN: 978 1 4081 11277

Annual. 2010 edition, published June 2009, £14.99.

A guide for freelance writers and artists. Details of English-language periodicals; of British, American and Commonwealth publishers; of British, American and Continental literary agents; and of press, art and photographic agencies. Practical information on such topics as copyright, libel and income tax; and on the Internet. Articles on writing for newspapers and the periodical press, on films, television, radio, artists, and markets for verse and drama.

6192

WRITERS' FORUM
PO Box 6337, Bournemouth BH1 9EH
Telephone: 01202 586848
Email: editorial@writers-forum.com
Web Site: www.writers-forum.com

Advertisement & PR Manager:
Wendy O'Brien, 40 Clyst Valley Road, Clyst St Mary, Exeter EX5 1DD
Telephone: 01392 873270
Email: wendy.obrien@virgin.net

Publisher: Tim Harris
Editor: Carl Styants
Advertising & PR Manager: Wendy O'Brien
Subscriptions Manager: Chris Wigg

11 issues a year. Subscription: UK £33; Worldwide £46.

Welcomes articles on any aspect of the craft and business of writing. Length: 800–2000 words. Payment: by arrangement. Administrators of Short Story Competition, plus poetry and short story competitions for subscribers in each issue. Founded 1993.
6.13 Training

6.13 TRAINING

6193

THE CENTRE FOR PUBLISHING STUDIES
University of Stirling, Stirling FK9 4LA
Telephone: 01786 467510
Fax: 01786 466210
Email: alison.scott@stir.ac.uk
Web Site: www.pubstud.co.uk

Directors: Prof Claire Squires
   James McCall *(Deputy)*
Lecturers: Helen Sun
   Frances Sessford

The Centre specializes in the study of and teaching about the publishing industry internationally. Centre staff have experience in North America, Africa, East Asia (especially China and Malaysia) and other areas, are engaged in editorial and marketing consultancy, and are active in publishing, training, and cultural organizations. There is current work on international book publishing.

The Centre runs a well-established one year full-time Mlitt course in Publishing Studies, with three main taught elements: contemporary publishing – publishing business, industry structure, authors, bookselling, marketing, financial, intellectual property (IP), group projects; editorial function – varieties of editing, practical skills in copy editing, proofreading; production – overview of manufacturing, design, desktop publishing, Internet Web pages, practical projects; handprinting, papermaking facilities; students research 20,000-word dissertations on individual topics; there are visiting trade speakers. Most students go into editorial or marketing jobs. There are also PhD research students. The Centre also offers short courses for businesses and organizations.

A specialist course, the MSc in International Publishing Management, began in January 2006.

6194

CENTRE FOR PUBLISHING, UNIVERSITY COLLEGE LONDON
Department of Information Studies, UCL, Gower Street, London WC1E 6BT
Telephone: (020) 7679 2473
Fax: (020) 7383 0557
Email: ma-publishing@ucl.ac.uk
Web Site: www.publishing.ucl.ac.uk

Directors: Prof Iain Stevenson *(Teaching)*
   Prof David Nicholas
   Dr Ian Rowlands *(Research)*
Industry Liaison: Prof Anthony Watkinson
Administrator: Ms Kerstin Michaels
Administration Secretary: Ms Lucy Lyons
Electronic Publishing: Dr Claire Warwick

Research and education in publishing. Offers a taught MA in Publishing with pathways in Publishing, Electronic Publishing and Magazine Publishing (from 2010). Also Mphil and PhD research in publishing.

6195

CITY UNIVERSITY
Department of Journalism and Publishing, Northampton Square, London EC1V 0HB
Telephone: (020) 7040 0100
Fax: (020) 7040 8594
Email: maryann.kernan.1@city.ac.uk
Web Site: www.city.ac.uk/journalism

Programme Director: Mary Ann Kernan
Visiting Lecturers: Max Adam
   Richard Balkwill
   Neil Dunnicliffe
   Brenda Stones
   Dominic Vaughan
   Stephen Mesquita

Offers a full-time one year Master's Degree (MA) in Publishing Studies to prepare entrants and re-entrants to the industry. Comprises nine taught units, a 5–6 week industrial placement and a dissertation. The department has close industry links and the course is supervised by leading industry professionals.

Also conducts research into publishing and supervises research students.

The MSc in Electronic Publishing offers a practical introduction to digital media, information management and multi-media production. Please contact Dr Vesna Brujic-Okretic in the Department of Infomatics: (020) 7040 8551 or v.brujic-okretic@city.ac.uk.

6196

GERMAN TUITION – BARBARA CLASSEN
2 Blackall Street, London EC2A 4AD
Telephone: (020) 7613 3177
Email: barbara@germantuition.com
Web Site: www.germantuition.com

Director/Tutor: Barbara Classen
Co-Tutors: Nicole Nagel
   Itamar Groisman
   Eva Friedrich
   Marina de Quay
   Janka Troeber

The company offers lively German tuition at all levels and specializes in German for the book trade. Students can choose between one-to-one tuition or small groups of 4–6. German Tuition also offers short-term tailor-made intensive courses.

Tutors are professional, experienced native speakers and offer free consultations with trial lesson. Students may work towards one of many recognized exams.

Clients include publishers, booksellers, journalists and other professionals.

Classes are held in the central London German Tuition office or in client's office/home 7 days a week.

German Tuition London has a small branch in Freiburg, Germany, offering tailor-made German language holidays and Business German courses for the book trade, usually over one week.

6197

LONDON COLLEGE OF COMMUNICATION
Elephant & Castle, London SE1 6SB
Telephone: (020) 7514 6569
Fax: (020) 7514 2035
Email: info@lcc.arts.ac.uk
Web Site: www.lcc.arts.ac.uk

Head of College: Sandra Kemp
Marketing Manager: Anne Nicholls *(Head of Marketing & Communications)*

Parent Company:
UK: University of the Arts, London

MA, BA Hons Publishing, Postgrad Dip/Cert Publishing.

LCC offers a range of full and part-time courses in publishing, printing and media. These include postgraduate, undergraduate and Further Education courses.

A range of short courses and part-time programmes is also offered. These cover almost every aspect of the printing and publishing industry.

6198

MARKETABILITY (UK) LTD
12 Sandy Lane, Teddington, Middx TW11 0DR
Telephone: (020) 8977 2741
Fax: (020) 8977 2741
Email: rachel@marketability.info
Web Site: www.marketability.info

Director: Rachel Maund

Current and recent clients for training include:
Australia: Australian Publishers Association; Victorian Law Foundation
China: Elsevier; Higher Education Press
Mexico: CANIEM (Mexican Publishers' Association)
Republic of Ireland: CLÉ (Irish Book Publishers Association)
Russia: Guild of Book Dealers
Singapore: National Book Development Council; Singapore Book Publishers' Association; Taylor & Francis; Wiley Asia; World Scientific
UK: ALPSP; Ashgate Publishing; Birlinn; A & C Black; Blackwell's UK; CABI Publishing; Cambridge University Press; Centre for Alternative Technology; City University; Continuum; Crown House Publishing; Edinburgh University Press; Elsevier; Granada Learning; HarperCollins Publishers; Hodder Education; Institute of

Physics; Learning Matters; Little, Brown Book Group; London College of Communications; Lonely Planet; Macmillan; McGraw Hill; NCVO (National Council for Voluntary Organisations); Nelson Thornes; Osprey Publishing; Oxford Brookes University; Oxford University Press; Palgrave Macmillan; Pearson Education; Primal Pictures; Publishing Scotland; Publishing Training Centre; Random House Group; Sage Publications; Specialist Schools and Academies Trust; Taylor & Francis Group; University College London; Welsh Books Council; John Wiley & Sons; Wiley-Blackwell

Marketability provides practical training to publishers, both through its small-group open workshop programme and through tailored in-house training. These flexible courses can be devised to cover a wide range of publishing issues. All tutors are actively working for publishers in the areas they are training in.

The open course programme includes: academic marketing, e-marketing, copywriting, copywriting for the web, schools marketing, direct mail, marketing to the book trade, marketing planning, introduction to marketing in publishing, publicity, essential editorial skills, profitable commissioning. There are numerous in-house course options including market research, working with authors, grammar and proofreading.

Also provides marketing support and consultancy. See separate entry under Sales and Marketing Services.

6199

NAPIER UNIVERSITY, SCHOOL OF CREATIVE INDUSTRIES
Craighouse Campus, Craighouse Road, Edinburgh
EH10 5LG
Telephone: 0131 455 6133
Fax: 0131 455 6193
Email: de.allan@napier.ac.uk
Web Site: www.napier.ac.uk\sci

Programme Leader: Avril Gray *(MSc Publishing full and part-time)*

BA and MSc Publishing. Higher education full and part-time qualifications.

6200

OXFORD INTERNATIONAL CENTRE FOR PUBLISHING STUDIES
Oxford Brookes University, Buckley Building, Gipsy Lane, Headington, Oxford OX3 0BP
Telephone: 01865 484967
Fax: 01865 484082
Email: angus.phillips@brookes.ac.uk
Web Site: www.brookes.ac.uk/publishing

Director: Angus Phillips

The Centre for Publishing Studies offers a BA in Publishing and MAs in Publishing, International Publishing, Publishing and Language, and Digital Publishing. In addition, it provides evening and daytime short courses and bespoke training and consultancy for publishing companies and other organizations involved in publishing.

6201

OXFORD PUBLISHING CONSULTANCY
27 Forelands Field Road, Bembridge, Isle of Wight
PO35 5TR
Telephone: 01983 872304
Fax: 01983 872304
Email: Bembridge27@aol.com

Managing Director: Paul Richardson

The Oxford Publishing Consultancy offers strategic management consultancy and training to book publishers nationally and internationally. It has particular expertise in China, Russia and Central and Eastern Europe.

6202

THE PUBLISHING TRAINING CENTRE AT BOOK HOUSE
45 East Hill, Wandsworth, London SW18 2QZ
Telephone: (020) 8874 2718
Fax: (020) 8870 8985
Email: publishing.training@bookhouse.co.uk
Web Site: www.train4publishing.co.uk

Chief Executive: John Whitley

Managers: Orna O'Brien *(Course Administration)*
Edelweiss Arnold *(Marketing)*

The Publishing Training Centre was set up in 1979 as an educational charity for book and journal publishers.

It offers over 60 different courses, most of which are run several times a year. Courses are between one and five days long and cover a wide range of publishing and management skills.

Most courses are held at The Publishing Training Centre's London premises, though some are residential, and are based mainly in the Oxford area.

In addition, The Publishing Training Centre offers:
– in-company courses in the UK and overseas;
– distance learning courses in proofreading, editing, picture research, editorial project management and copywriting;
– consultancy service;
– training needs analysis;
– books.

The Publishing Training Centre is responsible for the development and updating of the industry-agreed standards for each job function specific to publishing.

6203

SOCIETY FOR EDITORS AND PROOFREADERS
Erico House, 93–99 Upper Richmond Road, London
SW15 2TG
Telephone: (020) 8785 5617
Fax: (020) 8785 5618
Email: admin@sfep.org.uk
Web Site: www.sfep.org.uk

Chair: Sarah Price
Company Secretary: Justina Utuka

One of the major aims of the Society for Editors and Proofreaders is to help editorial freelances and staff to improve and update their skills. It is gradually building up a wide range of one-day courses, from 'Introduction to Proofreading' to 'Project Management' and 'On-Screen Editing', as well as more specialized courses. Most of its courses are run in London. About twice a year, two or three courses are run in Edinburgh, York and Bristol. Discounts are offered to members of the SFEP and to SI and NUJ members. Current details can be found on our website.

7   Appendices

7.1   PUBLISHERS CLASSIFIED BY FIELDS OF ACTIVITY

The categories shown below are those in which the publishers listed have declared their interest. The list is intended to be neither exclusive nor comprehensive.

Packagers are shown in *italic* print.

ACADEMIC & SCHOLARLY

Acumen Publishing Ltd
Adam Matthew Digital Ltd
Adam Matthew Publications Ltd
Age Concern Books
Al-Furqan Islamic Heritage Foundation
Alban Books Ltd
Alpha Science International Ltd
American Psychiatric Publishing Inc
Amnesty International International Secretariat
Amolibros
Peter Andrew Publishing Co Ltd
Anglo-Saxon Books
Anshan Ltd
Apex Publishing Ltd
Archetype Publications Ltd
Arena Books (Publishers)
Ashgate Publishing Ltd
Ashmolean Museum Publications
Association for Learning Technology
Association for Scottish Literary Studies
Audio-Forum - The Language Source
Aurora Metro Publications Ltd
Austin & Macauley Publishers Ltd
Authentic Media
B & D Publishing
B Squared
Ruth Bean Publishers
Bedford Freeman Worth (BFW)
Berg Publishers
Berghahn Books
Joseph Biddulph Publisher
Black Ace Books
Blackhall Publishing
Blackstaff Press
Bodleian Library Publishing
Book Marketing Ltd
BookPower
Borthwick Publications
Bowker (UK) Ltd
Boydell & Brewer Ltd
British Association for Adoption & Fostering
British Library
British Museum Press
Business Education Publishers
CABI
Calypso Publications
Cambridge Archive Editions Ltd

Cambridge Publishing Management Ltd
Cambridge University Press
Canopus Publishing Ltd
Carnegie Publishing Ltd
Jon Carpenter Publishing
John Catt Educational Ltd
Cengage Learning EMEA
Centre for Economic Policy Research
Centre for Policy on Ageing
Chalksoft Ltd
Channel View Publications Ltd
Chartered Institute of Personnel & Development
Christian Education
The Chrysalis Press
Church of Ireland Publishing
CILT, the National Centre for Languages
James Clarke & Co
Clear Answer Medical Publishing Ltd
Coachwise Ltd
Coastal Publishing
Cois Life
Commonwealth Secretariat
Construction Industry Research & Information Association (CIRIA)
The Continuum International Publishing Group Ltd
Cork University Press
Countyvise Ltd
CQ Press
Crescent Moon Publishing
Crossbow Education Ltd
Dance Books Ltd
Darton, Longman & Todd Ltd
The Davenant Press
Richard Dennis Publications
J M Dent
Ashley Drake Publishing Ltd
Gerald Duckworth & Co Ltd
Dunedin Academic Press
Earthscan
Edinburgh University Press
Edward Elgar Publishing Ltd
Elsevier Ltd
Emerald Group Publishing Ltd
Energy Institute
English Heritage
Equinox Publishing Ltd
The Erskine Press
Ethics International Press Ltd
Evangelical Press & Services Ltd
Everyman's Library
Fabian Society
Facet Publishing
Feather Books
Five Leaves Publications
Floris Books
Four Courts Press
Friends of the Earth
Garnet Publishing Ltd
GeoCenter International Ltd
Geography Publications

Geological Society Publishing House
Gill & Macmillan Ltd
Global Oriental Ltd
Global Professional Publishing
Glyndwr Publishing
The Goldsmith Press Ltd
Gracewing Publishing
Granta Editions
Greenleaf Publishing
Greenwood Publishing Group
Guildhall Press
Gwasg Gwenffrwd
Hachette Livre UK Ltd
Hart McLeod Ltd
Hart Publishing
Harvard University Press
Hawthorn Press
Roger Heavens
Helion & Co Ltd
Hobnob Press
Hodder Education
Hodder Gibson
Holo Books
Human Kinetics Europe Ltd
C. Hurst & Co (Publishers) Ltd
Hypatia Publications
Icon Books Ltd
Imperial College Press
Imprint Academic
Institute for Fiscal Studies
Institute of Acoustics
Institute of Development Studies
Institute of Education (Publications), University of London
Institute of Employment Rights
Institution of Engineering and Technology (IET)
Intellect Ltd
Interactyx
International Medical Press
International Network for the Availability of Scientific Publications (INASP)
The Islamic Texts Society
Ithaca Press
IVP
IWA Publishing
James & James (Publishers) Ltd
Janus Publishing Co Ltd
Jarndyce Booksellers
Richard Kay Publications
Kew Publishing
Jessica Kingsley Publishers
Kogan Page Ltd
Kube Publishing Ltd
Peter Lang Ltd
Learning Matters Ltd
Libris Ltd
The Lilliput Press Ltd
The Littman Library of Jewish Civilization
Liverpool University Press
Living Time® Media International
Lund Humphries

The Lutterworth Press
McGraw-Hill Education
Macmillan Publishers Ltd
Manchester University Press
Maney Publishing
Melisende
Mentor Books
Mercier Press Ltd
The Merlin Press Ltd
Merlin Publishing/Wolfhound Press
Merrell Publishers Ltd
Merton Priory Press Ltd
Methodist Publishing
Microform Academic Publishers
The MIT Press Ltd
M&K Publishing
Multi Science Publishing Co Ltd
Myriad Editions
NATE (National Association for the Teaching of English)
The National Academies Press
National Children's Bureau
National Gallery Co Ltd
National Portrait Gallery Publications
The National Trust
The National Youth Agency
Natural History Museum Publishing
NHS Immunisation Information
NMS Enterprises Limited - Publishing
Oak Tree Press
On Stream Publications Ltd
Onlywomen Press Ltd
Open Gate Press
Open University Worldwide
Orchard Publishing
Oxbow Books
Oxfam Publishing
Oxford University Press
Packard Publishing Ltd
Palgrave Macmillan
Panaf Books
Paragon Publishing
Pathfinder Books
Pavilion Journals (Brighton) Ltd
PCCS Books Ltd
Pearson Education
The Penguin Group (UK) Ltd
Pennant Books Ltd
Phaidon Press Ltd
The Pharmaceutical Press
Pickering & Chatto (Publishers) Ltd
Pluto Books Ltd
The Policy Press
Polity Press
Portland Press Ltd
Princeton University Press
Professional Engineering Publishing
ProQuest
Rand Publications
The Richmond Publishing Co
Robinswood Press Ltd

Round Hall Ltd
Roundhouse Publishing Ltd
Routledge-Cavendish
Joseph Rowntree Foundation
Royal Collection Publications
Royal College of General Practitioners
Royal College of Psychiatrists
Royal Geographical Society (with Institute of British Geographers)
Royal Irish Academy
The Royal Society of Chemistry
Russell House Publishing Ltd
Sage Publications Ltd
Saint Albert's Press
St Jerome Publishing Ltd
Sandstone Press Ltd
Saqi Books
Save the Children
Schott Music Ltd
Scion Publishing Ltd
SCM-Canterbury Press Ltd
Scottish Text Society
SEDA Publications
Shaw & Sons Ltd
Shepheard-Walwyn (Publishers) Ltd
Sigel Press
Slightly Foxed
SLS Legal Publications (NI)
Smith Settle Printing & Bookbinding Ltd
Colin Smythe Ltd
Social Affairs Unit
The Society for Promoting Christian Knowledge (SPCK)
Society of Antiquaries of Scotland
The Society of Metaphysicians Ltd
Souvenir Press Ltd
Springer London
Stacey International
Stainer & Bell Ltd
Stott's Correspondence College
Studymates Ltd
Sussex Academic Press
Sussex Publications
The Swedenborg Society
Symposium Publications Literary & Art
I. B. Tauris & Co Ltd
Taylor & Francis
Taylor Graham Publishing
Thames & Hudson Ltd
Trentham Books
Troubador Publishing Ltd
TSO (The Stationery Office Ltd)
UCAS
University College Dublin Press
University of Exeter Press
University of Hertfordshire Press
University of Wales Press
Vallentine Mitchell Publishers
Veritas Publications
Victoria & Albert Museum Publishing

Voltaire Foundation Ltd
Wallflower Press
Warburg Institute
Waterside Press
Waterside Press
Paul Watkins Publishing
Whiting & Birch Ltd
Whittles Publishing
John Wiley & Sons Ltd
WIT Press
Wolters Kluwer Health (P & E) Ltd
World Microfilms
XPL Publishing
Yale University Press London
Zed Books Ltd

ACCOUNTANCY & TAXATION

Age Concern Books
Peter Andrew Publishing Co Ltd
Blackhall Publishing
BookPower
Cambridge University Press
The Chartered Institute of Public
    Finance & Accountancy
Corpus Publishing Ltd
Emerald Group Publishing Ltd
W. Foulsham & Co Ltd
Global Professional Publishing
Gower Publishing Co Ltd
Granta Editions
Harriman House
Hodder Education
How To Books Ltd
In Easy Steps Ltd
Institute for Fiscal Studies
Jordan Publishing Ltd
Kogan Page Ltd
McGraw-Hill Education
National Housing Federation
Nelson Thornes Ltd
Oak Tree Press
Palgrave Macmillan
ProQuest
Round Hall Ltd
Sigel Press
Adam Smith Institute
Thorogood Publishing Ltd
Trog Associates Ltd
TSO (The Stationery Office Ltd)
Which? Books
John Wiley & Sons Ltd
XPL Publishing

AGRICULTURE

Blackstaff Press
CABI
Cambridge University Press
Carnegie Publishing Ltd
Commonwealth Secretariat
The Crowood Press Ltd
Earthscan
Eco-logic Books
Edward Elgar Publishing Ltd
Food Trade Press Ltd
Granta Editions
Institute of Development Studies
Manson Publishing Ltd
The National Academies Press
The National Trust
Old Pond Publishing Ltd
Oxfam Publishing
Packard Publishing Ltd
ProQuest
Smith Settle Printing &
    Bookbinding Ltd
Merlin Unwin Books Ltd
Whittet Books Ltd
John Wiley & Sons Ltd

ANIMAL CARE & BREEDING

Amber Books Ltd
Amolibros
Austin & Macauley Publishers Ltd
BookPower
CABI
Calypso Publications
Capall Bann Publishing
Carroll & Brown Ltd
Chalksoft Ltd

Collins & Brown
Corpus Publishing Ltd
The Crowood Press Ltd
D & N Publishing
The Davenant Press
Findhorn Press Ltd
Focus Publishing (Sevenoaks) Ltd
Robert Hale Ltd
HarperCollins Publishers Ltd
Haynes Publishing
Hodder Education
Manson Publishing Ltd
The National Academies Press
New Holland Publishers (UK) Ltd
Octopus Publishing Group
Quiller Publishing Ltd
Regency House Publishing Ltd
Souvenir Press Ltd
Toucan Books Ltd
Whittet Books Ltd
John Wiley & Sons Ltd

ANTIQUES & COLLECTING

Antique Collectors' Club Ltd
Austin & Macauley Publishers Ltd
Ruth Bean Publishers
BLA Publishing Ltd
Bodleian Library Publishing
British Museum Press
Cameron Books
Carlton Publishing Group
Caxton Publishing Group Ltd
The Crowood Press Ltd
D & N Publishing
Richard Dennis Publications
W. Foulsham & Co Ltd
Granta Editions
Greenlight Publishing
Robert Hale Ltd
HarperCollins Publishers Ltd
Hodder Education
How To Books Ltd
Landmark Publishing Ltd
Lund Humphries
The Lutterworth Press
Milestone Publications
Miller's
Mitchell Beazley
The National Trust
Newpro UK Ltd
NMS Enterprises Limited -
    Publishing
Octopus Publishing Group
The Orion Publishing Group Ltd
The Penguin Group (UK) Ltd
Prestel Publishing Ltd
Quantum Publishing
Quiller Publishing Ltd
Royal Collection Publications
Scala Publishers Ltd
Shire Publications Ltd
Souvenir Press Ltd
Tartarus Press
Thames & Hudson Ltd
Third Millennium Publishing Ltd
Unicorn Press
Victoria & Albert Museum
    Publishing
John Wiley & Sons Ltd
Philip Wilson Publishers

ARCHAEOLOGY

Archetype Publications Ltd
Ashmolean Museum Publications
Batsford
Blackstaff Press
Borthwick Publications
Boydell & Brewer Ltd
British Museum Press
Brown & Whittaker Publishing
Cambridge Publishing
    Management Ltd
Cambridge University Press
Capall Bann Publishing
Carnegie Publishing Ltd
Construction Industry Research &
    Information Association (CIRIA)
Cork University Press
Cornwall Editions Ltd
Council for British Archaeology

The Davenant Press
The Dovecote Press
Gerald Duckworth & Co Ltd
Edinburgh University Press
Emerald Group Publishing Ltd
English Heritage
Equinox Publishing Ltd
Evangelical Press & Services Ltd
Ex Libris Press
Four Courts Press
Geography Publications
Glasgow Museums Publishing
Green Magic
Greenlight Publishing
Halsgrove
Heart of Albion Press
Hobnob Press
Hodder Education
Holo Books
The King's England Press
Logaston Press
Maney Publishing
Melisende
Mercier Press Ltd
Mercury Books
Merton Priory Press Ltd
Mitchell Beazley
The National Trust
Natural History Museum
    Publishing
NMS Enterprises Limited -
    Publishing
North York Moors National Park
The Orion Publishing Group Ltd
Oxbow Books
The Penguin Group (UK) Ltd
Prestel Publishing Ltd
Quantum Publishing
Reardon Publishing
Royal Irish Academy
Scottish Children's Press
Scottish Cultural Press
Sessions of York
Shire Publications Ltd
Smith Settle Printing &
    Bookbinding Ltd
Society of Antiquaries of Scotland
Souvenir Press Ltd
Stacey International
Sussex Academic Press
I. B. Tauris & Co Ltd
Taylor & Francis
Thames & Hudson Ltd
Twelveheads Press
University of Exeter Press
University of Wales Press
Warburg Institute
John Wiley & Sons Ltd
WIT Press
Yale University Press London

ARCHITECTURE & DESIGN

Antique Collectors' Club Ltd
Architectural Association
    Publications
Ashgate Publishing Ltd
Aurum Press
AVA Publishing (UK) Ltd
Duncan Baird Publishers
Batsford
Berg Publishers
Joseph Biddulph Publisher
A. & C. Black (Publishers) Ltd
Black Dog Publishing Ltd
Bodleian Library Publishing
Cambridge Publishing
    Management Ltd
Cambridge University Press
Cameron Books
Carlton Publishing Group
Caxton Publishing Group Ltd
Centre for Alternative Technology
    Publications
Conran Octopus
Construction Industry Research &
    Information Association (CIRIA)
Cork University Press
Countryside Books
Richard Dennis Publications
Donhead Publishing Ltd
Gerald Duckworth & Co Ltd

Earthscan
Eco-logic Books
English Heritage
Garnet Publishing Ltd
GeoCenter International Ltd
Gower Publishing Co Ltd
Gracewing Publishing
Graffeg
Graham-Cameron Publishing &
    Illustration
Green Books
HarperCollins Publishers Ltd
Haynes Publishing
Hayward Publishing
The Herbert Press
Historical Publications Ltd
IHS BRE Press
Intellect Ltd
Laurence King Publishing Ltd
Dewi Lewis Publishing
Liberties Press
The Lilliput Press Ltd
Frances Lincoln Ltd
Liverpool University Press
Logaston Press
Lund Humphries
The Lutterworth Press
McGraw-Hill Education
Macmillan Publishers Ltd
Manchester University Press
Maney Publishing
Melisende
Merrell Publishers Ltd
The MIT Press Ltd
Mitchell Beazley
Multi Science Publishing Co Ltd
The National Trust
NMS Enterprises Limited -
    Publishing
W. W. Norton & Company Ltd
The O'Brien Press Ltd
Octopus Publishing Group
Ovolo Publishing Ltd
Packard Publishing Ltd
Papadakis Publisher
Paragon Publishing
Pavilion
Phaidon Press Ltd
Prestel Publishing Ltd
Quadrille Publishing Ltd
Quantum Publishing
Random House UK Ltd
Redcliffe Press Ltd
Regency House Publishing Ltd
RotoVision SA
Roundhouse Publishing Ltd
Joseph Rowntree Foundation
Royal Collection Publications
Sansom & Co Ltd
Saqi Books
Scala Publishers Ltd
Sheldrake Press
Shire Publications Ltd
Stacey International
I. B. Tauris & Co Ltd
Taylor & Francis
Thomas Telford Ltd
Teneues Publishing UK Ltd
Thames & Hudson Ltd
Toucan Books Ltd
Tyne Bridge Publishing
Unicorn Press
Victoria & Albert Museum
    Publishing
Warburg Institute
Paul Watkins Publishing
David West Children's Books
John Wiley & Sons Ltd
Philip Wilson Publishers
WIT Press
World Microfilms
Worth Press Ltd
Yale University Press London

ATLASES & MAPS

AA Publishing
Ian Allan Publishing Ltd
Amber Books Ltd
The Belmont Press
British Geological Survey
Carel Press

Caxton Publishing Group Ltd
Collins Geo
Cork University Press
G. L. Crowther
Discovery Walking Guides Ltd
Earthscan
Encyclopaedia Britannica (UK) Ltd
Express Newspapers
Folens Ltd
Geddes & Grosset
GeoCenter International Ltd
The Geographical Association
Geography Publications
Alan Godfrey Maps
HarperCollins Publishers Ltd
Harvey Map Services Ltd
Haynes Publishing
Hodder Education
Instant-Books UK Ltd
Macmillan Education
Maney Publishing
Mercury Books
Michelin Maps & Guides
Monkey Puzzle Media Ltd
Moonlight Publishing Ltd
Myriad Editions
New Internationalist Publications
    Ltd
Octopus Publishing Group
Old House Books
The Penguin Group (UK) Ltd
Philip's
Quantum Publishing
Reardon Publishing
Royal Irish Academy
Tarquin Publications
Toucan Books Ltd
John Wiley & Sons Ltd

AUDIO BOOKS

Ashgrove Publishing
Austin & Macauley Publishers Ltd
Barefoot Books
BBC Audiobooks Ltd
Beautiful Books Ltd
John Blake Publishing Ltd
Bloomsbury Publishing Plc
Canongate Books
Cló Iar-Chonnachta
Cois Life
CSA Word
Day One Publications
Dref Wen Cyf/Ltd
Feather Books
Gatehouse Media Ltd
Hachette Children's Books
HarperCollins Publishers Ltd
Hodder Education
Hodder & Stoughton General
ISIS Publishing Ltd
Kube Publishing Ltd
Little, Brown Book Group
Little People Books
Macmillan Children's Books Ltd
Macmillan Publishers Ltd
Magna Large Print Books
Naxos Audiobooks
The Orion Publishing Group Ltd
The Penguin Group (UK) Ltd
Reardon Publishing
Scottish Cultural Press
Sigel Press
Simon & Schuster (UK) Ltd
Studymates Ltd
Summersdale Publishers Ltd
Sussex Publications
Topical Resources
Transworld Publishers Ltd
Virgin Books Ltd
Witherby Seamanship
    International

AVIATION

Air-Britain (Historians) Ltd
Ian Allan Publishing Ltd
Amber Books Ltd
Ashgate Publishing Ltd
Bene Factum Publishing Ltd
BLA Publishing Ltd
Bridge Books

Brooklands Books Ltd
Caxton Publishing Group Ltd
Conway
Countryside Books
Crécy Publishing Ltd
The Crowood Press Ltd
D & N Publishing
Focus Publishing (Sevenoaks) Ltd
Granta Editions
Greenhill Books / Lionel Leventhal Ltd
Grub Street
Halsgrove
Haynes Publishing
Hodder Education
Icon Books Ltd
Jane's Information Group Ltd
Landmark Publishing Ltd
McGraw-Hill Education
Multi Science Publishing Co Ltd
Osprey Publishing Ltd
Professional Engineering Publishing
Quantum Publishing
Regency House Publishing Ltd
Special Interest Model Books Ltd
Stenlake Publishing Ltd
Truran
TSO (The Stationery Office Ltd)
John Wiley & Sons Ltd
Worth Press Ltd

BIBLIOGRAPHY & LIBRARY SCIENCE

Ashgate Publishing Ltd
Bowker (UK) Ltd
British Library
Cambridge University Press
James Clarke & Co
The Continuum International Publishing Group Ltd
Facet Publishing
Galactic Central Publications
Greenwood Publishing Group
Gwasg Gwenffrwd
Hypatia Publications
Institute of Development Studies
International Network for the Availability of Scientific Publications (INASP)
Jarndyce Booksellers
LISU
Maney Publishing
The MIT Press Ltd
Nielsen Book
ProQuest
Sage Publications Ltd
Colin Smythe Ltd
Sussex Academic Press
Taylor Graham Publishing
Voltaire Foundation Ltd
Warburg Institute
Woodhead Publishing Ltd

BIOGRAPHY & AUTOBIOGRAPHY

Accent Press Ltd
Acumen Publishing Ltd
Ian Allan Publishing Ltd
Allison & Busby
Alma Books Ltd
Amolibros
Apex Publishing Ltd
Arcadia Books Ltd
Argyll Publishing
Ashgrove Publishing
Atlantic Books
Attic Press
Aureus Publishing Ltd
Aurum Press
Austin & Macauley Publishers Ltd
Authentic Media
Authorhouse UK Ltd
Back-In-Print Books Ltd
Barny Books
Bene Factum Publishing Ltd
Berghahn Books
Black Ace Books
Black Spring Press Ltd
Blackstaff Press

John Blake Publishing Ltd
Bloomsbury Publishing Plc
Bodleian Library Publishing
Book Castle Publishing Ltd
Marion Boyars Publishers Ltd
Brandon/Mount Eagle Publications
Nicholas Brealey Publishing
Breedon Books Publishing Co Ltd
Brewin Books Ltd
British Library
Brown & Whittaker Publishing
Business Education Publishers
Cambridge Publishing Management Ltd
Cambridge University Press
Camra Books
Canongate Books
Catcher Ltd
The Catholic Truth Society
Christian Focus Publications
The Chrysalis Press
James Clarke & Co
Cló Iar-Chonnachta
Colourpoint Books
Constable & Robinson Ltd
The Continuum International Publishing Group Ltd
Countyvise Ltd
Crescent Moon Publishing
Crimson Publishing
Cualann Press
Currach Press
Darton, Longman & Todd Ltd
The Davenant Press
Day One Publications
Richard Dennis Publications
Denor Press Ltd
J M Dent
The Dovecote Press
Ashley Drake Publishing Ltd
Gerald Duckworth & Co Ltd
Equinox Publishing Ltd
The Erskine Press
Essential Works Ltd
Evangelical Press & Services Ltd
Ex Libris Press
Express Newspapers
Faber & Faber Ltd
Family Publications
Feather Books
Filament Publishing Ltd
Flambard Press
Geography Publications
Gibson Square
Gill & Macmillan Ltd
Global Oriental Ltd
Glyndwr Publishing
The Goldsmith Press Ltd
Gomer
Gothic Image Publications
Gracewing Publishing
Granta Books
Granta Editions
Green Books
Greenwood Publishing Group
Guildhall Press
Gwasg Gwenffrwd
Gwasg Gwynedd
Hachette Scotland
Halban Publishers
Robert Hale Ltd
Halsgrove
Hammersmith Press Ltd
HarperCollins Publishers Ltd
Harvard University Press
Haynes Publishing
Highland Books
Hodder & Stoughton Faith
Hodder & Stoughton General
Alison Hodge Publishers
Holo Books
Honno (Welsh Women's Press)
Hypatia Publications
Icon Books Ltd
Independent Music Press
ISIS Publishing Ltd
Janus Publishing Co Ltd
Richard Kay Publications
Kingsway Publications
Libris Ltd
The Lilliput Press Ltd

Lion Hudson Plc
Little, Brown Book Group
The Littman Library of Jewish Civilization
Living Time® Media International
Luath Press Ltd
The Lutterworth Press
Macmillan Publishers Ltd
Mainstream Publishing Co (Edinburgh) Ltd
Maney Publishing
Maverick House Publishers
Mentor Books
Mercier Press Ltd
The Merlin Press Ltd
Merlin Publishing/Wolfhound Press
Merton Priory Press Ltd
Microform Academic Publishers
The MIT Press Ltd
Motor Racing Publications Ltd
Murdoch Books UK Ltd
John Murray Publishers
National Portrait Gallery Publications
The National Trust
Natural History Museum Publishing
New Island Books Ltd
NMS Enterprises Limited - Publishing
The O'Brien Press Ltd
The Oleander Press
Omnibus Press
On Stream Publications Ltd
Onlywomen Press Ltd
Orion Books Ltd
The Orion Publishing Group Ltd
Peter Owen Publishers
Oxbow Books
Pan Macmillan
Panaf Books
Pavilion
Pen Press
The Penguin Group (UK) Ltd
Pennant Books Ltd
Piatkus Books
Pipers' Ash Ltd
Piquant Editions
Plowright Press
Portobello Books Ltd
Profile Books
Quartet Books
Quiller Publishing Ltd
The Radcliffe Press
Robson Books
Roundhouse Publishing Ltd
Route Publishing Ltd
Royal Collection Publications
St Pauls Publishing
Salt Publishing Ltd
Sandstone Press Ltd
Saqi Books
SCM-Canterbury Press Ltd
Scottish Children's Press
Scottish Cultural Press
Seren
Sessions of York
Shepheard-Walwyn (Publishers) Ltd
The Shetland Times Ltd
Shire Publications Ltd
Short Books Ltd
Simon & Schuster (UK) Ltd
Slightly Foxed
Smith Settle Printing & Bookbinding Ltd
Colin Smythe Ltd
Souvenir Press Ltd
Stacey International
Stainer & Bell Ltd
Rudolf Steiner Press
Strong Oak Press
Sussex Academic Press
Tabb House
I. B. Tauris & Co Ltd
Telegram
Thames & Hudson Ltd
Thorogood Publishing Ltd
F. A. Thorpe Publishing
Thoth Publications
Transworld Publishers Ltd

Troubador Publishing Ltd
Truran
Tyne Bridge Publishing
Unicorn Press
United Writers Publications Ltd
University of Wales Press
Merlin Unwin Books Ltd
Upfront Publishing
Vallentine Mitchell Publishers
Veloce Publishing Ltd
Veritas Publications
Vertical Editions
Victoria & Albert Museum Publishing
Virgin Books Ltd
Vision
Voltaire Foundation Ltd
Warburg Institute
Waterside Press
Waterside Press
Weidenfeld & Nicolson
Whittles Publishing
John Wiley & Sons Ltd
Neil Wilson Publishing Ltd
Windhorse Publications
The Women's Press
Y Lolfa Cyf
Yale University Press London
Zymurgy Publishing

BIOLOGY & ZOOLOGY

Alpha Science International Ltd
Austin & Macauley Publishers Ltd
Bedford Freeman Worth (BFW)
Bender Richardson White
BLA Publishing Ltd
BookPower
Brown & Whittaker Publishing
CABI
Calypso Publications
Cambridge University Press
Clear Answer Medical Publishing Ltd
D & N Publishing
Earthscan
Focus Publishing (Sevenoaks) Ltd
HarperCollins Publishers Ltd
Harvard University Press
Hodder Education
Imperial College Press
Jones & Bartlett International
Kew Publishing
Letts and Lonsdale
McGraw-Hill Education
Macmillan Education
Macmillan Publishers Ltd
Manson Publishing Ltd
Mentor Books
The MIT Press Ltd
The National Academies Press
Natural History Museum Publishing
Nelson Thornes Ltd
NMS Enterprises Limited - Publishing
North York Moors National Park
W. W. Norton & Company Ltd
Open University Worldwide
Oxford University Press
Packard Publishing Ltd
Palgrave Macmillan
Portland Press Ltd
Princeton University Press
ProQuest
The Richmond Publishing Co
Royal Irish Academy
Scion Publishing Ltd
Studymates Ltd
Taylor & Francis
Ward Lock Educational Co Ltd
Whittet Books Ltd
John Wiley & Sons Ltd
WIT Press

CHEMISTRY

Alpha Science International Ltd
Anshan Ltd
Atlantic Europe Publishing Co Ltd
BBC Active
Bedford Freeman Worth (BFW)

BLA Publishing Ltd
Cambridge University Press
Elsevier Ltd
Energy Institute
Food Trade Press Ltd
HarperCollins Publishers Ltd
Hodder Education
Icon Books Ltd
Imperial College Press
Jones & Bartlett International
Letts and Lonsdale
McGraw-Hill Education
Macmillan Education
Macmillan Publishers Ltd
The National Academies Press
Nelson Thornes Ltd
W. W. Norton & Company Ltd
Open University Worldwide
Palgrave Macmillan
The Royal Society of Chemistry
Scion Publishing Ltd
Springer London
Studymates Ltd
Taylor & Francis
Ward Lock Educational Co Ltd
John Wiley & Sons Ltd

CHILDREN'S BOOKS

A.M.S. Educational Ltd
Acair Ltd
Accent Press Ltd
Aladdin Books Ltd
Alban Books Ltd
Albion Press Ltd
Allied Mouse Ltd
Amolibros
Andersen Press Ltd
Ann Arbor Publishers Ltd
Anno Domini Publishing (ADPS)
Antique Collectors' Club Ltd
Apex Publishing Ltd
Arcturus Publishing Ltd
Atlantic Europe Publishing Co Ltd
Aurora Metro Publications Ltd
Austin & Macauley Publishers Ltd
Australian Consolidated Press UK
Authentic Media
Authorhouse UK Ltd
Award Publications Ltd
b small publishing ltd
Barefoot Books
Barny Books
Nicola Baxter Ltd
BBC Active
The Belmont Press
Bender Richardson White
Bene Factum Publishing Ltd
Bible Reading Fellowship
BLA Publishing Ltd
A. & C. Black (Publishers) Ltd
Bloomsbury Publishing Plc
Bodleian Library Publishing
Book Street Ltd
Marion Boyars Publishers Ltd
British Association for Adoption & Fostering
British Museum Press
Brown Dog Books
Brown Wells & Jacobs Ltd
Cambridge Publishing Management Ltd
Cambridge University Press
Carlton Publishing Group
Catcher Ltd
The Catholic Truth Society
Caxton Publishing Group Ltd
Chalksoft Ltd
Chicken House Publishing Ltd
Child's Play (International) Ltd
Christian Education
Christian Focus Publications
Classical Comics Ltd
Cló Iar-Chonnachta
Coachwise Ltd
Cois Life
Constable & Robinson Ltd
Cornwall Editions Ltd
Corpus Publishing Ltd
Countyvise Ltd
Cowley Robinson Publishing Ltd
CRW Publishing Ltd

Cyhoeddiadau'r Gair
Day One Publications
Delancey Press Ltd
J M Dent
Ashley Drake Publishing Ltd
Dramatic Lines
Dref Wen Cyf/Ltd
Eddison Sadd Editions Ltd
Egmont UK Ltd
Emma Treehouse Ltd
Encyclopaedia Britannica (UK) Ltd
English Heritage
Evans Publishing Group
Everyman's Library
Faber & Faber Ltd
Feather Books
Five Leaves Publications
Floris Books
The Fostering Network
W. Foulsham & Co Ltd
Galore Park Publishing Ltd
Geddes & Grosset
Gill & Macmillan Ltd
Glowworm Books & Gifts Ltd
Gomer
Graham-Cameron Publishing & Illustration
W. F. Graham (Northampton) Ltd
Guildhall Press
Gwasg Gwenffrwd
Gwasg Gwynedd
Hachette Children's Books
Hachette Livre UK Ltd
Peter Haddock Publishing
Haldane Mason Ltd
HarperCollins Publishers Ltd
Hawthorn Press
Haynes Publishing
Highland Books
Holland Publishing Plc
John Hunt Publishing Ltd
Icon Books Ltd
Janus Publishing Co Ltd
The King's England Press
Jessica Kingsley Publishers
Kube Publishing Ltd
LDA
Letterland International Ltd
Letts and Lonsdale
Frances Lincoln Ltd
Lion Hudson Plc
Little People Books
Little Tiger Press
Living Time® Media International
Lomond Books Ltd
Luath Press Ltd
The Lutterworth Press
McCrimmon Publishing Co Ltd
Macmillan Children's Books Ltd
Macmillan Education
Macmillan Publishers Ltd
Mandrake of Oxford
Meadowside Children's Books & Gullane Children's Books
Mercier Press Ltd
Mercury Junior
Merlin Publishing/Wolfhound Press
Milet Publishing Ltd
Monkey Puzzle Media Ltd
Moonlight Publishing Ltd
MW Educational
The National Autistic Society (NAS)
National Gallery Co Ltd
The National Trust
Natural History Museum Publishing
Nelson Thornes Ltd
NMS Enterprises Limited - Publishing
North York Moors National Park
The O'Brien Press Ltd
Onlywomen Press Ltd
Orion Books Ltd
The Orion Publishing Group Ltd
Orpheus Books Ltd
Oxfam Publishing
Oxford University Press
Pan Macmillan
Pavilion
Pavilion Children's Books

Pen Press
The Penguin Group (UK) Ltd
Phaidon Press Ltd
Piccadilly Press
Pipers' Ash Ltd
Playne Books Ltd
Porthill Publishers
Positive Press Ltd
Tony Potter Publishing
Prestel Publishing Ltd
Quantum Publishing
Random House Children's Books
Random House UK Ltd
Ransom Publishing Ltd
Ravette Publishing Ltd
Reader's Digest Children's Publishing Ltd
Reardon Publishing
Regency House Publishing Ltd
Ripley Publishing Ltd
Rising Stars UK Ltd
Robinswood Press Ltd
Roundhouse Publishing Ltd
St Pauls Publishing
Save the Children
Scala Publishers Ltd
Scholastic UK Ltd
Scottish Children's Press
Scripture Union Publishing
Search Press Ltd
Seasquirt Publications
Sessions of York
SGC Books
Sharon House Publishing
Sheldrake Press
Short Books Ltd
Sigel Press
Simon & Schuster (UK) Ltd
Slightly Foxed
Solidus
Speechmark Publishing Ltd
Stacey International
Symposium Publications Literary & Art
Ta Ha Publishers Ltd
Tabb House
Tangerine Designs Ltd
Tangerine Designs Ltd
Tango Books Ltd
Tarquin Publications
Tate Publishing
Templar Publishing
Titan Publishing Group
Top That! Publishing Plc
Topical Resources
Toucan Books Ltd
Troubador Publishing Ltd
Tucker Slingsby Ltd
United Writers Publications Ltd
Usborne Publishing Ltd
Veritas Publications
David West Children's Books
John Wiley & Sons Ltd
Wordsworth Editions Ltd
Y Lolfa Cyf
Zero to Ten

CINEMA, VIDEO, TV & RADIO

Aurora Metro Publications Ltd
Aurum Press
Austin & Macauley Publishers Ltd
AVA Publishing (UK) Ltd
Berg Publishers
Berghahn Books
Black Dog Publishing Ltd
Black Spring Press Ltd
Blackstaff Press
Bloomsbury Publishing Plc
Marion Boyars Publishers Ltd
Carlton Publishing Group
The Continuum International Publishing Group Ltd
Crescent Moon Publishing
Currach Press
Essential Works Ltd
Faber & Faber Ltd
Gibson Square
Greenwood Publishing Group
Robert Hale Ltd
HarperCollins Publishers Ltd
Harvard University Press

Nick Hern Books
Hodder Education
Hodder & Stoughton General
Intellect Ltd
Living Time® Media International
Luath Press Ltd
Macmillan Publishers Ltd
Mainstream Publishing Co (Edinburgh) Ltd
Manchester University Press
Mentor Books
Merlin Publishing/Wolfhound Press
W. W. Norton & Company Ltd
The Orion Publishing Group Ltd
Peter Owen Publishers
Pan Macmillan
Pavilion
The Penguin Group (UK) Ltd
Phaidon Press Ltd
Pluto Books Ltd
Polity Press
Prestel Publishing Ltd
Reardon Publishing
Robson Books
RotoVision SA
Roundhouse Publishing Ltd
Charles Skilton Ltd
Sussex Publications
I. B. Tauris & Co Ltd
Telos Publishing Ltd
Titan Publishing Group
Transworld Publishers Ltd
United Writers Publications Ltd
University of Exeter Press
Virgin Books Ltd
Wallflower Press
David West Children's Books
World Microfilms

COMPUTER SCIENCE

Age Concern Books
Alpha Science International Ltd
Anshan Ltd
Austin & Macauley Publishers Ltd
Bernard Babani (Publishing) Ltd
BBC Active
BLA Publishing Ltd
BookPower
Business Education Publishers
Cambridge University Press
Carlton Publishing Group
Emerald Group Publishing Ltd
Global Professional Publishing
Haynes Publishing
Hodder Education
Imperial College Press
In Easy Steps Ltd
Institution of Engineering and Technology (IET)
Intellect Ltd
IOP Publishing
Jones & Bartlett International
Lawpack Publishing Ltd
McGraw-Hill Education
Macmillan Publishers Ltd
Market House Books Ltd
The MIT Press Ltd
Multi Science Publishing Co Ltd
Nelson Thornes Ltd
W. W. Norton & Company Ltd
Open University Worldwide
O'Reilly UK Ltd
Palgrave Macmillan
Paragon Publishing
Professional Engineering Publishing
Springer London
Taylor Graham Publishing
TSO (The Stationery Office Ltd)
Usborne Publishing Ltd
John Wiley & Sons Ltd
WIT Press

COOKERY, WINES & SPIRITS

Absolute Press
Accent Press Ltd
Antique Collectors' Club Ltd
Appletree Press Ltd
Arcturus Publishing Ltd

Ashgrove Publishing
Attic Press
Aurora Metro Publications Ltd
Aurum Press
Austin & Macauley Publishers Ltd
Australian Consolidated Press UK
Authorhouse UK Ltd
Duncan Baird Publishers
Blackstaff Press
John Blake Publishing Ltd
Bloomsbury Publishing Plc
Bossiney Books Ltd
Brown & Whittaker Publishing
Cambridge Publishing Management Ltd
Camra Books
Capall Bann Publishing
Carlton Publishing Group
Jon Carpenter Publishing
Carroll & Brown Ltd
Caxton Publishing Group Ltd
Collins & Brown
Conran Octopus
Copper Beech Publishing Ltd
Currach Press
Dedalus Ltd
Ashley Drake Publishing Ltd
Eddison Sadd Editions Ltd
Elliott & Thompson
Equinox Publishing Ltd
Ex Libris Press
Faber & Faber Ltd
A. & A. Farmar
Findhorn Press Ltd
Focus Publishing (Sevenoaks) Ltd
W. Foulsham & Co Ltd
Garnet Publishing Ltd
Geddes & Grosset
GeoCenter International Ltd
Gill & Macmillan Ltd
The Goldsmith Press Ltd
Graffeg
Granta Editions
Green Books
Grub Street
Hachette Scotland
Haldane Mason Ltd
HarperCollins Publishers Ltd
Ian Henry Publications Ltd
Hodder Education
Hodder & Stoughton General
Alison Hodge Publishers
How To Books Ltd
Kyle Cathie Ltd
Liberties Press
Frances Lincoln Ltd
Lomond Books Ltd
Luath Press Ltd
Macmillan Publishers Ltd
Mainstream Publishing Co (Edinburgh) Ltd
Merlin Publishing/Wolfhound Press
Mitchell Beazley
Murdoch Books UK Ltd
National Gallery Co Ltd
The National Trust
Need2Know
New Holland Publishers (UK) Ltd
New Internationalist Publications Ltd
NMS Enterprises Limited - Publishing
W. W. Norton & Company Ltd
The O'Brien Press Ltd
Octopus Publishing Group
On Stream Publications Ltd
The Orion Publishing Group Ltd
Papadakis Publisher
Paragon Publishing
Pavilion
Pen Press
The Penguin Group (UK) Ltd
Phaidon Press Ltd
Piatkus Books
Prospect Books
Quadrille Publishing Ltd
Quantum Publishing
Quiller Publishing Ltd
Random House UK Ltd
Robson Books
Roundhouse Publishing Ltd

Saqi Books
Scottish Children's Press
Scottish Cultural Press
Sheldrake Press
Simon & Schuster (UK) Ltd
Charles Skilton Ltd
Snowbooks
Special Interest Model Books Ltd
Summersdale Publishers Ltd
Top That! Publishing Plc
Transworld Publishers Ltd
Troubador Publishing Ltd
Truran
Tucker Slingsby Ltd
Merlin Unwin Books Ltd
Virgin Books Ltd
John Wiley & Sons Ltd
Neil Wilson Publishing Ltd
Y Lolfa Cyf
Zymurgy Publishing

CRAFTS & HOBBIES

Accent Press Ltd
Amber Books Ltd
Apex Publishing Ltd
Arcturus Publishing Ltd
Aurum Press
Australian Consolidated Press UK
Bernard Babani (Publishing) Ltd
Batsford
Ruth Bean Publishers
A. & C. Black (Publishers) Ltd
Black Dog Publishing Ltd
Book Street Ltd
Brown Wells & Jacobs Ltd
Calypso Publications
Cambridge Publishing Management Ltd
Capall Bann Publishing
Carlton Publishing Group
Carroll & Brown Ltd
Caxton Publishing Group Ltd
Collins & Brown
Conran Octopus
The Crowood Press Ltd
D & N Publishing
David & Charles Ltd
Eco-logic Books
Floris Books
Focus Publishing (Sevenoaks) Ltd
W. Foulsham & Co Ltd
Stanley Gibbons
Greenlight Publishing
Haldane Mason Ltd
Robert Hale Ltd
HarperCollins Publishers Ltd
Hawthorn Press
Haynes Publishing
The Herbert Press
Hodder Education
The Ilex Press Ltd
In Easy Steps Ltd
The Ivy Press Ltd
Kyle Cathie Ltd
Lomond Books Ltd
The Lutterworth Press
Macmillan Publishers Ltd
Melisende
Mitchell Beazley
Murdoch Books UK Ltd
New Holland Publishers (UK) Ltd
Octopus Publishing Group
Old House Books
The Orion Publishing Group Ltd
The Penguin Group (UK) Ltd
Quadrille Publishing Ltd
Quantum Publishing
Quiller Publishing Ltd
Random House UK Ltd
Regency House Publishing Ltd
Roundhouse Publishing Ltd
Search Press Ltd
Sigma Press
Snowbooks
Souvenir Press Ltd
Special Interest Model Books Ltd
Stenlake Publishing Ltd
Stobart Davies Ltd
Stott's Correspondence College
Summersdale Publishers Ltd
Tarquin Publications

Thames & Hudson Ltd
Top That! Publishing Plc
Toucan Books Ltd
Tucker Slingsby Ltd
Unicorn Press
Usborne Publishing Ltd
David West Children's Books
Willow Island Editions
Y Lolfa Cyf

CRIME

Accent Press Ltd
Allison & Busby
Alma Books Ltd
Amber Books Ltd
Apex Publishing Ltd
Arcadia Books Ltd
Arcturus Publishing Ltd
Atlantic Books
Austin & Macauley Publishers Ltd
Authorhouse UK Ltd
Back-In-Print Books Ltd
Bitter Lemon Press
Blackstaff Press
John Blake Publishing Ltd
Canongate Books
Carlton Publishing Group
Caxton Publishing Group Ltd
CBD Research Ltd
Constable & Robinson Ltd
Countyvise Ltd
Gerald Duckworth & Co Ltd
Express Newspapers
Feather Books
Five Leaves Publications
Flambard Press
W. Foulsham & Co Ltd
Guildhall Press
Hachette Scotland
Robert Hale Ltd
HarperCollins Publishers Ltd
Haynes Publishing
Hodder & Stoughton General
Honno (Welsh Women's Press)
Icon Books Ltd
ISIS Publishing Ltd
Janus Publishing Co Ltd
Jordan Publishing Ltd
Little, Brown Book Group
Living Time® Media International
Luath Press Ltd
Macmillan Publishers Ltd
Mainstream Publishing Co
 (Edinburgh) Ltd
Mandrake of Oxford
Maverick House Publishers
Mentor Books
Merlin Publishing/Wolfhound
 Press
New Holland Publishers (UK) Ltd
Onlywomen Press Ltd
The Orion Publishing Group Ltd
Pen Press
The Penguin Group (UK) Ltd
Pennant Books Ltd
Piatkus Books
Profile Books
Random House UK Ltd
Robson Books
Sandstone Press Ltd
Severn House Publishers Ltd
Simon & Schuster (UK) Ltd
Snowbooks
Social Affairs Unit
Telos Publishing Ltd
Transworld Publishers Ltd
Troubador Publishing Ltd
Vision
Waterside Press
Waterside Press
Neil Wilson Publishing Ltd
The Women's Press
Zymurgy Publishing

DO-IT-YOURSELF

Caxton Publishing Group Ltd
Centre for Alternative Technology
 Publications
Collins & Brown
The Crowood Press Ltd

D & N Publishing
David & Charles Ltd
Express Newspapers
Focus Publishing (Sevenoaks) Ltd
Granta Editions
Green Books
HarperCollins Publishers Ltd
Haynes Publishing
Hodder Education
Janus Publishing Co Ltd
Lawpack Publishing Ltd
Murdoch Books UK Ltd
New Holland Publishers (UK) Ltd
Octopus Publishing Group
Ovolo Publishing Ltd
Pen Press
The Penguin Group (UK) Ltd
Quadrille Publishing Ltd
Quantum Publishing
Random House UK Ltd
Search Press Ltd
Stobart Davies Ltd
John Wiley & Sons Ltd

ECONOMICS

Adam Matthew Publications Ltd
Peter Andrew Publishing Co Ltd
Arena Books (Publishers)
Ashgate Publishing Ltd
Atlantic Books
Berghahn Books
Blackhall Publishing
BookPower
Nicholas Brealey Publishing
Cambridge University Press
Jon Carpenter Publishing
Centre for Economic Policy
 Research
The Chartered Institute of Public
 Finance & Accountancy
Commonwealth Secretariat
The Continuum International
 Publishing Group Ltd
Council of Mortgage Lenders
J M Dent
Earthscan
Edward Elgar Publishing Ltd
Emerald Group Publishing Ltd
Euromonitor International Plc
Fabian Society
Garnet Publishing Ltd
Gill & Macmillan Ltd
Global Professional Publishing
Green Books
Greenwood Publishing Group
HarperCollins Publishers Ltd
Harriman House
Harvard University Press
Hodder Education
Icon Books Ltd
Imperial College Press
Institute for Fiscal Studies
Institute of Development Studies
Institute of Employment Rights
Ithaca Press
Janus Publishing Co Ltd
Jarndyce Booksellers
Kube Publishing Ltd
McGraw-Hill Education
Macmillan Publishers Ltd
Manchester University Press
Mehring Books
Mentor Books
The Merlin Press Ltd
Microform Academic Publishers
The MIT Press Ltd
National Extension College Trust
 Ltd
Nelson Thornes Ltd
W. W. Norton & Company Ltd
Open University Worldwide
Oxfam Publishing
Oxford University Press
Palgrave Macmillan
Pathfinder Books
Pickering & Chatto (Publishers) Ltd
Pluto Books Ltd
The Policy Press
Princeton University Press
ProQuest
Rand Publications

Random House UK Ltd
Joseph Rowntree Foundation
Sage Publications Ltd
Shepheard-Walwyn (Publishers)
 Ltd
Adam Smith Institute
Social Affairs Unit
Spokesman
Sussex Academic Press
Taylor & Francis
Troubador Publishing Ltd
TSO (The Stationery Office Ltd)
Virgin Books Ltd
John Wiley & Sons Ltd
Yale University Press London
Zed Books Ltd

EDUCATIONAL & TEXTBOOKS

A.M.S. Educational Ltd
Acair Ltd
Accent Press Ltd
Acumen Publishing Ltd
Adamson Publishing Ltd
Age Concern Books
Aladdin Books Ltd
Alban Books Ltd
Philip Allan Publishers Ltd
Alpha Science International Ltd
American Psychiatric Publishing
 Inc
Anglo-Saxon Books
Ann Arbor Publishers Ltd
Anshan Ltd
Arcturus Publishing Ltd
Ashgate Publishing Ltd
Association for Scottish Literary
 Studies
Atlantic Europe Publishing Co Ltd
Aurora Metro Publications Ltd
Austin & Macauley Publishers Ltd
AVA Publishing (UK) Ltd
B & D Publishing
B Squared
Bernard Babani (Publishing) Ltd
Back-In-Print Books Ltd
Badger Publishing Ltd
Barefoot Books
Nicola Baxter Ltd
BBC Active
BEAM Education
Bender Richardson White
Berg Publishers
Bible Reading Fellowship
A. & C. Black (Publishers) Ltd
BookPower
Borthwick Publications
Brilliant Publications
Business Education Publishers
Butterfingers Books
Calypso Publications
*Cambridge Publishing
 Management Ltd*
Cambridge University Press
Capall Bann Publishing
Careers Europe
Carel Press
Catcher Ltd
The Catholic Truth Society
John Catt Educational Ltd
Cengage Learning EMEA
Centre for Alternative Technology
 Publications
Chalksoft Ltd
Channel View Publications Ltd
Chartered Institute of Personnel &
 Development
Chemcord Ltd
Christian Education
Christian Focus Publications
CILT, the National Centre for
 Languages
Claire Publications
Classical Comics Ltd
Clear Answer Medical Publishing
 Ltd
Cló Iar-Chonnachta
Coachwise Ltd
Cois Life
Collins Geo
Colourpoint Books

The Continuum International
 Publishing Group Ltd
Coordination Group Publications
 Ltd (CGP Ltd)
CQ Press
Crimson Publishing
Crossbow Education Ltd
Darton, Longman & Todd Ltd
The Davenant Press
Delta ELT Publishing Ltd
Diagram Visual Information Ltd
Ashley Drake Publishing Ltd
Dramatic Lines
Dref Wen Cyf/Ltd
Earthscan
Edinburgh University Press
Educational Planning Books Ltd
Edward Elgar Publishing Ltd
Elm Publications
Elsevier Ltd
Emerald Group Publishing Ltd
English Heritage
Equinox Publishing Ltd
Ethics International Press Ltd
Evans Publishing Group
Facet Publishing
Filament Publishing Ltd
First & Best in Education
Folens Ltd
The Fostering Network
W. Foulsham & Co Ltd
Freelance Market News
Friends of the Earth
Galore Park Publishing Ltd
Gatehouse Media Ltd
The Geographical Association
Geography Publications
Gill & Macmillan Ltd
Global Professional Publishing
Gower Publishing Co Ltd
*Graham-Cameron Publishing &
 Illustration*
Granada Learning
Granta Editions
Greenleaf Publishing
Greenwood Publishing Group
Guildhall Press
Gwasg Gwenffrwd
Hachette Children's Books
Hachette Livre UK Ltd
Haldane Mason Ltd
HarperCollins Publishers Ltd
Hart McLeod Ltd
Hawthorn Press
Ian Henry Publications Ltd
Hinton House Publishers Ltd
Hodder Education
Hodder Gibson
Holland Publishing Plc
Hopscotch Educational Publishing
How To Books Ltd
Human Kinetics Europe Ltd
Hypatia Publications
Icon Books Ltd
In Easy Steps Ltd
Institute of Development Studies
Institute of Education
 (Publications), University of
 London
Institution of Engineering and
 Technology (IET)
Intellect Ltd
Janus Publishing Co Ltd
Jolly Learning Ltd
Jones & Bartlett International
Hilda King Educational
Jessica Kingsley Publishers
Chris Kington Publishing
Kogan Page Ltd
Kube Publishing Ltd
LDA
Learning Matters Ltd
Learning Together
Letterland International Ltd
Letts and Lonsdale
Lexus Ltd
Lion Hudson Plc
Little People Books
The Littman Library of Jewish
 Civilization
Liverpool University Press
Living Time® Media International

The Lutterworth Press
McCrimmon Publishing Co Ltd
McGraw-Hill Education
Macmillan Education
Macmillan Publishers Ltd
Management Pocketbooks Ltd
Manchester University Press
Mentor Books
Merlin Publishing/Wolfhound
 Press
Methodist Publishing
Monkey Puzzle Media Ltd
MW Educational
NATE (National Association for the
 Teaching of English)
The National Academies Press
The National Autistic Society
 (NAS)
National Children's Bureau
National Extension College Trust
 Ltd
National Housing Federation
The National Youth Agency
Natural History Museum
 Publishing
Nelson Thornes Ltd
NHS Immunisation Information
NMS Enterprises Limited -
 Publishing
North York Moors National Park
Northcote House Publishers Ltd
Norwood Publishers Ltd
Oak Tree Press
Open University Worldwide
Optimus Professional Publishing
Orchard Publishing
Oxfam Publishing
Oxford University Press
Packard Publishing Ltd
Palgrave Macmillan
Paragon Publishing
Pearson Education
Pearson Education
Pen Press
Philip's
The Policy Press
Polity Press
Portland Press Ltd
Positive Press Ltd
Practical Pre-School Books
Princeton University Press
Radcliffe Publishing Ltd
Rand Publications
Ransom Publishing Ltd
The Richmond Publishing Co
Rising Stars UK Ltd
Robinswood Press Ltd
Round Hall Ltd
Routledge-Cavendish
The Royal Society of Chemistry
Russell House Publishing Ltd
Sage Publications Ltd
Save the Children
Scholastic UK Ltd
SchoolPlay Productions Ltd
SCM-Canterbury Press Ltd
Scripture Union Publishing
Shaw & Sons Ltd
Sigel Press
Social Affairs Unit
The Society of Metaphysicians Ltd
Southgate Publishers
Speechmark Publishing Ltd
Stacey International
Rudolf Steiner Press
Stokesby House Publications
STRI (Sports Turf Research
 Institute)
Studymates Ltd
Supportive Learning Publications
 (SLP)
Sussex Academic Press
Symposium Publications Literary &
 Art
Tango Books Ltd
Tarquin Publications
Taylor & Francis
Teachit (UK) Ltd
Thames & Hudson Ltd
Third Millennium Publishing Ltd
THRASS (UK) Ltd
Topical Resources

Trentham Books
Trotman Publishing
TSO (The Stationery Office Ltd)
UCAS
United Writers Publications Ltd
University of Hertfordshire Press
University of Wales Press
Veritas Publications
Wallflower Press
Ward Lock Educational Co Ltd
Waterside Press
Waterside Press
Whittles Publishing
John Wiley & Sons Ltd
Witherby Seamanship
    International
Young People in Focus

ELECTRONIC (EDUCATIONAL)

Adam Matthew Digital Ltd
Alpha Science International Ltd
Atlantic Europe Publishing Co Ltd
AVA Publishing (UK) Ltd
Bernard Babani (Publishing) Ltd
BBC Active
Bowker (UK) Ltd
Cambridge University Press
Carel Press
Catcher Ltd
Chalksoft Ltd
Claire Publications
Coachwise Ltd
Collins Geo
Commonwealth Secretariat
The Continuum International
    Publishing Group Ltd
Elm Publications
Emerald Group Publishing Ltd
Encyclopaedia Britannica (UK) Ltd
Ethics International Press Ltd
Evans Publishing Group
First & Best in Education
Folens Ltd
The Geographical Association
Global Professional Publishing
HarperCollins Publishers Ltd
Heart of Albion Press
Hodder Education
Human Kinetics Europe Ltd
Imperial College Press
Intellect Ltd
Jolly Learning Ltd
Kogan Page Ltd
Letterland International Ltd
Living Time® Media International
McCrimmon Publishing Co Ltd
McGraw-Hill Education
National Extension College Trust
    Ltd
National Gallery Co Ltd
Nelson Thornes Ltd
New Internationalist Publications
    Ltd
Open University Worldwide
Optimus Professional Publishing
Oxfam Publishing
Palgrave Macmillan
Paragon Publishing
ProQuest
Radcliffe Publishing Ltd
Ransom Publishing Ltd
Rising Stars UK Ltd
Robinswood Press Ltd
Royal Geographical Society (with
    Institute of British
    Geographers)
The Royal Society of Chemistry
Russell House Publishing Ltd
Sage Publications Ltd
The Society of Metaphysicians Ltd
Studymates Ltd
Summersdale Publishers Ltd
THRASS (UK) Ltd
John Wiley & Sons Ltd

ELECTRONIC (ENTERTAINMENT)

Bernard Babani (Publishing) Ltd
HarperCollins Publishers Ltd
The Ilex Press Ltd

Living Time® Media International
Summersdale Publishers Ltd

ELECTRONIC (PROFESSIONAL & ACADEMIC)

Adam Matthew Digital Ltd
Alpha Science International Ltd
Ashgate Publishing Ltd
Bernard Babani (Publishing) Ltd
Berghahn Books
Book Marketing Ltd
Bowker (UK) Ltd
Cambridge University Press
Centre for Policy on Ageing
The Continuum International
    Publishing Group Ltd
Earthscan
Emerald Group Publishing Ltd
Energy Institute
Equinox Publishing Ltd
Ethics International Press Ltd
Facet Publishing
Filament Publishing Ltd
Garnet Publishing Ltd
Global Professional Publishing
Gwasg Gwenffrwd
Hachette Livre UK Ltd
HarperCollins Publishers Ltd
Haynes Publishing
Hodder Education
Human Kinetics Europe Ltd
Imperial College Press
In Easy Steps Ltd
Institution of Engineering and
    Technology (IET)
Intellect Ltd
International Medical Press
International Network for the
    Availability of Scientific
    Publications (INASP)
IOP Publishing
IWA Publishing
Jane's Information Group Ltd
Jordan Publishing Ltd
Chris Kington Publishing
Kogan Page Ltd
McGraw-Hill Education
Macmillan Publishers Ltd
Maney Publishing
Methodist Publishing
Microform Academic Publishers
Multi Science Publishing Co Ltd
Myriad Editions
National Children's Bureau
National Gallery Co Ltd
Outsell Inc / EPS
Oxford University Press
Paragon Publishing
Pavilion Journals (Brighton) Ltd
Pearson Education
Pearson Education
The Pharmaceutical Press
Portland Press Ltd
Princeton University Press
ProQuest
Radcliffe Publishing Ltd
Round Hall Ltd
Routledge-Cavendish
Royal Geographical Society (with
    Institute of British
    Geographers)
The Royal Society of Chemistry
Russell House Publishing Ltd
St Jerome Publishing Ltd
Summersdale Publishers Ltd
Taylor & Francis
Teachit (UK) Ltd
TSO (The Stationery Office Ltd)
Voltaire Foundation Ltd
John Wiley & Sons Ltd
WIT Press
Witherby Seamanship
    International
Wolters Kluwer Health (P & E) Ltd
Woodhead Publishing Ltd

ENGINEERING

Alpha Science International Ltd
Peter Andrew Publishing Co Ltd
Anshan Ltd

Bernard Babani (Publishing) Ltd
BookPower
Cambridge University Press
Construction Industry Research &
    Information Association (CIRIA)
Conway
Earthscan
Emerald Group Publishing Ltd
Energy Institute
Geological Society Publishing
    House
Gower Publishing Co Ltd
IChemE
Imperial College Press
Institute of Physics & Engineering
    in Medicine
Institution of Engineering and
    Technology (IET)
IWA Publishing
McGraw-Hill Education
Macmillan Publishers Ltd
Maney Publishing
Multi Science Publishing Co Ltd
The National Academies Press
Nelson Thornes Ltd
Open University Worldwide
Palgrave Macmillan
Professional Engineering
    Publishing
Special Interest Model Books Ltd
Springer London
Taylor & Francis
Thomas Telford Ltd
TSO (The Stationery Office Ltd)
Tyne Bridge Publishing
Whittles Publishing
John Wiley & Sons Ltd
WIT Press
Woodhead Publishing Ltd

ENGLISH AS A FOREIGN LANGUAGE

Austin & Macauley Publishers Ltd
BBC Active
A. & C. Black (Publishers) Ltd
*Cambridge Publishing
    Management Ltd*
Cambridge University Press
Cengage Learning EMEA
Classical Comics Ltd
Folens Ltd
Gatehouse Media Ltd
The Goldsmith Press Ltd
*Graham-Cameron Publishing &
    Illustration*
HarperCollins Publishers Ltd
Hodder Education
Letterland International Ltd
Living Time® Media International
McGraw-Hill Education
Macmillan Education
Macmillan Publishers Ltd
Milet Publishing Ltd
Moonlight Publishing Ltd
New Island Books Ltd
Open University Worldwide
Oxford University Press
Paragon Publishing
Robinswood Press Ltd
Sandstone Press Ltd
Speechmark Publishing Ltd
Studymates Ltd
Symposium Publications Literary &
    Art

ENVIRONMENT & DEVELOPMENT STUDIES

Alpha Science International Ltd
Anshan Ltd
Ashgate Publishing Ltd
Atlantic Europe Publishing Co Ltd
Austin & Macauley Publishers Ltd
Berghahn Books
CABI
Cambridge University Press
Capall Bann Publishing
Jon Carpenter Publishing
Centre for Alternative Technology
    Publications
Channel View Publications Ltd

Commonwealth Secretariat
Construction Industry Research &
    Information Association (CIRIA)
Cork University Press
CQ Press
Earthscan
Eco-logic Books
Edward Elgar Publishing Ltd
Emerald Group Publishing Ltd
Energy Institute
Ethics International Press Ltd
Fabian Society
Friends of the Earth
Geological Society Publishing
    House
Granta Editions
Green Books
Greenleaf Publishing
HarperCollins Publishers Ltd
Hodder Education
IHS BRE Press
Imperial College Press
Institute of Development Studies
Intellect Ltd
Macmillan Education
Macmillan Publishers Ltd
Maney Publishing
The MIT Press Ltd
Multi Science Publishing Co Ltd
Myriad Editions
The National Academies Press
Nelson Thornes Ltd
New Internationalist Publications
    Ltd
North York Moors National Park
On Stream Publications Ltd
Open Gate Press
Open University Worldwide
Oxfam Publishing
Packard Publishing Ltd
Palgrave Macmillan
Paragon Publishing
Plowright Press
Pluto Books Ltd
Princeton University Press
Routledge-Cavendish
Royal Geographical Society (with
    Institute of British
    Geographers)
Sandstone Press Ltd
Alastair Sawday Publishing
Scottish Cultural Press
Sigel Press
Social Affairs Unit
The Society of Metaphysicians Ltd
Southgate Publishers
Stokesby House Publications
STRI (Sports Turf Research
    Institute)
Sussex Academic Press
Taylor & Francis
Thames & Hudson Ltd
John Wiley & Sons Ltd
WIT Press
Woodhead Publishing Ltd
Zed Books Ltd

FASHION & COSTUME

Amber Books Ltd
Antique Collectors' Club Ltd
Aurum Press
Austin & Macauley Publishers Ltd
AVA Publishing (UK) Ltd
Batsford
Ruth Bean Publishers
Berg Publishers
A. & C. Black (Publishers) Ltd
Black Dog Publishing Ltd
Carlton Publishing Group
Collins & Brown
Copper Beech Publishing Co Ltd
Essential Works Ltd
Glasgow Museums Publishing
Global Oriental Ltd
Granta Editions
The Herbert Press
Independent Music Press
The Ivy Press Ltd
Janus Publishing Co Ltd
Laurence King Publishing Ltd
Maney Publishing

Merrell Publishers Ltd
Mitchell Beazley
National Portrait Gallery
    Publications
The National Trust
Nelson Thornes Ltd
The Orion Publishing Group Ltd
Peter Owen Publishers
Oxbow Books
Papadakis Publisher
Pavilion
Phaidon Press Ltd
Prestel Publishing Ltd
Quadrille Publishing Ltd
Quantum Publishing
RotoVision SA
Royal Collection Publications
Charles Skilton Ltd
Stott's Correspondence College
Thames & Hudson Ltd
Unicorn Press
Victoria & Albert Museum
    Publishing
David West Children's Books
Yale University Press London

FICTION

Acair Ltd
Accent Press Ltd
Albyn Press
Allison & Busby
Alma Books Ltd
Amolibros
Apex Publishing Ltd
Arcadia Books Ltd
Arena Books (Publishers)
Argyll Publishing
Ashgrove Publishing
Atlantic Books
Aurora Metro Publications Ltd
Austin & Macauley Publishers Ltd
Authorhouse UK Ltd
Back-In-Print Books Ltd
The Banton Press
Barny Books
Beautiful Books Ltd
Birlinn Ltd
Bitter Lemon Press
Black Ace Books
Black Spring Press Ltd
Blackstaff Press
Bloomsbury Publishing Plc
Blue Sky Press
Marion Boyars Publishers Ltd
Brandon/Mount Eagle
    Publications
Canongate Books
Capuchin Classics
Catcher Ltd
Caxton Publishing Group Ltd
The Chrysalis Press
Classical Comics Ltd
Cló Iar-Chonnachta
Cois Life
Collins & Brown
Colourpoint Books
Constable & Robinson Ltd
Cornwall Editions Ltd
Countyvise Ltd
CRW Publishing Ltd
Dedalus Ltd
Delancey Press Ltd
Denor Press Ltd
J M Dent
Dref Wen Cyf/Ltd
Gerald Duckworth & Co Ltd
Elliott & Thompson
Enitharmon Press
Everyman's Library
Faber & Faber Ltd
Feather Books
Five Leaves Publications
Flambard Press
Freelance Market News
The Gallery Press
Garnet Publishing Ltd
Victor Gollancz Ltd
Granta Books
Guildhall Press
Hachette Children's Books
Hachette Scotland

Halban Publishers
Robert Hale Ltd
Harlequin Mills & Boon Ltd
HarperCollins Publishers Ltd
Ian Henry Publications Ltd
Hodder & Stoughton Faith
Hodder & Stoughton General
Honno (Welsh Women's Press)
John Hunt Publishing Ltd
Icon Books Ltd
ISIS Publishing Ltd
Ithaca Press
Janus Publishing Co Ltd
Jarndyce Booksellers
Legend Press
Libris Ltd
The Lilliput Press Ltd
Little, Brown Book Group
Living Time® Media International
Luath Press Ltd
Macmillan Publishers Ltd
Magna Large Print Books
The Maia Press Ltd
Mandrake of Oxford
Mentor Books
Mercier Press Ltd
Merlin Publishing/Wolfhound
 Press
Milet Publishing Ltd
John Murray Publishers
Myriad Editions
Myrmidon Books Ltd
New Internationalist Publications
 Ltd
New Island Books Ltd
Oneworld Classics
Onlywomen Press Ltd
Orion Books Ltd
The Orion Publishing Group Ltd
Peter Owen Publishers
Pan Macmillan
Paragon Publishing
Pen Press
The Penguin Group (UK) Ltd
Piatkus Books
Pipers' Ash Ltd
Piquant Editions
Portobello Books Ltd
Profile Books
Publishing House
Pushkin Press
Quartet Books
Random House UK Ltd
Ripley Publishing Ltd
Rising Stars UK Ltd
Robinswood Press Ltd
Route Publishing Ltd
Salt Publishing Ltd
Sandstone Press Ltd
Saqi Books
Scottish Children's Press
Seren
Severn House Publishers Ltd
Short Books Ltd
Sigel Press
Silver Moon Books
Simon & Schuster (UK) Ltd
Charles Skilton Ltd
Slightly Foxed
Snowbooks
Solidus
Spokesman
Sportsbooks Ltd
Tabb House
Tartarus Press
Telegram
Telos Publishing Ltd
Templar Publishing
Thorogood Publishing Ltd
F. A. Thorpe Publishing
Tindal Street Press
Transworld Publishers Ltd
Troubador Publishing Ltd
Truran
United Writers Publications Ltd
Upfront Publishing
Usborne Publishing Ltd
Voltaire Foundation Ltd
Waterside Press
Weidenfeld & Nicolson
Whittles Publishing
The Women's Press

Wordsworth Editions Ltd
Worth Press Ltd
Y Lolfa Cyf

FINE ART & ART HISTORY

Albyn Press
Antique Collectors' Club Ltd
Apex Publishing Ltd
Archetype Publications Ltd
Arcturus Publishing Ltd
Ashgate Publishing Ltd
Ashmolean Museum Publications
Aureus Publishing Ltd
Duncan Baird Publishers
A. & C. Black (Publishers) Ltd
Black Dog Publishing Ltd
Blackthorn Press
Bodleian Library Publishing
British Library
British Museum Press
*Cambridge Publishing
 Management Ltd*
Cambridge University Press
Cameron Books
Canongate Books
Caxton Publishing Group Ltd
Cork University Press
Crescent Moon Publishing
D & N Publishing
David & Charles Ltd
Richard Dennis Publications
Gerald Duckworth & Co Ltd
Four Courts Press
Gibson Square
Glasgow Museums Publishing
The Goldsmith Press Ltd
Gomer
Gothic Image Publications
Granta Editions
Green Books
Hachette Children's Books
Halsgrove
HarperCollins Publishers Ltd
Harvard University Press
Hayward Publishing
The Herbert Press
Alison Hodge Publishers
Hypatia Publications
The Ilex Press Ltd
Janus Publishing Co Ltd
Kew Publishing
Laurence King Publishing Ltd
Dewi Lewis Publishing
The Lilliput Press Ltd
Frances Lincoln Ltd
The Littman Library of Jewish
 Civilization
Liverpool University Press
Logaston Press
Lund Humphries
The Lutterworth Press
Macmillan Publishers Ltd
Mainstream Publishing Co
 (Edinburgh) Ltd
Mandrake of Oxford
Maney Publishing
Melisende
Merlin Publishing/Wolfhound
 Press
Merrell Publishers Ltd
The MIT Press Ltd
Mitchell Beazley
Monkey Puzzle Media Ltd
Moonlight Publishing Ltd
John Murray Publishers
National Extension College Trust
 Ltd
National Galleries of Scotland
National Gallery Co Ltd
National Gallery of Ireland
National Portrait Gallery
 Publications
The National Trust
Natural History Museum
 Publishing
NMS Enterprises Limited -
 Publishing
W. W. Norton & Company Ltd
Octopus Publishing Group
Open University Worldwide
The Orion Publishing Group Ltd

Phaidon Press Ltd
Piquant Editions
Porthill Publishers
Prestel Publishing Ltd
Quantum Publishing
Quiller Publishing Ltd
Random House UK Ltd
Redcliffe Press Ltd
RotoVision SA
Roundhouse Publishing Ltd
Royal Collection Publications
Sansom & Co Ltd
Saqi Books
Scala Publishers Ltd
Seren
Charles Skilton Ltd
Stacey International
Rudolf Steiner Press
Strong Oak Press
Sussex Academic Press
Sussex Publications
Symposium Publications Literary &
 Art
Tate Publishing
I. B. Tauris & Co Ltd
Thames & Hudson Ltd
Third Millennium Publishing Ltd
Toucan Books Ltd
Truran
Tyne Bridge Publishing
Unicorn Press
Victoria & Albert Museum
 Publishing
Warburg Institute
Paul Watkins Publishing
Philip Wilson Publishers
Yale University Press London

GARDENING

AA Publishing
Absolute Press
Age Concern Books
Amolibros
Antique Collectors' Club Ltd
Arcturus Publishing Ltd
Aurum Press
Austin & Macauley Publishers Ltd
Batsford
Bene Factum Publishing Ltd
*Cambridge Publishing
 Management Ltd*
Capall Bann Publishing
Caxton Publishing Group Ltd
Centre for Alternative Technology
 Publications
Chalksoft Ltd
Conran Octopus
Copper Beech Publishing Ltd
Crescent Moon Publishing
The Crowood Press Ltd
D & N Publishing
Dedalus Ltd
J M Dent
Eco-logic Books
Ex Libris Press
Express Newspapers
Floramedia UK Ltd
Floris Books
Focus Publishing (Sevenoaks) Ltd
W. Foulsham & Co Ltd
Friends of the Earth
GeoCenter International Ltd
Graffeg
Green Books
HarperCollins Publishers Ltd
Hawthorn Press
Haynes Publishing
Hodder Education
Alison Hodge Publishers
How To Books Ltd
Kyle Cathie Ltd
Frances Lincoln Ltd
Luath Press Ltd
Macmillan Publishers Ltd
Mitchell Beazley
Murdoch Books UK Ltd
The National Trust
New Holland Publishers (UK) Ltd
W. W. Norton & Company Ltd
Octopus Publishing Group
The Orion Publishing Group Ltd

Packard Publishing Ltd
Pan Macmillan
Papadakis Publisher
Pavilion
The Penguin Group (UK) Ltd
Quadrille Publishing Ltd
Quantum Publishing
Quiller Publishing Ltd
Random House UK Ltd
Search Press Ltd
SGC Books
Shire Publications Ltd
Slightly Foxed
Souvenir Press Ltd
Thames & Hudson Ltd
Top That! Publishing Plc
Toucan Books Ltd
Transworld Publishers Ltd
Truran
Tucker Slingsby Ltd
Whittet Books Ltd
John Wiley & Sons Ltd
Willow Island Editions

GAY & LESBIAN STUDIES

Arcadia Books Ltd
Aurora Metro Publications Ltd
Austin & Macauley Publishers Ltd
Cló Iar-Chonnachta
Cork University Press
Gibson Square
Guildhall Press
Manchester University Press
The MIT Press Ltd
Onlywomen Press Ltd
Peter Owen Publishers
Pen Press
Routledge-Cavendish
SCM-Canterbury Press Ltd
Silver Moon Books
Charles Skilton Ltd
Taylor & Francis
Thames & Hudson Ltd
Virgin Books Ltd
Vision
The Women's Press

GENDER STUDIES

Adam Matthew Digital Ltd
Adam Matthew Publications Ltd
Arcadia Books Ltd
Ashgate Publishing Ltd
Attic Press
Aurora Metro Publications Ltd
Berghahn Books
Cambridge University Press
Capall Bann Publishing
Commonwealth Secretariat
Cork University Press
Crescent Moon Publishing
Edinburgh University Press
Equinox Publishing Ltd
Garnet Publishing Ltd
Global Oriental Ltd
Greenwood Publishing Group
HarperCollins Publishers Ltd
Harvard University Press
Hawthorn Press
Hodder Education
Holo Books
C. Hurst & Co (Publishers) Ltd
Icon Books Ltd
Institute of Development Studies
Intellect Ltd
Ithaca Press
Karnac Books Ltd
Macmillan Publishers Ltd
Manchester University Press
The Merlin Press Ltd
Merlin Publishing/Wolfhound
 Press
The MIT Press Ltd
Myriad Editions
National Portrait Gallery
 Publications
New Island Books Ltd
W. W. Norton & Company Ltd
Onlywomen Press Ltd
Oxfam Publishing
Palgrave Macmillan

Pathfinder Books
PCCS Books Ltd
Piatkus Books
Plowright Press
Pluto Books Ltd
The Policy Press
Polity Press
Routledge-Cavendish
Russell House Publishing Ltd
Sage Publications Ltd
Saqi Books
SCM-Canterbury Press Ltd
Sheldon Press
Souvenir Press Ltd
Sussex Academic Press
I. B. Tauris & Co Ltd
Taylor & Francis
Trentham Books
University of Wales Press
Vision
The Women's Press
Yale University Press London
Zed Books Ltd

GEOGRAPHY & GEOLOGY

Albyn Press
Amolibros
Ashgate Publishing Ltd
Atlantic Europe Publishing Co Ltd
BBC Active
Bedford Freeman Worth (BFW)
Blackstaff Press
British Geological Survey
Cambridge University Press
Chalksoft Ltd
G. L. Crowther
D & N Publishing
Diagram Visual Information Ltd
The Dovecote Press
Dunedin Academic Press
Earthscan
Ex Libris Press
The Geographical Association
Geography Publications
Geological Society Publishing
 House
Global Oriental Ltd
Graffeg
HarperCollins Publishers Ltd
Hodder Education
Icon Books Ltd
Imray Laurie Norie & Wilson Ltd
Jones & Bartlett International
Letts and Lonsdale
Luath Press Ltd
McGraw-Hill Education
Macmillan Education
Maney Publishing
Manson Publishing Ltd
Mentor Books
Mercury Books
Monkey Puzzle Media Ltd
The National Academies Press
Natural History Museum
 Publishing
Nelson Thornes Ltd
NMS Enterprises Limited -
 Publishing
North York Moors National Park
W. W. Norton & Company Ltd
Old House Books
Open University Worldwide
Optimus Professional Publishing
Packard Publishing Ltd
Palgrave Macmillan
Roadmaster Publishing
Royal Geographical Society (with
 Institute of British
 Geographers)
Scottish Cultural Press
Stacey International
Supportive Learning Publications
 (SLP)
Sussex Academic Press
I. B. Tauris & Co Ltd
Taylor & Francis
Truran
TSO (The Stationery Office Ltd)
University of Hertfordshire Press
Ward Lock Educational Co Ltd
David West Children's Books

Whittles Publishing
John Wiley & Sons Ltd
WIT Press

GUIDE BOOKS

AA Publishing
Absolute Press
Accent Press Ltd
Age Concern Books
Albyn Press
Apex Publishing Ltd
Appletree Press Ltd
Argyll Publishing
Arris Publishing Ltd
Back-In-Print Books Ltd
Birlinn Ltd
Blackstaff Press
Bossiney Books Ltd
Bradt Travel Guides Ltd
British Geological Survey
Brown & Whittaker Publishing
Camra Books
Canongate Books
Capall Bann Publishing
The Catholic Truth Society
Cicerone Press Ltd
Collins Geo
Countryside Books
Crimson Publishing
Currach Press
D & N Publishing
Day One Publications
Discovery Walking Guides Ltd
The Dovecote Press
English Heritage
Everyman's Library
Ex Libris Press
Express Newspapers
FHG Guides Ltd
Findhorn Press Ltd
Footprint Handbooks
W. Foulsham & Co Ltd
Garnet Publishing Ltd
GeoCenter International Ltd
The Geographical Association
Gill & Macmillan Ltd
Gothic Image Publications
Gracewing Publishing
Graffeg
Granta Editions
Green Books
Guildhall Press
Harden's Ltd
HarperCollins Publishers Ltd
Haynes Publishing
Heart of Albion Press
Hobnob Press
Holo Books
How To Books Ltd
Instant-Books UK Ltd
Landmark Publishing Ltd
Frances Lincoln Ltd
Logaston Press
Lomond Books Ltd
Luath Press Ltd
Macmillan Publishers Ltd
Mainstream Publishing Co
   (Edinburgh) Ltd
Mentor Books
Merlin Publishing/Wolfhound
   Press
Michelin Maps & Guides
National Gallery Co Ltd
The National Trust
New Holland Publishers (UK) Ltd
New Island Books Ltd
NMS Enterprises Limited -
   Publishing
North York Moors National Park
The O'Brien Press Ltd
Old House Books
The Orion Publishing Group Ltd
Pan Macmillan
The Penguin Group (UK) Ltd
Prestel Publishing Ltd
Random House UK Ltd
Reardon Publishing
Roadmaster Publishing
Roundhouse Publishing Ltd
Royal Collection Publications

S. B. Publications
Alastair Sawday Publishing
Scala Publishers Ltd
Sheldrake Press
The Shetland Times Ltd
Shire Publications Ltd
Sigma Press
Simon & Schuster (UK) Ltd
Charles Skilton Ltd
Stacey International
Summersdale Publishers Ltd
I. B. Tauris & Co Ltd
Thames & Hudson Ltd
Third Millennium Publishing Ltd
Top That! Publishing Plc
Travel Publishing Ltd
Troubador Publishing Ltd
Truran
Twelveheads Press
Which? Books
John Wiley & Sons Ltd
Willow Island Editions
Neil Wilson Publishing Ltd
Y Lolfa Cyf

HEALTH & BEAUTY

Age Concern Books
Amberwood Publishing Ltd
Peter Andrew Publishing Co Ltd
Apex Publishing Ltd
Argyll Publishing
Ashgrove Publishing
Aurum Press
Austin & Macauley Publishers Ltd
Duncan Baird Publishers
A. & C. Black (Publishers) Ltd
Blackstaff Press
Bloomsbury Publishing Plc
Capall Bann Publishing
Carlton Publishing Group
Carroll & Brown Ltd
Class Publishing
Collins & Brown
Constable & Robinson Ltd
Paul H. Crompton Ltd
Diagram Visual Information Ltd
Eddison Sadd Editions Ltd
Essential Works Ltd
Express Newspapers
Findhorn Press Ltd
Floris Books
W. Foulsham & Co Ltd
Granta Editions
Green Books
Hachette Scotland
Haldane Mason Ltd
Hammersmith Press Ltd
HarperCollins Publishers Ltd
Harvard University Press
Hawker Publications
Haynes Publishing
Hodder Education
Human Kinetics Europe Ltd
Icon Books Ltd
The Ivy Press Ltd
Jessica Kingsley Publishers
Kyle Cathie Ltd
Liberties Press
Frances Lincoln Ltd
Macmillan Publishers Ltd
Mainstream Publishing Co
   (Edinburgh) Ltd
Mentor Books
Merlin Publishing/Wolfhound
   Press
Mitchell Beazley
Monkey Puzzle Media Ltd
Murdoch Books UK Ltd
Need2Know
Nelson Thornes Ltd
New Holland Publishers (UK) Ltd
Octopus Publishing Group
On Stream Publications Ltd
The Orion Publishing Group Ltd
Pan Macmillan
Pavilion
Pen Press
The Penguin Group (UK) Ltd
Piatkus Books
Quadrille Publishing Ltd
Quantum Publishing

Random House UK Ltd
Robson Books
Roundhouse Publishing Ltd
SGC Books
Sheldon Press
Simon & Schuster (UK) Ltd
Souvenir Press Ltd
Speechmark Publishing Ltd
Stott's Correspondence College
Temple Lodge Publishing
Top That! Publishing Plc
Transworld Publishers Ltd
Trog Associates Ltd
Tucker Slingsby Ltd
Virgin Books Ltd
John Wiley & Sons Ltd
The Women's Press

HISTORY & ANTIQUARIAN

Acair Ltd
Acumen Publishing Ltd
Adam Matthew Digital Ltd
Adam Matthew Publications Ltd
Al-Furqan Islamic Heritage
   Foundation
Albyn Press
Ian Allan Publishing Ltd
Allison & Busby
Amber Books Ltd
Amolibros
Anglo-Saxon Books
Appletree Press Ltd
Arcturus Publishing Ltd
Arena Books (Publishers)
Arris Publishing Ltd
Ashgate Publishing Ltd
Ashmolean Museum Publications
Atlantic Books
Atlantic Europe Publishing Co Ltd
Barny Books
Batsford
BBC Active
The Belmont Press
Bene Factum Publishing Ltd
Berghahn Books
Birlinn Ltd
Black Ace Books
Black Dog Publishing Ltd
Blackstaff Press
Blackthorn Press
Bloomsbury Publishing Plc
Bodleian Library Publishing
Book Castle Publishing Ltd
Borthwick Publications
Bossiney Books Ltd
Boydell & Brewer Ltd
Brewin Books Ltd
Bridge Books
British Library
Brown & Whittaker Publishing
Business Education Publishers
Cambridge Archive Editions Ltd
Cambridge University Press
Canongate Books
Capall Bann Publishing
Carlton Publishing Group
Carnegie Publishing Ltd
Jon Carpenter Publishing
The Catholic Truth Society
Christian Focus Publications
The Chrysalis Press
Church of Ireland Publishing
James Clarke & Co
Cló Iar-Chonnachta
Colourpoint Books
Columba
The Continuum International
   Publishing Group Ltd
Conway
Copper Beech Publishing Ltd
Cork University Press
Cornwall Editions Ltd
Countryside Books
Countyvise Ltd
Crécy Publishing Ltd
Cualann Press
Currach Press
D & N Publishing
The Davenant Press
Richard Dennis Publications
J M Dent

The Dovecote Press
Ashley Drake Publishing Ltd
Dramatic Lines
Gerald Duckworth & Co Ltd
Edinburgh University Press
Elliott & Thompson
English Heritage
Equinox Publishing Ltd
The Erskine Press
Evangelical Press & Services Ltd
Ex Libris Press
Family Publications
A. & A. Farmar
Five Leaves Publications
Four Courts Press
Garnet Publishing Ltd
Geddes & Grosset
Geography Publications
Gibson Square
Gill & Macmillan Ltd
Glasgow Museums Publishing
Global Oriental Ltd
Glyndwr Publishing
Alan Godfrey Maps
Gomer
Gothic Image Publications
Gracewing Publishing
Greenhill Books / Lionel Leventhal
   Ltd
Greenwood Publishing Group
Gresham Books Ltd
Guildhall Press
Gwasg Gwenffrwd
Hachette Scotland
Halban Publishers
Halsgrove
HarperCollins Publishers Ltd
Harvard University Press
Haynes Publishing
Heart of Albion Press
Helion & Co Ltd
Ian Henry Publications Ltd
Historical Publications Ltd
Hobnob Press
Hodder Education
Hodder & Stoughton Faith
Hodder & Stoughton General
Holo Books
Icon Books Ltd
Intellect Ltd
Ithaca Press
James & James (Publishers) Ltd
Janus Publishing Co Ltd
Richard Kay Publications
The King's England Press
Landmark Publishing Ltd
Letts and Lonsdale
Liberties Press
The Lilliput Press Ltd
Little, Brown Book Group
The Littman Library of Jewish
   Civilization
Liverpool University Press
Living Time® Media International
Logaston Press
Lomond Books Ltd
Luath Press Ltd
The Lutterworth Press
Macmillan Education
Macmillan Publishers Ltd
Mainstream Publishing Co
   (Edinburgh) Ltd
Manchester University Press
Maney Publishing
Mehring Books
Melisende
Mentor Books
Mercier Press Ltd
Mercury Books
The Merlin Press Ltd
Merlin Publishing/Wolfhound
   Press
Merton Priory Press Ltd
Meyrick Marketing Ltd
Microform Academic Publishers
Mitchell Beazley
Monkey Puzzle Media Ltd
Moorley's Print & Publishing Ltd
Murdoch Books UK Ltd
John Murray Publishers
National Archives of Scotland

National Portrait Gallery
   Publications
The National Trust
Nelson Thornes Ltd
New Island Books Ltd
NMS Enterprises Limited -
   Publishing
North York Moors National Park
W. W. Norton & Company Ltd
The Nostalgia Collection
Octopus Publishing Group
Old House Books
The Oleander Press
Open University Worldwide
Optimus Professional Publishing
The Orion Publishing Group Ltd
Osprey Publishing Ltd
Peter Owen Publishers
Oxbow Books
Palgrave Macmillan
Pan Macmillan
Pathfinder Books
The Penguin Group (UK) Ltd
Piatkus Books
Pickering & Chatto (Publishers) Ltd
Playne Books Ltd
Plowright Press
Polity Press
Portobello Books Ltd
Princeton University Press
Profile Books
ProQuest
Quantum Publishing
Quartet Books
The Radcliffe Press
Random House UK Ltd
Reardon Publishing
Redcliffe Press Ltd
Reflections of a Bygone Age
Roundhouse Publishing Ltd
Royal Collection Publications
Royal Irish Academy
S. B. Publications
Saint Albert's Press
Saqi Books
Scottish Children's Press
Scottish Cultural Press
Scottish Text Society
Sessions of York
Sheaf Publishing
Sheldrake Press
Shepheard-Walwyn (Publishers)
   Ltd
Shire Publications Ltd
Short Books Ltd
Slightly Foxed
Smith Settle Printing &
   Bookbinding Ltd
Society of Antiquaries of Scotland
Society of Genealogists
   Enterprises Ltd
Spokesman
Sportsbooks Ltd
Stacey International
Stainer & Bell Ltd
Stenlake Publishing Ltd
Strong Oak Press
Studymates Ltd
Summersdale Publishers Ltd
Supportive Learning Publications
   (SLP)
Sussex Academic Press
Sussex Publications
I. B. Tauris & Co Ltd
Taylor & Francis
Thames & Hudson Ltd
Toucan Books Ltd
Transworld Publishers Ltd
Troubador Publishing Ltd
Truran
Twelveheads Press
Tyne Bridge Publishing
Unicorn Press
University of Exeter Press
University of Hertfordshire Press
University of Wales Press
Vallentine Mitchell Publishers
Voltaire Foundation Ltd
Warburg Institute
Waterside Press
Waterside Press
Paul Watkins Publishing

David West Children's Books
John Wiley & Sons Ltd
Neil Wilson Publishing Ltd
Philip Wilson Publishers
World Microfilms
Yale University Press London

HUMOUR

Accent Press Ltd
Allison & Busby
Alma Books Ltd
Antique Collectors' Club Ltd
Apex Publishing Ltd
Appletree Press Ltd
Arcturus Publishing Ltd
Atlantic Books
Aurora Metro Publications Ltd
Aurum Press
Austin & Macauley Publishers Ltd
Authorhouse UK Ltd
Barny Books
Beautiful Books Ltd
Bene Factum Publishing Ltd
Birlinn Ltd
A. & C. Black (Publishers) Ltd
Blackstaff Press
John Blake Publishing Ltd
Bloomsbury Publishing Plc
Bodleian Library Publishing
Brown Dog Books
Canongate Books
Carlton Publishing Group
Constable & Robinson Ltd
Countryside Books
Countyvise Ltd
CRW Publishing Ltd
Currach Press
David & Charles Ltd
Delancey Press Ltd
Gerald Duckworth & Co Ltd
Essential Works Ltd
Exley Publications Ltd
Express Newspapers
Feather Books
W. Foulsham & Co Ltd
Gibson Square
Gill & Macmillan Ltd
Gothic Image Publications
Guildhall Press
Hachette Scotland
Robert Hale Ltd
HarperCollins Publishers Ltd
Ian Henry Publications Ltd
Hodder & Stoughton Faith
Hodder & Stoughton General
Holo Books
Icon Books Ltd
ISIS Publishing Ltd
Janus Publishing Co Ltd
Little, Brown Book Group
Lomond Books Ltd
Luath Press Ltd
Macmillan Publishers Ltd
Mainstream Publishing Co
(Edinburgh) Ltd
Maverick House Publishers
Mentor Books
Mercier Press Ltd
Merlin Publishing/Wolfhound
Press
John Murray Publishers
The National Trust
New Holland Publishers (UK) Ltd
New Island Books Ltd
Nightingale Press
The O'Brien Press Ltd
The Oleander Press
The Orion Publishing Group Ltd
Pen Press
The Penguin Group (UK) Ltd
Pennant Books Ltd
Piatkus Books
Porthill Publishers
Portico
Tony Potter Publishing
Quadrille Publishing Ltd
Quiller Publishing Ltd
Random House UK Ltd
Ravette Publishing Ltd
Reardon Publishing

Robson Books
Sandstone Press Ltd
Saqi Books
Sheldrake Press
Short Books Ltd
Simon & Schuster (UK) Ltd
Snowbooks
Souvenir Press Ltd
Summersdale Publishers Ltd
Supportive Learning Publications
(SLP)
Top That! Publishing Plc
Transworld Publishers Ltd
Troubador Publishing Ltd
United Writers Publications Ltd
Merlin Unwin Books Ltd
Virgin Books Ltd
Weidenfeld & Nicolson
John Wiley & Sons Ltd
Neil Wilson Publishing Ltd
Y Lolfa Cyf
Zymurgy Publishing

ILLUSTRATED & FINE EDITIONS

Absolute Press
Albyn Press
Ashgate Publishing Ltd
Bene Factum Publishing Ltd
Birlinn Ltd
Black Dog Publishing Ltd
Blackstaff Press
British Library
Canongate Books
Richard Dennis Publications
Enitharmon Press
The Erskine Press
Essential Works Ltd
Everyman's Library
Express Newspapers
Global Oriental Ltd
Gothic Image Publications
Granta Editions
Halsgrove
HarperCollins Publishers Ltd
The Herbert Press
The Ivy Press Ltd
Dewi Lewis Publishing
The Lilliput Press Ltd
Frances Lincoln Ltd
Lomond Books Ltd
The Lutterworth Press
Mainstream Publishing Co
(Edinburgh) Ltd
Manchester University Press
Maney Publishing
Melisende
Merrell Publishers Ltd
Mitchell Beazley
National Portrait Gallery
Publications
The Old Stile Press
The Orion Publishing Group Ltd
Phaidon Press Ltd
Piquant Editions
Quiller Publishing Ltd
Random House UK Ltd
Royal Collection Publications
Sandstone Press Ltd
Scala Publishers Ltd
Shepheard-Walwyn (Publishers)
Ltd
Charles Skilton Ltd
Slightly Foxed
Smith Settle Printing &
Bookbinding Ltd
Snowbooks
The Society for Promoting
Christian Knowledge (SPCK)
Stacey International
Tartarus Press
Thames & Hudson Ltd
University of Wales Press
Merlin Unwin Books Ltd
Veloce Publishing Ltd
Virgin Books Ltd
Weidenfeld & Nicolson
Whittet Books Ltd
Yale University Press London
Zymurgy Publishing

INDUSTRY, BUSINESS & MANAGEMENT

Accent Press Ltd
Peter Andrew Publishing Co Ltd
Arena Books (Publishers)
Ashgate Publishing Ltd
Atlantic Books
Aurelian Information Ltd
AVA Publishing (UK) Ltd
Barny Books
BCR Publishing Ltd
Bene Factum Publishing Ltd
Blackhall Publishing
BookPower
Nicholas Brealey Publishing
Business Education Publishers
*Cambridge Publishing
Management Ltd*
Cambridge University Press
Carnegie Publishing Ltd
Cengage Learning EMEA
Centre for Economic Policy
Research
Chartered Institute of Personnel &
Development
Commonwealth Secretariat
Construction Industry Research &
Information Association (CIRIA)
Crimson Publishing
Ashley Drake Publishing Ltd
Earthscan
Edward Elgar Publishing Ltd
Elm Publications
Emerald Group Publishing Ltd
Energy Institute
Ethics International Press Ltd
Euromonitor International Plc
Executive Grapevine International
Ltd
Filament Publishing Ltd
W. Foulsham & Co Ltd
Global Professional Publishing
Gower Publishing Co Ltd
Greenleaf Publishing
Greenwood Publishing Group
HarperCollins Publishers Ltd
Harriman House
Hawthorn Press
Hodder Education
How To Books Ltd
ICSA Information & Training Ltd
The Ilex Press Ltd
Imperial College Press
In Easy Steps Ltd
Institute for Employment Studies
Institute of Development Studies
Institution of Engineering and
Technology (IET)
IWA Publishing
James & James (Publishers) Ltd
Jane's Information Group Ltd
Jordan Publishing Ltd
Kogan Page Ltd
McGraw-Hill Education
Management Pocketbooks Ltd
Market House Books Ltd
Mentor Books
The MIT Press Ltd
The National Academies Press
Nelson Thornes Ltd
Oak Tree Press
Open University Worldwide
Oxford University Press
Palgrave Macmillan
Pen Press
The Penguin Group (UK) Ltd
Piatkus Books
Princeton University Press
Profile Books
Radcliffe Publishing Ltd
Round Hall Ltd
Roundhouse Publishing Ltd
Russell House Publishing Ltd
Sage Publications Ltd
Sessions of York
Sherwood Publishing
Sigel Press
Simon & Schuster (UK) Ltd
Social Affairs Unit
Souvenir Press Ltd

Studymates Ltd
Sussex Academic Press
Taylor & Francis
Thorogood Publishing Ltd
Trog Associates Ltd
Trotman Publishing
Troubador Publishing Ltd
TSO (The Stationery Office Ltd)
United Writers Publications Ltd
Weidenfeld & Nicolson
John Wiley & Sons Ltd
WIT Press
Witherby Seamanship
International
Woodhead Publishing Ltd
XPL Publishing
Zambezi Publishing Ltd

LANGUAGES & LINGUISTICS

Anglo-Saxon Books
Association for Scottish Literary
Studies
Audio-Forum - The Language
Source
b small publishing ltd
BBC Active
Berghahn Books
Joseph Biddulph Publisher
Brilliant Publications
Cambridge University Press
Carel Press
Channel View Publications Ltd
CILT, the National Centre for
Languages
Claire Publications
Cló Iar-Chonnachta
Cois Life
The Continuum International
Publishing Group Ltd
Delta ELT Publishing Ltd
Ashley Drake Publishing Ltd
Edinburgh University Press
Emerald Group Publishing Ltd
Equinox Publishing Ltd
GeoCenter International Ltd
Geography Publications
Global Oriental Ltd
Gomer
Gwasg Gwenffrwd
HarperCollins Publishers Ltd
Hodder Education
Icon Books Ltd
Intellect Ltd
Ithaca Press
Jarndyce Booksellers
Letts and Lonsdale
Lexus Ltd
Libris Ltd
Liverpool University Press
Luath Press Ltd
Macmillan Education
Macmillan Publishers Ltd
Manchester University Press
Maney Publishing
Mentor Books
Milet Publishing Ltd
The MIT Press Ltd
National Extension College Trust
Ltd
Nelson Thornes Ltd
The Oleander Press
Open University Worldwide
Oxford University Press
Packard Publishing Ltd
Palgrave Macmillan
Paragon Publishing
Portico
Royal Irish Academy
Scottish Children's Press
Scottish Cultural Press
Speechmark Publishing Ltd
Stacey International
Studymates Ltd
Ta Ha Publishers Ltd
Taigh na Teud Music Publishers
Taylor & Francis
Troubador Publishing Ltd
Truran
University of Wales Press
Usborne Publishing Ltd

Voltaire Foundation Ltd
Waterside Press
Paul Watkins Publishing
John Wiley & Sons Ltd
Y Lolfa Cyf
Yale University Press London

LAW

Amnesty International
International Secretariat
Peter Andrew Publishing Co Ltd
Ashgate Publishing Ltd
Atlantic Books
Bartsky Ltd
Bene Factum Publishing Ltd
Joseph Biddulph Publisher
Blackhall Publishing
Borthwick Publications
Business Education Publishers
Cambridge University Press
Class Publishing
Commonwealth Secretariat
Delta Alpha Publishing Ltd
J M Dent
Earthscan
Edinburgh University Press
Edward Elgar Publishing Ltd
Four Courts Press
Global Professional Publishing
Granta Editions
W. Green The Scottish Law
Publisher
Greenwood Publishing Group
Hachette Livre UK Ltd
Hart Publishing
Harvard University Press
Hodder Education
Holo Books
Incorporated Council of Law
Reporting for England and
Wales
Institute for Fiscal Studies
Institute of Employment Rights
The Islamic Texts Society
Ithaca Press
Jones & Bartlett International
Jordan Publishing Ltd
Jessica Kingsley Publishers
Kube Publishing Ltd
Law Society Publishing
Lawpack Publishing Ltd
Leatherhead Food International
Legal Action Group
McGraw-Hill Education
Macmillan Publishers Ltd
Manchester University Press
Market House Books Ltd
Merlin Publishing/Wolfhound
Press
National Extension College Trust
Ltd
National Housing Federation
Nelson Thornes Ltd
Oak Tree Press
Oxford University Press
Palgrave Macmillan
Pearson Education
Pluto Books Ltd
Princeton University Press
Round Hall Ltd
Routledge-Cavendish
Russell House Publishing Ltd
Shaw & Sons Ltd
SLS Legal Publications (NI)
Studymates Ltd
Sussex Academic Press
Taylor & Francis
Thomson International Legal &
Regulatory
Thorogood Publishing Ltd
Trentham Books
TSO (The Stationery Office Ltd)
Waterside Press
Waterside Press
Weidenfeld & Nicolson
Which? Books
Witherby Seamanship
International
Woodhead Publishing Ltd
XPL Publishing

LITERATURE & CRITICISM

Adam Matthew Digital Ltd
Adam Matthew Publications Ltd
Albyn Press
Allison & Busby
Amolibros
Arena Books (Publishers)
Ashgate Publishing Ltd
Association for Scottish Literary
    Studies
Atlantic Books
Austin & Macauley Publishers Ltd
Back-In-Print Books Ltd
Beautiful Books Ltd
Berghahn Books
Blackstaff Press
Blackthorn Press
Bloodaxe Books Ltd
Bloomsbury Publishing Plc
Bodleian Library Publishing
Marion Boyars Publishers Ltd
Boydell & Brewer Ltd
Brandon/Mount Eagle
    Publications
Cambridge University Press
Canongate Books
Carel Press
The Chrysalis Press
James Clarke & Co
Classical Comics Ltd
Cló Iar-Chonnachta
Cois Life
The Continuum International
    Publishing Group Ltd
Cork University Press
Crescent Moon Publishing
Dedalus Ltd
J M Dent
Dionysia Press Ltd
Ashley Drake Publishing Ltd
Gerald Duckworth & Co Ltd
Edinburgh University Press
Enitharmon Press
Everyman's Library
Faber & Faber Ltd
Feather Books
Four Courts Press
Freelance Market News
Garnet Publishing Ltd
Gill & Macmillan Ltd
Global Oriental Ltd
The Goldsmith Press Ltd
Gomer
Green Books
Greenwood Publishing Group
Guildhall Press
Gwasg Gwenffrwd
Halban Publishers
HarperCollins Publishers Ltd
Harvard University Press
Hippopotamus Press
Hobnob Press
Hodder Education
How To Books Ltd
Icon Books Ltd
Intellect Ltd
Ithaca Press
Janus Publishing Co Ltd
Jarndyce Booksellers
Liberties Press
Libris Ltd
The Lilliput Press Ltd
Little, Brown Book Group
The Littman Library of Jewish
    Civilization
Liverpool University Press
Living Time® Media International
Luath Press Ltd
The Lutterworth Press
Macmillan Publishers Ltd
Mainstream Publishing Co
    (Edinburgh) Ltd
Manchester University Press
Mandrake of Oxford
Maney Publishing
Mehring Books
Mercier Press Ltd
Mercury Books
Merlin Publishing/Wolfhound
    Press
Microform Academic Publishers

NATE (National Association for the
    Teaching of English)
National Portrait Gallery
    Publications
Nelson Thornes Ltd
New Island Books Ltd
Northcote House Publishers Ltd
W. W. Norton & Company Ltd
The Old Stile Press
The Oleander Press
Oneworld Classics
Onlywomen Press Ltd
Open University Worldwide
Peter Owen Publishers
Oxbow Books
Palgrave Macmillan
Pan Macmillan
Pen Press
The Penguin Group (UK) Ltd
Pickering & Chatto (Publishers) Ltd
Pipers' Ash Ltd
Pluto Press Ltd
Polity Press
ProQuest
Random House UK Ltd
Redcliffe Press Ltd
Roundhouse Publishing Ltd
Salt Publishing Ltd
Sandstone Press Ltd
Sansom & Co Ltd
Saqi Books
Scottish Cultural Press
Scottish Text Society
Seren
Charles Skilton Ltd
Colin Smythe Ltd
Souvenir Press Ltd
Stenlake Publishing Ltd
Studymates Ltd
Sussex Academic Press
Sussex Publications
The Swedenborg Society
Symposium Publications Literary &
    Art
Tabb House
Tartarus Press
Taylor & Francis
Thames & Hudson Ltd
Trog Associates Ltd
Troubador Publishing Ltd
University of Exeter Press
University of Hertfordshire Press
University of Wales Press
Voltaire Foundation Ltd
Waterside Press
John Wiley & Sons Ltd
The Women's Press
Wordsworth Editions Ltd

MAGIC & THE OCCULT

Aeon Books
Amolibros
Arcturus Publishing Ltd
Austin & Macauley Publishers Ltd
Duncan Baird Publishers
The Banton Press
Blue Beyond Books
Bossiney Books Ltd
Capall Bann Publishing
Caxton Publishing Group Ltd
Collins & Brown
Crescent Moon Publishing
Eddison Sadd Editions Ltd
W. Foulsham & Co Ltd
Geddes & Grosset
Godsfield Press Ltd
Gothic Image Publications
Green Magic
Robert Hale Ltd
HarperCollins Publishers Ltd
Heart of Albion Press
John Hunt Publishing Ltd
Janus Publishing Co Ltd
Luath Press Ltd
Mandrake of Oxford
Pen Press
Piatkus Books
Quadrille Publishing Ltd
Quantum Publishing
Reardon Publishing
Regency House Publishing Ltd

The Society of Metaphysicians Ltd
Souvenir Press Ltd
Rudolf Steiner Press
Temple Lodge Publishing
Thames & Hudson Ltd
Thoth Publications
Troubador Publishing Ltd
University of Hertfordshire Press
Warburg Institute
John Wiley & Sons Ltd
Zambezi Publishing Ltd

MATHEMATICS & STATISTICS

Al-Furqan Islamic Heritage
    Foundation
Alpha Science International Ltd
Anshan Ltd
Atlantic Books
Atlantic Europe Publishing Co Ltd
Bernard Babani (Publishing) Ltd
BBC Active
BEAM Education
Bedford Freeman Worth (BFW)
Blackstaff Press
Cambridge University Press
Carel Press
Chalksoft Ltd
Claire Publications
Global Professional Publishing
Hodder Education
Icon Books Ltd
Imperial College Press
The Institute of Mathematics and
    its Applications
IOP Publishing
Jones & Bartlett International
S. Karger AG
Letts and Lonsdale
McGraw-Hill Education
Macmillan Education
Macmillan Publishers Ltd
Mentor Books
The National Academies Press
National Extension College Trust
    Ltd
Nelson Thornes Ltd
W. W. Norton & Company Ltd
Open University Worldwide
Oxford University Press
Palgrave Macmillan
Princeton University Press
ProQuest
Sage Publications Ltd
Springer London
Studymates Ltd
Supportive Learning Publications
    (SLP)
Tarquin Publications
Taylor & Francis
TSO (The Stationery Office Ltd)
University of Hertfordshire Press
Ward Lock Educational Co Ltd
John Wiley & Sons Ltd
WIT Press

MEDICAL (INCL. SELF HELP & ALTERNATIVE MEDICINE)

Accent Press Ltd
Age Concern Books
Alpha Science International Ltd
Amberwood Publishing Ltd
American Psychiatric Publishing
    Inc
Amolibros
Anshan Ltd
Apex Publishing Ltd
Arcturus Publishing Ltd
Argyll Publishing
Ashgrove Publishing
Austin & Macauley Publishers Ltd
Duncan Baird Publishers
Barny Books
Bartsky Ltd
Bene Factum Publishing Ltd
BLA Publishing Ltd
Blackhall Publishing
Blackstaff Press
BookPower
CABI

*Cambridge Publishing
    Management Ltd*
Cambridge University Press
Capall Bann Publishing
Jon Carpenter Publishing
Carroll & Brown Ltd
Caxton Publishing Group Ltd
Class Publishing
Clear Answer Medical Publishing
    Ltd
Collins & Brown
Columba
Constable & Robinson Ltd
Corpus Publishing Ltd
Paul H. Crompton Ltd
D & N Publishing
Denor Press Ltd
Eddison Sadd Editions Ltd
Elsevier Ltd
The Erskine Press
Filament Publishing Ltd
Findhorn Press Ltd
Floris Books
Focus Publishing (Sevenoaks) Ltd
W. Foulsham & Co Ltd
Geddes & Grosset
Godsfield Press Ltd
Granta Editions
Green Magic
Greenwood Publishing Group
Hachette Livre UK Ltd
Haldane Mason Ltd
Hammersmith Press Ltd
HarperCollins Publishers Ltd
Hawker Publications
Hawthorn Press
Haynes Publishing
Ian Henry Publications Ltd
Hinton House Publishers Ltd
Hodder Education
Hodder & Stoughton Faith
How To Books Ltd
Human Kinetics Europe Ltd
Imperial College Press
Institute of Physics & Engineering
    in Medicine
International Medical Press
Janus Publishing Co Ltd
Jones & Bartlett International
S. Karger AG
Richard Kay Publications
Jessica Kingsley Publishers
Luath Press Ltd
McGraw-Hill Education
Macmillan Publishers Ltd
Mainstream Publishing Co
    (Edinburgh) Ltd
Mandrake of Oxford
Maney Publishing
Manson Publishing Ltd
Market House Books Ltd
Mitchell Beazley
M&K Publishing
The National Academies Press
National Extension College Trust
    Ltd
Need2Know
Nelson Thornes Ltd
NHS Immunisation Information
Open University Worldwide
Oxford University Press
Palgrave Macmillan
Pavilion Journals (Brighton) Ltd
PCCS Books Ltd
Pen Press
The Penguin Group (UK) Ltd
The Pharmaceutical Press
Piatkus Books
Portland Press Ltd
Professional Engineering
    Publishing
ProQuest
Publishing House
Quadrille Publishing Ltd
Quantum Publishing
Quintessence Publishing Co Ltd
Radcliffe Publishing Ltd
Round Hall Ltd
Roundhouse Publishing Ltd
Routledge-Cavendish
Royal College of General
    Practitioners

Royal College of Psychiatrists
Royal Society of Medicine Press
    Ltd
Russell House Publishing Ltd
Scion Publishing Ltd
Sheldon Press
Simon & Schuster (UK) Ltd
Social Affairs Unit
The Society for Promoting
    Christian Knowledge (SPCK)
The Society of Metaphysicians Ltd
Souvenir Press Ltd
Speechmark Publishing Ltd
Springer London
Rudolf Steiner Press
Stokesby House Publications
Studymates Ltd
Taylor & Francis
Temple Lodge Publishing
Troubador Publishing Ltd
TSO (The Stationery Office Ltd)
Merlin Unwin Books Ltd
Whiting & Birch Ltd
John Wiley & Sons Ltd
Windhorse Publications
WIT Press
Wolters Kluwer Health (P & E) Ltd
XPL Publishing
Zambezi Publishing Ltd

MILITARY & WAR

A.M.S. Educational Ltd
Adam Matthew Digital Ltd
Air-Britain (Historians) Ltd
Ian Allan Publishing Ltd
Amber Books Ltd
Anglo-Saxon Books
Apex Publishing Ltd
Arcturus Publishing Ltd
Ashgate Publishing Ltd
Atlantic Books
Aurum Press
Austin & Macauley Publishers Ltd
Back-In-Print Books Ltd
Barny Books
Bene Factum Publishing Ltd
Berghahn Books
Birlinn Ltd
BLA Publishing Ltd
Blackstaff Press
Bloomsbury Publishing Plc
Bodleian Library Publishing
Boydell & Brewer Ltd
Brewin Books Ltd
Bridge Books
Brooklands Books Ltd
Business Education Publishers
*Cambridge Publishing
    Management Ltd*
Carlton Publishing Group
Caxton Publishing Group Ltd
Chatham Publishing
Constable & Robinson Ltd
Conway
Countryside Books
Crécy Publishing Ltd
The Crowood Press Ltd
Cualann Press
D & N Publishing
David & Charles Ltd
The Dovecote Press
Ashley Drake Publishing Ltd
Gerald Duckworth & Co Ltd
Elliott & Thompson
English Heritage
The Erskine Press
Essential Works Ltd
Focus Publishing (Sevenoaks) Ltd
W. Foulsham & Co Ltd
Four Courts Press
Glyndwr Publishing
*Graham-Cameron Publishing &
    Illustration*
Greenhill Books / Lionel Leventhal
    Ltd
Greenwood Publishing Group
Grub Street
Hachette Scotland
Robert Hale Ltd
Halsgrove
HarperCollins Publishers Ltd

Harvard University Press
Haynes Publishing
Helion & Co Ltd
Hodder & Stoughton General
C. Hurst & Co (Publishers) Ltd
Icon Books Ltd
Jane's Information Group Ltd
Janus Publishing Co Ltd
Richard Kay Publications
Little, Brown Book Group
Luath Press Ltd
The Lutterworth Press
Macmillan Publishers Ltd
Mainstream Publishing Co
   (Edinburgh) Ltd
Maney Publishing
Maritime Books
Maverick House Publishers
Mercury Books
Microform Academic Publishers
Middleton Press
John Murray Publishers
Myriad Editions
NMS Enterprises Limited -
   Publishing
W. W. Norton & Company Ltd
The Nostalgia Collection
The Orion Publishing Group Ltd
Osprey Publishing Ltd
Pathfinder Books
Pen Press
The Penguin Group (UK) Ltd
Piatkus Books
Quantum Publishing
Quiller Publishing Ltd
The Radcliffe Press
Rand Publications
Random House UK Ltd
Reardon Publishing
Regency House Publishing Ltd
Ripping Yarns.com
Roundhouse Publishing Ltd
Scottish Cultural Press
Shire Publications Ltd
Sigel Press
Charles Skilton Ltd
Souvenir Press Ltd
Spokesman
Stacey International
Strong Oak Press
Studymates Ltd
Sussex Academic Press
I. B. Tauris & Co Ltd
Taylor & Francis
Thames & Hudson Ltd
Third Millennium Publishing Ltd
Thorogood Publishing Ltd
Transworld Publishers Ltd
Troubador Publishing Ltd
Truran
Tyne Bridge Publishing
Unicorn Press
United Writers Publications Ltd
University of Wales Press
Merlin Unwin Books Ltd
Virgin Books Ltd
Vision
David West Children's Books
Whittles Publishing
John Wiley & Sons Ltd
Neil Wilson Publishing Ltd
Worth Press Ltd
Yale University Press London

MUSIC

Amolibros
Appletree Press Ltd
Arc Publications Ltd
Arcturus Publishing Ltd
Ashgate Publishing Ltd
Atlantic Books
Attic Press
Aureus Publishing Ltd
Aurum Press
Beautiful Books Ltd
BLA Publishing Ltd
A. & C. Black (Publishers) Ltd
Black Dog Publishing Ltd
Black Spring Press Ltd
Blackstaff Press
John Blake Publishing Ltd

Bloomsbury Publishing Plc
Blue Beyond Books
Blue Sky Press
Marion Boyars Publishers Ltd
Boydell & Brewer Ltd
Cambridge University Press
Canongate Books
Capall Bann Publishing
Carlton Publishing Group
Chalksoft Ltd
Cló Iar-Chonnachta
Collins & Brown
The Continuum International
   Publishing Group Ltd
Cork University Press
Crescent Moon Publishing
Currach Press
Dance Books Ltd
J M Dent
Elliott & Thompson
Equinox Publishing Ltd
Essential Works Ltd
Faber & Faber Ltd
Feather Books
Focus Publishing (Sevenoaks) Ltd
Four Courts Press
GeoCenter International Ltd
Granta Editions
Greenwood Publishing Group
Gresham Books Ltd
Guildhall Press
Hachette Scotland
Robert Hale Ltd
HarperCollins Publishers Ltd
Hawthorn Press
Haynes Publishing
Independent Music Press
Libris Ltd
The Lilliput Press Ltd
Little, Brown Book Group
The Littman Library of Jewish
   Civilization
Luath Press Ltd
McCrimmon Publishing Co Ltd
Macmillan Publishers Ltd
Mainstream Publishing Co
   (Edinburgh) Ltd
Market House Books Ltd
Merlin Publishing/Wolfhound
   Press
The MIT Press Ltd
Mitchell Beazley
Moonlight Publishing Ltd
Moorley's Print & Publishing Ltd
W. W. Norton & Company Ltd
Omnibus Press
Ovolo Publishing Ltd
Peter Owen Publishers
Oxford University Press
Packard Publishing Ltd
Pavilion
PC Publishing
Pen Press
The Penguin Group (UK) Ltd
Pennant Books Ltd
Phaidon Press Ltd
Piatkus Books
Portico
ProQuest
Quantum Publishing
Quartet Books
Random House UK Ltd
Ravette Publishing Ltd
Robson Books
RotoVision SA
Roundhouse Publishing Ltd
SchoolPlay Productions Ltd
Schott Music Ltd
SCM-Canterbury Press Ltd
Scripture Union Publishing
The Shetland Times Ltd
Simon & Schuster (UK) Ltd
Souvenir Press Ltd
Spartan Press Music Publishers Ltd
Stainer & Bell Ltd
Rudolf Steiner Press
Sussex Academic Press
Sussex Publications
Taigh na Teud Music Publishers
Taylor & Francis
Thames & Hudson Ltd

Transworld Publishers Ltd
University of Wales Press
Usborne Publishing Ltd
Virgin Books Ltd
Ward Lock Educational Co Ltd
David West Children's Books
Wild Goose Publications
John Wiley & Sons Ltd
Neil Wilson Publishing Ltd
Y Lolfa Cyf
Yale University Press London

NATURAL HISTORY

AA Publishing
Antique Collectors' Club Ltd
Arcturus Publishing Ltd
Argyll Publishing
Arris Publishing Ltd
Atlantic Books
Aurum Press
Austin & Macauley Publishers Ltd
Duncan Baird Publishers
Bender Richardson White
BLA Publishing Ltd
A. & C. Black (Publishers) Ltd
Blackstaff Press
British Museum Press
Brown & Whittaker Publishing
Calypso Publications
*Cambridge Publishing
   Management Ltd*
Cambridge University Press
Cameron Books
Capall Bann Publishing
Carlton Publishing Group
Carnegie Publishing Ltd
Caxton Publishing Group Ltd
Chalksoft Ltd
Cornwall Editions Ltd
Countyvise Ltd
The Crowood Press Ltd
D & N Publishing
David & Charles Ltd
The Dovecote Press
The Erskine Press
Ex Libris Press
Focus Publishing (Sevenoaks) Ltd
Graffeg
*Graham-Cameron Publishing &
   Illustration*
Granta Editions
Green Books
Haldane Mason Ltd
Robert Hale Ltd
Halsgrove
HarperCollins Publishers Ltd
Harvard University Press
Hodder Education
Alison Hodge Publishers
Icon Books Ltd
Logaston Press
Lomond Books Ltd
Luath Press Ltd
The Lutterworth Press
Macmillan Publishers Ltd
The MIT Press Ltd
Mitchell Beazley
Monkey Puzzle Media Ltd
Moonlight Publishing Ltd
The National Academies Press
The National Trust
Natural History Museum
   Publishing
New Holland Publishers (UK) Ltd
Newpro UK Ltd
NMS Enterprises Limited -
   Publishing
North York Moors National Park
W. W. Norton & Company Ltd
Octopus Publishing Group
Old House Books
Open University Worldwide
Optimus Professional Publishing
The Orion Publishing Group Ltd
Oxbow Books
Packard Publishing Ltd
Papadakis Publisher
The Penguin Group (UK) Ltd
Philip's
Princeton University Press
Quantum Publishing

Quiller Publishing Ltd
Random House UK Ltd
Reardon Publishing
The Richmond Publishing Co
Roundhouse Publishing Ltd
Royal Collection Publications
S. B. Publications
Scottish Children's Press
Scottish Cultural Press
Sessions of York
SGC Books
The Shetland Times Ltd
Shire Publications Ltd
Souvenir Press Ltd
Stacey International
Stobart Davies Ltd
Subbuteo Natural History Books
Thames & Hudson Ltd
Top That! Publishing Plc
Toucan Books Ltd
Troubador Publishing Ltd
Truran
Merlin Unwin Books Ltd
Usborne Publishing Ltd
David West Children's Books
Whittet Books Ltd
Whittles Publishing
John Wiley & Sons Ltd
Willow Island Editions
Yale University Press London
Zymurgy Publishing

NAUTICAL

Adlard Coles Nautical
Ian Allan Publishing Ltd
Amber Books Ltd
Amolibros
Austin & Macauley Publishers Ltd
The Belmont Press
BLA Publishing Ltd
A. & C. Black (Publishers) Ltd
Brown, Son & Ferguson, Ltd
Chatham Publishing
Conway
Countyvise Ltd
Crécy Publishing Ltd
The Crowood Press Ltd
Ex Libris Press
Focus Publishing (Sevenoaks) Ltd
Glyndwr Publishing
Granta Editions
Haynes Publishing
Imray Laurie Norie & Wilson Ltd
Jane's Information Group Ltd
Janus Publishing Co Ltd
Landmark Publishing Ltd
Middleton Press
The National Academies Press
W. W. Norton & Company Ltd
The Nostalgia Collection
The Orion Publishing Group Ltd
Oxbow Books
Professional Engineering
   Publishing
Quantum Publishing
Quiller Publishing Ltd
Reardon Publishing
Roadmaster Publishing
Scottish Cultural Press
Special Interest Model Books Ltd
Stenlake Publishing Ltd
Truran
TSO (The Stationery Office Ltd)
Twelveheads Press
Tyne Bridge Publishing
Unicorn Press
United Writers Publications Ltd
Paul Watkins Publishing
Whittles Publishing
Neil Wilson Publishing Ltd
Witherby Seamanship
   International

PHILOSOPHY

Acumen Publishing Ltd
Alban Books Ltd
Amolibros
Apex Publishing Ltd
Arcturus Publishing Ltd
Arena Books (Publishers)

Ashgate Publishing Ltd
Atlantic Books
Austin & Macauley Publishers Ltd
Duncan Baird Publishers
Black Ace Books
Black Dog Publishing Ltd
Blue Beyond Books
Marion Boyars Publishers Ltd
Boydell & Brewer Ltd
Cambridge University Press
Canongate Books
Capall Bann Publishing
Jon Carpenter Publishing
James Clarke & Co
The Continuum International
   Publishing Group Ltd
Cork University Press
Crescent Moon Publishing
Darton, Longman & Todd Ltd
Gerald Duckworth & Co Ltd
Dunedin Academic Press
Edinburgh University Press
Emerald Group Publishing Ltd
Equinox Publishing Ltd
Everyman's Library
Fabian Society
Floris Books
Four Courts Press
Gibson Square
Global Oriental Ltd
Gothic Image Publications
Gracewing Publishing
Green Books
Greenwood Publishing Group
Halban Publishers
Harvard University Press
Heart of Albion Press
Hodder Education
John Hunt Publishing Ltd
Icon Books Ltd
Imprint Academic
Intellect Ltd
Janus Publishing Co Ltd
Letts and Lonsdale
The Littman Library of Jewish
   Civilization
Living Time® Media International
The Lutterworth Press
McGraw-Hill Education
Macmillan Publishers Ltd
Mandrake of Oxford
The MIT Press Ltd
W. W. Norton & Company Ltd
Open Gate Press
The Orion Publishing Group Ltd
Oxford University Press
Palgrave Macmillan
Pathfinder Books
Pen Press
The Penguin Group (UK) Ltd
Pipers' Ash Ltd
Pluto Books Ltd
Polity Press
Princeton University Press
Random House UK Ltd
Roundhouse Publishing Ltd
Routledge-Cavendish
St Pauls Publishing
Saqi Books
SCM-Canterbury Press Ltd
Shepheard-Walwyn (Publishers)
   Ltd
Short Books Ltd
The Society of Metaphysicians Ltd
Souvenir Press Ltd
Spokesman
Rudolf Steiner Press
Sussex Academic Press
Taylor & Francis
Temple Lodge Publishing
Thames & Hudson Ltd
Troubador Publishing Ltd
University of Wales Press
Merlin Unwin Books Ltd
Veritas Publications
Voltaire Foundation Ltd
Warburg Institute
Weidenfeld & Nicolson
John Wiley & Sons Ltd
Windhorse Publications
Yale University Press London

PHOTOGRAPHY

AA Publishing
Arcadia Books Ltd
Aurum Press
AVA Publishing (UK) Ltd
Black Dog Publishing Ltd
Blackstaff Press
Cló Iar-Chonnachta
Collins & Brown
Cork University Press
Crescent Moon Publishing
Currach Press
D & N Publishing
David & Charles Ltd
Essential Works Ltd
Flambard Press
Focus Publishing (Sevenoaks) Ltd
Freelance Market News
Garnet Publishing Ltd
GeoCenter International Ltd
Gomer
Gothic Image Publications
Graffeg
Guildhall Press
Robert Hale Ltd
HarperCollins Publishers Ltd
Haynes Publishing
Hayward Publishing
Alison Hodge Publishers
The Ilex Press Ltd
In Easy Steps Ltd
Dewi Lewis Publishing
Libris Ltd
The Lilliput Press Ltd
Luath Press Ltd
Lund Humphries
Mainstream Publishing Co
   (Edinburgh) Ltd
Mentor Books
Merlin Publishing/Wolfhound
   Press
Merrell Publishers Ltd
Meyrick Marketing Ltd
The MIT Press Ltd
Mitchell Beazley
National Galleries of Scotland
National Portrait Gallery
   Publications
New Internationalist Publications
   Ltd
Newpro UK Ltd
Papadakis Publisher
Pavilion
The Penguin Group (UK) Ltd
Phaidon Press Ltd
Prestel Publishing Ltd
Quadrille Publishing Ltd
Quantum Publishing
Random House UK Ltd
RotoVision SA
Roundhouse Publishing Ltd
Royal Collection Publications
Saqi Books
Stacey International
Tate Publishing
Teneues Publishing UK Ltd
Thames & Hudson Ltd
Third Millennium Publishing Ltd
Truran
Unicorn Press
Merlin Unwin Books Ltd
Victoria & Albert Museum
   Publishing
Weidenfeld & Nicolson
John Wiley & Sons Ltd
Yale University Press London
Zymurgy Publishing

PHYSICS

Alpha Science International Ltd
Anshan Ltd
Atlantic Europe Publishing Co Ltd
BBC Active
Bedford Freeman Worth (BFW)
BLA Publishing Ltd
Cambridge University Press
Canopus Publishing Ltd
HarperCollins Publishers Ltd
Hodder Education
Icon Books Ltd

Imperial College Press
Institute of Physics & Engineering
   in Medicine
IOP Publishing
Jones & Bartlett International
Letts and Lonsdale
McGraw-Hill Education
Macmillan Education
Macmillan Publishers Ltd
Multi Science Publishing Co Ltd
The National Academies Press
National Extension College Trust
   Ltd
Nelson Thornes Ltd
W. W. Norton & Company Ltd
Open University Worldwide
Oxford University Press
Palgrave Macmillan
ProQuest
Studymates Ltd
Taylor & Francis
Ward Lock Educational Co Ltd
John Wiley & Sons Ltd

POETRY

A.M.S. Educational Ltd
Acair Ltd
Accent Press Ltd
Albyn Press
Alma Books Ltd
Amolibros
Anglo-Saxon Books
Anvil Press Poetry Ltd
Apex Publishing Ltd
Arc Publications Ltd
Arcturus Publishing Ltd
Association for Scottish Literary
   Studies
Atlantic Books
Authorhouse UK Ltd
Barddas
Joseph Biddulph Publisher
Blackstaff Press
Bloodaxe Books Ltd
Blue Beyond Books
Blue Sky Press
Brown & Whittaker Publishing
Canongate Books
Catcher Ltd
Cló Iar-Chonnachta
Cois Life
Countyvise Ltd
Crescent Moon Publishing
Enitharmon Press
Ex Libris Press
Express Newspapers
Faber & Faber Ltd
Feather Books
Five Leaves Publications
Flambard Press
W. Foulsham & Co Ltd
Freelance Market News
The Gallery Press
The Goldsmith Press Ltd
Gomer
Green Books
Guildhall Press
Gwasg Gwenffrwd
Hachette Children's Books
HarperCollins Publishers Ltd
Hippopotamus Press
Icon Books Ltd
ISIS Publishing Ltd
Janus Publishing Co Ltd
Jarndyce Booksellers
The King's England Press
Libris Ltd
Living Time® Media International
Luath Press Ltd
Macmillan Children's Books Ltd
Macmillan Publishers Ltd
Mandrake of Oxford
Mentor Books
Mercier Press Ltd
Merlin Publishing/Wolfhound
   Press
Methodist Publishing
Moorley's Print & Publishing Ltd
New Island Books Ltd
NMS Enterprises Limited -
   Publishing

W. W. Norton & Company Ltd
The Old Stile Press
The Oleander Press
Oneworld Classics
Paragon Publishing
Pen Press
The Penguin Group (UK) Ltd
Pentathol Publishing
Pipers' Ash Ltd
ProQuest
Random House UK Ltd
Redcliffe Press Ltd
Route Publishing Ltd
Saint Albert's Press
Salt Publishing Ltd
Saqi Books
Scottish Children's Press
Scottish Cultural Press
Scottish Text Society
Seren
Sessions of York
Charles Skilton Ltd
Spokesman
Stenlake Publishing Ltd
Studymates Ltd
Summer Palace Press
Symposium Publications Literary &
   Art
Tabb House
Triumph House
Troubador Publishing Ltd
University of Wales Press
Upfront Publishing
John Wiley & Sons Ltd
Wordsworth Editions Ltd
Y Lolfa Cyf

POLITICS & WORLD AFFAIRS

Acumen Publishing Ltd
Amnesty International
   International Secretariat
Amolibros
Apex Publishing Ltd
Arcadia Books Ltd
Arena Books (Publishers)
Arris Publishing Ltd
Ashgate Publishing Ltd
Atlantic Books
Attic Press
Austin & Macauley Publishers Ltd
Berghahn Books
Blackstaff Press
Bloomsbury Publishing Plc
Brandon/Mount Eagle
   Publications
Cambridge Archive Editions Ltd
Cambridge University Press
Canongate Books
Jon Carpenter Publishing
Centre for Economic Policy
   Research
Commonwealth Secretariat
The Continuum International
   Publishing Group Ltd
Conway
CQ Press
Ashley Drake Publishing Ltd
Gerald Duckworth & Co Ltd
Dunedin Academic Press
Earthscan
Edinburgh University Press
Ethics International Press Ltd
Faber & Faber Ltd
Fabian Society
Garnet Publishing Ltd
Gibson Square
Gill & Macmillan Ltd
Global Oriental Ltd
Gothic Image Publications
Granta Books
Green Books
Greenwood Publishing Group
Guildhall Press
Gwasg Gwenffrwd
Halban Publishers
Robert Hale Ltd
HarperCollins Publishers Ltd
Harvard University Press
Hodder Education
Hodder & Stoughton General
C. Hurst & Co (Publishers) Ltd

Icon Books Ltd
Imprint Academic
Institute of Development Studies
Institute of Employment Rights
Ithaca Press
Jane's Information Group Ltd
Janus Publishing Co Ltd
Richard Kay Publications
Liberties Press
Little, Brown Book Group
The Littman Library of Jewish
   Civilization
Liverpool University Press
Luath Press Ltd
The Lutterworth Press
McGraw-Hill Education
Macmillan Publishers Ltd
Mainstream Publishing Co
   (Edinburgh) Ltd
Manchester University Press
Maverick House Publishers
Mehring Books
Melisende
Mentor Books
Mercier Press Ltd
The Merlin Press Ltd
Merlin Publishing/Wolfhound
   Press
Microform Academic Publishers
The MIT Press Ltd
Monkey Puzzle Media Ltd
Myriad Editions
Nelson Thornes Ltd
New Holland Publishers (UK) Ltd
New Internationalist Publications
   Ltd
New Island Books Ltd
W. W. Norton & Company Ltd
The O'Brien Press Ltd
Open Gate Press
Open University Worldwide
The Orion Publishing Group Ltd
Oxfam Publishing
Oxford University Press
Palgrave Macmillan
Panaf Books
Pathfinder Books
Pen Press
The Penguin Group (UK) Ltd
Pluto Books Ltd
The Policy Press
Polity Press
Portobello Books Ltd
Princeton University Press
Profile Books
ProQuest
Publishing House
The Radcliffe Press
Rand Publications
Random House UK Ltd
Roundhouse Publishing Ltd
Routledge-Cavendish
Joseph Rowntree Foundation
Sage Publications Ltd
Sandstone Press Ltd
Saqi Books
Save the Children
Seren
Sessions of York
Shepheard-Walwyn (Publishers)
   Ltd
Simon & Schuster (UK) Ltd
Adam Smith Institute
Social Affairs Unit
Spokesman
Stacey International
Rudolf Steiner Press
Studymates Ltd
Sussex Academic Press
I. B. Tauris & Co Ltd
Taylor & Francis
Temple Lodge Publishing
Transworld Publishers Ltd
Trentham Books
Troubador Publishing Ltd
TSO (The Stationery Office Ltd)
University of Wales Press
Vallentine Mitchell Publishers
Virgin Books Ltd
Vision
Weidenfeld & Nicolson
John Wiley & Sons Ltd

The Women's Press
Y Lolfa Cyf
Yale University Press London
Zed Books Ltd

PSYCHOLOGY & PSYCHIATRY

American Psychiatric Publishing
   Inc
Ann Arbor Publishers Ltd
Anshan Ltd
Ashgrove Publishing
Atlantic Books
Austin & Macauley Publishers Ltd
Beautiful Books Ltd
Bedford Freeman Worth (BFW)
Blackhall Publishing
Nicholas Brealey Publishing
British Association for Adoption &
   Fostering
Cambridge University Press
Capall Bann Publishing
Channel View Publications Ltd
Columba
Constable & Robinson Ltd
Currach Press
Darton, Longman & Todd Ltd
Delancey Press Ltd
Ashley Drake Publishing Ltd
Emerald Group Publishing Ltd
The Fostering Network
Gill & Macmillan Ltd
Global Oriental Ltd
Gothic Image Publications
Greenwood Publishing Group
HarperCollins Publishers Ltd
Harvard University Press
Hawthorn Press
Heart of Albion Press
Hinton House Publishers Ltd
Hodder Education
Human Kinetics Europe Ltd
John Hunt Publishing Ltd
Icon Books Ltd
Imprint Academic
Jones & Bartlett International
S. Karger AG
Karnac Books Ltd
Jessica Kingsley Publishers
Letts and Lonsdale
Little, Brown Book Group
Living Time® Media International
McGraw-Hill Education
Macmillan Publishers Ltd
Market House Books Ltd
The MIT Press Ltd
M&K Publishing
The National Academies Press
The National Autistic Society
   (NAS)
National Extension College Trust
   Ltd
Nelson Thornes Ltd
W. W. Norton & Company Ltd
Open Gate Press
Open University Worldwide
Oxford University Press
Palgrave Macmillan
Pavilion Journals (Brighton) Ltd
PCCS Books Ltd
The Penguin Group (UK) Ltd
Piatkus Books
Pipers' Ash Ltd
ProQuest
Royal College of Psychiatrists
Russell House Publishing Ltd
Sage Publications Ltd
St Pauls Publishing
Sheldon Press
Sherwood Publishing
The Society for Promoting
   Christian Knowledge (SPCK)
Souvenir Press Ltd
Speechmark Publishing Ltd
Sussex Academic Press
Taylor & Francis
Troubador Publishing Ltd
United Writers Publications Ltd
University of Hertfordshire Press
Whiting & Birch Ltd
John Wiley & Sons Ltd
The Women's Press

REFERENCE BOOKS, DIRECTORIES & DICTIONARIES

Acumen Publishing Ltd
Adam Matthew Publications Ltd
Adamson Publishing Ltd
Age Concern Books
Alban Books Ltd
Albyn Press
Ian Allan Publishing Ltd
Alpha Science International Ltd
Amber Books Ltd
American Psychiatric Publishing Inc
Anglo-Saxon Books
Antique Collectors' Club Ltd
Apex Publishing Ltd
Appletree Press Ltd
Arcturus Publishing Ltd
Ashgate Publishing Ltd
Atlantic Books
Atlantic Europe Publishing Co Ltd
Aurelian Information Ltd
Aurora Metro Publications Ltd
AVA Publishing (UK) Ltd
Duncan Baird Publishers
Bender Richardson White
Bene Factum Publishing Ltd
Joseph Biddulph Publisher
BLA Publishing Ltd
A. & C. Black (Publishers) Ltd
Blackstaff Press
Bloomsbury Publishing Plc
Bodleian Library Publishing
Book Marketing Ltd
Bowker (UK) Ltd
Boydell & Brewer Ltd
British Association for Adoption & Fostering
British Museum Press
Calypso Publications
Cambridge Publishing Management Ltd
Cambridge University Press
Camra Books
Canopus Publishing Ltd
Carel Press
Caxton Publishing Group Ltd
CBD Research Ltd
Chambers Harrap Publishers Ltd
Church House Publishing
James Clarke & Co
Collins & Brown
Commonwealth Secretariat
The Continuum International Publishing Group Ltd
Countryside Books
CQ Press
Crimson Publishing
D & N Publishing
Delta Alpha Publishing Ltd
J M Dent
Diagram Visual Information Ltd
Gerald Duckworth & Co Ltd
Earthscan
Edinburgh University Press
Edward Elgar Publishing Ltd
Encyclopaedia Britannica (UK) Ltd
Energy Institute
Equinox Publishing Ltd
Euromonitor International Plc
Evangelical Press & Services Ltd
Executive Grapevine International Ltd
Express Newspapers
Facet Publishing
Folens Ltd
Food Trade Press Ltd
W. Foulsham & Co Ltd
Friends of the Earth
Geddes & Grosset
GeoCenter International Ltd
Geography Publications
Stanley Gibbons
Gill & Macmillan Ltd
Global Professional Publishing
Glyndwr Publishing
Gomer
Granta Editions
Green Books
Greenwood Publishing Group
Gwasg Gwenffrwd

Hachette Children's Books
Peter Haddock Publishing
Robert Hale Ltd
Harden's Ltd
HarperCollins Publishers Ltd
Harvard University Press
Haynes Publishing
Hemming Information Services
Hodder Education
How To Books Ltd
Icon Books Ltd
In Easy Steps Ltd
International Network for the Availability of Scientific Publications (INASP)
IVP
IWA Publishing
Jane's Information Group Ltd
Jarndyce Booksellers
Richard Joseph Publishers Ltd
Richard Kay Publications
Kogan Page Ltd
Kyle Cathie Ltd
Lawpack Publishing Ltd
Letts and Lonsdale
Dewi Lewis Publishing
Lexus Ltd
The Lilliput Press Ltd
LISU
Logaston Press
Lomond Books Ltd
The Lutterworth Press
McGraw-Hill Education
Macmillan Education
Macmillan Publishers Ltd
Manchester University Press
Market House Books Ltd
Mentor Books
Mercury Books
Merlin Publishing/Wolfhound Press
Milet Publishing Ltd
The MIT Press Ltd
Mitchell Beazley
Multi Science Publishing Co Ltd
National Children's Bureau
National Housing Federation
The National Trust
Natural History Museum Publishing
New Holland Publishers (UK) Ltd
New Internationalist Publications Ltd
Old House Books
The Oleander Press
On Stream Publications Ltd
The Orion Publishing Group Ltd
Oxford University Press
Packard Publishing Ltd
Palgrave Macmillan
Pen Press
The Penguin Group (UK) Ltd
Philip's
Piquant Editions
Portico
Portland Press Ltd
Princeton University Press
ProQuest
Quiller Publishing Ltd
Radcliffe Publishing Ltd
RotoVision SA
Round Hall Ltd
Roundhouse Publishing Ltd
Royal Irish Academy
The Royal Society of Chemistry
Sage Publications Ltd
SCM-Canterbury Press Ltd
Scottish Cultural Press
Shaw & Sons Ltd
Social Affairs Unit
Stacey International
Stainer & Bell Ltd
STRI (Sports Turf Research Institute)
Tartarus Press
I. B. Tauris & Co Ltd
Taylor & Francis
Thames & Hudson Ltd
Top That! Publishing Plc
Toucan Books Ltd
Trotman Publishing
Truran

TSO (The Stationery Office Ltd)
UCAS
Unicorn Press
University of Wales Press
Merlin Unwin Books Ltd
Usborne Publishing Ltd
Veloce Publishing Ltd
Virgin Books Ltd
Voltaire Foundation Ltd
Waterside Press
Waterside Press
Which? Books
Whittles Publishing
John Wiley & Sons Ltd
Witherby Seamanship International
The Women's Press
Wordsworth Editions Ltd

RELIGION & THEOLOGY

Acumen Publishing Ltd
Al-Furqan Islamic Heritage Foundation
Alban Books Ltd
R. L. Allan & Son Publishers
Anno Domini Publishing (ADPS)
Apex Publishing Ltd
Arcturus Publishing Ltd
Arena Books (Publishers)
Ashgate Publishing Ltd
Ashgrove Publishing
Atlantic Books
Atlantic Europe Publishing Co Ltd
Austin & Macauley Publishers Ltd
Authentic Media
Authorhouse UK Ltd
Duncan Baird Publishers
The Banner of Truth Trust
The Banton Press
BBC Active
Bender Richardson White
Berghahn Books
Bible Reading Fellowship
BLA Publishing Ltd
Blackstaff Press
Blue Beyond Books
Borthwick Publications
Bryntirion Press
Cambridge Publishing Management Ltd
Cambridge University Press
Capall Bann Publishing
The Catholic Truth Society
Christian Education
Christian Focus Publications
Church House Publishing
Church of Ireland Publishing
James Clarke & Co
Columba
The Continuum International Publishing Group Ltd
Countyvise Ltd
Crescent Moon Publishing
Paul H. Crompton Ltd
Cyhoeddiadau'r Gair
Darton, Longman & Todd Ltd
The Davenant Press
Day One Publications
Gerald Duckworth & Co Ltd
Eagle Publishing Ltd
Edinburgh University Press
Equinox Publishing Ltd
Evangelical Press & Services Ltd
Family Publications
Feather Books
Findhorn Press Ltd
Floris Books
W. Foulsham & Co Ltd
Four Courts Press
Garnet Publishing Ltd
Global Oriental Ltd
Godsfield Press Ltd
Gothic Image Publications
Gracewing Publishing
Graham-Cameron Publishing & Illustration
Green Magic
Greenwood Publishing Group
Gresham Books Ltd
Gwasg Gwenffrwd
Hachette Livre UK Ltd

Halban Publishers
HarperCollins Publishers Ltd
Harvard University Press
Hawthorn Press
Heart of Albion Press
Highland Books
Hodder Education
Hodder & Stoughton Faith
John Hunt Publishing Ltd
C. Hurst & Co (Publishers) Ltd
Icon Books Ltd
Imprint Academic
The Islamic Texts Society
Ithaca Press
IVP
Janus Publishing Co Ltd
Jessica Kingsley Publishers
Kingsway Publications
Kube Publishing Ltd
Liberties Press
Frances Lincoln Ltd
Lion Hudson Plc
The Littman Library of Jewish Civilization
The Lutterworth Press
McCrimmon Publishing Co Ltd
Macmillan Publishers Ltd
Mandrake of Oxford
Maney Publishing
Melisende
Mercier Press Ltd
Merlin Publishing/Wolfhound Press
Methodist Publishing
Microform Academic Publishers
Moorley's Print & Publishing Ltd
National Extension College Trust Ltd
Nelson Thornes Ltd
The Open Bible Trust
Open Gate Press
Open University Worldwide
Oxford University Press
Palgrave Macmillan
Paragon Publishing
PCCS Books Ltd
Pen Press
The Penguin Group (UK) Ltd
Pickering & Chatto (Publishers) Ltd
Pipers' Ash Ltd
Piquant Editions
ProQuest
Redemptorist Publications
Sage Publications Ltd
Saint Albert's Press
St Pauls Publishing
Saqi Books
SCM-Canterbury Press Ltd
Scottish Children's Press
Scottish Cultural Press
Scripture Union Publishing
Sessions of York
Shepheard-Walwyn (Publishers) Ltd
The Society for Promoting Christian Knowledge (SPCK)
Souvenir Press Ltd
Stacey International
Stainer & Bell Ltd
Rudolf Steiner Press
Studymates Ltd
Sussex Academic Press
The Swedenborg Society
Ta Ha Publishers Ltd
I. B. Tauris & Co Ltd
Taylor & Francis
Temple Lodge Publishing
Thames & Hudson Ltd
Tharpa Publications
Thoth Publications
Trinitarian Bible Society
Triumph House
University of Wales Press
Vallentine Mitchell Publishers
Veritas Publications
Voltaire Foundation Ltd
Warburg Institute
Ward Lock Educational Co Ltd
Wild Goose Publications
John Wiley & Sons Ltd
Windhorse Publications
Worth Press Ltd

Yale University Press London

SCIENCE FICTION

Apex Publishing Ltd
Atlantic Books
Austin & Macauley Publishers Ltd
Authorhouse UK Ltd
Carlton Publishing Group
Catcher Ltd
Constable & Robinson Ltd
Gerald Duckworth & Co Ltd
Victor Gollancz Ltd
Greenwood Publishing Group
HarperCollins Publishers Ltd
Hodder & Stoughton General
Icon Books Ltd
ISIS Publishing Ltd
Janus Publishing Co Ltd
Little, Brown Book Group
Liverpool University Press
Living Time® Media International
Macmillan Publishers Ltd
Orion Books Ltd
The Orion Publishing Group Ltd
Pan Macmillan
Paragon Publishing
Pen Press
Pipers' Ash Ltd
Random House UK Ltd
Sandstone Press Ltd
Severn House Publishers Ltd
Sigel Press
Simon & Schuster (UK) Ltd
Snowbooks
Transworld Publishers Ltd
Troubador Publishing Ltd
United Writers Publications Ltd

SCIENTIFIC & TECHNICAL

Alpha Science International Ltd
Anshan Ltd
Archetype Publications Ltd
Atlantic Europe Publishing Co Ltd
Bernard Babani (Publishing) Ltd
BookPower
British Geological Survey
CABI
Calypso Publications
Cambridge University Press
Canopus Publishing Ltd
Chalksoft Ltd
Commonwealth Secretariat
Construction Industry Research & Information Association (CIRIA)
J M Dent
Donhead Publishing Ltd
Earthscan
Elsevier Ltd
Energy Institute
English Heritage
Forensic Science Society
Geological Society Publishing House
Granta Editions
Greenleaf Publishing
HarperCollins Publishers Ltd
Haynes Publishing
Hodder Education
Human Kinetics Europe Ltd
IChemE
Icon Books Ltd
IHS BRE Press
Imperial College Press
Imprint Academic
In Easy Steps Ltd
Institute of Acoustics
Institute of Food Science & Technology
Institute of Physics & Engineering in Medicine
Institution of Engineering and Technology (IET)
Intellect Ltd
IOP Publishing
IWA Publishing
Jones & Bartlett International
Kew Publishing
Leatherhead Food International
Letts and Lonsdale
McGraw-Hill Education

Macmillan Publishers Ltd
Maney Publishing
Manson Publishing Ltd
Market House Books Ltd
Mentor Books
The MIT Press Ltd
Monkey Puzzle Media Ltd
Multi Science Publishing Co Ltd
The National Academies Press
Natural History Museum
    Publishing
Nelson Thornes Ltd
NMS Enterprises Limited -
    Publishing
Open University Worldwide
Packard Publishing Ltd
Palgrave Macmillan
Paragon Publishing
PC Publishing
The Pharmaceutical Press
Pickering & Chatto (Publishers) Ltd
Portland Press Ltd
Princeton University Press
Professional Engineering
    Publishing
ProQuest
Radcliffe Publishing Ltd
The Richmond Publishing Co
The Royal Society of Chemistry
Sage Publications Ltd
Scion Publishing Ltd
The Society of Metaphysicians Ltd
Stobart Davies Ltd
STRI (Sports Turf Research
    Institute)
Studymates Ltd
Taylor & Francis
Taylor Graham Publishing
Thomas Telford Ltd
TSO (The Stationery Office Ltd)
Usborne Publishing Ltd
David West Children's Books
Whittles Publishing
John Wiley & Sons Ltd
WIT Press
Witherby Seamanship
    International
Woodhead Publishing Ltd

SOCIOLOGY & ANTHROPOLOGY

Acumen Publishing Ltd
Age Concern Books
Arena Books (Publishers)
Ashgate Publishing Ltd
Austin & Macauley Publishers Ltd
Berg Publishers
Berghahn Books
Blackhall Publishing
British Association for Adoption &
    Fostering
British Museum Press
Cambridge University Press
Jon Carpenter Publishing
Centre for Policy on Ageing
Channel View Publications Ltd
Countryside Books
Crescent Moon Publishing
Dunedin Academic Press
Earthscan
Edinburgh University Press
Emerald Group Publishing Ltd
Equinox Publishing Ltd
The Fostering Network
Garnet Publishing Ltd
Global Oriental Ltd
Greenwood Publishing Group
Gwasg Gwenffrwd
Harvard University Press
Heart of Albion Press
Hodder Education
C. Hurst & Co (Publishers) Ltd
Icon Books Ltd
Imprint Academic
Institute of Development Studies
Institute of Education
    (Publications), University of
    London
Intellect Ltd
Ithaca Press
Janus Publishing Co Ltd

Jarndyce Booksellers
Jessica Kingsley Publishers
Learning Matters Ltd
Letts and Lonsdale
The Littman Library of Jewish
    Civilization
Liverpool University Press
McGraw-Hill Education
Macmillan Publishers Ltd
Manchester University Press
Mandrake of Oxford
The Merlin Press Ltd
Microform Academic Publishers
National Extension College Trust
    Ltd
Nelson Thornes Ltd
NMS Enterprises Limited -
    Publishing
Open University Worldwide
Oxbow Books
Palgrave Macmillan
Panaf Books
Pathfinder Books
Pavilion Journals (Brighton) Ltd
Pennant Books Ltd
Piatkus Books
Plowright Press
Pluto Books Ltd
The Policy Press
Polity Press
Princeton University Press
Joseph Rowntree Foundation
Russell House Publishing Ltd
Sage Publications Ltd
Saqi Books
Save the Children
Scottish Cultural Press
Shire Publications Ltd
Social Affairs Unit
Souvenir Press Ltd
Spokesman
Rudolf Steiner Press
Studymates Ltd
Sussex Academic Press
I. B. Tauris & Co Ltd
Taylor & Francis
Thames & Hudson Ltd
University of Hertfordshire Press
University of Wales Press
Vision
Waterside Press
Waterside Press
Whiting & Birch Ltd
John Wiley & Sons Ltd
Zed Books Ltd

SPORTS & GAMES

Absolute Press
Ian Allan Publishing Ltd
Amber Books Ltd
Amolibros
Peter Andrew Publishing Co Ltd
Apex Publishing Ltd
Appletree Press Ltd
Arcturus Publishing Ltd
Atlantic Books
Aureus Publishing Ltd
Aurum Press
Austin & Macauley Publishers Ltd
A. & C. Black (Publishers) Ltd
Blackstaff Press
John Blake Publishing Ltd
Breedon Books Publishing Co Ltd
Brown Dog Books
Butterfingers Books
Cambridge Publishing
    Management Ltd
Carel Press
Carlton Publishing Group
Christian Focus Publications
Cicerone Press Ltd
Coachwise Ltd
Collins & Brown
Copper Beech Publishing Ltd
Corpus Publishing Ltd
Countyvise Ltd
Paul H. Crompton Ltd
The Crowood Press Ltd
Cualann Press
Currach Press
D & N Publishing

Diagram Visual Information Ltd
Ashley Drake Publishing Ltd
Elliott & Thompson
Essential Works Ltd
Express Newspapers
FHG Guides Ltd
Filament Publishing Ltd
Focus Publishing (Sevenoaks) Ltd
Footprint Handbooks
Gomer
Granta Editions
Greenwood Publishing Group
Hachette Scotland
Haldane Mason Ltd
HarperCollins Publishers Ltd
Hart McLeod Ltd
Harvey Map Services Ltd
Haynes Publishing
Roger Heavens
Hodder Education
Hodder & Stoughton General
Alison Hodge Publishers
Human Kinetics Europe Ltd
Icon Books Ltd
Imray Laurie Norie & Wilson Ltd
Janus Publishing Co Ltd
Jones & Bartlett International
Jessica Kingsley Publishers
Know the Score Books
Kyle Cathie Ltd
Letts and Lonsdale
Dewi Lewis Publishing
Liberties Press
Frances Lincoln Ltd
Little, Brown Book Group
Luath Press Ltd
The Lutterworth Press
Macmillan Publishers Ltd
Mainstream Publishing Co
    (Edinburgh) Ltd
Maverick House Publishers
Mentor Books
Merlin Publishing/Wolfhound
    Press
Mitchell Beazley
Monkey Puzzle Media Ltd
Motor Racing Publications Ltd
Multi Science Publishing Co Ltd
Nelson Thornes Ltd
New Holland Publishers (UK) Ltd
W. W. Norton & Company Ltd
The O'Brien Press
Octopus Publishing Group
Old House Books
The Oleander Press
The Orion Publishing Group Ltd
Packard Publishing Ltd
Pan Macmillan
Paragon Publishing
Pen Press
Pennant Books Ltd
Pipers' Ash Ltd
Portico
Quantum Publishing
Quiller Publishing Ltd
Raceform Ltd
Random House UK Ltd
Ripping Yarns.com
Robson Books
Roundhouse Publishing Ltd
Russell House Publishing Ltd
Sandstone Press Ltd
Scala Publishers Ltd
Scottish Children's Press
Short Books Ltd
Sigma Press
Simon & Schuster (UK) Ltd
Smith Settle Printing &
    Bookbinding Ltd
Snowbooks
Soccer Books Ltd
Souvenir Press Ltd
Sportsbooks Ltd
STRI (Sports Turf Research
    Institute)
Summersdale Publishers Ltd
Supportive Learning Publications
    (SLP)
Sussex Academic Press
Taylor & Francis
Transworld Publishers Ltd
United Writers Publications Ltd

University of Wales Press
Merlin Unwin Books Ltd
Usborne Publishing Ltd
Veloce Publishing Ltd
Vertical Editions
Virgin Books Ltd
Weidenfeld & Nicolson
David West Children's Books
John Wiley & Sons Ltd
Y Lolfa Cyf
Yore Publications

THEATRE, DRAMA & DANCE

Amolibros
Peter Andrew Publishing Co Ltd
Ashgate Publishing Ltd
Association for Scottish Literary
    Studies
Aurora Metro Publications Ltd
Austin & Macauley Publishers Ltd
Ruth Bean Publishers
Berghahn Books
A. & C. Black (Publishers) Ltd
Blackstaff Press
Bloomsbury Publishing Plc
Marion Boyars Publishers Ltd
Brown, Son & Ferguson, Ltd
Cambridge University Press
Capall Bann Publishing
Carel Press
Classical Comics Ltd
Cló Iar-Chonnachta
Cois Life
Collins & Brown
The Continuum International
    Publishing Group Ltd
Crescent Moon Publishing
Cressrelles Publishing Co Ltd
The Crowood Press Ltd
D & N Publishing
Dance Books Ltd
Ashley Drake Publishing Ltd
Dramatic Lines
Faber & Faber Ltd
Feather Books
Filament Publishing Ltd
Five Leaves Publications
Focus Publishing (Sevenoaks) Ltd
Samuel French Ltd
The Gallery Press
Granta Editions
Greenwood Publishing Group
Guildhall Press
Hanbury Plays
Ian Henry Publications Ltd
Nick Hern Books
Human Kinetics Europe Ltd
Intellect Ltd
Janus Publishing Co Ltd
Kenyon-Deane
The Littman Library of Jewish
    Civilization
Luath Press Ltd
Macmillan Publishers Ltd
Manchester University Press
Market House Books Ltd
Mercier Press Ltd
J. Garnet Miller
Moorley's Print & Publishing Ltd
NATE (National Association for the
    Teaching of English)
Nelson Thornes Ltd
New Island Books Ltd
New Playwrights' Network
Northcote House Publishers Ltd
W. W. Norton & Company Ltd
The Old Stile Press
Open University Worldwide
Peter Owen Publishers
Palgrave Macmillan
Paragon Publishing
Pavilion
Pen Press
Pipers' Ash Ltd
Playne Books Ltd
The Playwrights Publishing Co
ProQuest
Robson Books
RotoVision SA
Roundhouse Publishing Ltd
Russell House Publishing Ltd

SchoolPlay Productions Ltd
Scottish Cultural Press
Seren
Charles Skilton Ltd
Colin Smythe Ltd
Souvenir Press Ltd
Spokesman
Stainer & Bell Ltd
Rudolf Steiner Press
Studymates Ltd
Supportive Learning Publications
    (SLP)
Sussex Academic Press
Taylor & Francis
Thames & Hudson Ltd
Trentham Books
Troubador Publishing Ltd
University of Exeter Press
University of Hertfordshire Press
Victoria & Albert Museum
    Publishing
Waterside Press
Waterside Press
Joseph Weinberger Ltd
Yale University Press London

TRANSPORT

AA Publishing
Albyn Press
Ian Allan Publishing Ltd
Amber Books Ltd
Ashgate Publishing Ltd
Atlantic Books
Aurum Press
Barny Books
The Belmont Press
Breedon Books Publishing Co Ltd
Brewin Books Ltd
Brooklands Books Ltd
Capital Transport Publishing
Carlton Publishing Group
Caxton Publishing Group Ltd
Chatham Publishing
Colourpoint Books
Conway
Copper Beech Publishing Ltd
Countryside Books
Countyvise Ltd
Crécy Publishing Ltd
The Crowood Press Ltd
G. L. Crowther
Currach Press
D & N Publishing
The Dovecote Press
Earthscan
Edward Elgar Publishing Ltd
Elm Publications
Essential Works Ltd
Ex Libris Press
Express Newspapers
Focus Publishing (Sevenoaks) Ltd
Friends of the Earth
GeoCenter International Ltd
Glasgow Museums Publishing
Gomer
Haynes Publishing
Ian Henry Publications Ltd
Imray Laurie Norie & Wilson Ltd
Irwell Press Ltd
Jane's Information Group Ltd
Kogan Page Ltd
Landmark Publishing Ltd
McGraw-Hill Education
Manchester University Press
Maney Publishing
Maritime Books
Merrell Publishers Ltd
Merton Priory Press Ltd
Middleton Press
Motor Racing Publications Ltd
NMS Enterprises Limited -
    Publishing
The Nostalgia Collection
Old House Books
Old Pond Publishing Ltd
Professional Engineering
    Publishing
Quantum Publishing
Quiller Publishing Ltd
Random House UK Ltd
Reflections of a Bygone Age

Roadmaster Publishing
Sheaf Publishing
Sheldrake Press
Shire Publications Ltd
Charles Skilton Ltd
Snowbooks
Soccer Books Ltd
Special Interest Model Books Ltd
Stenlake Publishing Ltd
Troubador Publishing Ltd
TSO (The Stationery Office Ltd)
Twelveheads Press
Veloce Publishing Ltd
David West Children's Books
WIT Press
Witherby Seamanship
International

TRAVEL & TOPOGRAPHY

AA Publishing
Absolute Press
Amolibros
Chris Andrews Publications Ltd
Appletree Press Ltd
Arcadia Books Ltd
Arena Books (Publishers)
Arris Publishing Ltd
Aurora Metro Publications Ltd
Aurum Press
Austin & Macauley Publishers Ltd
Beautiful Books Ltd
The Belmont Press
Berghahn Books
Black Dog Publishing Ltd
Blackstaff Press
Book Castle Publishing Ltd
Boydell & Brewer Ltd
Bradt Travel Guides Ltd
Brandon/Mount Eagle
Publications
Nicholas Brealey Publishing
Bridge Books
Calypso Publications
*Cambridge Publishing
Management Ltd*
Camra Books

Centre for Alternative Technology
Publications
Channel View Publications Ltd
The Chrysalis Press
Cicerone Press Ltd
Cló Iar-Chonnachta
Collins Geo
Constable & Robinson Ltd
Countryside Books
Crescent Moon Publishing
Crimson Publishing
Cualann Press
Currach Press
D & N Publishing
Day One Publications
Dedalus Ltd
Discovery Walking Guides Ltd
The Dovecote Press
Gerald Duckworth & Co Ltd
Eland Publishing Ltd
Elm Publications
English Heritage
The Erskine Press
Everyman's Library
Ex Libris Press
Express Newspapers
Footprint Handbooks
W. Foulsham & Co Ltd
Garnet Publishing Ltd
GeoCenter International Ltd
The Geographical Association
Gibson Square
Gill & Macmillan Ltd
Global Oriental Ltd
Gothic Image Publications
Graffeg
Granta Books
Granta Editions
Green Books
Green Magic
Gwasg Gwenffrwd
Robert Hale Ltd
Halsgrove
HarperCollins Publishers Ltd
Haynes Publishing
Historical Publications Ltd
Hobnob Press

Alison Hodge Publishers
Holo Books
How To Books Ltd
Imray Laurie Norie & Wilson Ltd
Instant-Books UK Ltd
The King's England Press
Know the Score Books
Landmark Publishing Ltd
Libris Ltd
Frances Lincoln Ltd
Little, Brown Book Group
Luath Press Ltd
Macmillan Publishers Ltd
Melisende
Mentor Books
Merlin Publishing/Wolfhound
Press
Meyrick Marketing Ltd
Michelin Maps & Guides
Mitchell Beazley
Monkey Puzzle Media Ltd
Murdoch Books UK Ltd
John Murray Publishers
The National Trust
New Holland Publishers (UK) Ltd
The O'Brien Press Ltd
Old House Books
The Oleander Press
The Orion Publishing Group Ltd
Pan Macmillan
Pavilion
Pen Press
The Penguin Group (UK) Ltd
Playne Books Ltd
Portobello Books Ltd
Prestel Publishing Ltd
Punk Publishing Ltd
Quiller Publishing Ltd
The Radcliffe Press
Reardon Publishing
Ripping Yarns.com
Roadmaster Publishing
Robson Books
Alan Rogers Guides Ltd
Roundhouse Publishing Ltd
S. B. Publications
Alastair Sawday Publishing

Scala Publishers Ltd
SCM-Canterbury Press Ltd
Sheldrake Press
Shire Publications Ltd
Sigma Press
Simon & Schuster (UK) Ltd
Charles Skilton Ltd
Slightly Foxed
Smith Settle Printing &
Bookbinding Ltd
Souvenir Press Ltd
Stacey International
Strong Oak Press
Summersdale Publishers Ltd
Sunflower Books
Teneues Publishing UK Ltd
Thames & Hudson Ltd
Thorogood Publishing Ltd
F. A. Thorpe Publishing
Toucan Books Ltd
Transworld Publishers Ltd
Travel Publishing Ltd
Trotman Publishing
Troubador Publishing Ltd
United Writers Publications Ltd
Weidenfeld & Nicolson
John Wiley & Sons Ltd
Willow Island Editions
Neil Wilson Publishing Ltd
Zymurgy Publishing

VETERINARY SCIENCE

BookPower
CABI
Luath Press Ltd
Manson Publishing Ltd
The National Academies Press
Old Pond Publishing Ltd
The Pharmaceutical Press
Quiller Publishing Ltd
Souvenir Press Ltd
TSO (The Stationery Office Ltd)
Whittet Books Ltd
John Wiley & Sons Ltd

VOCATIONAL TRAINING &
CAREERS

Austin & Macauley Publishers Ltd
Bene Factum Publishing Ltd
BookPower
Nicholas Brealey Publishing
*Cambridge Publishing
Management Ltd*
Cengage Learning EMEA
CILT, the National Centre for
Languages
Crimson Publishing
Emerald Group Publishing Ltd
Ethics International Press Ltd
Filament Publishing Ltd
The Fostering Network
Gower Publishing Co Ltd
Hawker Publications
Hodder Education
How To Books Ltd
In Easy Steps Ltd
Institute of Education
(Publications), University of
London
Jones & Bartlett International
Jessica Kingsley Publishers
Kogan Page Ltd
Lawpack Publishing Ltd
Letts and Lonsdale
McGraw-Hill Education
Macmillan Education
National Extension College Trust
Ltd
National Housing Federation
Need2Know
Nelson Thornes Ltd
Optimus Professional Publishing
Palgrave Macmillan
Radcliffe Publishing Ltd
Russell House Publishing Ltd
Southgate Publishers
Trotman Publishing
UCAS
Which? Books
John Wiley & Sons Ltd

7.2 INDEX OF ISBN PREFIXES

7.3   INDEX OF PERSONAL NAMES

7.4 INDEX OF COMPANIES & IMPRINTS

LONDON & SOUTH-EAST ENGLAND

Brighton
BN1 1WZ **3042**
BN1 9RE **2396**
BN1 9RF **2393**
BN2 1GJ **2587**
BN3 1AS **2582**
BN3 1DD **2643**
BN3 1FL **2514**
BN7 2NS **2385, 3026**
BN11 1BE **2063**
BN23 6NT **2432**
BN24 9BP **2736**
BN25 2UB **2667**
BN41 1WR **2645**
Bromley
BR2 9JF **2081**
BR3 5JS **2153**
Canterbury
CT20 2WP **2302**
Croydon
CR0 4PA **2271**
CR2 6NZ **2775**
CR5 2YH **2416**
CR9 5YP **2509**
Dartford
DA1 4BZ **2686**
Guildford
GU3 1LP **2720**
GU5 9SW **2224**
GU7 2EP **2362**
GU9 7HS **2564**
GU9 7PT **2046, 2312, 2466**
GU21 6LQ **2540**
GU29 9AZ **2499**
GU32 2EW **2347**
GU34 1HG **2216**
GU34 3HQ **2633**
GU47 9DD **2067**
Harrow
HA3 5ZH **2141**
HA3 8RU **2086**
HA8 7BJ **2794**
HA9 9EA **2604**
Hemel Hempstead
HP10 8EU **2428**
HP17 8NT **2278**
HP20 2NQ **3028**
HP23 5AH **3005**
Ilford
IG7 6DL **2419**
IG8 8HD **2372**
Kingston-upon-Thames
KT3 3AB **2622**
KT5 9SP **2754**
KT11 1LG **2125**
KT12 4RG **2016**
KT14 7HX **2757**
KT22 7RY **2445**
London
E1M 5QL **2415**
E2 6DG **2579**
E8 3BH **2475**

E9 5LN **2491**
E14 4JP **2189, 2307, 2503, 2505, 2550, 2593**
E14 5LB **2059**
E14 9TP **2753**
EC1A 9PN **2673**
EC1M 4AR **2665**
EC1M 5NP **2447**
EC1M 5QL **2760**
EC1M 5UX **2256**
EC1M 6BF **2235**
EC1M 6PE **3038**
EC1M 7BA **2710**
EC1N 8QU **2486**
EC1N 8RT **2793**
EC1N 8TS **2121**
EC1N 8XA **2238**
EC1R 0DU **3021**
EC1R 0HT **2019, 2339**
EC1R 0JH **2613, 2694**
EC1R 4QB **2116**
EC1R 4QL **2243**
EC1R 4SX **2568**
EC1V 0AT **2259, 2668**
EC1V 0BB **2433, 2562**
EC1V 0DG **2156**
EC1V 1LR **2429**
EC1V 1NG **2519**
EC1V 3QP **2157**
EC1V 4JX **2700**
EC1V 7QE **2520**
EC1V 9BP **2191**
EC1Y 1SP **2657**
EC2A 3AR **2096**
EC2A 3DU **2762**
EC3R 6AE **2263**
EC3R 8DU **2405**
EC4A 2HS **2484**
EC4Y 0DY **2458, 2594**
N1 1EW **2299**
N1 2LZ **2223**
N1 3JT **2082**
N1 6ND **2817**
N1 7JQ **2286**
N1 9JB **2431**
N1 9JF **2832**
N1 9JN **2435, 2705, 3011**
N1 9PA **2591**
N1 9PF **3003**
N1 9RW **2470, 2576**
N1 9UN **2446**
N3 1DZ **2722**
N6 5AA **2601**
N7 8PL **2365**
N7 9BH **3034**
N7 9DP **2382**
N12 8ZR **2226**
N19 4PT **2134**
N22 6TZ **2501**
NW1 0ND **2058**
NW1 1DB **2669**
NW1 2DB **2123**

NW1 3BH **2333, 2334, 2367, 2369, 2370, 2512**
NW1 4DF **2809**
NW1 4ND **2618**
NW1 7HP **2437**
NW1 8PR **2595**
NW3 3PF **2761**
NW3 5HT **2424**
NW5 2DU **2252**
NW5 2RZ **2455**
NW5 2XL **2453**
NW5 4QH **3018**
NW6 1DZ **2560**
NW6 1LU **2055**
NW6 3HR **2697**
NW6 6RD **2148**
NW8 6WD **2054, 2727, 2737, 2825**
NW10 3YB **2338**
NW11 7DL **2481**
SE1 0HX **2493**
SE1 0JF **2800**
SE1 0UP **2767**
SE1 2BH **2249**
SE1 2EJ **2042**
SE1 3AW **2441**
SE1 7HR **2173**
SE1 7JN **2592**
SE1 7NX **2192**
SE1 8HA **2282**
SE1 8RD **2821**
SE1 8UG **2539**
SE1 8XX **2354**
SE10 8RF **2035**
SE11 5AY **2150**
SE11 5SD **2617**
SE19 3RY **3010, 3012**
SE23 3HZ **2810**
SE24 0PB **2375, 2609**
SE27 9NT **2740**
SW1A 1JR **2649**
SW1H 0QS **2414**
SW1H 9BN **2265**
SW1H 9JJ **2612**
SW1P 3AZ **2170**
SW1P 3BL **2703**
SW1P 4PG **2747**
SW1P 4ST **2688, 2708**
SW1V 2SA **2028, 2628, 2799**
SW1V 2SS **2358**
SW1X 7DL **2449**
SW1X 8PG **2651**
SW1Y 5HX **2188**
SW3 4AH **2015, 2699**
SW5 0RE **2570**
SW6 1RU **2423**
SW6 6AW **2459**
SW6 6JD **2342**
SW7 1PU **2650**
SW7 2AR **2652**
SW7 2RL **2798**
SW7 3WS **2734**
SW7 5BD **2529**
SW8 5WZ **2087**

SW11 2JW **2253**
SW11 3AS **2660**
SW11 5DH **2351**
SW11 6SS **2327**
SW12 0DA **2689**
SW14 8ER **2690**
SW15 1AZ **3041**
SW15 1DQ **2207**
SW15 1NL **2112**
SW15 2PE **2212**
SW15 2TG **2511**
SW16 4ER **2011**
SW18 1YW **2069**
SW18 4JJ **2217**
SW19 1JQ **2161**
SW19 3NN **2773**
W1A 3FB **2589**
W1B 1AH **2383**
W1B 5DL **2084**
W1B 5SA **2707**
W1D 3HB **2360**
W1D 3QY **2009, 2097, 2104**
W1F 7BB **2671**
W1F 9JW **2337**
W1G 0AE **2655**
W1G 0DD **2287**
W1G 7AR **2250**
W1G 8DH **2077**
W1J 6HE **2222**
W1S 4EX **2638**
W1T 2LD **2620, 2822**
W1T 3JJ **2808**
W1T 3JW **2145**
W1T 3LJ **2555**
W1T 3QT **2545**
W1T 4EJ **2021**
W1T 5DX **2411**
W1T 5HJ **2040**
W1T 5JR **2285**
W1T 6DF **3001**
W1U 6BY **2417**
W1U 6NR **2258**
W1W 7AB **2039**
W1W 8AF **2802**
W1Y 0RA **2581**
W2 2EA **2534**
W2 4BU **2624, 2748**
W2 4QS **2179**
W2 5BP **2739**
W2 5RH **2664, 2752**
W4 5TF **2316**
W4 5YD **2744**
W5 4YX **2010**
W5 5SA **2627, 2770**
W6 7NF **2068**
W6 7NJ **2399**
W6 7PA **2177, 2420**
W6 8JB **2346**
W6 9ER **2190**
W8 4BH **2142, 2721**
W8 4PL **2013**
W8 6SA **2242**
W10 5ST **2558**
W11 2LW **2093**
W11 4QR **2317, 2607**

W12 8QP **2361**
W14 0RA **2078, 2184, 2193, 2580, 2605, 2641**
W14 9PB **2102**
WC1A 2QA **2610**
WC1A 2TH **2596, 2738**
WC1B 3DA **2264**
WC1B 3DP **2829**
WC1B 3ES **2041**
WC1B 3JH **2152, 2489, 2490**
WC1B 3PA **2418**
WC1B 3PD **2714**
WC1B 3PL **2379**
WC1B 3QQ **2124**
WC1E 7AE **2266, 2394**
WC1E 7DS **2108**
WC1E 7EY **2349, 2504**
WC1H 0AB **2803**
WC1H 0AL **2397**
WC1H 9HF **2680**
WC1N 2BX **2047, 2245**
WC1N 3JZ **2051**
WC1R 4LR **2154**
WC1V 6NY **2525**
WC1V 7QX **2758**
WC1X 0DW **2026**
WC1X 8HB **2698**
WC1X 9DH **3019**
WC1X 9NG **2095**
WC2A 1PL **2440**
WC2A 1PP **2390**
WC2B 4PJ **2199**
WC2H 0HE **2526**
WC2H 0LS **2619**
WC2H 7HH **2523**
WC2H 9EA **2227, 2309, 2565, 2566, 2807**
WC2H 9HE **2386**
WC2N 6DF **2344**
WC2N 6RL **2162**
WC2R 0LX **2298**
WC2R 0RL **2079, 2588**
Luton
LU6 2ES **2120**
Medway
ME2 4HN **2024**
ME5 9AQ **2639**
ME14 5XU **2204**
Portsmouth
PO8 9JL **2500**
PO14 1BU **2105**
PO19 1RP **2733**
PO19 7DN **2574**
PO19 8SQ **2814**
Reading
RG1 4QS **2291, 2412**
RG8 8LU **2559**
RG9 4PG **2052**
RG14 5DS **2200**
RG20 6NL **2623**
RG20 8AN **2578**
RG21 4EA **2001**
RG21 6XS **2085, 2473, 2575**

RG21 6YR **2294**
RG27 0JG **2805, 3040**
Redhill
RH4 1DN **2755**
RH10 7WD **2729**
RH12 9GH **2630**
RH17 5PA **3033**
RH18 5ES **2723, 2756**
RH19 3BJ **2111**
RH19 3BT **2804, 3008**
RH19 4FS **2195**
Romford
RM1 4LH **2359**
Slough
SL1 4AA **2283**
SL2 3PQ **2135**
SL2 3RS **2635**
SL6 2QL **2469**
SL9 8XA **2704**
SL9 9QE **2114**
Southall
UB9 5NX **3007**
UB9 6AT **2830**
Southampton
SO23 8RY **2071**
SO24 0BE **2378**
SO24 9JH **2477**
SO40 7AA **2819**
Southend
SS1 1EF **2400**
SS3 0EQ **2468**
SS9 2LB **2513**
St Albans
AL1 3BN **2395**
AL1 4EG **2827**
AL1 4JL **2745**
AL1 4LW **2137**
AL6 9EQ **2530**
AL8 6HG **2261**
AL10 9AB **2789**
Sutton (Surrey)
SM1 1DF **2683**
Tonbridge
TN2 3DR **2678**
TN4 9AT **2033**
TN11 8HL **2012**
TN13 3AJ **3022**
TN16 1BZ **2279**
TN17 1HE **2642**
TN18 5AD **2303**
TN30 6BW **2290, 2326**
TN35 4PG **2711**
Twickenham
TW1 3QS **3039**
TW1 4HX **2057**
TW2 5RQ **2233**
TW7 6NH **2833**
TW9 1SR **2345**
TW9 2LL **2022, 2557**
TW9 2ND **2206, 2776**
TW9 3AE **2427**
TW9 3HA **2066**
Watford
WD6 3PW **2163, 2322**
WD17 1JA **2497**
WD19 4BG **2262**

WD25 9XX **2384**

SOUTH-WEST ENGLAND

Bath
BA1 2BT **2002**
BA1 3JN **2297**
BA1 5BG **2075, 3035**
BA1 5DZ **3016**
BA2 3AF **2239**
BA2 3BH **2080**
BA2 3DZ **2280**
BA2 3LR **2126, 2541**
BA2 4JT **2751**
BA2 7EJ **2743**
BA2 7JF **3037**
BA6 8AE **2132**
BA6 8XR **2311**
BA11 1DS **2165**
BA11 4EL **2364**
BA11 4LW **3020**
BA13 4JE **2237**
BA14 0AA **2608**
BA22 7JJ **2353**
Bournemouth
BH15 3SY **2716**
BH20 6AE **2182**
BH21 4JD **2231**
Bristol
BS1 4ND **2139**
BS1 6BE **2407**
BS1 6JS **2421**
BS8 1QU **2602**
BS3 3EA **2632, 2663**
BS16 3JG **2403**
BS21 7HH **2160**
BS41 9LR **2666**
Dorchester
DT1 1TT **2795**
DT7 3LS **2656**
Exeter
EX1 1NX **2443**
EX4 4QR **2788**
EX5 5HY **2387**
EX17 4LW **2713**
EX32 9HG **2616**
EX38 8ZJ **2422**
Jersey
JE2 3LD **2260**
Plymouth
PL2 2EQ **2831**
PL6 7PP **2771**
PL14 4EL **2482**
PL15 8LD **2110**
PL19 9NQ **2544**
PL23 1EQ **2197**
PL28 8BG **2741**
Salisbury
SP3 5QP **2496**
SP3 6FA **2366**
SP7 9LY **2230**
Swindon
SN2 2GZ **2251**
SN2 2NA **2527**
SN5 7YD **2166**
SN7 7DS **2538**
SN8 2AA **2006, 2007**
SN8 2HR **2209**
SN8 2LH **3017**
SN11 8YE **2811**
SN15 4BW **2597**
Taunton
TA4 1NE **2140**
TA4 1QF **3004**
TA7 9AR **2320**
TA19 0LE **2225**
TA21 9PZ **2340**
Torquay
TQ9 6EB **2319**
TQ9 7DL **2615**
TQ12 4PU **2219**
TQ13 8PA **2551**
Truro
TR4 8ZJ **2781**

TR5 0RA **2778**
TR18 4AW **2380**
TR20 8BG **2786**
TR20 8XA **2371**

MIDLANDS

Birmingham
B9 4AA **2766**
B29 6LB **2167**
B80 7LG **2118**
B80 7NT **2434**
B91 1UE **2357**
Coventry
CV8 2GN **2169**
CV21 3HQ **2381**
CV34 4XE **2600**
CV37 1EP **2065**
CV47 0FB **2389**
Derby
DE6 1HD **2438**
DE7 5DA **2508**
DE21 4SZ **2117**
Dudley
DY8 3XY **2640**
Gloucester
GL5 1BJ **2352**
GL6 7RL **2712**
GL7 3QB **2211**
GL15 6YD **3015**
GL50 2JA **2244**
GL50 2JR **2719**
GL50 9AN **2631**
GL52 3LZ **2783**
GL53 7TH **2532**
GL56 0YN **2045**
Hereford
HR3 6QH **2463**
HR3 8QU **2546**
HR6 0QF **2313**
HR6 8NZ **2220**
HR9 5LA **2584**
Leicester
LE5 3GJ **2528**
LE7 7FU **2763, 2784**
LE8 0LQ **2777**
LE11 1UD **2679**
LE11 3TU **2457**
LE11 5DN **2764**
LE16 9BE **2355**
LE67 9SY **2436**
Milton Keynes
MK2 2EB **2677**
MK7 6AA **2561**
MK9 2BE **2062**
MK13 9HG **2717**
MK18 1NT **2363**
MK40 4FB **2577**
MK43 7LP **2083**
MK45 4BE **2408**
Northampton
NN3 6AP **2060**
NN3 6RT **2315**
NN5 7JU **2229, 2392**
NN7 3JB **3031**
NN12 6BT **2025, 2517, 2626**
NN12 9AR **2178**
NN14 4BW **2547**
NN17 4HH **2273**
Nottingham
NG1 9AW **2274**
NG6 0BT **2718**
NG7 2RD **2676**
NG7 3HR **2413**
NG12 5GG **2122**
NG12 5HT **2634**
NG14 5AL **2599**
NG17 2HU **2780**
NG32 2BB **2076**
Oxford
OX1 1AP **2479**
OX1 1ST **2406**
OX1 2EW **2571**

OX1 2JW **2348**
OX1 2PH **2048**
OX1 3BG **2106**
OX1 3HJ **2373**
OX1 5RP **2267**
OX2 0ES **2409**
OX2 0LX **2030**
OX2 0PH **2567, 2693**
OX2 0UJ **2460**
OX2 6DP **2573**
OX2 6JX **2801**
OX2 7DR **2456**
OX2 8DP **2325**
OX2 8EJ **2586**
OX2 9RU **2202**
OX3 0BP **2049**
OX4 1AW **2088**
OX4 1BW **2535**
OX4 1RE **2089**
OX4 2JY **2572**
OX4 2JZ **2023**
OX4 3PP **2471**
OX5 1GB **2247**
OX5 1RX **2376**
OX7 3PH **2147**
OX7 6RU **3002**
OX10 8DE **2133**
OX12 8JY **2507**
OX14 1AA **2625**
OX14 3FE **2090**
OX14 4RN **2647, 2749**
OX15 0SE **2017**
OX15 4FF **2672**
OX18 4XN **2218**
OX20 1TW **2611**
OX28 4AW **3030**
OX29 8SZ **2439**
Shrewsbury
SY3 0WN **2269**
SY4 1JA **2621**
SY4 4UR **2731**
SY5 5JX **2462**
SY6 9WZ **2391**
SY8 1DB **2791**
Stoke-on-Trent
ST4 5NP **2772**
ST17 0TE **2208**
Worcester
WR9 7EE **2343**
WR9 7RP **2029**
WR13 6RN **2205, 2426, 2502, 2537**

EAST ANGLIA

Cambridge
CB1 1JT **2554**
CB1 2NT **2176, 2467**
CB2 1JZ **2410**
CB2 1UR **2603**
CB2 8HN **2521**
CB2 8RU **2136**
CB3 9ND **2563**
CB4 0WF **2654**
CB4 1ND **2318**
CB4 3BW **2695**
CB5 8DT **2818**
CB5 8SW **2614**
CB21 5DH **2661**
CB21 6AH **2823**
CB23 1HJ **2356**
CB23 7AY **2448**
CB23 7NU **3013**
CB25 9HP **3025**
Chelmsford
CM6 2PP **2149**
CM8 1WF **2324**
CM15 9TB **2510**
CM20 2JE **2585**
CM23 2EJ **2636**
Colchester
CO1 2TW **2276**
CO2 8HP **2606**
CO3 3HU **2670**

CO6 1JE **2174**
CO15 5WN **2036**
Ipswich
IP1 3RP **3009**
IP1 5LT **2552**
IP12 1AP **2768**
IP12 1BL **2151**
IP12 2QW **3029**
IP12 3DF **2113**
IP12 4SD **2034**
IP25 6QH **2583**
IP33 2BL **2043**
IP33 3PH **2255**
Norwich
NR2 3AD **2785**
NR3 1PD **2779**
NR3 3AX **2008**
NR14 7UR **3006**
NR16 2PB **2254**
NR26 8NB **3024**
NR29 3ET **2726**
Peterborough
PE2 6SG **2495**
PE2 6XP **2792**
PE2 9JX **2531, 2774**
PE11 1NZ **2158, 2684**
PE11 4TA **2806**
PE21 8EU **2425**
PE27 5BT **2388**
PE28 0AE **2569**
PE28 2NJ **2246**
PE28 5XE **2221**
PE37 7XG **2031**
Stevenage
SG1 2AY **2402**
SG1 4SU **2070**
SG8 5NJ **2826**
SG9 9AJ **3036**
SG12 9HJ **2824**
SG14 2JA **2691**

NORTH-EAST ENGLAND

Bradford
BD1 3PT **2143**
BD16 1AU **2728**
BD16 1WA **2248**
BD23 2QR **2797**
BD23 4ND **2474**
Darlington
DL3 0PH **2257**
DL8 4AY **2746**
Doncaster
DN35 8HU **2706**
Durham
DH4 5QY **2131**
DH8 7PW **2306**
Harrogate
HG1 1BX **2281**
HG4 5DF **2107**
Leeds
LS3 1AB **2480**
LS6 4NB **2027**
LS8 2SP **2288**
LS12 4HP **2181**
LS19 7XY **2702**
LS28 6AT **2377**
Newcastle-upon-Tyne
NE1 1SG **2275**
NE1 3DY **2515**
NE6 2HL **2834**
NE43 7TN **2005**
NE48 1RP **2103**
NE70 7JX **2032**
NE99 1DX **2782**
Sheffield
S1 2BS **2485**
S1 4BF **2295**
S3 7WL **2687**
S3 8GG **2323**
S8 0XJ **2516**
SO23 9EH **2629**
S32 1DJ **2241**
S41 0FR **2494**

S63 9BL **2430**
S80 3LR **2064**
Wakefield
WF3 2AP **2498**
WF4 4PX **2815**
WF5 9AQ **2685**
WF8 4WW **2646**
York
YO10 5DD **2109**
YO10 5DX **2658**
YO16 6BT **2336**
YO18 8AL **2100**
YO24 1ES **2401**
YO30 6WP **2648**
YO30 7BZ **2198**
YO31 9HS **2682**
YO62 5BP **2543**

NORTH-WEST ENGLAND

Carlisle
CA2 5AU **2144**
CA3 9HZ **2598**
CA12 5AS **2506**
Chester
CH3 8JF **2765**
CH41 9HH **2201**
Lancaster
LA1 4SL **2146**
LA7 7PY **2172**
LA12 9QQ **2759**
LA17 7WZ **2194**
Liverpool
L3 5SD **2398**
L69 7ZU **2461**
Manchester
M1 1JB **3023**
M13 9NR **2478**
M22 5LH **2203**
M23 9HH **2659**
Oldham
OL14 6DA **2038**
Preston
PR1 8JP **2210**
PR3 5LE **2769**
PR9 0QT **2750**
Stockport
SK4 4ND **2450**
SK14 4SH **2442**
Warrington
WA4 9DE **2292**

WALES

Cardiff
CF5 1GZ **2314**
CF10 4UP **2790**
CF14 2EA **2234**
CF14 7ZY **2232**
CF31 3AE **2681**
CF31 4DX **2129**
CF32 0TN **2056**
CF37 5PB **2091**
CF46 6SA **2004**
CF71 9AY **2305**
Llandudno
LL12 7AW **2119**
LL13 7NS **2590**
LL14 5HL **2735**
LL18 9AY **2730**
LL21 9WZ **2331**
LL26 0EH **2330**
LL53 5YE **2332**
LL53 6SH **2215**
Mid-Wales
LD7 1UP **3027**
SY20 9AZ **2155**
SY23 3GL **2374**
SY24 5HE **2828**
Newport (Gwent)
NP25 4TN **2553**
Swansea
SA6 6AE **2074**
SA18 3HP **2696, 2725**

SA44 4JL **2310**
SA62 5AU **3032**

SCOTLAND

Aberdeen
AB12 3RT **2637**
AB34 5LP **2404**
Dumfries
DG10 9SU **3014**
Edinburgh
EH1 1JF **2542, 2709**
EH1 1TE **2138**
EH2 1ND **2465**
EH1 3QB **2236**
EH1 3UG **2476**
EH1 3YY **2518**
EH2 4PS **2321**
EH4 3BL **2014**
EH4 3DS **2522**
EH7 4AY **2159**
EH8 9LF **2240**
EH9 1QS **2092**
EH11 1SH **2277**
EH12 6EL **2072**
EH15 1JG **2228**
EH22 3LJ **2674, 2675**
EH52 5LH **2304**
EH52 5NF **2464**
EH54 8SB **2820**
Falkirk
FK16 6BJ **2350**
Glasgow
G2 3DH **2813**
G2 6TS **2018**
G12 8QH **2050**
G13 1BQ **2816**
G40 2AB **2451**
G41 2SD **2127**
G53 7NN **2301**
G64 2QT **2185**
G74 2JZ **2164**
Inverness
IV15 9SS **2020**
IV15 9WJ **2662**
IV20 1TW **2168**
IV36 3TE **2272**
IV42 8PY **2742**
Kilmarnock
KA5 6RD **2724**
KA27 8SB **2073**
Kirkcaldy
KY12 7XG **2213**
Motherwell
ML11 9DJ **2293**
Orkney
KW6 6EY **2812**
Paisley & Isles
HS1 2QN **2003**
PA1 1NB **2335, 2368**
PA1 1TJ **2270**
PA22 3AE **2044**
PA75 6PR **2128**
Perth
PH2 1AU **2094**
PH20 1BU **2715**
Shetland
ZE1 0PX **2692**

NORTHERN IRELAND

Belfast
BT3 9LE **2099**
BT5 6NW **2444**
BT7 1AP **2037**
BT9 5AU **2732**
BT9 5BS **2701**
BT23 4YH **2186**
BT48 0LZ **2328**